Women Writers of the Seventeenth Century

Women Writers of the Seventeenth Century

EDITED BY

KATHARINA M. WILSON

AND

FRANK J. WARNKE

The University of Georgia Press

ATHENS AND LONDON

Set in Mergenthaler Sabon
The paper in this book meets the guidelines for permanence and durability of the Committee on Production Guidelines for Book Longevity of the Council on Library Resources.

Typeset by The Composing Room of Michigan
Printed and bound by Thomson-Shore

Printed in the United States of America
93 92 91 90 89 5 4 3 2 1

Library of Congress Cataloging in Publication Data

Women writers of the seventeenth century / edited by Katharina M. Wilson and Frank J. Warnke.
p. cm.
Includes bibliographies and index.
ISBN 0-8203-1111-1 (alk. paper).
ISBN 0-8203-1112-X (pbk.:alk. paper)
1. Literature—Women authors—History and criticism. 2. Literature—17th century—History and criticism. I. Wilson, Katharina M. II. Warnke, Frank J.
PN471.W57 1989
808.8'99287—dc19 88-24994
CIP

British Library Cataloging in Publication Data available

IN MEMORIAM

He loved language. He played with it, used it as an instrument to tease out shades of meaning, infinitesimal tonal variances. He was an incorrigible punster, occasionally punning in several languages.

He loved his work. A born teacher and scholar, he delighted in sharing his mind, his knowledge, and his experience with students and young colleagues. He worked steadily, never letting a day go by without six hours at his typewriter.

He loved people. Jealousy, mistrust, envy were concepts alien to his personality. He was kind and he was generous. Tolerant and always eager to help everyone, he devoted a good portion of his time and creative energies to helping younger faculty crystallize their ideas, their methodologies.

His death cut short an academic career nothing short of brilliant. Born in Marlborough, Massachusetts, on November 3, 1925, Frank Warnke received his B.A. in English from Yale University and his M.A. and Ph.D. in English and comparative literature from Columbia University. He was the author of *John Donne, European Metaphysical Poetry, Versions of Baroque: European Literature in the Seventeenth Century,* and *Three Women Poets: Renaissance and Baroque,* as well as articles on such varied topics as modern American poetry, Baroque drama and poetry, the comparatist's canon, and Italian opera. In addition, he was the editor of the *Encyclopedia of Poetry and Poetics, Princeton Handbook of Poetic Terms* (both with A. Preminger and O. B. Hardison), and *John Donne, Poetry and Prose.* He held Fulbright professorships to Germany twice, was resident scholar at the Rockefeller Center in Bellagio, and received grants from the American Council of Learned Societies and the American Philosophical Society. He was a Morse Fellow at Yale University and the recipient of the Cristo-Loveanu Prize in Comparative Literature.

Frank Warnke died tragically on June 27, 1988, in a car accident.

KATHARINA M. WILSON

Contents

The seventeenth century was also a great age of epistolary writings. Mme de Sévigné, perhaps the most prolific *epistolière* of the age (there are over fifteen hundred extant letters penned by her) gives us a lively account of the glorious reign of Louis XIV and provides us with her intimate personal views on subjects as diverse as religion, children, gambling, travel, syphilis, medicine, literature, court intrigues, and wars.

If the conflict between the traditional symbolic and the emerging scientific world views is one of the factors conditioning the Baroque mentality, another of equal significance is surely the religious controversy between Catholic and Protestant, Anglican and Puritan, and Lutheran and Calvinist that left so heavy and tragic a mark on the age.[13] Catharina von Greiffenberg, an Austrian Protestant noblewoman reared a generation before the Habsburgs had effectively imposed Catholicism on all their realms, was obliged to flee her estate for the sanctuary of Lutheran Nuremberg (where she was warmly welcomed by her fellow poets). She planned a trip to Vienna to convert the emperor to Lutheranism but, fortunately for her, was dissuaded. On the other hand, in what must have been one of the best-publicized events of the century, Queen Christina of Lutheran Sweden renounced her crown, converted to Catholicism, and played a significant role in the Counter-Reformation. In Hungary the Lutheran noblewoman Kata Szidónia Petrőczi heroically resisted the Catholicizing tendencies of the Habsburgs; Mary Ward fled England to escape the religious persecution of Catholics, only to occasion vituperative criticism by the Catholic clergy who attempted to suppress the schools for girls she founded throughout Europe; and the staunchly Calvinistic Anna Maria van Schurman, disillusioned by the doctrinal rigidities of the church, abandoned her intellectual and literary aspirations to join a persecuted pietistic sect.

Baroque society was not hospitable to the artistic and intellectual endeavors of women, its authoritarianism and increased centralization having tightened the grip of traditional conservative attitudes.[14] Mary Ward faced constant criticism and persecution by the clergy; Anne Bradstreet was regarded as an oddity; and Margaret Cavendish, the Duchess of Newcastle, was widely viewed as mad. (In relatively tolerant Holland, Tesselschade had better fortune.) Neither Protestantism, with its hectic and neurotic concern for doctrinal purity, nor Counter-Reformation Catholicism, with its paranoid fear of heresy, could provide an ambience like that of the High Renaissance. In its sophistication and relative openness to the arts, the Renaissance permitted—and in some cases even fostered—the work of such women as Vittoria Colonna, Gaspara Stampa, Louise Labé, and Marguerite de Navarre, and it made possible the protests of the very same literate women whom it sought to oppress.[15] Joan Kelly remarks: "Feminist theorizing arose in the fifteenth century, in intimate association with and in reaction to the new secular culture of the modern

European state. It emerged as the voice of literate women who felt themselves maligned and newly oppressed by that culture, but who were empowered by it at the same time to speak out in their defense."[16] Despite the hostile atmosphere, and in some instances in dialectical opposition to misogyny, seventeenth-century women wrote their works, displaying a marked flair for the great and difficult Baroque styles.[17]

Not all seventeenth-century writers, male or female, can justly be classified as Baroque; an adversarial stance toward patriarchal authority induced in some an avoidance of what was, in effect, the style of the establishment. The Baroque was a current in the art of the period, albeit the most important one. One might argue that Aphra Behn flourished after the English sensibility had become Neoclassical rather than Baroque. *La Princesse de Clèves* is justly regarded as a masterpiece of Neoclassicism, although some scholars would contend that Mme de LaFayette, like her contemporary Jean Racine, epitomizes a *baroque dompté* (the term is Helmut Hatzfeld's) in which classical *bienséance* cannot conceal the turbulence of Baroque passion. The Danish countess Leonora Christina and the Italian Camilla Faà Gonzaga practice, in their gripping memoirs, a style that does not even attempt the fashionable devices of the Baroque; they write straightforward, highly personal prose guided by no principles apart from their own genius and firm convictions. Camilla Faà, indeed, sees the process of writing as the only path left to (re)establish her identity—to recollect, rectify, and justly preserve the story of her life which her husband, Duke Ferdinand, had misrepresented. Finally, the memoirs of Queen Christina of Sweden, while rhetorical and occasionally ebullient, preserve in an essentially personal prose a fascinating individual's struggle to achieve her ambitions.

Even when composing in the traditional genres and forms of Baroque letters, women writers were autodidacts by necessity and often stood outside the mainstream. Unable to attend universities and rarely permitted to join literary societies, they were forced to work in relative isolation—a phenomenon at least partially responsible for the noted independence and "modernity" of their thought, form, and style.

Scholarship and learning, as well as belles lettres, attracted many women during the seventeenth century. The learned lady, as Natalie Zemon Davis observes, "struggled to establish a role herself: the female schoolteacher became a familiar figure, whether as spinster or as an Ursuline."[18] Frequently labeled "bluestockings," often distrusted or even ridiculed, women scholars voiced ardent concerns for the position, education, and educability of women; they advocated serious intellectual training and sustained study. "Not to find pleasure in serious reading," wrote Mme de Sévigné in 1689, "gives a pastel coloring to the mind," and her sentiments seem to have been shared by scores of seventeenth-century women.

Introduction

KATHARINA M. WILSON AND
FRANK J. WARNKE

> Let me with *Sappho* and *Orinda* be
> Oh ever Sacred Nymph, adorn'd by thee;
> And give my Verses Immortality.

Aphra Behn thus interrupts her translation of the final volume of Cowley's *Six Books of Plants* by wishing to associate herself not with a male genius but with two immortal women poets—one of the Greek past, the other of the English present.[1] Aware of the continuous line of illustrious women poets and wishing, in her thirst for poetic fame, to be remembered as part of that tradition, Behn epitomizes the emerging consciousness of the Early Modern woman writer.[2]

The seventeenth century witnessed a great surge of literary activity by women. It has been estimated that four hundred women wrote between 1640 and 1700 in England alone and that their writings constituted approximately one percent of the texts published.[3] A large portion of the works penned by women in the Early Modern era, as in the Middle Ages and the Renaissance, were devotional or religio-political in nature; but the ratio of religious to secular texts became a great deal more balanced as time progressed. Analogously, women scholars, while still considered oddities, did increase in number in the 1600s; the mid- and late seventeenth century therefore witnessed an unprecedented number of women who decided to write polemically and with a collective awareness of their gender in order to address the subject of women's condition and potential, thus partaking in the philosophic/theological debate concerning the spiritual equality of the sexes.[4] Men, too, participated in the debate on both sides of the issue,[5] and the numerous catalogs of good (or famous) women and essays in defense of (or attacking) the female sex proliferated during the period and bear witness to the fervor of the controversy.[6] As Moira Ferguson remarks, "Fostered by the influence of Cartesian, Lockean, and spiritual egalitarian views of the world, . . . several sturdy defenses of women . . . launched forthright feminist essays on a surprised public."[7] "The human animal is," Marie de Gournay wrote in 1622, "neither male nor female. . . . And if I am allowed to jest a little in passing, I have a joke that is not altogether irrelevant: nothing resembles a male cat on a windowsill more than a female cat."[8] And Rachel Speght argued similarly, though less wittily, in a 1621 poem:

> Both man and woman of three parts consist,
> Which Paul doth bodie, soule, and spirit call:
> And from the soule three faculties arise,
> The mind, the will, the power; then wherefore shall
> A woman have her intellect in vaine,
> Or not endeavour Knowledge to attaine.[9]

Some women scholars of the period advanced the idea that the education of women is for the benefit of men as well. Bathsua Makin, for instance, suggests that women's education will act as an incentive to men to keep up their studies. Keeping women ignorant, she asserts, is simply a tool of domination: "Let women be fools, and then you may easily make them slaves."

The equation of learning with at least limited power made it politically wise, even essential, that Early Modern women scholars circumscribe the field of application as well as the extent and availability of education for women. Almost invariably they limited their advocacy of learning to women "of estate"; they pled for private (as opposed to public) instruction; they often reassured their audience that they did not wish to hinder "good housewifery"; and they usually linked the support of education to moral probity.

In the realm of belles lettres, the seventeenth century also saw a great flowering of women's art, giving us several women who—either by necessity or by choice—lived by their pen. Whether conforming to Baroque sensibilities or deliberately avoiding them, seventeenth-century women writers left us both with a legacy of feminist aesthetics (marginal in some cases, but surprisingly pronounced in others) and with a complex picture of female experience in the wide range of intellectual perspectives that they chose to provide. Perhaps the most important aspect of this legacy was the growing collective awareness of gender not only as a determining factor of individual identity but also as the parameter of most tenets of social, political, and intellectual endeavor. While during the Middle Ages and the Renaissance, as Merry E. Wiesner observes, women by and large succeeded in intellectual pursuits when they simultaneously rejected the world of women, several Early Modern women writers gave public expression to the recognition "that women as a group suffered discrimination and should be given rights and privileges because of, not despite, their femaleness."[10] The rights and privileges which Early Modern women sought involved remedying the long tradition of patriarchal suppression; their goal was a degree of sexual egalitarianism. One should judge a person by his or her accomplishments, early feminists argued, not by gender. Leonora Christina, the Danish princess imprisoned for her husband's alleged crimes, remarks, for example: "The mind pays no heed to sex and is not changed through external form or figure. . . . often women acquit themselves heroically. How often does one not see effeminate hearts in men's bodies and, on the contrary, virile strength in weak vessels. It is unfair to measure the deed by the person and not to esteem the person by the deed."[11] Her courageous conduct in and out of prison, one should add, bears ample testimony to the "virility" of her mind.

This new awareness that women can succeed *qua* women contrasts most clearly with the perception of medieval writers. Patristic theology and Church tradition predicated the notion of the baptismal equality of the sexes, an equality to which women could rise by embracing virginity and becoming, in St. Jerome's words, "like men." The female ideal as a male clone thus pervaded the consciousness of many medieval women writers. Not surprisingly, therefore, the large majority were single women either confessed in vows (like men) or widowed or abandoned by their husbands. Women writers of the Early Modern era, on the other hand, most typically were married and did not necessarily aspire to the male ideal in their creative efforts. Consequently, seventeenth-century women writers often succeeded in creating female heroes (not heroines who were appendages to men) in an effort to valorize the female experience and women's contributions to society.

The sense of gender-collectivity is also reflected in the modes and models of discourse women writers chose for expression. With some frequency, Early Modern women writers modeled their texts on their female predecessors: the Spaniard María de Zayas y Sotomayor used Marguerite de Navarre's *Heptameron* as a source for her *novelas;* Polish author Elzbieta Druzbacka patterned her fantastic tale of a young prince's life in fairyland, the *Fabula o Ksiazeciv Adolfie, dziedzicu Roksolanii,* after Mme d'Aulnoy's *L'Histoire d'Hypolite, Comte de Duglas;* and Mme d'Aulnoy used Mme de LaFayette as her model for the *Histoire,* to mention a few examples. The works of women scholars of the Early Modern era also bear eloquent testimony to their awareness of shared, gender-specific experience and ideas. Many corresponded with one another, and most were aware of and built upon the works of their female contemporaries. Bathsua Makin and Marie de Gournay both corresponded with Anna Maria van Schurman; Makin incorporated some of Schurman's ideas into her own pedagogical manifesto; Mme de LaFayette's first published work was a literary portrait of her friend Mme de Sévigné; and Ana Caro composed a eulogy for the preface of María de Zayas y Sotomayor's *Novelas*. Moreover, in many of the seventeenth-century women's texts, the same sense of collectivity is felt in the almost inevitable catalogs of famous virtuous/heroic women of the past and the present, whose examples are presented to support the view that women's suppression and supposed inferiority are by no means historic, philosophic, or ethical absolutes.

Yet this female self-consciousness among seventeenth-century authors is complex and at best ambiguous. Some of the women writers are outright misogynists when discussing public positions sought by women or public protests for reform voiced by women. Some deliberately embrace a class- rather than a gender-consciousness when faced with controversial issues. Even the passionately vocal defenders of women's right to education often hasten to provide assurances that female education is to be limited to the nonpublic, nonprofessional spheres and is only to be pursued if servants can discharge household duties.

The new self-consciousness about gender is most clearly pronounced in the writings of the polemicists (such as Makin, de Gournay, and Schurman) and in works of women *not* members of the aristocracy. Aristocratic women appear to view themselves as aristocrats first and women second; some, like the Duchess of Newcastle, deliberately distance themselves from their lower-class and militantly reformist sisters. The self-consciousness also appears to be more pronounced with successful writers: Aphra Behn, María de Zayas y Sotomayor, and Ana Caro, for instance, repeatedly emphasize this awareness of a gender-bond, whereas Camilla Faà Gonzaga, who wrote furtively and produced only one work, does not.

Confessional allegiance does not seem to have been much of a conditioning factor in the literary creativity of seventeenth-century women. Catholic Spain and Poland produced their share of literary women, but so did Lutheran Denmark and Sweden. The most staunchly Calvinistic centers—Geneva or, early in the century, the Palatinate—may have stifled female artistic activity with more than customary vigor, but then one must consider predominantly Calvinistic Holland, where Maria Tesselschade and others flourished. Dutch Calvinism, however, was less hostile than the Genevan variety to belles lettres as a whole, because of the firm links between the burghers and the local aristocracy, the relative openness of a maritime commercial culture, and the degree of religious tolerance granted, albeit grudgingly. An atmosphere in which one is reminded of the existence of options may have played a role in fostering female artistic activity. England and Holland were *relatively* tolerant; Austria and Hungary, at least early in the century, had not forgotten religious diversity in the face of the Habsburg insistence on orthodoxy; and even in the repressively Catholic society of Louis XIV's France, some court intellectuals had not altogether forgotten the heritage of Henri IV or of Montaigne.

The present volume offers selections from the works of seventeenth-

devotion—themes often to be found in the work of the same author. The Baroque is one of the great ages of Western mysticism; at the same time, it is the age in which the scientific world view of Galileo, Kepler, Bacon, Descartes, and Newton definitively ousted the traditional world view—symbolic, poetic, ordered, and hierarchical—that had prevailed since classical antiquity. In an era of such intellectual ferment, it is not surprising that literature itself was keenly intellectual.

The Baroque literary imagination achieved its greatest triumphs in lyric poetry and drama, although one must not forget that it also produced *Don Quijote* and *Paradise Lost.* In both the lyric and the drama, one encounters notable contributions by women writers: Catharina von Greiffenberg, the Austrian mystic and religious poet who achieved remarkable heights of intellectual exaltation; Kata Szidónia Petrőczi, the Hungarian lyric poet and translator of German pietistic writings whose passionately personal poems were not discovered until the nineteenth century; Sibylle Schwarz, the sensitive German lyric poet and dramatist who enjoyed great contemporary popularity; Ludamilia Elisabeth von Schwarzburg-Rudolstadt, whose devotional poems contributed to the formation of the religious vernacular in Germany; the Dutch poet Maria Tesselschade, learned, witty, and much respected by her contemporaries; Ana Caro, one of Golden Age Spain's outstanding playwrights; and Aphra Behn, lyric poet, productive and distinguished dramatist, and one of the founders of the English novel. Even though prose fiction is not one of the dominant genres of the Baroque, the seventeenth century did have its share of glorious novelistic triumphs; the century opened with the *Quijote* and closed with *La Princesse de Clèves* by Mme de LaFayette, perhaps the first true novel in French and certainly one of the greatest.

In whatever genre they chose to write, Baroque authors seem to have been obsessed by two venerable *topoi*—the world as theater, and life as a dream. The relevance to the general preoccupation with appearance versus reality is obvious, and that preoccupation itself may to some extent explain the great efflorescence of dramatic literature in the seventeenth century. In the novelistic genre, on the other hand, the appearance/reality question is frequently bonded with a strong didactic concern, as evidenced by the many "exemplary novels" popular in the seventeenth century. The masterful collections of María de Zayas y Sotomayor and Mariana de Carvajal employ the form to convey their essentially feminist aesthetics, clothed in the conventional topos of the dichotomy between illusion (delusion) and reality, a dichotomy that is frequently presented in a gender-specific manner. The fables of Mme d'Aulnoy, didactic and escapist at the same time, also formulate new and surprisingly feminist perspectives by assigning nontraditional roles to males and female—for example, the nurturing, passive role to man and the guarding, fighting, active role to woman.

century women writers of widely diverse national, social, and educational backgrounds. As one might expect, a high proportion were members of the privileged class—queens, duchesses, countesses, and great court ladies. Also represented, however, are their bourgeois sisters, particularly from countries such as England and the Netherlands in which, by mid-century, the middle classes had consolidated some degree of economic and political power. The writers differ as well in their concerns, perspectives, and literary accomplishments. Some write to satisfy creative aspirations or to express heartfelt piety and devotion. Others take up the pen to vindicate themselves, to record their misery, or to depict society as they see it. Still others are polemicists, who write to persuade or refute. Their biographies and works are a paean to the seventeenth century's diversity in female flesh.

THE BAROQUE is the dominant style of the literature and art of the seventeenth century. To most authorities, that great style—or complex of styles—manifested itself first in Italy and France in the 1580s, and later extended to termini in the various national cultures. It shaded into Neoclassicism in France and England during the 1660s; continued rather later in Spain, Latin America, and the German-speaking world; and lasted well into the eighteenth century in Russia and Eastern Europe.[12] Some historians posit a period of Mannerism that intervened between the Renaissance and the Baroque and included such figures as Montaigne, Cervantes, and Donne. From the comparatist's point of view, however, it is perhaps wise to think of Mannerism as one of the many currents within the Baroque rather than as a separate period.

What then is the Baroque? In technique it is distinguished by devices of extravagance, ingenuity, playfulness, and exaggeration. Sometimes relying heavily on sensuous effect, Baroque authors often go to the opposite extreme and favor forms of expression so intellectualized as to approach the abstract. When Baroque art is sensuous, however, it aims not at the careful mimesis typical of Renaissance art but rather at a kind of frankly artificial phantasmagoria. Whether sensuous or stern, Baroque literature characteristically derives its features from a strenuously active intellect—an intellect aware of the contradictions of experience (above all, the problem of appearance versus reality). Hence Baroque authors extensively use the figures of contradiction: irony, paradox, ambiguity, antithesis. Over their work hovers always the faculty of wit (Italian *ingegno,* Spanish *ingenio,* French *esprit*), which the seventeenth century defined as the ability to discern the similarities among apparently dissimilar phenomena.

Struck by the contradictions of life, Baroque authors thirst for the divine and transcendent unity that they believe must lie beyond those contradictions. Sometimes they seek it in sexual love, sometimes in religious

While the fifteenth-century *querelle des femmes* never disappeared entirely from the literary scene (and was vigorously sustained by the women humanists of Renaissance Italy), it flared up again with renewed vigor after the publication of Jacques Olivier's *Alphabet of the Imperfection and Malice of Women* in 1615. Among the illustrious participants in the debate were Europe's leading women scholars: France's Marie de Gournay; Holland's Anna Maria van Schurman; Italy's Lucrezia Marinella; England's Bathsua Makin, Margaret Cavendish, and Aphra Behn; and Spain's María de Zayas y Sotomayor. More than their fifteenth- and sixteenth-century predecessors, these seventeenth-century women addressed many of the philosophical and theological issues raised by misogyny: Is woman, indeed, an incomplete version of the male? Are men and women equally prone to sin? Are women capable of bettering their lot? Will women be resurrected in female form after the last day of judgment?[19]

Early Modern women scholars advocate boldly and often uncompromisingly the spiritual and intellectual equality of the sexes in their early works. Anna Maria van Schurman, perhaps the most famous (though certainly not the most militant) among them, formulates her views in a syllogistic manner:

> 1) Nature has given every human being the principles or the potential to grasp the principles of all arts and sciences. Women, too, have been given their principles; therefore, women are capable of grasping the arts and sciences.
>
> 2) Whoever has a desire for pursuing the arts and the sciences (cf. Aristotle, Metaphysica I:2), can do so. Women as members of the human species do have this desire; therefore, women are capable of pursuing the arts and sciences.[20]

Schurman's defense of education for women is firmly anchored in ethical concerns; it rejects the prevalent view of the dangers posed by women's learning—namely, the tendency to heresy, pride, and sexual infidelity.[21] Within the Renaissance tradition of More and Vives,[22] who advocated women's education as a means to moral improvement, Schurman insists that education, the study of letters, leads to "the true greatness of soul."[23] She differs from her Renaissance predecessors in her unwillingness to ascribe intrinsic value to household activities[24] and her firmly optimistic view of the inevitable social and intellectual results of the education of women. In her devaluation of exclusively domestic, ornamental occupations for women, Schurman is joined by her English contemporary, Bathsua Makin. Makin argues in her introductory remarks to *An Essay to Revive the Antient Education of Gentlewomen:*

> Before I mention the Objections, I shall state the Propositions I have endeavoured to prove; That which I intend is this, That Persons of competent

> natural parts, indifferently inclin'd and disposed to Learning, whom God hath blessed with Estates, that are not cumbred in the World, but have liberty and opportunity in their Childhood; and afterwards, being competently instructed in all things now useful that concern them as Women, may and ought to be improved in more Polite Learning, in Religion, Arts, and the knowledge of things, in Tongues also as subservient to these, rather than to spend the over-plus time of their youth, in making Points for Bravery, in dressing and trimming themselves like *Bartholomew*-Babies, in Painting and Dancing, in making Flowers of Coloured Straw, and building Houses of stained Paper, and such like vanities.[25]

Unlike Lucretia Marinella and the more radical writers who advocated woman's superiority to man or delivered sweeping defenses of sexual egalitarianism, Schurman represents the more widespread view of seventeenth-century feminists writers: the potential equality of male and female, a potentiality which can be realized through equal education, social acceptance, and public opportunity.

While Schurman is deeply religious and cerebral in the logic of her defense of women, her French contemporary Marie de Gournay is polemical and delightfully irreverent. On the subject of the masculine identity of Christ (and therefore of priests), the Catholic de Gournay argues that Jesus' incarnation as a male is no special distinction bestowed upon the male sex, but simply a matter of historic convenience. "If men pride themselves," she says, "on the fact that Jesus Christ was born of their sex, the answer is that this was necessary for the sake of decency, for if he had been a woman, it would have been impossible for Jesus to go out at all hours of the day and the night and mingle with the crowds to convert them and to help and save mankind, without creating a scandal, especially in the face of the malice of the Jews."[26] A correspondent and admirer of Schurman and a noted philological scholar herself, de Gournay presents her readers with a display of satiric pyrotechnics when faced with male scholars' disregard for female scholarship and art. Speaking of women collectively, de Gournay delivers a moving plea for equality. At the beginning of "The Ladies' Grievance," which she dedicated to the competent French regent Anne of Austria, de Gournay expresses her outrage at patriarchial prejudices by addressing the quintessential concern of women since time immemorial—freedom: "Happy are you, reader, if you do not belong to this sex to whom all good things are forbidden, since to us freedom is forbidden; and whom they [men] prevent from acquiring almost all virtues by keeping us away from power. . . . Happy are you, therefore, for whom it is no crime to be intelligent and learned, since the mere fact that you are a man allows you to think and do as you please and makes whatever you say right, and other people will believe you or at any rate listen to you."[27]

Freedom, of course, is a protean term: ambiguous at best, constantly changing, and almost impossible to define in absolute as opposed to relative terms. Ever since Joan Kelly's pioneering work over a decade ago, scholars have believed that the freedom of Renaissance and Early Modern women declined in the context of an increasing disjunction between the public and private spheres of life through a restricting of female activity to the domestic sphere.[28] More recently, Merry Wiesner has argued that, for Renaissance and seventeenth-century women, freedom specifically meant the ability to participate in public life.[29] Margaret Cavendish, Duchess of Newcastle, for example, wrote in 1656: "Thus by an Opinion, which I hope is but an Erroneous one in Men, we are shut out of all Power and Authority, by reason we are never Imployed either in Civil or Martial Affairs, our Counsels are Despised, and Laught at, the best of our actions are Trodden down with Scorn; by the Over-weening conceit Men have of Themselves, and through a Despisement of us."[30] Demanding equal education for women, Margaret Cavendish defines freedom as access to the means and tools of power, the opportunity of full participation in public and intellectual life. Her French contemporary Marie de Gournay addresses the question of freedom in broader and more psychological terms, a definition that seems to hold true for most seventeenth-century women writers. Freedom, she asserts, is the phenomenon of being taken seriously, of having the opportunity for intellectual and artistic fulfillment and success—aspirations not very different from recent efforts by women scholars to establish a policy of anonymous submissions for publication. In her advocacy of equal opportunities for men and women, de Gournay goes one step further by suggesting that the victims of patriarchal chauvinism are ultimately men as well as women. Concluding her tract, she warns of the dangers presented by the ignorance of prejudice: "Men will find out, moreover, that in order to pay them back, women are seeking to acquire that same fine habit they have of wanting to belittle our sex without even listening to us or reading our writings, for we have listened to them and read their works. They should also remember a dangerous expression of excellent origin: only the less able can live content with their own wisdom, looking over their shoulder at that of others, and ignorance is the mother of presumption."[31]

The present volume is a florilegium of the works of seventeenth-century women writers; it is also a sampler of the emerging feminine aesthetics of early authors who cautiously explore their identities both as poets and as women. Like a sampler, the volume contains different textures, different designs of varying degrees of sophistication, self-awareness and confidence, ranging from the deferential to the self-assured. In selecting the texts, we opted for variety, rather than unity, attempting to present the reader with a diapason of the manifold and varied contributions women made to seventeenth-century intellectual and cultural history.

NOTES

1. Abraham Cowley, *Six Books of Plants,* trans. Aphra Behn (London, 1689), 6:143.

2. On that emerging consciousness and the sense of collectivity, see Moira Ferguson, *First Feminists* (Bloomington, Ind., and Old Westbury, N.Y.: Indiana University Press and The Feminist Press, 1985), 32–37, and *Female Scholars,* ed. J. R. Brink (Montreal: Eden, 1980).

3. For the statistics see Elaine Hobby's unpublished paper "Breaking the Silence," cited by Ferguson, *First Feminists,* 42.

4. A new series edited by Elisabeth Gössman, *Archiv für Philosophie- und Theologie-Geschichtliche Frauenforschung* (Munich: Indiana, 1984–), has assembled many of the texts. Volume 1., *Das Wohlgelehrte Frauenzimmer* (1984), prints selections from the main texts of the seventeenth-century Querelle des Femmes; volume 2, *Eva, Gottes Meisterwerk* (1985), presents texts from the seventeenth and eighteenth centuries; the *Catalogues of Learned Women,* volume 3 (1986), reprints the whole of Johann Caspar Eberti's *Eröffnetes Cabinet dess Gelehrten Frauen-Zimmers* (1706).

5. See, for example, Johannes Bergmann, *Disputatio philosophica mulieribus* (1629); Wilhelm Ignatius Schütz, *Num foeminae christianae conveniat studium litterarum?* (1648); Wilhelm Ignatius Schütz, *Ehren-Preiss dess Hochlöblichen Frauen-Zimmers* (1663); Johannes Gorgias, *Gestürzter Ehren Preiss des hochlöblichen Frauen-Zimmers* (1666). Jacob Thomasius, *De foeminarum eruditione* 1671/1676, all in *Das Wohlgelehrte Frauenzimmer.*

6. Eberti's catalog, for example, contains over five hundred essays on learned women.

7. Ferguson, *First Feminists,* 33.

8. See *The Equality of Men and Women,* p. 19 of this volume.

9. *Mortalities Memorandum* with a *Dreame Prefixed,* in *The Paradise of Women: Writings by Englishwomen of the Renaissance,* ed. B. Travitsky (Westport, Conn.: Greenwood, 1981), 132.

10. Merry E. Wiesner, "Women's Defenses of Their Public Role," in *Women in the Middle Ages and the Renaissance,* ed. Mary Beth Rose (Syracuse, N.Y.: Syracuse University Press, 1986), 15.

11. *Hæltinners Pryd,* ed. Christopher Maaløe (Copenhagen: Reitzel, 1977), 20–21.

12. Among the most important treatments of the Baroque are R. Wellek, *Concepts of Criticism* (New Haven: Yale University Press, 1963), 69–127; Helmut Hatzfeld, *Estudios sobre el barroco* (Madrid: Gredos, 1964); Odette de Mourgues, *Metaphysical, Baroque, and Précieux Poetry* (Oxford: Oxford University Press, 1953); Peter Skrine, *The Baroque* (New York: Holmes and Meier, 1978). Frank J. Warnke's view is expressed in his *Versions of Baroque* (New Haven: Yale University Press, 1972).

13. The Counter-Reformation, largely the work of the Jesuits, was very successful; by the seventeenth century the Catholic Church had managed to stop the spread of Protestantism in France, to reclaim large parts of Hungary and Poland, and to maintain itself in Austria, Bavaria, Ireland, the southern Netherlands, Spain, Portugal, and Italy. Protestantism, on the other hand, retained its sway over England, the Scandinavian countries, Germany, the northern Netherlands, and Switzerland.

14. The process had started earlier and derived from several changes in the position of women. As Joan Kelly remarks, "One was the loss of power women of rank suffered as states eroded the military, juridicial and political powers of aristocratic families. The other was the formation of the preindustrial patriarchal household as the basic social unit, as well as the economic unit of postfeudal society. State legislation in the fifteenth and sixteenth centuries strengthened the household as an instrument of social control. Laws concerning the poor and laws against vagrants, prostitutes, witches, and even religious orders in Protestant countries herded people into households for their livelihood and placed unpropertied males—

and all women—under the governance of the household 'master.' Both these processes weakened traditional supports for female authority and subjected women to patriarchal power in the family and the state" ("Early Feminist Theory and the *Querelle des Femmes,* 1400–1789," *Signs: Journal of Women in Culture and Society* 8 [1982]:23).

15. For a good discussion of the limits on female scholarship and composition, see Margaret P. Hannay, ed., *Silent but for the Word: Tudor Women as Patrons, Translators, and Writers of Religious Works* (Kent, Ohio: Kent State University Press, 1985).

16. Joan Kelly, "Early Feminist Theory and the Querelle des Femmes," *Signs* 84 (1982):5.

17. Women were faced with social and economic restrictions as well. Natalie Z. Davis argues in *Society and Culture in Early Modern France* (Stanford: Stanford University Press, 1975): "As it turned out, women suffered for their powerlessness in both Catholic and Protestant lands in the late sixteenth to eighteenth centuries as changes in marriage laws restricted the freedoms of wives even further, as female guilds dwindled, as the female role in middle level commerce and farm direction contracted, and as the differential between male and female wages increased" (p. 94).

18. Ibid.

19. Kelly, "Early Feminist Theory," 6.

20. Schurman, quoted in *Das Wohlgelehrte Frauenzimmer,* 48.

21. See Gossman, introduction to Eberti's *Eröffnetes Cabinet,* xv.

22. For a summary of the views of Vives on female education, see Valerie Wayne, "Some Sad Sentence: Vives' *Instruction of a Christian Woman,*" in *Silent but for the Word,* 15–29.

23. Schurman, *Opuscula* (Leiden, 1648; 2d ed., 1650), 45.

24. J. R. Brink, ed., *Female Scholars: A Tradition of Learned Women Before 1800* (Montreal: Eden Press, 1980), 73.

25. See *An Essay to Revive the Antient Education of Gentlewomen,* pp. 294–95 of this volume.

26. See *The Equality of Men and Women,*" p. 22 of this volume.

27. See *The Ladies' Grievance,* p. 23 of this volume.

28. See Joan Kelly, *Women, History and Theory,* introduction by Blanche W. Cook et al. (Chicago: University of Chicago Press, 1984).

29. Wiesner, "Women's Defenses," 3.

30. Margaret Cavendish, quoted in "Philosophical and Physical Opinions," in *First Feminists,* 85.

31. See *The Ladies' Grievance,* p. 26 of this volume.

PART ONE

France

EDITOR OF MONTAINE

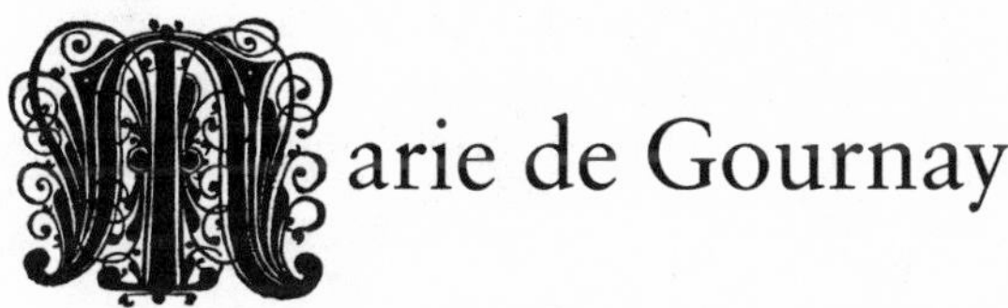

Marie de Gournay

MAYA BIJVOET

She was the only woman whose work appeared in the *Parnasse Royal* of 1635 published in honor of Louis XIII and was among the seventy most famous women of all time celebrated in Jean de la Forge's *Circle of Learned Women* of 1663. Yet it was not until the beginning of the nineteenth century, when the Romantics reexamined the literary development of the early 1700s, that Marie de Gournay (1565–1645) was taken seriously as a philologist and literary critic. Sainte-Beuve realized that there was much "raison et justice" in her defense of Ronsard and the Pléiade and recommended that all academicians read her collected works.[1] Before this deserved rehabilitation as a writer and scholar in her own right, Marie de Gournay had been known mostly as Montaigne's "adopted" daughter and the editor of his *Essays*. Numerous contemporary satires and pamphlets ridicule her as a vain, rather plain (or outright ugly) and prudish bluestocking, so arrogant as to want to emulate the best of men in learning and so pedantic as to voice her ideas with great self-assurance. She was, it seems, the type of person whom opposition makes only more steadfast in her own qualities and opinions.[2]

In addition to eleven different editions of her beloved Montaigne's *Essays* Marie de Gournay produced one short novel; translations from Virgil, Ovid, Cicero, Tacitus, Sallust, and others; numerous poems devoted to people or public occasions; essays on the French language, on poetry and the theory of translation, as well as on education, morality and religion; plus two interesting "feminist" tracts—all published during her lifetime. Her collected works, in fact, saw several reprints in a relatively short period of time.[3]

Though she came from a noble family, Marie de Gournay was far from well-to-do and had to rely on money from printers and from wealthy patrons like the king or Richelieu. She was not "a princess, or a great lady dabbling in literature," but a professional writer.[4] The fact that she never married also set her apart, because secular celibacy for women was still regarded as very eccentric.[5] As an autodidact and a scholar of international reputation, she became an advocate of women's right to education and intellectual fulfillment. In France, she was also the most scholarly female critic before Mme de Staël.[6]

Marie de Gournay was born in Paris on October 6, 1565, the oldest of six children of Guillaume le Jars, who held important functions in the king's household, and Jeanne d'Hacqueville.[7] In 1568, her father bought the estate of Gournay-sur-Aronde in Picardie. He died young in 1577. As the religious wars (six before 1577) made serious inroads on the family's resources and the debts multiplied, Madame le Jars found it necessary to exchange their expensive Parisian life for the more reasonable ways of the country and moved her children to Gournay in 1580. Here, Marie spent all her free time reading and studying in secret. There were very few books available in the castle, yet the girl managed to teach herself Latin and to translate Diogenes Laertius's *Life of Socrates,* which inspired many of her noble ideas. At the age of eighteen or nineteen, she read Montaigne's *Essays.* The book was then hardly known, and Marie's elders regarded her fervent enthusiasm for it as madness. Henceforth, Marie dreamed of meeting the man whose writing had revealed her to herself. During a visit to Paris with her mother in 1588, she learned that Montaigne was there too, wrote him a letter, and was invited to meet with him personally. A deep friendship developed between the fifty-five-year-old mayor of Bordeaux and the young woman from Picardie. Montaigne's stay at Gournay some time thereafter must have been the happiest time of Marie's life. Immediately after his departure she set to work on the novel *Le Proumenoir de M. de Montaigne* (Promenade with M. de Montaigne), and sent the manuscript to him as soon as it was finished. Montaigne never returned it, nor did he ever comment on it. Instead, his wife sent the manuscript back to Marie in 1594, along with Montaigne's manuscript of the *Essays.*

Madame le Jars died in 1591, leaving her oldest daughter with grave family responsibilities. Marie provided generously for her brothers and sisters and kept only a small portion of the estate for herself. Refusing an offer to live with wealthy friends, she decided instead to move back to Paris and live there alone—a controversial decision for which she was severely criticized. A letter from Justius Lipsius in 1593 informed her that Montaigne had died in September 1592. His last letter to Marie had apparently been lost en route. The news caused Marie intense grief, though the package containing her novel and the manuscript of the *Essays* helped revive her spirits. *Le Proumenoir* was published in 1594, and the following year she printed her first edition of the *Essays* with a lengthy preface examining and refuting all criticism leveled against the work. Toward the end of 1595, Marie undertook the dangerous journey to Bordeaux. She stayed at the château of Montaigne for sixteen months, in which time she developed an intimate friendship with his wife and his daughter Léonore. To promote the sales of the *Essays* in the Low Countries and perhaps also in the hope of meeting Lipsius, she traveled north in 1598 and was given an honorable reception in Brussels and Antwerp. There is no evidence that she met Lipsius there.

Then followed a period of struggle for independence. Although Marie had decided to devote her life to letters and to live by her pen, she also wanted to live a life befitting her birth and status but did not have the money for it. She tried, without much success, to secure royal patronage for herself. She took up alchemy, buying expensive equipment and materials, but lost money on it. Gradually, however, she made her way into court circles, particularly the court of Marguérite de Valois, the divorced wife of Henri IV, whose home in Paris became the center of the intellectual elite. Marie must have met there all the important poets and intellectuals of her time. She won the favor of the duc de Névers, who presented her to Henri IV. The latter's assassination in 1610, however, shattered her hopes of securing a royal pension. With her *Defense of the Jesuit Fathers* (vindicating those accused of responsibility for the king's murder) she unwisely entered the field of religious controversy and was slanderously attacked in the *Anti-Gournay,* a publication that sullied her name for a long time to come. But in the privacy of her small apartment over the next few years, she received distinguished visitors from many places and continued to study, vituperate, and write.

A fourth of her collected works, *L'Ombre de la demoiselle de Gournay* (The Shadow of Miss de Gournay), published in 1626, consists of studies on language and poetry which are "a genuine contribution to French literary scholarship."[8] Marie preferred epic and heroic verse, and her basic concept of poetry was that of the Pléiade. She loathed the exaggerated purism and new classicism of the court poet Malherbe and his followers. Unfortunately, she was not much of a poet herself, which must have been a deep personal disappointment. Her religious poems, mostly interpretations of texts from the Latin Missal, are probably the best she wrote. Her poetic efforts must not have gone unrecognized, however, for her verses appear in a number of contemporary collections.

Because she was eager to display her learning, a very unfeminine thing to do at the time, and because she lacked the grace and beauty which might have made men more accepting of her and her ideas,[9] she may have suffered more acutely than other women—the *précieuses,* for example—from the treatment she received on account of her sex. At any rate, she manifests a sense of mission and a devotion to the cause of feminism we do not find in the fashionable learned ladies of the salons.

Her last years passed in relative peace and comfort. She gained Richelieu's favor and most likely received aid from the royal exchequer, so that she could afford a slightly more comfortable life. Some say that the French Academy had its beginnings in her salon in these years.[10] Her collected works appeared for the second and third time, under the title *Les Advis ou les présens de la demoiselle de Gournay* (The Opinions and Writings of Miss de Gournay).[11] She kept revising and changing her own texts, just as she kept working on the *Essays*. The last edition she supervised appeared in 1635 with a dedication to Richelieu, who had made the publication possible. Richelieu died in 1642, Louis XIII in 1643, and she herself at the age of eighty on July 13, 1645.

The eighteenth century, basing its literary theory and praxis on the foundations laid by Malherbe and his school, judged Marie de Gournay even more severely than her contemporaries. They condemned, among other things, her archaism and stubborn defense of the art and poetry of the past. She has also been accused of making too much of the great Montaigne's affection for her, which she supposedly exploited merely to further her own fame and fortune. In part because of a very warm tribute which appeared in the first posthumous edition of the *Essays* and which she later retracted, her editorial integrity has been severely questioned. In book 2, chapter 17 of the 1595 edition, Montaigne states:

> I have taken pleasure in publishing in several places the hopes I have of Marie de Gournay le Jars, my adopted daughter: and certainly beloved by me with much more than paternal love, and wrapped up with me in my solitude and retirement as one of the best parts of my own being. I am no longer concerned for anything in the world but her. If a man may presage from her youth, her soul will one day be capable of the finest things, and among others, of the perfection of that most sacred friendship to which we do not read that any of her sex has ever yet been able to mount: the sincerity and solidity of her character are already sufficient for it, and her affection toward me more than super-abundant, and such, in short, that there is nothing more to be wished, if not that the apprehension she has of my end, because of my five and fifty years when she met me, might not so cruelly afflict her. The judgment she formed of the first Essays, though a woman, and in this age, and so young, and isolated in her province, and the well-known impetuosity with which she long sought my friendship and acquaintance solely on the strength of the esteem she had conceived for me through the Essays, before she ever saw my face, is a circumstance very worthy of consideration.[12]

This passage does not figure in a second manuscript annotated by Montaigne, generally known as the Bordeaux Copy and therefore is assumed to have been written by Marie herself. The assumption, however, "implies a kind of arrogance and deceit for which there is no warrant in our knowledge of the lady's character." In the second and later editions Marie toned down this praise by omitting certain expressions. Some critics have seen such changes as a silent avowal of guilt; others have felt that "it is perfectly easy to understand how, after being exposed . . . to the gibes of the wits, she should have yielded to the pressure of the new decorum and employed an editor's licence in the interest of personal modesty."[13] Montaigne's wishes as to the posthumous publication of the *Essays* are for the most part unknown, but it is clear that he explicitly assigned Marie the main part in this charge. A meticulous study of the Bordeaux Copy and Marie's first edition has indicated that, although she allowed herself liberties which no modern editor would dare take, she was—given the editorial conventions of her day—a most careful and faithful editor, sincerely devoted to rendering the intentions of her "father" with the greatest accuracy possible.[14]

In the seventeenth and eighteenth centuries, the term *d'alliance,* denoting an elective kinship, was used frequently in the case of a special intellectual affinity between two writers or scholars: la Boétie was Montaigne's "brother," Lipsius called Marie his "sister," etc. Yet the terms of Montaigne's eulogy bespeak genuine love, and it has been suggested that the friendship pact masks a violent passion on Montaigne's part.[15] Marie's severe depression following his death may indicate that these feelings were mutual. The relationship remained platonic, however.

Montaigne's work may have inspired or influenced most of what Marie herself wrote, though her originality and creative talent must not be underestimated. The *Proumenoir,* a story she once told Montaigne and then wrote down at his suggestion, is considered one of the first psychological novels in French.[16] Marie took the plot from a 1533 novel by Claude de Taillemont, but she infused the action with a different spirit and introduced her own favorite themes. Her heroine is an unmarried girl who risks her reputation and accepts hardships in order to escape a marriage of convenience and follow the man of her choice. The long digressions in the manner of Montaigne disturbed many of her contemporaries, yet in later editions Marie added onto them. Fundamentally a moralist, she was in fact more interested in the digressions than in the tale itself. Contrary to the commonly held belief that in order to remain chaste women should not be allowed to know too much, she insists that for women, as for men, the basis of virtue is knowledge.

Marie was not a feminist in the modern sense, of course. She was not even so radical as the male feminist Poullain de la Barre (1647–1723), whose writings questioned the conventional notion of male superiority with Cartesian rigor and advocated concrete social and political reform.[17] Marie simply made intelligent, highly readable, and entertaining contributions to the debate concerning women's rights and roles. The fifteenth-century *querelle des femmes* had never really died, and around 1615 it flared up again in full force, ignited by a pamphlet by Jacques Olivier called *Alphabet of the Imperfections and Malice of Women.*

As the "feminists" made their demands and challenged the still-prevailing Renaissance notion of woman, and as traditionalists and misogynists reiterated the arguments used for centuries to justify the status quo, theologians searched the Bible and other religious authorities for answers to some key questions of the debate. Were women truly human beings? Were they, like men, made in God's likeness? Was the female a perfect creation of God or merely an imperfect version of the male? Would she be allowed to participate in the resurrection in the form of a woman, or as a man, or as some sexless being? Were men and women equal before God? Were they equally prone to sin?[18] The view, derived from Plato's *Timaeus* and other works, of the womb as a sort of animal eager to bring forth, and of woman as prey to almost boundless lust to satisfy the cravings of her womb, still persisted widely and justified the strictures imposed on the female sex.

In *The Equality of Men and Women* and *The Ladies' Grievance,* Marie, somewhat prudishly perhaps, completely avoids the medical and biological aspect of the problem and in fact underplays—if not altogether ignores—the physical differences between the sexes. Instead, she focuses on the theological questions and searches the philosophers for evidence in favor of Eve's equality, for ideas to counter the low regard in which women's intelligence was generally held. Since the vast majority of the female population of France at the time was completely illiterate, it is no wonder that women were equated with ignorance, incompetence, and mere physicality. Marie herself, however, provided living proof that education could make a woman intelligent, rational, articulate, and also independent. As opposed to many other advocates of women's rights, Marie de Gournay does not claim that women are superior to men; she believes that, given the opportunities, privileges, and education usually granted to men, women can equal men's accomplishments. The discrepancy in intelligence and achievements between men and women results from differences in education, circumstances, and attitudes, not from an inherent, predestined intellectual inequality. While these ideas are almost commonplace today, they were still outlandish in Marie's time, and she needed to enlist the support of all great minds ancient and modern to make a legitimate case for them.

The *Equality of Men and Women* was first printed in 1622. Marie's originality in this treatise is that she does not try to demonstrate her contentions by reasons (for they are always debatable) nor by examples (for anything can be proven by example) but by the authority of the philosophers, the Church fathers, and Holy Scripture. In the *Republic,* she says, Plato and Socrates pay generous tribute to the female sex and acknowledge women's accomplishments in the arts and in public life. If Socrates, in Xenophon's *Symposion,* makes a few negative comments about the ignorance of women, he does so in full awareness of its causes and without excluding the possibility of exceptions. Considering the nature of the education most women receive, Marie is surprised that their ignorance and incompetence are not worse. The fact that French and English ladies are quite accomplished in social graces and polite conversation compared to Italian women, who are not given the same opportunities for practice, shows that even a little exposure, training, and respect can make a difference. Therefore, if women were to receive the same instruction as men in the sciences and humanities, there is no reason why the gap between the sexes would not close. Both Plutarch and Seneca deny that there is any difference in virtue or talent between men and women. As for their modern counterpart Montaigne, Marie cannot find in his writings an affirmation of her idea; forcing the issue considerably, she notes that the great essayist at least did not categorically condemn women to a secondary role. In reality, Montaigne seems to have subscribed to the traditional belief about the intellectual and moral inferiority of women which disqualifies them for involvement in public life.[19] We also know that he left the education of his daughter Léonore entirely up to his wife and that the girl hence was brought up in the traditional manner. Without openly contradicting her master—and fumbling a bit to save his face—Marie de Gournay asserts her independence from him in this regard. The education of women is the only area where they did not agree.

Aristotle, too, is presented as a champion of female equality, as well as Erasmus, Politian, and Castiglione. Since all the great minds of the past and present acknowledge the merits of women, those men who do not must lack intelligence. In ancient Rome, the Amazons were as venerated as male gods like Theseus or Tantalus. The Salic law which excluded females from succession to a throne was born of demographic necessity, not of prejudice. French peeresses held the same privileges as their husbands, and female regents held as much authority as a king. Marie de Gournay hails the invention of the regency, without which the French nation would have disintegrated. Even very primitive people like the Gauls and the various Germanic tribes respected women, bringing them dowries or consulting with them on both private and public matters. The implied moral for the "civilized" French male of the 1600s is clear.

Man and woman, Marie argues, are above all complementary, created differently for the sake of procreation only. In most things they are alike and similarly endowed. To take the Scripture so literally as to deny that woman was made in the image of God is simply ludicrous.[20] If Saint Paul excluded women from the priesthood and forbade them to raise their voices in the Church, it is not because he despised them but because he feared (with good reason) that priestesses might distract male worshipers with their beauty and feminine charms. The Church venerates female saints like Petronella and Magdalene; moreover, God singled out two women, Judith and Joan of Arc, for a very special mission. Having thus shown the equity of God, the Church, and the Apostles in such matters, Marie then contradicts herself and unwittingly presents Christianity as more profoundly antifeminist than paganism, pointing out that all ancient pagan peoples granted women access to the priesthood. Yet Marie correctly perceives the psychological motivations underlying these Christian customs.

Marie de Gournay was not a systematic philosopher; her method has severe weaknesses. To accuse her of "bad faith," however, is to ignore her context.[21] Most writers of her day, especially the writers of pamphlets, drew from their sources only arguments appropriate to their cause. Still, the effect of her already-quite-conventional arguments is indeed muted by obvious contradictions.

When Marie de Gournay gets very angry, she writes great prose. In the much shorter and more vehement tract *The Ladies' Grievance,* written in 1626, she gives full rein to her satirical talent. A supplement to Montaigne's essay "The Art of Conversation" (3:8), it deals with one aspect of conversation which Montaigne ignores: ladies' participation. Here Marie gives vent to her frustration, which she must have confronted daily, over most men's refusal to engage in a serious discussion with a woman—just as many male authors refused to read the work of their female colleagues. The tract is a passionate plea for intellectual equality and a satirical representation of the way women, in Marie's opinion, were treated in conversation. She proves her psychological insight by showing that the responses of the male participants in this imaginary debate—responses that appear as gestures of politeness, mercy, and tolerance—are in fact evasions motivated by unconscious insecurities and the fear that women indeed may be equal. As a writer, Marie was especially outraged by the prejudices and the repressive system which stunted women's intellectual and moral growth. Her essay ends on an ominous note: one day women will have their revenge. Since they have read the books written by men and know their minds, they also know how little it takes to rise above them.

The issue of mixed conversation was widely debated in the early part of the seventeenth century; indeed, many moralists considered it dangerous for men to converse with women. Marie's feelings of bitterness may not have been shared by all women of her time, but her *Grievance* may well have contributed to the resolution of the question. It was eventually settled in favor of women's free participation in conversation. In the second half of the century very little was written that questioned the morality or pleasantness of mixed social intercourse.[22]

A year after Marie de Gournay's death, Anna Maria van Schurman, her learned friend from the Netherlands who was called "the star of Utrecht" on account of her extraordinary knowledge and artistic talents, published a French translation of her famous treatise on the subject of education for women entitled *Question célèbre* (first printed in Latin in 1641). The question was whether it was appropriate and morally advisable for a girl to devote herself to the study of literature and scientific subjects. Schurman answered the question in the affirmative, using much the same arguments as Marie de Gournay and acknowledging her debt to *Equality*. Unlike Marie de Gournay, however, Anna Marie van Schurman was deeply religious, a staunch Calvinist for whom God and theology became so important that in her last years she abandoned her "frivolous" scholarly pursuits altogether. Schurman also later toned down her "feminist" ideas, stressing that only for women of wealth and leisure was time for study appropriate. She openly expressed her reservations about Marie de Gournay's essay, almost as if she were ashamed of her earlier enthusiasm.

No two women could be more different than the modest, withdrawn Anna Maria van Schurman with her interest in mysticism and pietism and the querulous, skeptical, satirical Marie de Gournay, although both decided to remain unmarried partly because of their love of learning. They apparently admired each other and for many years exchanged polite letters in which their differences are manifest. One such letter, written by Marie de Gournay on October 20, 1639, clearly illustrates her shrewdness and arrogance.[23] Following the conventions of the period she begins with a modesty topos, assuming the posture of almost servile humility and respect:

> Miss,
>
> I would do injustice to the legitimate purpose of my letter if I were to talk about other things in addition to my deep gratitude which your generous favors have so greatly deserved; otherwise, what opportunities wouldn't I have to praise you? Certainly, I will readily admit that to represent them as they deserve surpasses the true limit of my ability, the price of so few services paid by me to the Muses. Therefore, accept this act of gratitude which I only consider worthy of being received by you in these lines because I made the solemn vow that my heart will celebrate it forever.

After this rather tortuous introduction whose only object is to flatter and arouse benevolence in the addressee, Marie de Gournay suddenly drops all pretense. Going straight to the point, she bluntly accuses Schurman of wasting her time on the study of Hebrew and other languages and then concludes politely with a flattering compliment:

> Could I, in passing, be so bold as to give you, philosophically, a little piece of my mind: the study of languages can occupy too much and too long a mind capable of other and better things like your own, nor is there a point in saying, as you do, that you want to read everything in the original because translations are not as good, for whatever books contain that is truly worth the attention of a soul like yours I can find in Latin, or in the most extreme case in Greek, to which languages you can with little trouble add English, Spanish, and above all French, which language the *Essays* have made a necessity for all the universe. If I live another couple of years, I will send you a new edition of my *Advis* in which your name will be mentioned.
>
> Remaining meanwhile with all my heart,
> Miss,
>
> Your very humble and faithful servant,
>
> GOURNAY.

Marie de Gournay's skepticism was typical of the intellectuals of Catholic seventeenth-century France. It was shared by thinkers like Descartes, who also considered reading the Bible in the original a complete waste of time. When Descartes expressed this opinion to Anna Maria van Schurman, she was no longer keen on his friendship. To Marie de Gournay she replied:

> As to your opinion that I amuse myself too much studying languages, I can assure you that I devote to them only my free time and sometimes with long intervals; if only you allow me to make an exception for the Holy language. For besides having as subject the word of God which must be the primary object of our thoughts, and besides the fact that no translation can render the simple meaning of its holy mysteries, it has qualities and ornaments which all the elegance and grace of the Latin and Greek language cannot match. The words of Saint Hieronymus: "let us learn here on earth those things whose knowledge will stay with us until in heaven," certainly apply to Hebrew, the usefulness of which (in the opinion of the wisest of men) will last until the other life.[24]

This deep religious feeling was alien to Marie de Gournay. Anna Maria van Schurman was undoubtedly a greater scholar, with more modesty and tact than Marie de Gournay, but she lacked the imagination and the fire which make much of Marie's writing so appealing.[25]

Recent studies of Marie's literary ideas suggest that her predilection for the poetry of the Pléiade, especially Ronsard, and for the metaphors of a poet like Du Perron cannot be dismissed simply as proof of her old-fashioned, anticlassical taste. Though her love of learning, the classics, and Reason made her a "daughter of the Renaissance," she was also a product of the Baroque age. She shared the Baroque writer's love of the unexpected and admired the Pléiade particularly for its conception of poetry as a dynamic, free creation of genius—in other words, its specifically Baroque element.[26] Even her feminism is in some ways allied to the Baroque period. Feminism played an important part in French literature of the first half of the seventeenth century, especially during the age of Louis XIII and Anne of Austria, to whom *Equality* is dedicated; its popularity as a theme contributed to, and perhaps even influenced, the development of Baroque literature.[27] For these reasons, though she was old-fashioned and attached to the past in certain ways, Marie de Gournay was also very much a woman of her time.

Except for incidental lines translated by critics for the purpose of quotation, this is the first time that parts of Marie de Gournay's work have appeared in English. The translations are based on Mario Schiff's 1910 edition, *La Fille d'alliance de Montaigne: Marie de Gournay.* Schiff uses the 1622 edition of *The Equality of Men and Women* and the 1626 edition of *The Ladies' Grievance.*

NOTES

1. Sainte-Beuve, *Tableau de la poésie française au XVI*[3] *siècle,* 274–82.
2. Alan Boase, *The Fortunes of Montaigne,* 57.
3. The volume comprising over 1,200 pages appeared in 1624, 1634, and again in 1641.
4. Boase, *The Fortunes of Montaigne,* 55.
5. Ian Maclean, *Women Triumphant,* 88.
6. Domna Stanton, "Women as Object and Subject of Exchange: Marie de Gournay's *Le Proumenoir* (1594)," 11.
7. The details of Marie de Gournay's life, long shrouded in darkness except for a few stories related ad infinitum by the satirists, have been gathered and set forth with objectivity and respect by Wellesley professor Marjorie Ilsley, who has done much to rehabilitate Marie. The following biographical information is based on Ilsley's *A Daughter of the Renaissance.*
8. Ilsley, *A Daughter of the Renaissance,* 145.
9. Mario Schiff considered this one major cause of her lack of popularity (*La Fille d'alliance de Montaigne,* 37).
10. Ilsley treats the question of Marie's possible role in the foundation of the French Academy extensively (*A Daughter of the Renaissance,* 220–41).
11. The title of the first edition of 1626, *L'Ombre de la demoiselle de Gournay,* by which she meant to convey both the insignificance of the work and its faithful representation of her own views, was changed to the less pretentious *Les Advis ou les présens* on the recommendation of the printer.
12. Jacob Zeitlin, trans., *The Essays of Michel de Montaigne,* 577.
13. Ibid., 433–34.
14. Most recent commentators agree on this point. See Ilsley, *A Daughter of the Renaissance,* 44–47; Boase, *The Fortunes of Montaigne,* 63; Jean Morand, "Marie le Jars de Gournay," 53.
15. Morand, "Marie le Jars de Gournay," 54.
16. See especially Ilsley, *A Daughter of the Renaissance,* 48–60, and the article by Domna Stanton.

17. Poullain de la Barre wrote three books: *L'Egalité des deux sexes* (1673), *De l'education des dames* (1674), and *De l'excellence des hommes* (1675), which were mostly unsuccessful with both male and female readers.

18. See Maclean, *Woman Triumphant,* 2–8.

19. *Essays* 1:27, 2:8, 2:9, 3:3, 3:5.

20. Saint Paul's comment, in 1 Cor. 11:17, on these verses in Genesis (1:26–27) seems to suggest that woman in fact is *not* made in the image of God.

21. Rowan, "Seventeenth-Century French Feminism, 276.

22. Maclean, *Woman Triumphant,* 143–51.

23. My translation. The letter is in the Royal Library in The Hague, Nr. 861023 HSS.

24. My translation from a quote in A. H. M. Douma, *Anna Maria van Schurman en de studie der vrouw* (Amsterdam: H. J. Paris, 1924), 27.

25. The friendship between the two women deserves further study. It has been discussed by Schiff, *La Fille d'alliance de Montaigne,* 117–21, and by Ilsley, *A Daughter of the Renaissance,* 212–15.

26. Peggie Holmes, "Mlle de Gournay's Defense of Baroque Imagery," 129 and passim. Marie's most interesting philological essays have been edited by Anne Uildriks, *Les Idées littéraires de Mlle de Gournay.* See also Heinrich Lausberg, "Marie de Gournay et la crise du langage poétique."

27. Maclean, esp. pp. 264–65.

The Equality of Men and Women

TO THE QUEEN[1]

Madame:

Those who devised for the King, your father, the emblem of a sun with the words: "For me the Sun never sets," did more than they realized, for by so symbolizing the greatness of this Prince of the Stars, who can be seen at work on one of his estates almost all the time without even a night's interruption, they made the emblem hereditary for Your Majesty and foretold your virtue as well as the happiness of the French people under your august presence. Indeed, Madame, the light of virtue will never falter in Your Majesty, nor will the fortune and happiness of the people it shines upon. Since you are still at the dawn of your years and your virtue, dare to take courage, Madame, and strive to attain simultaneously the noon of both the former and the latter; I am talking about those virtues which mature only with time and inner refinement, for you have already reached, early in the morning, the noon-hour of some other highly recommendable virtues, among them faith, charity toward the poor, and conjugal love. But, to be sure, the endeavor requires courage as great and powerful as Your Majesty herself, however great and powerful she may be, for kings fall victim to that unfortunate, infernal plague of flatterers, who always manage to find their way into the palaces and make it infinitely more difficult for sovereigns than for persons of lower status to attain virtue and the clarity of thought which is virtue's guide and nurse. I know of only one sure means by which Your Majesty may hope to reach the noon of both at the same time and that is the serious study of good prudent and moral books, for when a prince has educated his mind in this way he will be more astute than the flatterers and they will no longer dare take advantage of him. Only the dead can teach rulers and kings useful lessons, for the living consist of two groups, those who are mad and mean like the flatterers in question, who can nor want to speak sensibly in the presence of a king, and those who are wise and good and who are both capable and willing to speak sensibly, but afraid to do so. Indeed, Madame, it is in virtue that persons of your status must seek true highness and the Crown of Crowns, especially since they have the power, though not the right, to violate the laws and justice and will encounter as much danger and more shame than other human beings when they do this. Hence a great king himself teaches us that the greatness of the king's daughter is all inside. But how rude of me! While all other people address their princes and kings with adulation and praise, I am so bold as to approach my queen with a sermon! Forgive me my zeal nonetheless, Madame, for I can't wait to hear France applaud and exclaim wherever Your MAJESTY, new Sun of virtue, passes: "For me the light will never go out." I am eager to see you become, as your worthy beginnings have given me hope you will, the living evidence of the thesis I offer here in humility, according to which men and women are equal. Because of your unique greatness, bestowed upon you by birth and marriage, you will serve both as an example for our sex and as an object of emulation for all men in the entire universe, if you rise to the level of virtuousness, I mean. And, Madame, as soon as you decide to shine with this beautiful and precious luster, all of our sex will sparkle in the splendor of your rays. I am, Madame, Your Majesty's humble and obedient servant and subject,

GOURNEY

Most writers who take up the cause of women against men's arrogant belief in their own superiority pay them back in full and claim that women are superior. I flee all extremes and am content to make women equal to men, Nature opposing superiority as much as inferiority in this respect. Yes, for some men it is not even enough to place themselves above women; they also judge it necessary to limit women's activities to the distaff and to the distaff alone.[2] But women may take solace in the fact that this disdain comes only from those men they would least want to resemble, people who, if they belonged to it, would lend probability to the ugly things vomited about the female sex, and who feel in their heart that they have nothing to recommend themselves but the fact that they belong to the other. They have heard it blazoned out in the streets that women lack dignity and intelligence, even the temperament and organs necessary to acquire intelligence, and their eloquence triumphs when preaching these maxims, especially since *dignity, organs,* and *temperament* are such handsome words. These men have not learned, on the other hand, that the most important quality of an inept person is to rely on popular belief and hearsay. See how such minds compare the two sexes: for them, the highest point of excellence to which a woman may aspire is to resemble the most ordinary of men. It is as difficult for us to imagine that a great woman could call herself a great human being as to acknowledge that a man could rise to the level of a god. These men are braver than Hercules himself, for he defeated twelve monsters in twelve battles, while they undo half of the world's population by one single word. Yet who will believe that people who strive to elevate themselves and strengthen their position through the weakness of others are capable of elevating and strengthening themselves on their own? The funny thing is that they think they are clear of impudence when they refrain from vilifying our sex, yet they are guilty of the same thing when they praise and glorify themselves, whether in particular or in general, and no matter how falsely, as if the veracity of their boasts received its measure and quality from their impudence. God knows that I have seen joyous vaunters like that, whose inflated phrases soon became some of the most cutting statements disparaging women. But if these men are truly intelligent and gallant, which they claim they are as if by law, then why don't they officially lower the status of women by a second law stating the opposite? Though I think very highly of the moral and intellectual capacities of the ladies, I will not claim at this time that I can prove my point by means of arguments, for they can always be refuted, nor with examples, since that is much too common, hence only by referring to the authority of God Himself and of the pillars of His Church and of the great men who served as guiding lights to the universe. Let us start first with these glorious witnesses and reserve God and the holy Church fathers for later, like a treasure.

Plato, whose divinity remains undisputed, and hence also Socrates, his interpreter in his writings and the spokesman of his ideas (if they did not originate with Socrates, his most divine preceptor, himself), in the *Republic* and elsewhere attribute to women the same rights, faculties, and functions as to men.[3] They maintain, moreover, that women have often surpassed the men of their country, and women indeed have invented some of the highest arts and surpassed men, as monumental and sovereign examples even, in all kinds of accomplishments and virtues in the most celebrated cities of antiquity, among them Alexandria, first of the Empire after Rome.[4] Consequently, it could happen that these philosophers, miracles of Nature, to add distinction to the truly important speeches in their books, put them in the mouths of Diotima and Aspasia: Diotima, whom the latter does not hesitate to call his mistress and teacher in the highest branches of learning, while he himself is the preceptor and master of the human race.[5] Theodoret acknowledges this so readily in his Oration of Faith that it is likely, it seems to me, that he was in favor of a positive view of our sex.[6] After this evidence of Socrates' respect for women, one can see well enough that if in Xenophon's *Symposion* he comments negatively here and there on the wisdom of women in comparison with that of men, he is aware that their ignorance and lack of experience is due to their upbringing, or in the worst case he means this in a very general sense, leaving ample and frequent opportunity for exceptions, which is something the garrulous talkers we are concerned with completely fail to do.

It is true that women attain a high degree of intelligence less frequently than men do, but it is a miracle that the lack of good instruction, the very abundance even of bad talk and teaching, does not produce worse results or prevent them from acquiring intelligence altogether. Is there a greater difference between men and women than among women themselves, depending on their education and according to whether they were brought up in the city or in a village or according to the nation to which they belong? Why couldn't women overcome the gap that usually exists between the minds of men and their own, if they were given the same instruction as men in practical affairs as well as in letters? For a good education is as important as the cultivation of one of its aspects, grace in social intercourse, for example, which French and English ladies have ample opportunity to acquire while Italian ladies receive none, so that the latter are generally far surpassed by the former in this respect. In general, I say, for in certain individual cases Italian women can sometimes excel. After all, we got from them two queens, to whose wisdom France is deeply obliged. Why, really, cannot education play a decisive role and bridge the distance we observe between the intelligence of men and women, considering that in this example here the worst surpasses the best with the aid of just one of its parts, that is, as I said, grace and intelligence in conversation; for the appearance of Italian women is more subtle and more suitable to refine the mind, as is evident in their men when compared with Frenchmen and Englishmen. Plutarch maintains in his treatise about the virtuous deeds of women, that men and women are equally virtuous. Seneca, on the other hand, says in his *Consolations* that Nature has not treated the ladies ungratefully or limited or diminished their virtues and intellect more than the moral character and intelligence of men, but rather has endowed us with the same vigor and with the same capacity for honest and praiseworthy deeds. Having considered these two, let us now see what that third master of the triumvirate of human and moral wisdom thinks in his *Essays*. It seems to him, he says, even though he does not know why, that one rarely finds women who are worthy of governing men. Doesn't he mean that in particular cases women may be the equal of men and admit that, if he is not speaking in general, it is for fear of being wrong, even though he could blame his restriction on the poor and uncomely education our sex generally receives? Elsewhere in the same work he does not forget to quote and discuss, incidentally, the authority which Plato attributes to women in his *Republic*, and he also says that Anthistenes denies that there is a difference between the two sexes in talent and virtue. As for the philosopher Aristotle, stirring heaven and earth, he did not look negatively in a general sense, as far as I know, upon the female sex; instead, he was rather positive, relying no doubt on the judgment of his spiritual father and grandfather, Socrates and Plato, as on something permanent and unchanging because coming from individuals through whose mouths, we cannot deny this, the entire human race and indeed Reason itself have pronounced their verdict.[7] Is it necessary to quote the numerous other ancient and modern thinkers of illustrious renown—among the latter, Erasmus, Politian, or the honest and pertinent preceptor of the courtiers[8]—and so many other famous poets who all disagree with these detractors of the female sex and believe in her qualities, aptitude, and suitability for every function and for every recommendable and worthy activity? To tell you the truth, women console themselves with the thought that those who scorn their merits cannot really be intelligent if all these great minds are. An intelligent man can never say, even if he believes it, that moral qualities and talents are in short supply in women, unless he first has all these scholars nominated buffaloes by a decree in order to invalidate their opinions which do not agree at all with his own feelings of depreciation.[9] But then entire nations, even the most sublime, would have to be dubbed buffaloes, like the people from Smyrna in Tacitus who at that time in Rome claimed that they were descendants of Tantalus, son of Jupiter, or of Theseus, grandson of Neptune, or of an Amazon, whom they hence regarded as highly as these gods, in order to obtain precedence in nobility over their neighbors. As for the Salic law which deprives women of the crown, it exists only in France and was invented at the time of Pharamond solely in the interest of the wars against the Empire whose yoke our fathers managed to shake off, the female sex being probably physically less fit to bear arms and having to bring forth and nourish children.[10] However, we must also mention that as the peers of France were created at first as a sort of associates of the kings, as their name indicates, the peers' wives have the same rank, privileges, and votes as the peers. Similarly, the Lacedemonians, a virtuous and generous people, consulted their women on all matters private and public. It has been good for the French that they created the regency and female regents with the same authority as the kings, for without that how many would not have lost control over their state? We know now very well from experience how necessary such a remedy is in case of the king's minority. Tacitus relates that the Germanic tribes, bellicose people who were finally vanquished rather than defeated after more than two hundred years, brought dowries to their wives and not the other way around. Some tribes among them, moreover, were always ruled by our sex. And when Aeneas gave Dido the scepter of Ilion, the scholiasts say that this was because the oldest daughters, which this princess was too, of yore ruled over royal houses. Could one wish for two more beautiful arguments against the Salic law—if that law can tolerate two counter-arguments at all? Neither our old Gauls nor the Carthaginians despised women; when they were united in Hannibal's army to cross the Alps, they appointed the wives of the Gauls to arbitrate in cases of conflict between them. Even though men in many places have deprived our sex of its share of the best advantages, this larceny and the suffering it causes is clearly due to the difference in physical strength rather than to a lack of mental capacities or moral worth on our part. And physical strength is such a low virtue that there is a greater difference between man and beast than between man and woman in this respect, animals being both the strongest and the lowest. If the same Latin historiographer tells us that, where force rules, equity, probity and modesty itself are the attributes of the conqueror, are we then surprised to find that intelligence and human qualities in general are defined in terms of men, at the exclusion of women?

The human animal, moreover, is, to be precise, neither male nor female, the sexes having been created not for their own sake but *secundum quid*, that is for the purpose of propagation only. What differentiates man from the other animals is the human soul. And if I am allowed to jest a little in passing, I have a joke that is not altogether irrelevant: nothing resembles a male cat on the windowsill more than a female cat. Man and woman are so completely one that, if man is more than woman, then woman is more than man. Man was created male and female, say the Scriptures, considering the two as one.[11] Hence Jesus Christ is called the Son of Man, even though he was born of a woman. The great Saint Basil later said: "Man and woman are equally virtuous, because God has created them in the same way and endowed them equally; *masculum et foeminam fecit eos*. Hence, if their nature is one and the same, they will behave similarly, and whenever the deeds are the same, they must be evaluated and praised the same way."[12] That is the opinion of this powerful pillar and venerable witness of the Church. It is useful to remember in this respect that certain ancient cavilers have gone so far as to deny that the female sex, as opposed to the male sex, is made in the likeness of God, which likeness they must have taken to be, as far as I can tell, in the beard.[13] On top of that, and as a result, these people also had to deny that women resemble men, since they cannot resemble men without resembling Him whom men resemble.

God Himself has granted women the prophecy to the same degree as men, and has made women judges, instructors, and leaders of his people, loyal in peace and in wartime, and what is more, He has made them triumph in the great victories women have often won in different parts of the world. And over what kind of people, do you think? Over Cyrus and Theseus and also over Hercules, whom they gave a good beating even if they did not defeat him. Penthesilea's fall was the very culmination of Achilles' glory.[14] Hear how Seneca and Ronsard speak of him:

> He vanquished the Amazon, last terror of the Greeks,
> flinging Penthesilea into the dust.

Have women, moreover (this is only an incidental remark), excelled less in loyalty, which involves all the most important virtues, than in intelligence, magnanimity, or fighting spirit? Paterculus tells us that at the time of the Roman proscriptions, the loyalty of the children was nil, that of the freedmen weak, but that of the women very strong. Hence, if Saint Paul, to continue my journey through the testimonies of holy men, excludes women from the priesthood and forbids them to speak in the Church,[15] he clearly does not do this out of contempt for women but rather out of fear that they would lead some men into temptation if they showed so publicly and openly the beauty and grace they have in greater measure than men, which would be inevitable when ministering and preaching. I believe it is clear that contempt is out of the question here, for this apostle mentions a woman, Thesbé, as his coadjutor in the service of our Lord—not to mention Saint Petronella's profound influence on Saint Peter.[16] Saint Magdalene is considered in the Church the equal of the apostles *par apostolis*.[17] Indeed, the Church has allowed an exception to that rule of silence for the woman who preached in the cave near Marseilles for thirty years while all of Provence listened to her. If anyone should question this evidence of predications by women, we can ask him what it was that the Sibyls did but preach through divine inspiration to the entire universe about the future coming of Jesus Christ. All ancient nations allowed women to be priestesses on the same basis as men. The Christians are at least forced to acknowledge that women can administer the sacrament of baptism. But if we were justly given the capacity to administer that sacrament, then which faculty necessary to administer the others do we justly lack? One could say that the fact that dying babies need to be baptized has forced the ancient fathers to establish this custom in spite of themselves, but there is no doubt they would never have believed that emergency situations would justify their doing wrong to the point of allowing the sacred ritual of a sacrament to be violated and calumnized. And yet, since they did grant women the right to administer this sacrament, it is clear that the only reason for forbidding them to administer the other sacraments must be to keep authority in the hands of men, either because they belong to the same sex or to make sure that, rightly or wrongly, there is peace between the two sexes by making one of the two weak and inferior. Surely, what Saint Jerome writes on our account is wise, namely that in matters of religious service a person must be judged on the basis of his faith and knowledge of doctrine, not his sex: a judgment which, if we interpret it as being of general application, provides the more reason to give the ladies access to all honorable activities and branches of learning. That is exactly the intention of this saint, who personally has much regard for women and considers them very capable. Then there is Saint John the Eagle, most beloved of the evangelists, who did not despise women any more than Saint Peter or Saint Paul or the two Church fathers Saint Basil and Saint Jerome, for he addresses his epistles specifically to them.[18] I won't even mention the numerous other saints and fathers who speak to the same effect in their writings. As for Judith, I would not dare mention her, any more than I bring up other examples of this caliber, even though there are many of them, all as heroic in one way or another as the most illustrious men—I would not mention Judith if her conduct had been inspired exclusively by her own motivation and will.[19] I will give no isolated examples here for fear that they will be perceived not as proof of the qualities and talents of our sex but as the fruits of my imagination and enthusiasm. Judith's case, however, deserves a place here, because the truth is that what she did, as a young woman in the midst of so many cowardly and weakhearted men, in such extremity, something so sacred and difficult, with such an important result as the safety of a people and a city loyal to God, all this seems a question of divine inspiration and of God's powerful benevolence toward women rather than a purely voluntary human deed. The same seems true for the feats of the virgin of Orleans, which happened in more or less the same circumstances but were of wider and greater usefulness, involving something as important as the safety of a great kingdom and its prince.

This illustrious Amazon, instructed in the cares of Mars,
Mowing down squadrons, defying fate,
A sturdy breastplate over her round breast,
The purple tip sparkling with divine grace,
To crown her chief with glory and laurels,
This virgin dares confront the most famous warriors.[20]

Let me add that Saint Magdalene is the only soul to whom the Redeemer ever promised this august favor, saying the words: "In all places where the Gospel will be preached, they shall speak of you."[21] Jesus Christ also revealed his wondrous and glorious resurrection first to the women in order to make them, as one venerable father says, apostles to his apostles, with the message: "Go to the Apostles, He said, and tell them and to Peter what you have seen."[22] I must remind you, though, that He revealed His new birth to both women and men in the person of Anna, daughter of Phanuel, who recognized him at the same time as that good old man Saint Simeon.[23] And this birth had been predicted among the Gentiles only by the aforementioned Sibyls, a unique privilege of the female sex. What an honor for us women was also Pilate's story of a dream which appeared to one of us, at the exclusion of all men, and in such important circumstances.[24]

If men pride themselves on the fact that Jesus Christ was born of their sex, the answer is that this was necessary for the sake of decency, for if he had been a woman, it would have been impossible for Jesus to go out at all hours of the day and the night and mingle with the crowds to convert them and to help and save mankind, without creating a scandal, especially in the face of the malice of the Jews. Besides, whoever is so stupid as to imagine God to be either masculine or feminine openly shows that he is as bad a philosopher as a theologian. His name does have a masculine ring to it, but that does not necessarily mean that we should accept one sex rather than the other. Moreover, the advantage men have because of His incarnation in one of their sex (if, considering the explanation just given, they can indeed derive a sense of superiority from that at all) is compensated for by the fact that He was conceived in the body of a woman, because of the complete perfection of this woman, who is the only one among all human beings since the fall of our first parents to bear the title perfect and unique among mankind through her assumption into heaven.[25] Finally, if the Scriptures declare that the husband is the master of his wife, the worst stupidity a man can commit is to conclude that therefore he is worthy of being his wife's master.[26] On the basis of the examples, authorities, and reasons enumerated here, by which the equality of God's favors and benevolence toward the two species or sexes and even their very unity has been proven, and considering that God proclaims: "The two will be but one," and also says: "The man will leave his father and mother to follow his wife," we must conclude that this statement was motivated only by the need to promote peace in marriage.[27] This would no doubt require that one party yield to the other, and the male with his physical strength and his power could not bear to submit himself. But even if it were true that woman was forced to submit to man in punishment for the sin with the apple, as some people maintain, that still is in no way an argument in favor of this alleged superiority of men. Suppose we believed that the Scriptures indeed order woman to submit to the authority of man because she cannot think as well as he can, see here the absurdity that would follow: women would be worthy of having been made in the likeness of the Creator, worthy of taking part in the most holy Eucharist, of sharing the mysteries of the Redemption, Paradise, worthy of the vision, even possession, of God, but not of the status and privileges of men. Wouldn't we be saying then that men are more precious and sacred than all these things, and wouldn't that be the most grievous blasphemy?

The Ladies' Grievance

Happy are you, reader, if you do not belong to this sex to whom all good things are forbidden, since to us freedom is forbidden; and whom they [men] prevent from acquiring almost all virtues by keeping us away from power, in the moderation of which most virtues are formed, to leave us as our only form of happiness and as our only sovereign virtues: ignorance, foolishness, and subservience. Happy are you, therefore, for whom it is no crime to be intelligent and learned, since the mere fact that you are a man allows you to think and do as you please and makes whatever you say right, and other people will believe you or at any rate listen to you. But not to talk about the other grievances of our sex, let me ask you about the insolent manner in which we are ordinarily treated in conversation, to the extent that we participate in conversation at all. I have so little, or actually it would be more correct to say, so much pride that I am not afraid to admit that I know about this from experience. Even though the ladies had the powerful arguments of Carneades, there is not even the puniest of men who does not rebuke them, with the assent of most of those present, when with just a smile or a nod of the head, his silent eloquence proclaims: It is only a woman speaking.[28] This man here will dismiss it as spite or aggravation or at least as mere obstinacy when a woman disagrees with his opinion, no matter how discreet she tries to be, either because he does not believe that women can disturb his precious mind by any means other than spite and obstinacy or because he feels deep inside his heart that he is poorly prepared for the battle and needs to start a silly quarrel about nothing in order to get out of it. And don't think that I am inventing something crazy when I relate this estoppel to his encounter with some minds he might perhaps find difficult to defeat. Another one will give up for sheer weakness halfway through the conversation, pretending he does not want to importune anyone of our sex, and will be considered both the winner and a gentleman. Yet another, though convinced (he says) that women are capable of holding their own in a debate, does not think that his sense of propriety allows him to challenge such a mind in a legitimate duel, especially since his sense of propriety is based on the worthy opinions of the majority of men who have great disdain for our sex, as I have pointed out before. Could we stretch the meaning of the following lines from Horace to contain a reproach about this kind of longing and fear for undue popular approval or reprobation?

> Anyone who has ever cherished or feared
> False honor or false shame,
> Must have coveted in his heart
> Lies and falsehood.

A slavish and worthless type of intelligence is the kind which only can, and only wants to, act and be in accordance with the opinions of a mass of fools and idiots, for that is what we should call the majority of people. Even more worthless and sickening, however, is the kind of justice which gives satisfaction to others only when it is in its own interest. It is far from leading an ordinary person by the nose to pretend that he is leading us by the nose. But let us continue.

That man who pronounces thirty stupidities will nonetheless win the prize on account of his beard or because of the pride he takes in some presumed ability which he and the whole company measure according to his wealth and social status without thinking that often these things are the result of the person's being more of a buffoon and a more successful flatterer than his friends, or a result of his mean submissiveness or some other vice, or the result of the favors and generosity of people who would not grant a place in their hearts, or be on intimate terms with, anyone more capable than he. This one here will be hit if he does not have the intelligence to perceive the hurling blow of a female hand. Another one, who is aware of it, tries to elude the blow by mocking the conversation and turning it perpetually into meaningless prattle, or he will change the topic and steer the conversation in another direction and begin to vomit pedantically all sorts of very pretty things which no one has asked him for; or he will complicate and distort the arguments with some juggling of logic and foolish ostentation, convinced that he will dazzle his antagonist with the brilliance of his intelligence and the various ways in which he can display it. There are also people, on the other hand, who know how easy it is to take advantage of the ear of the listeners, who are very rarely able to evaluate the order and development of a debate and conversation or the strength of the discussants, and who are also very rarely able to remain unimpressed by the pseudo-knowledge these people spit up as if they had to account for all of their schooling, and therefore cannot determine when such gallantries are an escape or a victory. Hence, all these gentlemen need to do to win the prize is flee the blows, and then they can harvest as much glory as they are willing to save themselves work. These few words must be said about the particular part women play in conversation, for the art of conversation in general and its perfections and deficiencies have already been discussed in a most complete and excellent manner.[29] Let me add to this that not only the lower ranks among the literati stumble like this, putting down women, for even among the authors, alive and dead, who have acquired quite a literary reputation in this century, sometimes with very serious works, I have known some who thoroughly despised all books written by women without even bothering to read them to see of what stuff they are made, and without wanting to find out first whether they themselves could produce books worthy to be read by all kinds of women. This indeed is a convenient habit in accordance with popular taste which enhances the brilliance of their intelligence. For in order to be respected by general opinion, that many-headed beast, especially at court, all a man needs to do is despise a few people here and there and swear that as far as he is concerned he is the *prime del monde*, just like that poor fool who thought she was a picture of beauty and ran through the streets of Paris with her hands on her hips, shouting: "Come and see how pretty I am." But to be charitable, I wish these people had given us more evidence of their flexibility and demonstrated to us that their intelligence is superior to ours in every individual case everywhere, or at least that it equals that of their neighbors, yes even ordinary neighbors. Then we would not be obliged to read, in the books of those among the gang who have the guts to write, horrible translations of good authors whom they have no business translating, or insipid and unimportant ideas, when they take it upon themselves to philosophize. The only spice in such works consists in a certain varnish of language over very meager subject matter, the fluff of whipped egg whites. Which reminds me of a prefatory epistle I chanced upon the other day, written by a certain person belonging to that group of men who are proud that they never spend their time reading anything written by a woman. My God, you should see the number of diadems, the amount of glory and Orient, of splendor and Palestine fetched from a hundred miles beyond the river Jordan! And, good Lord, the host of paragraph marks, which the author regards as so many symbols of unfathomable depth! Aren't authors who seek appropriate ornamentation in exaggerated and pompous words very far from finding it, especially in prose? Those whom nature has given a thin, gaunt body, says a man of great merit, tend to fill it up with padding, and those who lack imagination and whose ideas are dry dress them up with words. What a shame that France regards the talents of her writers with such a dark eye and such poor judgment that she has bestowed an outstanding literary reputation on an author who, just like the father of this epistle, never had any recommendable qualities but this varnish and a little knowledge of scholasticism. Since the man is dead, I have no reason to mention his name. Finally, to wish my fellow beings well again, I would also desire that some of that flock of scholars and writers who despise this puny and ill-treated sex would stop employing the printers and so leave us at least in doubt as to whether they can write a good book, for they take this doubt away from us when they build their work with the labor of others, in details as well as in general, for fear that this honest man, whom the *Essays* have ridiculed for the same reason while their author was still alive, should remain without company. If I had the courage to take the trouble to defend the rights of the ladies, I would quickly have found supporters in Socrates, Plato, Plutarch, Seneca, Antisthenes, and also in Saint Basil, Saint Jerome, and other such minds, whom these pseudo-scholars so liberally contradict and denounce when they make a difference, and a universal one at that, between the merits and talents of the two sexes. But besides being sufficiently punished by showing that they are unaware of their stupidity, condemning the particular through the general (granted that the mental capacity of women is inferior in general), and by being so stupid as to ignore audaciously the judgment of great men like this (and I don't even mention the modern thinkers or the eternal decree of God Himself, who created both sexes from one and has also endowed women with all the gifts and favors he bestows upon men, as I have set forth more extensively in *The Equality of Men and Women*), they will let us say to them, if they like, that we do not know whether they are capable of defeating women by the sovereign law of their good pleasure which condemns us to stupidity, or whether they experience glory in their efforts to erase us with their disdain. But we do know several women who would never pride themselves on such a small accomplishment as outshining men, and I don't mean that they do this with that cheap kind of disdain of which men make their insulting lightning bolts, but rather by exerting their own talents. Men will find out, moreover, that in order to pay them back, women are seeking to acquire that same fine habit they have of wanting to belittle our sex without even listening to us or reading our writings, for we have listened to them and read their works. They should also remember a dangerous expression of excellent origin: only the less able can live content with their own wisdom, looking over their shoulder at that of others, and ignorance is the mother of presumption.

NOTES TO THE TRANSLATIONS

1. Anne of Austria (1601–1666), daughter of Philip III of Spain, the king mentioned in the opening line of the dedication. Anne of Austria was the mother of Louis XIV, for whom she ruled from 1643 to 1652. She was looked upon as a model by many feminist writers including Marie de Gournay.

2. In her *Question célèbre,* Anna Maria van Schurman says, echoing Marie: "I know that in order for us to be useful, they give us a needle and a distaff and tell us that this must be the only occupation of our sex." See Schiff, *La Fille d'alliance de Montaigne,* 62.

3. There is indeed a passage in the *Republic* where one interlocutor seems to suggest that men and women are equally suited for all forms of political activity (*Republic* 5 and 7; also *Laws* 7 and *Meno* 72A–73C).

4. In the editions of 1634 and 1641, Marie de Gournay inserts here a long paragraph with examples supporting her thesis: Hypathia; Themistoclea, Theano, and Damo (the sister, wife, and daughter of Pythagoras); Cornelia; Laelia; Arete; and of course Anna Maria van Schurman ("new star" in the firmament). See Schiff, *La Fille d'alliance de Montaigne,* 79–80. Such listings of strong or intelligent women ("femmes fortes") became something of a convention in feminist writings of the time.

5. Diotima is the fictional name of a priestess at Mantinea in Plato's *Symposion,* from whom Socrates claims to have learned his ideas of love. Aspasia played an unusual role in intellectual circles in Athens. Pericles divorced his wife to marry her.

6. Saint Theodoret was a bishop, theologian, and church historian of the fifth century.

7. See *Politics* 1.1.9 and *Economics* (attributed to Aristotle at the time) 1.3.

8. Angelo Poleziano (1454–1494), Italian scholar and poet. Castiglione (1478–1529) was the author of the famous *Il Cortegiano.*

9. Instead of "buffaloes," Marie de Gournay uses elsewhere the less incongruous "dreamers."

10. Pharamond was a legendary chief of the Franks. The *Lex Salica,* legal code of the Salic Franks, contained a rule excluding females from the line of succession to a throne. The issue of Salic law was much discussed in the reign of Anne of Austria, both in imaginative literature and in pamphlets. Marie tries to explain it in terms of demographic necessity. See Maclean, *Woman Triumphant,* 58, 60–61.

11. Genesis 2:24.

12. Saint Basil's commentary on Genesis in *Homiles* 1 provides one of the most striking arguments in favor of the equality of women and men.

13. Marie ridicules the general opinion on this question which was derived in part from Saint Paul (1 Cor. 11:7). See n. 20 above.

14. In Greek mythology Penthesilea, daughter of Ares and Otrera, queen of the Amazons, helps Priam and is killed by Achilles after a glorious battle.

15. 1 Cor.14:34.

16. The legendary pious daughter of Saint Peter, who was struck with palsy by her father and later restored to health by him. She died after a self-imposed fast, to escape an unwanted suitor. *Acta SS.* May, 3. 10–11; 7. 420–22.

17. According to the Greek church calendar, Magdalene is a saint equal to the apostles. The Greek church teaches that Magdalene accompanied Mary to Ephesus and that her remains are in Constantinople. She was one of the Galilean women who followed Jesus and supported him (Luke 8:2). Magdalene was an eyewitness of His crucifixion and entombment on Easter morning (John 20:11–18). She has been associated, on the one hand, with the nameless sinner of Luke 7:37–50 and, on the other, with Maria of Bethany. About the sinner developed the legend of a repenting Magdalene who spent the rest of her life as a hermit in the Sainte Beaume cave near Marseilles, where she apparently led a penitential life

for thirty years, preaching to the people of the area, and where her remains are now venerated. Marie de Gournay considers the Magdalene of the Greek and the Western churches as one and the same.

18. That is, to women. His second epistle is addressed to the "Lady chosen by God, and her children," claimed by some to have been a specific woman. It is more likely a symbolic title for the universal church of a special Asia Minor community.

19. Judith (*Apocrypha,* bk. 4) is described as a beautiful, pious widow who entices and brutally assassinates Holofernes, the Assyrian general besieging her hometown, Bethulia. Thus she delivers her people from the enemy with courage and cunning.

20. Here Marie is quoting from her own translation of book 1 of Virgil's *Aeneid.*

21. Matt. 26:13; Mark 14:9.

22. John 20:11–18.

23. Luke 2:25–38.

24. Matt. 27:19. Pilate's wife sent a message to the procurator to have nothing to do with Jesus, a holy man on whose account she had suffered much in a dream that day.

25. The argument that it is a great honor for the female sex that a woman gave birth to Jesus, *quod homo non potuit* (of which man is incapable), was a very common one at the time.

26. See, for example, Eph. 5:23; Gen. 3:16.

27. See, for example, Gen. 2:24; Eph. 5:31.

28. Carneades, a Greek philosopher (213–126 B.C.), was famous for his convincing speeches as a political emissary to Rome.

29. By Montaigne, *Essays,* 3:8.

BIBLIOGRAPHY

Primary Works

de Gournay, Marie. *Le Proumenoir de Monsieur de Montaigne.* Paris: Abel l'Angelier, 1594.

———. *Bien-Venue de Monseigneur le Duc d'Anjou.* Paris: Fleury Bourriquant, 1608.

———. *Adieu de l'Ame du Roy de France et de Navarre, Henry le Grand à la Royne,* with *La Défense des Pères Iésuites.* Paris: Fleury Bourriquant, 1610.

———. *Versions de quelques pièces de Virgile, Tacite et Saluste,* with *L'Institution de Monseigneur, frère du Roy.* Paris: Fleury Bourriquant, 1619.

———. *Eschantillons de Virgile,* n.p., n.d.

———. *Egalité des hommes et des femmes.* Paris: n.p., 1622.

———. *Remerciment au Roy.* Paris: n.p., 1624.

———. *Préface* to the *Essais* of Montaigne (appeared in the editions of 1595, 1599, 1617, 1625, 1635; shortened in the editions of 1598, 1600, 1694, 1611, 1617).

———. *L'Ombre de la Demoiselle de Gournay.* Paris: Jean Libert, 1626.

———. *Les Advis ou les Présens de la Demoiselle de Gournay.* Paris: Toussainct Du-Bray, 1634.

———. *Les Advis ou les Présens de la Demoiselle de Gournay* (contains many new additions). Paris: Du-Bray, 1641.

Related Works

Baader, Renate. "Streitbar und unzeitgemäss: Die Moralistik der Marie de Gournay." In *Die Französische Autorin vom Mittelalter bis zur Gegenwart,* 77–89. Wiesbaden: Akademische Verlagsgesellschaft Athenaion, 1979.

Boase, Alan. "Marie de Gournay." In *The Fortunes of Montaigne,* 48–76. New York: Farrar, Straus & Giroux, 1970.

Casevitz, Thérèse. "Mademoiselle de Gournay et le féminisme." *Revue Politique et littéraire* 13 (1925): 768–71.

Holmes, Peggie P. "Mlle de Gournay's Defense of Baroque Imagery." *French Studies* 8 (1954): 122–31.

Ilsley, Marjorie H. *A Daughter of the Renaissance: Marie le Jars de Gournay, Her Life and Works*. The Hague: Mouton, 1963.

Lausberg, Heinrich. "Marie de Gournay et la crise du langage poétique." In *Critique et création littéraires en France au XVII*e *siècle,* edited by Marc Fumaroli, 117–24. Colloques Internationaux du CNRS 557. Paris: CNRS, 1977.

Maclean, Ian. *Woman Triumphant: Feminism in French Literature 1610–1652*. Oxford: Clarendon Press, 1977.

Michel, Pierre. "Une Apôtre du féminisme au XVIIe siècle: Mademoiselle de Gournay." *Bulletin de la Société des Amis de Montaigne* 27 (1971): 55–58.

Morand, Jean. "Marie le Jars de Gournay: La 'Fille d'Alliance' de Montaigne." *Bulletin de la Société des Amis de Montaigne* 27 (1971): 45–54.

Rowan, Mary M. "Seventeenth-Century French Feminism: Two Opposing Attitudes." *International Journal of Women Studies* 3 (1980–81): 273–91.

Sainte-Beuve, C. A. *Tableau de la poésie française au XVI*e *siècle* (1828). Paris: Alphonse Lemerre, 1876.

Schiff, Mario. *La Fille d'alliance de Montaigne: Marie de Gournay.* Paris, 1910. Reprint. Geneva: Slatkine, 1978.

Stanton, Domna C. "Woman as Object and Subject of Exchange: Marie de Gournay's *Le Proumenoir* (1594)." *L'Esprit Créateur* 23, no. 2 (1983): 9–25.

Uildriks, Anne. *Les Idées littéraires de Mlle de Gournay.* Diss., Groningen, 1962.

Zeitlin, Jacob, trans. *The Essays of Michel de Montaigne.* Vol. 2. New York: A. Knopf, 1935.

“EPISTOLIÈRE” OF THE SPLENDID CENTURY

Madame de Sévigné

JEANNE A. OJALA AND
WILLIAM T. OJALA

Marie de Rabutin-Chantal, the marquise de Sévigné, has left to a grateful posterity a lively account of an entire epoch, the glorious and elegant Age of Louis XIV, the Sun King. Over fifteen hundred of her letters are extant, covering the period from 1648 to 1696; through the eyes of this intelligent, observant, independent, and robust aristocratic woman the reader is immersed in the glittering and cultured *beau monde* of the Splendid Century. Grand fêtes, brutal executions, court intrigues, wars and rebellions, and intimate family affairs are all recorded in a vivid, witty, and at times earthy style. Her aristocratic status in the fairly rigid social hierarchy of the time is reflected in her attitudes and interests; only “people of quality” were worth consideration, but she could marvel, along with the unwashed Parisian rabble, as a notorious female criminal endured torture and abuse before being executed in a public square. Life was precarious and often short, but whatever happened was God’s Will, or Providence, as she expressed it. Unlike many of the fragile, protected upperclass women of her time, Mme de Sévigné lived a full, healthy, self-governed life. Her letters form a chronicle of this classical era in which the King dictated cultural style and taste, and harmony and order prevailed in the arts. The independent, often unruly nobility lived refined and cultured lives amidst the wretched masses, inferior beings created by God to labor and to serve their “betters.” The Catholic church enjoyed a prolonged period of spiritual rejuvenation in the seventeenth century under the leadership of such men as Vincent de Paul and François de Sales; Mme de Sévigné’s paternal grandmother, Jeanne de Chantal, abandoned her family to enter religious life and was the foundress of over one hundred convents of the Order of the Visitation.[1] On the other hand, worldly prelates lived luxuriously and often neglected their duties.

The lack of newspapers made letter writing an important means of disseminating news, and Mme de Sévigné's letters were eagerly read and passed around among interested friends or family members. Sometimes humorous, sometimes poignant, always interesting, never banal, Mme de Sévigné's vast correspondence provides a spirited and immediate picture of her life and times. Unlike *mémoires,* which attempt to recapture and re-create times past, letters describe the present, its events, moods, tone, and concerns. Mme de Sévigné recorded it all: from the civil wars to the triumph of the regal young monarch, through the creation of the most sumptuous court in Europe and a magnificent culture to the years of war that depleted the country's resources and turned the aging monarch from worldly pleasures to a dreary, not always convincing piety.

Marie de Rabutin-Chantal was born in the elegant townhouse of her maternal grandfather, Philippe de Coulanges, on the fashionable Place Royale (now Place des Vosges) in Paris on February 5, 1626. Her father, Celse-Bénigne de Rabutin-Chantal, was from an old, illustrious Burgundian family which traced its ancestry to at least the twelfth century. When this boisterous, adventuresome young noble married the wealthy daughter of a former tax-farmer, the Rabutins scorned the union that they regarded as a *mésalliance,* refusing to sign the marriage contract or attend the wedding ceremony. However, Celse-Bénigne's mother, Jeanne de Chantal, and her brothers approved of the marriage: debt-ridden aristocratic families were often forced to "manure their fields" (an expression Mme de Sévigné used) by allying themselves with the monied, magisterial classes.

The marquis de Chantal had made a favorable impression at the court of Louis XIII, but his repeated participation in illegal duels and his friendship with those who schemed and plotted against the King's formidable minister, the cardinal de Richelieu, soon turned both King and minister against him. Hoping to recoup his reputation and to show his loyalty to the monarchy, Chantal volunteered to join a military expedition against the English on the Ile de Ré; he was fatally wounded in battle and died there in 1627. Marie's grandfather Coulanges was appointed her guardian, and the child remained in the warm, happy, and tightly knit Coulanges household. However, when her mother died at the age of thirty, the seven-year-old orphan became the center of a family conflict. The Rabutins demanded that the rich heiress be put in their charge. There is little doubt that, if they had won their legal suit, Marie would have been relegated to a convent under the watchful eye of her avaricious aunt, Mme de Toulongeon; her fortune would have been used to provide dowries for her aunt's two daughters and to further the career of her cousin, Roger de Rabutin, comte de Bussy. Fortunately, she was saved from this fate by her indomitable paternal grandmother, the saintly Jeanne de Chantal, whose firm intervention guaranteed a loving, carefree childhood for Marie among the easy-going and worldly, but prudent, Coulanges.

After the death of her grandparents she was placed in 1637 under the guardianship of her uncle, Philippe II de Coulanges, and his wife, with whom she lived until her marriage at age eighteen. Brought up among uncles, aunts, and cousins of all ages in a secure and luxurious environment, the young girl evidently did not suffer from the loss of her parents and grandparents.

Born and reared in the Marais quarter of Paris, the future Mme de Sévigné lived there during and after her marriage and, in fact, until she died, an active member of upperclass society. The open, relaxed atmosphere of her youth provided a foundation for her personality and disposition as an adult: optimistic, confident, and loving, Marie did not fear life, for she lived forever surrounded by numerous relatives and friends. Her uncle Christophe de Coulanges, abbé de Livry, was her constant companion for over forty years and managed her financial affairs with great success, thus assuring her a secure future. A cousin, Philippe-Emmanuel de Coulanges, called the "chansonnier," was also a favorite. "Mon petit," as Mme de Sévigné affectionately called him, grew older, but never grew up. Perhaps it was his childlike innocence and unrestrained enjoyment of society which endeared him to everyone.

The education of young Marie was truly remarkable for her sex and her time. Under the direction of the pedantic, pompous Gilles Ménage and the cultured Academician Jean Chapelain, both friends of the Coulanges, Marie studied languages and French literature. She became fluent in Italian, knew Spanish, and easily read Latin authors in the original. A substantial sum was set aside for her education and for the singing, dancing, and riding lessons considered essential for a cultivated aristocratic woman. Little formal or systematic intellectual training was necessary, since "learned" women were not greatly admired but rather classed as "curiosities." Mme de Sévigné never claimed to be learned, but the world of books was part of her daily life, staving off boredom, sloth, and mental rigidity. "To be ignorant is a great blunder," she believed.[2] Her first teachers were probably the *religieuses* of the Convent of the Visitation near her home in the Marais. However rudimentary her training may have been from these simple women, Marie developed a sincere religious faith without the ferocious commitment of her grandmother Chantal; still, her beliefs comforted her and gave order and purpose to the world. Equally important in her education was her freedom to explore, to expand her mind, and to cultivate her interests. Her love of reading lasted throughout her life: history, philosophy, poetry, religion and theology, even romances, and works by her contemporaries Molière, Corneille, La Fontaine, Racine, Mme de LaFayette, and Mlle de Scudéry, filled her quiet hours. "Not to find pleasure in serious reading gives pastel colorings to the mind," she wrote in 1689.[3] This broad education prepared her to be self-confident, to live in a less than perfect world, and to find comfort and small joys in her own self-created daily environment. She remained open to new ideas, even those not approved of by the King or the Church. Travel was also a part of education, and like reading, it broadened her perspective even into old age. If education was intended to develop self-reliance and provide a modicum of happiness, it certainly achieved its purpose in her case.

On August 4, 1644, at age eighteen, Marie de Rabutin-Chantal married twenty-one-year-old baron Henri de Sévigné of old Breton aristocracy (marquis was his courtesy title). The abbé de Coulanges, Marie's beloved uncle, whom she called le Bien Bon, and the infamous future cardinal de Retz, a relative of Henri, had arranged the marriage between the two young orphans. It was not an altogether happy choice; Henri was handsome and charming, but also extravagant, flighty, promiscuous, and an incorrigible duellist. The first months of their marriage were spent at his estate of Les Rochers in Brittany, the Sévigné residence for over two hundred years. It later became a retreat for Mme de Sévigné, far from expensive Paris society and the court of Versailles. Narrow, dull provincial life did not appeal to Henri, however, and after eighteen months the couple returned to Paris. Their residence was modest by aristocratic standards, well beneath the manner in which Mme de Sévigné had been accustomed to living. Finally freed from a grim, lonely childhood, Henri threw himself into the lavish, hedonistic society. His wife, brought up in this environment, was more at ease than Henri in the sophisticated aristocratic and magisterial circles of the capital.

Henri's passion for society led him to neglect his wife, and it was not long before the young cavalier was involved in a series of love affairs. It is doubtful that Marie expected her husband to settle into marriage without first having his fling in society; however, Henri was indiscreet and thoughtless, though not malicious. The beautiful Ninon de Lenclos[4] took him as a lover for her normal period of three months and then dismissed him like a servant. This famous courtesan later shared her bed with Mme de Sévigné's son, and amazingly, even with her grandson. Years later Mme de Sévigné generously recalled that Ninon had not ruined her husband, only spoiled him.[5] Far more serious was Sévigné's affair with the lovely, mindless Mme de Gondran, "la belle Lolo," which degenerated into a ridiculous *ménage à trois* that amused and mildly scandalized society.

The marquis's sexual ventures were not the only problem that plagued the young couple. There was a chronic shortage of money caused by their overly lavish lifestyle, spiraling inflation, and irregular, decreased payments on investments. The Franco-Spanish War (1635–1659) and the civil wars (the Frondes, 1648–1652) had created an unstable economic situation in France, while poor harvests and escalating taxes reduced the profits from the Sévignés' estates which were often inefficiently managed. Diminished revenues forced them to live at Les Rochers in Brittany for about half their married life in order to economize. At her husband's death, Mme de Sévigné had to repay several loans and other debts, including two years' rent on their Paris residence, servants' wages, and other large household bills.

During the civil wars, it was not surprising that Sévigné threw himself into the fracas on the side of the rebels against the child-king, Louis XIV. The unruly nobles, both men and women, plotted and fought, blithely changed sides as suited their momentary interests, and brought chaos and misery to their country and its poor inhabitants. They paid dearly for their lawless acts as soon as the King came of age; Louis never forgot or forgave the disloyalty of his nobility and forever branded them *frondeurs*. Mme de Sévigné was never personally involved in these rebellions; she had no interest in political intrigue and spent most of these unsettled times in Brittany.

Henri's amorous and rebellious adventures were not unusual for a man of his rank and background at this time. Loyalty and obedience to the King's will and laws and faithfulness in arranged marriages among the aristocracy were rare. Sévigné, however, sullied his reputation in society and forfeited the respect of his wife with his untempered passion for "la belle Lolo," which led to a fatal duel with the chevalier d'Albret on February 4, 1651; Sévigné died the next day on his wife's twenty-fifth birthday. There is no firm evidence of Mme de Sévigné's feelings at the time, but her cousin Bussy claimed she had loved Henri and sincerely regretted his death. Many of her friends were surprised that she was not simply relieved at being rid of a man she did not respect. The caustic, melancholic La Rochefoucauld's *maxime* stated that "there are good marriages, but no delicious ones." One can assume that his widowed friend agreed with his assessment.

Mme de Sévigné and her two small children retired to Les Rochers for a proper period of mourning, and the abbé de Coulanges set about reorganizing her finances. The young widow would not follow the example of her pious grandmother Chantal and withdraw from society. Instead she moved into a large house in Paris with her aunt La Trousse. Cautious but not prudish in her relations with men, she carefully protected her reputation. This was not easy for a young woman in seventeenth-century Paris, but the determined widow kept her numerous admirers and suitors at a safe distance. She definitely enjoyed the company of men and even enjoyed being courted. It would appear from comments in her correspondence that she never regretted her decision not to remarry. She was free and had no illusions about marriage. "The state of matrimony is a dangerous disease: far better to take to drink in my opinion," she wrote after thirty-eight years of widowhood.[6] Moreover, she still had her family, her children, and a large circle of devoted friends. In this secure environment Mme de Sévigné created a life of her own choosing, a life that did not revolve around or depend on a husband.

Mme de Sévigné was a wealthy, well-born woman, having inherited a fortune from her mother's family and a distinguished name and numerous estates from her father; as a widow she received her husband's châteaux and lands in her own right. A member of the privileged class in France, she had entrée to Court and the right to own property. It was not necessary that a male legal guardian be appointed by the courts to oversee her affairs. Women were considered capable of making their own decisions, and Mme de Sévigné did. As a landowner she had a voice in provincial assemblies, collected rents and fees from her tenants, and paid taxes. Of course women did not hold office, but they could own land and be legally responsible for their affairs. Aristocratic women were not considered inferior to men of their class; birth and property gave women status. Mme de Sévigné was actually head of the Rabutin family—a fact she frequently pointed out to her cousin Bussy, who was a member of the cadet branch of their family.

The Sévignés' ill-matched marriage lasted less than seven years and produced two children who were the center of their mother's world as long as she lived. Françoise-Marguerite de Sévigné was born in Paris in October 1646; the "prettiest girl in France," she was also cold, reserved, aloof, and at times openly exasperated by her mother's smothering attentions and passionate adoration. She was Mme de Sévigné's delight and anguish. Very early in life, it was obvious that this "dry stick of a girl" was preferred to the son born two years later. No expense was spared to present her at court where she could attract a suitable husband. Much to Mme de Sévigné's dismay, her daughter was twenty-three years old before she finally married the twice-widowed, thirty-seven-year-old François Adémar de Monteil, comte de Grignan, in January 1669. Mme de Sévigné and her family approved of M de Grignan, though her cousin, Bussy-Rabutin, very early sounded a cautious concern about Grignan: "There is only one thing that makes me nervous . . . and that is that Grignan, who is not yet old, has already reached his third wife—he wears them out nearly as fast as his clothes, or at any rate his carriages."[7] Mme de Sévigné could not have been unaware or unconcerned about the possibility that Grignan had venereal disease (he had syphilis). He was from an old aristocratic

Provençal family and was also presumed to be fabulously wealthy.[8] It was hoped that he would be appointed to some lucrative position at Court so that the couple could remain in Paris. Instead, the King named Grignan lieutenant-general (governor) of Provence, and in the spring of 1670 he left Paris for his new post. Mme de Grignan remained with her mother to await the birth of her child (she had had a miscarriage at the abbey of Livry in November 1669). To the family's disappointment, a daughter, Marie-Blanche, was born in November 1670. Grignan already had two daughters from his first marriage but no sons, and providing dowries for several girls was beyond the financial means of the family. Much to Mme de Sévigné's dismay, Marie-Blanche at age five was packed off to a convent in Aix-en-Provence where she spent the remainder of her life.

Leaving the infant with her mother, Mme de Grignan set out a few months later to join her husband in Provence. Mme de Sévigné was plunged into despair at this first separation from her daughter. This normally rational woman, to whom family losses were not unknown, suddenly became overwrought and almost obsessed with her daughter, whose health, lifestyle, beauty, and letters occupied her mother's thoughts for the rest of her life. Now the famous correspondence began. Letters to and from her daughter became as necessary to her well-being as going to Les Rochers or the abbey of Livry for periods of solitude and spiritual regeneration. Twice weekly Mme de Sévigné posted her long letters filled with declarations of love, torrents of advice, and news of trifling or important events and people. Encumbered by debts and frequently pregnant, Mme de Grignan caused her mother constant anxiety, conjuring up "gray-brown thoughts." The contrast in their personalities also created a strain in their relationship. Concern for Mme de Grignan's visibly deteriorating health brought on a stream of pleas to avoid the annual pregnancies that drained her energy and destroyed her beauty. "I shall not come to Provence if you are pregnant," Mme de Sévigné bluntly threatened before a grandson was born a few months later.[9] Throughout their turbulent reunions and wrenching separations, however, Mme de Sévigné tenaciously reaffirmed her adoration for Mme de Grignan. "Your love is the very breath of my existence," she wrote in 1671.[10] This was not literary hyperbole; it was true and remained a constant theme.

For over twenty-five years Mme de Sévigné seemed able to find new ways of expressing this sentiment. She realized that her love was excessive, but her usual self-control and common sense could not restrain her emotions in this case. Even when refused absolution by her priest for loving her daughter more than her Creator, Mme de Sévigné was unable to moderate her feelings. She was never realistic about her daughter, whose faults kept Mme de Sévigné in a constant state of alarm. Mme de Grignan's gambling, pregnancies, neglect of health and beauty, quasi-royal lifestyle, and obvious preference for her son irritated Mme de Sévigné and caused tension between them. Indeed, Mme de Grignan lived as she pleased and as befitted the high position of her husband in the King's service. But Mme de Sévigné was not a woman to suffer in silence or to mince words when she had an opinion on anything. It must have been difficult for Mme de Grignan to live under such close scrutiny and constant interference in her most private affairs. In language that would normally strain, or even sever, relations in a close family, Mme de Sévigné even reproached her son-in-law for not protecting his wife's well-being:

> I am addressing myself to you, dear comte, for you are reported to have said that my daughter's confinements were models of what confinements should be, and that the more frequently she does it the better. Dear God! She never does anything else. I must, however, warn you that unless you call a halt to this business out of common humanity, and if this poor machine is never allowed a pause, you will destroy it utterly, which would be regrettable. I am putting this to you for your serious consideration—the subject can scarcely be called hilarious.[11]

There is little doubt that Mme de Grignan contracted syphilis from her husband, evidenced by the birth of several sickly, deformed children and by her own deteriorating health. Mme de Sévigné, who was usually robust and lively, suffered from bouts of "black melancholy" as she witnessed her daughter's physical decline. Perhaps she felt guilty for arranging this marriage, which brought prestige and an illustrious name but also the fatal consequences of venereal disease that likely caused the early deaths of Grignan's first two wives. It was a harsh reality that the distraught mother was never able to accept with equanimity.

In contrast to this obsession with her daughter, Mme de Sévigné had an easy, open relationship with her son Charles. Mild-mannered, unambitious, and charming, Charles muddled through life, never finding a profession that suited his temperament or a mistress he could satisfy. For her part, Mme de Sévigné forever scolded him for his dissipation and loved him for his openness and humor. She had a friendly rapport with her son, who responded with genuine affection. Furthermore, Charles never made outrageous demands for attention or for money, and he loved the solitude of Les Rochers as much as his mother did.

Charles thoughtlessly frittered away his youth chasing women, carousing about Paris with his idle, dandified young companions, and indulging in sexual adventures that provided hearty laughter for his mother and her friends. Charles's embarrassment over momentary impotence during a rendezvous with the actress Champmeslé (an interpreter of Racine's plays) was related to an amused gathering, and Mme de Sévigné, in turn, described the incident to her daughter:

> The young *Merveille* [the actress Champmeslé] has not broken with him as yet, but she will soon, I believe. I know now why your brother came yesterday from the farther end of Paris to see me. He wanted to acquaint me with an accident that had befallen him. He found a favorable opportunity; and in the meantime, do I dare say it? *Son dada demeura court à Lérida* [His little gee-gee remained short of reaching Lérida.][12] It is a strange thing! the poor damsel never had been so entertained in her life. The disconcerted cavalier retired, thinking himself bewitched. And what is better still, he could not be easy till he had acquainted me with his disaster. We laughed very heartily at him; I told him I was overjoyed to find him punished where he had sinned. . . . He said the most extravagant things in the world, and so did I. It was a scene worthy of Molière. . . . In short, this affair makes me laugh, and I wish sincerely it may be the means of weaning him from a state so offensive to God, and dangerous to his own soul!

Mme de Sévigné was obviously amused, and she refrained from condemning or sermonizing about his social mishaps. At this same time (spring 1671) a brief and rather stormy liaison with his father's former mistress Ninon ended abruptly, bringing on another scene with his mother:

> Ninon has left him; when she loved him he was dissatisfied, now that she loves him no longer he is in despair, to add to which, she hasn't a good word to say for him. . . . She says "His spirit is made of pap, his body of chewed string, and his heart a pumpkin fricasseed in snow. . . ." He recounted his follies to M de La Rochefoucauld who . . . agrees with what I say, that my son errs less from the head than from the heart. . . . We ended by laughing heartily, in which your brother joined, who is ever the best company in the world, and agrees with everything that is said.[13]

Eventually his amorous escapades resulted in Charles's contracting venereal disease; without a reproach, Mme de Sévigné accompanied her errant son to Paris to undergo the painful treatment which probably left him sterile. These terrible infectious diseases affected a shockingly large number of people at the time but were not cause for social ostracism. Cheating at cards was considered a more serious social sin than contracting syphilis.

Although not so generous as she was with her daughter, Mme de Sévigné spent a large sum of money to buy an army commission for Charles as ensign in the Gendarmes-Dauphin. Despite his sincere efforts to obtain promotion, he had risen only to sub-lieutenant when he sold his post about nine years later. His mother was disappointed that he would no longer have a place at Court where he could represent his and the family's interests. However, Charles was content to be a country gentleman, living quietly at Les Rochers. He took part in provincial affairs that required his attention but much preferred to spend his days reading and visiting neighbors.

It was never in Mme de Sévigné's character to be a recluse, to withdraw from society and her familiar circles of friends. She lived in Paris when she could afford it, and at Les Rochers when she was forced to conserve her resources: "Reason says Brittany, but affection Paris. Sometimes you have to give in to that tyrant reason."[14] Life in Brittany was not always one of quiet contemplation, letter writing, reading, and walking in the woods. As an important landowner, Mme de Sévigné had social and political obligations; in Rennes she met with the local Estates, attended ceremonies, paid social visits, and dined with her provincial neighbors. She complained, however, of being deprived of her solitude and having to spend large sums of money on fashionable dress and on entertaining in a suitable manner. These meetings made heavy demands on her, and she soon grew weary of social intercourse: "I long most passionately to be out of here, where they are doing me too much honor; I am hungry for fasting and silence. I have not much intelligence, but here I seem to be spending what I have in small change, which I throw away and distribute in silly little things, and that is ruining me. . . . Oh Lord, when shall I be able to die of hunger and hold my tongue? I can't say another word: here come a thousand people."[15] In Paris social engagements were not considered obligatory and she could refuse invitations if she needed to be alone, a frequent and at times urgent need. To be too much of this world did not leave time for contemplation, serious reading, and setting one's life right with God. No doubt this periodic withdrawal from the world helped to conserve her energy and prolong her life.

Mme de Sévigné much preferred small gatherings with close friends, such as the frail novelist Mme de LaFayette and her intimate companion of twenty-five years, the gouty, mordant duc de La Rochefoucauld; the worldly, unrepentant ex-frondeur, the cardinal de Retz; and the gentle, homely romance writer, Mlle de Scudéry. Aristocratic friends and relatives who held high positions in the King's government also formed part of her social circle; they shared similar lifestyles, interests, attitudes, and values. Moreover, she was a loyal friend even to those who incurred the displeasure of the King. The cardinal de Retz was sent into exile for his traitorous conduct during the Fronde; Roger de Bussy, Mme de Sévigné's cousin and lifelong correspondent, spent seventeen years in exile for arousing the wrath of Louis XIV by publishing an outrageous lampoon of persons at Court, including Mme de Sévigné, in his *l'Histoire amoureuse des Gaules*. She eventually forgave him for this affront, but she never forgot his unflattering portrait. Bussy may have been unbearably proud and acerbic at times, even maleficent, but the two cousins shared the gregarious Rabutin character and the witty, elegant style, the easy-flowing expressiveness known as *rabutinage*. Another of Mme de Sévigné's friends and admirers was Superintendent of Finance Nicolas Fouquet. In 1661, he was arrested for misappropriation of government funds, his papers seized and brought to the King. Among them were several letters from Mme de Sévigné, which fortunately were innocent enough not to tarnish her reputation. After a three-year trial Fouquet was found guilty and sentenced to life in prison. Mme de Sévigné remained openly loyal to him and his family. She was not blind to Louis XIV's faults and abuse of power in dealing with his nobility, but she also was not so foolish as to denounce his decisions. The fate of de Retz, Bussy, and Fouquet had a direct bearing on the future of Mme de Sévigné and her children because she had counted on them to represent her interests at Court. Although she managed well on her own, she was repeatedly disappointed that her son and son-in-law were not better rewarded for their services to the King.

Parisian society appreciated the charm, humor, and affectionate nature of the lively widow. Respected by both men and women, she moved easily among the intellectual literary circles of the capital and in rustic, sometimes humorously pretentious provincial society. Mme de Sévigné loved Paris, especially the Marais where most of her friends lived. This fashionable quarter was supplanted in the second half of the seventeenth century by the more exclusive Saint-Germain quarter in the western part of the city, but Mme de Sévigné never abandoned the Marais. This does not mean, however, that her world was restricted by narrow geographic or social boundaries.

She traveled extensively for a woman of her time. Frequent visits to Brittany, Burgundy, and Provence brought her into contact with a great variety of provincial customs and traditions which she found interesting and stimulating. Travel by coach was slow, uncomfortable, even dangerous, but in spite of formidable inconveniences, Mme de Sévigné undertook many long, tedious journeys. Travel, like reading, kept at bay the two evils she dreaded most—boredom and sloth. Occasionally she attended functions at Court, participating in the elegant fêtes and celebrations for which the Sun King was famous. She admired the King and appeared to enjoy the attention given her by a court society which basked in the radiance of their *roi soleil:*

> I was on Saturday at Versailles [she wrote to her daughter]. . . . You know the ceremony of attending on the Queen at her toilette, at mass, and at dinner. . . . At three the King and Queen, Monsieur, Madame, Mademoiselle, the Princes and Princesses, Madame de Montespan [Louis's mistress *en titre*] and her train, the courtiers and the ladies, in short, the whole Court of France, retire to that fine apartment of the King's which you know. It is furnished with the utmost magnificence. . . .

> I bowed to the King in the way you taught me, and he returned my salutation as if I were young and beautiful. The Queen talked to me of my illness [rheumatism] as if it were a confinement. . . . Monsieur le duc [de Condé] paid me a thousand of those meaningless compliments which he bestows so liberally. You know what it is to receive a word from everyone who passes you.[16]

Both mother and daughter were admired at Court for their beauty and grace and their ability to sing and dance. After her daughter's marriage and her son's purchase of a commission in the army, Mme de Sévigné chose to attend Court less often, but she never lost contact with people who could keep her informed of events at Versailles. She remained a friend of the remarkable widow Scarron who cared for the King's bastard children and finally married, morganatically, the middle-aged, sexually satiated Louis XIV.[17] La Grande Mademoiselle, the richest woman in France and first cousin to the King, welcomed the sympathetic ear of Mme de Sévigné after Louis XIV refused to allow her to marry M de Lauzun, an ambitious, insignificant nobleman (see letter 1). In fact, Mme de Sévigné's letters describing this affair are much more interesting and lively than the actual episode itself. Any misalliance was open to ridicule and biting insult, but this one involving the cousin of the haughty, arrogant King was simply too delicious to pass by. Among the generally fashionable, ornamental ladies of the Court, the King's sister-in-law, Elizabeth-Charlotte, a large, gruff German woman, stood out as an amazon; she was married to Monsieur,[18] who was handsome, effeminate, and blatantly bisexual. Mme de Sévigné liked the frank young woman and appreciated her common sense and matter-of-fact conversation. Of Monsieur she says less; it was not prudent to talk about his foppish behavior because the King loathed homosexuality. Mme de Sévigné was an excellent listener, able to discern and complement the mood of people around her. She empathized well, always saying the appropriate words at the right time. In this she was a typical courtier, but not a fawning sycophant.

The King's mistresses, like his family, received intense scrutiny from high society. Mme de Sévigné recorded the rise and fall, the pregnancies, the titles, favors, and estates bestowed on a long line of young women. They were the celebrities of the time, rising from obscure, though noble, backgrounds, being presented at Court as "mistress in title," living sumptuous, though shallow, lives, and eventually being discarded and replaced as the King tired of them. It is obvious that Mme de Sévigné felt a certain sympathy for these women, whose lives were restricted by and totally devoted to their master, their King. Everything they had they owed to him. Certainly she never expressed any envy of their positions or their wealth. These women were not free, a situation that Mme de Sévigné had assiduously avoided after her unsatisfactory marriage. Being the King's mistress was even less secure than being the wife of a promiscuous, spendthrift husband during this period. Not surprisingly, when the beautiful Françoise-Marguerite de Sévigné was one of the centerpieces of the young King's court and it was merely suggested that she might find "official favor" with Louis, her protective mother refused even to consider the possibility. Mme de Sévigné was not flattered by the suggestion, but she was not offended either.

Paying homage to Louis le Grand at Versailles and maintaining a noble lifestyle in Paris were prohibitively expensive, and as family obligations and high taxes depleted her resources, Mme de Sévigné spent more time at her Brittany estate. In her rather modest château about three miles from Vitré, she asserted her independence from her children and friends, and from the demands of society. She indulged her love of gardening and reading; she enjoyed solitude and nature as few women of her time did. She supervised the planting of oak and chestnut trees which lined interlocking walkways where she strolled every day, accompanied by a servant because wolves still roamed the wild countryside. Her favorite time was twilight, when one could not distinguish "entre chien et loup" (between a dog and a wolf) and when her thoughts might turn "gris-brun"; but gloom never lasted long amidst the inexpressible beauty of her cloistered woods. Indeed, there is a freshness, a sprightliness in her letters from Les Rochers. Her freedom to do as she pleased and the change of scene seemed to renew her spirits. Le Bien Bon often accompanied her when she traveled, and they spent long periods together at Les Rochers and at his abbey of Livry in the Bondy forest near Paris. From early childhood, on holy days and during Lent, she retired to the abbey to revitalize her relationship with God and reflect on the transitory nature of human life. "I accomplish more there [at Livry] in one day than I do in a fortnight here [in Paris]. I prayed, read a great deal, discoursed on the next world and on the means of grace."[19] When le Bien Bon died in 1687, the King appointed another abbé at Livry, and Mme de Sévigné lost her familiar haven. She was "overcome with sorrow to say adieu forever to that pleasant solitude I loved so much; after having wept for the Abbé, I wept for the Abbey."[20]

Mme de Sévigné had already relinquished ownership of Les Rochers three years earlier when in 1684 le Bien Bon arranged for Charles to marry a delicate, wealthy Breton girl of good family. After assigning to Charles his share of the de Sévigné estates, Mme de Sévigné was once again forced to economize. Worse still, she was replaced as mistress of her beloved Les Rochers—"The property I possess is no longer mine."[21] Perhaps because of her reduced circumstances and the surrender of part of her former security, she described her daughter-in-law in less than flattering terms:

> My daughter-in-law has very few moments of gaiety. . . . She changes her face a hundred times a day without finding a good one. She is extremely delicate and scarcely ever stirs out of doors. She is always cold. By nine o'clock at night she is completely exhausted. The days are too long for her, and the need she has to be idle makes her leave me quite at liberty . . . with which I assure you I am very much pleased. . . . I take my walks alone, but I dare not trust myself in the time between the dog and the wolf [twilight] for fear of bursting into tears and lamentations. Darkness is very bad for me in my present condition; if my soul can fortify itself, I will sacrifice this melancholy amusement for fear of offending you.[22]

Frankly, Mme de Sévigné did not know what to think of this quiet young woman who was now mistress of Les Rochers and companion to her son. "She has good points, I suppose, but up to the present I am disposed . . . [to say] she is not this, nor that, nor the other, but the day may come when I shall say she is the other."[23] In contrast to the utter joy she claimed to experience in the company of her cold, reserved daughter, Mme de Sévigné accepted the presence of her daughter-in-law as long as it did not interfere with her routine and interrupt her thoughts about the comtesse de Grignan.

Eventually Mme de Sévigné came to admire and respect her son's wife who suited Charles's increasingly sedentary habits, and no great changes had to be made to accommodate her into their lives at Les Rochers. The friendly, lighthearted banter between mother and son slowly gave way to meditation and reflection on more somber subjects. Fewer delightful evenings were devoted to reading Molière, religious works replaced the variety of light literature previously read, and a curiously solemn calm pervaded Les Rochers. Despite her more restricted circumstances and diminished role at the château, Mme de Sévigné stubbornly refused to alter her daily routine. "I take my walks by myself . . . and am thankful for my freedom," she told her daughter.[24] Charles and his wife evidently had a good marriage, which relieved his mother's worse fears that he would squander his inheritance and make a ridiculous figure in society. The pious couple ended their days in retirement at a monastery in the Faubourg Saint-Jacques in Paris—not what one would have expected from a descendant of the adventurous, rambunctious Henri de Sévigné or the poetic, witty Rabutin warriors. The couple had no children, and the Sévigné name died with them.

In many ways Mme de Sévigné was unique in her time: her love and appreciation of nature and of reading, her enjoyment of travel despite the discomfort and dangers, and her unabashed love of life. A good Catholic, she eschewed the religious conflicts of both Jesuits and Jansenists[25] in France. She praised the thought-provoking sermons of Father Louis Bourdeloue, severely criticized worldly bishops and abbés, and found spiritual stimulation in the Jansenist works of Pascal and the gentle Nicole. Her faith was simple and practical, providing comfort and solace, and she never expressed the need to delve into theological complexities. An unfaltering belief in Providence helped her accept what she could not change in life. "One must be prepared for the ordinary inconveniences of mankind; God is the Master, [and] I submit to His will. . . . As for Providence, I would not live in peace if I did not often think about it; it is consolation for the sad states of life, it cuts short all complaints, it mitigates all sorrows, it determines all thoughts."[26] There is a certain resignation here, an acceptance of life as it was, combined with a gratitude that it was not worse.

A sympathetic observer of life around her, Mme de Sévigné managed to retain her optimism and *joie de vivre* into old age. Melancholia might occasionally cloud her otherwise orderly life, but only for a brief time. An even disposition and a benevolent view of human nature protected her from dwelling on the darker, seamier side of life. Reasonable (except in her love for her daughter), open-minded, self-confident, and trusting, she faced each day as it came, never regretting a past she could not change or fearing a future she could not control. She was what the French call a *primaire* personality—one who lives in the present: "Life is too short for us to dwell long upon the same sentiment; one must take time as it comes. I feel myself [to be] of this happy humor."[27] Her mother, father, and husband are scarcely mentioned in her letters, for they no longer affected her life. Even her happy childhood and the generosity and care she received from her family were in the past and not relevant to the present. Only once, after the death of le Bien Bon, did she recall in some detail all that he had meant in her life: "it is to him I owe the comfort and security of my days."[28] Few dates were important enough to be recalled or celebrated. The first anniversary of her daughter's wedding warranted a notation alongside the date of her letter, but no long discourse on the event. As she remarked to Bussy many years later: "I had only retained the dates of my birth and of my marriage, but without increasing the number I will forget the year when I was born which saddens me [she was then sixty], and I will put in its stead that of my widowhood, and the commencement of an existence which has been sufficiently pleasant and happy, without triumphs and without distinction; but it will finish in a more Christian manner than if it had been disturbed by great events, and that truly is the chief thing."[29]

Unlike many women of her time, Mme de Sévigné had the good fortune not to be plagued with debilitating, though fashionable, bouts of "vapors" and imbalanced "humors." At age fifty she suffered her first real illness, a severe attack of rheumatism which immobilized her for several months. Purgings, bleedings, and herbal ointments failed to relieve the pain in her swollen limbs. Unable to care for herself, hounded by doctors, and distressed by her daughter's latest pregnancy, Mme de Sévigné reacted rather petulantly to her condition: "By indulging her [meaning herself] . . . you can show your love for your mother; you can visit her, comfort her for being sick, and above all, because she has lost the charming illusion that she is immortal. She has become skeptical, full of doubts, and so lowered in her own estimation, she conceives it possible that one fine day she may find herself crossing the Styx in the same boat as the rest of humanity; for Charon shows no favors."[30]

As soon as she was able to travel, however, she went to the spa at Vichy to take the waters; her spirits revived, and she regaled her correspondents with descriptions of her cure: "Today I started the showers which serve as a good rehearsal for purgatory."[31] She would be cured—of that she had no doubt. Even when enduring the discomfort of her rather unfashionable illness and ingesting the nasty-tasting restorative mineral waters of Vichy, she could not suppress her obvious pleasure at being there. Complaints about the treatment were tempered with gaiety and good humor—no more dour, self-pitying complaints about the cure or the rheumatic attack. Mme de Sévigné's strong constitution finally triumphed over her illness and over the bleedings, emetics, purges, and boiling hot baths which fortunately did not exacerbate her condition. "We all assemble and drink and make wry faces; for just think to yourself that [the waters] are boiling hot and have a very nauseous taste of sulfur. We walk to and fro, we chat, we go to mass, we work off the waters, and everyone speaks without hesitation of the effects they produce."[32]

Without becoming depressed or obsessed with old age and infirmity, she realized that she was as vulnerable as the rest of mankind to the inevitable passage of time. But she was grateful to benevolent Providence, for "it is day to day that we grow old; we are today as we were yesterday, and tomorrow as today; thus we grow old without being conscious of it, and this is one of the miracles of that Providence that I adore."[33] It has been said that "this tranquil comprehension of one's own life in the span is one of the rarest of human faculties. . . . Mme de Sévigné had a gusto for living, and in that gusto is comprehended the best and the worst of her. To the cynic she appears foolish and to the unhappy, superficial."[34] One might add that, to the realist, she appears not to have been intimidated or frightened by an unknown future; "I try to dwell on what I owe to God for leading me in so gentle a manner to my appointed end, for encouraging me to spend my days in preparing for it, and for not being tempted to drain the cup of life to the dregs. Extreme old age is ugly and humiliating."[35] Living in the present had its blessings, and believing her fate to be safely in the hands of God kept her from being overwhelmed by the sorrows and pains which afflicted all mankind.

There was a "wholesomeness" to her life which "extended to everything she saw with her eyes or considered with her mind. Her nature was an ocean so large and so rich in purifying salts that all the sewage of the world could not pollute it."[36] She was sensitive, tender, and affectionate, yet nothing that affected mankind appalled or embittered her. Only her beloved daughter whose life was burdened with debts and deteriorating health caused her deep sadness; even this "gross infatuation," however, could not destroy her equanimity. Mme de Sévigné "saw the Universe . . . as a sublime compromise, and being a woman of the world, sane to the tips of her fingers, she understood, accepted and appreciated a compromise when she met it. Life inspired her with no fear and with little reverence; it was something to use, to manipulate and to enjoy."[37] There is no doubt that she enjoyed life; she left a full account of it in her letters. And Mme de Sévigné fortunately never suffered the humiliation and ugliness she associated with old age. In 1696, at age seventy, she contracted a "fever"; twelve days later she died at her beloved daughter's château of Grignan in Provence and was buried there in the family vault of the church.

NOTES

We would like to thank the Camargo Foundation for the fellowship in Cassis, France, which enabled us to complete our work on Mme de Sévigné.

1. In 1600 Jeanne de Chantal was left a widow with four children. Her family urged her to remarry, but she refused. To show her determination, she branded the name of Jesus on her left breast with a hot iron. Her decision was firm: she stepped over the prostrate body of her weeping young son Celse-Bénigne, as she walked through the door of her home. A woman of great energy and strong will, she was not a mystic nor did she indulge in ecstatic devotions. Jeanne de Chantel was made a saint in 1767.
2. Letter to Mme de Grignan from Les Rochers, Sunday, December 11, 1689.
3. Letter to Mme de Grignan from Les Rochers, Wednesday, November 16, 1689.
4. The most famous courtesan of the century. She was refined, wealthy, and intelligent. Her house in the Marais quarter of Paris was a gathering place for people of wit and culture. The newly married Sévignés were among her friends. Ninon died at age 85.
5. Letter to Mme de Grignan from Paris, Friday, March 13, 1671.
6. Letter to Mme de Grignan from Les Rochers, Sunday, December 18, 1689.
7. Letter to Mme de Sévigné from Roger de Bussy-Rabutin, from Chaseu, Saturday, December 8, 1668.
8. Letter to Bussy from Paris, Tuesday, December 4, 1668.
9. Letter to Mme de Grignan from Les Rochers, Wednesday, December 2, 1671.
10. Letter to Mme de Grignan from Paris, Wednesday, April 22, 1671.
11. Note to the comte de Grignan from Les Rochers, Wednesday, March 4, 1676.

12. These are words from a song referring to a check received by le Grand Condé's forces in front of Lérida, Spain, in 1647. Letter to Mme de Grignan from Paris, April 8, 1671.

13. Letter to Mme de Grignan from Paris, Wednesday, April 22, 1671.

14. Letter to Mme de Grignan from Paris, Friday, March 25, 1689.

15. Letter to Mme de Grignan from Rennes, Brittany, Wednesday morning, August 7, 1680.

16. Letter to Mme de Grignan from Paris, Wednesday, July 29, 1676.

17. Françoise d'Aubigné, Mme Scarron, was the widow of the crippled poet and satirist, Paul Scarron. She was governess to the King's illegitimate children by Mme de Montespan. Discreet and pious, she was given the château of Maintenon not far from Paris and the title of marquise by the grateful King. After the death of Marie-Thérèse in 1683, Mme de Maintenon secretly married Louis XIV, though she was never queen of France.

18. Monsieur was the title of the King's brother, Philippe d'Orléans. His wife was referred to as Madame. Elizabeth-Charlotte was his second wife.

19. Letter to Mme de Grignan from Paris, Friday, October 16, 1676.

20. Letter to Bussy from Paris, Thursday, November 13, 1687.

21. Letter to Mme de Grignan from Les Rochers, November 15, 1687.

22. Letter to Mme de Grignan from Les Rochers, Wednesday, September 27, 1684.

23. Letter to Mme de Grignan from Les Rochers, Sunday, October 1, 1684.

24. Ibid.

25. The Jesuit preachers of the time were popular and influential in French society and at Court. The Jansenists were a heretical Catholic sect associated with the abbey of Port-Royal. The "Puritans" of the French Catholic Church, they were actively persecuted by Louis XIV. Blaise Pascal's *Lettres Provinciales* and *Pensées* are among the most famous Jansenist writings.

26. Letter to Mme de Grignan from Les Rochers, Wednesday, July 13, 1689.

27. Letter to Bussy from Paris, Tuesday, May 14, 1686.

28. Letter to Bussy from Paris, Tuesday, September 2, 1687.

29. Letter to Bussy from Paris, Tuesday, June 17, 1687.

30. Letter to Mme de Grignan from Paris, Friday, April 10, 1676.

31. Letter to Mme de Grignan from Vichy, Thursday, May 28, 1676.

32. Letter to Mme de Grignan from Vichy, Wednesday, May 20, 1676.

33. Letter to Moulceau from Paris, Monday, January 27, 1687. Philippe de Moulceau was President of the Chambre des Comtes in Montpellier. Mme de Sévigné had met him at Grignan. They were friends and correspondents.

34. L. L. Irvine, *Ten Letter Writers,* 123.

35. Letter to Moulceau from Paris, written on Feast of the Epiphany, 1687.

36. Irvine, *Ten Letter Writers,* 118.

37. Ibid., 120.

Letter 1

Paris, Monday, December 15, 1670

TO M DE COULANGES[1]

I am going to tell you the most astonishing thing, the most surprising, the most marvelous, the most bewildering, most triumphant, most astounding, most outrageous, most singular, most extraordinary, most unbelievable, most unforeseen, the greatest, the smallest, most rare, the most common, the most talked about, the most secret until today, the most brilliant, the most enviable, in short, a thing of which one finds only one example in past centuries,[2] and yet that example is not accurate; a thing nobody can believe in Paris (how can one believe it in Lyon?);[3] a thing that makes everyone cry for mercy; a thing that fills Mme de Rohan and Mme de Hauterine[4] with joy; finally a thing that will happen on Sunday and those who see it will fancy they are seeing visions—a thing which will happen on Sunday and which perhaps will not happen on Monday. I cannot make up my mind to say it. Guess what it is; I give you three guesses. Do you give up? Very well, it is necessary to tell you: M de Lauzun[5] is marrying on Sunday at the Louvre—guess who? I give you four guesses, I give you ten, I give you a hundred. Mme de Coulanges will be saying: That is not very difficult to guess; it is Mlle de La Vallière[6]—Not at all, Madame. Mlle de Retz then?[7] Not at all. You are very provincial. How silly we are, you say. It is Mlle Colbert?[8] Still less close. It is surely Mlle de Créquy?[9] You are not there yet. I shall have to tell you in the end: he marries, on Sunday, in the Louvre, with the King's permission, Mademoiselle, Mademoiselle de . . . Mademoiselle . . . guess the name. He marries Mademoiselle, my word! by my word! my sworn word! Mademoiselle, la Grande Mademoiselle; Mademoiselle, daughter of the late Monsieur;[10] Mademoiselle, granddaughter of Henri IV; Mademoiselle d'Eu, Mademoiselle de Dombes, Mademoiselle de Montpensier, Mademoiselle d'Orléans; Mademoiselle, first cousin of the King; Mademoiselle, destined for a throne; Mademoiselle, the only match in France worthy of Monsieur.[11] There is a fine subject for discourse. If you shout out loud, if you are beside yourself, if you say that we have lied, that it is false, that we are making fun of you, that this is a good tale, that it is too insignificant to be imagined; if, in short, you insult us, we shall say that you are right. We did the same as you.

Adieu, the letters carried by this post will show you if we are telling the truth or not.

Letter 2

Paris, Sunday, April 26, 1671

TO MME DE GRIGNAN

This is Sunday, April twenty-sixth; and this letter will not go out until Wednesday, but it is not so much a letter as a story that I have just learned from Moreuil[12] of what happened at Chantilly[13] concerning Vatel.[14] I wrote to you last Wednesday that he had stabbed himself; here are the details of the affair.

The King arrived on Thursday evening. Hunting, lanterns, moonlight, a gentle walk, supper served in a place carpeted with daffodils—everything was perfect. They had supper. There was no roast at one or two tables because of several unexpected guests which upset Vatel, and he said more than once, "I am dishonored; this is a humiliation I cannot bear." He said to Gourville,[15] "I am bewildered; I haven't slept for twelve nights. Assist me giving orders." Gourville comforted him as best he could, but this roast missing, not from the King's table but from the twenty-fifth down, was constantly on his mind. Gourville told all this to Monsieur le prince who went to Vatel's room and said to him, "Vatel, everything is all right; nothing was so perfect as the King's supper." "Monseigneur, your kindness is overwhelming," he replied, "but I know that there was no roast at two tables." "Not at all," said Monsieur le prince, "don't upset yourself; all is going splendidly." Night falls. The fireworks are a failure owing to fog, and they cost 16,000 francs. By four in the morning Vatel was rushing around everywhere, finding everyone wrapped in slumber. He met a small purveyor who had only two loads of fish. "Is that all?" he asked. "Yes, Sir." He did not know that Vatel had sent men around to all the seaports. Vatel waited a short time, and other purveyors did not arrive; he lost his head and thought there would be no more fish. He found Gourville and said, "Sir, I shall never survive this disgrace; my honor and my reputation are at stake." Gourville laughed at him. Vatel went to his room, put his sword up against the door and ran it through his heart . . . only on the third attempt, for the first two were not mortal. Then he fell dead. At that moment fish was coming in from all quarters. They looked for Vatel to distribute it, went to his room, broke in the door, and found him lying in his own blood. They rushed to Monsieur le prince, who was terribly upset. Monsieur le duc[16] wept, for his trip to Burgundy depended on Vatel. Monsieur le prince told the King very sadly, explaining that it was a matter of too fine a sense of honor; he was greatly praised. His courage was both praised and blamed. The King said that he had been putting off his visit to Chantilly for five years because he was aware of what trouble it would be and told Monsieur le prince that he ought to have only two tables and not undertake all the rest. He swore that he would not allow Monsieur le prince to do so again, but it was too late for poor Vatel. However, Gourville tried to make up for the loss of Vatel, which he did in great measure. There was an elegant dinner, light refreshments, and then supper, a walk, cards, hunting, everything scented with daffodils, everything enchanting. Yesterday, Saturday, the same thing, and in the evening the King went on to Liancourt, where he ordered *medianoche;*[17] he is to stay there today.

That is what Moreuil told me, to be passed on to you. I don't know how to end this, not that I know anything about it. M d'Hacqueville,[18] who was present, will no doubt tell you the tale, but as his writing is not as legible as mine I am also writing. I have given a lot of details but I am sending them because on a similar occasion I should like them myself.

Letter 3

Les Rochers, Sunday, May 31, 1671

TO MME DE GRIGNAN

At last, my child, we are at our dear, old Les Rochers. How can I see these walks again, these ornaments, this little secluded room, these books, this chamber, and not die of sadness? Some recollections are agreeable; but there are others again so real and so tender that they are hardly supportable. Such are mine with respect to you. And you may easily guess the effect this is likely to produce in a heart like mine.

If you continue staying well, my dear child, I believe I shall not come to see you until next year. Brittany and Provence are not compatible. Long journeys are strange things. If we were always feeling as we do at the end of a journey, we should never stir from the place where we are. But Providence, in kindness to us, causes us to forget. It is much the same with women in childbirth. God bestows this forgetfulness so that the world should not come to an end and that one may make journeys to Provence. Mine therefore will give me the greatest joy I can have in my life, but how sad a thought to see no end to your stay there [in Provence]! I admire and applaud your good sense. Although, to tell you the truth, I am greatly touched by this impossibility [of the Grignans living in Paris], yet I hope time will make us see things in a different light. We must hope so, for without that consolation there would be nothing to live for. I sometimes have such melancholy moments in these woods that I return more shaken than if I had had a fever.

It seems to me that you had a good time in Marseille. Do not forget to tell me how you were received at Grignan. The people here had arranged a sort of triumphal entry for my son; Vaillant [bailiff at Les Rochers] had drawn up more than fifteen hundred men under arms, all well turned out with new ribbons around their necks, and had marched them within a league of Les Rochers. But guess what happened! our Abbé [her uncle le Bien Bon] had written that we should be there on Tuesday and afterwards forgot to mention it to us. Accordingly, these poor people waited on Tuesday until ten o'clock at night, when they returned home very much chagrined at their disappointment; we quietly arrived on Wednesday without dreaming that an army had been put in the field to welcome us. We were a good deal vexed but what could be done? That is how we started.

Mademoiselle du Plessis[19] is exactly as you left her. She has formed a new acquaintance with a woman at Vitré of whom she is very proud because she is a bluestocking who has read all the novels and has had two letters from the princess de Tarente.[20] I was naughty enough to get Vaillant to say I was jealous of this new friend, that it had given me great uneasiness, though I had not let anything show. All she said about it was worthy of Molière. It is highly amusing to see how artfully she handles me and how carefully she avoids speaking of my supposed rival in front of me. I, too, play my part very well.

My little trees are astonishingly beautiful. Pilois[21] is raising their stately heads to the skies. In short, nothing is so beautiful as these walks you saw being planted. You know I once gave you a sort of motto which was very suitable. Here is something I wrote on a tree for my son when he came back from Candia [on Crete]: *vago de fama;*[22] isn't that pretty, notwithstanding its conciseness? Only yesterday I had another inscribed in honor of idlers, *bella cosa far niente.*[23] Alas, my dear, how dreary my letters are! Where is the time when I talked of Paris like other people? Now you will hear of nothing but myself, and such is my conceit that I am persuaded you prefer that to any other.

I am highly pleased with my company here. Our Abbé is ever more admirable; my son and La Mousse[24] get on very well with me and I with them. We are always looking for one another; and when business takes me from them they are in despair and think I am absurd to prefer a farmer's accounts to the tales of La Fontaine. They are all passionately devoted to you, and I think they will be writing to you. So I am making the first move, for I do not like talking to you in a crowd. My dearest girl, always love me, for love is my life and my soul. As I told you the other day, it constitutes all my joy and all my sorrow. I declare that the rest of my life is overshadowed with gloom and sadness when I think that I must spend it so far away from you.

Letter 4

Paris, Wednesday, March 16, 1672

TO MME DE GRIGNAN

You refer to my departure. Ah, my dear daughter, I am clinging to that pleasant hope. Nothing now stops me but my poor aunt[25] who is dying of grief and dropsy; it breaks my heart to see her sufferings and all the affectionate and sensible things she says to me. Her courage, patience, and resignation are all admirable. M d'Hacqueville and I watch her decline from day to day. He sees my inmost heart and knows the pain I feel at not being free at present. I am following his advice, and we shall see between now and Easter whether her illness gets worse as it has done since I have been here. If it does, she will die in our arms, but if she shows any improvement and is likely to languish for any length of time, I shall then set out as soon as M de Coulanges [her cousin] comes back. Our poor Abbé is in despair as I am. . . . This is all I can think about. You can't be as anxious to see me as I am to embrace you. . . .

You ask me, my dear child, if I am as fond of life as ever. I admit that I think it has some acute sorrows. But I am even more unhappy at the thought of death, and I feel that I am so unfortunate to have to finish all this by death that I should desire nothing better, if it were possible, than to begin life again. I find myself in the midst of an undertaking that embarrasses me; I was launched upon life without my consent. I must leave it and that overwhelms me. For how shall I leave it? In what manner? Through which door? At what time? In what frame of mind? Am I to suffer a thousand pains and die in a state of despair? Shall I lose my senses? Am I to die in an accident? How shall I stand with God? What shall I have to offer to Him? Will fear or necessity bring me back to Him? Shall I have no other emotion than that of fear? What have I to hope for? Am I worthy of paradise? Do I deserve only the torments of hell? What an alternative! What a puzzle! Nothing is so silly as to place one's salvation in uncertainty, but nothing is more natural, and the stupid life I lead is the easiest thing in the world to understand. I am buried in thoughts of this nature, and I find death so terrible that I hate life more for leading me to it than I do for all the thorns that are strewn in its way. You will ask me then if I would wish to live forever. Not at all, but if I had been consulted, I would have liked to die in my nurse's arms; it would have spared me many troubles and brought me to heaven safely and easily. But let us speak of other things.

I am quite provoked that you have received *Bajazet*[26] from others rather than me. It is that wretch Barbin[27] who has served me this trick out of spite because I do not write *Princesses de Clèves* and *de Montpensier.*[28] You form a very just and true judgment of *Bajazet* and you will see that I share your opinion: I wish I could send you Champmeslé [the actress] to enliven it for you. The character of Bajazet lacks life. The manners and customs of the Turks are badly observed—their marriages have less ceremony. The denouement is not at all well prepared, and no reasons are given for so much slaughter. Of course, there are some good things in it, but nothing superlative, nothing perfect, none of those fine speeches of Corneille that thrill you. My dear, let us be cautious not to compare Racine to him, let us appreciate the difference. There are cold and feeble parts, and he will never be able to surpass his *Alexander* and *Andromache*. Many persons consider *Bajazet* as inferior to these, and it is my opinion also, if I may be so bold to give it. Racine is writing plays for Champmeslé and not for posterity. If ever he grows old and ceases to be in love, it will not be the same thing. Long live our old friend Corneille! Let us overlook some bad lines for the sake of those divine and sublime sallies that transport us, those masterly strokes that bid defiance to imitation. Despréaux[29] has more to say about this than me, and this is the opinion of everyone of good taste; let us therefore maintain it. . . .

I love you dearly for not being pregnant. Console yourself with being *uselessly beautiful* with the pleasure of not being ill [her word for pregnant] all the time.

I cannot pity you for having no butter in Provence because you have admirable oil and excellent fish. Ah! my dear, I can easily judge how people like you must employ their time and thoughts in the middle of your Provence. I shall think of it as you do, and pity you from my soul for being obliged to spend so many of your finest years there. I am so little desirous of making a figure at your court in Provence, and I can form a just conception of it from what I know of that in Brittany . . . that after three days of being in Vitré I wished for nothing but to return to Les Rochers. I swear to God that the sole object of my desires is to spend summer with you at Grignan.

Farewell, my child; I am rambling on and on. I defy you to understand how much I love you.

Letter 5

Les Rochers, Sunday, September 29, 1675

TO MME DE GRIGNAN

I wrote to you, dear child, from every place where I have been able to do so. And as I have not taken as much care with respect to our dear d'Hacqueville and my other friends, they have been very uneasy about me, for which I am really obliged to them. They did the Loire [River] the honor to suppose that it had swallowed me up. Alas, poor creature! I am sure I should have been the first it had ever served in this bad way; I found no inconvenience from it other than its waters were too shallow. M d'Hacqueville writes me that he does not know what to say to you of me, and that he fears his silence respecting me will alarm you. Are you not too good, dear child, in having appeared so solicitous about me that we are anxious to spare you about trifling things? You have so thoroughly convinced me of this that I have thought of nothing but writing to you punctually.

I left Silleraye the day after I wrote to you, which was on Wednesday; M de Lavardin put me into my carriage, and M d'Harouys[30] loaded me with provisions of all kinds. We arrived here on Thursday. The first person I met was Mademoiselle du Plessis [a Breton neighbor], more hideous, more foolish, and more impertinent than ever. Her liking for me does me no credit. I swear *here and now on my honor* not to encourage it by the least complaisance, friendship, kindness, or mark of approbation. I say the rudest things possible to her, but unfortunately she turns everything into a joke. . . . She is constantly at my elbow, but at present, indeed, she is taking the drudgery of the house off my hands; at the moment, she is cutting out table napkins for me.

I found my woods of inexpressible beauty and melancholy; the trees which you saw planted have grown very large, beautiful, and straight. They have spread out and now form a delightful shade; they are from forty to fifty feet high. Is there not something of maternal pride in giving you these details, and remember I planted them myself. As M de Montbazon [Molière's character] used to say of his children, "I first saw them when they were only so high." This lovely place is made for dreaming. . . . If thoughts are not made black by it, they are at least tinged with a dark gray. I think of you constantly, I regret your absence, I long for your company, then your health, your affairs, your long, protracted absence, and you can imagine how all this gathers at dusk when the light begins to fade. Do you remember these lines?

Under what unlucky star was born
The object of such tender love? [Racine]

It requires the most perfect submission to God's will to endure the future without despair, but I shall say no more lest I weary you. . . .

My health is as good as it was six years ago, and I cannot conceive whence comes this perpetual spring; I can only suppose I have an adaptable temperament. I read, I amuse myself. If I have anything to do, I do it in front of the Abbé as if he were not in the room. This agreeable unconstraint, together with a little hope, prevents me from being at the expense of a rope to hang myself. I found a letter of yours the other day in which you called me your good mamma. It was written at Sainte-Marie's [a convent] when you were ten years old, and you related to me the story of Madame Amelot, who fell head over heels from her parlor to the cellar. Your style was good even then. I found several other letters to Mademoiselle de Sévigné. All these circumstances bring you to my mind. . . . I received no letters from you by the last post which makes me sad. . . .

Adieu, beloved child. I frequently hear from your brother; he is very much concerned at not being able to get rid of his wretched *guidonage*,[31] but he should consider that there are a number of persons who must be provided for first, and who indeed have merited it by their services; these will always be preferred to one who is absent and considered as already provided for, and who has besides had no opportunity of showing himself by anything except his boredom in being so long a simple subaltern about whom no one cares. Well! this is precisely what we used to say: after a long and wearisome voyage, we found ourselves nine hundred leagues from where we were going, and so on!

Letter 6

Vichy, Thursday, May 28, 1676

TO MME DE GRIGNAN

I have just received two letters from you, one from Paris and the other from Lyon. You are deprived of a great pleasure in never having your own letters to read. . . . You write with a grace and propriety that I meet with nowhere else. You judge well in believing that I write without effort and that my hands are better [she had rheumatism]; they will not yet close, and the palms and fingers are very swollen. This makes me tremble, and gives an ill grace to my hands and arms; but one circumstance that consoles me a little is that I hold my pen without difficulty.

Today I started the showers which serve as a good rehearsal for purgatory. Stark naked one stands in a little subterranean hole where there is a hose of boiling hot water from the spring which an attendant directs wherever you choose. This state of nature, without so much as a fig leaf, is very humiliating. I had wanted to bring my two serving maids to keep me company. Behind a curtain a person sits to support your courage. In my case, it is a physician from Gannat [a small village near Vichy] whom Madame de Noailles[32] always takes with her; she likes him, a very genteel young man, not a charlatan, she says, and whom she sent to me out of pure friendship. I am keeping him though it might cost me my last penny, for the physicians here are unbearable, and this one diverts me. He is not of the genus apothecary. . . . He has wit and honesty, and is a man of the world: in short, I am perfectly satisfied. He talked to me throughout my martyrdom. Think of a jet of boiling water pouring over one or the other of your most vulnerable parts, at first applied to every part of the body in order to stir the senses, and then to the affected joints. But when it comes to the neck, the heat catches you unawares which is impossible to describe. This, however, is the main point. It is necessary to endure, one does endure; one emerges unscathed and is then put into a warm bed to sweat profusely, and this is the cure. My physician is very kind to me, for instead of leaving me for two hours to the tediousness of such a situation, I make him read to me, and that diverts me. This is the life I shall lead for seven or eight days, during which I expect to drink the waters also. But this, I am told, would be too much; my stay, therefore, will be rather longer than I expected.

It was to bid adieu to my rheumatism . . . that I came here. I find it was necessary. I feel as if I were taking a new lease on life. And if I could see and embrace you once more in the tenderness and joy of my heart, you might perhaps still call me your *bellissimi madre,* and I should not renounce the title of *mère beauté* M de Coulanges [her cousin] once gave me. It lies in your hands to bring about this transformation.

I am ordered to take chicken broth every day; nothing is more simple, nor more refreshing. I wish you would take some to prevent being burned up [by the heat and sun] at Grignan. . . . I am still uneasy about the health of our Cardinal [de Retz]. He exhausts himself with reading. Good heavens! has he not read everything that was to be read? I am delighted, my child, when you speak with confidence of the affection that I have for you; I assure you, you cannot believe too firmly that you constitute all the happiness, all the pleasure, and all the sorrow of my life.

Letter 7

Paris, Thursday, November 13, 1687

TO THE COMTE DE BUSSY-RABUTIN

I have just received a letter from you, dear cousin, the most delightful and affectionate that ever was. I have never seen friendship expressed so naturally and so persuasively. In a word, you have persuaded me, and I believe that my life is necessary to the preservation and the enjoyment of yours. Therefore, I am going to give you an account of it to please you and show you the state I am in.

I keep going back to the last days of my dear uncle the Abbé to whom, as you well know, I was under infinite obligations. I owed him all the sweetness and repose of my life, and it is to him you owe the joy I brought into your society. Without him, we should never have laughed together; you owe him for all my gaiety, my good humor, sprightliness, the gift I had of understanding you, the intelligence which made me comprehend what you have said and guess what you were going to say; in short, the good Abbé rescued me from the abyss in which M de Sévigné left me, restored me to what I was, to what you have seen me, worthy of your esteem and friendship. I draw a veil over your faults which are great, but I must forget them and tell you how keenly I have felt the loss of this lovable source of all the peace and repose of my life. He died after a fever of seven days, like a young man, with the most Christian sentiments that touched me deeply; for God has given me a foundation of religion which has made me look carefully at this last act of life. His life lasted for eighty years. He lived with honor, and he died a Christian. God grant us the same mercy. It was at the end of August that I wept bitterly for him.

I would have never left him if he had lived until the day of my death. But finding myself too free by the fifteenth or sixteenth of September, I resolved to go to Vichy at least to cure my imagination about some kinds of spasms in my left hand and a suggestion of vapors which made me fear apoplexy. This proposed journey made the duchesse de Chaulnes[33] want to do it too. I joined her, and as I wanted to go on to Bourbon [a fashionable spa], I remained with her. . . . I sent for a quantity of Vichy water which is excellent when heated in the wells of Bourbon. I took some of these, and then some of the Bourbon waters; a very good mixture. The two rivals were reconciled to each other until they were of one heart and soul. Vichy reposes on the bosom of Bourbon and warms herself at its fireside, that is to say, in the bubblings of its fountains. I have been so well that when I asked for a shower [of mineral waters], it was refused. They derided my fears, treated them as vague imaginings, and sent me away as a person in perfect health. They positively assured me of this, so that I believed it and now consider myself upon this footing. My daughter is delighted for she loves me, as you know.

Such, my dear cousin, is my situation. As your health depends on mine, here is an important proposal for you. Look after your cold, and in this way, make me continue well too. We must go on together and not leave each other.

I returned from Bourbon three weeks ago. Our pretty little Abbey [of Livry] was not yet given away, and we spent twelve days there. Now it has been given to the former bishop of Nîmes, a very holy prelate. I left there three days ago, upset at saying adieu forever to that delightful solitude I loved so much. After weeping for the Abbé, I wept for the Abbey.

I know you wrote to me during my journey to Bourbon. I have not taken time today to answer you, but have given in to the temptation to talk about myself at full speed, without reticence or limitation. I ask you to pardon me, and I assure you that I will not give way to so much liberty another time, for I know, and Solomon says it, that to judge how much we bore others by talking about ourselves, we have only to think how much others bore us when they talk about themselves. This rule is general enough, but I think I can exempt myself today, for I should be glad if your pen were as inconsiderate as mine, and delighted if you would talk to me for a long time about yourself. This feeling has persuaded me to enter into this terrible discourse, and with that confidence, I shall make no apologies; so I embrace you, dear cousin, and the charming Coligny [Bussy's daughter]. I return to Madame de Bussy [his wife] a thousand thanks for her compliments. I would let myself be killed rather than be made to write a word more.

Letter 8

Les Rochers, Wednesday, October 12, 1689

TO MME DE GRIGNAN

. . . I must tell you what Madame de LaFayette writes to me in the tone of a decree from a council on high, first from herself, then from Madame de Chaulnes and Madame de Lavardin,[34] threatening to love me no longer if I refuse to return immediately to Paris, saying that I shall be ill here, that I shall die, that my mind will decay, that, in short, I must make no opposition but come, and that she will not even read my frivolous reasons to the contrary. My dear, there is a vivacity and friendship that pleases me. These are the plans she proposes to me. I am to go to Malicorne in my son's equipage; Madame de Chaulnes is to dispatch the duc de Chaulnes's [carriage] there to meet me. I will arrive in Paris and live with the duchesse [de Chaulnes]. I am to buy no horses until spring. And this is the best of all: I am to find a thousand écus in my coffer from someone who has no need for the money, who will lend it to me without interest and will not press me to repay it. And that I must set out *immediately.* This is a long letter from someone who just recovered from a fever. I responded with gratitude, but treating it as a jest, assuring her that I would be only moderately bored with my son, his wife, some books, and the hope of returning to Paris this summer, without being lodged outside of my own house, without needing an equipage because I shall then have one, and without owing a thousand écus to a generous friend, whose good soul and magnanimous conduct would distress me more than all the bailiffs in the world; moreover, I gave her my word not to be ill, not to grow old, nor foolish, [knowing] that she will always love me in spite of her threat. This is the way I responded to these three good friends. Someday I will show you that letter; it will please you. Good heavens, what a proposal! not to be in my own house, to be dependent, to have no carriage, and owe a thousand écus! Truthfully, my dear child, I would infinitely rather be here. The horror of winter in the country is worse in prospect than reality. Tell me whether you approve of my conduct. If you were in Paris, ah! that might indeed shake my resolution, but you are not there. I have taken my time and my measures accordingly, and, if by some miracle you were now to fly there like a bird, I do not know whether my reason would not entreat yours, with the permission of our friendship, to let me complete certain little payments this winter, which will constitute the repose of my life. I could not refrain from relating to you this trifle. . . .

Your dream has surprised me. You believe it a false one, because you did not perceive a single tree before the door [in back of the château of Les Rochers]; that made you laugh. There is nothing more true: my son cut down all, I say all, the trees two years ago. He prides himself on having a fine view, just as you have dreamed, and carries this to such a length that he wants to build a wall around the parterre and turn the tennis court into a bowling green leaving only the road, and make there a moat and a low wall. It is true that if he does this, it will be a great improvement and add much to the beauty of the parterre; it is made after the design of M Le Nôtre,[35] and the Place Coulanges is planted with orange trees. You must have seen the future in your dream, as you have seen the past there before. I preserve your letters and your dream for my son and his wife, who will be charmed with your remembrances.

Letter 9

Grignan, Monday, November 13, 1690

TO THE COMTE DE BUSSY-RABUTIN

When you see the date of this letter, my cousin, you will take me for a bird. I have passed courageously from Brittany into Provence. If my daughter had been in Paris, I should have gone there, but knowing she would spend the winter in this beautiful country, I resolved to come and spend it with her, enjoy her fine sunshine, and return with her to Paris next year. I decided that after having given sixteen months to my son, it was right to give a few to my daughter, and this plan, which appeared difficult to execute, has not caused me much trouble. It took me three weeks to make the journey by litter, and upon the Rhône [River]. I even took a few days of rest. And, at last, I was received by M de Grignan and my daughter with such cordial affection, such sincere joy and gratitude, that I thought I had not come far enough to see such excellent people, and that the hundred and fifty leagues had not at all fatigued me. This house [the château de Grignan] is one of grandeur and beauty and has magnificent furnishings which I will describe to you someday. I wished to inform you of my change of climate, so you would no longer write to me at Les Rochers but here, where I feel the sun by its gentle warmth will make me feel young again. We must not neglect these little assistances, my dear cousin. I received your last letter before I left Brittany; but I was so overwhelmed with business that I deferred answering it until I came here.

We learned the other day of the death of M de Seignelay.[36] How young! how wealthy! how well established! Nothing was lacking for his happiness: it seems to us that it is splendor that is dead. What surprised us was that Mme de Seignelay has renounced society because her husband owed five million [livres]. That shows that large revenues are useless when one spends two or three times as much. In a word, my dear cousin, death makes us all equal. It is where we await the fortunate people.[37] Death brings down their joy and their pride and thus consoles those who are less fortunate. A little word on Christianity would not be amiss at this point, but I do not wish to make a sermon; I only want to write a letter of friendship to my dear cousin, to ask him his news and that of his dear daughter, to embrace them both with all my heart, to assure them of the esteem and respect of Madame de Grignan and her husband who desire me to do so, and implore you to love me always; it is not worthwhile to change after so many years.

NOTES TO THE TRANSLATIONS

1. Her cousin, Philippe-Emmanuel de Coulanges, whom Mme de Sévigné affectionately called "le petit Coulanges."

2. Marie of England, widow of Louis XII of France, married the Duke of Suffolk three months after her husband's death.

3. M and Mme de Coulanges were in Lyon at this time.

4. Both of these women had formed *mésalliances,* for which they were ridiculed.

5. Antoine Nompar de Caumont, duc de Lauzun, was a flamboyant soldier and adventurer who had a brief romantic liaison with the Grande Mademoiselle. Lauzun fell into disgrace and spent several years in prison at Pignerol. Freed but not allowed to return to Court, he resided in England until James II fled. Lauzun accompanied the King's wife and son to exile in France (1688). It is uncertain whether he ever married the Grande Mademoiselle, but presumably he did. Two years after she died, he married a young woman and lived to the age of ninety.

6. Louise de LaVaillière, first of Louis XIV's official mistresses who held sway at Court.

Replaced by Mme de Montespan, she retired to a convent in Paris and took the name Sister Louise de la Miséricorde.

7. Paule-Marguerite de Gondi, the fifteen-year-old niece of cardinal de Retz.

8. Henriette-Louise Colbert, second daughter of the King's minister. She married Paul de Beauvillier in 1671, having been betrothed to him in 1667.

9. The eldest daughter of the duc de Créquy, who married the duc de Némouille.

10. Gaston d'Orléans, brother of Louis XIII, called Monsieur. His daughter was one of the wealthiest people in France.

11. This Monsieur refers to Philippe, brother of Louis XIV, who had married Henriette-Anne, daughter of Charles I of England; she died in 1670.

12. Moreuil, First Gentleman of the Condé household. He was secretary to de La Rochefoucauld, then became his brother-in-law, and wrote his *Mémoires*.

13. A medieval fortress that was rebuilt in the sixteenth century and further embellished under Louis XIV and Louis XV; the home of Condé.

14. Major-domo to the Grand Condé. He had been in the employ of Fouquet (former Superintendent of Finance).

15. Jean Hérauld de Gourville. He had been a servant of the La Rochefoucauld family, then rose to steward, secretary, and financier to the duc de La Rochefoucauld. Involved with the financial scandals surrounding Fouquet, he was sentenced to death. He fled France, but returned eight years later. Gourville enriched himself by working for Condé. He helped La Rochefoucauld when he needed money and remained a loyal and faithful friend to his former employer.

16. Son of the prince de Condé.

17. Word (originally Spanish) meaning a meal of meat which is eaten immediately after midnight when a fast day is followed by a meat day.

18. Abbé d'Hacqueville, King's Councillor and close friend of Mme de Sévigné.

19. A pretentious neighbor who lived near Les Rochers; Mme de Sévigné disliked and often mocked her.

20. Princess Amélie de Tarente was a German princess, daughter of William V, Landegrave of Hesse-Cassel. She married Henri-Charles de La Trémouille who went by the name of prince de Tarente. She was a good friend and *suzeraine* of Mme de Sévigné in Brittany, and aunt of Madame, second wife of the King's brother. She remained Protestant and went into exile after the revocation of the Edict of Nantes in 1685.

21. The gardener at Les Rochers. The tree-lined walks still exist at the château.

22. Love of glory or love of fame.

23. It is a lovely thing to have nothing to do.

24. Abbé de La Mousse. Illegitimate son of Mme de Sévigné's uncle and guardian, Philippe II de Coulanges, he was raised as part of the family. He also tutored Françoise-Marguerite de Sévigné.

25. Henriette de Coulanges, marquise de La Trousse. Older sister of Mme de Sévigné's mother.

26. A new play by Racine.

27. A famous Paris publisher.

28. This is not clear; *La Princesse de Clèves,* written by Mme de LaFayette, was not published by Barbin until March 1678; she never admitted to writing *La Princesse de Montpensier,* which was not published until 1662.

29. The writer, Nicolas Boileau-Despréaux, and Jean Racine had been appointed royal historians by Louis XIV. Mme de Sévigné did not think much of their abilities as historians and believed a soldier/writer like her cousin Bussy would have been a better choice.

30. She had stayed at her friend Lavardin's château on her way to Brittany. Guillaume d'Harouys, seigneur de la Silleraye, was treasurer of the Breton Estates and brother-in-law of Philippe-Emmanuel de Coulanges, cousin of Mme de Sévigné.

31. Charles's commission as ensign in the Gendarmes-Dauphin; he had not been promoted after years of service. His mother obviously blamed him for his lack of success.

32. Wife of duc de Noailles, Lieutenant-General in Auvergne.

33. Wife of the Governor of Brittany and a close friend.

34. Mme de Lavardin was a close, longtime friend of Mme de Sévigné with whom she engaged *en Barvardin* (from *bavarder,* to gossip or to chat).

35. André Le Nôtre, a master gardener of the time. He laid out the gardens of Versailles and the Tuileries Gardens in Paris.

36. The son of the Grand Colbert; he died at age thirty-nine at Versailles on November 3, 1690.

37. The "we" refers to herself, age 65, and her cousin Bussy, over 72 years of age. In the next few years she lost many of her friends; Bussy died in 1693, the same year as Mme de LaFayette, friend to Mme de Sévigné for forty years.

BIBLIOGRAPHY

Primary Works

Duchêne, Roger, ed. *Madame de Sévigné: Correspondance.* 3 vols. Paris: Gallimard, 1972–1978.

Hammersley, Violet, ed. *Letters from Madame la Marquise de Sévigné.* New York: Harcourt, Brace and Company, 1956.

The Letters of Madame de Sévigné. 7 vols. Carnavalet Edition. Philadelphia: J. P. Horn and Company, 1927.

Madame de Sévigné: Selected Letters. Translated by Leonard Tancock. Harmondsworth, Eng.: Penguin, 1982.

Related Works

Aldis, Janet. *The Queen of Letter Writers: Marquise de Sévigné, Dame de Bourbilly, 1626–1696.* London: Methuen and Company, 1907.

Allentuch, Harriet Ray. *Madame de Sévigné: A Portrait in Letters.* Baltimore: Johns Hopkins Press, 1963.

Aubenas, J. A. *Histoire de Madame de Sévigné, de sa famille, et de ses amis.* N.p., 1842.

Bailly, Auguste. *Madame de Sévigné.* Paris: Fayard, 1955.

Boissier, Gaston. "Mme de Sévigné." *Les Grands Ecrivains français.* 5th ed. Hachette, 1901.

Combes, F. *Madame de Sévigné historien: le siècle et la Cour de Louis XIV.* Paris: Emile Perrin, 1885.

Duchêne, Roger. *Madame de Sévigné ou la chance d'être femme.* Paris: Fayard, 1982.

Faguet, E. "Madame de Sévigné." *Les Femmes Illustres.* N.p., 1910.

Irvine, Lyn Lloyd. *Ten Letter Writers.* London: L. and V. Woolf, 1932.

Jouhandeau, Marcel. "La vraie Sévigné." *Ecrits de Paris* (September 1959): 76–84.

Lamartine de Prat, M. S. A. de. *Madame de Sévigné.* N.p., 1864.

Lemoine, Jean M. P. J. *Madame de Sévigné, sa famille et ses amis.* Paris, 1926.

Madame de Sévigné and her Contemporaries. 2 vols. London: Henry Colburn, 1841.

Marcu, Eva. "Madame de Sévigné and Her Daughter." *Romanic Review* 51 (October 1960): 182–91.

Noyes, Alfred. "The Enigma of Madame de Sévigné." *Contemporary Review* 189 (March 1956): 149–53.

Puliga, comtesse de. *Madame de Sévigné: Her Correspondents and Contemporaries*. London: Tinsley Brothers, 1873.

Richie, Anne Isabella (Thackeray). *Madame de Sévigné*. Philadelphia: J. P. Lippincott and Company, 1881.

Saint-René Taillandier, M. *Madame de Sévigné et sa fille*. Paris, 1938.

Stanley, Arthur. *Madame de Sévigné: Her Letters and Her World*. London: Eyre and Spottiswoode, 1946.

Tilly, Arthur A. *Madame de Sévigné. Some Aspects of Her Life and Character*. Cambridge: Cambridge University Press, 1936.

Walckenaer, C. A. baron. *Memoirs touchant la vie et les ecrits de Marie de Rabutin-Chantal, Dame de Bourbilly, Marquise de Sévigné*. 5 vols. Paris: Didot, 1843–1856.

Williams, Charles G. S. *Madame de Sévigné*. Boston: Twayne Publishers, 1981.

ANATOMIST OF THE HEART

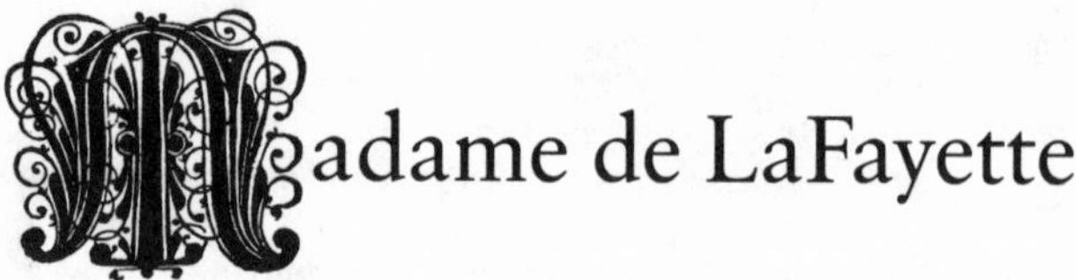

Madame de LaFayette

RONALD BOGUE

At the literary salon of the Hôtel de Nevers she was known as *le brouillard* (the fog). No one knows for certain why, but it would seem that Mme de LaFayette (1634–1693) struck casual acquaintances as somewhat reserved, aloof, and enigmatic. Those who knew her well valued her company but seldom characterized her in terms that contradicted this impression of distance, praising her most often for her intelligence and judgment. Those who were familiar with her efforts at court on behalf of her husband, and later on behalf of her sons, knew her as an indefatigable proponent of her family's interests who could manipulate the court's complicated networks of personal influence with considerable skill and success. But seldom does one glimpse in her contemporaries' remarks any sign of what the inner woman was like.

Mme de LaFayette clearly worked to protect her privacy, and it is significant that her literary activities were among the secrets she kept from the world. In part she hid her writing to avoid the stigma incurred by female authors in seventeenth-century aristocratic circles.[1] But one suspects that she would have protected her anonymity even if her authorship had been socially acceptable, for her fiction seems a central part of that private life she kept separate from her public existence. This cool, reasonable woman was one of her century's most penetrating chroniclers of the sufferings of passion and the heart's self-deceptions. She was acutely aware of the need to shield one's psychological being from the scrutiny of the world, since in all her fiction it is her heroines' failure to hide their inner selves from others that leads to their downfall.

Of Mme de LaFayette's early life little is known.[2] She was the firstborn child of Marc Pioche, sieur de La Vergne, and Isabelle Pena, both of the lowest ranks of the nobility. On March 18, 1634, she was baptized Marie-

Madeleine, Pioche de la Vergne, in the Saint-Sulpice church, just a few blocks from the Petit Luxembourg palace, where her father had taken up residence after accepting the post of governor of Richelieu's nephew, the marquis de Brézé. Soon after her birth, her father built a house on the rue de Vaugirard, near the Petit Luxembourg, and here he received such prominent intellectual figures as Chapelain, Voiture, and the abbé d'Aubignac. (Mme de LaFayette later inherited the house, which served as her principal residence for most of her adult life.) Her father saw military duty against the Spanish in 1636 and 1640 and took the post of lieutenant-governor of Le Havre in 1645. In 1649, when Marie-Madeleine was fifteen, her father died. Her two younger sisters, Eléonor-Armande and Isabelle-Louise, entered a convent, and her mother, one year after her husband's death, married the chevalier Renaud-René de Sévigné, whose rank, despite his connections with the *frondeurs,* considerably elevated the social standing of Isabelle Pena and her daughter.

Around the time of her father's death, Marie-Madeleine began to frequent polite society. She visited the Hôtel de Rambouillet—somewhat in decline during the Fronde—and there made the acquaintance of Mme de Sévigné, who was to become one of her closest friends. In 1650 she gained entree to the Louvre through the influence of her godmother, the duchesse d'Aiguillon, joining the ranks of Anne of Austria's ladies-in-waiting. The somewhat pedantic but learned Gilles Ménage courted Marie-Madeleine for a time, teaching her some Latin and Italian, introducing her to Petrarch and Tasso, and procuring for her copies of the popular multivolume romances *Le Grand Cyrus* and *Clélie.* Ménage never won her heart, but he gave her a taste of gallantry and the rudiments of a literary education, and he introduced her to some writers, most notably the minor figures Huet and Segrais, who solicited her first published literary work, a brief portrait of Mme de Sévigné, published in 1659.

By 1654 she had also become a friend of the ten-year-old Henriette-Anne Stuart (known as Henriette d'Angleterre), the daughter of Charles I of England and his impoverished widow, Henriette-Marie de France (daughter of Henri IV and Marie de Médicis). Mother and daughter were residing at the Convent of the Visitation in Chaillot, where Marie-Madeleine also met her future sister-in-law, Louise-Angélique de LaFayette, the convent's future mother superior. Marie-Madeleine's young friend was later to become a major figure at court, for after her brother Charles II's restoration to the English throne, she married Louis XIV's brother, Philippe de France, duc d'Orléans. Mme de LaFayette served her as friend and confidante at court.

On February 15, 1655, Marie-Madeleine married Jean-François Motier, comte de LaFayette, a widower twenty-eight years her senior and a member of a distinguished provincial family in somewhat straitened circumstances.

After their marriage, the couple settled at her husband's château in the Auvergne. Despite claims in her correspondence that she loved her husband greatly and that her provincial life was "a very happy one,"[3] her marriage was clearly an arranged alliance and her country existence a form of exile. After giving birth to two sons (Louis in 1658 and Armand in 1659), Mme de LaFayette returned to Paris with her husband; in 1660 M de LaFayette left for Auvergne alone. Gradually, M and Mme de LaFayette reached a tacit and amicable agreement that he would oversee the family estate while she resided in Paris at the rue de Vaugirard (which Mme de LaFayette had inherited on her mother's death in 1656). This arrangement not only was more agreeable to Mme de LaFayette, but it also allowed her to tend to her husband's complicated legal suits, several of which she was able to conclude favorably in 1662.

During the 1660s, Mme de LaFayette continued to rise in social standing and became increasingly involved in literary pursuits. Her friendship with Henriette d'Angleterre (always referred to at court simply as "Madame" following her marriage to the duc d'Orléans in 1661) gave her the entree to court society, and she became a regular at the Hôtel de Nevers, an important center of intellectual, political, and social life of the period. In 1662 her first work of fiction appeared anonymously, a novella titled *La Princesse de Montpensier*. The work was quite popular; in ensuing years it was often cited as an exemplum of *vraisemblance* and an alternative to the cumbersome and improbable romances of Mlle de Scudéry and La Calprenède, so popular during the 1640s and 1650s. Though set in the sixteenth century, this story of the illicit passion of the princesse de Montpensier for the duc de Guise was clearly modeled on Henriette d'Angleterre's love for the comte de Guiche.[4] Apparently Henriette did not notice the resemblances (although some contemporaries did), for she continued to confide in Mme de LaFayette and in 1665 asked for the latter's assistance in writing her memoirs. That year they set to work, Mme de LaFayette transcribing Henriette's recollections in the evening and the two of them revising the text the following morning. They discontinued their work later that year but resumed the project in 1669.

In the meantime, Mme de LaFayette had made the acquaintance of La Rochefoucauld. She found the noble frondeur fascinating, although she thought after reading his *Maximes* that he must have considerable corruption "in heart and mind to be able to imagine all that";[5] by 1668 they had become intimate friends. (Neither her contemporaries nor later historians have been able to determine whether they were lovers.) In 1669 she enlisted the aid of La Rochefoucauld and Segrais in composing a romance about Moors and Christians in medieval Spain. Segrais was responsible for the plot, Mme de LaFayette for the psychological development of the characters, and La Rochefoucauld for the refinement of the style. The first volume of the novel, titled *Zaïde,* appeared under the name of Segrais in 1670, the second volume following in 1671. It was a considerable success and, despite the collaborative nature of the work, bore clear signs of being more Mme de LaFayette's than anyone else's.

In June 1670, Mme de LaFayette witnessed the sudden and unexpected death of Henriette d'Angleterre, whom she had visited at Saint-Cloud on Saturday, June 28. The next day Henriette was stricken with a severe pain in her side, and within nine hours she was dead. This loss, wrote Mme de LaFayette, was "such as can never be consoled, and which leaves a bitterness spread over all the rest of one's life." Mme de LaFayette was deeply shaken. Her projected life of Henriette d'Angleterre came to an abrupt end, for "the death of this princess left me with neither the means nor the desire of continuing this history, and I wrote down only those circumstances surrounding her death to which I was a witness."[6]

Following Henriette d'Angleterre's death, Mme de LaFayette's court connections were greatly curtailed, but she continued to attract a distinguished group to the rue de Vaugirard. She may have begun work on her masterpiece, *La Princesse de Clèves,* as early as 1671, but the novel was long in forthcoming. She assiduously researched the historical background of the novel, and she devoted considerable time to promoting her sons' careers and restoring the morale of an increasingly depressed La Rochefoucauld. After several years' labor, *La Princesse de Clèves* was published in 1678. Even before being printed, its circulation in manuscript had made it the center of conversation in polite circles. The novel's unusual confession scene, in which the princesse de Clèves tells her husband of her love for the duc de Nemours in order to enlist his aid in fighting this passion, provoked the *Mercure Galant* to solicit letters of opinion from its readers as to whether the princess had acted wisely. A tragedy based on the novel was performed by the end of the year, and a full-scale critique of the work was published in December 1678 (to which Mme de LaFayette responded, through the agency of Jean Antoine, abbé de Charnes).

La Princesse de Clèves was the last work of Mme de LaFayette to be published in her lifetime. Shortly after its publication, her closest companion, La Rochefoucauld, fell ill and died on March 17, 1680. Although Mme de LaFayette was to say late in life that "one does not die of anyone else's death,"[7] she apparently suffered greatly at the loss. "Poor Mme de LaFayette no longer knows what to do with herself," wrote Mme de Sévigné. "She has had a great shock. Everyone will be consoled, except her."[8] She continued to busy herself with the advancement of her sons' careers throughout the 1680s, and following the death of her husband in 1683 she took charge of administering the family estate. "Never has a woman, without leaving her room, conducted business so well," wrote

Mme de Sévigné. "She has a hundred arms, she reaches everywhere; her children are greatly appreciative and thank her daily for possessing such a winning nature."[9] Sometime during this decade she may have written the novella *La Comtesse de Tende,* which was found among her elder son's papers on his death and published in 1724. She also composed a modest history of court affairs at the end of the decade that was published posthumously in 1731 under the title *Mémoires de la Cour de France pour les années 1688 et 1689.* In her final years, Mme de LaFayette turned her thoughts to religion, eventually cutting herself off from the world. During the last year of her life, she wrote no letters and received no one. On May 22, 1693, she went into a coma and died on May 25. Two days later she was buried in Saint-Sulpice, the church in which she had been baptized.

There is no question that *La Princesse de Clèves* is Mme de LaFayette's masterpiece. It has continued to enjoy a position of unvarying eminence in French letters, having received the praise of such writers as Voltaire, Stendhal, Saint-Beuve, Taine, Barbey d'Aurevilly, Camus, and Butor. It was translated into English only one year after its French publication, and other English translations followed in 1720, 1777, 1891–92, 1925, 1946, 1950, 1961, and 1979.[10] Contemporary scholars have insisted that traditional claims concerning the author's originality and influence have been exaggerated, for she did not invent the French novel. Instead, they claim, she made use of fictional forms current in the 1660s and 1670s, and her work was not emulated directly by many writers. Yet *La Princesse de Clèves* clearly stands as the finest French novel of the seventeenth century, and one of the great psychological novels of world literature.

The novel, set in the sixteenth century during the reign of Henri II, tells the story of the young and dazzling princesse de Clèves, a woman who accedes willingly to her arranged marriage with the prince de Clèves but soon falls passionately in love with the duc de Nemours. Eventually she finds that she cannot conceal the signs of her love from the many inquisitive eyes at court and, after retiring to the country, confesses to her husband that she has succumbed to a passion for another; she begs him to help her fight this passion so that she may remain faithful to him. Unfortunately, the duc de Nemours has gone to the country to catch a glimpse of his beloved and, while hiding in the woods outside the house of the princess, overhears her confession to her husband. The duc de Nemours recounts this singular incident, without mentioning any names, to a close friend, and soon the story is common knowledge at court. When the prince and princess hear the story, each accuses the other of betraying a confidence. The prince gradually discovers the identity of the princess's beloved and has the duc de Nemours followed. When he learns that the duke has again traveled to the country where his wife is staying, the prince flies into a jealous rage and refuses to hear the rest of his spy's report testifying to his wife's innocence. (The duc de Nemours had once again simply hidden in the woods and admired the princess from afar.) Shortly thereafter the prince becomes ill and, on his deathbed, accuses his wife of causing his death through her infidelity. The princess is deeply affected by his death; although innocent of any wrongdoing and free to marry, she refuses the duc de Nemours's proposal and spends her remaining days in a convent.

The greatness of the novel lies in its detailed and subtle presentation of the inner workings of its characters. Although Mme de LaFayette displays the neoclassical penchant for discovering the universal within the particular, relating only those events and thoughts that contribute to the tragic conflict between love and duty, her probing of the characters' psyches often reveals divided motives, implicit ambiguities, and deflected desires. The singularity of the princesse de Clèves's actions in confessing to her husband and refusing the hand of her beloved has fueled, from the work's first publication, endless speculation concerning her motives. Modern readers have been particularly struck by scenes such as the one in which the duc de Nemours, hiding in the woods, spies on the princess in her country house—she lovingly wrapping ribbons around his cane while gazing on his fetishized portrait, he enjoying the voyeur's pose that later in the novel virtually becomes a constituent of their desire.[11] The novel's world is one of glittering surfaces and deceiving appearances, a society whose members have little privacy and spend most of their time trying to penetrate one another's disguises. Time and again Mme de LaFayette shows that the public world of history, generally considered in her age to be the guarantor of truth, is an illusory cover for the inner reality that only fiction can explore.[12]

The great success of *La Princesse de Clèves* has assured Mme de LaFayette a place of eminence in literary history, but unfortunately it has also cast her other works into undeserved obscurity (particularly in English-speaking countries, where, with the exception of a 1666 London translation of *La Princesse de Montpensier,* they have remained untranslated). One cannot deny the preeminence of *La Princesse de Clèves,* but, even if she had not written that novel, she would still be an important seventeenth-century writer.

La Princesse de Montpensier, Mme de LaFayette's first piece of fiction, did enjoy a considerable, albeit short-lived, reputation in the seventeenth century for a *vraisemblance* that heroic romances earlier in the century lacked. Like *La Princesse de Clèves, La Princesse de Montpensier* is set in the sixteenth century and concerns a woman who finds passion after an arranged marriage and comes to an unhappy end. Psychological characterization in this novella, although astute, is less detailed than in *La Prin-*

cesse de Clèves, largely because it focuses more consistently on the complex relations between the public and personal spheres in court society. By choosing actual historical personages for her characters and integrating the action of the love plot with the political struggles of the age, Mme de LaFayette not only creates *vraisemblance* but also shows how affairs of state, social ambitions, and affairs of the heart impinge on one another. Nowhere else does Mme de LaFayette so convincingly demonstrate parallels between the disorders of the state and the devastation of passion.

Zaïde also was well received in the seventeenth century and in the eighteenth was often judged the equal of *La Princesse de Clèves.* In the nineteenth century it fell from favor; for modern audiences, it remains the least accessible of Mme de LaFayette's works of fiction. *Zaïde* is a romance, replete with all the improbabilities standard in fiction of the earlier seventeenth century: shipwrecks, mistaken identities, miraculous reunions, mysterious portraits, and extended debates about love. Yet the characterization is often complex and the psychological portraits compelling (for example, the obsessively jealous Alphonse and the self-centered seducer Alamir). *Zaïde* suffers from the limitations of its genre, but given those limitations, it is a surprisingly interesting work.

Perhaps the most underrated of Mme de LaFayette's writings is *La Comtesse de Tende,* published posthumously in 1724 and seldom given the attention it deserves.[13] Most often it has been treated as an early, abandoned sketch of what was later to become *La Princesse de Clèves,* yet little evidence supports this conclusion. There are certain stylistic similarities between *La Comtesse de Tende* and *La Princesse de Montpensier,* but the former's ironic use of zeugma and period clichés and its acerbic and laconic tone are unparalleled in Mme de LaFayette's earlier writings. Both *La Princesse de Clèves* and *La Comtesse de Tende* eventuate in a wife's confession of wayward passion to her husband, but a devoted wife's appeal to her husband for aid in fighting passion is a far cry from a wife's admission that she's pregnant with another man's child. It seems most likely that *La Comtesse de Tende,* the harshest, most realistic, and least sentimental of Mme de LaFayette's tales, was also her last.

The assertion that *La Comtesse de Tende* is a rudimentary draft could be maintained only through a cursory and careless examination of the work. Its style is terse and clipped, but intentionally so. It is a masterpiece of compression and economy, each detail added with the deft control of an experienced craftsman. With pitiless rigor, Mme de LaFayette exposes the weaknesses of her characters: the comte de Tende, "rich, handsome, more likely to make himself esteemed than to please"; the chevalier de Navarre, inspired in his passion "half by love and half by ambition"; and the comtesse de Tende, dissuaded from suicide by "nature and Christianity." In a few brief episodes, she traces the trajectory of a life and dissects the basic contradictions of a social world, with its public ambitions, its private desires, and its ubiquitous and protean vanities. In *La Comtesse de Tende*, the world of Mme de LaFayette's fiction is reduced to its baser truths. It is a sexist world in which women, though weak and vain, are nevertheless victims of callous and self-serving lovers (such as the chevalier de Navarre) and of self-righteous and vindictive husbands (such as the comte de Tende). Mme de LaFayette sympathizes with her heroine to an extent, yet ultimately views her plight with the detachment of one who is facing life's harsher realities with an unflinching eye.

Of her nonfictional works, *L'Histoire de Madame Henriette d'Angleterre* is easily the most interesting. Much of the history reads like one of Mme de LaFayette's novels—Madame continually engaged in intrigues and liaisons of a labyrinthine and often improbable complexity. But the most impressive portion of the work is the concluding narration of her death, a prime example of neoclassical restraint and simplicity in the presentation of material charged with intense emotion.

Though not an especially beautiful woman, Madame possessed a charm and sweetness that many at court found appealing. She participated fully in court life, aspiring briefly for the king's heart, and retained her spirit and good nature despite eight pregnancies (including six miscarriages) in nine years and despite marriage to a weak, jealous man whose homosexual proclivities occasioned Mme de LaFayette's oblique remark that "the miracle of inflaming the heart of this prince was reserved to no woman in the world."[14] Her death in 1670 was totally unexpected and left many at court in shock.

Mme de LaFayette was deeply moved, yet she responded to this dire event not with cries of lamentation but with the barest of narratives, a scrupulously detailed account of the minute circumstances surrounding Madame's death. The resulting document is a fascinating record of medical practices of the period, life at court, the role of the king, and the nature of marriage among the aristocracy. But it is also a touching and dramatic portrayal of suffering, loss, and dignity, one whose power and force stem from its very lack of emotional expression.

The translation of the *Histoire de Madame Henriette d'Angleterre* is based on the 1720 edition, reprinted in Claudine Herrmann's edition of the *Histoire*. The translation of *La Comtesse de Tende* follows the manuscript edition of Micheline Cuenin, rather than the 1724 edition which shows clear signs of revision after Mme de LaFayette's death.

NOTES

1. Upon learning that Huet had revealed her authorship of *La Princesse de Montpensier,* Mme de LaFayette wrote Huet that "indeed I gave you a *Princesse de Montpensier* for Araminte, but not as one of my works. She will believe that I am a true professional author, to give my books like that. Please try to repair what this might have spoiled in the opinion that I want her to have of me" (Mme de LaFayette, *Correspondance,* 1:175).

2. The standard biographies of Mme de LaFayette are Beaunier's *La Jeunesse de Madame de La Fayette* and *L'Amie de La Rochefoucauld,* and Magne's *Madame de LaFayette en ménage* and *Le Coeur et l'esprit de Madame de LaFayette.* The best introduction to the life and works of Madame de LaFayette in English is Haig's exemplary volume, *Madame de LaFayette.*

3. Mme de LaFayette, *Correspondance,* 1:69.

4. The parallels between *La Princesse de Montpensier* and the life of Madame Henriette d'Angleterre are pointed out by Magne, *Le Coeur et l'esprit,* 19–20, and Beaunier, *L'Amie de La Rochefoucauld,* 259ff.

5. Mme de LaFayette, *Correspondance,* 1:219.

6. Mme de LaFayette, *Histoire de Madame Henriette d'Angleterre,* ed. Herrmann, 24.

7. Mme de LaFayette, *Correspondance,* 2:203.

8. Mme de Sévigné, *Correspondance,* 2:891–92.

9. Ibid., 3:158, 847.

10. For more information on English translations of *La Princesse de Clèves,* see the preface to Greene's translation, 17–20.

11. On the couple's latent voyeurism, see Butor's "Sur *La Princesse de Clèves.*"

12. For a thorough treatment of the theme of appearance and reality in *La Princesse de Clèves,* see Kreiter, *Le Problème du paraître dans l'oeuvre de Mme de LaFayette.* On the relationship between history and truth in the novel, see Rousset, "La Princesse de Clèves." Useful studies in English of this work include Turnell, *The Novel in France,* 27–47, Weinstein, *Fictions of the Self,* 66–83, and Kamuf, *Fictions of Feminine Desire,* 67–96.

13. See Scott, "Criticism and 'La Comtesse de Tende,'" for a history of the reception of *La Comtesse de Tende* and for an intelligent commentary on the story.

14. Mme de LaFayette, *Histoire de Madame Henriette d'Angleterre,* 43.

From The History of Madame Henriette d'Angleterre

(A large part of *The History of Madame Henriette d'Angleterre* concerns the events surrounding Madame's life at court from roughly 1660 to 1665. The final section of the *History,* from which these excerpts are taken, abruptly shifts from 1665 to Madame's last days in June 1670. In May 1670, Louis XIV had sent Madame to England to assist in the negotiation of the Treaty of Dover. As sister-in-law of Louis XIV and sister of Charles II, she was a natural choice for intermediary. Her mission was deemed a success, and she returned from England in June 1670 at the height of her prestige. Her diplomatic triumph, however, further strained her strife-ridden marriage; her husband was jealous of her sudden prominence in state affairs, but also of the opportunity Dover had provided her of seeing a former ardent admirer, the Duke of Buckingham.

On Friday, June 24, 1670, she and her husband went to their palace at Saint-Cloud, roughly five miles from the center of Paris. Mme de LaFayette joined Madame at Saint-Cloud the next day. Madame had been complaining since Friday of an ache in her side, and Mme de LaFayette thought that Madame looked rather pale. At midday on Sunday, June 29, Madame and others were offered a glass of chicory water, a popular drink of the period.)

[Madame] drank it, and while putting the cup back in the saucer with one hand, she held her side with the other, and said in a tone expressing extreme pain: "Oh! my side! oh! what pain! I can't stand it!"

She turned red while uttering these words, and, in the following moment, a livid paleness came over her that surprised everyone; she continued to cry out, and asked to be carried since she could no longer stay on her feet.

We held her under her arms; she could scarcely walk, and she was all bent over. Her maids undressed her in an instant. I supported her while she was being unlaced; she was still moaning, and I noticed that she had tears in her eyes. I was astonished and moved, for I knew her to be the most patient person in the world.

I said to her, while kissing the arms that I held, that she must be suffering greatly. She answered that it was inconceivable; she was placed on the bed, and as soon as she was situated there she screamed again more loudly than before, and threw herself from one side to the other, like someone suffering infinitely. Her first doctor, M. Esprit, was immediately sent for. He came, and said that it was colic and ordered the customary remedies for such illnesses; yet her pains were inconceivable. Madame said that the pain was much worse than they thought, that she was going to die, that someone should go seek a confessor.

Monsieur [Madame's husband] was beside her bed; she embraced him, and said with a sweetness and a look capable of softening the most barbarous of hearts: "Alas, Monsieur, you have ceased loving me for some time; but that is unjust; I have never been unfaithful to you." Monsieur seemed very touched, and all who were in the room were so moved that the only sounds to be heard were the sobs of people weeping.

All that I have just related took place in less than half an hour. Madame continued to cry out that she felt terrible pains in the hollow of her stomach; suddenly she said that someone should look at the glass from which she drank, that it contained poison, that perhaps someone had mistaken one bottle for another, that she had been poisoned, that she could feel it, and that she should be given an antidote.

I was beside the bed near Monsieur, and, although I believed him quite incapable of such a crime, an understandable astonishment at the thought of human malignity made me observe him attentively. He was neither moved nor embarrassed by the opinion of Madame.[1] He said that some of the drink should be given to a dog; he concurred with Madame that oil [often recommended in cases of arsenic poisoning] and an antidote should be sent for in order to help Madame rid herself of such a dreadful thought. Madame Desbordes, her first chamber lady, who was absolutely loyal to her, told her that she had prepared the infusion and had drunk some, but Madame still insisted on having oil and an antidote; she was given both. Sainte-Foi, Monsieur's first *valet de chambre,* brought her some viper's powder [believed to be an effective counter-poison]. She told him that she would take it from his hand since she trusted him. She was given several drugs to counteract a possible poison, and it is possible that they served more to hurt than to soothe her. The antidotes she had been given made her vomit; she had already wanted to several times before anything had come up, but her vomit was defective, and she was able to bring up only phlegm and a portion of the food that she had eaten. The convulsions brought on by these remedies and the excessive pains that she suffered induced a torpor that resembled repose; but she told us that we should not be fooled, that her pains were still the same, that she no longer had the strength to scream, and that there was no cure for her illness.

It seemed that she was completely certain of her death, and that she was resigned to it as to something indifferent. By all appearances, the thought of poison was fixed in her mind, and, seeing that the remedies had been useless, she no longer thought of living, and concentrated only on enduring her suffering with patience. She began to grow very apprehensive. Monsieur summoned Madame de Gamaches to take her pulse; the doctors had not thought of it; she left the bed terrified, and told us that she could find no pulse, and that all Madame's extremities were cold. That frightened us; Monsieur seemed scared. Monsieur Esprit [Monsieur's doctor] said that this was a common occurrence with colic, and that he would vouch for the life of Madame. Monsieur flew into a rage and said that he had vouched for Monsieur de Valois [Monsieur and Madame's infant son] and that he had died; that he was vouching for Madame, and she was dying too.

[Madame asked that the curé de Saint-Cloud attend her, and Monsieur sent for two of the king's doctors, MM Yvelin and Valet. Madame was bled from the arm and administered a senna enema, but her condition did not improve. She was then moved to a pallet on the floor so that her bed could be cleaned.]

Monsieur asked her if she were being bothered. "Oh, no, Monsieur!" she said, "nothing can bother me any more; I won't be among the living tomorrow morning, you will see." She was given some bouillon, since she had eaten nothing since dinner; as soon as she swallowed, her pains redoubled and became as violent as they had been when she drank the chicory infusion. Death was written on her face, and one could see it in her cruel sufferings, although she did not seem perturbed.

The king had sent for news several times, and she had always replied that she was dying. Those who had seen her told him that she was indeed very ill, and M de Créqui, who had passed by St.-Cloud on the way to Versailles, told the king that he believed she was in great danger, so that the king decided to come see her, and arrived at St.-Cloud at eleven o'clock.

When the king arrived, Madame was suffering the intensified pains caused by the bouillon; it seemed as if the doctors were enlightened by his presence; he summoned them to a private conference to hear what they thought of her case, and these same doctors, who, two hours earlier, had vouched for her life and had claimed that cold extremities were common symptoms of colic, began saying that her case was beyond hope, that cold limbs and weak pulse were the signs of gangrene, and that she must receive the last rites of Our Savior.

The queen and the comtesse de Soissons had come with the king; Madame de la Vallière and Madame de Montespan[2] had come together. I spoke to the countess; Monsieur called me, and in tears told me what the doctors had just said; I was surprised and touched, and I told Monsieur that the doctors had lost their minds, and that they cared neither about her life nor about her salvation, that she had spoken to the Curé de St.-Cloud for only an hour, and that someone must be summoned for her. Monsieur said that he would give orders that M de Condom [Bossuet, bishop of Condom, a major writer of the period] be found; I agreed that a better choice could not be made, but I suggested that while waiting for him, we should call Monsieur Feuillet, a canon whose merit was well-known.

Meanwhile, the king had gone to see Madame. She told him that he was losing the most faithful servant he would ever have. He said that she was not in such great danger, but that he was astonished at her fortitude, which he found to be considerable; she answered that he knew well that she had never feared death, but that she had only feared losing his good graces.

The king then spoke with her of God; afterward, he came back toward the spot where the doctors were gathered; he found me in despair that they had given her no remedies, above all no emetics. He did me the honor of saying that they had lost their wits, that they did not know what they were doing and that he was going to try to put them back in their right minds. He spoke to them, and then drew near Madame's bed, telling her that he was no doctor, but that he had just suggested thirty remedies to the doctors. They had responded that they would have to wait. Madame uttered a few words, and said that one had to die according to the proper forms.

The king, seeing that by all appearances there was no hope, in tears said goodbye to Madame. She prayed him not to cry, which moved him, and told him that the first news he would have the next day would be of her death.

The maréchal de Grammont came near her bed. She told him that he was losing a good friend, that she was going to die, and that she had believed at first that she had been poisoned by mistake.

When the king left, I was beside her bed; she said to me, "Madame de La Fayette, my nostrils are already closed." I could only answer with tears; for what she had said was true, and I had not yet noticed. She was then moved back to the large bed, and she began having hiccups. She told M Esprit that they were the hiccups of death: she had already asked several times when she would die; she asked again, and although she was answered as a person who was not near death, one could clearly see that she had no hope of recovery.

She never turned her thoughts to life; never a word of reflection on the cruelty of her destiny, which had seized her in the flower of her youth; no questions of the doctors to learn whether it was possible for her to be saved; no eagerness for remedies, even though the violence of her pains must have made her long for them; a peaceful countenance mid the certitude of death, the conviction of being poisoned, and sufferings that continued to be cruel; finally, a courage without example, beyond representation.

The king departed, and the doctors declared that there was no hope. M Feuillet came; he spoke to Madame with a thoroughgoing austerity; but he found her in a frame of mind that went far beyond his austerity. She was a little apprehensive that her past confessions had been worthless, and begged M Feuillet to help her make a general confession; she did so with sincere piety, and with the firm resolution of living a Christian life should God restore her to health.

I drew near her bed after her confession; M Feuillet was beside her, as was a capuchin, her usual confessor. This good father wanted to speak with her, and launched into matters that fatigued her. She looked at me with eyes that communicated what she was thinking, and then fixing them on the capuchin, she said, with an amazing sweetness, as if she were afraid of hurting him, "Let M Feuillet speak, my father; you may speak after him."

At this moment the English ambassador [William Ralph Montagu] arrived. As soon as she saw him, she spoke to him of her brother the king [of

England], and of the grief he would feel at her death; she had already spoken of this several times at the beginning of her illness. She begged him to write the king that he was losing the person who loved him most in the world. The ambassador then asked her if she had been poisoned. I do not know whether she said that she had been, but I do know that she told him that he must mention nothing in that vein to her brother the king, that he must be spared that grief, and that above all he must not dream of seeking vengeance; that the king was not guilty, that no one must be angry with him.

She said all this in English, and, since the word "poison" is the same in French as in English, M Feuillet understood it and interrupted the conversation, saying that she must sacrifice her life to God and think of nothing else.

She received the last sacrament. Then, Monsieur having retired for the night, she asked if she was never to see him again. He was sent for; he came and in tears embraced her. She begged him to go to bed, and told him that he had touched her heart.

In the meanwhile she continued steadily to decline, and from time to time fits of weakness attacked her heart. M Brager, an excellent doctor, arrived. He did not despair of her at first; he set about consulting with the other doctors. Madame called for them; they said that they wanted to be left to themselves for a little while, but she sent again for them. They gathered around her bed; it had been suggested that she be bled at the foot. "If you wish to do so," she said, "there is no time to lose: my head is growing confused, and my stomach is feeling full."

They remained surprised at such great fortitude, and, seeing that she continued to desire a bleeding, they had it done; but no blood came, and little had come the first time they had bled her. She thought she was going to die while they had her foot in the water; the doctors told her that they were going to prepare a remedy, but she replied that she wanted extreme unction before taking anything.

M de Condom [Bossuet] arrived while she was receiving extreme unction.[3] He spoke with her of God, in keeping with her state, and with that eloquence and that spirit of religion that was evident in all his works; he had her perform those acts that he judged necessary; she entered into all that he said with an astonishing zeal and presence of mind.

While he spoke, her first maid approached her to give her a few things that she needed; she said to her in English, so that M de Condom would not understand, conserving to the brink of death her considerate nature: "When I am dead, give M de Condom the emerald ring that I had made for him."

While he continued to speak to her of God, a desire to sleep came over her, which was actually only a failing of nature. She asked him if she could not have a few minutes' rest; he said that she could, and that he was going to pray for her.

M Feuillet remained at the head of her bed, and, almost in the same instant, Madame asked him to call M de Condom back, saying that she was certain that she was about to die. M de Condom drew near and gave her the crucifix; she held it and kissed it with fervor. M de Condom continued to talk to her the whole time, and she answered with the same clarity of mind, as if she had not been ill, holding the crucifix against her mouth all the while; only death made her let it go. Her strength failed her; she let it fall and ceased speaking and living at almost the same time; her agony lasted but a moment, and, after two or three small convulsive movements of her lips, she died at two-thirty in the morning, eight hours after her illness had begun.[4]

La Comtesse de Tende

Mademoiselle de Strozzi,[5] daughter of the marshal and close relative of Catherine de Médicis, married, during the first year of the regency of that queen, the comte de Tende, of the house of Savoy, rich, handsome, more likely to make himself esteemed than to please, the noble at court who lived with the greatest splendor. Nevertheless, his wife loved him at first with passion. She was quite young; he regarded her as a child, and he was soon in love with someone else. The comtesse de Tende, lively, and of Italian descent, grew jealous; she could find no repose and left none for her husband; he avoided her company and no longer lived with her as one lives with one's wife.

The countess grew more beautiful; she showed a great deal of spirit and intelligence; everyone looked on her with wonder; she became occupied with her own affairs and imperceptibly was cured of her jealousy and her passion.

She became the intimate friend of the princesse de Neuchatel, young, beautiful and the widow of the prince of that name, who in leaving her that title made her the most elevated and the most brilliant match of the court.

The chevalier de Navarre, descended from former sovereigns of that realm, was also young then, handsome, full of spirit and pride; but fortune had given him nothing more than his birth. He cast his eyes on the princesse de Neuchatel, with whose temperament he was acquainted, as on a person capable of a violent attachment and able to make the fortune of a man such as himself. Toward that end, he devoted himself to her, without being in love himself, and won her affection: he was admitted to her company, but he found himself still quite far from the success that he desired.

His plan was unknown to virtually everyone; he had confided in only one of his friends and that friend was also an intimate friend of the comte de Tende. He made the chevalier de Navarre agree to confide his secret to the count, in hopes that he could enlist the count's aid with regard to the princesse de Neuchatel.

The comte de Tende already liked the chevalier de Navarre; he spoke of him to his wife, for whom he was beginning to have greater consideration, and persuaded her to do what was desired. The princesse de Neuchatel had already confided her affection for the chevalier de Navarre; the countess tried to strengthen it.

The chevalier came to see her; he arranged meetings and strategems with her; however, upon seeing her, he was seized with a violent passion for her, but he did not give way to it immediately. He saw the obstacles that these feelings, inspired half by love and half by ambition, would put in the way of his plans; he resisted, but, in order to have succeeded, he would have had to see the comtesse de Tende less often; consequently, he fell madly in love with the countess.

He could not entirely hide his passion; she noticed it; her vanity was flattered, and she began to feel a violent love for him.

One day, while she was speaking with him of the great fortune of marrying the princesse de Neuchatel, he said to her while looking at her in a way that completely declared his passion: "And do you believe, madame, that there is no fortune that I would prefer to that of marrying the princess?"

The comtesse de Tende was struck by the glances and words of the chevalier; she looked at him, and confusion and silence arose between them, more eloquent than words.

From that day forward, the countess was so agitated that she was deprived of all repose; she felt the remorse of taking from her intimate friend the heart of a man whom she was going to marry solely for the sake of being loved, whom she was marrying with the disapproval of everyone, and at the expense of her high station.

This betrayal horrified her. Thoughts of the shame and evils of a love affair filled her mind; she saw the abyss into which she was rushing and she resolved to avoid it. She kept her resolutions poorly.

The princess had almost decided to marry the chevalier de Navarre; nevertheless, she was not satisfied with the passion he had for her and, despite the passion she had for him and the care which he took to fool her, she discerned the lack of fervor in his feelings.

She complained of him to the comtesse de Tende. The countess reassured her, but the complaints of Mme de Neuchatel managed to upset the countess; they made her see the extent of her treason, which would perhaps cost her beloved his fortune.

The countess warned him of the princess's suspicions. He said that he was indifferent to everything except being loved by her; nevertheless, he restrained himself by her orders and he so reassured the princesse de Neuchatel that she informed the comtesse de Tende that she was entirely satisfied with the chevalier de Navarre.

Jealousy then seized the countess. She feared that her beloved truly loved the princess; she saw all the reasons he had for loving her.

Their marriage, which she had wished for, horrified her; she did not want him to break with her, however, and she found herself caught in a bitter state of uncertainty.

She let the chevalier see all her feelings of remorse toward the princess; she only resolved to hide from him her jealousy and believed in fact that she had done so.

The princess's passion finally overcame her irresolution; she decided to marry and she resolved to do so secretly and not to announce it until it was done. The comtesse de Tende was close to dying of grief.

The same day that was set aside for the marriage, there was a public ceremony; her husband was present. She sent all of her attendants to the ceremony; she had them say that she could not be seen and she shut herself in her room, stretched out on a divan and abandoned herself to the most painful feelings that remorse and jealousy could arouse.

While she was in this state, she heard a hidden door of her room open and saw before her the chevalier de Navarre, more handsomely dressed and charming than she had ever seen him. "Chevalier, where are you going?" she cried. "What are you looking for? Have you lost your mind? What's become of your marriage? Have you no thought for my reputation?" "Don't worry about your reputation," he answered. "No one knows. It is not a question of my marriage; it is no longer a matter of my fortune; it is only a question of your heart, Madame, and of being loved by you; I renounce all the rest. You have let me see that you do not hate me, but you have tried to hide from me the fact that I am so favored in your eyes that my marriage grieves you. I have come to tell you, Madame, that I renounce it all, that this marriage would be torture and that I only want to live for you.

"I am expected even as I speak to you, all is ready, but I am going to call it all off, if, in doing so, I do something that pleases you and that proves to you my passion."

The countess fell back on her divan, raised herself halfway and, looking at the chevalier with eyes full of love and tears, said, "Do you want me to die? Do you think that a heart can bear all that you have made me feel? Abandon because of me the fortune that awaits you! I can hardly stand the thought. Go to the princesse de Neuchatel, go to the greatness that is destined for you; you will have my heart at the same time. I will do with my remorse, my indecision and my jealousy—since I must confess them to you—all that my weak reason advises, but I will never see you again if you do not immediately conclude your marriage. Go, do not wait here another moment, but, for love of me and of yourself, renounce this unreasonable passion which you have declared to me and which will perhaps lead us into horrible misfortunes."

The chevalier at first was carried away with joy at seeing himself so truly loved by the comtesse de Tende; but the horror of giving himself to another soon came fully before his eyes. He wept, he mourned, he promised her all that she asked, provided that she see him again in the same place.

She wanted to know, before he left, how he had come in. He told her that he had confided in a squire in her service who had formerly been attached to him, and that this man had led him through the stable courtyard to the small stairway that led to her room and that also led to the squire's quarters.

Meanwhile, the hour of the wedding grew near, and the chevalier, at the urging of the comtesse de Tende, finally was forced to leave, but he went as to his torture to the greatest and most desirable fortune to which a noble without means had ever been elevated.

The comtesse de Tende passed the night, as one might imagine, in restless agitation. She called for her attendants at dawn and, a short time after her rooms were opened for visits, her squire, whose name was Lalande, approached her bed and put a letter on it without being perceived by anyone else.

This letter made her heart beat, both because she recognized it as coming from the chevalier de Navarre, and because it was so unlikely that, during this night that was to have been his wedding night, he would have caused or encountered some obstacle to his marriage. She opened the letter with great emotion and found there roughly the following words:

> I think only of you, madame, I am concerned only with you; and in the first moments of the legitimate possession of the most elevated match in France, hardly has the day begun but I leave the bedroom where I spent the night in order to tell you, Madame, that I have already repented a thousand times of having obeyed you and of not having abandoned everything to live for you alone.

This letter, and the moments during which it was written, noticeably touched the comtesse de Tende; she went to dine with the princesse de Neuchatel who had asked for her. The marriage had been announced. She found a vast crowd in the princess's room, but as soon as the princess saw her, she left everyone and asked the countess to come with her into her study.

They had barely taken their seats when the face of the princess became covered with tears. The countess thought that it was the effect of the announcement of her marriage and that she had found it more difficult to bear than she had imagined it would be; but she soon saw that she was mistaken. "Ah! madame," said the princess, "what have I done? I have married a man out of passion; I have made an unequal marriage, one that all disapprove and that demeans me, and he whom I have preferred to all others loves someone else."

The comtesse de Tende thought she would faint at these words; she felt that the princess could not have fathomed the passion of her husband without also uncovering its cause; she was unable to respond.

The princesse de Navarre, as she was called after her marriage, did not notice and continued: "The prince de Navarre, Madame, far from showing the eagerness which the conclusion of our marriage vows should arouse, did nothing until evening. He came without joy, his mind occupied and troubled; he left my room at the break of day on some slight pretext. But he had gone to write someone; I could tell by his hands. To whom could he write except a mistress, why did he hesitate, and what troubled him so?"

At this moment the conversation was interrupted by the arrival of the princesse de Condé. The princesse de Navarre left to receive her but the comtesse de Tende remained distraught.

She wrote that night to the prince de Navarre to warn him of his wife's suspicions and to beseech him to control himself.

These dangers and obstacles did not make their passion subside; the comtesse de Tende could find no repose, and sleep no longer came to her eyes.

One morning, after she had called her servants, the squire Lalande approached and told her very softly that the prince de Navarre was in her study and that he urgently entreated her to let him tell her something that was absolutely necessary for her to know.

One easily gives way to what is pleasing; the comtesse de Tende knew that her husband had gone out; she said that she wanted to sleep; she ordered her attendants to close her doors and not to enter unless she called for them.

The prince de Navarre entered from the study and threw himself on his knees before her bed. "What do you have to say to me?" she asked. "That I love you, Madame, that I adore you, that I cannot live with Mme de Navarre. The desire to see you seized me this morning with such violence that I could not resist. I have come here risking everything and without even a hope of speaking with you."

The countess at first scolded him for compromising her so impulsively, and then their passion led them into so long a conversation that they were still together when the comte de Tende returned from the city.

He went to his wife's rooms; he was told that she was not up yet. It was late. He did not restrain himself from entering her bedroom,[6] and he found the prince de Navarre on his knees before her bed as he had been initially.

Never has astonishment been so great as the comte de Tende's, and never has confusion been the equal of his wife's.

The prince de Navarre alone conserved his presence of mind, neither growing flustered nor rising from his knees. "Come, come," he said to the comte de Tende, "help me obtain a favor that I seek on my knees and that I am refused."

The tone and air of the prince de Navarre suspended the astonishment of the comte de Tende. "I do not know," he replied in the same tone as that with which the prince had spoken, "whether a favor that you ask of my wife when I am told that she is asleep and I find you alone with her, and without your carriage at the door, is of the sort that I would wish her to grant you."

The prince de Navarre, reassured and free of the initial confusion of the moment, arose, and, completely at ease, took a seat. The comtesse de Tende, trembling and upset, was able to hide her confusion in the shadows of that part of the room where she found herself.

The prince de Navarre said to the count:

"I am going to surprise you, you will blame me, but I must nevertheless seek aid.

"I am in love with and loved by the most charming person at court; I slipped away last night from the princesse de Navarre and all of my servants to go to a rendezvous with her. My wife, who has already discerned that I am occupied with something other than her, and who has been paying special attention to my activities, learned from my servants that I had left them; she is sunk in a jealousy and despair which nothing can approach.

"I told her that the hours that are causing her such distress were passed at the house of the maréchale de Saint-André, who is indisposed and who sees almost no one, and I told her that the comtesse de Tende alone was there and that she could ask the countess if she had not seen me there all evening. I decided to come and confide in the countess. I went to La Châtre's, which is only a few steps from here; I made sure that no one saw me leave. I was told that the countess was awake. I found no one in her antechamber and I impetuously rushed in. She refused to lie for my sake; she told me that she did not want to betray her friend and she reprimanded me very judiciously—in the same terms I have used to rebuke myself, but to no avail. Madame de Navarre must be spared the distress and jealousy that she is suffering, and I must escape the deadly embarrassment of her reproaches."

The comtesse de Tende was hardly less surprised by the prince de Navarre's presence of mind than she had been by the arrival of her husband; she regained her equilibrium.

The comte de Tende no longer held the slightest doubt. He joined his wife in pointing out to the prince the abyss of evils into which he was falling and all that he owed the princess, and the comtesse de Tende promised to tell her everything that her husband wanted her to say.

As he was leaving, the comte de Tende stopped: "As recompense for the services that we are going to do for you, at the expense of the truth, tell us at least," he said, "who this lovely mistress is. She cannot be a very estimable person to love you and to continue an affair with you, when she sees you attached to someone as beautiful as the princesse de Navarre, when she sees you married to her, and when she recognizes all that you owe her. That person must be devoid of intelligence, courage, and sensitivity, and, in truth, she does not deserve your disturbing as great a good fortune as yours and making yourself so ungrateful and guilty for her sake."

The prince was unable to respond; he pretended to be in a hurry. The comte de Tende showed him to the door himself so that no one would see him. The comtesse de Tende continued to be wildly distraught at the danger she had run, the thoughts that the words of her husband had brought to mind, and the sight of the evils to which her passion was exposing her.

But she did not have the strength to extricate herself from the situation. She continued her affair with the prince de Navarre. She sometimes saw him through the agency of Lalande. She thought herself to be, and in fact was, one of the most miserable women in the world. Every day the princesse de Navarre confided in her the jealousy of which she was the cause; that jealousy filled her with remorse, and, when the princesse de Navarre was satisfied with her husband, the countess was lost in jealousy herself.

A new torment was added to those she already possessed: the comte de Tende became as infatuated with her as if she had never been his wife; he never left her side and wanted to resume the rights that he had earlier scorned.

The countess opposed him with a strength and bitterness that approached contempt and outright refusal: predisposed toward the prince de Navarre, she was wounded and offended by any other passion than his.

The campaign approached; the prince de Navarre soon would have to leave for the army. The comtesse de Tende began to feel the torments of his absence and to fear the perils to which he would be exposed; she resolved to flee from the constraint of ceaselessly hiding her affliction and decided to spend the summer months on an estate of hers which lay thirty leagues from Paris.

She carried out her plans; the farewell of the countess and the prince was so painful that both took it as a bad omen. The comte de Tende stayed near the king, as required by his office.

The members of court had to move close to the army; the house of Mme de Tende was not far away; her husband told her that he would come there for one night only on some military operations he had undertaken. He did not want her to think that he was coming to see her: he felt toward her all the resentment of which the passions are capable.

In the beginning Mme de Tende had found the prince de Navarre so full of respect, and she had felt herself to be so virtuous that she distrusted neither him nor herself. But time and circumstances had triumphed over virtue and respect, and, a short time after she had arrived at her house, she discovered that she was pregnant.

One has only to reflect on the reputation that she had acquired and maintained, and on the state of her relations with her husband, to judge the extent of her despair.

Several times she felt compelled to commit suicide; however, she placed some slight hope in the trip that her husband was to make in her vicinity, and she resolved to await the outcome.[7]

In this state of depression, she had the further misery of learning that Lalande, whom she had left behind in Paris to pass on her letters and those of her lover, had died after a few days, and she found herself deprived of all assistance at a time when she had such great need of it.

In the meantime, the army engaged in a siege. Her passion for the prince de Navarre filled her with new fears. She learned of the end of the siege, but she also learned that the prince de Navarre had been killed the final day of the operation.

She lost her discretion; she lost her reason; she was often deprived of both. This excess of misery seemed to her in these moments to be a kind of consolation. She no longer feared for her peace of mind, her reputation, or her life; death alone seemed desirable to her; she hoped for it in her agony, or she resolved to inflict it on herself.

A residue of propriety obliged her to say that she was ill and was undergoing extreme physical pain, so that she might offer a pretext for her cries and her tears.

If thousands of adversities made her turn against herself, she saw that she deserved them, and nature and Christianity dissuaded her from killing herself and suspended the execution of what she had resolved to do.

She had not been long in such violent agony when the comte de Tende arrived. She thought she knew all the feelings that her miserable state could inspire; but the arrival of her husband instilled in her a new distress and confusion.

He knew on arriving that she was ill, and as he had always maintained a certain decency in the eyes of the public and of his domestics, he saw her first in her room. She seemed distracted and wild, and she could not restrain her cries and tears, which she attributed all the while to the pains that tormented her.

The comte de Tende was touched by the state in which he found her; he became tender toward her. Hoping to offer her some diversion from her pains, he spoke to her of the death of the prince de Navarre, and of his wife's affliction. Mme de Tende could not bear this subject, and her cries and tears redoubled, to such an extent that the comte de Tende was surprised and nearly enlightened.

He left her room full of distress and agitation; it seemed to him that his wife's state was not being caused by physical pains.

Her redoubled tears when he had spoken of the prince de Navarre's death struck him, and, all at once, the incident involving the prince on his knees at her bedside came to his mind. He remembered the actions she had taken toward him when he had wanted to return to her; and finally he thought that he saw the truth, but there remained nonetheless that doubt which self-love always leaves us concerning those things which are too costly to believe.

His despair was extreme, and all his thoughts were violent; but as he was a prudent man, he restrained his first impulses. He resolved to leave the next morning at dawn without seeing his wife, trusting time to give him greater certainty and to dictate what further resolutions he might make.

However engulfed in misery, Mme de Tende could not avoid noticing the little power she had over herself and the expression on her husband's face when he left her room. She suspected a part of the truth and, no longer feeling anything for her life but horror, she decided to lose it in a manner that would not deprive her of hope for the life to come.

After considering what she should do, with mortal agitation, penetrated by suffering and repentance at the course of her life, she finally made up her mind and wrote these words to her husband:

> This letter is going to cost me my life, but I deserve death and I want it. I am pregnant. He who is the cause of my misfortune is no longer in this world, as is true as well of the only man who knew of our affair; the public has never suspected it. I had resolved to end my life by my own hands, but I offer it to God and to you for the expiation of my crime. I have not wanted to dishonor myself in the eyes of the world since my reputation concerns you: preserve it out of love for yourself. Hide the shame and make me die when you wish and as you wish.

The day had begun to break when she wrote this letter, perhaps the most difficult that anyone has ever written; she sealed it, sat by the window, and, since she saw the comte de Tende in the courtyard ready to board his coach, sent one of her servants to carry it to him and to tell him that it was nothing urgent and that he could read it at his leisure.

The comte de Tende was surprised by this letter; it gave him a sort of presentiment, not of all that he would find within it, but of some of the things which he had already thought about the day before.

He boarded the carriage alone, full of distress, without even daring to open the letter, despite his great impatience to read it. He finally did so and learned of his misfortune; but what could he think after having read it! If there had been witnesses, his violent state would have made one believe that he was deprived of his reason or near death. Jealousy and well-founded suspicions usually prepare husbands for their misfortune; they always have some doubts, but they do not have the certainty that an avowal brings, greater than that which our intellect alone can give us.

The comte de Tende had always found his wife quite lovely, although he was never loved equally in return; but she had always appeared to be the most estimable woman he had ever seen; thus, he felt no less astonishment than fury and, mingled with both these emotions, he still sensed, despite himself, a sorrow tinged with a certain measure of tenderness.

He stopped at a friend's house along the road, where he spent several days, grieved and distraught, as one might imagine. At first he thought everything it is natural to think in such circumstances: he longed only to have his wife killed. But the deaths of the prince de Navarre and of Lalande, whom he easily recognized as the confidant, slackened his fury a bit.

He did not doubt that his wife had told him the truth in saying that their affair had never been suspected; he imagined that the prince de Navarre could have fooled everyone, since he had fooled him after the most damning evidence had been presented before his eyes.

The public's complete ignorance of his misfortune pacified him somewhat; but the circumstances, which forced him to see to what extent and in what manner he had been duped, stabbed at his heart, and he breathed only vengeance.

Nevertheless, he thought that, if he were to have his wife killed and it were discovered that she was pregnant, the truth would easily be guessed. As he was, of all those at court, the man most jealous of his reputation, he took the course that would best serve his honor and resolved to let nothing be seen by the public. With that thought in mind, he decided to send a gentleman to the comtesse de Tende with this note:

> The desire to inhibit the display of my shame at present prevails over my vengeance; I shall see, in the course of time, how I shall decide your

unworthy destiny. Conduct yourself as if you had always been what you should have been.

The countess received the note with joy; she thought it was her death warrant, and when she saw that her husband would allow her to reveal that she was pregnant, she felt fully the extent to which shame is the most violent of the passions. She had found herself in a sort of calm in believing herself assured of death and in seeing her reputation safe. She no longer thought of anything other than preparing for death, and as she was an individual whose feelings were always intense, she embraced virtue and penitence with the same ardour as that with which she had followed her passion.

Her soul was steeped and drowned in affliction; she could not rest her eyes on anything in this life that did not seem more bitter than death itself, so that she saw no remedy for her misfortunes other than in the termination of her miserable life.

She passed some time in this state, appearing to be more a dead than a living person.

Finally, toward the sixth month of her pregnancy, her body succumbed, she came down with a continuous fever, and she went into labor because of the violence of the illness. She had the consolation of seeing her child born alive [so that he could be baptized], and of being assured that he would not live and that she would not be giving her husband an illegitimate heir.

She died a few days later and greeted death with a joy which none has ever known. She charged her confessor with the duty of carrying the news of her death to her husband, of asking his pardon, and of begging him to obliterate her memory, which he could only find detestable.

The comte de Tende received the news without insensitivity, and even with some sense of pity, but nevertheless with joy. Although he was quite young, he never wanted to remarry; women filled him with horror, and he lived to a very advanced age.[8]

NOTES TO THE TRANSLATIONS

1. Mme de LaFayette remained convinced that Monsieur had poisoned Madame. Conclusive evidence is not available, but it seems most likely that Madame died of natural causes.

2. Olympe Mancini, the comtesse de Soissons, had been the king's lover some years before. Madame de la Vallière had been the king's mistress since 1661, but in 1669 Madame de Montespan had begun to replace her in the king's favor. Madame de la Vallière was eventually disgraced and entered a convent in 1673.

3. One of Bossuet's best known works is his funeral oration for Madame, in which he expresses the court's shock at the death of Madame in lines well-known to most French

schoolchildren: "Oh disastrous night! Oh terrifying night! when suddenly, like a clap of thunder, the overwhelming news resounded: Madame is dying, Madame is dead! Who among us did not feel himself struck by this blow, as if some tragic accident had desolated his family? At the first sounds of this unexpected evil, people hurried to Saint-Cloud from all parts; everything declared dismay, except the heart of that princess. Everywhere one heard cries, everywhere one saw sadness and despair, and the image of death. The king, the queen, Monsieur, all the court, all the people, all were struck down, all were heartbroken, and it seemed to me that I saw the fulfillment of those words of the prophet [Ezekiel 7:27]: The king shall mourn, and the prince shall be clothed with desolation, and the hands of the people shall be troubled" (*Oraisons funèbres*, ed. Jacques Truchet [Paris: Garnier, 1961], 171).

4. In his memoirs, Philibert de la Mare gives an interesting account of Madame's last moments: "It had been said that Monsieur the bishop of Condom did not hate the now deceased Madame and that this feeling was reciprocal, and that having sent for him when she was first attacked by the illness of which she died, he grew faint when he saw her in that condition and that she said to him: I did not have you sent for to move my heart but to console me in the state I am in. He assisted her, however, with courage up until her death and after he had closed her eyes, the same faintness seized him. She charged him as she was dying with telling Monsieur that she had had a few youthful infatuations, but that she had never done anything against that fidelity which she owed him. During the final period of her illness there was in her room a Jansenist priest—I do not know whether or not he was the curé de Saint-Cloud—who questioned her in front of everyone who was in the room regarding that subject [her fidelity to Monsieur] with the greatest cruelty in the world; finally she died, holding in her arms a little dog named Mimi which had come from the comte de Guiche and which she did not want to let go of" (cited in Marie-Thérèse Hipp's edition of the *Vie de la Princesse d'Angleterre* [Geneva: Droz, 1967], 203).

5. The events of the story are fictional, but three of the principals bear the names of historical personages. Clarice Strozzi, daughter of Pierre Strozzi, maréchal de France, married the comte de Tende in 1560. She died without offspring in 1564. Honorat de Savoie, comte de Tende (1538–1572), was governor of Provence. Jacqueline de Rohan, married in 1536 to François d'Orléans-Longueville, prince de Neuchatel, became a widow in 1548 and died unmarried in 1586. The chevalier de Navarre is an imaginary individual and title.

6. Mme de LaFayette clearly disapproves of the comte de Tende's breach of manners in entering his wife's apartments unannounced.

7. Perhaps the countess hoped that conjugal relations with her husband would hide the actual paternity of her child.

8. The real comte de Tende did remarry and died at an early age, poisoned for having refused to execute the king's order of extending the Saint Bartholomew massacre into Provence.

BIBLIOGRAPHY

Primary Works

LaFayette, Mme de. *Correspondance de Madame de LaFayette*. Edited by André Beaunier. 2 vols. Paris: Gallimard, 1942.

———. *Histoire de la Princesse de Montpensier, Histoire de la Comtesse de Tende*. Edited by Micheline Cuénin. Geneva: Droz, 1979.

———. *Histoire de Madame Henriette d'Angleterre, La Princesse de Montpensier, La Comtesse de Tende*. Edited by Claudine Herrmann. Paris: Ed. des Femmes, 1979.

———. *The Princess of Cleves*. Translated by Mildred Sarah Greene. University, Miss.: Romance Monographs, 1979.

Related Works

Beaunier, André. *L'Amie de La Rochefoucauld*. Paris: Flammarion, 1927.
———. *La Jeunesse de Madame de La Fayette*. Paris: Flammarion, 1921.
Butor, Michel. "Sur *La Princesse de Clèves*." In *Repertoire I*, 74–78. Paris: Minuit, 1960.
Doubrovsky, Serge. "*La Princesse de Clèves:* Une Interpretation existentielle." *La Table Ronde,* no. 138 (June 1959): 36–51.
Haig, Stirling. *Madame de LaFayette*. New York: Twayne, 1970.
Kamuf, Peggy. *Fictions of Feminine Desire: Disclosures of Heloise*. Lincoln: University of Nebraska Press, 1982.
Kreiter, Janine Anseaume. *Le Problème du paraître dans l'oeuvre de Mme de LaFayette*. Paris: Nizet, 1977.
Magne, Emile. *Le Coeur et l'esprit de Madame de LaFayette*. Paris: Emile-Paul Frères, 1927.
———. *Madame de LaFayette en ménage*. Paris: Emile-Paul Frères, 1926.
Rousset, Jean. "La Princesse de Clèves." In *Forme et Signification,* 17–44. Paris: José Corti, 1962.
Scott, J. W. "Criticism and 'La Comtesse de Tende.'" *Modern Language Review* 50 (1955): 15–24.
Sévigné, Mme de. *Correspondance*. Edited by Roger Duchêne. 3 vols. Paris: Pléiade, 1972–78.
Turnell, Martin. *The Novel in France*. New York: New Directions, 1951.
Weinstein, Arnold. *Fictions of the Self: 1550–1800*. Princeton: Princeton University Press, 1981.

WRITER OF FANTASY

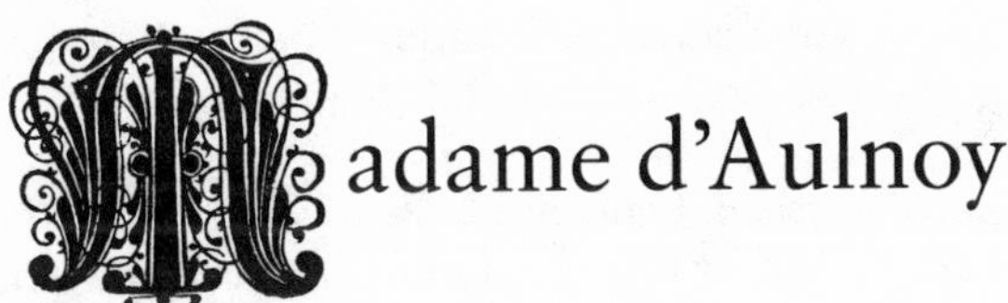adame d'Aulnoy

GLENDA K. MCLEOD

Marie-Catherine le Jumel de Barneville, baronne, comtesse, or simply Madame d'Aulnoy,[1] is in many ways as fascinating for what we do not know about her as for what we do. A talented but shadowy figure whose entire literary production took shape in just fourteen short years, she belongs chronologically to the dawn of the French Enlightenment. Yet stylistically, and especially in her *contes de fées,* she shows decidedly Baroque traits, traits that she subtly exploits to deconstruct traditional views of feminine potential and place.

Like most women writers, her reception has been riddled with ambiguities. Remembered primarily for her fairy tales, she and her work have often been overshadowed by the considerable attention accorded Charles Perrault, who occasionally usurps her position as the first author of a published *conte de fées.*[2] Although she was one of the most popular writers of her time, we do not even possess a complete bibliography of her works, despite her own efforts to leave us one.[3] She wrote the single most famous seventeenth-century French account of a journey into Spain, yet the greatest debate on her works is whether she ever went there.[4] Finally, though her historical novels, memoirs, and fairy tales clearly manifest a subversive and surprising vein of social criticism, this important aspect passed virtually undetected until quite recently while critical commentary focused instead upon long-dead scandals and questions of possible plagiarism.

The life of Mme d'Aulnoy was indeed fascinating. She was born at Barneville-la-Bertrand in 1650 or 1651, the only daughter of Nicholas-Claude le Jumel, seigneur of Barneville and Pennedepie, and Judith-Angelique Coustelier, who called herself "de Saint-Pater." Though her education appears to have been minimal, she possessed a gift for witty, elegant, and easy conversation; moreover, her written French, influenced by *préciosité* and the speech of refined Parisian society, was used to remarkable effect in her works. She also knew at least the rudiments of Spanish and English and was familiar with some classical literature, Spanish Baroque drama, parodic Renaissance verse, medieval French lays and *fabliaux,* and standard popular fare.

On March 6 or 8, 1666, she wed François de la Motte, the baron d'Aulnoy, at Saint Gervais in Paris.[5] At the age of only fifteen or sixteen, she was matched with a forty-six-year-old husband who had once served as the valet, footman, and possibly lover of César Vendôme. The marriage was probably arranged without Marie-Catherine's consent; it was certainly a marriage of convenience, linking her aristocratic line with d'Aulnoy's ready cash. Unfortunately, it was not a success.

A scant three years after the wedding, her widowed mother, Mme de Gudanes, and three Norman gentlemen tried to separate the baron from his money through a trumped-up charge of high treason. Although d'Aulnoy was arrested and imprisoned in the Bastille, the plot was discovered, and two of the Norman accomplices were executed. Mme de Gudanes discreetly disappeared, later to surface in Spain as a double agent of the French and Spanish governments. However, her daughter's complicity in the plot, as well as her activities after its failure, remains a mystery to this day. Although numerous apocryphal stories of midnight escapes or nocturnal arrests have been advanced, no solid proof has ever been found to explain her complicity.

Mme d'Aulnoy herself was nothing if not cryptic on the subject, occasionally claiming that she had spent these years traveling through Europe. On the basis of her claims, Jeanne Roche-Mazon proposed a possible itinerary, without, however, presenting conclusive evidence.[6] In fact, during the past century, scholars have become increasingly convinced that these supposed voyages are, at least in part, fabrications. If the baroness did leave Paris she did not remain away for long, for her fifth child was born there on October 13, 1676. Furthermore, her claim to have visited England, made in *Mémoires de la Cour d'Angleterre* (1695), has been seriously undermined by that book's numerous historical inconsistencies[7] and by the suspicious absence of her name in English memoirs and diaries of the period. The most famous of her trips—a visit to Spain—was also challenged by Raymond Foulché-Delbosc, although his case is considerably weaker than the arguments against her English voyage. What is certain is that she dropped from sight for a period of almost twenty years but by 1690 was back in Paris and writing.

At this point her career as an author truly began. Her first novel was published later that year, and thereafter book followed book at a dizzying speed. By the close of the decade, she was a respectable and best-selling author, one of only nine French women holding membership in the venerable Accademia dei Ricovvati of Padua.[8] In just over a decade, twenty-eight volumes flowed from her pen, a collection including novels, *novelles,* fairy tales, histories, edifying verse, travel books, memoirs, and a collection of letters. Freed from the stigma of the earlier scandal involving her husband, she left the convent and entered Parisian society. She maintained a fashionable salon in the Faubourg Saint Germain.

In 1699, however, a curious event once more robbed her of respectability when an unknown assailant attacked the husband of a friend and left him for dead at his own doorstep. His wife, who was suspected of plotting the crime, was rumored to have been at Mme d'Aulnoy's on the day of its execution. Arrested, tortured, brought to trial, and finally executed, this friend once more brought the baroness under suspicion. The now-famous author retired into semi-seclusion.

On August 21, 1700, the baron, now a comptroller in the household of the prince of Condé, died at the age of eighty, apparently having excluded his estranged wife entirely from his will.[9] She died in Paris five years later, on January 13, 1705, survived by four of her six children and shrouded in the same mystery which surrounds so much of her life.

For at least a century after her death, her novels lived on, finding a large and interested audience. Her fairy tales have continued to charm for almost three hundred years. Yet despite this success, only now are critics beginning to take her work seriously, directing their comments less toward the events of her life than toward her literary production. If viewed chronologically, this body of work demonstrates that Mme d'Aulnoy was in fact a surprisingly innovative writer who explored not only different genres but also the potential for feminine characterization inherent in those genres. If some of her works betray unmistakable signs of hasty composition, others clearly indicate her abundant talent and energy and the subtle but emphatic social critique that suffuses her work.

Her literary debut of 1690 took the form of a novel, a genre that would continue to interest her throughout her short career. Of the four novels that she eventually wrote, the first one, *Histoire d'Hypolite, Comte de Duglas,* a story of love and adventure told on a vast, rambling scale, is by far her most original and artistically satisfying production. It also contains her first published fairy tale, the "Ile de la Félicité (The Blessed Isle)," whose appearance predates Perrault's book of fairy tales by seven years.

The story follows Julie and Hypolite, two star-crossed lovers playing out their destiny against the historical background of Henry VIII's England. In following this pattern, Mme d'Aulnoy conforms to the model set earlier by Mme de LaFayette in *La Princesse de Montpensier.* Using a short narrative, she grafts a sentimental plot with realistic psychology and action onto the events of political history.[10] Unlike Mme de LaFayette, however, Mme d'Aulnoy does not make the historical setting a primary focus; indeed, it receives little attention aside from the initial pages. Instead, she inserts intriguing echoes from her own life and in Julie establishes a pattern of wholesale victimization and passive suffering that was to be reiterated in almost all the feminine protagonists of her novels. Among other trials, Julie is imprisoned, threatened with death by a tyrannical and corrupt legal system, and immured in a convent against her will by her cruel older husband.

The values espoused in *Hypolite* concern fidelity in love and loyalty to one's vows, a recurrent theme in Mme d'Aulnoy's work. Devotion to the loved one is the key to the nobility of both Hypolite and Julie; it also enables Julie to achieve an elevated station by remaining true to her self-defined conception of integrity, a conception defended against husband, stepparents, and society.

For a new novelist, this first book was an auspicious beginning, one that attracted the attention of the most prestigious bookseller of the day. Claude Barbin, the publisher of Mme de LaFayette, La Fontaine, Racine, and Molière, would later bring out most of Mme d'Aulnoy's subsequent work, to the considerable profit of both, for the baroness proved to be a sharp judge of public taste. Her next books, the *Mémoires de la Cour d'Espagne* (Memoirs of the Spanish Court, 1690) and the *Relation du Voyage d'Espagne* (The Report of a Trip to Spain, 1691), capitalized on the interest aroused by the mysterious death of Marie Louise d'Orléans, the Bourbon princess who had recently wed Spain's king. Her devotional verse, *Sentimens d'une Ame penitente* (The Sentiments of a Penitent Soul, 1691) and *Le Retour d'une Ame à Dieu* (The Return of a Soul to God, 1692), quickly established her in the required role of public penitent, allowing her to reenter the social mainstream.

Her second novel, *Histoire de Jean de Bourbon* (1692), showed her eclectic interests. Set against a colorful historical background, *Jean de Bourbon* demonstrated its author's familiarity with medieval lays and romances and with the chronicle of Froissart, which served as an important source.[11] Published less than five months after the Spanish accounts, and not more than a year and a half after her first novel, it betrays signs of hasty composition. The novel is set in medieval Europe and sprawls over a vast geographic range—Arabia, France, Italy, and Spain. The typical d'Aulnoy heroine, Léonide, is depicted as passive, faithful, suffering, and trapped—caught in the jaws of circumstance and an unfair social system. But there is a new female character type as well, one that later surfaces frequently in Mme d'Aulnoy's fairy tales. This heroine, exemplified in *Jean de Bourbon* by the Queen of Fez and Casilda, is neither passive, suffering, nor particularly moral, but she does fascinate in her intricate plotting and desperate struggles with jealousy. Here both women of this type suffer tragic fates. After she kills the passive heroine, Léonide, Casilda is killed by Jean; the queen, who had hoped to gain the French hero and her lost kingdom, loses both. Like its predecessors, *Jean de Bourbon* was a financial success. It gave rise to two new editions the year of its publication and fueled d'Aulnoy's growing popularity. Today, however, it is the least inviting of the d'Aulnoy novels and is rarely read.

In the meantime, Mme d'Aulnoy's powers as a prose writer continued to mature. *Jean de Bourbon* was followed by an interesting experiment in short narrative prose, the *Nouvelles Espagnolles* (Spanish Short Stories, 1692), a series of six narratives varying in length from 40 to 134 pages.[12] These stories usually focus upon a young, beautiful heroine embroiled in various romantic complications such as unhappy marriages or clandestine love affairs. Secret messages, hidden passages, duels, kidnappings, and threats of exile to the convent abound. Heroines are passive, constant, and suffering, and love is an ambiguous and dangerous passion. Unlike the historical novels, however, the narratives in *Nouvelles Espagnolles* have contemporary settings and reveal Mme d'Aulnoy's genuine talent for verisimilitude. They also demonstrate an unexpected flair for comedy, which later found expression in her *contes de fées*.

In 1693, Mme d'Aulnoy published her seventh book, *Nouvelles ou Mémoires historiques*, a history of the war of Louis XIV against Holland. Compiled primarily from news dispatches and memoirs of participants, this very derivative work is of little interest today. It does, however, present a creditable account of the Sun King's forays into Holland. It also features Mme d'Aulnoy's complaint that books she hadn't written were being issued in Holland under her name. Her listing of her works to date, which appears in the preface, is the only authoritative bibliography we possess from her own hand.

In her later years, Mme d'Aulnoy returned to England as an exotic locale for her fiction and to the novel as a genre. Although her *Mémoires de la Cour d'Angleterre* (1695) claimed to relate the romantic intrigues of real personages—Lord Arran and the dukes of Monmouth and Buckingham—its stories were fictive. Flirtatious and witty, these tales evince Madame d'Aulnoy's growing talent for comedy. They present love not as a malady or an ennobling passion, as in her other works, but rather as a game that renders both male and female players ridiculous. Many of the adventures, in fact, approach deftly drawn farce.[13]

Le Comte de Warwick (1703), her last novel, was self-styled a *roman à clef*, an appellation rejected today by most critics.[14] Though it returns to a historical English setting similar to that of *Hypolite*, it connects the themes of love and power in a new and more direct way than in any of her previous books. Its plot portrays a secret love affair as the true motive behind Warwick's lust for making and unmaking kings. As in her first novel, the leading female protagonist is delineated chiefly by her heroic constancy, her loyalty to her own conception of honor. As in the second novel, she suffers a tragic death. Finally, as in the *contes de fées,* reality (in this case historic fact) is twisted to allow her heroines a wider arena for action and social influence. Still, despite the numerous motifs from earlier works, *Le Comte de Warwick* cannot match *Histoire d'Hypolite* for spontaneity, audience interest, or artistic skill. In her novels, at least, Mme d'Aulnoy's debut was her most impressive performance.

Despite the popularity of these works in her own time, today Madame d'Aulnoy's fame rests principally upon two collections of fairy tales written in the middle of her career: *Les Contes des Fées* (1697) and *Les Contes Nouveaux, ou les Fées à la mode* (New Tales or Fashionable Fairies, 1698). These collections, jointly containing twenty-five separate tales, demonstrate that among all the different prose forms to which Mme d'Aulnoy turned her hand, the fairy tale was the most sympathetic to her talent. It provided room for the free play of her imagination, a setting in which her heroines could assume active, powerful roles, and an opportunity to utilize her comic and satiric gifts. Most important, it allowed her to critique existing social structures with impunity.

These fairy tales were written not for children but for the fashionable ladies of Parisian society.[15] As in her novels nearly all the stories describe a young love threatened by obstacles, though the passivity and fatalism permeating her other prose works are conspicuously absent here. In fact, the *contes de fées* can most accurately be characterized as stories of maturation and growth in which the phenomenon of change plays a prominent part. Metamorphosis is a recurrent motif, used to suggest a variety of themes. Outer changes may mirror inner stages in the protagonists' struggles toward maturity,[16] or they may express discordancy—an uncertainty and unease or a doubt about self-identity. The latter, more Baroque application is often tied to a veiled refutation of gender-specific role definitions and to the characters' attempts to unite their inner beings with the outer appearances imposed by an often hostile world.

In the metamorphoses of this latter sort, the appearance/reality conflict, a favorite *topos* of seventeenth-century literature, is used to explore tensions between self-identification and socially defined gender roles. Mme d'Aulnoy questions these definitions in a number of ways, often generating new fictional situations and symbols by the fusion of traditional male and female types. "Belle-Belle ou le chevalier Fortuné," for example, features a woman disguised or transformed into a male knight. While the disguise motif is not unique, its presentation is. Belle-Belle, the feminine incarnation, is more active, more athletic, and more adventurous than her male counterpart, Fortuné, who becomes the passive pawn of other women's love intrigues. In fact, Fortuné, not Belle-Belle, reenacts the long-suffering, passive role reserved for heroines in Mme d'Aulnoy's novels.

Similarly, in the tale translated for this volume, "L'Abeille et l'oranger," the metamorphosis of a woman into a bee and a man into a flowering orange tree playfully but deliberately combines traditionally male and female characteristics within one protagonist. The active role of the bee is taken by the Princess Aimée; the passive role of the blooming, seductive orange tree is given the prince. The former guards her lover; the latter pledges undying constancy. She brings about their escapes and metamorphoses; he waits patiently for her to develop plans and to return. In both protagonists, the characteristics traditionally associated with one gender exist in perfect harmony within the body of the other, thus refuting arbitrary limitations imposed on either sex by society's conceptions of male and female identity.

The same social critique also found expression in Mme d'Aulnoy's innovative use of the tales' concluding morals, morals that often contradict or ignore the very stories they purport to explain.[17] A reader confronted with these discordant endings experiences a sharp, satiric jab or a more gentle impulse to thoughtful meditation in place of the self-satisfied closure usually associated with a concluding *sententia*. In "L'Abeille et l'orangier," for example, the moral advising prudent young women to refrain from sexual experiences before marriage is at frank odds with the heroine's blatant sexual pleasure as a bee. Under metamorphosis, Aimée nestles at night within the fragrant petals of her lover's flowers. The traditional implication of this moral—that women bear ultimate responsibility for the success of a union—also clashes with the tale's repeated insistence that both Aimé and Aimée should have equal responsibility for their marriage.[18]

Such discordancy between tale and moral, like the discrepancies introduced in some of the metamorphoses, reflects an underlying tension between private experience and authoritative interpretation. Yet despite the displacement of gender-specific role models, the stories do not so much reverse as fuse more conventional portraits. Aimée may guard her lover with her stinger in the male role of protector, but she also cares for his wounds in the female role of nurturer. Similarly, he may feed her with his pollen, but he also protects her with his flowers. Even more striking, of course, are the obvious physical aspects of the metamorphosis, in which a woman, complete with phallic stinger, nestles at night for protection within the blossoms of the male orange tree. Clearly the elasticity of the fairy tale and its loose ties with social realism provided Mme d'Aulnoy with an opportunity for unique character study and veiled social commentary.[19]

The genre also suited her particular gifts as a writer. Her style contrasts in almost every respect with Charles Perrault's and often harkens back to an earlier literary period.[20] She implies more often than states, elaborates rather than excises, and is fond of color, oddity, and new and exotic words. One critic has noted that she writes with the verve and the rich vocabulary of a "féminin Rabelais." Also blessed with a playful gift for rhyme and rhythm, she often coins humorous words and employs onomatopoeia to remarkable effect.[21] Though satiric in many ways, the tales never fail to move with lightness and an easy humor that have endeared them to three centuries of readers.[22] It is thus no surprise that their popularity was immediate and lasting. They went through innumerable French editions, if one counts impressions of single tales; fourteen issues of the complete works appeared in the eighteenth century alone. One translation into English was also made in the nineteenth century, though it unfortunately assumes that the tales are children's stories.

When Mme d'Aulnoy's corpus is considered as a whole, she is clearly far from the leading stylist of her day. But she also deserves attention for more than her unusual, mysterious life. Her works evince humor, a talent for rapid narration and parody, and an ability to analyze the emotions with delicacy and finesse. Moreover, in her characterizations of women, she raised one of the first voices to protest a moral code that would deny individual human liberty. This protest takes different forms in different genres. In the novels and memoirs, historical restrictions on women engender a fatalistic attitude and the passive stoicism of innocent victims. Heroism in these works is measured by stubborn stasis—the protagonist's refusal to be swayed—and resistance is registered negatively by an ability to say no. In the fairy tales, however, with their dazzling succession of metamorphoses, more optimistic portrayals predominate. Released from social realism, Mme d'Aulnoy could introduce characters capable of acts unthinkable in her own social milieu. Both male and female, these protagonists function effectively as courtiers, lovers, soldiers, and rulers who work to change their own lives and their society. Their uneasy search for a stable identity that will unite inner need and social duty, their questionings and quests trace an exploration of new and different ways to delineate the female protagonist in relationship to her society. While not a utopia, the world of Mme d'Aulnoy's *contes de fées* does provide an alternative to the more limited world of her other literary production and prepares the way for new forms.

The translation of "L'Abeille et l'orangier" is based on the text of the tale found in *Les Contes des Fées* (Paris: Mercure de France, 1956). This story illustrates clearly Mme d'Aulnoy's use of the metamorphoses and quest motifs and reveals her frustration with traditional character types. In addition, it embodies her typical humor, a humor that resides in a complicity between reader and author, an unspoken agreement that there is more to the tale than meets the eye. Behind these apparently simple stories is a complexity, derived in part from their ambiguous moral stance. Mme d'Aulnoy's monsters can be charming: they can mother, and they can be touched by beauty. But, as this tale shows, their teeth are sharp—a fact never forgotten by those who encounter these creatures, as the author continually reminds us. Mme d'Aulnoy's fairy tales are clearly for adults. Like her novels, they keep the tenuousness of a life lived under such circumstances always and alarmingly before the reader.

NOTES

1. She styled herself all three ways in her lifetime. Although her husband was a baron, they appear to have separated and thus her claim to the title "baronne" and especially "comtesse" is questionable. The first recorded instance of the latter is on the title page of *Relation du voyage d'Espagne.*

2. Her first published fairy tale was included in *Histoire d'Hypolite* (1690).

3. Madame d'Aulnoy did give a partial listing of her books in her history of Louis XIV's war against Holland. The bibliography compiled by Foulché-Delbosc, however, is still recognized as authoritative.

4. For the principal arguments in this debate see Raymond Foulché-Delbosc, "Madame d'Aulnoy et l'Espagne," 1–151, and Jeanne Roche-Mazon's response in "Madame d'Aulnoy, n'aurait-elle pas été en Espagne," 724–36.

5. Foulché-Delbosc records the marriage date as March 8; Roche-Mazon in *En Marge de l'oiseau bleu* as March 6.

6. Roche-Mazon, *En Marge de l'oiseau bleu,* 112–13.

7. She mentions, for example, meeting the French ambassador Barillon. His tenure at the court of Saint James, however, didn't begin until 1677, two years after the date she gives for her trip. For a discussion of this and other discrepancies, see James Beeler, *Madame d'Aulnoy, Historical Novelist of the Late Seventeenth Century.*

8. Madame d'Aulnoy was granted the name of Clio, the muse of history. Other honorees recorded in Eugiène Asse's monograph *Un Nièce du Grand Corneille: Mademoiselle Bernard* include Mlle de Scudéry (Sappho), Mme Dacier (Terpsicore), Antoinette de Salvan (Euterpe), La Présidente de Bretonvilliers (Melpomene), Mme le Camus de Melson (Uranie), Mlle de la Force (Thalie), Mlle Cheron (Erato), and Mlle Bernard (Calliope).

9. Foulché-Delbosc quotes a somewhat ironic letter of condolence from Saint-Evremond that leads the reader to suspect the baroness received no money from her husband's estate ("Madame d'Aulnoy et l'Espagne," 37).

10. Beeler, *Madame d'Aulnoy,* 82.

11. The crusade of Nicopolis, for example, provides the dramatic setting at the start of the novel, and many of the descriptive details can be traced to Froissart's account.

12. See Beeler, *Madame d'Aulnoy,* 225.

13. Ibid., 243.

14. Beeler mentions that no real persons have been found to fit the circumstances surrounding the characters of this novel (*Madame d'Aulnoy,* 243).

15. The popularity of fairy tales among the aristocratic ladies of Paris has been studied in James Barchilon, *Les Contes merveilleux français de 1690 à 1790.*

16. This aspect is traced in Amy DeGraff's *The Tower and the Well.* DeGraff is antici-

pated in some of her conclusions by Renée Hubert, "Le Sens du voyage dans quelques contes de Madame d'Aulnoy."

17. See Barchilon, *Les Contes merveilleux,* 38, for further comments on Mme d'Aulnoy's role as a "moraliste."

18. Marcelle Welch also maintains that the theme of shared love is a recurrent one in the tales, and that the emphasis upon shared responsibility and healthy feminine sexuality is part of a larger pattern of feminine libertinage ("La femme, le mariage et l'amour dans les contes de fées mondains du XVIIème siècle français," 47–58). See also Maya Slater, "Madame d'Aulnoy and the Adult Fairy Tale," 69–75.

19. See Welch for insights into Mme d'Aulnoy's critique of marriage.

20. Barchilon, *Les Contes merveilleux,* 31.

21. Ibid., 47–49.

22. The comic touch and flair for parody can be seen in the tale translated for this volume. In the original French, the dwarf's speech is delivered in a parody of ancien français. The author draws attention to this aspect by having the dwarf identify the picture she is holding as a portrait of "Merlinus," referring to Merlinus Coccaius (Teofilo Folengo) of Mantua whose "opus macaronicorum" is the masterpiece of this type of macaronic poetry.

The Bee and the Orange Tree

Once upon a time there was a king and queen who lacked nothing for their happiness but children. The aged queen had already given up hope for any when she became pregnant and gave birth to the most beautiful little girl ever seen. The joy in the royal palace was limitless. Everyone eagerly sought a name for the princess that would express what they felt for her. In the end, she was called Aimée, the loved one. The Queen had "Aimée, daughter of the king of the Blessed Isles" engraved on a turquoise heart. She hung this around the neck of the princess, believing that the turquoise would bring her happiness and good luck.

But the rule in this case did not live up to its reputation; for one day, in the most beautiful weather of the summer, when they had carried Aimée on a small boating trip to amuse the nurse, a frightful tempest suddenly arose and made it impossible to land. As the little princess was in a small boat used only for short trips along the seashore, it was soon shattered into a million pieces. The nurse and all the sailors perished. The small princess, asleep in her cradle, remained afloat on the waters until the sea finally washed her on the shore of a country that, while pleasant enough, had been nearly deserted since the ogre Ravagio and his wife Tormentine had come to live there. These two ogres, as ogres are wont, had eaten everyone there, because ogres are terrible people and once they've tasted fresh meat (their name for humans) they almost never eat anything else. Tormentine always found a secret way of bringing them victims because she had fairy blood.

She smelled the poor little princess from a league away, and she hastened to the shore to find her before Ravagio could. She and her husband were both greedy, and no creature was ever more hideous than they, with their squinting eye in the middle of their foreheads, their mouths gaping as wide as the mouth of an oven, their wide and flat noses, their long asses' ears, their bristling hair (which stood on end), and their two hunchbacks, one in the front and the other in the back.

Yet when she saw Aimée in her rich cradle, wrapped in her swaddling clothes of gold brocade, playing with her little hands, with her cheeks like carnations mixed with white roses, and with her little red mouth, laughing and half-opened, seeming to smile at this hideous monster who had come to devour her, even Tormentine was touched by a pity she had never before felt. She decided that she would feed her and that, if she *would* eat her, at least she wouldn't do so immediately.

She took her in her arms, tied the cradle on her back, and being thus outfitted, returned to her cavern.

"Ravagio," she said to her husband, "here is some well-fattened, very tender fresh meat, but by my head, you won't touch so much as a tooth to it, for it is a beautiful little girl and I want to feed her. We will marry her to our young ogrelet and they will produce little ogre offspring of an extraordinary character to divert us in our old age."

"Well said," replied Ravagio. "You are as wise as you are big. Let me see the child; it seems wonderfully beautiful to me."

"Don't go eating her," Tormentine told him, placing the small one in his large claws.

"No, no," he answered, "I'd rather die of hunger." And then, lo and behold, Ravagio, Tormentine, and the ogrelet caressed Aimée in so human a fashion that it was a kind of miracle.

But the poor child, who saw only these deformed apes around her, and who didn't see the breast of her nurse, began to pout. Then she cried with all her might, making Ravagio's cavern echo with the noise. Tormentine feared that this would anger her husband, so she took her and carried her into the woods with the ogrelets following. She had six of them, each more frightful than the last.

As I have said, she was part fairy, and her science consisted of holding an ivory wand while wishing for something. She took the wand and said, "I wish, in the name of the royal fairy Trusio, that the most beautiful hind in our forests might come, sweet and tame, leaving her fawns behind to nurse this dainty creature whom fortune has given me." At that very moment, a hind appeared. The ogrelets welcomed her. She approached and let herself be suckled by the princess; then Tormentine carried Aimée back to the grotto and the hind ran after, skipping and gamboling. The child watched and caressed her, and when she was in her cradle and cried, the hind's milk was ready, and the little ogres rocked her. . . .

[The princess thus spends her childhood among the ogres. Many years later, the grieving king and queen choose Aimé, a cousin of Aimée, to succeed to the throne. A delegation is sent to the kingdom of the king's brother to collect the handsome eighteen-year-old prince, and he departs with them.]

Let him go forth and may Fortune guide him. Let us return to Ravagio to see how our young princess is occupying herself. She has grown in beauty as well as in age, so one can indeed say that love, the Graces, and all the goddesses combined never had so many charms. When she was in the deep cavern with Ravagio, Tormentine, and the ogrelets, it seemed that the sun, the stars, and the heavens had descended among them. The cruelty she observed in these monsters only made her gentler. Indeed, she would have felt the full force of their savagery in the end if the ogrelet had not cherished her as dearly as his one eye. Oh! What can love not do? For this little monster had taken on a softer aspect in watching and loving the beautiful princess. . . .

[The princess is distressed, however, at the prospect of her future husband. She is now young, beautiful, and, although ill-educated, virtuous and gentle. She strides the woods like a young Diana, and, on the excuse of hunting her own food, often goes to a cavern near the sea to lament her fate. When *shipwrecked* sailors are washed up by the sea, she offers them assistance and warns them about the ogres. One day a most interesting young man is washed ashore. She runs to help him, and, although he appears near death, revives him. Both are astonished at the beautiful appearance of the other and are unaware that they are related. The man is, of course, the Prince Aimé.]

. . . In this mutual wonder, they continued to speak without understanding each other. Their gestures served as interpreters of their thoughts. The princess spent several minutes in this way, but suddenly, reflecting upon the peril to which this stranger was soon to be exposed, she fell into a melancholy and despondency that immediately showed on her face. The prince, fearing she might faint, hastened near her and wanted to take her hands, but she pushed him away and showed him, as well as she could, that he must flee from her. She began to run before him; she retraced her steps and indicated with signs that he was to do the same. He fled and returned. When he came back she was vexed, but she took her arrows and pointed them at his heart, to signify that he would be killed. He thought that she wanted to kill him, so he knelt on the ground and awaited the blow. When she saw that, she no longer knew what to do nor how to make her meaning clear, and, gazing at him tenderly, thought, "Alas, will you be the victim of my horrible hosts? With these very eyes that now have the pleasure of gazing at you, will I see you ripped to pieces and devoured without mercy?" She cried, and the bewildered prince was at a complete loss to explain her actions.

Nevertheless, she succeeded in making him understand that she didn't want him to follow her. She took him by the hand and led him to a rock with a cave opening onto the seashore. It was very deep; she went there often to weep for her misfortunes. Sometimes she slept there when the sun was too hot to return to the cavern, and as she had great skill and sense of propriety, she had furnished her cave with a web of butterfly wings of various colors. Upon twisted canes, braided one on top of another to form a sort of bed, she had spread a covercloth of sea rushes; she had also placed flowering boughs in large, deep shells which she filled with water to preserve her bouquets. There were a thousand pretty things that she had made, some with fishbone and shells, some with sea rushes and canes; and these little pieces of handiwork, despite their simplicity, had so delicate an air that it was easy to judge from them the princess's good taste and skill.

The prince, surprised by so much cleverness, believed that this was the place where she slept. He was overjoyed to find himself there with her, and although he wasn't fortunate enough to be able to make her understand the feeling of admiration which she inspired in him, it already seemed that he preferred seeing and living near her to all the crowns to which his birth and the will of his relatives called him.

She forced him to sit down. To show him that she wanted him to remain there until she could bring him something to eat, she, detaching the cord that held back part of her hair, attached it to the arm of the prince and tied him to the little bed. Then she left. He longed to follow her but feared to displease her, and so he began to abandon himself to thoughts from which the princess's presence had distracted him.

"Where am I?" he said, "In what country has fortune led me? My boats are lost, my men drowned; I have nothing left. I find, in lieu of the crown offered me, a dismal rock where I must seek shelter! What must become of me here? What people will I find? If I judge them by the woman who has come to my aid, they are divinities; but her fear lest I follow her, that rough and barbaric speech, which sounds so ill-suited in her pretty mouth, make me fear more somber adventures than those which have already befallen me!" Then he applied his whole attention to reviewing in his mind the incomparable beauties of the young savage. His heart chafed, and he grew impatient at her failure to return. Her absence seemed the greatest evil of all to him.

She returned with all possible speed; she had not stopped thinking of the prince and, being so new to tender sentiments, was not on guard against those which he inspired in her. She thanked heaven for saving him from the dangers of the sea and asked it to keep him from those he ran in being so close to the ogres. She was so preoccupied, and she walked so rapidly, that in arriving she felt a bit oppressed by the heavy tiger's skin that served her as a mantle. She sat down, and the prince rose to his feet, strongly moved by what she'd suffered. He was assuredly sicker than she. At last she recovered from her faint, and immediately showed him all the small ragouts she had brought—among others, four parrots and six squirrels baked by the sun, strawberries, cherries, raspberries, and other fruits. The plates were cedar and eaglewood; the knife was of stone; the napkins were great tree leaves which were very soft and pliable; a seashell was brought for drinking, and another contained beautiful water.

The prince expressed his gratitude with all the signs of head and hand that he could give her, and she, with a sweet smile, let him understand that all he did was agreeable to her. But the hour of separation had come. She made him so thoroughly understand she was leaving that both began to sigh and hide their tears from each other. Each cried tenderly. She arose and wanted to leave; the prince gave a great cry and threw himself at her feet, begging her to stay. She saw very well what he wanted, but she resisted him with a little air of severity. He knew that he must accustom himself to obeying her.

[Both spend terrible nights, and Aimée is terrified that the smell of fresh meat will attrack the ogres.]

. . . These various alarms kept her awake all night; she arose with the day and took the road along the seashore. She ran to the cave; she flew, laden with parrots, apes, and a bustard, with fruit, milk, and all the delicacies she could think of. The prince had not undressed, but he had suffered so much from his fatigue at sea and he had slept so little that towards daybreak he had fallen into a light doze.

"What's this!" she said, waking him, "I've thought of nothing but you since I left you; I haven't even closed my eyes, and you are capable of sleeping?" The prince looked at her, listening without understanding. He talked to her in his turn. "What joy, my darling," he said to her, kissing her hands, "what joy to see you again! It seems a century to me since you left this rock." He talked to her for a long time, forgetting that she couldn't understand him; when he remembered, he sighed sadly and fell silent. She spoke and told him that she had suffered cruel anxieties lest Ravagio and Tormentine discover him, and that she dared not hope he would be safe in this cave for long, that his absence would kill her but that she consented to it rather than expose him to being eaten, that she begged him to flee. At this point her eyes disappeared beneath her tears; she joined her hands before her in a pleading manner. He did not understand what she wanted. He was in despair of it and threw himself at her feet. At last she showed him the road so often that he understood a part of her signs, and made her understand in his turn that he'd rather die than leave her. . . .

[Aimée is so moved that she gives the prince her little turquoise heart. When Aimé reads the inscription, examines his cousin's face and his own feelings, he becomes convinced of her identity. To Aimée's astonishment he weeps, kisses her hands and returns the trinket, asking for a lock of her hair instead. Four days pass, and they continue to enjoy each other's companionship.]

. . . One evening when she had returned rather late, expecting the terrible Tormentine would scold her, she was very surprised to receive a favorable welcome from her and to find a table groaning with fruits. She asked permission to take some, and Ravagio told her they were for her; that the ogrelet had gone to hunt them for her; that, in a word, it was time to make him happy, and he wanted her to marry him in three days. What news! Could there have been anything in the world sadder for the lovely princess? She thought she should die from the fright and grief, but, hiding her affliction, she replied that she would obey them without repugnance, provided they put off the wedding date a little. Ravagio grew angry and cried, "Why should I not eat you now?!" The poor princess fell in a faint of fear between the claws of Tormentine and the ogrelet, who loved her greatly and who begged Ravagio so hard that he was appeased.

Aimée did not sleep one moment; she awaited daybreak impatiently. As soon as it appeared she was at the rock, and, when she saw the prince, she gave a dismal cry and spilled a river of tears. He stood nearly immobile; his passion for the beautiful Aimée had progressed in four days as much as ordinary passions do in four years. He was dying to ask her what was wrong. She knew very well that he would not understand her. She didn't know how to make him understand. At last she untied her long hair, placed a crown of flowers on her head and touching the hand of Aimé with her own, made a sign to him that she was to act thus with another. Then he understood the misfortune that threatened him—she was to be wed to another.

He was on the point of expiring at her feet; he knew neither the road nor the means to save her, and neither did she. They wept; they gazed at each other, and they mutually signaled that it would be better to die together than to separate. She stayed with him until evening. But as night came earlier than expected, and as she was deep in thought, she didn't mind the path that she took. She entered into an unfamiliar part of the woods, where a long thorn pierced her foot through and through. Fortunately for her, it was not far to the cavern. She had great difficulty reaching it; her foot was completely bloody. Ravagio, Tormentine, and the little ogrelets helped her; she suffered great pain when they pulled out the thorn; they crushed some herbs and placed these on her foot, and she went to bed with an anxiety for her dear prince that can well be imagined.

"Alas," she said, "I won't be able to walk tomorrow. What will he think when he doesn't see me? I made him understand that I'm going to be married; he'll think that I couldn't keep myself from it; who will feed him? In one way or another he is going to die; if he comes to look for me, he is lost; if I send the ogrelet to him, Ravagio will learn about him." She burst into tears; she sighed and wanted to rise early, but it was impossible for her to walk. Her wound was too great; and Tormentine, who saw her leaving, stopped her, and told her that if she stirred a step, she would eat her up. . .

[The Prince becomes anxious at her absence, and finally, determined to die rather than be without her, he goes to look for her. He finds the path and the cave and enters, looking for information.]

. . . Ravagio seized him suddenly with a frightful force and would have devoured him if the cries he made in defending himself had not reached the ears of his beloved. Hearing his voice, she no longer felt anything which could stop her. She left her alcove and entered the one where Ravagio held the poor prince. As pale and trembling as if she herself were about to be eaten, she threw herself on her knees before him and begged him to save this fresh meat for her wedding day with the ogrelet when she promised him to eat it. At these words, Ravagio was so happy to think that the princess wanted to acquire their customs that he let the prince go and shut him up in the alcove where the young ogres slept.

Aimée asked permission to feed him well so that he might not grow thin and dishonor the feast. The ogre consented. She carried the prince the best of everything that she could find. When he saw her enter, transports of joy diminished his pain; but when she showed him the wound on her foot, his despair was renewed. They wept together a long time; the prince could not eat, but his dear mistress cut such delicate tidbits with her own hands—tidbits she presented with such a pretty grace—that it was impossible for him to refuse.

She made the young ogres bring fresh moss which she covered with a coverlet of bird feathers, and she made the prince understand that this was his bed. Tormentine called her, and she could not bid farewell in any way but by holding out her hand to him. He kissed it with transports of tenderness that can't be described. She left it to her eyes to express what she felt.

Ravagio, Tormentine, and the princess slept in one of the alcoves of the cave; the ogrelet and five small ogres slept in another where the prince also slept. But it was the custom of ogredom that at night, the ogre, ogress, and little ogres slept with a beautiful golden crown on their heads.

Here was their only splendor, but they would have preferred being hanged and strangled to doing without it.

When everyone was asleep, the princess, who was thinking of her lover, suddenly had second thoughts. Despite the promise Ravagio and Tormentine had given not to eat Aimé, if they were hungry during the night (which they almost always were when they had fresh meat in the house), he was done for. The anxiety occasioned by this thought worked her to such a fever pitch that she thought she would die of fear. After some reflection, she rose, hastily covered herself with the tiger's skin and, tiptoeing soundlessly, went to the cavern where the young ogres slept. She took the crown of the first one she found and put it on the head of the prince, who was totally awake but didn't dare appear to be for he did not know who was performing this ceremony. Then the princess returned to her small bed.

She had hardly covered up again when Ravagio, who had been dreaming of the good meal he would make of the prince and whose appetite was growing with every thought, rose in turn and went to the alcove where the ogrelets were sleeping. As he could not see clearly and feared lest he make a mistake in the darkness, he groped with his hand and threw himself on the one who had no crown. He devoured him like a chicken. The poor princess heard him crunching the bones of the unfortunate one he was eating and grew faint from the fear that it was her lover; and the prince, on his side, being still closer to him, felt all the alarm one can experience on such an occasion.

The daylight ended a terrible night for the princess. She hastened to seek the prince and make him know by signs her fears and her impatience to see him safe from the murderous teeth of these monsters. She spoke kindly to him, and he would have been a thousand times kinder to her if the ogress, who had come to see her children, had not seen the blood covering the cavern and discovered that she was missing her youngest. She gave a horrible cry; Ravagio understood well enough the mistake he'd made, but the evil was impossible to remedy. He whispered in her ear that, being hungry, he had mistaken his choice and that he had believed he was eating fresh meat. Tormentine pretended to calm down, for Ravagio was cruel; and if she had not accepted his excuse in good faith, he possibly would have eaten her. . . .

[The two lovers spend much time together, and Aimée shows Aimé the cradle and swaddling clothes in which she was wrapped. That night, the princess again places the crown on Aimé's head.]

. . . The princess had never been better inspired than when she placed the crown on Aimé's head. Without this precaution, he would have died. The barbaric Tormentine awoke with a start, dreaming of the prince whom she considered as beautiful as the day and a tasty morsel to boot.

She greatly feared that Ravagio would eat him all by himself and deemed it better to do so before him. She glided soundlessly into the cavern of her children. Gently she touched those with crowns (including the prince), and one of the ogrelets was gone in three mouthfuls. Aimé and his mistress heard it all and trembled with fear, but Tormentine, having accomplished her purpose, wanted nothing further but to go to sleep; they were safe for the rest of the night.

"Heavens help us!" said the princess. "Show me what I must do in such an urgent extremity!" The prince didn't pray any less frantically, and sometimes he wanted to attack the two monsters and fight them. But what hope did he have of gaining an advantage? They were as tall as giants and their skin was proof against bullets; he thought, quite prudently, that only ingenuity could save them.

As soon as it was day and Tormentine found the bones of her ogrelet, she filled the air with horrible cries. Ravagio did not appear any less despairing. A hundred times they were ready to throw themselves on the prince and princess and devour them without mercy; the two hid in a small, dark corner of the cavern, but the eaters of fresh meat knew only too well where they were; of all the risks they ran, this one appeared the most obvious.

Aimée, reflecting and racking her brains, suddenly remembered that the ivory wand Tormentine used worked all kinds of marvels and that Tormentine herself couldn't say why. "If such surprising things happen, despite her ignorance, why will my words not have as much power?" Filled with this idea, she ran into the cavern where Tormentine slept; she searched for the wand, which was hidden in the bottom of a hole, and when she found it, cried: "In the name of the royal fairy Trusio, I wish that I could speak the same language as that of my lover." She would have made many other wishes but Ravagio entered and the princess fell silent, replacing the wand. She returned very quietly to the prince.

"Dear stranger," she said to him, "your pains affect me more strongly than my own." At these words, the prince stood astonished and confused.

"I understand you, adorable Princess," he said. "You speak my language, and I can hope that you understand in your turn that I suffer less on my account than on yours; that you are dearer to me than my own life, the light, and all that is most cherished in nature."

"My expression is simple," replied the princess, "but no less sincere. I feel that I would give all I have in my cave by the sea—my sheep, my lambs, finally all I own—for the sole pleasure of seeing you." The prince thanked her a thousand times for her kindnesses and implored her to tell him how in so short a time she had learned all the words and niceties of a language unknown to her until recently. She told him of the power of the enchanted wand, and he told her of her birth and their relation. The princess was transfixed with joy; since she was gifted with a wonderful mind by nature, she said so many fine and well-phrased things that the prince felt a violent increase in his passion for her.

There was no time to lose in gaining control of their situation. It was a matter of fleeing these irrational monsters and of immediately seeking a safe haven for their innocent love. They pledged to love each other forever and to unite their destinies as soon as they were in a position to marry. The princess told her lover that, when she was sure Ravagio and Tormentine were asleep, she would go seek their camel. They would mount it and flee to wherever it might please God to lead them. The prince was so happy that he could hardly contain his joy. Whatever reasons he still had for fear, the charming prospect of the future effaced many of his present woes.

The greatly desired nightfall arrived. The Princess took flour and kneaded it with her white hands into a cake in which she placed a bean. Then while holding the ivory wand she said, "O bean, small bean, I wish in the name of the royal fairy Trusio, that you might speak, when necessary, until you are cooked."

[She places the cake under the embers, gets the prince, and they leave.]

. . . Tormentine, meanwhile, who was filled with vexation, tossed and turned sleeplessly. She stretched out her arms to feel whether the princess was already in her small bed. Not finding her she cried out in a voice of thunder, "Where are you then, my darling?"

"Here. I'm near the fire," answered the bean.

"Are you coming to bed?" asked Tormentine.

"Soon," said the bean, "sleep, sleep." Tormentine feared to wake Ravagio and talked no more, but two hours later she felt the bed of Aimée and cried, "What? You little jade! You don't want to go to sleep?"

"I'm warming myself as much as I can," answered the bean.

"I wish you were in the middle of the fire for your pains," added the ogress.

"I'm there," said the bean, "One couldn't be nearer."

They had many other conversations which the bean kept up like a very clever bean. The conclusion was that, towards morning, Tormentine called the princess again, but the bean was cooked and did not respond. This silence alarmed her; she arose very angrily, searched, called, looked everywhere. No princess, no prince, no small wand. She cried out with such force that the woods and valleys echoed with the noise. "Arise my poppet, arise my beautiful Ravagio, your Tormentine has been betrayed! Our fresh meat has taken flight."

Ravagio opened his eye and jumped into the middle of the cavern like a lion; he roared; he bellowed; he howled; he foamed. "Quick, quick," he said, "fetch me my boots of seven leagues, seven leagues that I might follow our fugitives. I will give them a good chase and swallow them warm before long." He put on his boots which enabled him to advance seven leagues at a stride. Alas! how could they go fast enough to escape such a runner? Perhaps you are surprised that, with an ivory wand, they didn't go still faster than he; but the beautiful princess was new to the art of fairydom, and she didn't know all she could do with such a wand. Only great emergencies brought her sudden flashes of inspiration.

Lulled by the pleasure of being together and of understanding each other, and by the hope of not being pursued, they were making their way onward when the princess, who saw the terrible Ravagio first, cried, "Aimé, we are lost! See this frightful monster coming at us like a thunderbolt!"

"What are we going to do?" asked the prince. "What will become of us? Oh if I were alone, I wouldn't regret the loss of my life, but yours too, my darling, is exposed!"

"I'm defeated," replied the princess. "If the wand doesn't save us, we must resolve ourselves to die. I wish," she said, "in the name of the royal fairy Trusio that our camel might become a pond, the prince a ship, and I an old woman guiding it." At that very moment, the pond, the boat, and the old woman formed, and Ravagio arrived at the shore. He cried: "Hallo, mother! Haven't you seen a young man, a girl, and a camel passing by?"

The old woman in the middle of the pond placed her glasses on her nose. Examining Ravagio, she indicated that she had seen them. They had passed through the meadow. The ogre believed her and took the left path. . . .

[They return to their original forms and continue, hoping to meet someone who will be able to direct them to the Blessed Isles.]

. . . They lived off the fruits of the land, drank the water from the fountains, and slept under trees, quite anxious lest the savage beasts come to devour them. But the princess had her bow and arrows, by which she could try to defend herself, and the danger didn't frighten them enough to crush their pleasure in having escaped the cavern and in being together. Since Aimée had learned Aimé's language, they had said the most beautiful things in the world to each other. Love always quickens the wits. However, in their case, they had no need of such assistance, having a thousand natural accomplishments and a facility for continually producing new and novel ideas.

The prince showed his princess his great impatience to arrive at his or her father's palace, since she had promised him that, with their consent, she would receive him for a husband. What you won't believe, perhaps, without difficulty is that while waiting for this happy day, he lived with her in the forest, in the solitude, master of all he could have wanted, in so respectful and prudent a manner that there has never been found so much passion and virtue together.

After Ravagio had scoured the mountains, forests, and plains, he returned to his cavern where Tormentine and the ogrelets awaited him impatiently. He was laden with five or six persons who had unfortunately fallen under his claws. "Aha," Tormentine cried to him, "have you found and eaten them—those fugitives, those thieves, those fresh meats? And did you save me neither hand nor foot?"

"I believe they must have flown away," answered Ravagio. "I ran like a wolf everywhere without meeting them, and I only saw an old woman in a boat on a pond who gave me some news of them."

"And what did she say?" asked the impatient Tormentine.

"That they had turned to the left," added Ravagio.

"By my head," she cried. "You were their dupe! I suspect you were speaking to Aimé and Aimée themselves. Return, and if you trap them, don't give them a moment's grace."

Ravagio oiled his boots of seven leagues and left, running like a lunatic. Our young lovers were leaving a woods where they'd passed the night. When they saw him, they froze with fear.

"My Aimée," said the prince, "here is our enemy. I feel courageous enough to fight him; won't you be courageous enough to flee alone?"

"No!" she cried, "I won't abandon you, cruel one! Do you doubt my love then? But let's not lose a moment. Maybe the wand will assist us," she said. "In the name of the royal fairy Trusio I wish that the prince might change into a portrait, the camel into a column, and I into a dwarf."

The change was accomplished, and the dwarf began to blow its horn. Ravagio, who was proceeding with giant strides, said to him, "Tell me, you little abortion of nature, have you seen a handsome young man and a beautiful girl pass by with a camel?"

"Yea, I will tell thee," the dwarf said. "I knowest that thou quest for a gentle squire, a most wondrous ladie and their beastie. I espied them yestere'en at this very hour, disporting happily and rejoicing. This very squire didst receive the praise and guerdon of the jousts and tournaments that be held in honor of Merlusine, whose likeness thou seest painted here. Many nobles and gentlemen didst break their lances on haubert, helmet, and shield. The combat was fierce and the guerdon a most beauteous clasp of gold, wrought with pearls and diamonds. As they left, the unknown lady spake to me: 'Dwarf, my friend, without long parley, I beseech a gift of thee, by the name of thy fairest lady-love.' ('It shall not be denied,' quoth I to her, 'except it be not in my power.') 'If,' said she, 'thou meetest the great and wondrous giant who carries his eye in the midst of his forehead, beseech him most courteously to go in peace and leave us be.' Thereupon she whipped her palfrey and departed."

"Where?" asked Ravagio.

"By yon green meadows on the skirt of the wood," said the dwarf.

"If you are lying," said the ogre, "be assured, small toad, that I'll eat you, your column, and your picture of that stock fish."

"Neither falsehood nor knavery dwelleth in me," said the dwarf. "My mouth doth not lie; no living man canst find fraud in me; but go with speed if thou seekest to kill the two before sunset."

The ogre left; the dwarf regained Aimée's features and tapped the prince and the pillar, who both became again what they should be.

What joy for the lover and his mistress! "Never have I felt such keen anxiety, my dear Aimée," said the prince. "As my passion for you gains strength with every moment, my anxieties grow when you are present."

"And I," she said, "it seems to me I had no fear because Ravagio never eats pictures. I alone was exposed to his fury, and my appearance was not very appetizing. Finally I would give my life to save yours."

Ravagio ran to no end; he found neither lover nor mistress. Tired as a dog, he retraced his steps to his cavern. "What? You return without our prisoners?" cried Tormentine, tearing out her bristling hair. "Don't come near me, or I'll strangle you!"

"I met only a dwarf, a picture, and a column," he said.

"By my head," she said, "that was them! I'm a fool indeed to entrust you with responsibility for my vengeance, as if I were too little to take it upon myself! Now, *now* I go myself; I want to boot up in turn, and I won't go less carefully than you!"

She put on the boots of seven leagues and left. How could the prince and the princess go fast enough to escape these monsters with their cursed boots of seven leagues? They saw Tormentine coming, dressed in a snake-skin of various and amazing colors. She carried on her shoulders a terribly heavy iron club; as she was carefully looking everywhere, she would have noticed the prince and the princess if they hadn't been at the bottom of a woods.

"This situation is irreversible," Aimée said, crying. "Here is the cruel Tormentine, whose sight chills my blood; she is cleverer than Ravagio. If one of us talks to her, she'll recognize us and eat us up without further ado; it will all be over soon, as you can well imagine."

"Love, Love!" cried the prince, "don't abandon us. In your empire are there any hearts more tender or loves more pure than ours? Oh, my beloved Aimée!" he continued, taking her hands and kissing them ardently. "Are you destined to perish in such a barbarous fashion?"

"No," she said. "No, I feel the stirrings of a courage and firmness that reassures me; come, little wand, do your duty. I wish in the name of the royal fairy Trusio that the camel were a pot; that my dear prince were a beautiful orange tree and that I were changed into a bee to fly always around him." She tapped each of them the customary three times with her wand, and the change took place so fast that Tormentine, who had just arrived on the spot, didn't notice it.

The frightful shrew was winded, so she sat beneath the orange tree. The princess gave herself the pleasure of stinging her in a thousand places, and, although her skin was thick, the sting pierced it and made Tormentine cry out. To see her rolling about and beating herself against the grass, one would have thought that she was a bull or a young lion afflicted with flies. This one bee, you see, was worth a hundred others. The prince was dying of fear lest his love be caught and killed; but at last Tormentine, bloodied from head to foot, went away, and the princess prepared to return to her original form. Unfortunately, some travelers had passed through the woods and, seeing the ivory wand, which was very attractive, had picked it up and carried it away. There could hardly have been a more vexatious setback than this. The prince and the princess had not lost their use of language; but this helped little in their present state. Overwhelmed by grief, the prince voiced lamentations that greatly increased his beloved Aimée's grief. Often he cried:

The hour approached when Aimée my sweet
Would crown and make my love complete.
How dear to me this fond conceit!

O Love, whose powers aid the few,
Whose mighty passions none can quell,
Let Aimée's heart to mine be true,
Let Aimée dear in safety dwell.

Despite the changes you espy,
The proof our fortune's gone awry,
Let Aimée love me till we die.

"How wretched am I," he continued, "locked beneath the bark of a tree. Here I am—an orange tree deprived of movement. What will become of me if you leave me, my dear bee! But," he added, "what need to leave? You'll find a pleasant den in my flowers and a liquor sweeter than honey on which you can feed. My leaves will provide you a bed where you'll have no need to fear the malice of spiders!"

As soon as the orange tree ceased its lament, the bee replied to him:

My prince, don't fear I'll ever leave;
My heart is firm and strong and true.
Your noble heart should never grieve;
Forever mine belongs to you.

She added to this: "Don't worry that I'll ever leave you. Not lilies nor jasmines nor roses nor the most charming flowers on earth could ever tempt me to such an infidelity. You will always see your bee flying around you, and you will know that the orange tree is not any less dear to the bee than the prince was to the princess." Indeed she closed herself within one of the biggest flowers, as within a palace, and true love, which is never without resources, didn't neglect to provide them in this instance. . . .

[The woods are the favorite haunt of the Princess Linda, a young lady who has renounced marriage for fear she won't find a faithful lover. When she sees the tree, she is enchanted.]

. . . Linda, ravished by the beautiful perfume of the tree, sat beneath it. When about to reenter the palace, she was going to gather some flowers, but the vigilant bee sailed out from beneath the leaves where she had remained on guard and stung the princess with such force that she thought she would faint. There was no more discussion about stripping the orange tree of its blossoms. Linda returned home very ill.

When the prince could speak in liberty to Aimée, he asked her: "What made you so angry with the young Linda? You stung her cruelly."

"How can you ask me such a question?" she replied. "Have you not sufficient delicacy to understand that you must have sweets only for me, that all which is yours belongs to me, and that I defend my wealth when I defend your flowers?"

"But," he said to her, "you see them fall without pain. Would it not be the same to you if a princess decorates herself with them? If she puts them in her hair or places them on her breast?"

"No," the bee said to him in a rather sharp tone. "That is not the same thing to me. I know, ingrate, that you feel more for her than for me. There is a rather large difference between a refined person who is richly dressed and holds a high rank and an unfortunate princess whom you've seen covered in a tiger's skin in the midst of monsters who could only give her coarse and barbarous manners and whose beauty is too mediocre to hold you." She cried at this point as well as a bee could weep; several flowers of the orange tree were moistened by her tears, and his grief at having angered the princess went so far that all his leaves turned yellow, several branches withered, and he thought he might die of grief.

"What have I done, beautiful bee?" he cried. "What have I done to draw your anger? Oh you wish, without doubt, to leave me; you are already weary of having attached yourself to an unfortunate one such as I!" Thus the night passed—in reproaches. But at daybreak, an obliging west wind who had overheard them induced them to be reconciled. It could not have rendered them a more pleasing service.

Meanwhile, Linda, who was dying to have a bouquet of orange blossoms, rose early. She descended into her garden and flew to gather them. But, as she put forth her hand, she felt herself stung so violently by the jealous bee, that her heart failed her. She returned to her bedroom in a very bad humor. "I don't understand what this tree is that we've found." she said, "for as soon as I want to gather the smallest bud, the insect who guards it pierces me with stings!"

One of her ladies who was bright and very lively said to her, smiling: "I advise you, madam, to dress yourself as an Amazon and follow the example of Jason when he won the Golden Fleece. Courageously take the most beautiful of the flowers from that pretty tree."

Linda found something amusing in the idea. Immediately she had a helmet covered with feathers, a light cuirass and gauntlets made; and, to the sound of trumpets, drums, fifes, and oboes, she entered the garden, followed by all her ladies, who were armed in a similar fashion and who called this fête "The War of the Insects and Amazons." Linda drew her sword most gracefully; then, striking the most beautiful branch of the orange tree, she cried, "Come forth, terrible bee, come forth; I come to defy you! Will you be valiant enough to defend that which you love?"

But what became of Linda and all who accompanied her, when they heard a pitable "Alas" issue from the trunk of the orange tree, followed by a deep sigh and the sight of blood flowing from the cut branch? "Heavens!" she cried. "What have I done? What miracle is this?" She took the bloody branch and tried vainly to reattach it to the tree; she felt herself seized with fright and an overpowering alarm.

The poor small bee, in despair at the sad adventure of her beloved orange tree, thought to come forth to seek death on the point of the fatal sword, for she wanted to avenge her dear prince. But she preferred to live for him and, musing on the remedy he required, implored him to let her fly to Araby to collect a balm. Indeed, after he'd consented and they'd said a tender and moving farewell, she went to that part of the world where instinct alone guided her. But to speak more precisely, it was Love who led her and, since Love goes more rapidly than the most diligent insects, he enabled her to make this long journey quickly. She carried the balm back on her wings and the bottoms of her small feet, and with it she cured the prince. . . .

[The prince is cured, mostly by his joy in Aimée's concern. The princess had cut off one of his fingers, however, a loss that the bee blames on herself. Linda, puzzled, summons fairydom with handsome gifts to help her solve the riddle of the tree.]

. . . The Queen Trusio was one of the first to come. Never was any fairy more learned in the arts of fairydom. She examined the branch and the orange tree; she smelled the flowers and detected a human odor that surprised her. She didn't neglect spells either; and she spun them so well that suddenly the orange tree disappeared, and they saw a prince more handsome and well made than any other. At this sight, Linda stood motionless; she felt struck with wonder. She felt something very particular for him, so much so that she had already lost her first indifference by the time the young prince, thinking of his charming bee, threw himself at Trusio's feet. "Great Queen," he said to her, "I am infinitely indebted to you for giving me my life and returning me to my original form. But if you want me to owe you my peace and happiness as well—much more than the life to which you have called me—give me my princess!" In finishing his speech, he produced the small bee, who had never left his sight. "You will be happy," replied the generous Trusio. She began her spells again, and the Princess Aimée appeared with so many charms that there wasn't one of the ladies who didn't envy her.

Linda hesitated in her heart as to whether she should be happy or vexed at such an extraordinary adventure, particularly the part about the bee; but in the end, reason got the better of her passion, which was only in its infancy. She embraced Aimée a thousand times, and Trusio asked her to tell her adventures. The princess was too obligated to her to refuse her wishes. The graceful and easy way with which she spoke interested all the assembly; when she told Trusio that she had done so many marvelous things by virtue of the wand and her name, a great cry of joy was raised in the room, and each implored the fairy to complete the great work.

Trusio, on her side, felt a great pleasure at all she'd heard; she humbly enclosed the princess in her arms. "Since I was so useful to you without knowing it," she said, "consider, charming Aimée, now that I know you, how inclined I am to your service. I am a friend of your father the king and your mother the queen. Let us go swiftly in my flying chariot to the Blessed Isles where both of you will be received as you deserve."

Linda implored them to remain with her for a day while she presented them with rich gifts, and the Princess Aimée abandoned her tiger's skin for clothes of incomparable beauty.

Now let us imagine the joy of our two lovers—yes, let us imagine it if we can; but to do so we would have had to experience the same misfortunes, to have been among the ogres, and to have been metamorphosed several times.

At last they left. Trusio carried them through the air to the Blessed Isles, and they were received by the king and queen as those people in the world whom they least expected to see and whom they saw with the greatest satisfaction. The beauty and wisdom of Aimée, added to her wit, made her the wonder of her age. Her dear mamma loved her passionately. The good qualities of Prince Aimé were no less charming than his handsome appearance. They were married. Nothing was ever so luxurious as their wedding. The Graces attended in festive attire. The Loves were there without even having been asked, and, by their express order, the eldest son of the prince and princess was named Faithful Love.

He has added many titles since then to this one, but under all these names, it is very difficult to find again such a one as the eldest born of this charming marriage. Happy is the person who meets him without mistaking him for another.

Alone with Aimé in the wood,
Our princess was always discreet.
She clung to the prudent and good
And kept her love kind and sweet.

So, beauties, for capturing hearts,
Great pleasures alone will not do.
From revels love often departs.
Be faithful, be strict in his view
And to you he will always be true.

BIBLIOGRAPHY

Primary Works

d'Aulnoy, Marie-Catherine. *Contes des Fées.* 2 vols. Paris: Plon, 1956. (Also includes tales from second collection, *Contes Nouveaux*). First editions: *Contes des Fées.* Paris: Chez Claude Barbin, 1697. *Contes Nouveaux, ou les Fées à la mode.* Paris: Chez Claude Barbin, 1698.

———. *Le Comte de Warwick.* Paris: Compagnie des Libraries Associez, 1703.

———. *Histoire d'Hypolite, Comte de Duglas.* Paris: Chez Claude Barbin, 1690.

———. *Histoire de Jean de Bourbon.* Paris, 1729.

———. *Nouvelles Espagnolles.* A La Haye: Chez Jean Alberts, 1693.

———. *Nouvelles ou Mémoires Historiques.* Paris: Chez Claude Barbin, 1693.

———. *Mémoires de la Cour d'Angleterre.* A La Haye: Chez Meyndert Uytwerf, 1695.

———. *Mémoires de la Cour d'Espagne.* A La Haye: Adrian Moetjans, 1691.

———. *Relation du Voyage d'Espagne.* Paris: C. Klincksieck, 1926.

———. *Le Retour d'une Ame à Dieu.* Paris, 1692.

———. *Sentimens d'une Ame penitente.* Paris, 1691.

Related Works

Asse, Eugiène. *Un Nièce du Grand Corneille: Mademoiselle Bernard.* Paris: Revue biblio-iconographique, 1900.

Barbey d'Aurevilly, Jules-Amédée. *Femmes et moralistes.* Paris: A. Lemerre, 1906.

Barchilon, Jacques. *Le conte merveilleux français de 1690 à 1790.* Paris: H. Champion, 1975.

Beeler, James R. "Madame d'Aulnoy, Historical Novelist of the Late Seventeenth Century." Ph.D. diss., University of North Carolina, 1964.

DeGraff, Amy. *The Tower and the Well.* Birmingham, Ala.: Summa, 1985.

Foulché-Delbosc, Raymond. "Madame d'Aulnoy et l'Espagne." *Revue Hispanique* 67 (June 1926): 1–151.

Hubert, Renée. "Poetic Humor in Madame d'Aulnoy's Fairy Tales." *L'Esprit Créateur* 3 (1963), 123–49.

———. "L'Amour et la féerie chez Madame d'Aulnoy." *Romanische Forschungen* 75 (1963): 1–10.

———. "Le sens du voyage dans quelques contes de Madame d'Aulnoy." *French Review* 46 (April 1973): 931–37.

Jal, Auguste. *Dictionnaire critique de biographie et d'histoire*. Paris: H. Plon, 1872.

Jones, Shirley. "Examples of Sensibility in the Late Seventeenth Century Feminine Novel in France." *Modern Language Review* 61 (April 1966): 199–208.

Mitchell, Jane. *A Thematic Analysis of Madame d'Aulnoy's Contes de Fées*. Oxford, Miss.: Romance Monograph Series, 1978.

Roche-Mazon, Jeanne. *En Marge de l'oiseau bleu*. Paris: Livres de l'Artisan, 1930.

———. "Madame d'Aulnoy, n'aurait-elle pas été en Espagne?" *Revue de la littérature comparée* 7 (October–December 1927): 724–36.

———. *Autour des contes de fées*. Paris: Didier, 1968.

Slater, Maya. "Madame d'Aulnoy and the Adult Fairy Tale." *Newsletter for Seventeenth Century Studies* (1982): 69–75.

Storer, Mary. *Un episode littéraire de la fin du XVIIème siècle: La mode des contes de fées*. Paris: Champion, 1928.

Streckenback, Marie. "Madame d'Aulnoy: Ihre Novellen und Romane." *Romanische Forschungen* 43 (1931): 146–256.

Welch, Marcelle. "La femme, le mariage, et l'amour dans les contes de fées mondains du XVIIème siècle français." *Papers on French Seventeenth Century Literature* 10 (1983): 47–58.

PART TWO

taly

THE ITALIAN MEMORIALIST

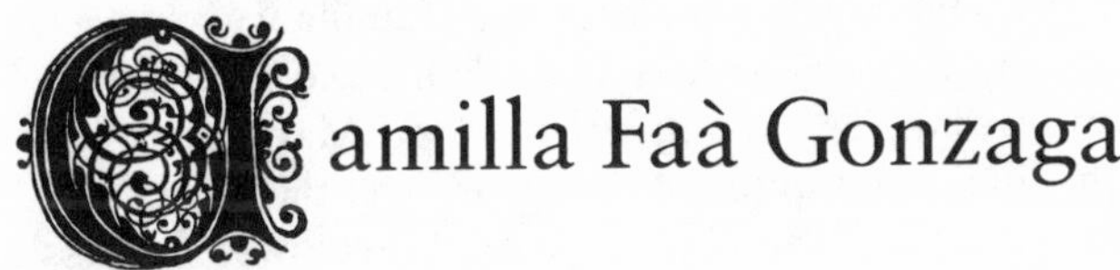

Camilla Faà Gonzaga

VALERIA FINUCCI

Born in 1599, Camilla Faà Gonzaga belongs chronologically to the Baroque period. She seems to be outside her time, however, in every respect. Her name does not appear in any anthology or critical compendium focusing on those years, or in collections specifically reserved to women; moreover, her very existence as a writer has only recently been discovered. Her sole work, a memoir written in 1622, lay dormant for over 270 years until published in 1895 by Giuseppe Giorcelli in a journal devoted to the literary, historical, and artistic output of the Piedmont city of Alessandria. Giorcelli titled it "Storia di donna Camilla Faa di Bruno Gonzaga." It was published again in 1918 by Fernanda Sorbelli-Bonfà under the title "Historia della Sig. ra Donna Camilla Faa Gonzaga."[1] The narrative has yet to receive critical attention, although some studies may be forthcoming. Costa-Zalessow has recently called it "the first female autobiography in Italy."[2]

The Faàs were a family from Monferrato who rose to nobility in the first half of the sixteenth century. Camilla's father, Ardizzino II (called Arduino by Sorbelli-Bonfà), was the first in his family to choose a military career and was employed as an army captain by the Gonzagas. He later became their ambassador to both Turin and Milan. At the death of his brother Ortensio, Ardizzino inherited the fief of Bruno, previously given to the family by Duke Vincenzo I. Together with the land brought in dowry by his wife Margherita Fassati, the new property rendered him one of the most influential men in the region. The exact number of his children is unknown. In addition to Camilla, documents show the existence of three sons, Ortensio, Bonifacio, and Ferdinando, and of a younger daughter, whose name has been lost. Camilla was still a child when her mother died. She was subsequently sent to live with a paternal aunt, a nun in an Alessandrian convent. Ardizzino chose this course to ensure a proper education for his daughter and to protect her from the gossip which would inevitably grow around a young female living in a household where paternal absences were frequent.[3] Giorcelli writes that Camilla was thirteen when Duchess Margherita of Savoy, wife of Duke Francesco II Gonzaga, took her as a lady-in-waiting. The young girl followed Margherita first to Mantua during the final ten months of the duke's life, then to Goito, and finally to the Savoy seat in Turin, where the newly widowed duchess retired. Camilla stayed only briefly at the Turinese court. As the political relationship between the Savoys and the Gonzagas soured, she was sent back to Mantua together with the full contingent of ladies-in-waiting who had escorted Margherita to her native land. The new Duke Ferdinando Gonzaga, Francesco II's younger brother, retained the women at court in Mantua pending the outcome of his marriage negotiations with his former sister-in-law Margherita. Had the match been successful, it would have had profound political implications for the Gonzagas—broadening their power, while reining in Savoy ambitions. No compromise was ever reached.

Camilla Faà had been back at court for nine months when Duke Ferdinando saw her for the first time. The date was September 1615, and he was preparing for his investiture as ruler of Mantua, a ceremony which took place with great pomp in January of the following year. Camilla was sixteen and a "nobilis et venustissima puella" with "rara pulchritudine."[4] The rest is tersely narrated in her memoir. Ferdinando and Camilla secretly married on February 19, 1616. The news of their nuptials stirred disbelief and controversy at court. Such a nonpolitical tie was not only unusual but also dangerously open to public criticism and legal review. To assuage Ardizzino's concern about his daughter's future, the duke gave Camilla the marquisate of Mombaruzzo, a property which later proved valuable by providing her with a steady income. Harmony between the two was short-lived, though not for personal reasons. Faced with the harsh realities of politics on the peninsula, Ferdinando knew that he needed strong allies if he wanted to retain his power. He was also pragmatic enough to see the wisdom in his courtiers' insistence on a political marriage to solve his political problems. Although worried about Camilla's future (she was pregnant at the time), he slowly started to distance himself. Next, he petitioned the Vatican to have their marriage annulled and to receive dispensation to wed the woman chosen for him, his niece Caterina de' Medici. Besides her large dowry, he sought the support of her powerful family in order to win his new war against the Savoy to reconquer the Monferrato. Pope Paul V allowed Ferdinando to carry out his plan not by issuing a papal bull but by refusing to consider the validity, or even the possibility, of his first marriage. He simply granted dispensation for two blood-related petitioners to marry.[5] The papal exemption arrived while the Gonzaga court was trying to collect on its own sufficient doctored proof and sanitized depositions to demonstrate the illegality of Ferdinando and Camilla's match, in the event that Paul V was unwilling to tamper with what had voluntarily taken place a few months earlier. The matrimonial code required that the ceremony be officiated, for example, by a parish priest, but Ferdinando and Camilla had been married by the court bishop. Also, a number of irregularities had been committed on purpose by the only witness, Alessandro Ferrari. These records are filed today in the Curia Vescovile in Mantua as "Protocol of examined witnesses" and dated February 1, 1617.[6]

The new wedding ceremony took place six days later, on February 7, two months after Ferdinando and Camilla's son, Giacinto, was born. It was evident that the duke regarded his new union as strictly political and that his heart was still with "la bella Ardizzina," as Camilla was called in Mantua. Together with some members of his court, he had visited her just before Giacinto's birth and had stayed on until his baptism, which was solemnized by the local dignitary, the Archbishop of Casale. The former spouses could not remain close for long, however. The new Gonzaga duchess Caterina, who was later described as a "vivid, discontented woman, imperious, fiery and sterile,"[7] had no interest in allowing Camilla to retain influence at court. She convinced the duke—by all accounts an eternally indecisive man—to force a choice on his former wife: marry a courtier, or embrace a life in the cloister. Either solution would have been perfect for Caterina; in order to erase Camilla's tenure at court, she needed to pass her rival off to a man or to a religious order—to anybody, in fact, but Ferdinando. Untethered, Camilla would have been a constant reminder that the duke had once married her and that their son could claim right to a title in the future.

Camilla stubbornly resisted pressures for five years. She gave up only when, already exiled in Ferrara, she saw no hope for any sort of restoration. The religious vows were hurriedly administered on May 22, 1622, the customary period of novitiate waived thanks to a timely exemption from the new pope, Gregory XV. Camilla, now Sister Caterina Camilla Gonzaga, a Clarissa nun, wrote her memoir a few months later to satisfy a request from her mother superior, Sister Bradamante Brasavola, who was curious to know her side of the story after so much slander had circulated in the duchy. She kept her ties with the Gonzagas in order to have news of her son, who had been taken from her a few months after his birth to be educated at court. He died early, in 1630, a victim of the plague brought to northern Italy by the invading German mercenary troops. Camilla passed away on July 14, 1662, forty years after she became a nun. Her body is buried in the Church of the Convent of the

Corpus Domini in Ferrara. The Latin inscription which her nieces had engraved on the tombstone uses her correct title, "Camillae Catherinae Gonzagae Fae Marchionissae." Since there was no doubt in her mind concerning her rightful name, Camilla kept using it more or less illegally throughout her lifetime. Even her mother superior, Sister Livia Rosalba Andreassi, referred to her in this fashion when she informed the new Duke of Mantua, Carlo II, of her death.

Documents on the life of Ferdinando Gonzaga are plentiful. Born in April 1587, he was destined by his family to become a cardinal and was sent to Rome. Upon his brother's death, however, he renounced the mitre and was invested sixth Duke of Mantua and fourth Duke of Monferrato. More a humanist than a condottiere or a politician, Ferdinando took time off from state responsibilities to cultivate a range of scholarly interests such as alchemy, literature, music, and theater.[8] Educated in Ingolstadt and Pisa, his name appears on the list of the members of the Accademia degli Invaghiti, under Rinato. According to Bellonci, Ferdinando was a rebel, "only too prone to moods of exhaltation and delicate torments, [his manner] delicate and gallant, . . . made up of Lombard graces and Spanish charm."[9] Sorbelli-Bonfà describes him as a "fervent lover, refined like a Renaissance prelate, extremely elegant and prodigal."[10]

Clearly he was in love with Camilla; had he not been thoroughly charmed, he would hardly have gone to the length of formally persuading Ardizzino to give him his daughter in marriage. Apart from Giacinto, Ferdinando had no other children. At his death in 1626, power went to his brother Vincenzo II and soon after to the French branch of the family, the Nevers—a devolution that incurred Austrian and Spanish wrath and contributed to the descent of the imperial armies into Italy. Their ravages and looting opened a painful, degrading chapter in Italian history, one graphically described by Manzoni in *I promessi sposi*.

CAMILLA FAÀ's real-life drama became at times the subject of literary exercises. Her vicissitudes were known to contemporaries, and she is mentioned in a compassionate and brief account as early as 1637 by the Gonzaga historian Antonio Possevino in a folio titled *Historia Belli Monferratensis* (History of the Monferrato War). As one would expect, her story became popular during the Romantic period. Paolo Giacometti wrote a historical drama in three acts titled *Camilla Faà da Casale*, which was first performed in Florence on October 20, 1846, and published in 1850. A few years earlier, in 1844, Carlo D'Arco had included an account of her life in his *Racconti patrii* (Native Tales) under the melodramatic title of "Degli amori sfortunatissimi di Camilla Faà." His choice of a plural reference to her loves, which no document pertaining to Camilla's life corroborates, was intended perhaps to titillate a readership in search of easy gratifications. The most thorough and romanticized rendering of Camilla's unfortunate story can be found in the historical novel *La bella Ardizzina* by Giambattista Intra, first published in 1881 and again in 1889. Here 869 pages review, dramatize, and embellish Camilla's case. The 1895 study by Giorcelli is shorter and more factual than the 1918 book by Sorbelli-Bonfà; both contain a reprint of Camilla's memoir as an appendix to the commentary.

Needless to say, each writer—historian, dramatist, or novelist—sees in the story what he wants to see. The first three books make little attempt at historical accuracy: D'Arco portrays Camilla as virtuous and haughty; Giacometti finds her a romantic figure; and Intra depicts her as partly unyielding and partly resigned. Sorbelli-Bonfà offers a sort of debunking of Camilla's memoir. She finds it too reticent, the author's memory too often faulty; yet at times she uses records that Camilla could hardly have had available in her seclusion. Sorbelli-Bonfà concludes that the writer did not do herself justice in her memoir because her reserve made her too disengaged and suggests that we should look into the extant historical documents for a better perception of the human, compassionate side of Camilla's unfortunate life.

THE MANUSCRIPT COPY of the "Storia" is kept today in the private archives of the convent in which Camilla spent so many years of her life. According to Intra, the original was copied by L. C. Volta; copies made subsequently are now in the Biblioteca Comunale of Mantua, the Gonzaga capital, and in Casale, property of the Faà heirs.[11] My translation uses the first published edition, the one printed by Giorcelli in *Rivista di Storia, Arte, Archeologia della provincia di Alessandria.*

The "Storia" offers a closeknit, concise reading. Its chronological development covers seven years, from the time Camilla enters womanhood with her official betrothal to a court knight, Ottavio Valenti, to the time she leaves active life by taking religious vows. Those years carried Camilla through constant changes of fortune, her destiny determined by the will of others, her avenues restricted by her sex. What is clear in reading the recollections is that Camilla's sense of propriety left Ferdinando no choice but to marry her; later, her total lack of political power opened the way to defeat and exile. Had she been interested in practical advantages, Camilla would have asked for different rewards (land grants for herself, for example, or social advancement for her brothers) than marriage; had she been willing to negotiate her worth, she would have avoided some painful rationalizations.

The memoir starts with the allusion to Ardizzino's choice of a husband for his daughter, a choice that at first seemed to please the duke. The next day, however, during a ball organized for all members of his retinue, he surprised Camilla by declaring a newly aroused passion for her. His arguments were persuasive—he was proposing marriage, after all, though at some vague time in the future—yet Camilla had lived enough at court to know how to decipher court language. She thanked him for his interest and laughed at his proposal. The flirtation would probably have ended had the duke not been her political superior and had he not lived at a time in which rulers could comprehend no limitations to their power. Camilla writes that Ferdinando acted quite properly at the beginning. Still, to prevent her escaping his courtship or questioning his assertions, he asked her father first to postpone indefinitely her preannounced marriage and then convinced him to leave Mantua to settle some private business in Monferrato. Ferdinando thus had more license to plead his case in earnest. Camilla gave in, however, only after her father agreed, only when his explicit approval made Ferdinando's desires for her legal. The two were secretly married at night in the duke's private chapel, a bishop ratifying the marriage vows and a chamber valet witnessing the rite. Camilla recalls that something in the ceremony did not seem proper, yet the duke's declaration of marriage intent, which he had written and signed beforehand, appeared serious enough to her. She also thought that a sovereign's signature automatically turned documents into laws. Soon, however, plotting began behind her back, and Ferdinando started to evade her. Although pregnant, she chose to leave the court for awhile and to wait for decisions on her future in her brothers' house, Ardizzino having recently died.

At first, Ferdinando seemed uncertain about his course. He eventually claimed state responsibilities and remarried (or rather, married for the first time, since, with a total disregard for her testimony—a befuddled Camilla notes—their own marriage was quietly dismissed). This marriage inaugurated a period of manipulation in the young woman's life, with her son's destiny serving as the wager each time. Outraged, Camilla dodged the solutions offered to silence her voice permanently: first, she rejected the idea of marrying again, since she thought herself already legally married; next, she rebuffed the cloister, claiming that her religious beliefs were not strong enough for such a drastic step. Eventually, her son was taken away from her, all documents with the duke's signature in her possession were confiscated, and she was kept more or less isolated in a convent. All possible alternatives slowly disappeared. By taking the vows in the end she adopted the most viable course: the whole court could see that she was choosing permanent seclusion in a cloister rather than marriage to protect her reputation. Opting for a husband would have made others forget that, despite the record in public documents, she was already lawfully married. For herself, for her family, and for her son's future she had to set the record straight. This she did as her most compelling duty in the first months of her life as a nun. Her memoir is unsigned.

Camilla does not name herself in the narrative, although she writes in the first person and introduces each player in her vicissitudes with the correct name and title. Naming is reserved for the most influential person in her life, the duke, who calls her "Donna Camilla" when he proposes marriage. The memoir carefully defines where power lies: with her father first of all, since as *pater familias* he is responsible for her marriage; with her brothers later, as new heads of the Faà household after Ardizzino's death; with the duke, when he becomes her lawful husband; and with her mother superior at the end, as the recognized authority in the convent. Throughout, Camilla is powerless. The memoir also explores the development of her womanhood. Thus we see her as an obedient daughter anxious to bow to Ardizzino's authority, as a questioning maid when Ferdinando starts to pursue her, as a dutiful wife demanding her matrimonial rights when her status is challenged, and as a concerned mother when her son's future is at stake. She is always proud, even when choosing conventual isolation.

Of course, it is possible to read the "Storia" negatively. After all, Camilla's adamant moral position as Ferdinando's legal—and only—wife compromised her chance to lead a good life, no matter how clandestine, with the man she wanted. But there is another, more interesting reading, perhaps closer to the truth. In this reading, Camilla's narrative of loss becomes an example of assertive biography, the statement of a candid "I" who refuses to be muffled. Exiled from the Mantuan court, spurned by friends, possibly abandoned by her brothers after the duke's will declared her marginality, Camilla cannot remain silent. Ironically she is able to pick up the pen only when, as a nun, she no longer has a name or a secular identity and has vowed to restrain her voice permanently. Camilla's narration is sedate, yet forceful in her exposure of the role she was forced to play and in the strength of her rebellion against a destiny whose course she had found written by others. There are no petty revenges in "Storia": Ferdinando is not punished, nor is the court chastised. In fact, it is precisely because she refuses to revictimize herself while writing of her victimization that Camilla is eventually able to recover her self-respect and to reclaim her honor. She also rectifies the record, even if only in her mother superior's eyes.[12] She knew that public vindication would eventually come, post mortem.

NOTES

1. The accent on "Faà" seems to be a modern trait. Her surname was not spelled with an accent in either edition of the "Storia," yet the mark is present in all later citations.

2. p. 14. Costa-Zalessow mentions Camilla's "Storia" in the introduction to her anthology but fails to reserve room in her text for the writing itself.

3. As for education, Camilla's could not have been sufficient, since she was taken out of the convent at thirteen. Her case was fairly typical, however. For more on female education during the Renaissance, see Kelso, *Doctrine for the Lady of the Renaissance.* For a specific study of female education in Renaissance Italy, see Blade, *Education of Italian Renaissance Women.*

4. Possevino, *Historia Belli Monferratensis.* Quoted in Giorcelli, "Documenti storici del Monferrato," 76.

5. See Grottanelli, "Caterina de' Medici," 318.

6. Catalogued as D. II, 70, and D. II, 20.

7. This sour, probably undeserved, description is in Bellonci, *A Prince of Mantua,* 303.

8. According to some historians, he was also a generous ruler. For Giorcelli, who quotes from Possevino, Ferdinando was less taken with the care of his wars than with enjoying himself "con ampliare od abbellire le ville, colla caccia, colla pesca, con spettacoli teatrali, accademie, e persino colle fisime dell'alchimia" (through widening or embellishing his villas, hunting, fishing, theatrical shows, academic gathering, and even with the fancy of alchemy), "Documenti storici del Monferrato," 75.

9. Bellonci, *A Prince of Mantua,* 270, 258. Bellonci's book, which focuses on Ferdinando's father, Vincenzo I, sheds some light on the events which took place in Mantua during those years.

10. The Italian reads: "appassionato amante, raffinato come un monsignore del Rinascimento, elegantissimo e prodigo" (*Camilla Gonzaga Faà,* 21).

11. The information is given in a note on p. 44.

12. For a detailed critical study of Faà's "Storia," see my "Remembering the 'I': Faà Gonzaga's 'Storia' (1622)."

The Story of Donna Camilla Faà of Bruno Gonzaga

Count Ardizzino Faà, my father, had been in Milan three years as ambassador to the Most Serene Ferdinando Duke of Mantua and Monferrato, when he came to Mantua to pay homage to His Highness being he in command of his deputation. Since I was then sixteen and a lady-in-waiting at that court, my father took the occasion to draw up a marriage contract between me and Sig. Ottavio Valenti, a qualified and rich knight. His Highness was informed of the matter, was happy for it, and was particularly pleased about this relationship.

The day after, it happened by chance that a ball was given at the Tea Palace. By His Highness's orders, we ladies-in-waiting went as well. During the dance His Highness came to invite me. He started by telling me that he had organized that ball with the express purpose of creating an occasion to talk to me because he had to say something important, but he wanted me to promise him first to say nothing about it to anybody. I gave him my word to be quiet, and he began: "You should know that I find myself very much obliged toward His Majesty, the Catholic king, for the protection he has given to my interests in these past wars.[1] Now, my time having come to get married, duty requires that this marriage be satisfying to him. To do so, however, I am faced with many impediments. Still my subjects plead with me daily about it. To satisfy everybody I am advised to take for a wife a woman who is my subject, of good moral habits and pleasing to me. A year had already gone by since I first started to be urged on the issue when one day, during a consultation on the matter, Madama di Ferrara, who was there, again recommended to me to resolve to marry. I answered her: 'Madam, since this is what is required for my own interests and for those of my states, I will do it, but Your Highness should be so kind as to find herself the woman I should take for a wife, since I do not have any particular one in mind.'[2] Madama accepted the office willingly and a few days later she proposed to me Madam N. N., her lady-in-waiting, whom you know very well. I would have settled down quite nicely with her, if I had not been advised that this young woman had an incurable disease. For this reason nothing more was done. Meanwhile it has been a long time since I first placed my thoughts upon you and I have managed to arrange things in a way that it is possible for me to take you for my wife. Lately circumstances have changed, though, and I find it now difficult to accomplish what once seemed easy. However, I have not lost hope that this can be done. Do not feel surprised, therefore, if I do not allow Valenti to marry you too soon. I wanted to inform you of this good will of mine because, if by chance the desired result does not come, you will still know how much you are esteemed by me. I also did not put this obstacle before your marriage in order to have you lose a good fortune, but only in case I have my hopes realized."

I laughed, thinking that for sure he was saying these things jokingly and in order to find out whether I could be easily duped. Therefore, I answered: "Sir, it would be a great favor for me simply to serve Your Highness's wife. I take your words as being said to while away this hour of dance because, thank God, I have brain enough to know I have no such merits to raise myself to those high ranks." He replied with many other things and the dance ended.

Four or six days later he told my father to feel free to go to Monferrato to speed up his business there. Also he said that he did not want him to marry me off until his return.

My father left and soon after His Highness wrote to him personally about the matter and of his own good will. To this purpose he wrote four letters during the time in which my father was away. Until October, I did and said whatever was possible to convince His Highness to take such a thought off his mind, and God knows it well since I could plainly foresee, if not completely at least in part, the misfortunes hanging over me.

In the month of October His Highness called my father back to Mantua. He came and a few days later, with an excuse, His Highness had someone in the court tell Valenti to find himself another woman to become his wife because he did not want his marriage to me to take place. Having done this, it seemed that His Highness was changing his mind and wanted to have me for his lover rather than his wife. When I realized this, I defended myself and said words full of resentment. He answered that he did not want to die because of me and that I would not be the first woman to be a prince's lover. He would treat me in such a manner that any great knight would be grateful to have me for a wife. Also I had to remember that I was in his house, and that I should not disparage his sense of decency (moderation) because, were he to fancy otherwise, he could change his way of acting toward me as well. Moreover, if I was reluctant to accede to his wishes for fear of my father, he would take care of that and, if his loving solicitude were to no avail, he could have my father's head cut off.

I replied: "Sir, Your Highness should believe me when I say that no man ever died for love, and you will not either. Even if I were not the first woman to have been mistress to a prince, I would still be the first to disgrace our house and God should take my life away from me if, because of me, my relatives need to go about with their heads down. If getting married to a knight were enough to keep me away from lasting dishonor, that could be understood, but His Highness should keep in mind the honor of other people, and know that nothing in this world could restore to me what would be taken away. It is true that the love I hold for my father is great, or rather is extraordinary, yet I do not worry about him in this circumstance, only about my soul and my reputation. I know well that His Highness respects me little if he thinks that what ties me up is just the fear of doing something wrong. Also, he should not resort to provoking my father in order to further his aims because he would simply deceive himself. Whereas now I have to uphold my own honor, I would then be obligated both to the honor and to the person who has lost his life for me without reason."

I asked my father to find a means to take me away from the court and bring me home; that, as for me, I had thought to follow a course of action which would satisfy my own honor—and maybe that of His Highness as well—by becoming a nun. Also I told him to remain assured that God would take care of this affliction, being myself resolute to die rather than do anything disgraceful.

As soon as he could answer, my dear father was moved to cry because he realized how much I was settled in my proposal.

Two hours later His Highness was somehow aware of what I had said to my father. He looked for him and told him that he knew very well what I had decided to do. This thought had amused him so much that, without having in mind any of his interests, he had determined not to deprive himself of me. He wanted me as a wife and soon my father would see the result of his decision.

He later came to my place together with the Bishop of Cesarea, who was then Abbot of Santa Barbara. He brought also Gregorio Carbonelli, a Neapolitan, and a certain Alessandro Ferrari, his chamber valet. He said to me: "Donna Camilla, the resolution you have reached to take the vows in order to save your reputation, together with the fact that I relish the idea itself, obliges me so much that I have resolved to marry you right now, upon your consent. To this end I brought along the Bishop of Diocesarea and Alessandro, who will act as a witness."

When I heard this I said: "Sir, you are a cautious person and for this reason I pray you to look after yourself. Please keep in mind what is best for your house and your state and do not jeopardize your chances just to satisfy a whim, because relationships acquired through marriage may help you to solve many problems. Think about it so that you will not find yourself unhappy after."

He answered: "Your words oblige me even further since I see that you are more concerned about my own interests than yours, and I know what I can do. Therefore, come this way to the chapel, which is next to the room where I used to live, because I want to marry you."

We went to the tribune in the chapel. When we arrived there His Highness said to the bishop: "Monsignor, you know very well the reason why I brought you along. Therefore, give Donna Camilla this script which I wrote with my own hand to better reassure her and then ask her whether she is pleased to have me for a husband. As for me, I am more than happy to have her for my wife."

The monsignor gave me the document, then asked that question. He had my consent and the wedding ceremony followed. Later His Highness said to me, while still holding my hand: "Do you believe me this time?" I answered: "How couldn't I now that our Blessed God is between us?"

Having done this, His Highness left and went to see my father in his rooms. He told him what had happened and added: "Now I cannot publicize this matter for the best because it is necessary that I reach an agreement with my brother and Madama di Ferrara. However, this should not worry you because the thing has been done. Were I to change my mind, I pray God not to let me kiss the Cross at my death and thus have my soul damned."

Before His Highness's departure I asked him whether he would mind me saying a word to the bishop. He agreed and then went to see my father, as I said, followed by his assistant, who was present at the event.

I said to the bishop: "Monsignor, there is something annoying me in this wedding ceremony, that is, whether your very reverend self can perform this task being a bishop rather than a parish priest." He answered: "Madam, do you believe that a person in my position would act without having the authority for doing so? You disparage me if you think I am a bad priest. Live happily and peacefully because I am the court parish priest as a result of a privilege that the Church of Santa Barbara has received among many others. To confirm it, your ladyship should remember that during Easter, when everybody goes to his own parish to receive the Holy Communion, the whole court comes to take the Communion in Santa Barbara and a badge is given in recognition of the fact that this is the court parish. As an abbot of this church, I can perform all functions pertaining to parish priests."

I was satisfied at these words since I knew very well that he was saying the truth, because I had seen this happen under my own eyes.

The monsignor then went away. Four days later I asked him again the same question when my father and Giovanni Baruto were present, and he gave the same answer.

During the time we were together I was not in the position of a duchess, but I was treated very differently from all other court ladies.

In May His Highness fell sick with high fevers and a form of head abscess and his life was in doubt. Having grown worse, he called the aforementioned bishop, my father and me. He said that, since he was ailing and was unable to know what God had in store for him, he had resolved to call most of his family to his bed and to tell those gathered that I was his wife, so that the people who had seen him treat me in certain ways would not come up with strange thoughts about the relationship and pass judgment on him and on me. When they came into the room, he had the bishop himself say how things were. Then, holding my hand, His Highness added: "This woman should be recognized as my wife by all of you. However, do not refer to the matter openly, because I do not want it publicized until my brother and I have come to a compromise. This will be done very soon."

It would all have been true if the prince's secretary, instigated by Madama of Ferrara's promises, had not put an end to the agreement. He meted out punishment for it, however, because he went to prison (for another reason) and there he stayed throughout the duke's lifetime.

To get back now to the problem between His Highness and his brother, they did not come to an understanding.[3] In fact, they even fought over the issue until August when the prince married the Princess of Bozzolo.

Everybody knows that because of this Madama di Ferrara and the counselors started to pester His Highness. They had the Queen of France write fiery letters in order to persuade him to leave me and marry a princess and brought forward to this purpose all the reasons one can imagine.

It should be added that my father fell ill at just about this time and died within ten days. His Highness went to see him in his final hours and told him many things. Among others, the following: that he wanted him to die happily because he was giving him his word that, as soon as possible and by all means, I would be placed in the position which was due to me. Also that he was sorry my father was unable to see his immediate descendants, since I was pregnant then, but one had to be satisfied with whatever God was pleased to grant.

My father died, as I said, and it had just happened that my enemies realized this was the occasion they needed since now I was alone, young, without advice, and unfamiliar with this sort of business. They started to beg His Highness to make up his mind and find some problems with our marriage in order to remarry and mend the imbroglio created by the prince (Vincenzo), his brother. In the meantime Madama di Ferrara continued to do as much as possible to persuade His Highness to consent to her wish.

The gallant bishop (may God forgive him) was not the last to be against me, and he should really be given the most blame because he had to tell me the truth when I asked him, or defend his actions with all his strength.

I was told by some of the duke's friends what was being plotted against me. I also became aware of what was going on from the behavior of the duke himself who, in seeing me, would change color and seemed no longer able to find his way to where I was. One morning I decided to meet him in order to know something. He seemed surprised and used a thousand excuses and pretenses to say that there was no remedy to his brother's foolishness and that he was receiving letters from the Queen of France, his aunt, instigating him on the matter.

I cannot repeat his precise words, but I perceived very well what was being plotted against me, even though his discourse was embellished with a number of excuses easy to imagine.

Having therefore understood it all, I decided to leave Mantua. Since His Highness had changed his mind, I had to change my own behavior, which would have been impossible while I was in Mantua.

I asked his permission to go to Monferrato to the house of my brothers, and I obtained it with great difficulty. I left the same day and spent the night in Marmirolo. The day after, before leaving, His Highness came to see me. Among other things he told me: "I asked the Bishop to study our case very well in order to see what I am to do, because I do not want to throw my hands up in the future and say: 'Poor me! I had children and I renounced them.' "

I replied: "Sir, you know a lot and do not need others to study things for you. By examining your conscience you will know what to do. You should remember that when you will be before God's tribunal you cannot excuse yourself with your ignorance. As for my own person, it is of great comfort to realize that both God and the world know the truth. I hope that I will not die any lower than I was at birth, and this will be more than enough for me."

During my trip I was very well escorted, this both to keep an eye on me and to honor me. He also wanted me to leave one of my brothers behind in Mantua.

I went directly to Bruno, which was under the jurisdiction of my eldest brother, and stayed there three weeks together with the people who had escorted me.

One morning a courier sent by His Highness arrived in a coach. He brought a note written by His Highness himself in which I was told to go immediately to Casale. To that purpose he had written to Sig. Alfonso D'Avalos, who was then his Governor General for Monferrato, to come and pick me up with two companies of mounted horsemen. I immediately left for Casale and there I stayed for a few months, always treated very well.

The moment of delivery came and Sig. Don Giacinto was born. He was baptized by Monsignor Pascale, bishop of the city, in the chapel inside the castle. His Highness, who had arrived in Casale a few days earlier, was present together with a good many of the nobility.

His Highness left almost immediately. Not too long after, the aforementioned Bishop of Casale came with an order from Sig. N. N. to examine me concerning the facts. During the examination I told him the whole truth, but the notary did not write it. I am positive about it, since I believe that the truth of the matter was never told to His Holiness. I heard that they sent a document to Rome with my signature. It must have been counterfeited, since I never undersigned any document.

After this His Highness went to Florence and those very serene people entreated him to recover from me the marriage pact mentioned above. However, either because he did not know how to get it back from me or because he did not want to upset me further, he neither wrote about it nor had others mention it to me. I heard that, in order to achieve his purpose, he made a similar one and presented it there, swearing that it was the one recovered from me.

He then married Madama Caterina de' Medici and brought her to Mantua.

A few months went by when—in the name of His Highness, of Madama di Mantua and of Madama di Ferrara and also with personal letters from him—I began to be petitioned and beseeched to go to Mantua with my son. I answered that he was the master of my son, but that, as for my going there myself, I was not going to do it because it hardly appeared convenient to me. Moreover, my coming would not quite be cheered before problems would arise. No matter what I said or did, however, I had to go, thus ordered with private letters, as I said, by all masters.

I left Casale for Mantua with a very good escort. When I arrived there, Sig. Giacinto was brought to court and I entered a monastery where I remained for a year and three months. During this time I was annoyed by requests to marry again, but I resisted them all.

One day His Highness came personally to see me together with four counselors. He earnestly pleaded with me to get married. I answered as best I could because my saying absolutely no to him would have meant pronouncing my own death sentence. Before leaving, His Highness sent those gentlemen ahead in order to be alone with me, and said: "Beware that I am serious when I say that you should remarry because I gave my word for you in Florence." I answered: "Sir, the person who married twice can marry a third time to keep his word, but I have no intention of marrying since my conscience does not allow it. If it has been possible for you to do it because you said that the first time you did it in jest, it is not possible for me now since I did it seriously then. Even if I could, I would rather let myself be cut to pieces than get married again."

He added: "If you will not do it for love, we will have you do it by force." And I: "I will not mind if you are able to have me marry by constraint."

And he: "Enough, and you will see."

Two days later, he sent a handwritten note which I still keep with me. With that he ordered me—in the name of the authority which he has over me as my prince—to get married without further objection. I answered that I was not thinking for the moment about getting married and that I wanted him to command me in a better form. Also that it would have been better to follow another course of action in this predicament since I could foresee how foolish they were going to appear before the world. This put the matter to rest for the moment.

While I was there it came to be known (and it was His Highness for sure who said it) that the document forwarded to Florence was not the real one, but a copy. A new torment, therefore, was added to my other ones when I was solicited to give up the original together with many other letters. Such a request was made because there were notes in which His Highness undersigned himself "Your Servant and Husband the Duke of Mantua."

I was firm in saying that I had given these writings back to His Highness and that, therefore, I could not give them again. I would never have changed words or facts, were it not for the love of my son because, as soon as I would refuse to consent to whatever was asked of me, my son's life was put in jeopardy. To keep him alive, therefore, I did not care to injure myself or to deny my will, as long as my own reputation was not questioned. This is why I gave the document away.

My own life was at issue here, but I could not care because my son was more important to me than myself.

Meanwhile, since my earlier fear that the sojourn in Mantua would bring about problems proved right, I started to petition His Highness to grant me permission to retire to a monastery in Casale, my city, or to one in Alessandria, where I was raised, since a sister of my father, a nun, lived there. They did not comply with my suggestion and proposed instead my coming to Ferrara. I did not want to follow that advice and some time went by with this quarrel. In the end, I accepted because I would have gone anywhere as long as I were not to stay in Mantua.

I was in Ferrara in secular clothes until 1622, continually asked in the meantime to remarry, a solution which I had very well resolved not to take, even if my son's life were at stake.

When they finally realized how persistent I was in my resolution, they started to suggest that I become a nun. I answered that this was something for which I never had any inclination. However, since I wanted His Highness to see that when the issue was not my reputation I would do anything to serve him and make him happy (many thought that, if I had changed my status, things would have turned for the better, which I never believed), I took the nun's habit on May 12. I professed the faith on the same occasion through a special dispensation from His Holiness Pope Gregory XV.

As soon as the function ended, I went to the little window in the church, as it is the custom. Among other people, I saw Sig. Possevino, who had been sent by His Highness to be present at the ceremony. I said to him: "Signor Antonio, you may tell His Highness that I have sacrificed my freedom over the altar of obedience in order to serve him, since everyone believes that on this resolution of mine depends the peace and happiness of his house. God grant it to be so for our common benefit. I have only my life left now and this too I offer to serve His Highness, if necessary. More I cannot give, and I do not long for anything.

The good Possevino did not answer me; he shrugged his shoulders and tears came to his eyes.

This is the tale of my unhappy tragedy. I beg to be forgiven for my mistakes and failings and please understand my desire to obey those who can order me. I beseech also to graciously consent that this writing not be shown, because it deals with known people and truth often generates hate. Moreover, I would not want my ignorance to be mocked.

NOTES TO THE TRANSLATION

1. Maria de' Medici, Queen of France, and her husband King Henry IV took a great interest in their nephew Ferdinando Gonzaga and helped him throughout his brief reign.

2. Madame Her Serene Highness of Ferrara was at the head of a strong nationalist party of nuns and friars and made her imperious will count whenever her nephew Ferdinando strayed or laid aside dynastic duties.

3. Vincenzo, Ferdinando's brother, had a twisted, extravagant, and depraved personality. He brought a scandal by marrying Isabella di Novellara (the Princess of Bozzolo), eighteen years his senior and mother of many children. When he fell in love with his niece Maria Gonzaga, however, he accused Isabella of having charmed and confused him. Vincenzo died young.

BIBLIOGRAPHY

Primary Works

Faà Gonzaga, Camilla. "Storia di donna Camilla Faa di Bruno Gonzaga." *Rivista di Storia, Arte, Archeologia della provincia di Alessandria.* Vol. 10, no. 4 (1895):90–99. Republished with only slight variations by Sorbelli-Bonfà as "Historia della Sig.ra Donna Camilla Faa Gonzaga" in *Camilla Gonzaga Faà: Storia documentata.*

Related Works

Bellonci, Maria. *A Prince of Mantua: The Life and Times of Vincenzo Gonzaga.* Translated by Stuart Hood. London: Weidenfeld and Nicholson, 1956.

Blade, Melinda. *Education of Italian Renaissance Women.* Mesquite, Tex.: Ide House, 1983.

Costa-Zalessow, Natalia. *Scrittrici italiane dal XIII al XX secolo.* Ravenna: Longo, 1982.

D'Arco, Carlo. "Degli amori sfortunatissimi di Camilla Faà." *Racconti patrii.* Mantua: Negretti, 1844.

Finucci, Valeria. "Remembering the 'I': Faà Gonzaga's 'Storia' (1622)." *Italian Quarterly* 28 (1987): 21–32.

Giacometti, Paolo. *Camilla Faà da Casale.* Florence: Libreria Filodrammatica, 1850.

Giorcelli, Giuseppe. "Documenti storici del Monferrato." *Rivista di Storia, Arte, Archeologia della provincia di Alessandria* 10.4 (1895):69–89.

Grottanelli, Luigi. "Caterina de' Medici Duchessa di Mantova." *Rassegna Nazionale* 16 (November 1894).

Kelso, Ruth. *Doctrine for the Lady of the Renaissance.* Urbana: University of Illinois Press, 1956.

Intra, Giambattista. *La bella Ardizzina.* Milan: Stabilimento Tipografico della Perseveranza, 1881. Reprint. Mantua: Stabilimento Tipografico Eredi Segna, 1889.

Possevino, Antonio. *Historia Belli Monferratensis.* Mantua, 1637.

Sorbelli-Bonfà, Fernanda. *Camilla Gonzaga Faà: Storia documentata.* Bologna: Zanichelli, 1918.

PART THREE

he Netherlands

A WOMAN OF MORE THAN LETTERS

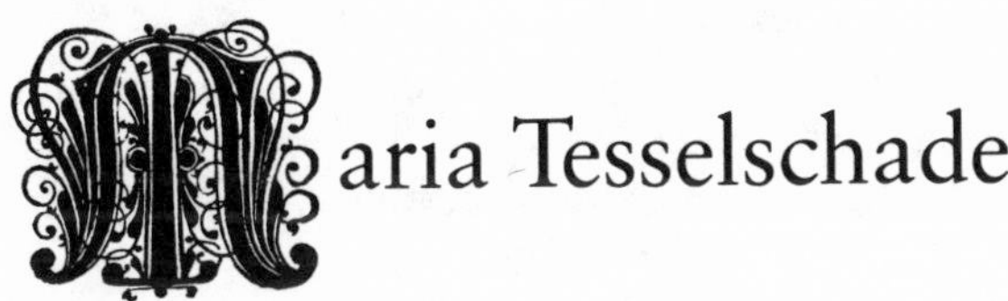

Maria Tesselschade

RIA VANDERAUWERA

Maria Tesselschade Roemersdochter was born in Amsterdam in 1594, the youngest daughter of the wealthy grain merchant and poet Roemer Pieterszoon Visscher. She derived her curious but sonorant middle name from the fact that her father suffered heavy losses following a storm off the Frisian island of Texel three months before her birth. To commemorate the sad event, Roemer Visscher named his daughter Tesselschade (*Tessel,* "Texel"; *scha,* "damage")—a most appropriate name for someone who would turn out to be a devotee of clever wordplay. By the time Maria Tesselschade died in 1649, she had lived through the first half of the remarkable era that entered history as the Dutch Golden Age. In a relatively short period of time, the Dutch Republic of the United Provinces had become a powerful political entity, rooted in the Reformation in defiance of its Catholic sovereign, Spain. Political power was matched by economic prosperity and intense cultural activity. It was the heyday of Dutch Renaissance literature, which developed late in comparison with that of southern Europe but produced several exquisite poets.

Mostly written on the occasion of, or as a reaction to, private and public events, Tesselschade's poems and letters contain fine examples of Dutch Renaissance literature; they also offer valuable insight into the bustling intellectual and religious climate of the young Dutch republic. Among her friends were some of the great Dutch writers and intellectuals of the time.

Tesselschade grew up in the friendly and stimulating atmosphere described by the poet Vondel as "the blessed house of Roemer, of which the floor was trodden and the doorstep worn by painters, artists, singers, and poets."[1] In addition to being a grain merchant, Roemer Visscher was the author of light, satirical verse,[2] and, above all, the amiable host of salonlike gatherings. Here artists and intellectuals passed their time with erudite, witty, and gay conversation; here they listened to performances of singers and to readings of one another's works.

Two of Roemer's daughters, Tesselschade and her elder sister Anna Roemers Visscher, like Maria artistically gifted,[3] became frequent and highly esteemed hostesses at their father's parties. The education Roemer Visscher had given his daughters must have gone beyond the usual training in domestic skills, a modicum of French and music that the young ladies of the merchant classes received at the time. The sisters knew both French and Italian, the vernacular languages considered the exciting, new vehicles of culture. They learned how to sing, draw, paint, and engrave. They decorated wine glasses—rummers or, as they were called in Dutch, *roemers,* which made for many puns on their father's name. The sisters also knew the art of calligraphy and did needlework. They read foreign authors, translated works, and wrote verse themselves. They apparently learned how to swim in their father's garden as well.

Roemer Visscher died in 1620, only a few months after his wife. In 1623 Tesselschade, whose charm and accomplishments had attracted the poets and artists at her father's house, married Allard Crombalgh, a naval officer with no literary or artistic pretensions. If we can believe Vondel, Tesselschade must have been so impressed with Crombalgh that she lost consciousness the first time she saw him in church.[4] The couple moved to Alkmaar. The union was short (Crombalgh died in 1634) but apparently very happy, judging from references to Crombalgh in his wife's writings. They had two daughters, both of whom died during Tesselschade's own lifetime.

While her sister's contact with the Amsterdam literary community faded (Anna had married the following year and moved to the provinces), Tesselschade always kept up a lively correspondence—especially with her lifelong friend, the poet, historiographer, and member of the judiciary Pieter Corneliszoon Hooft. Even more important, she became an esteemed guest of the *Muiderkring,* the Muiden Circle. This loose group of literati, scholars, merchants, and public officeholders—the best-trained and most cosmopolitan members of early seventeenth-century Dutch society—gathered at Hooft's castle at Muiden in summer or at his house on the Keizersgracht in winter to entertain and be entertained by poetry, music, and learning. These were a more refined continuation of the early meetings at Roemer Visscher's place. Tesselschade was undoubtedly the most welcome woman visitor among this cultured lot. Hooft's correspondence indicates that he often assured himself of Tesselschade's coming before inviting other guests, luring them with the grace and skills of *zoetemelxhart* (sweetmilkheart), as he would occasionally call her. Time and again he referred to Tesselschade's beautiful singing. Her engraving work must have pleased him as well, for he gave her a number of orders for rummers; and her poetry deserved his praise: "I am already drunk with the aroma of your poems though I can only scent them on paper. How will it be then when Your Honor inspires them with her own living voice?"[5] Once, when Tesselschade was already close to fifty, Hooft was only too eager to apologize to his friend, the classic scholar and medical doctor Barlaeus (Van Baerle), for the "sober entertainment" of a past meeting at Muiden in the hope of offering better amusement at another time, "when Tessela will be the sauce."[6]

Tesseltjen, to use the playful diminutive by which she was sometimes called, most certainly joined in some of the wilder pastimes of the cultured yet mirth-loving Muiden crowd. They once robbed a neighbor of some artichokes. Hooft later received twelve artichokes from the injured party and an accompanying letter in which the latter likened his forgiving spirit to that of Romulus granting asylum to criminals; he sent half of the delicious vegetables on to Tesselschade, with—how could it be otherwise?—a witty elaboration on the matter.

Between their meetings, Hooft's visitors engaged in an animated epistolary and literary exchange inspired by the most trivial events and the most tragic. They also liked to submit their work to one another for *betutteling*, correction or comments in which they patronizingly dotted *i*'s and crossed *t*'s. They played clever literary games, such as the exercise of composing various sonnets on the same rhymes and rhyme schemes.[7] Though much of Tesselschade's work has not survived, we may gather from her friends' correspondence that she was a most active contributor to the literary activities of the Muiden Circle. A true child of her time, she cleverly explored the possibilities of the vernacular, making use of various rhyme schemes and prosodic patterns. She had a predilection for complex imagery, ingenious wordplay, and obscure allusions. An admirer of the Italian poet Marino,[8] whom she had read with Hooft, Tesselschade did not keep her own work free from frivolous puns and mannerisms. It is no surprise that she urged her friend, the poet-diplomat Constantijn Huygens, to translate Donne or so Huygens suggested in his dedication of his Donne translations to her. Vondel, thoroughly disliking their obscurity, called them "a banquet . . . for our sweet little comrade Tesselscha."[9]

On various occasions, Tesselschade became the center of much heated writing activity among the Muiden members. Her cheerfulness and youth had endeared her to the men at Muiden; as a widow in her forties, still very attractive, she was courted in earnest by Barlaeus and somewhat in jest by Huygens, both of whom had been widowed as well. Barlaeus wrote many poems in Tesselschade's honor, mostly in Latin, which she could only read with difficulty. Some were probably conventional poems of love and idolatry (of which Barlaeus wrote many);[10] but the scholar's high-flown conception of the Alkmaar widow as the ideal of feminine perfection is worth quoting because it seems to have found its way into later literary history.[11] The following lines are part of a dialogue between Hooft and Barlaeus.[12] At the beginning, Hooft wonders why his friend is so well dressed. The answer is obvious: the scholar is just back from Alkmaar,

> where the famous *Tesselschade* is living, she who outstrips her sex in lucidity of mind, in many virtues and artistic skills. . . . There is nothing more divine and sublime than her mind. She understands what ordinary minds cannot comprehend. . . . she does not try to fabricate witty phrases, but such phrases flow out of her mouth naturally. . . . [Then follows a catalog of her skills.] Her conversation is marked by persuasion and admirable beauty. Her eyes betray virtue, her gait modesty, her gestures benevolence and composure.[13]

Barlaeus also believed that Tesselschade compared favorably to a well-known contemporary, the learned Anna Maria van Schurman. Hooft told Tesselschade of Barlaeus's regard and apparently took great pleasure in acting as go-between: "[Barlaeus] has recently told me . . . that he considers Your Honor's mind to be far above the mind of Miss Schurman, for her work smells of the schoolroom, whereas yours smells of a sublime intelligence and is pregnant with supernatural ideas."[14] It may be tempting to side with Barlaeus and fall for Tesselschade's scintillating wit and creative mind, while condemning Schurman to the uninspired state of bluestocking (a trap some later scholars fell into all too eagerly).[15] In reality, Barlaeus's observation probably says as much about his attitude toward women as about the qualities of his celebrated Tessela.

The couple was much teased and encouraged by their friends at Muiden. At one point Hooft tried to spur on the "cool Penelope," quoting a line from a French poem: "Faites, avec les fleurs, renaistre les amours" (Let love, along with flowers, blossom again).[16] Tesselschade retorted with a didactic and overwrought sonnet in honor of the second anniversary of her husband's death. The "swift soul," which wants "calm joy," disagrees with the "unwieldy body," which wants to persist in its "duty to sigh." But on the anniversary of Allard's death, "a stronger mind" (Christ's? Allard's? Tesselschade's strengthened mind?) "lifted" her body from the earth, encouraging her to abandon "fruitless bitterness" and tend to other duties. In the accompanying letter, Tesselschade pretended not to have understood Hooft's allusion to Barlaeus's advances, and she interpreted Hooft's French lines as follows: "Let love *for poetry*, along with flowers, blossom again." Perhaps writing or poetry were the other duties mentioned in the sonnet. The poem was significantly signed *Elck zyn Waerom* (to each his why), Tesselschade's motto, emphasizing her independent mind in this matter.[17]

On another occasion—for Hooft was insistent—Tesselschade's answer was equally firm, though she playfully chided her meddlesome friend: "My confidence in Your Honor's friendship will be the magic herb which protects me against the mermen's [sic] singing. Let them wheedle as much as they like, I'll keep them off my bed; let them content themselves with lesser feathers than the eagle's company. *E dal nodo gentil non mi discolsi may.*"[18] (The "eagle's company" is Tesselschade, the Dutch word for "eagle" being *adelaar,* Tesselschade's pun on her husband's name *Allard. Adelaar* can also be read as *adel aard,* "noble nature." The Italian quotation states "and from that node I have never come loose.")

Perhaps Tesselschade's demure manner inspired Hooft's anagram of her name: *Sachtesedeles,* "mild moral lesson." Faithful to her husband's memory, Tesselschade never gave in to her suitors. Huygens related an amusing incident in which the Alkmaar widow spent a night in his guest room: "On top the widow, beneath the widower, what do you think Barlaeus? What keeps the two of us apart? My ceiling cold, her virtue cool."[19] Tesselschade remained cool indeed, sending Huygens and Barlaeus levelheaded and often witty replies—perhaps not altogether devoid of coyness.

In 1641 or 1642, Tesselschade converted to Catholicism, a courageous act of faith at a time when Roman Catholics had become an unpopular minority in the United Provinces. Catholicism was officially banned, and practicing it depended on the goodwill of the local authorities. Conversions back to the Roman church were, nevertheless, not entirely uncommon in a religious climate that was still very much in flux. Though Tesselschade's conversion characteristically gave rise to a spirited debate with and among her friends, her surviving letters and poems never make her real motives very clear.

Religious issues and the invariably related political issues were, however, hard to avoid in the young Dutch republic. Tesselschade's very aversion to intolerance ("to each his why") may have turned her away from rigorous Calvinism, which, in her opinion, was seriously curtailing the freedom of the republic's citizens. Long before her actual conversion, she argued that a person's allegiance to his town (and, by extension, to the republic and its citizens' liberties) took priority over his allegiance to a particular church. Consequently, preachers who questioned that civil bond posed a serious threat to the well-being of the republic. (See her poem answering Vondel's question below.)

Two pietistic poems, of which the beautifully solemn "Maria Magdalena, Aen de voeten van Jesus" (Mary Magdalen, at the Feet of Jesus) has been included here, may also shed some light on Tesselschade's motivation. Her emphasis on man's repentance and God's mercy suggests her discontent with the very strict interpretation of predestination expounded by the Synod of Dort in 1619—that God has predetermined from eternity who will be saved and who will be damned, regardless of one's merit. The more sympathetic attitude of Rome on this matter—that one can play a role in one's own salvation—may well have influenced Tesselschade's decision to return to the old church. Whatever her reasons, fanaticism was not one of them; her writing after her conversion hardly ever shows signs of religious fervor or, for that matter, bigotry.

Many of her friends were sophisticated Calvinists, who were apparently never bothered by the incompatibility between Calvinist austerity and the epicurean pleasures of Muiden. Among them, only Huygens ("I do not spare the rod, I love the child too much")[20] relentlessly launched sharp attacks on Tesseltje. Using Hooft and Barlaeus as intermediaries, Tesselschade countered Huygens's sometimes vicious criticism with remarkable serenity and occasional playfulness (see the translated section on religion). Still, it is difficult to know how seriously to regard this witty and clever exchange of letters; to some extent, it served as an intellectual and literary diversion for the Muiden group.

While Tesselschade's cheerfulness and grace made her the undeniable darling of the Muiden Circle, it was her stoic composure and remarkable courage in times of grief (her own and others') that must have impressed the Renaissance men and women at Muiden most. The letters and poems in the section on grief show us Tesselschade as a brave woman who found strength in the quiet acceptance of the blows of fate and urged others to find it. In one of her most accomplished poems, a sonnet written on the death of Huygens's wife, she implored her friend to "confide to paper not to memory," since "paper was the weapon with which I fought the wish to die ere heaven could reclaim me." She had indeed been severely grief-stricken herself in 1634 when her nine-year-old daughter and her husband had died within days of each other. On that occasion she wrote Hooft that such a "fierce and frantic blow" tried her "patience to the utmost on the touchstone of life's suffering." Yet she was bearing her misery with "tearless eyes," while "reconciling myself to the will of the All-Mighty against which nothing can be willed." Hooft's reply betrays how much his favorite guest commanded his respect. "Slaving away" at finding a means to console her, he realizes that nothing can be of any avail—only to see how Tesselschade, permeated with "unbelievable courage," teaches him that the study of "true wisdom" (stoic doctrine) has the power to make a woman endure with equanimity the "sharpest arrows of Fortune." The tears she cannot shed will be "wrenched from his eyes," tears not of grief but of delight, at the sight of her noble and courageous heart.[21] Huygens was also deeply impressed by Tesselschade's comforting sonnet, which he would still remember as "Tesselschade's wise teaching" more than forty years later.

As time carried on, death and illness struck more of Tesselschade's friends. Hooft died in 1647, Barlaeus in 1648. Tesselschade herself had fallen ill during the winter of 1648, but she found the courage to address a poem of comfort to one of Barlaeus's students. Faithful to her stoic persuasion, she reproached him for his "unwise" tears for, after all, Barlaeus had passed on to a higher and happier region. Around the same time, she made a profound impression on a young poet and admirer who had come to show to "this widow I visit more than the young women of this town" his elegies on Barlaeus, for which "our heroine . . . bearing with utmost patience her illness and its burdens" had still shown much interest and attention.[22] Tesselschade died in June 1649 in Amsterdam and was buried in the Oude Kerk. In true Muiden style, Huygens portrayed her in his obituary poem as a woman transcending all (ap)prais(al).[23] Though Tesselschade's beauty and talents had been sung extensively in poetry and prose during her lifetime, only a few of her poems had actually been printed. More verse was published in various anthologies later in the century, but on the whole relatively little survived.[24] Her work on a translation of Tasso's *Gerusalemme Liberata* is entirely lost except for one stanza. One portrait of Tesselschade is known to us. The drawing, now in the Museum Fodor in Amsterdam, is dated 1612 and signed by Goltzius, the famous Haarlem painter and engraver.

Whereas much of the literature of the Golden Age, Tesselschade's included, was forgotten during the Enlightenment, the Romantic era marked a new interest in the past glory of the nation and the literature that accompanied it. Editors and anthologizers began to collect and include work by Tesselschade and her sister Anna. *Anna en Maria Tesselschade, de dochters van Roemer Visscher* (1808), a slim volume of work by both sisters, is particularly noteworthy for its "feminist" introduction. The editor, Jacobus Scheltema, dedicated his anthology to all Dutch women. He presented it as a contribution to the knowledge of Dutch literature but, above all, as a tribute to the remarkable women who "have passed into oblivion" and "contributed so much to the honor of your sex."[25] Scheltema further expressed the hope that his collection would launch new interest in "tracing and making known the merit of other deserving learned and artistic women in the Netherlands whose memory has more often than not been far too long neglected"[26]—a curious feminist "use" of the seventeenth-century poetess (at the wrong period and by the wrong sex), given the fact that Tesselschade has hardly ever managed to catch the attention of present-day women's studies scholars in the Netherlands.[27]

The "clever and modest poetess Tesselschade"[28] caught the imagination of male scholars all the more. The nineteenth-century writer and critic Edmund Gosse referred to Tesselschade, rather than to one of her better-known and more prolific contemporaries, in a general introduction on the Dutch Golden Age.[29] For Gosse, Tesselschade had apparently become some sort of ideal woman intellectual: wise but gentle, beautiful but modest, skilled but not too accomplished (she could not even read Latin!), and certainly not a bluestocking like Anna Maria van Schurman. Barlaeus's distinction had made history. Though not necessarily an insurmountable handicap, lack of knowledge of Latin in an otherwise well-accomplished and educated woman—at a time when Latin was an important vehicle of culture and scholarship—should at least be considered surprising. But it seems that for some scholars Tesselschade's flaws "fortunately" saved her from being too bright.

In the first decades of the twentieth century, Tesselschade scholarship peaked. Worp's text edition of 1918 is still the main locus for her work. Recent studies on Tesselschade are few and far between, but she continues to figure in work on Hooft and Huygens and in editions of their writings as one of their closest personal and literary friends. Tesselschade's charming presence at Muiden has also given rise to some spicier stories. Guards at Muiden Castle (turned into a museum) like to mention the existence of a secret passage between Hooft's and Tesselschade's bedrooms; a known incident when Tesselschade forgot her slippers at Muiden apocryphally ends with the host's finding them under his own bed.[30]

Although Tesselschade's limited body of poems is probably too small to place her among the century's literary great, her writings do reveal the strength and singularity of her personality. The poems and letters in which she fought off her "suitors" or the attacks on her conversion reveal a good-humored nature, unique social grace, and sound intelligence. Her motto, "to each his why," was an unmistakable sign of her deeply independent mind and tolerance towards others. Her attitude toward grief bespeaks a courageous and life-loving woman. It is no surprise that she was a sought-after guest at Muiden. Hooft, Huygens, and particularly Barlaeus were probably too complimentary of their lady friend, but Tesselschade must nevertheless have been a woman whose friendship they valued highly.

Sometimes overwrought and too manneristic for present literary taste, Tesselschade's work remains of interest today as one of the few testimonies of a highly intelligent, sensitive, witty woman who participated, apparently with great zest, in the exciting cultural life of the Netherlands' most illustrious age. We can only deplore that not more of her poems and especially her letters have come down to us.

What unmistably emerges from the surviving poems is that Tesselschade must have had considerable fun fashioning her clever puns and allusions. In my translations, I have tried to convey her playful, witty, complex tone and ideas. Rhyming couplets and blank verse proved particularly suitable to her various rhyme schemes, prosodic patterns, and reasoning poetry. I took the liberty of translating one sonnet ("To the Poet Boetius van Elslandt") into rhyming couplets, because Tesselschade's train of thought seemed too complex for the concise sonnet form in another language. The other sonnet (one of her best) I left in sonnet form. Her "Distinction Between a Wild and a Tame Singer," an often anthologized and much-praised poem, is missing here. This crafted illustration of the *ars naturae aemula* theme would have needed too much reshaping and intrusion by the translator to convey a similarly rich sound effect.[31]

Selecting a representative cross section of Tesselschade's work, I have preferred a thematic to a chronological grouping. The first translation section serves as an introduction; the second, third, and fourth deal respectively with religion, suitors, and grief. I have also followed the example given in the text editions by Worp and Van der Heijden and added introductory paragraphs explaining the circumstances in which the poems and letters originated.

NOTES

Quotations from Tesselschade's work and that of her literary friends are mainly taken from *'t Hoge huis te Muiden. Teksten uit de Muiderkring*, ed. M. C. A. Van der Heijden (1978), a selection of work by poets belonging to the so-called Muiden Circle. A few other quotations are from *Een onwaerdeerlycke Vrouw. Brieven en verzen van en aan Maria Tesselschade*, ed. J. A. Worp (1918), an almost complete collection of Tesselschade's poems and letters, which also contains many writings by her friends.

The translations are mine.

1. Worp, *Een onwaerdeerlycke Vrouw*, 29.

2. Roemer Visscher's poetry was collected by his friends in *Brabbeling* (1614). His *Sinnepoppen* (1614) is a collection of prose and emblemata.

3. The accomplishments of Anna Roemersdochter Visscher (1583–1651) include a new edition of her father's emblemata *Sinnepoppen* (1620), to which she added moralizing couplets, the translation into Dutch of the Huguenot poet Georgette de Montenay, and her own contribution to an anthology of Zealand poets entitled *Zeeusche Nachtegael* (1623).

4. See Worp, *Een onwaerdeerlycke Vrouw*, 52.

5. Van der Heijden, *'t Hoge huis te Muiden*, 152.

6. Ibid., 283.

7. The "schonckensonnetten" (1621)—after the first rhyme, *schoncken*—were a series of Muiden sonnets. Hooft, Tesselschade, and her sister were among the contributors. See Damsteegt, "De schonckensonnetten."

8. Most notably, one of the lines in her well-known and often praised poem "Onderscheydt tusschen een wilde, en een tamme zangster" (The Distinction Between a Wild and a Tame Singer)—the clever contrast of "Een zingend veedertje en een ghewieckt gheluydt" (a singing feather and a feathered sound)—is a literal borrowing from Marino. See Minderaa, "Een omstreden gedicht van Tesselschade," 121.

9. Van der Heijden, *'t Hoge huis te Muiden,* 175.

10. See Van Gool, "Tessela—Thessala—Tesselschade."

11. See, for example, Gosse, "A Dutch Poetess of the Seventeenth Century"; Brachin, "Tesselschade, femme savante"; and, especially, Worp's text edition *Een onwaerdeerlycke Vrouw,* which perpetuated the myth of Tesselschade's excellence and exquisiteness.

12. Although Worp included the writings of many friends to and about Tesselschade, he did not mention this dialogue. The "Casparis Barlaei Dialogi aliquot nuptiales" were part of a larger collection of work, "Faces Augustae, sive Poematia, quibus Illustriores Nuptiae . . . jam a Caspare Barlaeo et Cornelio Boyo Latino Carmine celebrantur . . . Dordraci, 1643." (See Sterck, "Tessalica," 255). Sterck translated part of the relevant dialogue between Hooft and Barlaeus into Dutch.

13. Sterck, "Tessalica," 256–57.

14. Van der Heijden, *'t Hoge huis te Muiden,* 234.

15. For example: "The blue-stockings of the day, like Anna Maria van Schurman, talked Greek and wrote Arabic, and were prigs of the most appalling intensity; but the daughters of Roemer Visscher, though possessing the finest feminine intellects of their age, could not even read Latin" (Gosse, "A Dutch Poetess of the Seventeenth Century," 240–41); "She knew a few foreign languages, read a lot, even wrote poetry, but was certainly not a bluestocking; on the contrary, she would sometimes violate spelling rules" (Worp, *Een onwaerdeerlycke Vrouw,* xliv); "Educated and brilliant, she was nothing of a bluestocking. She does not hide at all the fact that she does not know Latin" (Brachin, "Tesselschade, femme savante," 20).

16. Van der Heijden, *'t Hoge huis te Muiden,* 204. The French poem was written by a cousin of Hooft.

17. Ibid., 206–7.

18. Ibid., 253.

19. Ibid., 298.

20. Ibid., 270.

21. Ibid., 184–85.

22. Henrick Bruno, in Worp, *Een onwaerdeerlycke Vrouw,* 340.

23. "Haer onwaerdeerlickheit" (ibid., 318).

24. The most important anthology was *Verscheyde Nederduitsche Gedichten* (Several Dutch Poems), 1653, by Geeraerdt Brandt, who published eleven of Tesselschade's poems.

25. Scheltema, ed., v.

26. Ibid., v–vi.

27. A recent book by Keesing, *Het volk met lange rokken,* is a noteworthy exception.

28. Brandt, *Het leven van Pieter Corn. Hooft en de Lykreeden,* 32.

29. Gosse, "A Dutch Poetess of the Seventeenth Century."

30. See Sterck, "Vondel—Eusebia—Tesselschade," 2.

31. Two noteworthy attempts to translate this poem were made in *Batavian Anthology,* eds. J. Bowring and Harry S. van Dyk, and by Gosse in his article "A Dutch Poetess of the Seventeenth Century."

Letter to Barlaeus

(The following letter and poem are a good introductory example of the kind of literary exchange that took place between the members of the Muiden Circle. The letter is addressed to Barlaeus and refers to a poem he wrote on a portrait of the daughter of the king and queen of Bohemia. The royal couple had been living in The Hague since their expulsion from their country. Barlaeus encouraged Tesselschade to compose a similar poem, but, apparently lacking inspiration, she wrote a laudatory poem on Hooft instead.)

Dear Sir,

I have been trying to fulfill Your Honor's wish concerning the daughter of the queen of Bohemia, but nothing at all comes to my mind; indeed another mind—dear Hooft—keeps crossing it. This is the resulting sketch. Your Honor,[1] please receive it instead, and pronounce your judgment. Return it to me with interest,[2] and I'll send it back to you, copied by my daughter, who sends her greetings to you and your children. So does your friend,

TESSELSCHADE ROEMERS

To Amsterdam

Behold that mind of Hooft.[3] It is a sketch
minute of all your body's parts and limbs.
He will reveal no dark and gloomy omens,
but makes the sun through numerous ages
go back for you on history's pages.[4]
He is your captain, steering clear of sunken
reefs, providing light[5] for others' journeys,
poet immortal, feeding a thousand echoes,[6]
fed himself at the twin-topped mountain's[7] source.

On Religion

(In 1630, amid religious disturbances, Vondel put a series of questions from "the Amsterdam academics to all poets of the United Netherlands, lovers of the golden freedom," and offered a prize for the best answer. The members of the Nederduytsche Academie, founded in 1617 to promote both science and drama, had taken a firm stand against the lack of tolerance of some Contra-Remonstrant ministers. [Contra-Remonstrants or Gomarists represented the militant faction within Dutch Calvinism, asserting that other groups—Catholics, Protestants, and Jews alike—should be restricted, if not penalized.] Vondel's main questions were: What are the best and wisest tongues? Is one saved by truth or semblance? Does the harassment of pious souls [all those who are not orthodox Calvinists] not lead to the destruction of the republic? Is freedom for all religious factions, not just one, no longer the reason for the rebellion against

Spain? For Vondel and many members of the ruling class in Holland, the so-called Regents, the rebellion had been first and foremost a fight for political freedom. For the Contra-Remonstrants, however, the rebellion had been basically a fight for the victory and imposition of Calvinism.

In the 1620s, there had been some dispute as to whether members of the towns' militia who also belonged to the Reformed church could take the oath that pledged them to their towns, for they might be called upon to act against their fellow Calvinists—Contra-Remonstrants who were involved in heavy rioting at the time.

In this atmosphere of religious unrest, Vondel put forward his basic questions. Like him, the pragmatic patrician's daughter Tesselschade gave priority to freedom and the interests of town and state.)

Answer to Vondel's Question

The finest tongue that voices forged
sang praise to God and peace to man.
The tongue[8] that, silent, showed its virtue forth
gave Christ's disciples crowns of fire.
Earth's most wicked tongue[9] made man desire
parts of the hidden truth of God;
the tongue most angry[10] spoke in heaven: "to
the power supreme my power be equal."
On men who speak their faith in deed
God builds his power and his reign,
but semblance is a fickle thing
that leads its followers astray.
Holland's tender soil cannot endure
God-fearing souls waylaid in the dark.
In Brussels Roman beggars joined
men of other faiths to sign the paper
that of the emperor's daughter
requested freedom of the land.[11]
Mutineers, who despise peace, are
banned by states where order reigns.
Towns where burghers storm their neighbors' walls
cannot survive through time.
All earthly gods are pledged by oaths;
none stronger than the oath armed burghers
pledge to the safety of their towns.
Preachers that dare untie that bond
cut the knot that holds the seven arrows.[12]

To each his why.[13]

(At Tesselschade's request, Vondel sent her poem to Hooft for "editing purposes." Hooft wrote her that, "if I were contending for the Academy's prize, I would maintain that the best tongue is Mrs. Tesselschade's." He mentioned that his wife was full of praise for the poem as well, and the letter further indicates that he "corrected" Tesselschade's poem. He urged her to send it on to the Academy or, alternatively, to her sister, who was supposed to engrave the prize rummer . . . for "the rummer might not have been inclined to leave the family of Roemer."[14]

Publication of the replies to Vondel's questions was later forbidden, for many were apparently not so serene and balanced as Tesselschade's. In fact, it was feared that publication would refuel friction and feelings of hate.)

Mary Magdalen, at the Feet of Jesus

Do you unrobe or robe yourself, Mary
Magdalen, when you unbraid your tresses,
throw aside the glittering stones, tear up
that string of pearls, despise appearances,
rate as sham or fake whatever makes
you find refuge on stumbling blocks and keeps
your tender youth forever barred from heaven?
Pious woman, you clasp a wall of steel
that will give no way to passing time or hours
of grief;[15] you twine from down below your curly
vines around a stabler base; and thank
the Savior who made you rise from earthly mud.
And though you speak but from your inner self,
a mind turned inward understands the pearls
that from your eyes come down on scarlet red,
and cleanse away the crimson stains of sin.
Therefore, my Soul, look into the mirror,
throw out that lying tool, or hang it on
a column from where it will—by heaven
guided, and always kept before your eyes—
arouse in you repentance. Thus vanity
contrives forgiveness for your sins—the things
that pleased you once: honor, world, and country.
May this sketch and telling face give you further hope.[16]

You, who bar despair that comes with sin,
who, silent, praise virtue, and silently
obtain, more than just a silent speaker—

living proof that God forgives the sins
of those who act, not mean to act, like you.

(The following "song" (*deuntje,* little air) is Tesselschade's reply to a sonnet by Huygens entitled "The Second Tesselschade." Worried about her conversion to Roman Catholicism, Huygens began his poem with "Is Tesselschade on her way from Geneva to Rome?"[17] Elaborating on Huygens's imagery, she responded that she was on the right road, in spite of what he thought.)

Song

John spoke to Mary: "Did you go
to *mass* again? And hang out with
the reckless crowd, those assessors
of the fish?"[18] Mary answers this:
"My dear husband, they sail straight unlike
your crowd; and on Saint Peter's ship[19]
not a single mate goes overboard.
They have helm and rudder,[20] you are
sailing hit or miss. John, sweetheart,
what I am hearing is the truth,
what you're a*mass*ing is all wrong."

(Though friction between Tesselschade and Huygens had apparently cooled down, Tesselschade's conversion remained a difficult point. Witness the following letter to Barlaeus with its clear hints that the subject of religion had not receded.)

Letter to Barlaeus

Dear Sir,

My cousin Sammer[21] is expecting Your Honor, though with growing impatience. The poem[22] is finished, though, in two ways: it is awaiting your arrival to be chosen or denounced. I believed the issue[23] had died a long time ago,

> *For if, by the grace of God, we cannot choose,*
> *preaching: "do good, reject evil"—what's the use?*

Those capable of preaching understand this very well.

And what good is it to tell the pious crowd
that the truth which in the Testament is vowed
about Hoc[24] *etc. . . . is false? And all those yeas*
and nays[25] *which my mind is failing to appraise?*

Every single church-child knows its father, that is the way it is, but one who knows both his father and his mother is much better off, for a mother cannot produce a bastard according to common law.[26] On this point I am awaiting your opinion, unless we decide to have the matter rest.

Send my greetings to Mr. Hooft and all the friends of your house. Tell Mrs. Hooft to reassure her husband in my name for, drawing on my experience with father and husband, I can say that the fever from which her beloved is suffering is not lethal. Tell her furthermore that all the bitter things I swallowed from his hand while at Muiden are now rewarding me with a state of perfect health, which I wish him likewise with all my heart, remaining a friend to you both,

TESSELSCHA ROEMERS

(Barlaeus sent the question on to Huygens, who jumped at the opportunity offered and extended Tesselschade's imagery in a poem serving as response: it is no big deal to have a mother "tricked out with finery" and affected by "whore's pox"[27]—the traditional Protestant vision of the decadence of Rome. Tesselschade's answer, sent to Hooft, was lost. Judging from Huygens's sharp reply, she must have suggested that his attitude toward her conversion was not necessarily inspired by his own sincere beliefs but by other less honorable circumstances—namely, Huygens's position as a diplomat in the service of the House of Orange, which supported the cause of Calvinism against the moderate leading political class, the Regents. It must have been one of the rare occasions on which Tesselschade countered vicious attack by vicious reply.)

On Suitors

("Answer of Stone" is Tesselschade's reply to a poem by Huygens, in which the writer compared himself to Mohammed, whose body, according to ancient folk belief, is kept suspended in an iron coffin above the mosque of Medina, where it is held in equilibrium by magnets. In Huygens's vision the magnets are two widows [Maria Tesselschade and Maria van Treslong]. They had both been present at a party at Muiden in 1643, and Huygens had not been able to choose between them, or so he pretended. In her levelheaded answer, Tesselschade takes up the image of Huygens suspended between the two widows, warns him against making a choice, and expresses their willingness to keep him safely balanced.

The "stone" in the title refers to the magnets. Huygens had written that his body was buried and suspended *tusschen steen en steen* [between stone and stone].)[28]

Answer of Stone

Such sweet and gentle woe and sorrow
none can endure but us who know
the boldness of the speaker-poet.
O mind profound, do not let
any tongue reproach you with new
mourning.[29] Let those who know true
choice, know fear; you know neither.
But not very content either
with this sight of gracious grieving,
we will cure you of this swaying,
lest from the widows you choose one,
for balance rests on hesitation.
Thus Inconstant,[30] do not move or stir,
the choice you'd think the best, dear Sir,
might drop you right away. O never
lying prophet, remain forever
poised; between earth and heaven's light
suspended, we'll keep you still and quiet.

(The following short poem was written in reply to a poem and letter received from Barlaeus. He had sent Tesselschade a copy of his Latin oration "de coeli admirandis" [On the Marvels of Heaven], together with an accompanying poem, one of the very few he wrote in Dutch. In this poem he referred to Tesselschade as *Thessaliaanse Vrou* [Thessalian woman], thus punning on her name and Tessalia, a region in Greece associated with magic and sorcery in antiquity. Like a Tessalian witch, our poet is said to move sun, moon, and stars with her sweet rhymes and to enchant men like Huygens, Hooft, and Admiral Reael, for whom her pen, tongue and mind concoct magic potions. Barlaeus laments: "If they can be great through your name, is it then a surprise that I too seek to rise through your fame?[31] Once again Tesselschade's answer is demure and practical; the last two lines of her poem contain a request for the translation of Barlaeus's oration into Dutch, because she knew little or no Latin.)

To the Honorable Professor Barlaeus, on the Occasion of Sending Me His Oration on the Marvels of Heaven

Thessalian art, which makes the light of moon
descend through witty craftiness, did never
fall on Tesselscha. But you can call to
earth the whole of heaven and keep it straight
through wondrous power springing from the soul.[32]
If of your words you could translate the gracious traces,
I might retain some of the light of higher places.

(The playful Tesselschade is at work in the following poem. A captain has apparently robbed her of a brooch [the "harness" of the first line]).

Challenge (for M.D.)

Gone is the thing that was my harness,
yet I still possess the prowess
to call out the crooked charmer
who spirited away my armor,
which I had given to him freely,
then had offered him genteelly
to reveal its secret, yet how!
And why! This captain—yet how!—
commander, sir, and Christian could
he not return the borrowed good,
artlessly lent, yet gained with art,
playing Delilah's flattering part?
Beware, my power is not genteel,
no sweet and honeyed tongue but steel,
a cutting tool at my command which
will, instead of slimy speech,
be my revenge, wage war on one
who breaks a tranquil peace, on one
whose deeds undo his words. On this
cutting steel,[33] which can break glasses,
which can through crystal cut and stitch,

I do swear that the thing with which
you ran away, you will, dear Sir,
return—*ce qui n'est point mon coeur.*

On Grief

Letter to Hooft on the Death of His First Wife, Christina van Erp

Dear Sir,

Since I was overpowered by thoughts too potent to be withstood by propriety, I venture to express the hope that the heavenly virtues of our *patrona,* whose presence the unworthy earth enjoyed for too long, may revive in me (if you deem me worthy of them), as much as they may die in Your Honor.[34] She should have been snatched away from us long ago to the kingdom of Heaven where she belonged and deserved to be, and whereto she only recently ascended. With great regret I have learnt of your mourning and, sick at heart myself, I fully sympathize with your feelings, though I cannot believe them to be yours. How could you, dear Sir, who stored so much steadfast wisdom, be made miserable by worldly necessity? Pray, Your Honor, solve this problem, while in the meantime I remain your faithful friend and servant.

TESSELSCHA ROEMERS

Should it be your pleasure to reply, my brother will kindly send your letter together with his own wrapped around it.

Letter to Hooft on the Death of Her Husband and Daughter

Dear Sir,

My pen could not possibly express the vividness of the impression made on more experienced minds of the fierce and frantic blow dealt to me by grim fate, trying my patience to the utmost on the touchstone of life's suffering (a proof indeed that grief never descends alone on those that God wishes to put to the test).

It had therefore been my intention to lock my grief into my heart (so as not to confront Your Honor's joy and happiness with such a ghastly picture). Yet your sweet daughter, Susanna, unlocked my grief, and there was the occasion of cousin Sammer's[35] departure. He will inform Your Honor of the character of the illness, the sudden death, and other circumstances which I bore with a weeping soul, heavy heart and mourning mind, though with tearless eyes, and all the while, in that sad and wretched night, bereft of the sun of my soul, I had no other thought but of my beloved and alas, all too loving Allard, my eagle,[36] who on wings of love followed his beloved Tadea to heaven, exchanging mortal life for life immortal and leaving low-spirited me in the company of his beloved other half,[37] so that looking at her, as if in a mirror, I may constantly remember his dear figure, reconciling myself to the will of the Allmighty against which nothing can be willed.[38]

TESSELSCHA ROEMERS

(The lady of Sulekom in the following poem is Suzanna van Baerle, wife of Huygens. Hooft passed on the poem to Huygens, who was greatly impressed by the line "stel syn leed te boeck, zoo heeft hij 't niet t'onthouwen" [confide to paper, not to memory] and wrote: "Tesselschade has never risen above herself so much as with this one line." More than forty years later, long after Tesselschade's death, the elderly Huygens still remembered the line and the thought expressed in it, and celebrated Tesselschade in a poem called "Tesselschade's wijs onderwijs, 1637" [Tesselschade's Wise Teaching, 1637]. The epithet attached to Tesselschade was *kloeck,* "courageous.")[39]

To Hooft on the Passing Away of the Lady of Sulekom

She that's thought a beacon in a sea of grief,
whose stem and branch are lopped,[40] yet on with life must go,
does send to you this modest token of relief
for one who is drowned in a lake of utter[41] woe.

Tell Constant[42] to believe in paper's might,
if verse could tell his inner misery,
eaglelike to stare in his beloved's light,
confide to paper not to memory.

Beg him to lend meter to his mournful thought.
Paper made me win and oust the enemy;

paper was the weapon with which I fought
the wish to die ere heaven could reclaim me.

May his own writing teach him true relief,
for numbers cannot be so fierce as grief.[43]

(The following is probably Tesselschade's last poem. It is addressed to a student of the deceased Barlaeus.)

To the Poet Boetius van Elslandt

Your graying youth[44] from early on
did pledge us stuff believed by none
to have its present vigor. Now
on Barlaeus's fragrant marrow
have you been feasting with ambition
and put to use that good nutrition.
In you shines the master's splendor
which in spite of envy's slander
did not fade. His mind traverses
through the wisdom of your verses.
Did he not well behave when death
bereft him of his friend and breath—
dear Hooft? So friendly was his nature,
so loyal, that with gentle pressure,
it made him move away from here
to a higher and much happier sphere.
Does shedding tears improve his rise
to bliss? Why then this grief unwise?
Does not Athenian Amsterdam[45] embrace
Boetius, you babe well-nursed, to fill his place?

To each his why.

NOTES TO THE TRANSLATIONS

1. Notice the particular way in which the members of the Muiden Circle addressed one another in their letters: "U.E.," for "Uwe Edelheid," which is roughly equivalent to "Your Honor."

2. With corrections.

3. In Dutch *hoofd* (pronounced in the same way as Hooft) means "head," and the pun here was unmistakably intended by Tesselschade. What follows is praise for Hooft's work

(the product of his head, his mind) on the history of the Dutch fight for independence (see following note).

4. Reference to Hooft's *Nederlandsche Historiën* (1628–1647), in which the author described the history of the Dutch rebellion against Spain. Tesselschade's reference is hyperbolic, since Hooft really covered contemporary history. "Sun" also alludes to Hooft's emblem which accompanied his motto, *omnibus idem.*

5. Insight.

6. Imitators, followers.

7. Parnassus.

8. The Holy Ghost at Pentecost.

9. The serpent in Paradise.

10. Lucifer.

11. Tesselschade refers to the so-called Petition of the Nobles (1566) presented to the then-governess of the Netherlands, Margaret of Parma (daughter of the emperor Charles V). It contained a request for relaxation of the measures imposed against Calvinists and other Protestants. The request was signed by both the Catholic and the Protestant lower nobility. They received the nickname *Gueux* (beggars). Hence Tesselschade's *de Roomse Geus* (Roman Beggar).

12. A lion's claw holding seven arrows figured in the coat of arms of the seven United Provinces.

13. Tesselschade's motto, *Elck zyn Waerom.*

14. Van der Heijden, *'t Hoge huis te Muiden,* 117.

15. An English translation of this part of the poem also figures in Edmund Gosse's "A Dutch Poetess of the Seventeenth Century" (273).

16. Perhaps an indication that the poem was inspired by a sketch or a painting.

17. Van der Heijden, *'t Hoge huis te Muiden,* 265.

18. John calls the Catholics reckless (*brodroncke*) since they are convinced of being in the right. They know the exact meaning of everything (cf. *schatters,* assessors). "Fish" alludes to both Saint Peter's profession and fish (Greek *Ichtus,* a symbol for Christ).

19. The Roman Catholic Church.

20. Mary is referring to the centralized authority of Rome, nonexistent in the Protestant churches.

21. Relative of Tesselschade's husband, Allard Crombalgh.

22. It is not clear what poem Tesselschade is referring to.

23. The issue of free will.

24. Reference to "Hoc est enim corpus meum" (this is my body), the words of the Consecration in the Roman Mass. The notion of transubstantiation is rejected by Protestants.

25. The differences of opinion among various Protestant factions and churches.

26. Every church knows its father (God), but a church that knows father and mother ("Our Mother the Holy Church" in Catholic theology) is better off, for that church cannot be a bastard. Tesselschade probably had in mind that the Catholic church directly descends from Christ, whereas Protestantism comprises various churches founded by various people. All Protestant churches are thus bastard churches. See Van der Heijden, *'t Hoge huis te Muiden,* 285.

27. Ibid., 286.

28. Ibid., 270–71.

29. Huygens had been widowed in 1637. Tesselschade is warning him here against a second period of mourning—mourning about his pretended inability to make a choice.

30. Pun on Huygens's motto *constanter* (steadfast, unwavering), based on his first name, Constantijn. Tesselschade often used the Dutchified synonym *Vastaert* (also occasionally *Vasthart*) to refer to Huygens. Here the original reads *Onvastaert* (Inconstant).

31. Van der Heijden, *'t Hoge huis te Muiden,* 202–3.

32. Tesselschade is referring to Barlaeus's work as a scholar, meaning "you can explain heaven and earth."

33. Tesselschade's engraving needle which could indeed break the glasses on which she was working.

34. In other words, I wish that the virtues of your wife . . . may revive in me as much as the sadness of their memory may die in you (disappear).

35. See note 21.

36. In the Dutch original, Tesselschade refers to her husband as *Adelaert* (*adelaar* is Dutch for "eagle"), punning on his first name Allard and *adel aard* (noble nature, noble character).

37. The surviving daughter, Maria. Tadea is Teetje, who died of smallpox.

38. The syntax of the long sentence is somewhat shaky in the Dutch original. Tesselschade must have lost the thread.

39. Van der Heijden, *'t Hoge huis te Muiden,* 230.

40. Tesselschade is referring to her own grief, having lost a husband and a daughter.

41. The Dutch original reads here *Baerelycke,* meaning "utter" or "terrible." It is also a pun on Van Baerle, the maiden name of Huygens's wife.

42. *Vastaert* in the Dutch original (see note 30).

43. The Dutch line reads "Want queling op de maet en kan soo fel niet syn," which Tesselschade quoted literally from Huygens's translation of Donne's "The Triple Fool." Donne's line reads "grief brought to numbers cannot be so fierce."

44. You youth full of wisdom.

45. The Dutch reads "Amsterdams Athenen" (The Athens [place of wisdom] of Amsterdam). Tesselschade is referring to the Athenaeum Illustre, founded in 1632 as a more tolerant and less orthodox Calvinist counterpart of the University of Leyden.

BIBLIOGRAPHY

Primary Works

Van der Heijden, M. C. A., ed. *'t Hoge huis te Muiden. Teksten uit de Muiderkring.* 2d. ed. Utrecht: Prisma, 1978.

Worp, J. A., ed. *Een onwaerdeerlycke Vrouw. Brieven en verzen van en aan Maria Tesselschade,* 1918. Reprint. Utrecht: Hes Publishers, 1976.

Related Works

Bowring, John and Harry S. van Dyk, eds. *Batavian Anthology. Specimens of the Dutch Poets.* London: Taylor and Hessey.

Brachin, Pierre. "Tesselschade, femme savante." In *Etudes de littérature néerlandaise,* 9–30. Groningen: Wolters, 1955.

Brandt, Geeraerdt. *Het leven van Pieter Corn. Hooft en de Lykreeden.* 1677. Reprint, ed. P. Leendertz, Jr. 's-Gravenhage: Martinus Nijhoff, 1932.

Bruining, C. "Maria Tesselschade Visscher." *Onze Eeuw* 17 (1917), 3:161–96.

Damsteegt, B. C. "De schonckensonnetten." *Tijdschrift voor Nederlandse Taal en Letteren* 96 (1980): 101–32.

Flinn, John F. "La Préciosité dans la littérature néerlandaise. L'oeuvre de Maria Tesselschade." *Revue de Littérature Comparée* 40 (1966): 65–80.

Gedichten van C. van Baerle, J. van der Burgh, J. van Heemskerk, L. Reael, Anna en Maria Tesselschade Visscher, en anderen. Amsterdam: G. H. Arens, 1827.

Gosse, Edmund W. "A Dutch Poetess of the Seventeenth Century." In *Studies in the Literature of Northern Europe*, 230–77. London: Kegan, Paul, Trench & Co., 1879.

Keesing, Elisabeth. *Het volk met lange rokken*. Amsterdam: Querido, 1987.

Knuvelder, G. *Handboek tot de geschiedenis der Nederlandse Letterkunde*. 5th. ed. Vol. 2. 's-Hertogenbosch: L. C. G. Malmberg, 1971.

Michels, L. C. *Filologische Opstellen*. 4 vols. Zwolle: Tjeenk Willink, 1957–1964.

Minderaa, P. "Een omstreden gedicht van Tesselschade." In *Opstellen en voordrachten uit mijn hoogleraarstijd* (1948–1964), 79–96. Zwolle: Tjeenk Willink, 1964.

______. "Een geestige pennestrijd tussen Tesselschade en Huygens." *Tijdschrift voor Levende Talen* 33 (1967): 115–23.

Price, J. L. *Culture and Society in the Dutch Republic during the Seventeenth Century*. London: Batsford, 1974.

Scheltema, Jacobus, ed. *Anna en Maria Tesselschade, de dochters van Roemer Visscher*. Amsterdam: J. W. IJntema & Comp., 1808.

Sterck, J. F. M. "Vondel—Eusebia—Tesselschade." *Van Onzen Tijd* 11 (1910): 2 and 11.

______. *Oorkonden over Vondel en zijn kring*. Bussem: Paul Brand, 1918.

______. "Tessalica." *Tijdschrift voor Nederlandse Taal en Letteren* 40 (1921): 246–58.

Van Gool, A. "Tessela—Thessala—Tesselschade." In *Vondeljaarboek 1949*, 80–109. Amsterdam: Uitgeversmaatschappij "Joost van den Vondel," 1949.

Van Vloten, J., ed. *Tesselschade Roemers en hare vrienden*. Leyden: Brill, 1852.

LEARNED WOMAN OF UTRECHT

nna Maria van Schurman

JOYCE L. IRWIN

The only English-language biography of Anna Maria van Schurman, written by Una Birch in 1909, identified her in the subtitle as "Artist, Scholar, Saint." In Schurman's life (1607–1678), it is the middle term which gives significance to the others. The artwork of her youth, impressive as it may be, would not have earned her a lasting place among artists, nor would her later role as a follower of Jean de Labadie have been particularly noteworthy, had she not achieved international fame in early adulthood as the most learned woman of the age. Furthermore, the terms "artist" and "saint" used in reference to Schurman require some qualification and justification. Whereas she engaged in a wide variety of arts and crafts, she did not develop her skills to maturity. The detail of her paper cuttings is astonishing, especially in our day when this craft is no longer cultivated, but her self-portraits are remarkable more as evidence of her youthful vanity than of her ability in portraiture. Birch is surely correct in depicting her as an artistic dilettante: "Had Anna not been gifted with facilities so fatal as to preclude her working long enough at any one branch of art to become mistress of it, she might have become a distinguished painter. She tried to do too many things, and between making engravings of landscapes, waterfalls, hills, ships sailing on rivers, as well as studies and sketches of anything and everything that came into her horizon, she became excellent at nothing."[1]

The difficulty in applying the term "saint" occurs not in assessing the depth of her dedication nor the intensity of her commitment but rather in considering the object of that commitment. Jean de Labadie (1610–1674), who had left the Jesuit novitiate in France to become a Reformed preacher, was called to the Netherlands from Geneva in 1666 to serve the French-speaking congregation in Middelburg. The church had a strong contingent of reform-minded, mystically inclined members, but Labadie's criticisms of the ministry led him into conflict with the synod, which dismissed him after three years of controversy. The severity of his teaching was better suited to the separatist community which then formed around him than to the state church, but even most of those who wanted church reform regarded the Labadist community as a radical fringe element. Anyone associated with it was thereby thoroughly discredited. Even though Schurman's writings from her years as a Labadist remain quite moderate, especially in her disputes with the free-thinking Antoinette Bourignon, her canonization would be opposed with fervor by those who considered her deluded rather than saintly.

Of the three phases of her life, it was her middle period as a scholar which brought fame in her lifetime and earned her a lasting place in the history of learned women. For this reason, the emphasis here and in the following selections is on her intellectual life and her philosophy of education. Even the passages from the Labadist period were chosen with the intention of showing the changes in her attitude toward scholarship.

Anna van Schurman, at her birth in Cologne on November 5, 1607, inherited economic comfort and religious discomfort. Her father's parents had fled to Cologne from Antwerp during the persecutions of the Duke of Alva. There in 1602 her father, Frederick van Schurman, married a woman of like nobility and faith, Eva van Harf. When, in 1610, life in Cologne became unsafe for Reformed Protestants, the couple, now with two sons and daughter Anna Maria, moved to the family castle in Dreiborn. With their next move to Utrecht in 1615, they finally settled in Reformed territory but found the church embroiled in internal conflict with the Remonstrants. Educational opportunities for the boys caused the family to move again in 1623 to Franeker, but Frederick died within months after the move, and Anna and her mother returned a few years later to the family home in Utrecht. There Anna lived most of the rest of her life, taking charge of the household after her mother's death in 1637 and later caring for two nearly blind elderly aunts. For a few years she returned with them to Germany in order to reclaim their land after the Thirty Years' War. During this period in the vicinity of Cologne, where Reformed services were not available, Anna and her brother Johan Godschalck developed a form of house church with their aunts and came to value the close bonds of this tiny Christian community. The yearning to continue this mode of religious life after the death of the aunts in 1662 was undoubtedly one of the motivations which led Johan Godschalck, while on a trip to Switzerland, to urge Labadie to come to the Netherlands. The joy which Anna experienced in her life in the Labadist community had been foreshadowed and the taste cultivated during the years spent living closely with her aunts. Through renunciation of her material comforts, which she left behind for a life of austerity and external persecution, she found the religious comfort which had been so elusive during much of the rest of her life.

The academic prowess which in old age seemed so worthless to her nevertheless provided the literary skills that enabled her to reflect on her life and times in her autobiography, *Eukleria.* This work, though inspired by the values of a later period of life, is an unusually rich source of information concerning her life and deserves more thorough examination than is possible here.

Given Schurman's social and economic status, it is not unusual that she received tutoring and learned to read at an early age. Yet, as she later reported, she went far beyond the course of learning expected of girls, thanks to the encouragement of her father and the proximity of her brothers. Most notable were her achievements in language study: after learning Latin and the modern European languages, she progressed not only to Greek and Hebrew but also to such exotic languages as Arabic, Syriac, Aramaic, and Ethiopian, for the last of which she wrote a grammar. She absorbed also the content of the texts she read in these languages and thus was knowledgeable in all fields of humanistic study. H. C. M. Ghijsen sees in her striving toward universal knowledge the great Renaissance ideal of education.[2] When at the age of fourteen she wrote a poem in honor of the Dutch poet Jacob Cats, she drew attention to herself and entered a sphere of prominence in the learned world. Cats was only the first of many men who, impressed by her unusual intellectual accomplishments, corresponded with her and wrote poems in her honor over the next three decades. Among the most renowned were writer Constantin Huygens, philosophers René Descartes and Marin Mersenne, and theologian Gisbertus Voetius, but there were many more as well. The Dutch physician Johan van Beverwyck was inspired by her example to publish a sizable volume in praise of women, placing Schurman at the pinnacle of all the learned women, ancient and modern.[3]

Her exchanges with most of her admirers scarcely went beyond flowery compliments; even those letters which proceeded to issues of substance were enveloped in lengthy formalities. Yet there were those with whom she debated philosophical or theoretical issues. Beverwyck, during the time in which he was writing the history of learned women, was also corresponding with Schurman about the philosophical basis of medicine. Much as medical ethicists today attempt to define the limits of the physician's role, Beverwyck wondered whether life could be shortened or lengthened, particularly by medicine. Schurman's response, *On the Boundary of Life,* was sufficiently lengthy to be published as a separate short work both in Latin (*De vitae termino*) and in Dutch (*Paelsteen van den tijt onzes levens*). Her position, which regarded God as controlling life and death and the physician as God's helper in alleviating pain, was heavily influenced by Stoicism. She relied on numerous ancient writers who believed themselves in the power of God or fate.

The Stoic philosophy also provided the basis for Schurman's advice to the Englishwoman Dorothy Moor in the letter translated here. During this turbulent period in English political life, Schurman recommended a retreat from the troubles of the world to the repose of scholarship. This Stoic approach to life fit well with her restricted view of the value of learning for women, a topic which Schurman began to address in these same years around 1636 to 1640. Although in her view the subject matter should be unlimited, the goal of women's learning ought not extend to professional activity or employment. Nor should those with many domestic obligations neglect their duties for the sake of study. Rather, studies for women should have the value of enriching a life freed from other activity. Such a quietistic approach was less offensive to her contemporaries than the more sweeping defenses of sexual egalitarianism which had already appeared, for example, in Italy with Lucrezia Marinella[4] and in France with Marie de Gournay.[5] Nevertheless, her position was still unconventional enough to raise doubts among some and enthusiasm among others. André Rivet, a prominent Calvinist theologian of the time, was fully persuaded of Schurman's own ability and the appropriateness of her scholarly activities, but he feared too wide an involvement of women in such efforts. His lengthy correspondence with Schurman, which was published with her treatise in defense of women's education in 1638, focused on his misgivings concerning the democratization of education for women. Yet other letters in the volume of her collected writings published in 1648 make it evident that there was already an international network of women interested in pursuing and defending the intellectual life. Learned women from throughout Northern Europe wrote to her, and she responded with encouragement for their common cause. Her treatise, here entitled *Whether the Study of Letters is Fitting for a Christian Woman?* was translated into both French (*Question célèbre,* 1646) and English (*The Learned Maid,* 1659); among her English admirers were the antiquarian Simonds d'Ewes, a letter to whom is here translated from Latin, and the female scholar Bathsua Makin, who corresponded with Schurman in Greek.

Of Schurman's other female correspondents, the most enduring friend was Princess Elizabeth, daughter of Frederick of the Palatinate who became the "Winter King" of Bohemia. When ousted from his throne after a season, Frederick fled with his family to the Hague, where his wife continued to hold court long after his death in 1632. There Descartes found supporters for his new philosophical system and protection from the calumnies of his opponents. Until about 1640 Cartesianism had not been recognized as a serious threat to the Reformed scholastic theology taught in the Dutch universities, but by 1640 the opposition was sharp enough between the two camps to necessitate a break. This split was not yet apparent in Schurman's 1639 letter to Princess Elizabeth, in which her universalistic humanism manifests itself, but by the time of her 1644 letter she had clearly sided with the theologians who regarded Descartes' philosophy as a form of atheism. The fact that Descartes had just dedicated his *Principia Philosophiae* to Princess Elizabeth reveals the potential for a rift between the two women.

Whether Schurman had turned away from Descartes already in 1634 (as he claimed)[6] or around 1640 (as Ghijsen believed),[7] by 1644 she had definitely turned to the tutelage of the leading Reformed theologian Gisbertus Voetius, who had even made her the first female university student in the Netherlands by allowing her to attend lectures in a cubicle hidden from other students. Under Voetius's influence she became more concerned about the purity of the Dutch state church, manifested specifically in the extent of strict observance of the Sabbath. Nevertheless, the common search for truth drew both Schurman and Princess Elizabeth toward the same goal, in spite of the different routes they took along the way. Several decades later, as the Abbess of Herford, Elizabeth granted asylum to the beleaguered group of sectarians led by Jean de Labadie, of whom one was Anna Maria van Schurman.[8]

How two such highly educated women could become followers of a radical sectarian preacher—abandoning, in Schurman's case, her church, her intellectual aspirations, and her family home—is a question which disturbed supporters at the time and has continued to puzzle scholars.[9] That Schurman was aware of the potential consequences seems clear from the outset; that she felt personal and religious fulfillment can scarcely be doubted by any who read her autobiographical *Eukleria* or her letters of this later period. Historical research into Labadism has only recently begun to look beneath the sectarian and communitarian features of the movement to analyze its theological stance.[10] Whether Schurman's veneration of Labadie was "blind idolatry"[11] or a recognition of superior spiritual gifts will never be easy to determine; any judgment ought to be based on a fuller knowledge of the movement than is now available.[12]

What can be affirmed is that Schurman, in the stages of her life, embodied the intellectual currents of the seventeenth century. The broadly based humanism of the late Renaissance gave way during the Thirty Years' War to the hardening of ecclesiastical divisions and the systematization of theological doctrine in the form of Protestant scholasticism. The disillusionment which followed an indecisive war led to a search for new answers, new leaders, and new directions. The larger Pietist movement of which Labadism was a part attempted in its best moments not to create new, divided churches but to overcome the old doctrinal rigidities in a new emphasis on the simple gospel message of love. The historical judgment that this attempt was largely a failure should not hinder recognition of the idealistic vision which motivated it or the maturity of those who found in it the fulfillment of a lifelong search.

While Schurman's intellectual and spiritual journeys are most easily traced in the writings she left behind, it is also possible to observe phases in her personal, psychological development. Struggling to break ground for herself and other women through her intellectual pursuits, she nevertheless was bound by both social and religious convention. Her inner conflict between the desire for fame and recognition and the fear of offending proprieties may be glimpsed in the letter to Beverwyck. Although her letters are replete with humble protestations of her inadequacy, her later recollection of herself during this early period is of a person seeking worldly recognition. This inward conflict is complicated by her religious value systems: in the early period her conservative Calvinism encouraged broad humanistic learning but upheld bourgeois role models. The shift to Labadism entailed a rejection of both: intellectual endeavors as well as personal relationships were thought to be of value only insofar as they contributed to a more deeply spiritual life. Thus the adherence to Labadie freed her from the need for worldly recognition as well as from the fear of social disapproval. Some might wish to argue, on the basis of her unwavering defense and unadulterated praise of Labadie, that she had formed an unhealthy dependence on this charismatic leader. Yet an equally persuasive case might be made that through Labadie she attained release from artificial restraints imposed by her social class, enabling her to integrate her values and her mode of life to an extent not previously possible. Her choice of the "better life" made possible her personal maturation.

NOTES

1. Una Birch, *Anna van Schurman: Artist, Scholar, Saint,* 22.
2. Ghijsen, "Anna Maria van Schurman, 1607–1678," 380.
3. Johan van Beverwyck, *Van de Wtnementheyt des vrouwelicken Geslachts,* 171.
4. Lucrezia Marinella, *Le Nobiltà et Eccellenze delle Donne* (Venice, 1600).
5. Marie de Gournay, "*L'Egalité des hommes et des femmes* (1622), reprinted in Schiff, *La Fille d'alliance de Montaigne,* 61–77.
6. René Descartes, *Oeuvres,* published by Victor Cousin (Paris, 1824), 8:388.
7. Ghijsen, "Anna Maria van Schurman," 116.
8. On Princess Elizabeth, see the Baroness Blaze de Bury, *Memoirs of the Princess Palatine,* and Ludger Oeing-Hanhoff, "Descartes und Elisabeth von der Pfalz," 82–106.
9. See especially Mülhaupt, "Anna Maria von Schürmann, eine Rheinländerin zwischen zwei Frauenleitbildern," 161.

10. See S. van der Linde, "Anna Maria van Schurman en haar Eucleria."

11. This accusation was directed at Princess Elizabeth by Blaze de Bury; see *Memoirs of the Princess Palatine,* 321.

12. A recently announced work by Trevor Saxby, *The Quest for the New Jerusalem: Jean de Labadie and the Labadists* (Martinus Nijhoff, 1987), should be of considerable value in furthering our understanding of Labadie.

Early Letters

February 12, 1638, Utrecht

To Johan Beverwyck[1]

Those of the highest gifts of the Graces which we deem most fitting for a young woman, Distinguished Sir, namely modesty and silence, we seem scarcely to retain, at this time above all. Indeed such an outpouring of your kindness towards an undeserving one makes me uneasy, and you crown my lack of knowledge with publicity arousing such envy that I think I am not able to guard silence with modesty or modesty with silence. Through your most elegant letters you have caused me to be uncertain whether you have imprinted a more humble attitude of proper refinement on my soul or indeed a more remarkable opinion of you. But the fact that you have begun to keep an account of my name, whether led by some first attempts of my feeble intellect or by the persuasion of great men, was not at all sufficient to cause you to praise me so grandly, had that generosity of your remarkable spirit not urged you on. Meanwhile, nevertheless, I will not disguise how much it pleases me that I see you very much supporting my studies, and even approving the strange plan of my life with your judgment as if of Apollo. For there are today many who do not so easily submit to your opinion but rather decide that this more refined embellishment is not at all fitting to our sex, and that the access to the shrine of Minerva should not usually be open to us. And so you will find, if I am not mistaken, antagonists, and not men of the humblest seats, where you maintain these most incredible arguments (as men now judge them). Nevertheless, since the light of every kind of learning and ancient wisdom illuminates your way; and since your works clearly bear witness that you do not shrink from that free and Socratic method of philosophizing, I scarcely think anything will be more worthy of your attention than that you, by a certain public writing, claim its merit for our rank and that you kindle the nobler desires of women toward embracing this kind of life. Nor would I wish this so much for my sake as for the whole literary state of affairs, to which you have long since not hesitated to devote yourself fully. Wherefore we entreat you again and again that you take up this office in earnest and as soon as possible through all the sacred rites of the Muses. . . .

September 7, 1639, Utrecht

To the Princess of Bohemia

[Schurman discusses the study of the lives of the ancients by means of the biographies written by the classical historians Xenophon, Q. Curtius, Plutarch, Suetonius, and Tacitus.]

. . . If we wanted to proceed to the usefulness which results to us from this and to examine it in detail, we would find that it is almost infinite, notably in the livelier way the examples strike the imagination and the senses than the precepts of philosophy. Moreover, the knowledge of past matters which is acquired by this means is without partiality and without any sort of danger, which is almost inevitable to those who let themselves be led by experience alone. We can see there all the past centuries as in a clear mirror and make strong conjectures concerning those which are to come; and consequently we will succeed to that perfection of regarding nothing on the earth as new and we will say with the wisest of kings: "What has been done is what will be; and there is nothing new under the sun." It is indeed true that there is some difficulty in arriving at a particular application, mainly inasmuch as antiquity is commonly more rigorous and austere; but the essence of things remains the same, even though certain formalities and circumstances may be accustomed to change often. We can easily bring the required mediation if we know more closely the genius and temperament of their century and of ours. I. Lipsius outlined this method more fully in his book entitled *Admonitions and Political Examples,* showing to public personalities and to private individuals what application can be drawn from ancient and modern examples. And in fact, it seems to me that the latter are in no way inferior to the former if we consider not so much the force and eloquence of the historians as the material. I would dare to set a single Elizabeth in her life as Queen of England and a Jane Grey against all the illustrious women of ancient Greece and Rome. . . .

Physics is a little dry when we remain in its bare speculations: but there is one part (concerning which Saint Augustine has written in his twenty-first book, chapter four, of the *City of God;* also Cardan, Wecker, and several others) called "natural magic," which is more pleasant since it conjoins with the practical some works wonderful to the eye, and nevertheless it remains within the bounds of laudable curiosity. But astrology (I do not take this word for astronomy, as was customary in ancient times; that is a noble science and very worthy of our contemplation) goes further and usually degenerates into superstition because it attributes more to the secondary causes than the order and characteristics of nature permit. For to say that the human will and contingencies depend on the constitution of the heavens and on the appearance or conjunction of the planets is to introduce into the world a necessity greater than that of the Stoics. The causes which act freely and causally cannot be determined by natural causes, that is to say, by the influence of celestial bodies. But because of their excellence they are directly subordinate to the premier and sovereign cause. Moreover, it is a matter no less dangerous than vain to wish to predict future contingent matters, which belong properly to divinity alone, as we see in Isaiah 46:9–10, and is not communicable to creatures unless by extraordinary revelation. . . .

April 1, 1641, Utrecht

To Dorothy Moor[2]

Your letter seemed sweeter than nectar to me; and because I take great delight in your correspondence, I would have responded sooner had not my brother, who will bring this to you, long since intended to come to England. He will make known to you the manner of my life and will disclose the inner chambers of my heart to you. Nevertheless I can scarcely restrain myself from writing about the weightiest points of your letter.

You ask how I order and dispose my affairs so that I pass with least offense through the cares of this life, especially in this miserable age. Even if I owe the credit to your singular kindness and modesty that you consider my example not unworthy of imitation; still, if we were at some time permitted by the grace of God to enjoy one and the same companionship, I do not doubt that in such a union of minds and studies we could better encourage one another to virtue. However, I will tell you in a word not what I have always attained but what target I set for myself to be attained as nearly as possible. The polestar of heavenly truth shows us the short path and by far the safest; as was best stated by the great Count Mirandola, "Philosophy seeks truth, theology finds it, religion possesses it."

But in order not to digress further from the subject, I say not without cause along with the distinguished philosopher Epictetus that mortal affairs have two handles; not, however, as he, that one is suitable, the other unsuitable, but both as suitable, only that they are to be grasped properly and in order. Of course whatever pertains to living well and happily must be assigned either to divine providence or to our duty. Touching the first, I aim solely that, in those matters which are beyond our power, I may have one concern only—namely to throw all concerns onto God, according to that admonition of the Apostle, "Casting all your care on him, for he careth for you." Certainly the source of all our inquietude is that we are accustomed too anxiously to turn over in the mind the occurrences of things which depend solely on the will of the highest deity.

Our duty is what remains; only those parts which fall under our deliberation are to be regulated with our industry and prudence. Nothing so dislodges us from the bulwark of tranquillity, as the perverse example and the false attractions of this century, not to speak of the nuisances and annoyances which perpetually accompany the condition of those who take part in the theater of this world. But for this evil I find no other remedy more expedient than the retreat of studies. For indeed, since the most corrupt morals are practiced everywhere today, it is hardly possible for anyone to kindle in others as much enthusiasm for pursuing virtue as one yields of one's own enthusiasm when engaging in frequent interactions with people. Here, in this retreat, with those deceptions of this age removed, we judge more correctly of all things and we safely despise those things which fill the profane minds of men with admiration. Here one can direct the mind to higher things in the convenient leisure of the Muses and undertake the study of wisdom without impediment—about which more is written in the printed letter I am sending to you. I have added also my image depicted true to life with my own hand, by which I may become known to you in all ways, insofar as is possible. Farewell, immortal ornament of our sex, and continue to love in return her who is so fond of you.

January 26, 1644, Utrecht

To the Princess of Bohemia

. . . It is true that I have high regard for the scholastic doctors and that without doubt they could provide me with beautiful occasions for exercising my spirit if I were not frequently diverted from them by more necessary exercises. I do not wish to deny that they sometimes go astray through vain and dangerous speculations, which have brought upon them the censure of many learned people of our time. Nevertheless that ought not prejudice either the solidity or the excellence of their ideas which we are accustomed to admire in their works when it is a question either of clarifying the secrets of philosophy or of sustaining the highest points of the Christian religion against secular skeptics and atheists. It would be hard to tell whether they have been more ingenious in conjuring up doubts and objections or more adept in resolving them; whether they have been more rash in undertaking lofty and difficult matters or more fortunate and capable in clearing them up. Thus, in my opinion, they have combined well these two qualities rarely associated, the subtlety of reality. And in fact it is not strange that they have arrived at such a high degree of perfection, inasmuch as they have not scorned the legacy from their predecessors nor the heritage of all the past centuries; and because it is easy, according to the rule of the philosophers, "to add something to the discoveries of others." It was enough glory for them to let themselves be led by those two great stars of the divine and human sciences, St. Augustine and Aristotle, whom none have been able to obscure, no matter what chaotic muddles of errors people have tried to set over against their brilliant light. . . .

October 31, 1645, Utrecht

To Simonds d'Ewes[3]

Long ago I joyfully received your letter, illustrious Sir, as was fitting for a letter alive with the spirit of pure sincerity and refined humanity. Indeed I would not have caused you to wait so long for my response had I not previously decided, for more than one reason, to write infrequently to my countrymen and very rarely to foreigners. Nevertheless, when I learned recently from the most noble and most faithful Lord Strickland[4] how much you excel in honor and in all kinds of learning, the maiden modesty to which I am accustomed to yield did not blush to defer to your affable and noble virtues. And so, fixed in contemplation of them, I have grasped the pen eagerly, by which I might offer them through a letter the reverence and honor they claim as if by right. I am impelled to this also by your most favorable opinion of our sex, which I wish that I were able to prove as easily by my example (which you indeed judge too kindly) as by arguments. But that you write that the matron Bathsua Makin has so grandly praised my industry in higher studies and even that you have reckoned in addition with an unbelievable desire to encourage us, we accept it fully both with its unmerited kindness toward me and also with your ease in agreeing. To be sure, you attribute to me such renown in letters which, if I should admit willingly, I should sin greatly against the rules of truth and modesty. Nevertheless I shall not deny that I take great delight in the best and even the highest matters, even though they may sometimes exceed my powers of comprehension. Wherefore take care not to think me too little affected by the turmoil in your country, for whose welfare my prayers do not cease to wage war. . . .

January 26, 1647, Utrecht[5]

To Marie de Gournay

If I have testified to the sense I have of the advantages which your heroic qualities have procured for our sex, it has only been to discharge a duty which justice has rendered necessary for me. Indeed the letter which you have done me the honor of writing demonstrates well that your courtesy is not measured out according to its objects and that it accepts no limits other than its own. . . .

With regard to your opinion that I occupy myself too much with the study of language, I can assure you that I only contribute my leisure hours to them and sometimes after rather long gaps of time, if you permit me to make exception of the sacred language. Beyond the fact that it has as its subject the word of God, which ought to be the first object of our thoughts, and that there is no translation which can express so well the simplicity and dignity of these Holy Mysteries, it has the properties and ornaments which cannot be equaled by all the elegance even of Latin. The words of Jerome, "Let us learn those things on earth of which the knowledge will persist with us to the heavens" can well be applied to Hebrew, the use of which (according to the feeling of the most learned) will endure into the next life. Now it is an infallible proof of your good graces that you believe my spirit was born for the better things. As for me, if I cannot satisfy the grand designs which you have made of my abilities, at least I shall try to conform to your good advice. . . .

From Whether the Study of Letters Is Fitting for a Christian Woman?

And so let us show the limitations:[6]

First, of the subject itself, that at least a mediocre ability is predicated to our woman and that she not be utterly inept at learning.

Second, there must be the necessary means of instruction; nor must there be a pressing need in the home. This exception I also bring forth here because the good fortune befalls few that they have parents who want or are able to teach them themselves; and without the best of tutors, work in this area cannot be conducted.

Third, that the condition of time and fortune be such that it is possible sometimes to be free from a general or special vocation, certainly from the exercise of devotion or from the duties of the household. As follows easily, it will be preferable in childhood to have immunity and liberty from cares and duties; in more advanced age to have either celibacy or the attendance of servants who are accustomed to free wealthy women in great part from domestic duties.

Fourth, that her goal be not vain glory and show or a certain useless curiosity; but because of the general goal, that is, the glory of God and the salvation of one's soul, that she herself may go forth better and happier and may teach and direct the family (if that duty should rest upon her) and that she may be useful to her whole sex, inasmuch as it is possible to do so.

ARGUMENTS

I. Whoever is given by nature the first principles or the power of the principles of all arts and sciences is suited to study all arts and sciences: and to a woman these powers or principles are given by nature.

II. Whoever by nature has a desire for sciences and arts is suited to study sciences and arts. And women by nature have a desire for arts and sciences.

III. Whoever is created by God with sublime countenance and erect toward the heavens is suited for the knowledge and contemplation of things sublime and heavenly. But God created woman with sublime countenance and erect toward the heavens.

IV. Whoever longs greatly for a solid and enduring occupation is suited for the study of letters. And woman longs greatly for a solid and enduring occupation.

V. Whoever enjoys a more tranquil and free life is suited for the study of arts and sciences; and women for the most part enjoy a more tranquil and free life.

VI. Whoever is fit for the study of the principal sciences is also fit for the study of instrumental or adjunct sciences.

VII. Arts and sciences are fitting for those to whom all virtue in general is fitting.

VIII. Whatever perfects and adorns the mind of man is fitting to a Christian woman.

IX. Whatever by its nature contributes to exciting in us greater love and reverence for God is fitting for a Christian woman.

X. Whatever fortifies us against heresies and discloses their traps is fitting for a Christian woman.

XI. Those things which teach prudence without detriment to reputation and modesty are fitting to a Christian woman.

XII. Whatever leads to true greatness of soul is fitting for a Christian woman.

XIII. Whatever fills the mind of man with distinguished and honest delight is fitting for a Christian woman.

XIV. To whomever ignorance is not fitting, the study of letters is fitting.

LIMITATIONS OF THE PREDICATE

I limit that study of letters such that I think all honorable disciplines, or the universal circle of knowledge, as it is called, is appropriate to a Christian woman as a particular and general good or adornment of humanity; but that in accordance with the dignity and nature of the science or art and also in accordance with the girl's or woman's power of comprehension and fortune, that each may succeed during the course of learning in its own order, place, and time and that they be joined properly. First of all, let there be special regard for those sciences or arts which have the closest connection with theology and the moral virtues and serve them above all; we consider Grammar, Logic, and Rhetoric to be of this nature, especially logic, however, which is fitly called the key to all sciences; next, physics, metaphysics, history, etc. and also knowledge of languages, especially Hebrew and Greek, all of which can assist us toward an easier and fuller knowledge of Holy Scripture (to say nothing of other authors). Other things such as Mathematics (to which Music is also assigned), Poetry, etc., Painting and the like they may maintain as liberal arts as if they were extraordinary ornaments or pastimes. Finally, those studies which concern legal jurisprudence, military matters, the arts of speaking in church, court, or school, we do not urge in great measure, as they are less fitting or necessary. Meanwhile, nevertheless, we by no means concede that women should be excluded from the scholastic or theoretical knowledge (as it may be called) of those things, but above all from the knowledge of the most noble discipline of politics.

From Eukleria, or the Choice of the Better Part

I must go back to the first scene in my life and at this point give faithful testimony with childlike gratitude to my parents that they sought to educate me not only in humane letters but also in the faith insofar as they understood it.[7] This was a matter of such earnest concern to them that they had us instructed from childhood by an excellent domestic tutor, since we lived in the country. This met with such success that I, as a child of only three years (as was told to me later by others), could read German accurately and recite part of the catechism from memory. That I, or rather God, the cause of nature, contributed a special readiness to learn, I gladly recognize; but that no one may believe that I strove of my own accord or choice for things too exalted and out of the ordinary, I will here touch briefly on the trifling circumstance which led to the beginning of my studies.

When I was in my eleventh year (1618), it happened that my brothers (one of whom was two years, the other four years older than I) were given exercises in Latin and I in French by our father; I know not by what chance or, more likely, divine providence it occurred that I sometimes assisted them when they overlooked something, but I thus led my father to the thought that I might successfully be instructed with them in the same letters. And when he encouraged me to believe this and saw that I cheerfully followed his desire (surely only out of a wish to please him), he began from then on to initiate me in the study of letters.

In order, however, that I not be put off at the outset by the prickly points of grammar, he prudently set before me instead the philosopher Seneca (whom I enjoyed very much) to read and explicate, saying "the eagle catches no flies." The most essential elements he taught me thereafter, but only while playing or walking in the garden, so that I only tasted lightly of the bitter rudiments of study. Meanwhile, in order that the charms of this heathen writer not hinder Christian devotion (which is in conflict with all wisdom of the flesh), he had me moderate the reading of the former by combining it with the reading of Holy Scripture.

I said above that, through this delight in studies and arts, I was easily drawn away and made a stranger to children's games and other false amusements. Let me add also that I had been to a certain extent armed against other idle and worldly company, which was to entice me in subsequent years. This I owe to the instructions of my father (as well as the concern of my good mother) in the duties of godliness and also to his oft-repeated warnings, by which he deterred me from contamination by the spirit of the times and from the company of worldly people. And in order that I might not become imprudently entangled in the snares of this world, he warned me especially earnestly even up to his death to beware the inextricable, highly depraved bond of worldly marriage (as it commonly may be). I did not throw this fatherly advice to the winds when thereafter the world attempted in various ways to bind me to it by this method.

Only two or three things should be brought to light which reveal my former wanderings from the right path and my service to the world, although I appeared to many others to be wise and happy. First, as fame itself went before me (for it seemed I ought to keep that which was said kindly about me from being a lie), I turned my mind and efforts to too many different and idle—indeed worthless—matters. Second, that neither in respect to time nor to knowledge itself did I observe suitable proportions; I did not always give first place to the things which could best glorify God, edify my neighbor, and make my soul more pleasing to God.

Third, following mostly human instinct, which drew me more to human than to divine matters, I clung with too great intensity to various sciences and arts and in them sought, even if I did not find, some pleasure and repose. All this will easily be recognized by anyone who observes the course of my life.

In truth I was recently astonished at my earlier lack of moderation in studies; on the occasion of looking through my *Dissertation on the Learning of a Christian Woman,* which I wrote to A. Rivet, I became red-faced upon reading these words: "My feeling is that [the study of] all honorable disciplines or the universal circle of knowledge (as it is called) is appropriate to a Christian woman as a particular and general good or adornment of humanity." At that time I believed that I must learn everything that can be known in order, following the words I quoted there from the philosopher, "to escape from ignorance." But I did not want to recommend to others anything of which I myself was not fully persuaded. Yet how far my thoughts were then from the admonition of our Savior that "one thing is necessary," anyone can see from all that has been said.

Further, as far as the order and fitting proportion among my studies is concerned, I did indeed strive for it, but that I did not attain it can be seen from the following words of the same essay: "But let there be special regard for those arts and sciences which have the closest connection with theology and the moral virtues and serve them above all. . . ." [Schurman quotes here from the "Limitations of the Predicate" section of her *Dissertatio.*] It is evident from this that I did indeed subordinate everything to theology as preeminent but that this subordination extended almost *ad infinitum* before one would reach the goal of pure theology, since I considered so many and such different aids necessary for understanding Scripture that this study would easily overstep the bounds of this mortal life. In truth, had not the grace of God ordained otherwise, death would have overtaken me while still in these preparations.

The death of my dearly beloved mother who, not to mention her other virtues, was the best mother and housewife led me out of the too contemplative and literary life into a more active existence, as I now had to take care of the whole household almost entirely by myself. This gave me various opportunities to exercise so-called works of charity, such as visiting the sick, comforting the afflicted, instructing the ignorant, assisting the poor with alms, or also admonishing those who neglected their obligations and encouraging them to virtue and godliness. As sincerely as I tried to fulfill these duties as I understood them, I must confess that I made many mistakes. . . .

However, a more unusual and certain opportunity, divinely offered to me, for exercising a true work of love must not be overlooked here. There were, namely, still two of my mother's sisters living, who moved in with us partly because of the close blood and personal relationship and partly because of the general eruption of war in Germany. About twenty years before their deaths (the oldest died at the age of 91, the other at 89), God took their sight from them almost completely; for this reason my presence and help was so essential to them for this whole time, but especially in the last five to ten years, that I could scarcely be away from them for a day. Although caring for them and also for the household drew me from my usual studies and occupations almost completely, nevertheless I must recognize therein the remarkable grace of God toward us that he bound us together with such a close and sweet bond of love that so many years passed like a few days.

[Schurman and a "sister in Christ" followed Jean de Labadie to Amsterdam and sought in vain for housing close to Labadie's apartment. Their options, they concluded, were either to give up their intention or to spend considerable effort going back and forth between their lodging and his.]

When we discussed this inconvenience with Labadie and cast our eyes around his quite ample dwelling, this man of God showed us the lower part which was occupied only by a very honorable and elderly widow from Middelburg along with two unmarried daughters who took care of domestic matters; right away he graciously offered us a very comfortable room separated from the others.

Here it was necessary to make the best decision, not consulting either flesh and blood or human prudence. On the one hand we saw this as the best opportunity for our own edification; on the other hand we saw easily, if we were to move into Mr. de Labadie's house, what fury this would arouse in evil-minded people, especially those worldly minded preachers who had excluded from their communion this true servant of Christ as a scorner of their order and their opinion and thus turned everything which seemed to favor his cause into slander. Nor were we unaware how strong was the power and tyranny of custom, from which we would seem to be departing; for there is hardly a person who is not subordinate to it and obedient to its laws as to a dictator, an emperor, or a divinity. I also remembered the opinion of my old friend and counselor in cases of conscience, Dr. Voetius, which he had previously explained clearly enough in my presence when he disapproved the behavior of Paula, who with her daughter Eustachia followed Jerome to Palestine as the most learned teacher of his time—a behavior which I praised at the time. He disapproved it because thereby she made an evil name for herself among many, gave the world an unheard of and unparalleled example, and did not sufficiently observe the proprieties. . . .

But in truth these things held us back from the path of following Christ as little as if we had met a swarm of flies which one easily scatters and sends elsewhere. I do not deny that I had all my life placed much weight on bourgeois proprieties, customary manners, and a good name, as if true virtues: but in this case I paid no attention to them; I considered them transient in comparison with heavenly matters or as a heavenly gift and entrusted good which I could give back to God, just as everything which is mine belongs to God and has been given to me by God. Thus I decided to offer all this with generous spirit as a sacrifice to God, the giver of all.

We especially noted the wonderful workings of divine grace when, in our house meetings, the fundamental points of the Christian religion and of Christian life were handled in such a godly manner. . . . To all who made up our church was given the gift of lively repentance and sincere conversion. For as soon as they become inwardly aware of the power of these saving truths, which present to the heart first the shameful perversity of the world and its manner of struggling against God, and then the beauty of God, his all-sufficient goodness and his unending perfection, they are thereby bound quite strongly to the choosing of the best part; . . . We have seen clearly in all of them a complete denial of the world and scorn of all earthly things as well, on the other hand, as a true love of heavenly things and of Christ, a mortification of the old man and vivification of the new, so much so that there has occurred in our house community a general resurrection; this has brought forth among us all an unspeakable joy which the world does not know and which is not suited to the world, whether in its coarser or finer aspects.

The Princess [Elizabeth], who almost always attended these meditations, was thereby overcome with such wonder and love of these truths and this manner of teaching and was able to begin to distinguish true Christianity from its false imitations. More than once she praised the blessedness by which God had chosen her over others to provide accommodation and protection for his true church, gathered from true believers. But especially after Labadie had spoken close to her heart while she was ill, she assured me joyfully with the words of the Samaritan "that she believes from henceforth not because of my words or those of another, but because she herself heard and recognized" that these men were true servants of Christ taught by God. And how could it be otherwise, since she perceived the marvelous fullness of divine truth in their talks and the inexhaustible treasures which they brought forth from their heart on every occasion without any preparation or human studies. Others, on the contrary, she observed shaping their dry lectures artificially with great effort and study solely out of their brains or out of books and then repeating them mechanically. But those here, even when they treated the oldest and most common truths, always knew how to put them in a new light and yet to present them no less clearly than naturally. Not to speak of their simple, pure, free life which in fact was nothing other than a lasting evangelical sermon for those who observed it with an illuminated, unobscured sight.

March 14, 1677, Wiewerd in Frisia

Letter to J. J. Schütz

Since we hold Christ to be the only highest teacher instructing His true disciples through His Spirit and word, we depend on no teacher or particular writing when they taste either of human genius or academic technique or method, much less of the controversies of contentious educated parties.[8] The faithful servant of Christ, Mr. de Labadie, whom God used powerfully as an organ sanctified by his spirit for gathering and forming this church in the likeness of the first at Jerusalem, did not learn from the Jesuits nor the Jansenists nor the Calvinists (if one may thus label them); rather, even as a boy he first learned inwardly from God and drank those purest truths and, if I may add, love of God by which he was totally filled and to which the foremost of his teachers declared themselves enemies and, finally, persecutors. He did not see Calvin's writings until the age of forty, as I heard from his own mouth, but when he was already prepared to secede from the Roman Church, he wanted only to look into them to see whether those things were true which were attributed to this author and whether there was any justification for his adversaries to accuse him of Calvinism; yet he read nothing but [Calvin's] *Institutes of the Christian Religion*. Indeed he received the light of God with such humility and modesty, and he so reverently held all divine truths that no desire for disputing them or curiously inquiring into them ever came over him; but teaching them with so much light and heavenly unction, the words so penetrated the hearts of the listeners that no one who was not totally preoccupied with a contrary affection could fail to embrace them with full assent and love. . . .

. . . Therefore do not believe, dear brother, that among us thrives human and worldly erudition or the artifices of scholars or the concatenation of dogmas, or that our minds and hearts are entangled, bound up by the logical and rhetorical arts in systems of digests, or separated from others. It is indeed another kind of tie or chain which binds our congregation into one heart and mind, another principle which separates us from ourselves, from the world and the worldly; finally it is another kind of zeal by which we are aroused to resist those errors and faults in our path for the sake of each one's calling, rather than the drive of contention and human affection inflamed through the exercise of disputing.

NOTES TO THE TRANSLATIONS

1. This letter and those that follow can be found in their Latin and French originals in the 1650 edition of Schurman's *Opuscula,* on pages 184–86, 281–87, 195–99, 300–303, 217–19, 318–19. I would like to acknowledge the assistance of the late Professor Emeritus Robert Murray of Colgate University in the translation of difficult Latin passages.

The letter to Beverwyck protests her own unworthiness while encouraging Beverwyck in his public support of the cause of women. After Schurman had seen his book exalting women, she wrote another letter in 1639 containing a similarly cautious warning that his overexuberance might do the cause more harm than good. See Joyce Irwin, *Womanhood in Radical Protestantism, 1525–1675,* 146.

2. Dorothy Moor (Dorothea Moore) was widowed at age twenty-six by an English nobleman and thereafter immersed herself in language study—first Italian and French, then Latin and Hebrew. She and Schurman exchanged letters in Hebrew as well as the Latin from which this is translated. Beverwyck reported that Moor was so devout that, in addition to her language studies, she spent many hours reading and meditating on religious writings (*Van de Wtnementheyt des vrouwelicken Geslachts,* 498–99).

3. Sir Simonds D'Ewes (1602–1650), though trained as a barrister, devoted his life to the copying and analysis of historical manuscripts with the ambition, expressed as a young man, "to restore to Great Britain its true history—the exactest that ever was yet penned of any nation in the christian world" (quoted in *Dictionary of National Biography,* 5:901). Nevertheless, by the time of his death at the age of 49, most of his work remained in a miscellaneous collection of manuscripts. His autobiography was published from the manuscripts in 1845.

4. Walter Strickland was appointed agent of the English Long Parliament to the States General of the United Provinces in the 1640s and served in both councils of state appointed during the Protectorate of the 1650s.

5. The published date of this letter, January 26, 1647, cannot be correct, as Marie de Gournay died in 1645.

6. Schurman's *Dissertatio* was reprinted in her *Opuscula,* pages 28–56 of the 1650 edition. The selections presented here include portions of the prefatory definition of terms and all her arguments, stripped of their supporting material.

7. *Eukleria, seu melioris partis electio,* while autobiographical, is also an exposition of Schurman's theological position and that of the Labadist community. The work is therefore important not only in giving us her retrospections on earlier years but also in presenting an insider's account of Labadist beliefs and practices. The following selections can be found in the 1684 Dutch translation (reprinted 1978) on pages 10–11, 35–36, 42–45, 219–21, 242–48, 291–93, 295–96.

8. The lengthy correspondence between Schurman and Johann Jakob Schütz, friend of Philipp Spener in Frankfurt, is an important resource for studying the interrelationships among different pietistic thinkers and groups. The Basel University library manuscript of the letters was discovered by Johannes Wallmann and discussed in his *Philipp Jakob Spener und die Anfänge des Pietismus.* His response to Kurt Aland's criticism of that work appeared in "Spener-Studien," *Zeitschrift für Theologie und Kirche,* 69–105.

BIBLIOGRAPHY

Primary Works

Schurman, Anna Maria van. *Amica dissertatio inter Annam Mariam Schurmanniam et Andr. Rivetum de capacitate ingenii muliebris ad scientias.* Paris, 1638. Reprinted as *Dissertatio logica de ingenii muliebris ad doctrinam et meliores litteras aptitudine, cui accedunt epistolae aliquot (Schurmanniae ipsius et Riveti) ejusdem argumenti.* Leiden, 1641. English translation: *The Learned Maid, or, Whether a Maid may be a Scholar? A Logick Exercise written in Latine by that incomparable virgin Anna Maria a Schurman of Utrecht.* London, 1659.

———. *De vitae termino.* Leiden, 1639. Dutch version: *Paelsteen van den tijt onzes levens.* Dordrecht, 1639.

———. *Eukleria, seu melioris partis electio.* Altona, 1673. Dutch translation: *Eucleria of Uitkiezing van het Beste Deel.* Amsterdam, 1684. Reprinted Leeuwarden, 1978, with introduction by S. van der Linde.

———. *Eukleria II.* Dutch: Amsterdam, 1684. Latin: Amsterdam, 1685. German (with part I): German: Dessau, 1783.

———. *Mysterium magnum oder Grosses Geheimnis.* Wesel, 1699.

———. *Opuscula hebraea, graeca, latina, gallica, prosaica et metrica.* Leiden, 1648. (Includes first two works listed above.)

———. *Uitbreiding over de drie eerste Capittels van Genesis.* Groningen, 1732.

Related Works

Beverwyck, Johan van. *Van de Wtnementheyt des vrouwelicken Geslachts.* Dordrecht: Hendrick van Esch, 1639.

Birch (Pope-Hennessy), Una. *Anna van Schurman: Artist, Scholar, Saint.* London: Longmans, Green and Co., 1909.

Blaze de Bury, Marie Pauline Rose (Stewart), Baroness. *Memoirs of the Princess Palatine.* London: Richard Bentley, 1853.

Douma, Anna Margaretha Hendrika. *Anna Maria van Schurman en de Studie der Vrouw.* Amsterdam: H. J. Paris, 1924.

Ghijsen, H. C. M. "Anna Maria van Schurman, 1607–1678." *De Gids* 90, no. 1 (1926): 380–402; 90, no. 2 (1926): 105–28.

Irwin, Joyce L. "Anna Maria van Schurman: From Feminism to Pietism." *Church History* 46 (1977): 46–62.

———. "Anna Maria van Schurman: The Star of Utrecht." In *Female Scholars: A Tradition of Learned Women Before 1800,* edited by Jeanie R. Brink. Montreal: Eden Press, 1980.

———. "From Orthodoxy to Pietism: The Self-Reflections of Anna Maria van Schurman." *The Covenant Quarterly* 38, no. 1 (1980): 3–11.

———. *Womanhood in Radical Protestantism, 1525–1675.* New York: Edwin Mellen Press, 1979.

Linde, S. van der. "Anna Maria van Schurman en haar Eucleria." *Theologia Reformata* 21 (1978): 117–44.

Marinella, Lucrezia. *Le Nobiltà et Eccellenze delle Donne.* Venice: G. B. Ciotti, 1600.

Mülhaupt, Erwin. "Anna Maria von Schürmann, eine Rheinländerin zwischen zwei Frauenleitbildern." *Monatshefte für Evangelische Kirchengeschichte des Rheinlandes* 19 (1970): 140–61.

Mulvihill, Maureen E. "Anna Maria van Schurman." In *A Dictionary of British and American Women Writers, 1660–1800,* edited by Janet Todd. Totowa, N.J.: Rowman & Allanheld, 1985.

Oeing-Hanhoff, Ludger. "Descartes und Elisabeth von der Pfalz." *Philosophisches Jahrbuch* 91, no. 1 (1984): 82–106.

Schiff, Mario. *La Fille d'Alliance de Montaigne: Marie de Gournay.* Paris: H. Champion, 1910.

Schotel, Gilles Denijs Jacob. *Anna Maria van Schurman.* 's-Hertogenbosch: Gebroeders Muller, 1853.

Wallmann, Johannes. *Philipp Jakob Spener und die Anfänge des Pietismus.* Tübingen: J. C. B. Mohr (Paul Siebeck), 1970.

———. "Spener-Studien." *Zeitschrift für Theologie und Kirche* 77, no. 1 (1980): 69–105.

PART FOUR

pain

WRITER OF THE BAROQUE "NOVELA EJEMPLAR"

aría de Zayas y Sotomayor

PETER COCOZZELLA

According to reliable documentation by Manuel Serrano y Sanz, María de Zayas y Sotomayor was baptized in Madrid on September 12, 1590.[1] Many propitious circumstances accompanied her birth, which must have occurred in the same city just a few days before that date. Her lineage from a family of noble blood and high distinction insured for her a prominent position in society. Her birthplace, which remained the undisputed political and cultural capital of a powerful nation and a far-reaching empire, offered her the best opportunities available at the time for a complete education and acceptance into the select group of leading intellectuals of her day. Overwhelming evidence indicates that Zayas took full advantage of those opportunities, rebelling against the discrimination that she and other brilliant women faced within the passive role imposed upon them by Spanish society of the seventeenth century.

For a more substantial Zayas biography there is little solid information. Not even the date of her death is certain. Ironically, the problem stems from the discovery of two death certificates, dated 1661 and 1669, which bear the name of María de Zayas. Evidently, the name was common enough that it is impossible to determine which of the two documents, if either, applies to the writer in question.[2] Except for her Madrilenian origins, which Hispanists by and large do not dispute, practically everything else about her private life is open to conjecture. On the basis of the pan-Hispanic, cosmopolitan outlook manifested throughout Zayas's production, scholars have postulated that she knew firsthand those cities—Valladolid, Naples, Zaragoza, Barcelona, and others—that she describes with enthusiasm.

Internal evidence from her oeuvre reveals María de Zayas's personal traits: the rigorous training of her mind, her high level of education, her love of culture, her aristocratic bent and refined sensibilities—qualities that allowed her to move in the loftiest, if most rarefied, circles of her society. In addition, significant circumstantial evidence shows Zayas on familiar terms with some of the most brilliant literati of her day, such as the multitalented Ana Caro de Mallén, the poet Juan de Montalbán, the storyteller Alonso de Castillo Solórzano, and the "monstruo de la naturaleza" himself, the redoubtable Lope de Vega, who dedicated to Doña María some flattering verses in his *El laurel de Apolo*.[3] In contrast to the panegyric penned by Lope, there exists a burlesque portrait of Doña María. The noted seventeenth-century Catalan satirist, Francesc Fontanella, integrated that portrait with caricatures of other contemporary authors into a "vexamen," a jocular, semi-allegorical poem, dated March 15, 1643, from Barcelona. Kenneth Brown, who has recently edited this composition, draws upon information in the "vexamen" as well as circumstantial details to argue that Zayas, fully engaged in her literary pursuits, was living in Barcelona in 1643. Brown surmises that she was unable to return to Madrid for political reasons and continued to reside in the capital of Catalonia indefinitely, possibly until her death.[4]

Whether admired or satirized, Zayas won from her peers and has continued to win undisputed recognition for her achievements in the field of short fiction. Her fame rests primarily upon twenty short prose narratives (*novelas*) distributed evenly in two collections that were published in Zaragoza in 1637 and 1647.[5] Both volumes, *Novelas amorosas y exemplares* and *Parte segunda del sarao y entretenimiento honesto* (the latter also known as *Desengaños amorosos*), follow the model set forth by Boccaccio in the *Decameron,* in which stories are bound together by means of a common "frame."[6] Zayas exploits this device masterfully, not only to present and characterize her various narrators but also to describe the circumstances in which they tell their tales. In the exordium of her first collection (*Novelas amorosas y exemplares*), she introduces her principal artistic alter ego, the noblewoman Lysis, who has taken ill with quartan fever. From this simple incident, Zayas develops the "pretext" for an ambitious and ingenious plan. Having decided to hold soirees at Lysis's house throughout her convalescence, a group of friends (fair ladies and gentle gallants) propose as a key feature of their nightly entertainment the recounting of "maravillas"—events supposedly true or at least true to life, but astonishing nonetheless. In the second volume, *Desengaños amorosos,* the original plan undergoes a slight change; Lysis herself, fully recovered after a year-long illness, takes direct charge of organizing the soirees. From the beginning she chooses the narrators, who must be women, she says, in order to further the purposes of the *desengaños,* and establishes the order in which the ladies will tell their tales. After laying this groundwork for both her collections, Zayas fashions the superframe into a narration based upon Lysis's amatory experiences with Don Juan and later with Don Diego. This thinly woven plot concludes, pointedly, with Lysis's decision to abandon human love altogether in order to spend the rest of her life in a convent.

A fresh reading of Zayas's works confirms the praises that established scholars have lavished upon her literary merits. Zayas was able to put her personal stamp on the genre of the *novela*. No less formidable luminaries in Castilian literature of the "Golden Age" than Miguel de Cervantes and Lope de Vega brought their creative genius to bear upon collections entitled, respectively, *Novelas ejemplares* (1612) and *Novelas a Marcia Leonarda* (1624);[7] they gave the Italianate tale a renewed life in Hispanic letters. Zayas, though, had a genius and inventiveness of her own which came into full bloom in her distinctive *novelas*. Her originality is undimmed by the fact that it was attained only after she assimilated miscellaneous readings from several authors.[8] Scholars like Place, Vasileski, Foa, Peydro, to name but a representative few, do not tire in pointing out the extensive borrowings from Italian *novelisti* (Boccaccio, Piccolomini, Straparola, Bandello, Cinthio) and from French authors such as Marguerite de Navarre. Clearly, too, Zayas was conversant with the works of her most influential Spanish predecessors: for example, Juan de Timoneda's *Patrañuelo,* published in 1567, and the aforementioned volumes by Cervantes and Lope de Vega.[9]

I would contend that Doña María derived from Cervantes a fascination with the sheer protean character of the *novela*. Like Cervantes, she also emphasizes the marvelous; a fast-paced, action-filled plot; and the peculiarly Baroque time-eternity dyad, which Joaquín Casalduero sees as a leading strain in Cervantes's *Novelas ejemplares*.[10] Above all, despite Casalduero's insistence that we must not look for processes of psychological evolvement in Cervantes's works, we readily find Cervantian prototypes for the most prevalent and successful features of Zayas's art: her probings into the plight of women and her exploration of the female psyche.[11] In all probability, the Cervantes of such stories as "Las dos doncellas," "La fuerza de la sangre," and "La española inglesa"—all included in his *Novelas ejemplares*—provided Zayas with the inspiration to develop what we may call "psychological space." In this "inner theater of the psyche," the plight of her heroines (Camila, Roseleta, Elena, Lucrecia, to mention but a few) may be played out with dramatic intensity in the radical exorcising of emotions with pathetic, tragic, at times erotic, and always moralistic reverberations.[12] Cervantes's story of Dorotea, which consists of a series of episodes interwoven into the plot of the *Quijote,* also had a powerful influence on subsequent authors like María de Zayas.[13] We should bear in mind that Dorotea's poignant tale of moral fall and regeneration epitomizes an entire genre, the so-called *novela sen-*

timental (also of Italian origin), which found considerable diffusion in Spanish literature of the fifteenth century. Framed within Cervantes's felicitous version of the *novela sentimental,* the portrait of Dorotea forms one of the most memorable tales of love, deceit, and intrigue in the *Quijote.* It stands out as a point of departure for the kind of *novela* of sentiment, passion, and vicissitude that Zayas, in turn, created with striking success.[14]

Despite these general affinities with Cervantes's style, the overall orientation of Zayas's *novelas* differs from that of Cervantes. Because of temperament or education, Zayas could not take Cervantes's short narratives at their face value; she could not accept them as the highly accomplished, jewel-like products of a genius unsurpassed in recapturing a parcel of life "between parentheses."[15] Rather than follow Cervantes in pursuing the narrative as a mimesis of life in its baroque plenitude, Zayas seems to have taken more to heart Lope de Vega's critique in which the "monstruo" comments upon Cervantes's *novelas.* Recognizing, somewhat condescendingly, that "no le faltó gracia y estilo a Miguel de Cervantes" (Miguel de Cervantes did not lack elegance and style) and that the narratives in question "son libros de grande entretenimiento" (are books of great entertainment), the "monstruo" then turns these favorable observations into a backhanded compliment: the books "could be exemplary, like some of Bandello's *Tragic Histories,* if only they had been written by men of knowledge ('hombres científicos') or, at least, by some great courtiers, people who find in cases of disenchantment matter for noteworthy sententious sayings and aphorisms."[16] After a close analysis of Lope's ideologies, Walter Pabst explains that at the heart of Lope's tone of disappointment and lukewarm praise lies what Lope himself perceives as a basic deficiency in Cervantes's pieces: "the lack of that element that Petrarch and Castiglione had demanded in dogmatic terms, the absence, in the *novelas,* of a masterplan and social intention, the lack of a 'pointe.' "[17]

Lope's tendentious criticism of Cervantes could never apply to Zayas's *novelas* simply because Zayas went to great lengths to compensate for the "*pointe*-lessness" that only Lope would dare impute to the author of the *Quijote.* By making her *novela* conform to the principles that the Renaissance theoreticians promulgated as "canonical" for the work of fiction, Zayas strove for and mastered that *ciencia* (knowledge, expertise, technical know-how) implicit in Lope's concept of "hombre científico."[18] Beyond the acquisition of *ciencia* she reached for the development of *conciencia,* the authentic conscience or consciousness of an artist who is impelled—almost obsessed—by a dedication to the furtherance of a cause: in Zayas's case, the defense of women. As one of the signal champions in her epoch of the age-old tradition of *feminismo,* Zayas founded her art upon the equilibrium between *ciencia* and *conciencia.*[19] In that deft articulation between aesthetic and didactic concerns, she found, in fact, no match in Spanish literature of the Golden Age. We may say that she gave both Cervantes and Lope de Vega a goodly run for their novelistic money.

There can be no doubt concerning the exemplary dimension of Zayas's aesthetics. The *pointe* of her *novela* is stated boldly and uncompromisingly. Without sacrificing her consummate skills as a writer, she adapts her eclectic technique to advocating the God-given rights of women and to denouncing the abuses that a rampant, double-standard *machismo* perpetrates against the female members of the human species: the *inmensa mayoría* of wives, mothers, sisters, and daughters. This persistent focusing upon untold abuses, violations, injustices would give to any author—and it certainly does to Zayas—a peculiarly somber *Weltanschauung*. Her pessimistic world view, though adverse to the temperaments of Cervantes and Lope de Vega, is common in the Baroque age—in line with the streak of negativism in the writings of Mateo Alemán, Baltasar Gracián, Francisco de Quevedo and the paintings of Ribera, Zurbarán, Valdés Leal. Deviating from Cervantes's more optimistic orientation toward the immanence of the vital moment rooted in the here and now, Zayas's art manifests, in broad outline, a process of abstraction. It foreshadows Calderón's uniquely Baroque mimesis of human destiny—a literary vision that transcends unmediated, concrete experience and, to quote Casalduero, ends up conferring upon "life's mysteries the clear-cut outline of a problem."[20]

ONE OF Zayas's *novelas*, entitled "Tarde llega el desengaño" (Too Late for Disillusionment) and designated number four in the most recent edition of the *Desengaños*, is of paramount importance as an illustration of Zayas's masterful conjoining of aesthetics and didacticism, two foremost determinants of the overall consciousness of Phyllis, the female narrator.[21] "Desengaño 4" deserves a close reading precisely because it evolves from the convergence of an ideological intention and a psychological, intuitive concern. Phyllis, who plays an important role as a leading persona of Zayas herself, voices the discursive nucleus, which makes up the superframe of the *desengaño* proper, the rather long preamble and the much shorter final peroration. The well-controlled sway of Phyllis's rhetoric comes to a head in the two exhortations which she puts forth as a challenge to all women who will listen: 1) Women, open your eyes! Learn how to avoid being abused by studying the numerous examples of other women who, throughout the ages, have been deceived by men; and, 2) Women, stand on your own two feet! Learn how to compete with men in all the spheres of human activity. Defend yourselves and, if need be, do not hesitate to take up arms to redress your injuries!

As the wellspring of the entire narrative, Phyllis's first exhortation informs the *desengaño* proper, which unravels in a sequence of components, the first as a frame, setting, or context for the second, the second for the third, and so on, in accordance with a descending rank of observers and vantage points. At first, the reasoned discourse of the superframe is emblematic of the highest order of seeing: it shows Phyllis's capacity for the comprehensive vision of a master poet, comparable to that of an Olympian demigod. As Phyllis begins the narrative proper, the perspective of a general overseer becomes limited to the point of view of one person—Don Martin. Even though the third-person narrative reaffirms Phyllis's position as the supreme disposer of events, her omniscience is tempered by Don Martin's less privileged vantage point. In Don Martin's story, then, we have descended to a second level in the hierarchy of viewers. Moving down to yet a third level, we arrive at the domain of Don James's tale. Here the predominance of the two guests, the *vosotros* to whom Don James primarily addresses his story, lends to the narration a peculiar orientation—one that reflects the self-serving intention of the storyteller to put his best foot forward and a point of view that is narrow-minded, prejudiced, distorted, and disastrously erroneous. The key episodes recounted by Don James—his adventure with Lucretia, the catastrophic denouement of the affair, his involvement with Helen, his heeding the black woman's prevarications, his rash reaction to being totally deceived—illustrate, both figuratively and literally, that he is becoming hopelessly lost in the hellish realm of the dark, the very opposite of the lofty sphere of brightness from which Phyllis is able to observe and assess reality with unusual clairvoyance.

The story recounted by Phyllis brings home the salient points implicit in her exhortation, addressed to the female members of her audience, to open their eyes and see. It is perfectly natural, then, that the disposition of those events corresponds to a descending order of viewers—Phyllis herself, Don Martin, Don James—ranked according to their function in illustrating different degrees of conformity with Phyllis's challenge. The plot parallels a downward movement—an archetypal descent into hell—which hits bottom at the moment when Don James reacts so violently to the report of the Satanic slave woman. A bilious, rash temperament, an arrogant demeanor, an unyielding pride, and above all a warped sense of honor which he accepts unquestioningly as a sacred bequest from his culture are but a few of Don James's traits. Those flaws that pervert his character drive Don James inexorably to destroy the people who come into contact with him, even while he destroys himself. Finally, he succumbs to despair and incurable madness. As an earthy creature, victim of his raw passions, Don James can only see at the most superficial level—or rather, he cannot see at all in any meaningful way. Though struck by a woman's beauty as any man would be, he is incapable of transcending the primitive impulses of his eyes. In the context of Don James's inability to see—a flaw which stunts, in turn, his capacity to love and achieve any insight into the human condition—the symbolism of his being blindfolded during the first episode of his story will not be lost upon Zayas's attentive reader. Neither will that reader miss the profound irony in Don James's own words when he observes that, even with the blindfold removed, he senses no improvement because he is still in the dark: ". . . she took the blindfold from my eyes. She may as well not have done it, considering that darkness enveloped everything."[22] True to his tellurian nature, he wallows in the dark, in his carnal, passionate pleasures: "I let my sense of touch lead me to the knowledge of those things my eyesight could not perceive. Slowly did I fondle parts so temptingly bulging that in my imagination I envisaged her to be as shapely as any goddess."[23]

Quite effectively, Phyllis has led her audience to witness Don James's inexorable, gradual descent into his personal hell—a hell of non-seeing. Zayas, nevertheless, has not yet revealed fully the "pointe" of Phyllis's story. After describing the extreme measures he took to redress the affront he presumably received from Helen, his wife, Don James ceases his first-person account abruptly with his refusal to accept any advice from his guests. A significant shift occurs. As Phyllis resumes her third-person narration, tied to Don Martin's point of view, she calls our attention to some vivid scenes paraded before our eyes at a brisk pace: the black woman's confession and recantation, Don James's furious response, the discovery of Helen's inert body, Don James's insane behavior as the outcome of his inability to deal with his guilt. This turns out to be a tale of condemnation and salvation in which two sinners (the female slave and Don James) meet punishment while a saint (Helen) receives, in Heaven, the reward for her martyrdom. In the account of the wondrous workings of poetic justice and Divine Providence, we perceive the surge of a new dynamic of resolution which reverses the downward trend of Don James's moral fall and motivates the reassembling of the story-within-the-story. The black woman's confession fits, as a concluding episode, into Don James's story; this latches into the tale of Don Martin's adventures, which, in turn, dovetails nicely into the conclusion of Phyllis's discourse. That same dynamism impels the audience to follow the ascent back to the highest point of vision. Foreboding his eternal damnation, Don James's "blindness" and despair serve as a learning experience for Don Martin, while Don Martin's experience, which has deepened considerably his appreciation for human life, confirms Phyllis's wisdom. Now Phyllis has consummated the downward/upward pattern of her overall narrative. The *pointe* implicit in the superframe of the narrative has been brought out explicitly, having been given its artistic epiphany in the narrative itself. The first of Phyllis's two original exhortations to women concerning the necessity of keeping their eyes open is ready to make its impact upon the audience.

The technique of contrast is a major element of Zayas's style.[24] Lucretia and Helen, for example, are worlds apart in their attitudes toward their roles in society, their relationships with men, their rights as individuals. On all these issues Lucretia exhibits a position which must have appeared little short of revolutionary in Zayas's time. She is resolute and assertive enough not to have any compunctions about taking the initiative in her affair with Don James. Regardless of whether she may be capable of sublime love, she is well aware of her basic urges; capitalizing upon her advantages (wealth and rank), she aggressively seeks out the means to satisfy her desires. Lucretia's bold behavior and self-assurance set her at odds with the prevailing mores of her society. She is, nevertheless, no outcast, pariah, or lawbreaker, because she substitutes a subservience to the social code with an assertion of individual freedom and human rights—starting, of course, with her own rights and freedom. Though Zayas does not make an issue of the morality of Lucretia's unabashed, though discreet and cautious, coming-to-terms with her passionate nature, we may be sure that the guardians of conventional morality would not sanction her free spirit. However amoral or immoral she may be from the point of view of the "establishment," she remains a champion of a higher ethics—opponent of a status quo that, under the guise of a sacrosanct authority and unquestionable traditions, perpetrates hypocrisy, double standards, and abuses of all kinds. When faced with the prospect of disgrace, she does not hesitate to go on the offensive before the worst happens to her. Thus, she takes steps to eliminate her paramour (Don James) when his thoughtless actions become a threat to her well-being and good standing in society. In her, Don James has met his nemesis and his match. And why not? If men are allowed to trample on women's reputations, why should not women react violently toward men?

Doubtless, Lucretia stands out as the exemplary champion of María de Zayas's lifetime cause. A champion she certainly is and a feminist *avant la lettre*. A heroine she is not, however. Heroism and martyrdom shine forth in the emblematic portrait of Helen, brave Lucretia's saintly counterpart. Particularly striking, in contrast with Lucretia's authoritarian verve and dynamism, is Helen's passive endurance, a memorable version of stoic resignation. Helen is the victim par excellence, victim not only of an individual (her husband) but of an entire society as well. Both her husband and her society impose upon her a code of behavior as unjust as it is impossible to follow because of its absurd idealism: the mere presumption or suspicion of guilt suffices to condemn her to an ordeal that culminates in her death.

The Lucretia-Helen dyad reverberates with the tension of contrasts. At the same time, paradoxical though it may seem, those contrasts resolve themselves in a likeness between the two female personages. Not for nothing do Lucretia and Helen look so much alike that Don James, at first sight, mistakes one for the other: "I glimpsed, strangely enough, a living portrait of Lucretia, a woman who looked so much like her that a thousand fantasies came into my mind, and I imagined through wishful thinking that Lucretia had repented for abandoning me, as I have told you, and had decided to follow me around. This angel, in effect, was Helen."[25] In her presentation of the two women, Zayas creates a dilemma regarding exemplary courses of action. To be sure, Helen's conduct is appealing because it answers to the sublime call of Christian ethics. But the problem with saints like Helen is that their kingdom is not of this world and they often end up tortured and dead. Worse yet, Helen by her very presence seems to invite the treatment she receives from the likes of Don James and the perfidious maid, just as Desdemona's unsuspecting innocence creates an optimal breeding ground for Iago's malice and Othello's jealousy. Is Lucretia's brand of bold militancy to be preferred? Her unheroic stance and down-to-earth practicality leave much to be desired; Lucretia may command respect but not admiration. The dilemma could not be more clearly outlined: Helen's Stoic Christianity versus Lucretia's humanistic (hedonistic?) Machiavellianism. This dilemma Zayas posits in her writings cannot be solved by the powers of the intellect alone. True to the spirit of Baroque art, it can be transcended by the power of faith in Divine Providence and, on an aesthetic level, by an intuition which somehow can reconcile Phyllis's call to arms with the desiderata of Christian charity.

Thus, strictly from a temporal perspective, Zayas confronts the insoluble dilemma in human life, while within the context of eternity she preserves the integrity of Christian doctrine. Within "Desengaño 4," one can notice a subtle articulation of three essential concepts which give meaning to Zayas's version of the fundamental interplay between time and eternity. These concepts are identified by the three terms perhaps most laden with meaning in the context of the Spanish Baroque: *escarmiento, desengaño,* and *entendimiento.* Zayas dramatizes the terms by incarnating them in the *modus vivendi* of her leading personages.

Don Martin is the living exponent of *escarmiento,* the ability to learn from past experience. Epitomizing his process of maturation, the narrator describes Don Martin as "escarmentado en el suceso que vio por sus ojos" (so much the wiser . . . thanks to the events he witnessed with his own two eyes). He will live happily with his bride precisely because he has nurtured the sensibility necessary to learn from the tragedy he has seen develop before his very eyes.

Denoting a happy state of equanimity and freedom from deception and illusion—a condition "devoutly to be wished" for every human being—*desengaño* is much too fundamental in Zayas's lexicon to be restricted to only one character. It applies to every person who, sooner or later, must come to grips with the harsh realities of existence and must, therefore, learn to discern between "being" and "seeming," truth and falsehood. Lucretia, for instance, experiences her *desengaño* the moment she finally sees through the specious gallantries of Don James, recognizes his insensitive, selfish, "blind" temperament, and realizes that it is time to take action. Pathetic Helen suffers a traumatic *desengaño* when forced to witness the brutal murder of her cousin and sees herself dispossessed of all her worldly goods. Interestingly enough, Don James undergoes a false *desengaño* when he lets himself be tricked by the slave woman: "Como quedé, buenos amigos, el Cielo sólo lo sabe, y vosotros lo podéis juzgar" (Only God knows, my good friends, but you yourselves can surmise the state this news left me in). When he actually has to face reality, Don James, like Othello in a similar crisis, is completely devastated by the experience: "Mas, por cosas que hacían, no le pudieron aquietar, hasta que rematadamente perdió el juicio" (Nevertheless, despite their best efforts, they could not calm him down. He lost his mind completely and went raving mad!). With these very remarks the narrator seals up the "sound and fury" that constitute the story of Don James's life.

Entendimiento belongs to the highest echelon in Zayas's hierarchy of values; it indicates the most profound understanding, a necessary condition for true wisdom, which a valiant and enlightened individual can attain only after undergoing a *via purgativa* of sorts—that is, after traversing the strenuous road of *escarmiento* and *desengaño*. Not everyone reaches the virtuous condition of *entendimiento*. In "Desengaño 4," for instance, the adjectival phrase "bien entendido" or "bien entendida" (obviously pertaining to *entendimiento*), though used various times, is attributed only once in the plenitude of its appropriate meaning to Helen in the splendor of her youth and at the height of her good reputation. On one occasion Don James lets public opinion sway him to good purpose so that, ironically, he appreciates the true caliber of the maiden's virtues: "Era doncella, y sus virtudes las mismas que pude desear, pues al dote de la hermosura se allegaba el de honesta, recogida y bien entendida" (She was still unmarried and her virtues were as outstanding as I or anyone else could ever wish for. To the gifts of her natural beauty she added the traits of a chaste, modest, highly sensible person). Zayas suggests that, if Helen was acclaimed for her *entendimiento* even before her martyrdom, her later conduct substantiates the reputation she enjoyed early in her life and makes her even more worthy of acclaim as a champion of true wisdom.

Zayas fulfills her plan of joining the *delectabile* and the *utile* by placing her literary talents at the service of a dogmatic intention: the enlightenment of women. Even though she borrowed a great deal from her predecessors (especially from Cervantes and Lope de Vega), she developed her own distinctive narrative style.[26] A close reading of "Desengaño 4" reveals how Zayas fleshes out her vision of a well-integrated triad—*escarmiento, desengaño, entendimiento*—and transforms that vision into an organic artistic composition.

NOTES

1. For information about the parentage and early life of Zayas y Sotomayor, see Sarrano y Sanz, *Apuntes para una biblioteca de escritoras españolas desde el año 1401 al 1833,* 2:584–85. I have found indispensable Alicia Yllera's thorough, updated account of María de Zayas's life and works; see introduction to *Parte segunda del Sarao y entretenimiento honesto [Desengaños amorosos],* by María de Zayas, Letras Hispánicas, 179:11–110.

2. Serrano y Sanz (*Apuntes,* 585–86) transcribes the two documents in question.

3. See Yllera's introduction, 12–21. Lope's panegyric is quoted in Eduardo Rincón, introduction to *Novelas ejemplares y amorosas o Decamerón español,* by María de Zayas y Sotomayor, 2d ed., El Libro de Bolsillo, 109:18–19.

4. Professor Brown generously has made available to me a copy of his unpublished article, "María de Zayas y Sotomayor: Writing Poetry in Barcelona under Siege (1643)," in which he brings to light these hitherto unknown details about the latter period of Zayas's career.

5. Yllera (*Desengaños amorosos,* 64–93) presents a highly informative bibliography of Zayas's *novelas,* complete with a meticulous description of the early editions and an extensive list of the translations of Zayas's works into the main European languages.

6. Palomo proposes as a main determinant of Zayas's aesthetic of the narrative the fundamental dialectic between the "frame" and the *desengaños* proper (*La novela cortesana: forma y estructura,* especially 68–73).

7. *Novelas ejemplares,* ed. Harry Sieber, 5th ed., Letras Hispánicas, vols. 105–6 (Madrid: Cátedra, 1983). *Novelas a Marcia Leonarda,* ed. Francisco Rico, El Libro de Bolsillo, vol. 142 (Madrid: Alianza Editorial, 1968).

8. The following books, among others, include comprehensive reviews of Zayas's sources: Lena E. V. Sylvania, *Doña María de Zayas y Sotomayor. A Contribution to the Study of Her Works;* Edwin B. Place, *María de Zayas, an Outstanding Woman Short Story Writer of Seventeenth Century Spain;* Sandra M. Foa, *Feminismo y forma narrativa: estudio del tema y las técnicas de María de Zayas y Sotomayor.*

9. Yllera (*Desengaños amorosos,* 22–33), provides an illuminating, concise survey of this multifarious background that comes to bear upon Zayas's own production.

10. See Casalduero, *Sentido y forma de las novelas ejemplares,* especially the passage on p. 41: "El tiempo barroco es una cantidad abstracta—pasado, presente, futuro—puesta en relación constante con la eternidad. Los instantes, las horas, los días, los meses, los años, son instantes, horas, días, años de eternidad. El tiempo barroco es tiempo-eternidad."

11. A marked aversion to a psychological analysis of Cervantes's *novelas*—or, for that matter, of all Cervantes's works—transpires from Casalduero's entire study. For some particularly poignant remarks, see such passages as: "Tampoco debe buscarse en Cervantes el proceso psíquico, porque en el Barroco no puede encontrarse esa temporalidad decimonónica" (p. 41). Pages later, still in the same vein, Casalduero adds: "En el siglo XVII no

se puede concebir una aventura interior, es decir, una exploración psicológica del personaje" (p. 208).

12. As we will see presently, Elena (Helen) and Lucrecia are the protagonists of Zayas's "Desengaño 4," the *novela* translated here. Camila and Roseleta are the heroines of the second and third tales of the *Desengaños amorosos.*

13. For the story of Dorotea, see *Don Quijote,* pt. 1, chaps. 28–29, 36.

14. In another of his studies, Casalduero devotes to the Dorotea episodes a probing analysis which we may apply, also, to Zayas's portrayal of her leading female personages. See Casalduero, *Sentido y forma del Quijote,* 135–38.

15. See Harry Sieber's introduction to Cervantes's *Novelas ejemplares,* 1:15: "Casi todas las *Novelas ejemplares* presentan personajes en una situación, digamos, 'entre paréntesis.' "

16. Translation mine; for the original text of Lope's remarks, see F. Rico's edition of *Novelas a Marcia Leonarda,* 27–28.

17. Translation mine; see Pabst, *La novela corta en la teoría y en la creación literaria: notas para la historia de su antinomia en las letras románicas,* translated by Rafael de la Vega, 262–63.

18. Marcia L. Welles points out a definite relationship between the leading traits of Zayas's narrative and the prevailing literary "canons" of her age. See "María de Zayas y Sotomayor and Her *novela cortesana:* A Re-evaluation," 301–10.

19. For a brief history of *feminismo* before and during Zayas's lifetime, see Yllera, ed., *Desengaños amorosos,* 48–52, and Foa, *Feminismo y forma narrativa,* 13–100.

20. See Casalduero, *Sentido y forma de las novelas ejemplares,* 95; translation mine.

21. For my references to and quotations from "Desengaño 4," I make use of the text found in Yllera's edition, 227–55.

22. ". . . me desvendó los ojos; aunque fue como si no lo hiciera, porque todo estaba a oscuras" (p. 241).

23. ". . . empecé a procurar por el tiento a conocer lo que a la vista no podía, brujuleando partes tan realzadas, que la juzgué en mi imaginación por alguna deidad" (p. 241).

24. Foa (*Feminismo y forma narrativa,* 115–18) discusses additional examples of Zayas's technique of contrast.

25. ". . . vi, en fin, un retrato de Lucrecia, tan parecido a ella, que mil veces me quise persuadir a que, arrepentida de haberme puesto en la ocasión que he dicho, se había venido tras mí. Vi, en fin, a Elena" (p. 247).

26. I should mention here two specific cases of Zayas's indebtedness to Cervantes and Lope de Vega. Sandra M. Foa and Ricardo Senabre Sempere demonstrate convincingly that Cervantes's "El casamiento engañoso" (included in the *Novelas ejemplares*) and Lope's "Las fortunas de Diana" (one of the *Novelas a Marcia Leonarda*) serve as the basis for two of Zayas's stories ("El castigo de la miseria" and "El juez de su causa"), integrated into her *Novelas ejemplares y amorosas.* See Foa, "Humor and Suicide in Zayas and Cervantes," 71–83; and Senabre, "La fuente de una novela de doña María de Zayas," 163–72. In her other study (*Feminismo y forma narrativa,* 164–67), Foa identifies story 32 of Marguerite de Navarre's *Heptameron* as the principal source of Zayas's "Desengaño 4."

From Too Late for Disillusionment

All present listened with great pleasure to fair Phyllis, who, after acknowledging their thanks and feeling reassured that what she had rightfully requested would be granted, began with the following strains:

If you for all my griefs should find a measure,
you would not just find griefs but cause for glory.
Do you care to count them? You'll find it easier
to count the birds that fly high in the sky.

You might as well reduce the stars to a number
before you reach the count of all my griefs.
Could this be done? It would seem easier
to count the grains of sand around the sea.

Bereft of you, sweet captor of my heart,
I spend the night in longing for daylight
and when day comes, I wish the night were near.

I am pleased to send my plaints to where you are.
Though in pain, I feel great joy because of you
—a telltale sign that you are in my thoughts enshrined.

Now in hope, now in despair I moan and weep,
for without you, sweet sovereign,
the river tires me, the meadow makes me sad.

Will the day ever come
when I shall see you again, my lady sweet!

Until I see you again,
no joy shall be for me what joy should be!

With this song Don Martin tried to find diversion from his grief which was as intense as only a person who feels the pain of separation from a loved one can fully appreciate. Don Martin was a young man, still in early youth, of noble stock, gallant and of good intellect, native of the imperial city of Toledo, a man whose ambition to further his honor had kept him away from his fatherland and from a wholesome, beauteous young maiden, his betrothed, dearly beloved by him. Here we find him sailing on his journey back to Spain, his honor accrued by valiant deeds, his merits confirmed by invaluable services rendered in Flanders where he had served his Catholic king in the spirit of true heroism. From the king, Don Martin expected rewards worthy of these honorable deeds. After establishing contact with the court, he would, in the course of other ceremonies, commit himself willingly to the yoke of matrimony, a gentle and pleasant bond indeed for all those who gladly take it upon themselves. Nothing short of blissful was the marriage the noble youth envisaged for himself and his pretty cousin; with such anticipation, the journey delaying his enjoyment of that maiden's embraces seemed to him eternal. The prosperous winds that wafted the ship and made it fly appeared to him no better than a tedious stillness.

At this point, Lady Fortune (that cruel enemy of all peace and tranquility who never disposes of events in accordance with one's expectations) precipitated the darkest of nights, pitch-black, turbulent with frightening thunder and horrendous flashes of lightning mixed with violent rain. All of a sudden the favorable wind had turned into a furious tempest. The sailors, panic-stricken at the prospect of drowning, tried to lower the sails so that the ship would not collide with some crag and get smashed to pieces, but they were helpless and could do nothing. In whatever direction the ferocious wind happened to blow, there, totally out of control, the ship was pulled at top speed, to the great consternation of one and all who, resigning themselves to letting their bodies perish and seeing no other remedy, fell to their knees and called upon God to have mercy on their souls. As a last resort they set the rudder on a course toward Sardinia, realizing that they could do worse than reach the shores of that island; all had already given up any hope of ever weathering the storm alive, so that each one commended himself with great lamentations to the saint of his special devotion. Doubtless, if Don Martin had not urged them on so earnestly, their panic would have done them in. Thus, as a true son of Toledo who has to maintain an impassive countenance, whether faced with ill or good fortune, lest anyone find out what goes on within his heart, Don Martin put his trust in God and waited bravely for the outcome.

They floundered like this for three days. Stranded as they were in the dark, on high seas, they did not have the slightest indication as to where they were going. All this aggravated their fears that the ship would smash to pieces, an event which at least would save them from ending up in Moorish territories. When they sighted land on the fourth day shortly before dusk, their fears became even worse because, from what they actually saw—a group of mountains so ominously high—they could plainly predict the final disaster even before it occurred. Again they tried to lower the sails but again that was to no avail, for the ill-fated ship was tossed by the winds so furiously that, before they could carry out their attempts, the vessel hit the rocks and started to fall apart. By now, each and every man, seeing himself hopelessly near the end, was scampering to save his life as best he could, though each had the distinct sensation that his life was beyond saving.

Don Martin, who on other occasions in the course of his military exploits had found himself in similar close scrapes with death, took hold of a plank with spirited determination, and the other sailors tried to follow his example. Thanks to God's grace and Don Martin's leadership, they managed to settle in a relatively safe spot despite the surging waves. As soon as they set foot in this place, though they sensed danger lurking on every side because the fierce waves still swelled unrestrained as high as crag on which they stood, they gave thanks to God for the mercy he had shown them. Soon afterward, as everyone set out to search for the most secure shelter that could be found, and as members of the group thus spread out in different directions, Don Martin and a fellow voyager found refuge in a cavity or cleft within the rock, where, precisely because of the peculiar contour of this hollow space, the water could not reach them.

There they remained until the next morning, when the winds finally abated and all signs of menace disappeared from the sky. The sun came out, a happy change; the waves had retired to their blue mansions in the deep, and the broad daylight brought into view a strip of sandy beach, not more than ten feet wide, which provided a comfortable path at the foot of the jutting crags. Even while taking this sight in, Don Martin and his companion, anxious to find out where they were and painfully aware of their need for food (considering that they had not eaten since the morning of the previous day), became concerned lest they might have to spend another night in that place. Moving out of that not-so-safe-shelter, they set out to walk along the sandy path in search of some passage that would gain them access to the coast's highest level. They remained watchful all the while, fearing that they might be in Muslim territory where they ran the risk of losing their God-given freedom. This is not to say that they did not consider it much more vile to die of starvation. (I'll never know what sweetness we can ever find in this valley of tears that makes all of us cling to life, with its many mishaps and tribulations.)

Hunger caused Don Martin and his comrade much more misery than did the suspicion that they might be taken into captivity. They missed, to be sure, their garments and other fine cloths that went down with the ship, but what grieved them most was the fact that in the shipwreck they had also lost all their provisions. What Don Martin did not need was money because, in a coin purse which he carried in his pocket, were left, besides a gold chain, quite a few doubloons amounting to a goodly sum.

They must have spent at least half a day walking along the seashore when they came upon an out-of-the-way trail leading to the top of the cliff. They took it and, not without much strain, toward four o'clock in the afternoon reached the summit from which they could observe a wide plateau, delightfully variegated with cool shady groves, enclosing gardens truly lovely to the sight, and with many cultivated fields showing a scattering, here and there, of picturesque country houses. Nowhere, nevertheless, could they catch sight of even one person of the local population from whose demeanor they could surmise whether they were in a hostile country. At any rate, spurred on by the necessity of finding something to eat, even at the cost of surrendering themselves to whatever Lady Fortune had in mind for them, they continued their journey and, within the stretch of one league or thereabouts, around nightfall, they spied an imposing, wondrous castle in whose vicinity they noticed a man taking a stroll. From his stature, clothing, and bearing, he appeared to be a member of the nobility. Over a splendid, costly suit he wore a cloak of crimson velvet, adorned, in strict adherence to Spanish fashion, with a profusion of gold passementerie. The sight of this man brought no little joy to our wet, hungry wayfarers. They thanked God who, after so many hardships, had guided them to this place, obviously a Christian land, even though up to that point they had feared exactly the opposite would be true. They walked to meet the nobleman who, in his turn, had already stopped to wait for them, guessing the nature of their plight even by the way they moved toward him. As they stepped closer, they could see that he was a man no more than forty years old, of handsome features despite his rather swarthy complexion, with dark, somewhat curly hair and a mustache. When they finally came face to face with the nobleman, the latter, with an austere but not cheerless countenance, greeted them very courteously and then said: "I need not ask, gentlemen, what vicissitudes bring you here. Seeing that you travel on foot and noticing that your clothes are not quite dry yet, I surmise that you have escaped from a shipwreck—from a ship that, during the recent storm, must have sunk after smashing to pieces against those rocks below. Since you are still alive after going through all this, the heavens have shown you no little mercy. I know of many others who perished before they could touch dry land."

"You are absolutely right," answered Don Martin, after repaying the other man's courtesies. "I beg you, sir, would you be so kind as to tell me what country this is? Is there any place nearby where we may recover from the troubles we have been through and remedy the main cause of our exhaustion—hunger—because we haven't eaten for two whole days?"

"Gentlemen, you are on the Island of Grand Canary," replied the nobleman. "One must admit that, looking around at the place where you happened to come ashore, it would be quite difficult to recognize this part of the world. The main city is two leagues farther down the road. Since the day is about to end, you will not be able to get to the city and still have time to take care of all your needs. Besides, since you are new to these parts and do not know your way around, matters will not be easy for you. I know you need food and a good rest and am able to make out, by your speech, that you must be Spaniards. I myself take great pride in acknowledging that most of my lineage derives from Spain, that blessed land. So, I invite you to accept my house as a place where you can rest tonight or for as long as you please. Make use of my home as if it were your own, and I will consider it a great personal favor. In due time I will accompany you to the city, where I myself will have to go, as I usually do now and then; and, at that time you will be able to provide yourselves with whatever you need to proceed with your trip."

Don Martin and his comrade spared no courtesies in thanking the nobleman and, in view of their dire needs, decided to take him up on his compassionate offer. This decision having been made, the three men—together with some servants who had recently come out to join them—went into the castle and climbed toward the highest quarters, but not before drawing in the bridge and shutting the main gate, since it was a late hour and at the time the open fields were not secure from the assaults of bandits and highwaymen. Our two brave youths could not help noticing all the while that the nobleman had to be most distinguished and wealthy, because every hall in the castle was decked out with excellent canvases and rich tapestries and with other peculiar ornaments which announced that the owner was a man of means. In a place such as this, women servants could not be missing. A group of them came forth solicitously to attend to the lighting of the halls and to carry out the most minute instructions insuring the ultimate comfort of the two guests the master had brought in. At the master's call two damsels appeared and four white women slaves, branded in the face. He enjoined them to go to the lady of the house with the request to make ready a room with two beds for the two men and to prepare the supper immediately because these travelers needed to eat and rest.

While these preparations were underway Don Martin and his companion, who were left by themselves with the nobleman, harked back to the account of their trip and told him exactly how they had reached the island. By now the two understood that the nobleman was married, for in his order to the maids he had made reference to the lady of the household. When the supper was ready and the table had been set, two things struck the attention of the guests and left them so dumbfounded that they could not understand what was taking place before their eyes. What happened was that, as soon as the nobleman sat down, after requesting his guests to do the same, he took a key out of his pocket and gave it to a male attendant who used it, in turn, to open a minuscule door which could be seen encased in one of the walls. Through that tiny doorway the guests might have expected some hunting dogs or other similar animals to come out; but what actually came out, I can assure you, was a woman, in conspicuous contrast to another person of her sex who made her entrance, at the same time, through the common doorway which the servants had been using all along to enter and leave the dining hall. The appearance of either one of these women caused in Don Martin and his companion such astonishment that they lost track of what they were doing and paid no heed to their host who kept gesturing them to sit down.

The woman who had come out of the small door seemed no more than twenty-six years old. So exquisitely beautiful was she, despite the extreme abuses she apparently was subjected to, that, even though Don Martin had seen very attractive women throughout Flanders and Spain, he felt this woman surpassed all the others. So thin was she, nevertheless, and so wan that she looked more dead than alive or, rather, showed unmistakable signs of being near death. Over her snow-white, frail body, she wore nothing but a shift of coarse sackcloth. This garment, gathered at the waist by a simple piece of rope, served her as a chemise, gown, and dress all in one. Her hair, which looked more like a skein of yarn from Araby, was parted in the middle and tucked behind her ears in the so-called style of a peasant woman. Her only headdress was a rough linen scarf thrown loosely over her hair. In her delicate hands, which reminded one of flakes of snow, she carried a skull. Deeply moved after seeing her shed from her pretty eyes a stream of tears gleaming like pearls, Don Martin thought to himself that, if her mean apparel could not hide the radiance of her beauty, any other less unsightly attire would show her to be truly one of the great wonders of the world. She had already stepped over to the table and sat crouching beneath it.

By contrast, the other woman who had come into the hall through the common door was black, so jet black that ink would have looked white compared to her. On top of this, she had such a savage look on her face that Don Martin believed she had to be the devil incarnate or, at the very least, a portrait of the devil. She had a pug nose which gave her the appearance of a dog, one of those setters that today are held in such high esteem. Her wide mouth, with its protruding jaws and lips thick and heavy, seemed an imitation of a lion's muzzle. Her other features were of the same monstrous proportions. Don Martin had time to rivet his attention upon her ugly face and rich, resplendent clothes, because it took her awhile to get to the table. She was heralded by two maids, carrying in each hand a silver candleholder surmounted by a lit candle. This fierce, loathsome black woman wore a one-piece vestment with pointed sleeves: it was a gown of satin interlaced with gold filaments which brought out a tawny sheen. So stunning and rich was her attire that a queen herself could not wear any more impressive. Her wide necklaces and belt glittered with diamonds. There was a profusion of lily-white pearls all around her neck and wrists, and similar pearly ornaments dangled from her ears. On her head she sported a variety of flowers and jewels of precious stones. Equally priceless were the many rings that adorned her hands. The nobleman greeted her arrival with a cheerful smile; then he took her by the hand and helped to seat her at the table, saying: "We all bid you welcome, my dear lady."

Upon hearing these words, they all sat down. The black amazon was enthroned at the castellan's side, while Don Martin and his comrade, from their vantage point in front of the couple, were so bewildered and distracted by the sight of the woman that they could scarcely keep their minds upon their eating. The nobleman did perceive some signs of their distraction, but this did not stop him from caressing and indulging his fiendish, black ladylove, insisting upon spoonfeeding her with choice morsels taken from his own dish. As for the ill-fated beauty who sat hunched beneath the table, bones and bread crumbs that even dogs would find unappetizing were her only food. There she was, so lacking in sustenance, nibbling at scraps as if she herself were one of the household dogs.

When the supper was over, the black woman took leave of the two gentlemen and of her lover or husband—who could tell what he was to her?—and, exiting through the same doorway where they had seen her enter, she repeated the ceremony of having the two girls with the lit candles go before her. The ill-treated beauty, meanwhile, crawled from under the table, and one of the waiters who helped out with the service at mealtime poured some water into the skull she was carrying in her hands. After this, she went back to her dingy coop, whereupon the aforementioned attendant entrusted with the key, before giving it back to the master, used it to lock the woman in. All this took place while the servants gradually left the room to eat their own supper. The castellan noticed his guests deeply absorbed in reflections upon the strange occurrences they had been witnessing. Since they were reticent to ask questions, he took the initiative and spoke in the following fashion:

"My dear friends, I know full well that your troubles at sea call for peace and quiet rather than for the strain of having to listen to someone else's tale of woe. Yet I see you so dumbstruck about the things going on in my house that I presume you will not deem it such a heavy burden to hear about my story and about the background of the curious incidents you witness here. I have the feeling you will likely think you are listening to one of those fantastic tales of enchantments that people say used to take place when the world was still young. In order to free you from this amazement in which I find you, if you really would like to hear about me, I will tell you the incredible story of my life. I can only assure you that, among outsiders, you are the only ones to whom I will have told it and the only ones who have seen what occurs within this castle. In fact, since the day I left the city to retire within these walls, I have never allowed any of my relatives or friends who come to visit me to step beyond the first hall, and my servants will not dare—upon pain of death—reveal to anyone what takes place here."

"By all means, my good lord and friend," replied Martin, "please release me from the confusion in which I find myself. It is true that, as you say, my fatigue calls for a good rest, but I can have no greater satisfaction or relief than to hear about a life such as yours, steeped in such awesome mystery."

"Very well, then, since you ask me, I will tell you about myself," said the castellan. "Kindly lend me your attention and you will find out what has truly happened:

"My name is Don James of Aragon. This was also the name of my father, a native of Barcelona, in the kingdom of Catalonia, himself a distinguished nobleman of that city, as my family name clearly indicates. In the course of his courtship of a certain lady, my father ran into competition with some other noble youths, and, as luck would have it, this rivalry instigated the suitors to unsheathe their swords. The upshot of all this was that my father, realizing that, because of greater bravery or better luck, he had left one of his contenders gasping for dear life, took a horse and escaped to the kingdom of Valencia. From Valencia he sailed for Italy, where he remained a few years, residing in Naples. In this city, he—brave gallant that he was—rendered distinguished service to his king and attained the rank of captain. Eventually, tired of living abroad, he decided to return to his own country. During his return journey he was surprised by a storm and shipwrecked, just as you were, upon those very same rocks. He managed to save his life, just as you did; and, while recovering in the city from his many miseries, he happened to catch a glimpse of my mother, whose parents, already dead, had left her a well-to-do orphan when she was just a child. Finally, after two years of courtship, my father took her as his wife. I, the only offspring of their marriage, was educated by them until I reached the flourishing age of eighteen, at which time I felt such a natural disposition toward a military career that I asked my parents' permission to go to Flanders with a view toward spending a few years there while, at the same time, seeing something of the world. Though understandably affected by their parental concerns about me, they were well aware that an opportunity to gain honor in such a noble venture was not to be missed. After they supplied me with all the necessary equipment and gave me their blessings, I embarked for Flanders. There I installed myself in the military and took every appropriate action to discharge the duties of my rank. I spent six years doing this and, I believe, would still be in Flanders today if I had not been involved in a frightening incident, perhaps one of the most frightening you may have ever heard of.

"At that time I was twenty-four years old. My overall appearance was in full accord with my thriving age, for I wore the fetching uniform of a soldier and had the graceful bearing of a young man, not to mention the peculiar dash of nobility which I inherited with my blood. One day, while in the company of my cohorts and friends, fellow members of the guard corps, I was accosted by an elderly man who, by his mannerisms, appeared to be a squire. He took me aside and said that he wanted to have a word with me. So, I took leave of my friends and went with him. After making sure that nobody else had come with me, he stuck a handwritten piece of paper in my hand, asking me to read it and give him an answer. I then read the note which contained the following message: 'Your handsome appearance, my noble Spaniard, together with all the other attractions that Heaven has bestowed upon you, compel me to wish to speak to you. If you are brave enough to come to my house under the conditions my servant will spell out to you, you will not regret having made my acquaintance. May God be with you!'

"The note said nothing else. Seeing that I was to refer to the instructions to be delivered by the servant, I asked him what I was supposed to do in order to comply with the request contained in that note. He answered that for the time being he had no specific directions to give me, except that, if I had sufficient resolve to go with him, I should be at that very spot waiting for him to arrive at the stroke of ten. He would come to pick me up and would lead me to my destination. Youthful as I was and also being a soldier of fortune whose daring was corroborated by noble blood, I was totally unconcerned about running into risks, nor was I afraid of danger. It seemed to me I had nothing to lose, though I should ultimately descend to the depths of Hell. Since I knew no fear, I accepted the invitation and answered that I would be there waiting for him. The astute messenger assured me that I would not run into any risk whatsoever in this venture but warned me not to reveal the message to anyone. He urged me repeatedly not to say anything to either friend or comrade, adding that absolute secrecy was of the utmost importance for my own sake as well as for the sake of the person who had sent the note.

"Reassured I certainly was . . . reassured and also consumed with curiosity to get to the bottom of his mysterious affair so cautiously maneuvered. As soon as I saw that it was close to ten o'clock, I quickly stole away from my comrades and went straight to the appointed place. As the clock was striking the tenth hour, the messenger arrived on a spirited horse. The scene was visible enough, as it was a fairly clear night. He dismounted. After that the first thing he did was to blindfold me with a taffeta band which he brought expressly for that purpose. At moments a doubt would come to my mind: Was I really sure I could recognize that man's features? At other moments I would smile to myself: What about my own features so drastically transformed? After I mounted the horse, as he instructed me, he did the same and sat behind me astraddle the animal's haunches. So we began our horseback ride. From the duration of our journey I surmised we covered about two miles. Apparently, we rode through wide streets and narrow alleys and, at many points, since my blindfold did not allow me to view where we were going, I could have sworn we were retracing the stretch we had just traversed. At long last, at the end of a good hour or more, we arrived at a house and rode straight into a courtyard. There we dismounted. While I was still muffled in my blindfold, he took me by the hand and led me up the steps of a stairway. I must confess that I felt the twinge of fear on this occasion. I was beginning to have second thoughts about entering a situation which by its very nature—conceived as it was amid such wary machinations—aroused forebodings of some grave danger. I knew all the same that at this point I could not turn back and that my situation would have been even worse had I not brought with me a dagger and a sword, plus a small pistol which I usually carried in my pocket. With this in mind, I took heart. I had the means to defend myself. At least I would not die without inflicting death upon somebody else. By now we had reached the top of the stairway. As I was feeling my way along a balustrade—we were walking, it seemed to me, in the middle of a passageway—my guide, with a key which he must have carried with him all along, opened a door. As soon as we entered, he transferred my hand, which he held clasped in his own, to another person's hand, which by way of touch gave me a much more pleasing sensation than did the first one. Without uttering a word, my guide again closed the door and disappeared, leaving me even more baffled than before. The woman to whom he had delivered me—I could tell that the second person was a woman by the rustling noise of her silken garments—walked with me side by side through three more halls and, in the third, moved onto a dais, took a seat, and asked me to be seated also. I was greatly encouraged to hear the sound of her voice and went on to say to her:

"'I give thanks to God, my lady, for now I am quite sure I am in Paradise. I no longer fear, as I have feared, that someone might be taking me to the depths of Hell.'

"'What makes you think that this is Paradise?' she retorted.

"'The bliss I feel within my soul and the peculiar fragrance and overall sweetness of this blessed abode. Though I have been reduced to blindness there is nothing wrong with my mind. I now know that the hand I hold in my own cannot be but the hand of an angel!'

"'Oh, Don James!' she again replied. 'Is what I am doing, what you are witnessing, a token of lax conduct on my part? Do not judge it so. Think of it, rather, as the compelling power of love from which I have tried to find deliverance time and again, but to no avail. Though I have striven to gird myself with the best armor—my chastity and all the traits that I inherit with my noble blood—your gallantry and manliness have gained the upper hand. It is they that have won and have made me lay at your feet all the defenses I have attempted to muster. This is the reason why I have had you come here, flying in the face of all sense of propriety, in the elaborate manner which you yourself have experienced. I hope you understand that it is in your best interest as well as mine to proceed with the utmost caution and secrecy. Furthermore, if you really want to enjoy the bliss of our amorous relationship, I beg you: let no one find out about our trysts. I know you Spaniards have your share of faults, and not knowing how to keep a secret is not the least among them!'

"Saying this, she took the blindfold from my eyes. She may as well not have done it, considering that darkness enveloped everything. I told her how grateful I was for such supreme favors and, at the same time, emboldened by being alone with her in the dark, I let my sense of touch lead me to the knowledge of those things my eyesight could not perceive. Slowly did I fondle parts so temptingly bulging that in my imagination I envisaged her to be as shapely as any goddess.

"Until one o'clock in the morning I remained with her, enjoying the many pleasures she regaled me with—as many pleasures as could be enjoyed on one occasion. When she realized that it was time to end our blissful meeting, she handed me a large purse, quite heavy, so full that it could hardly be kept closed and then bade me goodbye, giving free rein to her most affectionate sentiments. She again tied a band around my head and over my eyes and, while begging me not to forget to be at the meeting spot the following night, she accompanied me to the same door through which I had entered, delivered me to the same guide who had brought me there, and locked the door behind us. The servant and I went down to the courtyard where our horse was waiting. We mounted the animal and, at the end of a horseback ride which lasted exactly as long as it had taken us to get over to the lady's palace, he left me in the same spot where he had come to meet me. When the servant went on his way, I headed for the barracks where I found my comrades all lying asleep. After I retired to my own room, I probably crossed myself a thousand times, astonished at the experience I had just had. I hastened to open the purse. In it I found a chain equivalent in size and quality to two hundred gold escudos, four pieces of jewelry studded with diamonds, and one hundred doubloons of the kind worth four escudos each. I stood there lost in amazement, thinking that the lady was in all probability a woman of great influence and harboring, throughout the night, feelings of gratefulness for my good luck. The next day, sporting a gold chain around my neck and huge, shining diamonds on my fingers, I went out, gambling heavily with my friends and lavishing money upon them. So impressive was my liberality that they began to ask me what part of the Indies I hailed from. I handily satisfied their curiosity by telling them that my father had recently sent me a great deal of money. When night fell, I was at the appointed spot waiting for my guide, who arrived punctually at the hour agreed upon and whom I greeted with open arms and with a generous compensation for his solicitous services. I, in my turn, was received by my lady as enthusiastically and was accommodated just as blissfully as I had been the night before, and at the end my efforts were handsomely rewarded, for she stuffed my pockets with so many doubloons that you would scarcely believe me if I told you the whole amount.

"This is the way I lived for more than a month; my guide did not miss a night, and every night without fail I enjoyed the favors of my-lady-from-a-land-of-fantasy who would also shower me with gifts of money and precious jewels. In the period that I have just mentioned she must have bestowed upon me, out of the goodness of her heart, more than six thousand ducats. With these resources I could and did live the life of a prince. All during this time she would never consent to being seen by me, and, whenever I insisted, she would point out that my proposal could be beneficial to neither of us. Seeing her, she said, would be tantamount to losing her.

"Happiness based upon vices and ephemeral pleasures cannot be long-lived. Fortune soon wearied of my run of luck and began reversing the turn of her wheel to my great detriment. What happened is that my friends and comrades, finding me so prosperous and acting rather arrogantly, became very suspicious, which was bad enough. Even worse, though, was their backbiting. They passed judgment on me and entertained long discussions as to how I could possibly have come up with so much jewelry and money. They concluded that I must have appropriated it in the most vile way. Word soon got around that I had to be either a bandit or a common thief. They went about saying these things unabashedly, behind my back, till their talk caught the ear of a real friend of mine named Don Balthazar. On many occasions this intimate companion, not minding the risks he was taking, had to stand up for me. He was disturbed at seeing my reputation denigrated in such a cowardly way, or perhaps even he was somewhat afraid that the others might be speaking the truth. One evening, after drawing me aside away from everybody, he took me out to the open country and said:

"'Don James, my good friend, it is impossible for me hide my feelings any longer. I must tell you why I brought you here. I am moved, believe me, by the affection I feel for you. I am extremely grieved when I hear people malign you—I mean all those people who know you well but have never seen you live so extravagantly. I must be frank. You surely realize that, upon seeing such frequent accumulations of funds, such luxurious clothes and expensive jewels as you have been displaying for quite a few days now without any compunction, your comrades in their conversations with one another indulge in speculations and snap judgments, each according to his own theory, about the origin of those goods. They say that you get them by some means I am ashamed even to mention. But this is not the time to beat around the bush. What they say, in so many words, is that you must be holding people up and robbing them clean. They deduce this because they see that you stay out all night long, every night. In coming to your defense I have had to put up with much unpleasantness. It has not been easy for just one person to contend with so many. I beg you, for the sake of the friendship that binds us even more strongly than kinship of blood, to spare me all these doubts and suspicions. I don't care if everybody else gets the wrong impression about you, just as long as I do not. After all, I too am a human being; and it may happen that, since I see you keep away from me and act cautiously toward me, I also will judge you wrongly as the others do. Knowing the truth, however, I certainly can put up a good fight to restore your good name and also preserve mine.'

"I reacted with a hearty guffaw to Don Balthazar's remarks. Then I started casting about for excuses, trying to put the best face on my circumstances while doing my utmost to keep in strict secrecy my relationship with that precious lady toward whom, by this time, I felt much more than a strong obligation for the many favors she had rendered me. Even though I still had not seen her, I was madly in love with her. But Don Balthazar kept dwelling upon the difficult position I was putting him in. So, at long last, asking him to swear absolute secrecy by the friendship that prevailed between us, I informed him of the great risk I was running and apprised him of everything that had happened and was currently happening to me. Don Balthazar listened attentively, giving signs now and again of his stupefaction. After pondering the case at great length, he said:

"'My good friend, don't you think it is perfectly reasonable, if only for your own safety, that we should know where this house is?'

"'I must say I have my doubts about being able to locate the house,' said I, 'if only because of the strange way they lead me there.'

"'Then let's put an end to your anxieties!' replied Don Balthazar. 'All you need to do is carry around, nicely concealed in a cup, a blood-soaked sponge. Whenever you go in or out you will leave a mark on the door by squeezing the sponge. The following day it will be a cinch to find the house.' "

"To make a long story short, that very night I took along a sponge and left a mark on the door. The next day Don Balthazar and I did not leave in the entire city a street or a plaza, a street corner or an alley, which we did not thoroughly search. We could not come upon that mark, however. Extremely fatigued and baffled by these results, we were on our way back to the barracks when we caught sight of the bloodstain on the portal of one of the most notable palaces in the city, hardly twenty houses away from our own quarters. This discovery added to our confusion and astonishment, but we thought it over and concluded that the main reason my guide took me on that meandering horseback ride was to disorient me, to make me believe that the mansion was quite far away indeed. We investigated the ownership of the house and found that it belonged to a great potentate of that kingdom, a prince well advanced in years, father of an only daughter who was the sole heir of his entire wealthy estate. This woman, one of the stunning beauties of the realm, was a widow, though still very young, since her father had married her off when she was practically a child. We surveyed the entire layout of the mansion and discovered that, even though there were grills over its many windows and balconies, each of these was fitted with a system of solid blinds and shutters which allowed a person to see through without being seen. We returned to our quarters to discuss this whole situation and, after eating supper, we went out. I hastened to my usual spot to await the coming of my guide, while Don Balthazar hid himself in some outside nook of that same mansion where he could remain until his curiosity had been satisfied. That night not only his curiosity but my own as well would be fully satisfied. My old 'seeing-eye dog' came as punctually as usual. I went along with the expectation of enjoying the bliss of my ecstasy in the dark; Don Balthazar waited out there until he saw me go in and then returned to the barracks. Left alone with my ladylove, I renewed my most tender caresses and my demonstrations of utmost devotion, and thanks to my insistence, though she demurred all the while, I managed to convince her to let me see her. She herself went to fetch some means of lighting and came back holding in her hand a lighted candle. What I saw was not a woman but a seraph from Heaven. She sat next to me and said:

"'Well, Don James, you may see me to your heart's content. I pray to God that this will not be the last time you do so. I am Madame Lucretia, Princess of Erne. After all this you cannot say that I have not consented to gratify your every whim. From now on, beware of what you do!'

"But youth, alas, is notorious for its disorderly conduct! Had I kept these words well-impressed upon my mind I would never have been reduced to the sorry state in which I find myself. My lady put out the candle and went on to say:

"'My father is very old and has no other heir except myself. Though I have many suitors, I do not and will not accede to matrimony until Heaven grants me the occasion in which I may take you as my husband.'

"I kissed her hands in gratitude for all the privileges she had granted me and was granting me still. At the end of our meeting, I went back to my room, filled with happiness and with gifts of money and deeply enamoured of comely Lucretia. I did not fail to give Don Balthazar a quick account of what had happened, not hiding my anxiety precipitated by a sudden awareness that when I left Lucretia looked sad and uneasy about something.

"In the morning I dressed even more elegantly and more meticulously than I had in previous days and, with my faithful companion, went out as we had done many times before. I, a young man very much in love but not very well behaved, aided and abetted by my friend, started to walk around the town, back and forth, peeking through windows, just to appease my eyes which could not refrain from looking for the beauty they once had seen. After we ate, we spent the afternoon and evening behaving in much the same manner. Alas, misfortune was by that time hot on my trail, and my good luck, quite tired of being my mate, was ready to part company with me! Since throughout the day we could not see in that house even the shadow of a woman, we decided to head back to our own quarters. On our way Don Balthazar stopped in at the billet of the guard corps while I remained standing at the portal. It was shortly before nightfall, at the twilight hour, as people say. All of a sudden, a woman dressed in the Flemish style and wearing a mask on her face ran over to me and addressed me in perfect Spanish—not an unusual occurrence, since practically all the inhabitants of that realm learn our language through their constant dealings with our fellow nationals.

"'Ill-advised young man,' she said, 'get out of this city at once! Beware: nothing less than your very life is at stake! Taking orders from the person who loves you the most, hired assassins are out to kill you tonight! The plight of such a handsome, vigorous young man as you has moved me to pity and so, even at the cost of incurring risks of my own, I have come to give you fair warning.'

"After blurting out these words, she dashed away, as swift as the wind, without waiting for a reply. I was not able to run after her because at that moment Don Balthazar, along with some other men who roomed with us, came to join me. Actually, to tell the truth, I don't think I would have been able to catch up with her even if they hadn't come. Her words left me absolutely thunderstruck and about to collapse, and I did not even catch onto the detail that the implacable judge who condemned me to that premeditated, imminent death was none other than my beloved lady. All this notwithstanding, I took some comfort in the company of my recently arrived friends. Soon after supper, I took Don Balthazar aside and told him about the incident. We must have weighed a thousand opinions pro and con. Now succumbing to our fears, now responding to our valor which spurred us to rise to the occasion, we protracted our discussion until about 9:45. Tired of these deliberations, I gave way to a flush of bravado born of my courageous spirit.

"'It's practically ten o'clock,' I exclaimed. 'Let's go, my friend, and let the world go hang! My life may be at stake, but I, for my part, will not leave this enterprise half finished!'

"So we left. I arrived at the usual spot, the clock struck ten, but the man I was waiting for did not appear. I waited until eleven, at which time giving up hope that he would come at all, I said to Don Balthazar:

"'Perhaps they don't want to come because they have seen that you are with me. Please step aside and hide yourself in that alleyway. Let's see what effect this will have!'

"No sooner had Don Balthazar moved away, as I had instructed, than six men, fully armed and wearing masks, rushed out of a house situated farther down the street from where I was standing. Two of them shooting with their pistols and the others brandishing their swords lunged toward me and soon had me completely surrounded. One of the gunmen missed me entirely because he aimed too high, but the other hit me squarely in the arm; and although the bullet did not go so far as to shatter my limb, it penetrated deep enough to cause a very serious wound. I jumped into the melee to defend myself. But what could I do? Slashing me with sword and dagger, they brought me down. Grievously wounded, I was at the brink of death. Aroused by the uproar of the fray, my friend ran to my aid; a group of neighbors came out into the street and so did some of my comrades who had not yet gone to sleep because they had been gambling. Meanwhile, those treacherous cowards, knowing what was good for them, took to their heels. If things had turned out otherwise, I am sure they wouldn't have fled, at least not before finishing me off. I was carried back to my room more dead than alive. They called in a physician and a priest to take care of my body and my soul. God was showing me no little mercy in keeping me alive, enabling me to benefit from their services. Finally, it appeared that I was about to breathe my last. But God did not wish, at that time, that my death sentence should be carried out.

"Since no treatment was spared to restore me to health—I had plenty of money to afford the best care—I recovered from all those wounds to the point where I could get up from my bed. As soon as I was able to stand on my feet, the general sent the sergeant-major to me with a message advising that I leave that foreign land and return to my own country. He made it clear that whoever had left me in those deplorable conditions did not consider himself yet fully avenged. The general had received this information as a warning transmitted through an anonymously written note that had come into his hands. The note said that what I had coming to me was a direct result of my extravagant behavior and of my being such a blabbermouth. It went on to admonish that I should disabuse myself of any farfetched explanations: a woman had had a hand, from the very beginning, in what had happened to me.

"Now I knew whence my punishment came. I did not wait for my health to improve further but took to the road and, with a great deal of trouble because of the weak state I was in, got back to my fatherland where I found out that wicked fate had severed the thread of my mother's life. Within a year, my father, quite old and very infirm, followed his beloved spouse to the grave. Suddenly I was very rich. I was then in the flower of youth, thirty-three or thirty-four years old. As might be expected, many opportunities of marriage with ladies of great and noble birth became available to me. Nevertheless, I was in no mood to marry, mainly because enshrined within my soul still lived the image of Madame Lucretia, my adored Lucretia, whom I lost the very day I set eyes upon her. Though she had made me the victim of so many ills, I could not forget, let alone detest, her. I felt this way until one Holy Week season when I went to our main church to take part in the religious services. That is when I saw the sun—no, what I viewed was an angel. I glimpsed, strangely enough, a living portrait of Lucretia, a woman who looked so much like her that a thousand fantasies came into my mind, and I imagined through wishful thinking that Lucretia had repented for abandoning me, as I have told you, and had decided to follow me around. This angel, in effect, was Helen, the selfsame wretched woman, identified by that name, whom you have seen gnaw the bones and other scraps that fall from my table. It would be inaccurate to say that I fell in love with her the moment I caught sight of her: the truth is that I felt I had already been in love with her. Actually, I adored her. Right then I resolved to make her my wife if there were no reasonable impediments. I wooed her persistently. I gathered information regarding her social standing and economic condition. I learned that she was of noble blood but was so poor that her economic condition could not even be described as middling. She was still unmarried and her virtues were as outstanding as I or anyone else could ever wish for. To the gifts of her natural beauty she added the traits of a chaste, modest, highly sensible person. She was bereft of father—he had been dead for a year—and her mother was an honorable, saintly woman.

"I could not have been more satisfied. Virtue and beauty combined! Were they not the greatest riches that a man could come upon? Surely, in Helen I would possess more riches than Midas himself could ever have had! I married her, thus winning the undying gratitude of both mother and daughter, as they themselves never tired of telling me. And, as my love for Helen grew by leaps and bounds, I considered myself the luckiest man on earth for having been worthy of such a wife. I raised Helen up from the direst misery to the grandest possible manner of life. How lofty this was you can imagine, having seen the black woman who sat at my table this evening. For her beauty as well as for the splendor which surrounded her in her public appearances, Helen was the envy of the most noble ladies in the Grand Canary. Her glamorous features were set off by her apparel and rich jewels, and everyone was fascinated by the sight of her, while I, whose love for her grew more intense day by day, would tirelessly try to find new tokens of my devotion that would obligate her to me more and more. So extreme was the tenderness of my love for her that every hour of her absence I would consider a century, and years in her presence would appear to me as moments. Helen was my heaven; Helen was my glory; Helen was my Garden of Delight! Helen, my enjoyment! Helen, my recreation! Alas, I can hardly blame you if you consider me demented, seeing how I rejoice in the name of Helen and how I abuse her now in the violent manner that you witnessed this evening! Well, Helen is the cause of my dread, my horror, my detestation. Helen was a woman and as a woman she was the occasion of her misfortunes and mine. Her mother died when Helen and I had been married for six years. I bemoaned that woman's death even more than did her own daughter. Oh, how I wish that she were alive today! Perhaps, in her presence, her daughter would have been to me the dutiful wife she ought to have been!

"Helen had a cousin, son of her father's sister, a dashing young gallant, wise in the ways of the world. He was, nevertheless, so wretchedly poor that he did not even have enough to support himself while studying to become a clergyman. I, who loved all things pertaining to Helen as if they were my own, took him into my house so that he could finish his education. He ate, bought his clothes, had his flings all at my expense. I would give him everything with the greatest pleasure: I considered him my son. Helen and I had then been married for eight years, and these years seemed to me but a short hour. Normally we lived in the city, but every summer we went to the castle to collect rent on our country estate, as all proprietors do. One summer, the fateful summer in which my misfortune began, Helen happened to feel indisposed. I took her discomforts to be the symptoms of pregnancy, a condition I desired so much, for I yearned to have a child with her. I would not allow her to come here. I decided to come by myself, but it was impossible for me to live without her. After remaining here for eight long days, the longing to see her filled me with anguish, so that I returned to the city in a state of jubilation that can hardly be imagined. With the same jubilation she opened her arms to me and gave me a delightful reception. Now, when I consider the treachery of a woman, I feel I could die! How cunningly she dissimulated when she caressed me. All the while, she kept begging me not to leave her behind if I had to return to the castle and kept saying that she could not live without me! Let us go back, for a moment, to the black woman you have already met. She was born, in this household, to a black man and a black woman, slaves who were married off while in the service of my parents. Well, that evening, as soon as I had settled down comfortably in my house, this black lady took me aside and, bursting into tears, said to me:

"'My kind lord, I do not feel it would be right to conceal from you the evil deeds that are taking place in your absence. I would be remiss in my gratitude for the bread I eat and for the fondness which you and your parents have shown in caring for my parents and me. God only knows the grief I feel in having to say this to you, but it is not fair that you should live, deceived and dishonored, unable to redress your injury, while I remain silent. I will not refrain from having my say even though I recall specific threats that have come my way and fear that my life will not last much beyond that moment when I am seen talking to you. To your great dishonor, my lady and her cousin have entered into the liaison of a most indecent love. While you are away, this cousin of hers usurps your bed. I had suspected all along and tried to keep a cautious watch on the sordid affair. The worst is that they have found out what I am doing. I, for my part, have advised you of the way they carry on behind your back. Now it is up to you to avenge yourself.'

"Only God knows, my good friends, but you yourselves can surmise the state this news left me in. A thousand horrid thoughts rushed to my mind at one time or another: Should I tear the tongue from the mouth of this vile messenger? Should I exterminate all signs of life in the entire household? Upon reflection I restrained myself. These acts would do nothing more than scare off my prey. So I disguised my wretched suffering. The next day, impatient to see with my own two eyes the cause of my dishonor, I made arrangements for all of us to come to this castle. Putting up the pretext that my business would require me to stay longer than usual, I sent ahead my entire retinue, including women servants and slaves, and then Helen and I, in our turn, left for the country. Helen seemed very pleased to follow my every pleasure, and I had to be cunning in concealing my true feelings. Cunning and dissimulation have become second nature to me now; I wish matters had turned out otherwise, for the honor of a husband is blemished even if the husband alone harbors suspicions of an offense and, of course, is tainted so much more by the presence of a person who has really witnessed that offense.

"Blinded with ferocious rage, the first thing I did as soon as I got here was to burn alive Helen's treacherous cousin. I took special pains to preserve his head so that it could be put to the use which you yourselves have seen. It was his skull that Helen was carrying in her hands. Let it serve as a cup from which she may partake of bitter drinks, just as formerly she imbibed sweet ambrosia from her paramour's lips! Afterwards, summoning the black woman who had revealed to me all those treacherous deeds, I presented her, in full view of Helen, with the entire array of Helen's jewels and other finery. In order to cause Helen even more hurt, I told the black woman that she would be my wife from that moment on and, as such, she could dispose of everything the way she wished. She was to be in charge of all my possessions and all my servants, both male and female. I told her she could sleep in my bed, but I have never consummated my union with her. First, I have to take away Helen's life also, as I intend to do before she dies a natural death. Helen wanted to speak out in her own behalf, but I did not allow her. I did not kill her on the spot, because a quick death is too small a punishment for a woman who has committed such a heinous crime against a man who, as I have already explained, snatched her from the direst misery and raised her up to the most splendid of social positions.

"In conclusion, I have held her penned up, in the condition that you have seen, for two years. She eats and drinks no more than that ration which was allotted to her today. A heap of straw is her only bed and the nook in which she stays is not any larger than the space occupied by her reclining body. I say this because her cramped quarters do not allow her to stand up. Her sole companion is the skull of her treacherous, beloved cousin. She is to remain in this condition until the moment of her death, witnessing day in and day out how the slave, whom she most despised, is now adorned with the finery that once belonged to her and is exalted to the position that she herself occupied at my table and at my side.

"This is the background of the events you have seen; this is the cause of your great amazement. Frankly, I am not asking for any advice, and, even if you were to give it to me, I would not take it. Please spare your efforts. If you tell me that it is extremely cruel for this woman to endure a living death, I know that very well, but I have planned her ordeal precisely to that effect. Perhaps you wish to tell me that it would be more merciful to do away with her once and for all. I agree, but it is precisely for that reason that I do not kill her: I want her to pay with her sufferings for the great harm she has caused me. Let the displeasures she is now enduring be a fit penalty for the pleasures she took away from me and she herself lost. Now that you know everything, go to bed please. Do not attempt to say anything to me because the thought of these unsavory events, the memory of which I have had to resurrect, makes me steam with deadly anger. Right now, just to feel the satisfaction of inflicting the punishment afresh, I wish that this were the day in which I found out about my disgrace. When you see me tomorrow, in all probability my passion will have abated to human bounds. At that time I will hear whatever you have to say, not because I am amenable to a change of heart but simply because I wouldn't want to be discourteous toward you."

With this, Don James got up from his seat and Don Martin and his companion followed suit. After charging one of his servants to take the two guests to the room where there beds had been prepared, Don James bade them good night and retired to his own sleeping quarters.

After listening to Don James's life story, Don Martin and his companion felt absolutely awestricken. They wondered how a gentleman of such noble blood, who was so sensible and was even a Christian, could have the temper to prolong to that excess such cruel vengeance wreaked upon a miserable, wretched woman whom he said he had loved so much. The thought occurred to them as it would to any person in his right mind:

what if that damnable slave woman had brought false testimony against her lady? One had to suppose, after all, that Don James had taken no time to investigate any incriminating evidence. Don Martin made up his mind that the next day he would raise that very point in his conversation with Don James. After finishing their discussion, the two men undressed for bed. Meanwhile, in the room where he usually slept, his nerves shattered (as he had indicated) by the revived memories of his shipwrecked life, Don James kept pacing back and forth, heaving huge sighs and wringing his hands. He gave every indication of being distraught.

At long last, God, who never forgets His creatures, who, as we will see presently, had already given Helen the reward for all her sufferings, decided that Helen's body, by the same token, should not be deprived of its due honors. God disposed of events as you shall hear. This is what happened: As soon as everyone in the castle had settled down to rest, the black woman began to utter loud yells, crying,

"Lord Jesus, I am dying! Is there a priest? I want confession!" She kept calling each of the housemaids by name, asking each one to summon the master at once. Thrown into considerable turmoil, the maids rushed into the black woman's room and found her writhing in the throes of her imminent death. Her face and entire body exuded the cold sweat of someone in agony, and she was shivering so much that her whole bed started to shake with her. Intermittently she would stretch out stiff as a cadaver—anybody would say she had given up the ghost. Then suddenly she would return to her spasms and yells, to her shiverings and cold sweats, enduring all at once. The servants took heed of what she was saying: would they call for her master? It was extremely important to her to talk to him before she departed from this world. So they went out to fetch him. Aroused by the great commotion in the household, the master, Don Martin, and Don Martin's companion had already come out of their respective rooms. The three of them, joined by a few male servants who had thrown on their clothes, burst into the black woman's bedroom. Don Martin noticed immediately the richness of the bed in which that abominable bulk of a woman was used to sleeping. It was covered mainly in blue damask, but the fringes of the canopy were of velvet, laden with silver frills and tassels. It did not take Don Martin long to guess that this must have been Helen's former bed; it, too, that ill-advised husband had put at the disposal of the black woman. Finding her master there, the dying beastly woman spoke out:

"My good lord, in the dire straits in which I find myself, I can no longer profit from lies or any other form of deception. I am under the great pressure of one who feels his time is running out. I was hale and hearty when I went to bed after eating a good supper, yet now I am practically finished. I am a Christian, though a bad one and, although I am black, I do not lack the reasoning ability to know that it is time for me to speak the truth, especially since I fear the threat of God's judgment. Just because in my lifetime I have never been afraid of the wrath of God, it does not follow that I will be as fearless in the hour of my death. I must tell you something: as sure as I am going through these excruciating pains, my lady is innocent! She has nothing to be blamed for, nothing that justifies the horrifying punishment to which you have condemned her. May God never forgive me if everything I told you about her was not false witness I bore against her. I never saw her do anything that in any way countered the reputation she had always enjoyed—that reputation of being a saintly, honorable, chaste woman. I tell you also that her cousin died an innocent man. The truth of the matter is that I fell in love with him and did my best to persuade him to be my lover. When I saw that he would not respond to my affections but would always be talking with my lady, that awful suspicion came to my mind that they must be lovers. The very day you returned from the country, my lady was upset with me and, in the course of our tiff, I started to make wild accusations about her goings-on with her cousin. She was indignant at the liberties I was taking with her and vented her displeasure upon me, scolding me vehemently and slapping me hard. Even while she was punishing me, in walked her cousin, who, once apprised of the situation, lent her a hand in mistreating me. At the end, they both swore in front of me that you would hear about this without fail. Dreading your punishment, I lost no time in getting to you first with my pack of lies, hoping that you would take your revenge on them both, as you certainly did. Now God does not want my wickedness to remain hidden any longer, but what's done is done. At this time I ask you to forgive me, and I hope you can convince my lady to do the same. All this I ask so that I myself may enjoy God's forgiveness. Please, I beg you, restore my lady to her former position, for I swear by the love of God that all her sufferings are due to no fault of her own."

"Yes, I'll do just that!" cried Don James in reply to the slave's last request. His eyes were feverishly red-hot with furious anger. "Let me show you the kind of forgiveness you deserve, you treacherous, wicked female! I wish to God you had more than one life. I would be more than happy to kill you over and over again!"

With these words he took a leap over to the bed and, drawing out his dagger, stabbed the woman three, four, or perhaps more times, until he made sure he had thoroughly killed her. This he did with such swiftness that no one present could stop him or even restrain him, although I think no one would have cared to intervene anyway, since everybody thought she fully deserved that final punishment.

The act done, Don James left the room and began pacing up and down the hall, lost in his thoughts and occasionally heaving one of his usual heavy sighs. Just then Don Martin went up to him and, beaming with satisfaction, said:

"What is the matter, sir? Think of today as the day of your renewed wedding with your beautiful Helen. On such a happy day in which you have regained honor and wife, you sulk excessively, wasting away the time that you should spend rejoicing in your lady's embrace. This is not right! Compose yourself and cheer up just like the rest of us here. Give me that special key and let us bring out that ill-fated, innocent lady."

The piteous man became somewhat calmer. He took out the key and gave it to Don Martin, who opened the narrow door and began calling to the lady inside:

"Come out, madame. At long last, the day of your deliverance is here!"

Seeing that these remarks elicited no response, he asked for a candle. His words were truly spoken, indeed, for Helen had found already her final deliverance. After crawling inside, he saw the unfortunate lady dead, her inert body lying on a squalid heap of straw. Her arms were folded over her chest. One of her hands, the left one, remained fully stretched while the right hand, by some peculiar positioning of its beautiful fingers, suggested a well-shaped cross. Her face, though woefully thin and wan, was so beautiful that it looked rather like the face of an angel. The skull of that poor wretch, her innocent cousin, could be seen next to her head, over to one side. Compassion got the better of brave Don Martin: tears welled up in his eyes. His tears fell even more profusely when he approached the woman, touched her hand, and found it dead and cold. Upon some reflection, he suspected that from her hellish prison she had heard her husband recount the sad story of her life. Apparently, her grief had been unbearable—that is to say, the grief of hearing her husband once more give full credit to a bold-faced liar had done what even the many years of torture had not been able to do: it had been more than enough to kill her, as simply as that. Don Martin saw, of course, that nothing could be done for poor Helen. He moaned amid his many tears:

"Bless you, dear Helen: your days of misfortune are over, but unfortunate you are all the same, for you did not even find out how Heaven came to side with your innocence. You could not even depart from this world with that one small consolation!"

He called to Don James and said to him:

"Come in, sir! Observe the inevitable consequences of your being so cruelly deceived. Come, I beg you! All we can do now is shed tears and give vent to our emotions. Helen has no need to receive from your hands the reward for her martyrdom. God has already given it to her in Heaven."

Don James did go in. He was so perturbed he could barely walk straight. Seeing the state to which Helen had been reduced, he started to weep as if suddenly he had turned into a frail, sniveling woman. Was this the same man who had had the heart of a fierce enraged animal? He fell upon Helen's body and, kissing her hands, said:

"Alas, dearest Helen! You have left me to my own devices! Why, dear lady, couldn't you wait to wreak your vengeance upon this treacherous man, who, rather than appreciate your virtues, preferred to give credit to a cheap lie? Ask God to work His justice, for I deserve the worst punishment!"

Alarmed by this man who was distraught with grief, Don Martin, fearing that the nobleman might try something desperate, was wise enough to run up to him and remove the dagger dangling from his belt. And Don James would surely have done something desperate, considering that he kept groping for that dagger with his hand. When he couldn't find it, he began striking himself with both his fists and tore at his beard and hair, while saying things that made little sense. All flocked around him—they were all in tears—and they almost had to drag him out of the room. Nevertheless, despite their best efforts, they could not calm him down. He lost his mind completely and went raving mad! This incident struck the final blow as the culmination of all the heartrending episodes they had witnessed. Everyone present expressed his grief without inhibition, crying out loudly. Each cried as bitterly as would anyone, bereft of the person whom he had loved most dearly from the depths of his soul. In particular, the maids and the female slaves of the deceased Helen wept bitter tears. They pressed around her sobbing, interjecting one plaintive exclamation after another, now extolling her good nature, now proclaiming her virtuous life—exclamations they would not have dared utter before that day, since they knew how much it would have displeased their master to hear them.

Don Martin took notice of all this confusion and ordered the women to go elsewhere. He and a group of male servants transported Don James bodily to his bed and forced him to lie down. They tied him down to prevent him from getting up and jumping out the window, as he again and again threatened to do. Don James kept beseeching them to let him take his own life for, he said, he wanted to be with Helen wherever she was. Don Martin knew better and gave two servants strict orders not to turn aside from Don James or leave him alone even for one second. Don Martin asked whether his host had relatives in the city. They told him that he had there a cousin, son of his mother's sister, a rich gentleman of noble lineage and good character. Don Martin took steps and dispatched a male servant with a letter addressed to that cousin, bidding him come by in order to do what he could to work out a satisfactory settlement after so many catastrophes. As soon as he received news of what had happened to Don James, Don Alexander [the cousin of Don James] informed himself as much as he could about the disastrous case; and then he and his wife went over to Don James's castle, accompanied by many other members of the household, including numerous servants, male and female, and by quite a few members of the neighboring gentry who had heard of the tragic events. In the castle all these people found many reasons to mourn, and mourn they did in chorus, their hearts touched to the quick, especially after they saw Helen who seemed to become more beautiful as each hour went by. When Don Martin thought it was the right moment—he would not allow anyone to touch Helen before he thought it appropriate—they took her body out of the cubicle and placed it in a casket that they had ordered from the city. First, they buried in the castle's chapel the cadaver of the black woman who, by now, really looked like Lucifer himself. Later Don James and all the people in his household moved to the city, to Don Alexander's house, where they also transferred Helen's body along with all the goods contained in the castle. Don Martin and his comrade went along and were greatly honored by everyone. After Helen's burial, an event that prompted yet another manifestation of profuse mourning, the most renowned physicians were called in to find a cure for Don James's illness, but they could do nothing for him.

Don Martin remained in town for a full month, waiting to see whether Don James was getting any better; but, noting that all remedies were futile, he took leave of Don Alexander and boarded a ship sailing for Spain. He reached his port of destination safe and sound and eventually made his way to the royal palace. His majesty recognized the many occasions in which he had been well served by Don Martin and granted him an appropriate reward. Thereupon, Don Martin returned to Toledo where he married his beloved cousin with whom he now lives happily. So much the wiser is he, thanks to the events he witnessed with his own two eyes. We may safely assume he is not going to let himself be deceived by sinister machinations of wicked maids and male servants. Wherever he goes, he is wont to tell the story that you have heard in much the same fashion that I have recounted it to you. In this story one may find a real substantiation for the opinion that, as far as cruel behavior is concerned in cases involving honor, men are indeed to be feared, for they let themselves be driven by their cruelest instincts without bothering to look at all the evidence. This story shows likewise that many women, although innocent, endure dire punishments. Let us bear in mind therefore that, contrary to what public opinion would have us believe, not all women deserve to be blamed, as they commonly are. Now I will let the ladies be the judges of one last consideration, which might lead to disillusionment. Ask yourselves the following question: If women who are not guilty of any offense end up paying with their lives, as Helen did, what payment should be exacted from those other women who, led astray by their nonsensical and whimsical love affairs, not only bring about their own punishment but also cause the defamation of all women? Not all women, I repeat, deserve such disgrace. Upon close analysis, we would do well to conclude that, in our time, men have such a low opinion of us women that we will neither win them over by our sufferings nor oblige them with our innocence.

Here fair Phyllis concluded her tale of disenchantment which moved deeply all those who had heard her recount how patiently Helen had endured her prolonged martyrdom. The gentlemen were grateful for the courtesy that Phyllis had shown toward them and they, in turn, acknowledged her kindness with courteous words. The participants in the soiree spent a good part of the evening giving their own opinions about the story, while the night swiftly ran its course towards journey's end, making way for the sun which was approaching just as swiftly in its flaming chariot. As time went by, the attendants brought out a costly repast, very elegantly served; since the party had lasted beyond the wee hours of the morning, Lysis had decided not to serve the regular supper. All the invited guests were advised to gather earlier for the session of the following evening in order to give themselves sufficient time to attend a sumptuous banquet, already scheduled to take place after the telling of the fourth tale. . . .

BIBLIOGRAPHY

Primary Works

Cervantes Saavedra, Miguel de. *Novelas ejemplares*. Edited by Harry Sieber. 5th ed. 2 vols. Letras Hispánicas, vols. 105–6. Madrid: Cátedra, 1983.

Vega y Carpio, Lope de. *Novelas a Marcia Leonarda*. Edited by Francisco Rico. El Libro de Bolsillo, vol. 142. Madrid: Alianza Editorial, 1968.

Zayas y Sotomayor, María de. *Novelas ejemplares y amorosas o Decamaerón español*. Edited by Eduardo Rincón. 2d ed. El libro de Bolsillo, vol. 109. Madrid: Alianza Editorial, 1980.

———. *Parte segunda del Sarao y entretenimiento honesto [Desengaños amorosos]*. Edited by Alicia Yllera. Letras Hispánicas, vol. 179. Madrid: Cátedra, 1983.

Related Works

Casalduero, Joaquín. *Sentido y forma de las novelas ejemplares*. Madrid: Editorial Gredos, 1962.

———. *Sentido y forma del Quijote (1605–1615)*. Madrid: Ediciones Insula, 1949.

Foa, Sandra M. *Feminismo y forma narrativa: estudio del tema y las técnicas de María de Zayas y Sotomayor*. Valencia: Albatros Ediciones—Hispanófila, 1979.

———. "Humor and Suicide in Zayas and Cervantes." *Anales Cervantinos* 16 (1977): 71–83.

Montesa Peydro, Salvador. *Texto y contexto en la narrativa de María de Zayas.* Madrid: Dirección General de la Juventud y Promoción Sociocultural, 1981.
Pabst, Walter. *La novela corta en la teoría y en la creación literaria: notas para la historia de su antinomia en las letras románicas.* Translated by Rafael de la Vega. Madrid: Editorial Gredos, 1972.
Palomo, María del Pilar. *La novela cortesana: forma y estructura.* Barcelona: Planeta, 1976.
Place, Edwin B. *María de Zayas, an Outstanding Woman Short Story Writer of Seventeenth Century Spain.* University of Colorado Studies, no. 13. Boulder: University of Colorado Press, 1923.
Rincón, Eduardo. Introduction to *Novelas ejemplares y amorosas o Decamerón español,* by María de Zayas y Sotomayor.
Senabre, Ricardo. "La fuente de una novela de doña María de Zayas." *Revista de Filología Española* 46 (1963): 163–72.
Serrano y Sanz, Manuel. *Apuntes para una biblioteca de escritoras españolas desde el año 1401 al 1833.* Vol. 2. Madrid: Tipografía de la Revista de Archivos, Bibliotecas y Museos, 1905. 2 vols, 1903–1905.
Sylvania, Lena E. V. *Doña María de Zayas y Sotomayor. A Contribution to the Study of Her Works.* New York: Columbia University Press, 1922.
Vasileski, Irma. *María de Zayas y Sotomayor: Su época y su obra.* Madrid: Playor, 1973.
Welles, Marcia L. "María de Zayas y Sotomayor and Her *novela cortesana:* A Re-evaluation." *Bulletin of Hispanic Studies* 55 (1978): 301–10.
Yllera, Alicia. Introduction to *Parte segunda del Sarao y entretenimiento honesto,* by María de Zayas y Sotomayor.

SPANISH POET AND DRAMATIST

na Caro

RUTH LUNDELIUS

"Man's world, woman's place"[1] declares the position of sexual dominance and subordination prevalent in society during most of Western history. In Hispanic cultures, more than in most, the public world, including the cultivation of letters, was the prerogative of men, while women were customarily confined to a narrow round of domestic life. Surprisingly, however, even a cursory perusal of Manuel Serrano y Sanz's *Apuntes para una biblioteca de escritoras españolas* reveals a considerable number of recognized female authors. Most of these women, though celebrated in their own time, now lie unknown and unread. So it is, too, with those who wrote for the stage, the most popular genre of the sixteenth and seventeenth centuries.[2] These plays or *comedias* usually revolve around a stereotyped development of the relationship of the sexes—romantic comedy.[3] Of the half-dozen or so female playwrights, the most talented as a dramatist was Ana Caro Mallén de Soto (c. 1600—c. 1650), whose life and works I will examine in light of the dictum laid down at the beginning of this paragraph.

Her manifest reputation among her contemporaries comes down to us from several sources. Rodrigo Caro, the sixteenth-century antiquarian, in his *Varones insignes de Sevilla* (Famous Men of Seville), describes her as a "famous poetess who has written many plays, presented with much applause in Seville and Madrid and other places, and other works of poetry, and participated in many literary contests, for which she almost always was awarded first prize."[4] The bibliophile Nicolás Antonio also praised her as "a Spanish poet of our times, whose *comedias* were never presented in public without applause."[5] One of her two extant plays, *El Conde de Partinuplés,* was praised by Matos Fragoso, a contemporary dramatist, in his *comedia* entitled *La corsaria catalana* (The Catalan Pirate):

Leon. What *comedias* do you bring?
Autor. Famous ones
From the miraculous pens
Of Spain . . .
La bizarra Arsinda, which is
By the ingenious Cervantes,
. . . .
El Conde Partinuplés.[6]

The epithet "tenth muse," a stock laudatory phrase for feminine writers, was bestowed on her by several contemporaries, among them the editor of the *Laurel de comedias de diferentes autores,* which included *El Conde de Partinuplés.*

Yet despite her contemporary reputation, the course of her life is but little illuminated in surviving documentation, most of which was originally collected in the pioneering compilation of Serrano y Sanz.[7] Likewise, time has not been kind to her literary manuscripts, some of which seem to have perished. It is certain, however, that the Caro family, of Andalusian origin, traced a distinguished lineage into the remote past, and that Ana was born in the latter part of the sixteenth century or around 1600.[8] Except for a short stay in Madrid, her life passed in and around her native Seville, itself an important literary, theatrical, and artistic center in her day. Her works contain numerous expressions of civic pride, as she invokes the beauty and grandeur of Seville, and loving reminiscences of her native countryside. The most detailed celebration of her city occurs in the play *Valor, agravio y mujer* (Valor, Offense, and Woman) where she fondly recalls, through the words of Don Juan, the "native land" with its palace, the gardens, the Guadalquivir River, and the cathedral—"the first wonder and the eighth of the seven."[9] Accordingly, one notes that all her early works, especially the long poetic narratives on local events, were published in Seville. These early efforts might best be considered ornate newsletters in poetry. She wrote in the highly embellished, metaphoric style of distorted syntax and studied obscurity, known in Spain as *culteranismo* or *gongorismo,* characteristic of the so-called Sevillian school of poetry. Serrano y Sanz includes selections or, at least, descriptions of these works, and several have now been reprinted in modern editions.

We may conjecture, from what we are told in our sources and from what is confirmed in her surviving works, that she had received an extensive education, certainly far superior to that of the average girl of that time. She was familiar with literature, languages, history, classics, rhetoric—in short, with the staples of humanistic learning of the age. That she was able to indulge her literary inclinations speaks for a life of financial ease and social prestige, not to mention a certain liberal tendency in the family attitude toward education.

In 1637 Ana Caro went to Madrid, where she was evidently received into the innermost literary and social circles of the capital.[10] Much has been said of her close association with the better-known short story writer María de Zayas, with whom she may have resided for a time. One recalls Zayas's outspoken feminism and may assume an ideological sympathy between them; in any case, both women overcame cultural restrictions and artificial barriers to develop their natural intellectual gifts. Indeed Ana often mentions her sex to plead the indulgence of her readers, but the manner and tone of this ploy hint at a form of self-confident pride in her achievements, sheathed though it is in the language of becoming humility.[11]

Testifying to her friendship with María de Zayas are the "Décimas a Doña María de Zayas y Sotomayor," part of the eulogistic prefatory material to the first edition of Zayas's *Novelas amorosas y ejemplares* of 1638. Alonso del Castillo, in his novel *La garduña de Sevilla* (The Filcher from Seville), praising the talent of María de Zayas, adds: "Doña Ana Caro de Mallén accompanies her in Madrid, a lady from our Sevilla, to whom is due no less praise, for with her pleasing and well-reasoned verses she amazes and delights whoever hears and reads them; this is proven by the verses that she has written for the fiesta that was celebrated in the Buen Retiro this Carnaval season."[12]

The verses to which he was referring are the *Contexto de las reales fiestas que se hizieron en el Palacio del Buen Retiro a la coronación del Rey de Romanos, y entrada en Madrid de la Señora Princesa de Cariñán.* These were verses recounting the ostentatious festivities in Madrid February 15–25, 1637, which celebrated the arrival in Madrid of María, the Bourbon princess of Cariñán (Carignano), and the election of Ferdinand III of Hungary, brother-in-law of Philip IV, to the succession of the Holy Roman Empire.[13] The piece has some historical interest as a description of the lavish and ruinously expensive spectacles produced at the Spanish court. Such extravagance, as Trevor Davies remarked, "was conducted on a scale that astonished Europe."[14] Oppressed, perhaps by the deceptions and jealousies of Baroque court life, and perhaps deeply wounded in some direct personal way, Ana's residence in Madrid was rather brief.[15]

Early in 1637 she was back in Seville, where, in fact, she wrote the *Contexto,* which circulated in manuscript until she was persuaded to publish it.[16] We hear indirectly of her other literary activities. Vélez de Guevara, her better-known fellow Andalusian playwright and poet, includes her in a fictitious "academia" in his picaresque novel *El diablo cojuelo* (The Lame Devil). This "academia" supposedly included "the greatest talents (*los mayores ingenios*) of Seville," and, in fact, featured several important historical literary figures including Ana, eulogized as "the tenth muse of Seville" (*décima musa sevillana*), who read a *silva* to the Fénix.[17] The historicity of their meeting place—on the street "de las Armas"—and of some of the members has persuaded scholars, including Willard King and José Sánchez, to conjecture that there is some historical substance behind Vélez's academy.[18]

The reader notes that much of Ana's poetry was closely tied to her native city of Seville. The "Loa sacramental" (a short verse drama performed in the streets on wagons or *carros* in celebration of Corpus Christi) dates from 1639. José Sánchez Arjona discovered in the municipal archives of Seville titles of two more *autos sacramentales* by Ana which have not survived: *La puerta de la Macarena* (The Macarena Archway), presented in 1641 by the company of Manuel de Vallejo, and *La cuesta de Castilleja* (The Hill of Castilleja), which was presented in 1642.[19] And again in 1645 another *auto,* the title of which is unknown, came from her hand. On this occasion, as well as for her other *autos,* she was paid three hundred *reales* for her work. Her last known production was a sonnet ("Soneto") in praise of Tomás de Palomares, notary of Seville, and of his recent book *Estilo nuevo de escrituras públicas* (The New Style of Public Writings), which appeared in 1645.[20] It seems likely that she died soon afterward, perhaps in the terrible plague which decimated Seville during the years 1649–1652.

Through the centuries, except for an occasional passing meritorious reference, usually in histories of distinguished Sevillians, Ana Caro's reputation sank into obscurity.[21] She is remembered now only as a very minor playwright, and principally on the basis of only one play, *El Conde de Partinuplés*. Nineteenth-century critical opinion on her tended to be cautiously neutral. Mesonero Romanos, in his edition of the *Biblioteca de autores españoles* (*BAE*), states that he included *El Conde de Partinuplés* for its merit relative to other chivalric plays, and also because the author was a woman, one who enjoyed considerable popularity in her time.[22] Her work has only recently begun to be studied by a few twentieth-century critics. Professor Frederick de Armas devoted a chapter of his book *The Invisible Mistress* to *El Conde de Partinuplés*.[23] Elizabeth Ordóñez, in her article "The Woman and Her Text," studies the dramatic work of Ana from a feminist perspective, while Matthew Stroud finds *Valor, agravio y mujer* to be an extremely traditional play.[24] In the following pages I offer an analysis of the two surviving plays, beginning with the better-known *El Conde de Partinuplés*. It is my contention that the author adheres to the values and structures of the patriarchal society of her day but, at the same time, fantasizes a reversal in the roles of the sexes and intimates a certain reorientation in the position of women in society. The reversal of roles she employs for dramatic effect, though as a consequence an implicit championing of a more liberalized status for women emerges throughout her dramatic creations.

The plot of *El Conde de Partinuplés* is a reworking of a popular medieval romance, the *Partonopeus de Blois*.[25] Both *comedia* and romance turn on the immemorial folk topos of the mysterious lover and the disastrous romantic consequences of the irrepressible curiosity of the other consort.[26] Ana, however, recasts the characters, motives, and destinies of her figures.[27] Her heroine, Rosaura, princess of Constantinople, lies under the shadow of a dangerous astral prognostication cast by her astrologer-father, Aurelio, that she will be dishonored and her country endangered at the hands of a faithless suitor. But on the other hand, circumstances oblige her to marry. In these foreboding difficulties, Rosaura turns to the magical powers of her cousin Aldora to entrap the most promising suitor possible. This choice falls on Partinuplés of Blois. The horoscope also had foretold that the kingdom could be saved by an *industria,* a stratagem or ingenuity, and it is the exercise of this ingenuity by the female protagonists that comprises the development of the plot. A love idyll, abetted by Aldora's magic and by Rosaura's cunning, ensues but is disrupted when the count, against his pledged word, seeks to discover the features of his invisible mistress. The dire horoscope seems on the verge of vindication: Rosaura has been deceived; her country is invaded by the forces of Lisbella, Partinuplés's vengeful ex-betrothed; and unwittingly Partinuplés has miserably failed the test Rosaura put to his fidelity. But the power of chivalric deeds, the curiosity and jealousy aroused by another disguise (that of the hero), and the initiative of Rosaura succeed in healing the breach between the two lovers.

The *comedia* concludes, as was customary, with the marriage of all the eligible partners in the plot. Marriages symbolized for the Golden Age spectator more than a pleasing emotional conclusion; they constituted a powerful reaffirmation of the institutions of the established social order and of their supposed foundations in nature itself. Astrology and magic, enchantment and disguise, impossible transformations and uncontrollable passions were common motifs that held a deep fascination for the imagination of the contemporary audience. It is Ana's handling of her characters and their motives that lifts *El Conde* above the level of the average chivalric play. Her most important innovation is the new twist she gives to the portrait of Rosaura, exemplifying a common type of *comedia* heroine who refuses to fall in love and marry. This heroine averse to romance—the conventional destiny of women—is typically motivated by misplaced vanity and arrogant disdain for men, and the whole dramatic action of the *comedia* in which she appears is to humble her pride, bring her to her senses, and reconcile her to her natural duty—marriage.[28] But Rosaura's coldness, as de Armas points out, is not grounded on indifference but instead stems from the fears of betrayal suggested by her father's horoscope.[29] Here Ana is able to turn the tables on the conventional perception of this character type and to shift the culpability from the ill nature of women to the flawed character and infidelity of the male. And in effecting this shift she is able, at the same time, to center the audience's sympathy on Rosaura and her not-so-feminine self-assertiveness against fate and duplicity. The tone of independence and the other attributes of masculine self-assertion common to this type—courage, initiative, a sense of position, and an openness to knowledge—are also characteristics of Ana's heroines. Yet Rosaura has many feminine qualities also, as evidenced by the strength of love she now feels. She convinces herself that if she won Partinuplés he would not break his word. Aldora's warning that he is already betrothed to Lisbella serves to inflame her jealousy and curiosity, both recognized as powerful catalysts of love in the *comedia.*

It is with a portrait, an image of Rosaura, brought magically before his eyes, that Partinuplés first falls in love. This is in keeping with the then-popular theory that love entered through the eyes and thus had a physiological basis; hence, too, love might come at first sight, almost instantaneously. But it is with the further aid of Aldora's magic that Rosaura fans the flames of Partinuplés's curiosity and desire in a scene where she alternately shows herself mysteriously transposed to a beast in the hunt and back again into a ravishing beauty before again mysteriously disappearing, leaving the challenge: "If you seek me you will find me."[30] The hunt, a common erotic symbol, may merge with the pursuit of knowledge or become an instructive chase, as it does here. Marcelle Thiébaux writes: "The pursued game acted as a lure, a guide, a psychopomp to draw the hunter ineluctably on his course into unfamiliar, unsuspected, or forbidden territory where a crucial contest would take place that would change his life."[31] In this way Rosaura keeps her presence alive in Partinuplés's imagination, tantalizing his curiosity while at the same time denying him her open countenance and love. In such an instance the author uses a common *comedia* ploy called the *burla,* a trick or illusion, in the course of unfolding her plot.

The *burla* is also employed in a pivotal scene, the banquet, basic in some form to all versions of the romance. Here the banquet takes place in an enchanted palace and is a mixture of low comedy with growing love and curiosity. The comic element, where Ana's talents shine forth, is provided through Gaulín, a servant-jester, with his constant references to hunger, his fears and suspicions, and his antifeminist jibes. The *burla* is played on the level appropriate to the social status of the hero and also that of the servant. Finally, urged on by the baser impulses of his servant, the count can no longer restrain his curiosity and brings a light. The flaw that precipitates the lovers' crisis is clearly shown to reside in the unbridled curiosity of the man.

Yet in her description of women in this popular genre of drama, the author still introduces the full gamut of traditional male fantasies concerning women, ranging from devil to angel. The count had questioned Rosaura, "monster, woman, or deity?" (p. 128). Logically, however, it is the *gracioso* who most often reiterates the commonplaces of misogyny: "demon, witch, monster" and "a woman or a serpent, which is the same thing" (p. 138). These and similar comments are the expression of stereotypical male fears of women and feminine power. The exotic figure of the mysterious, magically powerful princess is a particularly suitable presence to evoke the mystique of feminine control over nature and man, to excite the audience with the suggestion of forbidden knowledge, and to extol woman as a rational, assertive, self-sufficient individual equal to man and capable of directing her own life and the lives of others.[32] But her digression from the accepted proprieties of feminine behavior demonstrated through the preceding action of the play is ultimately resolved by the traditional course of the princess to the altar with the man of her choice.

Ana's other play, *Valor, agravio y mujer* is similar to *El Conde* in the characterization of the feminine protagonist, Leonor, who adopts an even more masculine stance than Rosaura in order to resolve her romantic crisis and to vindicate her honor. The role-reversal motif is immediately suggested in the title, which juxtaposes traditionally antithetical attributes, for valor—physical or moral—was a masculine quality not typically associated with women. The stage appeal of the woman dressed as a man was especially strong in the Spanish theater where, from earliest times, women played the female roles. An actress cross-dressing and mimicking male behavior was visibly displaying more of her form than custom normally sanctioned as well as opening up all manner of erotic and comic possibilities for the plot. Despite repeated ecclesiastical condemnations of this spectacle, the woman disguised as a man quickly became a popular stock character in the *comedia*.[33] The endless opportunities the role-reversal figure provided for romance, intrigue, confusion, mistaken identity, satire, and social criticism secured her an enduring popularity, so that even Lope de Vega's dry recommendation of this type is understated: "customarily / the masculine disguise has much appeal."[34] Of the catalogue of motives for assuming masculine attire compiled by Carmen Bravo-Villasante, the most common was the pursuit of love or the resolution of some romantic entanglement.[35] So it is that Doña Leonor abandons her skirts for the breeches and doublet of an officer, and, as Don Leonardo, sets out for Flanders where she intends to bring her errant lover, Don Juan, to heel after he has abandoned her. Again Ana Caro displays her talent for characterization, while at the same time using her character quietly to question the whole status of women in the society of the time. In this way she raises the interest of her drama above the level of the average run-of-the-mill "abandoned woman" play.

In the first scenes of the play all creation—both the world of nature and the world of men—seems to reflect the disorder, menace, and violence accompanying the perfidy of Don Juan. Out of this universal disharmony Ana weaves a picture of the weakness, passivity and social repression of women in contrast to the unrestrained will and freedom of men. When the play opens, two women are discovered just after they have been thrown from their runaway horses—a common symbol of unbridled sexual passion. They are shown alone and afoot amid a threatening storm in an unfamiliar, frightening forest surrounded by precipitous mountain peaks.[36] The symbolism is typically Baroque and masculine—the darkened forest, the frowning heavens, the threat from lightning and violent winds. The imagery of the whole situation is heavy with implicit danger to the women. The peril materializes in the next scene, when the women are on the point of being robbed by two bandits. At this juncture Don Juan, and his servant-*gracioso,* Tomillo, who have also been lost in the storm, appear on the scene, and Don Juan, with the impersonal gallantry of his class, rescues the ladies from their captors.

The scene soon shifts to Flanders, where all the characters have now been assembled. In a monologue Don Juan explains that he left Seville to try his fortune in a new setting, because he had tired of the lady he seduced. Just then, Don Leonardo arrives, accompanied by her lackey-*gracioso,* Ribete.

Leonor is so intent on replacing feminine diffidence with masculine assertiveness that she affirms to her servant that she *is* a man. "My offense changed my being" (p. 185).[37] The *burla* that betrayed her honor she will set aright by employing her masculine disguise. As she said, "In this suit I will recover my lost honor" (p. 185). Furthermore Leonor announces that she will capitalize on all the opportunities tradition reserved for men. She constantly appeals to her "reason"—by implication, an assertion of independence from the subordination of women to the "reason" and "will" of their patriarchical protectors. Her male clothing, which symbolizes the masculine rights and prerogatives she has taken up, serves, however, to keep before the audience the male/female ambiguity of her position. The *gracioso* dwells, with sensual enthusiasm, on the effeminate appearance of the disguised actress, but in mind, speech, and manner, Leonor aggressively moves to counter her effeminate appearance. She compares herself to the warlike women of classical mythology; she struts and swears with all the bluster of a seasoned soldier; and she draws her sword without hesitation to challenge the faithless Don Juan. The erotic element, especially evident in the visually oriented stage, is complemented with satire of male conceits and posturings.

Leonor's role reversal leads to a parody of the egocentric male who, when threatened in his honor, tended to reaffirm the full authority of his being and good name with the peculiarly Spanish declaration: "I am who I am." According to Leo Spitzer, the essence of the individual was expressed through the name: it was a sign of lineage, nobility, and self-worth, with echoes of identification with Christian tradition and decades of patriarchal status and pride.[38] The name served to give the male a tangible niche in the social and physical landscape. Leonor parodies this androcentric formula by appropriating and then inverting it: "Yo, ¿soy quien soy?" (I, am I who I am? [p. 185]). Her ambiguous position imparts a biting humor to this declaration. And, of course, her pronouncement underlines her disguise, for in her new persona she creates her own *burla* or deception that keeps everyone else in confusion and Leonor in control of each situation and person until her machinations come together in her final revenge.

The play is a tour de force in the use of dramatic irony, mistaken identities, misspoken conversations, and the baroque device of deceiving with the truth ("engañar con la verdad") in order to advance the action, to create comedy, and to focus the erotic attention of the audience. Appearances are never what they seem. Thus, when Leonor confronts Don Juan in her role as Leonardo and accuses him of dishonoring a certain Sevillian lady, Doña Leonor, she has Don Juan completely off balance, while she is in full control. "I know what I can do," she says, and "he will not go unless I wish it" (p. 195). She interrogates, accuses, and recriminates him in the high rhetoric of outraged innocence: ". . . you are / A treacherous, ungrateful, fickle, / Unjust, deceitful, false, / Perjurous, barbarous, facile / Godless, faithless breaker of promises" (p. 196). Although the depiction of the faithless lover was a very common motif, Ana deploys the full weight of her talents to indict man as the less moral, the less perfect of the sexes; in short, she inverts the order of contemporary prejudices on this issue. Through Leonor she rejects the double standard of morality and squarely denounces Don Juan's lapse from ethical responsibility as the primary agent in Leonor's dishonor. The onus of guilt falls not upon woman's weakness but upon Don Juan's misuse of masculine freedom and power.

Much of the third act of the play is a dramatic unfolding of this condemnation of the double standard of morality. Leonardo spreads the word that he is in love with Leonor, but says he knows that she has been deceived and he has come to kill the man who dishonored her, thus avenging dishonor so that he can marry her himself. As in so many *comedias* this tactic serves to provoke jealousy, and Don Juan's envy revives his former love. If this stratagem will ultimately lead to a reunion of the lovers and marriage, the immediate reaction of all the men, who hold the traditional bias against women, is a chorus of condemnations of the unfortunate woman. And Don Juan, the guiltiest, is loudest of all in execration, as he laments: "Ah, if only she had been an honest woman" (p. 210).

The ambiguity of Leonor's position is skillfully exploited by Ana to question the assumptions of inherent masculine superiority and to suggest a more even balance in the social status of the sexes. Northrop Frye points out that a common theme of comedy is a struggle between the old order and the new.[39] In the guise of "Leonardo" she insists on "his" honor and adds: "for I am master (mistress) of it (honor) and of Leonor also" (p. 210). She continues the fiction of speaking as a male character, but at the same time she is speaking self-referentially, as a woman. And in doing so she plainly fashions her own independence. She thus wrestles control of her own honor and of her own future away from patriarchal protection or guidance. Leonor's disguise gives her the advantage of manipulating each situation with the utmost ingenuity, creating hilarious confusion, misunderstanding, and double-talk until Don Juan has been reduced to nearly irrational confusion. In this comedy of errors the author "carries baroque theatrical devices to the limits of parody"[40] to expose the artificiality of the conventional distinctions between the sexes. Elizabeth Ordóñez suggests that the female protagonists of Ana Caro's plays "emerge as analogues of the playwright as they dispose the lives around them and experiment gleefully with the frequently absurd conventions of baroque theater. . . . Woman's near mastery of the unsuspecting male makes of him her actor in her play."[41] And in so doing the author reverses the stereotyping of the sexes. Thus men are depicted as weak, inconstant, untrustworthy, and false, while women are shown as creative, resourceful, self-assertive, and, most important, as possessors of knowledge and its uses. Yet this reevaluation of the relations of the sexes, and its implications, is never rebellious or strident in Ana's plays.

In a popular and public genre of literature like the *comedia*, commercial and artistic success were inextricably bound to pleasing the deeper instincts of the audience. So Ana Caro conformed externally to conventional formats of male-authored texts. She used the dramaturgical devices, plots, and conventions of the age. But she also adapted to her own ends two male fantasies of female character types—significantly, the woman apparently averse to marriage and the woman disguised as a man. These stock figures allow her to mimic and satirize male behavior, to show the artificiality of the grounds supposedly separating the sexes, and to discredit the double standard of the honor system. The illusion in both plays—the world of enchantment and magic in *El Conde de Partinuplés* and that of disguise and make-believe in *Valor, agravio y mujer*—provide an imaginary stage or world where the accepted social roles of the sexes are reversed. Here the preferences and desires of the woman are given paramount importance, and the claims of the female ego receive satisfaction. The ultimate wisdom of locating women's destiny in marriage is not questioned. But in the end, when the *burla* becomes *veras,* when the fiction turns to reality, we see not the subjugation of female to male but the happy acceptance by Rosaura and Leonor of the suitors they have freely chosen. The role reversal device here does not degenerate into the image of the "unruly" or "uncontrollable" or anti-social female, the topsy-turvy world of a disintegrating society—all reasons frequently advanced for the repression of women.[42] Rather, the women use the inversion of roles motif for entirely creditable purposes—to escape a cruel fate or to right a wrong done to them. Furthermore, the women in these self-assertive roles are not condemned or depicted as erring in any way; instead, they emerge entirely triumphant, so that at the conclusion it is the men who have been rendered repentant and wiser. Both sexes are implicitly shown to have much to gain in liberalizing woman's position in society. The author is careful to ensure the audience's sympathy with the female characters, and thereby she engages support for her perception of the equality between the sexes.

I have chosen selections from *El Conde de Partinuplés* for translation because it is probably the better known of Ana's two plays and it also exemplifies her literary treatment of a romance that remained popular for centuries. The first selection involves Rosaura's dilemma over her obligation to marry and her consideration of possible suitors. The second selection takes place in the enchanted palace where the count brings a light.

NOTES

1. Elizabeth Janeway, *Man's World, Woman's Place: A Study in Social Mythology.*
2. See La Barrera, *Catálogo bibliográfico y biográfico del teatro antiguo español.*
3. *Comedia* is the Spanish term used to designate a play during the sixteenth and seventeenth centuries. It refers to tragedies as well as comedies.
4. Caro, *Varones insignes de Sevilla,* 73.
5. *Biblioteca hispana nova,* 2:344.
6. See Serrano y Sanz, *Apuntes,* 1:179.
7. For further bibliography see Simón Díaz, *Bibliografía de la literatura hispánica,* vol. 7, nos. 5102–27; and for a brief bio-bibliographical review see the entry by de Armas in *Women Writers of Spain,* 66–67.
8. De Armas places her birthdate in the latter third of the sixteenth century (*Women Writers of Spain,* 66), but López Estrada believes she was born approximately in the first decade of the seventeenth century (*Homenaje a A. Pérez Gómez,* 58).

9. Serrano y Sanz, *Apuntes,* 1:183.

10. She tells us in the *Contexto de las reales fiestas* that she wished to see the Spanish court and arrived in Madrid on January 1, 1937, during a snowstorm (fol. 13r).

11. In the *Contexto* alone one finds here and there:

> Por muger ignorante . . . (1r).
> Que admita mis borrones le suplico, si por muger, como muger me ampara . . . (p. 12r).
> Suplícole, por de muger, reciba el don afectuoso (31v).

12. *Clásicos Castellanos,* ed. Federico Ruiz Morcuende, 67.

13. For more information see Alfred Morel-Fatio, *L'Espagne au XVI*[e] *et au XVII*[e] *siècle,* 606 ff.; Antonio Rodríguez Villa, *La corte y monarquía de España en los años de 1636 y 1637,* esp. 101 ff.; José Deleito y Piñuela, *El rey se divierte,* 211 ff.; and Martin Hume, *The Court of Philip IV.*

14. Trevor Davies, *Spain in Decline,* 104.

15. There are numerous indications in the *Contexto.* For example, near the beginning she describes the snowfall as "sad portent of my misfortunes" (p. 14v), and the third part contains such frequent references to disillusion and deception, hatred and envy that they seem to be more than baroque commonplaces.

16. In the brief "To the Reader" of the *Contexto,* she tells us that she had not originally planned to publish the piece; that some time elapsed between the composition and publication, during which time it probably circulated in manuscript; and that she was finally persuaded by friends or admirers to publish it (A3r). In the dedication to the Conde Duque of Olivares, preceding the second part, she tells us that she wrote the piece at Seville, that the Conde Duque saw it, and again that she had been urged to publish it (16r).

17. *El diablo cojuelo,* 185–87.

18. See *El diablo cojuelo,* 186, n. 3; also King, *Prosa novelística y academias literarias,* 82; and Sánchez, *Academias literarias del Siglo de Oro,* 215 ff. (Academia del Diablo Cojuelo) and 328 ff. (Academias de Sevilla).

19. *Anales del teatro en Sevilla,* 349–74; *El teatro en Sevilla en los siglos XVI y XVII,* 287, 311, 248–50.

20. Seville: Simón Fajardo Arias Montano, 1645.

21. The interested reader may consult the following: Diego Ortiz de Zúñiga, *Anales eclesiásticos y seculares de la muy noble y leal ciudad de Sevilla,* 586; Juan Bautista Cubíe, *Las mugeres vindicadas de las calumnias de los hombres, con un catálogo de las españolas, que más se han distinguido en ciencias y armas,* 84; Fermín Araña de Varflora, *Hijos de Sevilla ilustres en santidad, letras, armas, artes o dignidad,* 35; Angel Lasso de la Vega y Argüelles, *Escuela poética sevillana en los siglos XVI y XVII,* 205; and Francisco Torres Montes, *Dramaturgos andaluces del Siglo de Oro,* 46.

22. *BAE,* 49:xi.

23. De Armas, *The Invisible Mistress: Aspects of Feminism and Fantasy in the Golden Age.*

24. Ordóñez, "Woman and Her Text in the Works of María de Zayas and Ana Caro," 3–15; Stroud, "La literatura y la mujer en el Barroco: *Valor, agravio y mujer* de Ana Caro," 605–12.

25. For the sources and diffusion of the legend, in addition to *The Invisible Mistress,* the interested reader may consult Helaine Newstead, "The Traditional Background of Partonopeus de Blois," 916–46; and Joseph Gildea and Leon P. Smith, eds., *Partonopeus de Blois: A French Romance of the Twelfth Century.* Richard C. Smith's introduction to his editions of the 1497 Seville text in "Partinuplés, conde de Bles," DAI 38 (1977–78): 4872A, includes a detailed survey of the text tradition in Castilian and Catalán.

26. A misogynistic twist is exemplified in the interpolated story of Psyche and Cupid in

Apuleius's *The Golden Ass*. Psyche's curiosity is so great that she brings a lamp to gaze upon the sleeping Cupid, thereby causing disaster.

27. With the revival of chivalric literature in Spain during the sixteenth century, this romance became very popular, and many adaptations and traces appear in Golden Age plays and short stories. De Armas discusses traces in María de Zayas's "Tarde llega el desengaño" (*The Invisible Mistress,* 44–46).

28. McKendrick, *Woman and Society in the Spanish Drama of the Golden Age,* 145.

29. De Armas, *The Invisible Mistress,* 177.

30. *BAE,* 49:128. All further references are to this edition.

31. Thiébaux, *The Stag of Love: The Chase in Medieval Literature,* 56. See also pp. 104–5 for the Partonopeus legend.

32. Although it was undoubtedly the legend of Partinuplés and the role reversal that attracted Ana Caro, the influence of the legend of Psyche is an apt one here. As discussed by Erich Neumann, Psyche develops from the unknowing, passive, undifferentiated female archetype into the "female psyche," individuated, with ego and rational capability. It is precisely the latter characteristics that the author wishes to emphasize in Rosaura and Aldora. See *Amor and Psyche. The Psychic Development of the Feminine.*

33. Carmen Bravo-Villasante, *La mujer vestida de hombre en el teatro español. Siglos XVI–XVII;* reviewed by B. B. Ashcom, "Concerning 'La Mujer en Hábito de Hombre' in the Comedia." For a broader approach see McKendrick, *Woman and Society.*

34. A. Morel-Fatio, ed., *Bulletin Hispanique* 3 (1901): 381, ll. 327–28.

35. *La mujer vestida,* 223.

36. For an interesting discussion of imagery of confinement, see Sandra Gilbert and Susan Gubar, *The Madwoman in the Attic,* 83ff.

37. Serrano y Sanz, *Apuntes,* 1:185. All further references are to this edition.

38. "Soy quien soy," 113–27. Spitzer studies various influences that converge to give total meaning to the phrase, including the "sum qui sum" with which the Vulgate renders the words of Jehovah.

39. Frye, *Anatomy of Criticism,* 164.

40. Ordóñez, "Women and Her Text," 12.

41. Ibid., 13.

42. See Natalie Z. Davis, *Society and Culture in Early Modern France,* chapter 5, and Barbara A. Babcock, ed., *The Reversible World: Symbolic Inversion in Art and Society,* especially the introduction.

From El Conde de Partinuplés

ACT I

Rosaura. I am not, Aldora,
Content with my destiny,
I fear those prophecies
And I know not if I will choose
Some ingrate for a master;
For my soul warns me
That he may be barbarous.

I would like, my cousin,
To see and know first
These gentlemen whom
My vassals have proposed to me,
And, if one pleases me,
Manner, presence, and mind,
To know his temperament
And see within his soul,
His heart, his affability,
Discourse, and understanding,
Penetrate his intentions,
Examine the constitution
Of his heart, if it is peaceful
Or ambitious or foolish.
But if I can know
Nothing of this,
And will have to throw myself
Upon the deep and haughty sea
In selecting for master a man
Who will have free reign
Over the kingdom of my heart
Whether he be ambitious or blind,
What pleasure can I have
When, oh God, I contemplate myself
A slave, being a lady,
And vassal, being a mistress?
Aldora. Discreetly you speak,
But it's impossible
To penetrate the hearts
And the secrets of the soul.
The most that I can do for you today,
Since you know my genius
In regard to the magic art,
Is to show you first
In visible reflections
These proposed princes.
And if one presses to know
The causes by the effects,
By observing their activities
It will be easy
To know which one is understanding and informed,
Which arrogant or modest,

Which discreet or studious,
Which loving and which tender.
And thus it is possible
To lean toward one of them
Before, in their presence,
Your decorum is at stake,
Not daring to choose.

Rosaura. Oh, Aldora, how indebted I am to you!
If you will do what you say,
Make haste, cousin, make haste.
For you know that we women
Ordinarily sin through extreme curiosity.
Make known your portents,
Work your prodigious powers,
For I am dying to see them.

Aldora. Soon you will see them. Attention.

Rosaura. With all my soul I am concentrating.

Aldora. Unhappy spirits
That inhabit the frightful kingdom
Of those black flames,
Without light yet with fire,
I conjure, urge, and command you,
That you reveal all together at one time
In whatever pursuits they might be engaged,
The exalted princes,
Frederick of Poland,
Robert of Transylvania,
Edward of Scotland, from France
Partinuplés. Do these suffice?

Rosaura. Yes, cousin, I am amazed.

(The theater is changed and the four are revealed in the manner in which they are named.)

. . . .

Aldora. This one whom you see so gallant,
Who in the crystal of a mirror
Reflects the perfection
Of his handsome, resplendent body,
Is Frederick of Poland.

(Each one is revealed.)

This one who is reading,
Studious and absorbed,

Is Edward, of the kingdom
Of Scotland noble prince,
Wise, clever, and discreet,
Philosopher and astrologer.
That one who, with shining steel
Adorns his gallant chest,
Is the brave Robert,
Prince of Transylvania.
The one who is visible there
Pensive or absorbed, gazing at
The sun of a beautiful portrait
Is the famous Partinuplés,
Noble heir of France,
Nephew of his king,
Who offers to him in marriage
Lisbella, his cousin,
A noble prince, modest,
Gentle, courtly,
Valiant, spirited, and wise.
This one is more worthy of being
Among them all your master,
If his marriage were not
(As I have told you)
Arranged to Lisbella.
Rosaura. To Lisbella?
For that reason, Aldora, for that reason
I want that man.
Aldora. There is an obstacle,
As I told you.
Rosaura. Ay, Aldora, if there were not,
Another would please me, another would be
For my majesty a selection
Important to insist upon,
But if I see that he belongs to another
How is it possible,
Through envy or desire,
Not to attempt an impossibility
Even if his charm were less?
(The theater is changed as before and everything is covered.)
Now he has disappeared,
And his charming image is no longer
Before my eyes, and my soul remains,

Shall I say in sorrow or torment?
I will say in torment and in sorrow
Due to his absence and my jealousy.

ACT 3

Rosaura. How have you been?
Conde. Listen:
As without sun the day,
As without stars the night,
As without light the dawn,
Sad, in darkness, and uneasy.
And you, how have you been?
Rosaura. Listen:
As without rain the flowers,
As without flowers the meadows,
As without verdure the mountains,
Bewildered, grieved, and sad.
Gaulín. What a gush of hyperbata!
A poor lackey am I,
For I have disrupted the order
Of the farce, by not having
A lady to whom to speak words of love.
The poet overlooked this;
May you pardon her for it.
Rosaura. Be seated and tell me of the feats
Of your victory.
Gaulín. Is my master
Made of bronze?

(They sit down on cushions of the raised dais.)

Conde. Listen, now.
Rosaura. I am listening.
May you [yourself] be deaf, and may God forgive me.
Conde. We left, as you ordered,
Gaulín and I on two swift
Hypogriffs, that seemed to be
Two live flashes of lightning.
I found Paris surrounded
By enemy squadrons,
That were delighted to sight it
Without significant resistance.
Because my uncle, although he was acting,
Sometimes with pleas, sometimes with shouts,

As general,
Was putting his people in order
Without valor or strength,
His noble years drained
By reason of
Long years of invasions.
I broke the resistance
Of the enemy, and in the name
Of the French army
I attempted to bring
Its disorder under my command,
Instilling in the soldiers' hearts
So much of my valor and esteem,
That in three hours
We found ourselves the victors
Over the arrogant Scots and Britons.
My uncle and Lisbella arrived
And seeing me (do not be angered)
He was content, she surprised.
. . . Listen.

(She fell asleep!)

I say: Are you listening, my lady?
What an opportunity, Gaulín!
Gaulín. Well, Count,
Don't waste it; it would be madness.
Conde. In order to put an end to confusion,
Praise God, if I had a light
I would attempt, even though she might be angered
To know . . . Ah, my lady, are you asleep?
Gaulín. What are you waiting for? For her to snore?
Is she by chance a barmaid?
In those halls
A light can be obtained.
Shall I go for it?
Conde. Yes; no; are you listening?
Hurry, but no.

(He gets up.)

Gaulín. Make up your mind.
Isn't she a woman and you a man?
Is she going to kill you?
Conde. You are right.
Go and get it.
Gaulín. He made up his mind.

Let's resolve this puzzle.

(He leaves.)

Conde. How greatly I err, my love!
Desire obliges one to undertake many things
When pursuing a delusion.
Is it possible that I (heavens!)
Fail to live up to my obligations
To satisfy my desire?

(Gaulín comes out with a candle.)

Gaulín. Here is the light.
Conde. With this curiosity everything will be over.
I know that it portends my death,
But now I have the opportunity;
This time my word of honor will be broken.
Give me the candle.
Gaulín. Here it is.
Conde. Let us overcome fear, my love.
For heaven's sake, what beauty!
Such perfection and such harmony.
Heaven exceeded itself
Surpassing the beauty
Of nature in her.
Don't you recognize the beast of the forest,
Gaulín?
Gaulín. I am amazed.
What divine perfection!
Conde. Beautiful sphinx, even more perplexing
Is my life after seeing you;
You kill slowly asleep,
You conquer quickly awake.
Confused, my soul grapples with
Its anticipated harm;
For if unknown evils
One sun I saw in the past,
Now to foretell my death
I look upon two suns eclipsed.
Most beautiful creation
Of the supreme power,
What has it availed you
To insist on denying yourself?
Oh, fortunate indeed be the sleep
That suspended your cares!
They are now unnecessary deceptions,

For it augurs clear malice
To want to hide your face
If you kill with eyes closed.
Rosaura (Half asleep). Continue, count, continue.
Oh, God! What is this? Your treachery
Deceived me. What have you done, ingrate?

(She gets up.)

Gaulín. A daughter in the house
And bad nights are ours.
Rosaura. Wretched man,
Such double dealing with me?
False, treacherous, unfaithful,
What boldness urged
Your evil nature to such a monstrous
Offense, deceitful, weak!

(Aldora comes out.)

Aldora. What's the matter? Why are you shouting?
Beautiful Rosaura, what is this?
Rosaura. Aldora, that barbarous man,
Have him thrown off a precipice, as an ingrate,
Treacherous, deceitful, perverse.
Death to the count, this shall be,
Even though it breaks to pieces
My heart, which adores him
With pure and noble love.
This is necessary vengeance
Even though grief chokes me
Because now, doubtlessly,
Since I ill-bestowed my favors,
The fatal prophecy has been fulfilled
By the treacherous count.
May he die before my kingdom
Suffers him; from that tower
Have him thrown to the abyss
Since he offended with treachery
So much love.
Aldora. Grave offense!
He is French; you shouldn't be surprised,
For they never keep their word.
Conde. Listen.
Rosaura. There are no satisfactions
For such treachery, for such wrong.
Gaulín [to Aldora]. For heaven's sake, calm her,

Lady.
Rosaura. You also prattle,
Vile servant?
Gaulín. A curse upon my tongue, indeed!
Conde. Since you are deciding the punishment,
Heed . . .
Rosaura. What should I heed?
Conde. Love . . .
Rosaura. What satisfactions?
Conde. Remember . . .
Rosaura. Speak no more.
Conde. The happy favors . . .
Rosaura. What impudence! Quickly, Aldora,
For with his very words
He is inciting my ire
To take vengeance.
Get him out of my sight;
Be done with it, or I shall call
My guard . . .

BIBLIOGRAPHY

Primary Works

Caro de Mallén Soto, Ana. *El Conde de Partinuplés.* In *Laurel de comedias de diferentes autores. Quarta parte.* Madrid: Imprenta Real, 1653. Modern edition in the *Biblioteca de Autores Españoles.* Vol. 49. *Dramáticos posteriores a Lope de Vega,* ed. Ramón Mesonero Romanos, 125–38. Madrid: Sucesores de Hernando, 1924.

———. *Contexto de las reales fiestas que se hizieron en el Palacio del Buen Retiro a la coronación del Rey de Romanos, y entrada en Madrid de la Señora Princesa de Cariñán en tres discursos.* Madrid: Imprenta del Reino, 1637. Modern facsimile edition by Antonio Pérez y Gómez. Valencia: Talleres de Tipografía Moderna, 1951.

———. "Décimas a Doña María de Zayas y Sotomayor." In María de Zayas, *Novelas amorosas y ejemplares.* Zaragosa, 1638. Ed. Agustín de Amezúa. Madrid: Aldus, S.A. de Artes Gráficas, 1948.

———. *Grandiosa vitoria que alcançó de los Moros de Tetuán Iorge de Mendoça y Piçaña, General de Ceuta, quitándoles gran suma de ganados cerca de las mesmas puertas de Tetuán.* Seville: Simón Faxardo, 1633. Modern edition by Francisco López Estrada. In *Homenaje a Blecua,* 337–46. Madrid: Editorial Gredos, 1983.

———. *Loa sacramental, que se representó en el carro de Antonio de Prado, en las fiestas del Corpus de Seuilla, este año de 1639.* Seville: Juan Gómez de Blas, n.d. Modern edition by F. López Estrada. In *Revista de Dialectología y Tradiciones Populares (Homenaje a Vicente García de Diego)* 32 (1976): 263–74.

———. *Relación de la grandiosa fiesta, y octava, que en la iglesia parroquial de el glorioso*

San Miguel de la Ciudad de Seuilla, hizo don García Sarmiento de Sotomayor . . . Seville: Andrés Grande, 1635.

———. *Relación, en que se da cuenta de las grandiosas fiestas, que en el conuento de N. P. S. Francisco de la Ciudad de Seuilla se an hecho a los Santos Mártires del Iapón.*Seville: Pedro Gómez, 1628. Modern edition by F. López Estrada. In *Homenaje a Antonio Pérez Gómez,* 51–69. Valencia: Artes Gráficas Soler, 1978.

———. "Soneto." In Tomás de Palomares, *Estilo nuevo de escrituras públicas.* Seville: Simón Fajardo de Arias Montano, 1645.

———. *Valor, agravio y mujer.* Ed. M. Serrano y Sanz. In *Apuntes para una biblioteca de escritoras españolas,* 1:79–212.

———. *Valor, agravio, y muger. Comedia famosa.* Seville: Francisco de Leefdael, n.d. Singly printed text, University of Toronto Library.

Serrano y Sanz, Manuel. *Apuntes para una biblioteca de escritoras españolas.* 2 vols. 1903. Reprint, in *Biblioteca de Autores Españoles,* vol. 268. Madrid, 1975.

Related Works

Abel, Elizabeth, ed. *Writing and Sexual Difference.* Chicago: University of Chicago Press, 1982.

Antonio, Nicolás. *Biblioteca hispana nova.* Madrid: J. de Ibarra, 1783–88.

Araña de Varflora, Fermín. *Hijos de Sevilla ilustres en santidad, letras, armas, artes o dignidad.* Seville: Imprenta de Vásquez, 1791.

Ashcom, B. B. "Concerning 'La Mujer en Hábito de Hombre' in the *Comedia.*" *Hispanic Review* 28 (1960): 43–62.

Babcock, Barbara A., ed. *The Reversible World. Symbolic Inversion in Art and Society.* Ithaca: Cornell University Press, 1978.

Bautista Cubíe, Juan. *Las mugeres vindicadas de las calumnias de los hombres, con un catálogo de las españolas, que más se han distinguido en ciencias y armas.* Madrid, 1768.

Bravo-Villasante, Carmen. *La mujer vestida de hombre en el teatro español. Siglos XVI–XVII.* Madrid: Revista de Occidente, 1955.

Caro, Rodrigo. *Varones insignes en letras naturales de la ilustrísima ciudad de Sevilla. Epistolario.* Edited by Santiago Montoto. Seville, 1915.

Castillo Solórzano, Alonso de. *La garduña de Sevilla y anzuelo de las bolsas.* Edited by F. Ruiz Morcuende. Madrid: Espasa-Calpe, 1957.

Davis, Natalie Z. *Society and Culture in Early Modern France.* Stanford: Stanford University Press, 1975.

De Armas, Frederick. "Ana Caro de Mallén Soto." In *Women Writers of Spain: An Annotated Bio-bibliographical Guide.* Edited by Carolyn L. Galerstein. New York: Greenwood Press, 1986.

———. *The Invisible Mistress: Aspects of Feminism and Fantasy in the Golden Age.* Charlottesville: Biblioteca Siglo de Oro, 1976.

Deleito y Pinuela, Jose. *El rey se divierte.* Madrid: Espasa-Calpe, 1955.

Frye, Northrop. *Anatomy of Criticism: Four Essays.* Princeton: Princeton University Press, 1957.

Gilbert, Sandra and Susan Gubar. *The Madwoman in the Attic: The Woman Writer and the Nineteenth Century Literary Imagination.* New Haven: Yale University Press, 1979.

Gildea, Joseph and Leon P. Smith, eds. *Partonopeus de Blois: A French Romance of the Twelfth Century.* Villanova: Villanova University Press, 1967–70.

Hume, Martin. *The Court of Philip IV: Spain in Decadence.* New York: G. P. Putnam's Sons, 1907.

Janeway, Elizabeth. *Man's World, Woman's Place: A Study in Social Mythology.* New York: William Morrow and Co., 1971.

King, Willard. *Prosa novelística y academias literarias en el siglo XVII.* Anejos del Boletín de la Real Academia Española. Vol. 10. Madrid, 1963.

La Barrera y Leirado, Cayetano Alberto de. *Catálogo bibliográfico y biográfico del teatro antiguo español desde sus orígenes hasta mediados del siglo XVIII.* Madrid, 1860. Reprint, London: Tamesis Books, 1968.

Lasso de la Vega y Argüelles, Angel. *Escuela poética sevillana en los siglos XVI y XVII.* Madrid: Imprenta de la viuda e hijos de Galiano, 1871.

Lundelius, Ruth. "The *Mujer Varonil* in the Golden Age Drama." Ph.D. diss., University of Pennsylvania, 1969.

McKendrick, Melveena. *Woman and Society in the Spanish Drama of the Golden Age: A Study of the "Mujer Varonil."* Cambridge: Cambridge University Press, 1974.

Matulka, Barbara. "The Feminist Theme in the Drama of the *Siglo de Oro.*" *Romanic Review* 26 (1935): 191–231.

Morel-Fatio, Alfred. *L'Espagne au XVIe et au XVIIe siècle.* Paris, 1878.

Neumann, Erich. *Amor and Psyche: The Psychic Development of the Feminine.* Translated by Ralph Manheim. New York: Bollingen Series, Pantheon Books, 1956.

Newstead, Helaine. "The Traditional Background of Partonopeus de Blois." *PMLA* 61 (1945): 916–46.

Ordóñez, Elizabeth. "Woman and Her Text in the Works of María de Zayas and Ana Caro." *Revista de Estudios Hispánicos* 19, no. 1 (1985): 3–15.

Ortiz de Zúniga, Diego. *Anales eclesiásticos y seculares de la muy noble y muy leal ciudad de Sevilla.* Madrid: Imprenta Real, 1677.

Rodríguez Villa, Antonio. *La corte y monarquía de España en los años de 1636 y 1637.* Madrid: Luis Navarro, 1886.

Sánchez, José. *Academias literarias del Siglo de Oro.* Madrid: Editorial Gredos, 1961.

Sánchez Arjona, José. *Noticias referentes a los anales del teatro en Sevilla desde Lope de Rueda hasta fines del siglo XVII.* Seville: Imprenta de E. Rasco, 1898.

———. *El teatro en Sevilla en los siglos XVI y XVII.* Madrid: Establecimiento Tipográfico de A. Alonso, 1887.

Seidenspinner-Núñez, Dayle. "Symmetry of Form and Emblematic Design in *El Conde Partinuplés.*" *Kentucky Romance Quarterly* 30 (1983): 61–76.

Sentaurens, Jean. *Séville et le théâtre de la fin du moyen âge à la fin du XVIIe siècle.* Bordeaux: Presses Universitaires de Bordeaux, 1984.

Simón Díaz, José. *Bibliografía de la literatura hispánica.* Vol. 7. Madrid: Consejo Superior de Investigaciones Científicas, 1967.

Smith, Richard C. "Partinuples, conde de Bles," *DAI* 38 (1977–78): 4872A.

Spitzer, Leo. "Soy quien soy." *Nueva Revista de Filología Hispánica* 1 (1947): 113–27.

Stroud, Matthew D. "La literatura y la mujer en el Barroco: *Valor, agravio y mujer* de Ana Caro." *Actas del VIII Congreso de la Asociacion Internacional de Hispanistas.* Edited by David Kossoff, et al. Providence, R.I.: Brown University, 1983.

Thiébaux, Marcelle. *The Stag of Love: The Chase in Medieval Literature.* Ithaca: Cornell University Press, 1974.

Torres Montes, Francisco. *Dramaturgos andaluces del Siglo de Oro.* Seville, 1985.

Trevor Davies, R. *Spain in Decline: 1621–1700.* London: Macmillan and Co., 1957.

Vega Carpio, Lope Félix de. "Arte nuevo de hacer comedias en este tiempo." Edited by A. Morel-Fatio. *Bulletin Hispanique* 3 (1901): 365–405.

Vélez de Guevara, Luis. *El diablo cojuelo.* Edited by Rodríguez Marín. Madrid: Espasa-Calpe, 1969.

THE SPANISH STORYTELLER

Mariana de Carvajal

NOËL M. VALIS

Long before it was written down, the art of storytelling, as it emerged from that room where the spinning, weaving, and unweaving of cloth and words took shape in the same breath, assumed a feminine voice. Though the voice was largely anonymous and unowned, lacking the possessive spirit of authored texts, sometimes we heard a faint murmur, saw a figure shine for a moment before her trace was lost. And sometimes we found her again. Recovering the trace of one writer in particular, Mariana de Carvajal, is precisely the aim of this essay. We cannot grasp her significance, however, without first speaking of another seventeenth-century woman writer, whose work provides a frame of reference for our understanding of Mariana de Carvajal.

The rescue of this special feminine past in recent years has brought to light an exceptionally strong voice out of Spain's Golden Age: María de Zayas y Sotomayor. The stories in her *Novelas amorosas y ejemplares* (Exemplary Tales of Love, 1637) and *Desengaños amorosos* (The Deceits of Love, 1647) recast the conventional narrative frame and topoi of love and honor lost and sometimes regained by viewing them through a feminist—and feminine—discourse. As one critic observes, Zayas subverts the traditional *novela* (short prose narrative) form by shifting "the text's emphasis away from the work itself to its effect on the reader, especially the female reader, thereby creating a revisionary link if not a conspiratorial alliance between narrator and reader."[1] Zayas's unorthodox talent has often been paired in literary histories with Mariana de Carvajal y Saavedra, in a kind of binary opposition vibrating between dissent and conformity. Zayas was the aberration; Carvajal confirmed the rule. Yet this lesser talent is of no less interest to us today, for surely the quiet voice of womanly submission inscribed paradoxically upon the assertive act of writing itself also speaks a language worth learning, tells us something about ourselves and the cultural past out of which we still operate.

Not surprisingly, we know very little about Mariana de Carvajal—and most of that knowledge is gleaned from the surviving records of male members of her family. Thus her presence comes to us indirectly, much the way her voice, plain and unobtrusive, can be carefully sifted through the textual screen of an inherited male literary tradition. Lineage—both writerly and familial—assumes a central place in Carvajal's life and fiction, infusing both with a high sense of purpose and an awareness of station as the chief reason for being. Carvajal's writing, like her birth, can only be understood within the context of aristocratic values in which legitimacy and power are their own justification. Their absence when virtual (in both its accepted and rare meanings) brings about a crisis of male authority, one which Carvajal nearly always seeks to reestablish even as she undermines the very ground upon which it rests in her fiction. In the two stories translated here, feminine reliance upon masculine effectiveness and strength, though in the end recompensed and validated, is sorely tested by repeated male betrayal. Thus, while the traditional pattern of male rescue is never questioned, the underlying power base, when shown to be either impotent or corrupt, is subverted. It should, I hope, become evident that Carvajal, unlike María de Zayas, is no dissenter. Yet the plainness of her voice and narrative scheme is precisely the sort of reading experience which makes us see things most clearly by suggesting that we judge actions as they are being performed, whether basely or honestly. In this connection, I like to think of her writing within the nonliterary framework of the law. Like a lawyer, Carvajal simply presents the facts of her case. Though her defendant is nearly always a woman, thus precluding complete objectivity, she leaves it up to the reader to interpret actions and attribute the proper motives. In other words, she presumes the existence of a reader in the role of judge.

It is fitting then that our knowledge of her life can be compressed into a few legal documents. In examining her husband's last will and testament, her eldest son's birth certificate as well as his petition for membership in the Order of Santiago, and other papers, we learn she was born probably around the turn of the century in Jaén, raised in Granada, and married into an upperclass family like her own in the year 1635.[2] In 1640 she gave birth to the first of nine surviving children, six of them female. When her husband, the Licenciado Don Baltasar Velázquez, who worked in the royal treasury, died in 1656, he left his family in a precarious financial situation. Appealing to Philip IV for a widow's pension of two hundred ducats, in a rare document penned directly by Doña Mariana, she writes that her husband, "having served His Majesty for twenty-three years," died "without leaving any estate, but with three male children and six females, whereby the petitioner finds herself in great need and without the means to sustain and nourish her children."[3] The petition was granted. Serrano y Sanz surmises Doña Mariana may have died before 1664 (her stories had appeared in 1663), but another source puts her death around 1670.[4]

Carvajal's widowhood and the responsibility of a large family in straitened circumstances take on added significance as the necessary backdrop to her writing. Her knowledge of commercial and legal matters is evident in the stories and, indeed, as Julio Jiménez remarks, "We are struck by the grace and ease with which the author exploits such themes, even as metaphors."[5] Since her husband had appointed her his executrix and legal guardian of their children, one also suspects she was a strong-willed woman, highly competent within her restricted sphere of action. Perhaps too, she was impatient with excessive modesty and caviling, to judge from the narrator's remark in the seventh *novela,* "La Industria vence desdenes" (Industry Conquers Disdain), that a young woman's overly scrupulous resolve is "valiente aunque necia" (valiant but stupid).

Certainly this clearheaded, plainspoken person, ungiven to flights of fancy, is the voice we hear in her stories. Unlike her literary predecessor María de Zayas, with whom she is often unfavorably compared, Carvajal displays little imaginative bravura, and her personal passions are carefully guarded. Such restraint in style and theme must have affected not only the kind of readership she had but the numbers as well. Tracing the literary fortunes of her writing is, in one sense, fairly easy. The editions are few, the critical commentary small and unpretentious. But on the other hand, we do not really know how her work was received in the seventeenth century; and from our twentieth-century perspective, her subsequent neglect reflects not only her second-rate status within a much criticized genre but also her lowly position as a woman writer. In literary histories and elsewhere, she simply has not been given serious consideration. I doubt, for example, that most Hispanist scholars could do more than recognize her name. We know from the many editions of her work that María de Zayas enjoyed great success in her day and that she was esteemed by such luminaries as Lope de Vega and Juan Pérez de Montalbán.[6] We could not with confidence assert the same of Mariana de Carvajal.

Her only extant collection of *novelas* appeared in 1663 under the title *Navidades de Madrid, y noches entretenidas, en ocho novelas* (Christmas in Madrid, or Entertaining Nights, in eight tales).[7] Serrano y Sanz describes a second edition of 1668, which subsequent researchers have been unable to locate. A third appeared in 1728. The Biblioteca Nacional of Madrid owns four copies of the first edition and six of the eighteenth-century printing, a small indication perhaps of Carvajal's possible reading public. More recently, she has been reedited in the form of a dissertation in 1974. Since Julio Jiménez's critical edition of her stories easily represents the most accessible primary source for this study, I will be citing exclusively from his text.[8] In a preface to the reader, Doña Mariana asks her public "to forgive the defects of such a badly cut pen, in which you will find a greater desire to serve you with a book of twelve plays wherein you will see with what affection I desire it." But the plays, as well as a promised second part to her stories, are presumably lost or were never written.

On the whole, critical reception of Carvajal's work has not been enthusiastic. Serrano y Sanz says she is "inferior in invention, style and depiction of customs" to Zayas.[9] Amezúa calls her "insipid . . . dull and prosaic," seeing the decline of the *novela* form in Spain clearly manifested in the type of domestic tale Doña Mariana specialized in. A more balanced view is that of Caroline Bourland, who notes that Carvajal is less prolific, less imaginative and less clever with words than María de Zayas; on the other hand, she is also more spontaneous and artless, and her stories better structured. The German Hispanist Pfandl was quite sympathetic toward her, and Sainz de Robles thought her an excellent storyteller, "in control of her narrative skills, with a discreet and clear style." What has hindered our perception of Carvajal even more is the noncritical, purely positivistic approach to her writing. The best example is the work of Caroline Bourland, who takes Doña Mariana's stories literally, as firsthand sources of information about the domestic life and values of the seventeenth-century Spanish upper classes.[10]

Carvajal's case also reveals the more pervasive problem of implied blind critical acceptance of realism's tenets when clearly we are not dealing with mimetic fiction. Amezúa, for example, treats what he calls the *novela cortesana,* or courtly tale, as a reflection of real life, a position which novelist Juan Goytisolo felt compelled to attack as recently as 1972.[11] As codified, artificial constructs, according to Welles, the stories of María de Zayas and Mariana de Carvajal belong more properly to the world of romance.[12] They are not realistic fictions. Yet it is evident that a well-entrenched resistance to the genre itself in Hispanist circles has also restricted our understanding of such texts, as Peter Dunn's otherwise perceptive study of the prolific story writer Castillo Solórzano demonstrates. In analyzing the poor quality of second- and third-rate fiction of the period, he stresses such defects as "the low standard of the feeling evoked," the mechanistic plots, and "the faulty presentation of detail."[13] He is of course quite right to criticize the proliferation of bad writing, but in the process he makes certain assumptions which prejudice his presentation in favor of an unstated frame of reference: realistic fiction.

Scholars traditionally have difficulties dealing with escapist literature, in part because it cannot be fitted into the canon. Since the seventeenth-century Spanish *novela* was enormously popular, mass-produced, and consumer-oriented, the stories may very well have "catered for lower grades of response," as Dunn says. Nonetheless, most of them never expected to do more than entertain, the Horatian dictum aside.[14] Who after all was the reading public for such fiction? While some claim it was written for the nascent bourgeoisie and commercial classes of the period, others like Maxime Chevalier insist that the aristocratic values informing the courtly tale can only have been intended for aristocratic readers.[15] Chevalier further notes that socially the Spanish nobility was far more important than the middle class; even more significant, from an examination of personal libraries and wills we know that "the most active and well-off members of the bourgeoisie [bought] very few books of entertainment." Chevalier concludes that the readers of this early example of the literature of consumption had to be numerically small. For whatever reasons, the Spanish middle class had no time for such diversions, while at least some of the *hidalgos, caballeros,* and their hangers-on, the *letrados* and the high clergymen, had all the time in the world. One could easily argue, as Dunn and others have, that the subsequent decline of the genre into the sensational and formulaic after the high point of Cervantes's *Novelas ejemplares* (1613, Exemplary Novels) reflects an unstable, declining political power and an undynamic, stratified society. But try to imagine leisure. Consider the pursuit of pleasure through the dilatory and often digressive art of storytelling, in its oral and written traditions. The audience for both prized the verbally adept, as social amusement implied a level of social attainment not all could hope to possess. Even before the heyday of the *novela cortesana* in Spain (about 1620 to 1650), books existed to instruct the uninitiated in a few basic principles of good storytelling. Giovanni Della Casa's *Galateo; or The Book of Manners* (1558), for example, which would be adapted into Spanish by Lucas Gracián Dantisco (1582?), spells out in an admirably condensed passage "rules for telling stories in an unlaboured style which will please the hearer."[16] In a world of growing print consumption, the oral conventions of the narrative art had to be written down.

It is within this literary and social setting, already highly codified and nearly exhausted,[17] that Mariana de Carvajal published her stories. Indeed, one of the censors for her book would express surprise that anyone "in these times would spend his leisure in such an exercise" (p. 49). Yet Doña Mariana seems sublimely unaware that she represents the last gasp of a dying tradition, promising, like any good storyteller versed in whetting the appetite (and guaranteeing a built-in audience), a sequel to her tales. She also has no doubts about who her reader is. "I present you," she says in "To the Reader," "with a widow and an orphan; there is a necessary obligation in a noble breast to soften such a painful affliction, for the greatest virtue nobility enjoys is to take pride in consoling the sad of heart, protecting the poor and considering himself well served by the humble servant who . . . waits with affectionate loyalty on his esteemed master." Like her reading public, Doña Mariana's characters are also, unsurprisingly, aristocratic. Using the conventional frame-tale technique of combining several unrelated narratives as told by a group of friends gathered together to amuse one another, Carvajal further unifies the collection by situating it temporally and topographically within a defined space and time. The eight stories are narrated during the Christmas holidays in the house of the recently widowed and wealthy Doña Lucrecia de Haro.

As a still-attractive woman with only one son, Doña Lucrecia surely must have represented a form of wish fulfillment to the financially saddled mother of nine who created her.[18] Thus the consolation offered the fictional widow in these stories at the same time vicariously serves the real widow's need to be comforted. Writing for Doña Mariana may have stood for a "substitute gratification," as Freud maintained of all art. But whether or not she used literature to induce the desired dream, that dream—her writing—is founded on the principle of identity. From the very beginning she establishes a close sense of identification with Doña Lucrecia and her household of assorted noble friends. The seventeenth-century reader must have felt the same identification. The author after all makes a special plea in her preface that her audience sympathize with and comfort the unhappy widow. And the widow's friends expressly suggest storytelling as a way to lessen her grief. Thus it is appropriate not only that such storytelling take place within the home but also that most of the stories unfold in prescribed domestic spaces. Doña Mariana's deeply ingrained feeling for the hearth is natural and "feminine" as traditionally viewed. Moreover, it is logical that with few exceptions she should confine herself to restricted, closed-in spaces, because that is all a woman could know in her day.[19] But the interiority of settings stressed in *Navidades de Madrid* also reinforces a sameness. All the stories are told within the privacy of an inner room so that no breath of scandal can touch the recently widowed Doña Lucrecia. One of her friends remarks: "Since we are free from the gossip of neighbors and this room is far from the street, we'll have a little music and a little dancing as well." The reader too is invited to participate vicariously with his sympathy in entertaining the bereaved widow. We are all among friends, Doña Mariana seems to be telling us; so let's see how we can amuse ourselves by telling stories about people like us.

When like talk about like, we often call it gossip. And when such conversation takes place behind closed doors, the air of complicity simply heightens the slightly forbidden nature of secret chatter. Indeed at the end of "Love Conquers All," one of the two stories translated here, Doña Juana says that "'tomorrow I have a story to tell you about a lady from Toledo who in no way will serve as an example so that these ladies will not be badly affected, for it often happens that terrible women are unlucky, or perchance live unhappily married.' All agreed with what she was saying, mentioning some of the things they knew about their friends." The parallel between gossip and storytelling thus strengthens the notion of identification as a narrative principle upon which Carvajal relies.[20]

Fiction as gossip, moreover, is structured chiefly on patterns of relationships. When we put together the identity principle with a sense of relationships, we are seeing a feminine mind at work, for as Elizabeth Abel observes, the self a female child "develops and carries through her life is one of self-in-relationship." She also calls the concern with relationships "characteristically female," especially as it is manifested through friendship or collaborative bonding. Rather than complementarity which points to difference, identification is the dominant "psychological mechanism that draws women together."[21] Because it fosters a sense of community, we should not be surprised that women writers are often the standard-bearers of tradition. What happens, though, when tradition itself, the emblem of a patriarchal society, is shown through its figures of authority to be corrupt and even impotent? How does a writer like Mariana de Carvajal compensate for what we might call male inadequacies? I would suggest that, as a widow experiencing personal deprivation, Doña Mariana, like the fictional Doña Lucrecia, may very well have used friendship to lessen the acutely felt absence of male support. As a writer engaged in balancing power against the legitimate claims of desire, however, she leans most heavily on the principle of identity, establishing a form of solidarity with her women characters to offset deficiencies encountered elsewhere.

The first story translated here, "Quien bien obra, siempre acierta" (Virtue Is Its Own Reward), is illustrative of this technique. Although both the stories contain far more movement and exterior settings than most of Carvajal's fiction, they are nevertheless *novelas caseras,* or domestic *novelas,* in the sense that the author continues to detail relationships, both spoken and unspoken, and in the process reveals a latent psychological drama through her plainspoken (though obviously selective) presentation of the "facts." In "Virtue Is Its Own Reward," she begins her narration in straightforward fashion by presenting one of the principal characters: "After serving eight years in Flanders, a Cordovan gentleman named Don Alonso de Saavedra, with the royal peace ratified and armies withdrawn, asked permission of his general to return home." The narrator sets the soldier on his way home but then interrupts the journey with a sudden storm, which in turn is climaxed by Don Alonso's witnessing the attempted murder of a young woman. This pattern of events inverts the traditional *novela* structure, as Pfandl observes. "Instead of having the action progress slowly until the decisive moment, she places at the beginning an extraordinary and unexpected event, and from there, lets the dramatic interest little by little diminish."[22] Pfandl likens this movement to the concentric circles of waves produced when a large stone is tossed into a pool of water. The comparison is appropriate but inadequate. If we pursue the inversion, we see that Carvajal, in bringing us to the olive grove where Don Alonso rescues the young woman from certain death, displaces the focus of her *novela* from the soldier to Doña Esperanza. From this point on, it will be *her* story, as she relates through several pages the family difficulties which have brought her to such calamity.

Doña Esperanza is the victim of a skewed relationship. In love with Don Luis (who also happens to be Don Alonso's brother, for a nice coincidence), she finds herself in a quandary when her father, Don Alvaro, a town councilman like Don Luis, violently quarrels with her lover. To complicate matters, she must contend with an insufferably jealous bastard half-brother, the result of a backstairs liaison with a household slave. Thus Carvajal creates two sets of rivalries, and at the center of both is the father. As in the *comedia,* there is no mother. Truly shocking, however, is Don Alvaro's subsequent behavior when he tries to have his own daughter killed. In dealing with a father's betrayal, the author refrains from stating his intentions; nor does Doña Esperanza ever accuse her father directly of attempted murder. Carvajal neither interferes with her characters nor analyzes the psychological subtleties of such underlying feelings as sibling rivalry, hatred between father and child, or the sense of inferiority brought on by illegitimacy. Yet the motivations are implicit. Later, when both Don Alvaro and Don Luis are wounded after quarreling, Doña Esperanza says: "To tell you the pain I felt would be impossible, because all of my family became my enemy, and there was no one I could trust to find out how he [Don Luis] was." It doesn't occur to her to mention concern for her father's health. (She uses the plural "we" to indicate such worry.) Or when her lover suggests they elope, she readily agrees, noting that "once married my father would relent and in the event he did not, nothing else mattered except being with him [Don Luis]." One can only conclude that Doña Esperanza does not really care what her father thinks or feels. To make the story even more curious, Don Luis never actually appears. He is always the missing, but never forgotten, third party to a strange triangle of jealousy and corrupted authority.

If Doña Esperanza shows little affection for her father, he in turn gives all the appearance of a loving paternal presence. When her bastard brother Leonardo discovers the exchange of love letters and she runs off to a neighbor's house, Don Alvaro retrieves her; "as he embraced me, [he] said he couldn't be angry over such a small thing, not with a daughter whom he loved so very much." Yet that same night, on her father's orders, Leonardo and another slave take her to the olive grove to murder her. Why? First, there is revenge; Doña Esperanza's love affair with his enemy is for him unforgivable. But in entrusting Leonardo to do the murder, he reveals an additional motive: public recognition of his bastard son, though not of the son's slave mother. In essence, he prefers a son—even an illegitimate one of mixed blood—to a daughter. As a female, Doña Esperanza simply does not count.

During the legal proceedings, Don Alvaro steadfastly denies any guilt. What persuades him to accede to the magistrate's wishes is the thought that his secret connection with the slave Juliana might become public knowledge. Don Alvaro is released from his imprisonment not because he has been judged and found guilty—or innocent—but because the magistrate's superiors, out of deference to Don Alvaro's position and influence, have advised him to settle the case by patching up the quarrel and marrying off Doña Esperanza to Don Luis. In addition, Don Alvaro is forced to sell the female slave within fifteen days, outside the city limits, "because it wasn't seemly that a gentleman of quality should give such a bad example." Instead, he frees her and marries her off to an apprentice carpenter from Granada. Any sympathy this act might engender is negated by his peremptory, lordly manner toward Juliana, who has no time to reply.

By dealing with a powerful nobleman in this fashion, the magistrate—like the storyteller herself—maintains order, achieves a semblance of justice, and leaves the power structure unthreatened. Nor should we expect anything more from a text coming out of Counter-Reformation Spain. Yet in focusing the story on Doña Esperanza and her travails, Carvajal naturally shifts our sympathy toward the feminine side. Betrayal and corruption of authority emanate from the father. Don Alvaro's conduct represents a triple form of treachery. Socially, he has not behaved like a gentleman, in carrying on an affair with his slave (although in a class critique one might say, how like a gentleman); familially, he has sabotaged any chance of a father-daughter relationship; and legally, he has committed a crime. In all three dimensions, moreover, he is a liar; in all three, he has betrayed his aristocratic duties. And since character *is* social class in the *novela cortesana,* Don Alvaro's legal, social and familial infractions must be considered an indictment from the author. Carvajal's real-life experience with the law is especially noticeable in the closing section of her story as testimony is heard, statements are taken, and torture is threatened in order to elicit the proper confession. But this lawyerlike stance, apparent throughout her narrative, is precisely what condemns Don Alvaro. What is most sacred is the intricate network of relationships constituting the sense of community. In violating the social and legal code, Don Alvaro also ends up compromising justice itself; the magistrate, we read, "was troubled, since Don Alvaro was a powerful man and of such high birth." The magistrate, in truth, is cowed by Don Alvaro. Carvajal never questions the existing power structure and, indeed, praises an outcome which ensures social harmony. But her deceptive matter-of-factness in disclosing the corruption of authority also creates a sympathy toward the victims of abusive power: women.

The second story, "Zelos vengan desprecios" (Love Conquers All), is similarly structured around the characteristic Golden Age motif of rivalry. This time, however, the ritual of sexual competition is juxtaposed to friendship, and the feminine centerpiece—the Lady Narcisa—assumes prominence immediately. "Narcisa," Carvajal begins, "a Milanese lady and mistress over many, as illustrious of blood as she was conceited, was of such rare beauty that she surpassed all other women in her country." "Free of love's cares," she is also free of parental, or any familial, strictures. Unlike Doña Esperanza, she seems to move in a vacuum, rejecting suitors wholesale. Except for her companion (and cousin) Clori and her circle of friends, there is no network of binding relationships guiding her actions. Yet friendship between women plays a significant role in Carvajal's sixth *novela*. The emphasis placed on Narcisa's freedom and her female friendships may also explain why this particular story occurs in Milan, and not in Counter-Reformation Spain. Narcisa's mythological name, moreover, lends itself to an Italian setting.

Indeed it is her name, introduced at the very beginning, which first strikes the reader. Here is a conceited character, unloving and disdainful toward men—a type which Golden Age theater would also exploit in *la mujer esquiva*[23]—whose very nature we might expect to discourage audience responsiveness. But Doña Mariana offsets this potentially negative impression by introducing two suitors, the Duke Arnaldo and the Count Leonido, who are such irritating boobies that we can't help feeling amused sympathy over Narcisa's plight. Much of the story line consists of the various ineffective strategies both men employ to win her hand and defeat their most powerful rival, Narcisa's unknown suitor (the Spanish nobleman, Don Duarte), who conveniently steps in every time Leonido and Arnaldo become *de trop*. Don Duarte's valor, combined with his habit of casually dropping out of sight whenever interest starts to mount, propels Narcisa through a mild form of reverse psychology toward love and the eventual happy resolution of the tale. The action, in moving continually between the protagonist's Milanese home and her country villa, makes this *novela* one of Carvajal's liveliest, with enough swordfights, insults and mystery to satisfy readers who crave adventure and romance. As Bourland remarks, Doña Mariana's stories abound in youth and laughter, characteristics singularly lacking in other short story writers. This youthful atmosphere also links her work more closely to Golden Age theater, in itself unsurprising given the blurring of genre distinctions which prevailed in seventeenth-century Spanish literature.[24]

The somber mood of betrayal which dominated the fifth *novela* is scarcely noted in this story. Still, the pattern of male unreliability—in this case, male inadequacy and incompetence—prevails, although the treatment is essentially comic in the tradition of high romance. Indeed, when Narcisa complains to the viceroy of sexual harassment and threats to her honor, he replies that "he entirely agreed with her, she was quite right, but titled persons of that sort were so powerful he simply had to turn the other cheek and pretend not to see. And he advised her to act with prudence since she possessed so much of it. She was so disgusted that to vent her anger she treated them [Arnaldo and Leonido] with even harsher contempt." Once again, the impotence of legally constituted authority, when faced with the reality of socially determined power, demonstrates that recourse to the law is fraught with obstacles and sometimes no redress at all. When the viceroy advises *prudencia,* we are reminded of Carvajal's other story, in which Don Alvaro is similarly recommended for his prudence in obeying the magistrate's orders. The term, which appears repeatedly in Golden Age literature, suggests conformity to the existing state of affairs and extralegal measures to resolve conflict. It seems to have little to do with the efficacy of law itself, representing instead the legitimizing force of circumstance and unwritten custom, in which character as convention brings about change. (Thus Gracián says, "The wise man knows that the very polestar of prudence lies in steering by the wind."[25])

When Narcisa is frustrated in her attempts to obtain legal satisfaction, she turns instead to her friends. "Narcisa had a villa," we read, "a quarter of a league from Milan, an amusing place with pleasant gardens and situated close to a lovely grove well stocked for hunting. Her friends, especially two titled ladies, liked going there for relaxation sometimes, for Narcisa was beloved by all her women friends, something which is rarely seen. She prided herself on being as courteous and affable with the women as she was cruel with the men, and her loving affection allowed no room for envy." The evenhanded symmetry of style to portray her feelings is misleading, however, for Carvajal, like Zayas, engages the reader to take sides and identify with her feminine protagonist, here through the recognition of emotional kinship.[26]

What Doña Mariana stresses is a sense of comradeship, of solidarity among women. Narcisa is "beloved" and there is "no room for envy," despite the fact that we may assume her hostility toward men is not shared by all. Indeed her "loving affection" disproves the implied narcissism of her character. Unlike the *mujer esquiva* or "reluctant bride" of Golden

Age drama, whose vanity and arrogant pride were often condemned, especially by Lope,[27] Carvajal's Narcisa, though conceited, possesses other traits that modify the convention. While Doña Mariana's story largely fits the established pattern—disdain turns to love, which ends in matrimony—variations within the norm are significant. Narcisa says at one point: "If I was born free of love, I am not free of having been born a woman." The double-edged bias of this statement—unspoken dissent within conformity—quietly subverts womanly submission while yielding in the end to the prescribed dictates of nature.

Most significantly, Narcisa's initial dislike of men is counterbalanced by her loving relationship with women, though it would be risky to interpret an implied lesbianism in this case. Certainly Carvajal is too much the traditionalist to espouse defiance of social and sexual norms. We simply cannot know with any confidence what writers like Doña Mariana thought of female homosexuality, a phenomenon which has been mostly "subterranean" in character.[28] One suspects nevertheless that Doña Mariana may be playing with surreptitious knowledge which she uses as a reader tease. It hardly matters whether Narcisa really is what a twentieth-century audience might think her. But her "loving affection," combined with the specular sameness reflected in her name, paradoxically excludes narcissism by pointing to an identification with that which is similar to oneself.

Thus the self-in-relationship mirrored in Narcisa's name and apparently inconsistent character also suggests that within the commonality of female friendship there exists a complementarity or difference which strengthens bonding rather than tearing it apart.[29] Debra Andrist, in noting the "scanty development of female friendships and [their] incomplete dynamics" in the *Quijote,* emphasizes differentiation based on social inequality (a lady and her maid, for example).[30] But here we see how class unites, even when Narcisa's exceptional character separates her from most of her female contemporaries. As Gardiner remarks, commonality/complementarity (sameness/oppositeness) should be regarded as "fluid processes." In essence this means that differences tend to merge and the principle of identity prevails.

I have stressed the importance of female friendship in Carvajal's story not only for its thematic role but also for its influence on narrative structure. The back-and-forth movement between Milan and the country is occasioned as much by her women friends as by Narcisa's desire to avoid scandal. They miss her and find that her country villa offers not only relaxation and entertainment but friendship as well. Thus Carvajal writes in one passage that "Narcisa's friends . . . felt her absence and, as the place was so nearby, they wanted to pay her a visit." And in another: "Her friends wrote her, telling her of the duke's absence and begging her to come back to Milan, because they found themselves very lonely without her." The particular rhythm of physical movement in this sixth *novela* suggests an inner vacillation between female friendship and male attraction. As with Don Alonso in the fifth story, Don Duarte provides the expected narrative resolution through his decisiveness and daring. But, on the other hand, the unstated loyalties of Narcisa's women friends should not be underestimated. When faced with the treachery of Arnaldo and Leonido, she may be rescued by Don Duarte, but she is also comforted by her friends' moral support.

In the end, of course, both Arnaldo and Leonido escape the consequences of their acts, as social order is restored and the status quo maintained through the conventional device of matrimony. One cannot help noticing, nevertheless, Narcisa's very public way of showing her relief and joy over the Duke Arnaldo's marriage to his cousin: "Narcisa became so cheerful that she wanted to show her pleasure. So she ordered that a window near the duke's be rented, dressed in court finery, and, accompanied by her cousin and friends, she went to see the revelry." Doña Mariana's heroine is clearly rubbing it in. Her public demonstration of satisfaction as she gloats over the duke's defeat can be interpreted as the proverbial last word. In such a fashion, Carvajal turns womanly submission into feminine triumph.[31]

NOTES

1. Ordóñez, "Woman and Her Text in the Works of María de Zayas and Ana Caro," 6.

2. These and other details of Carvajal's life are largely taken from Serrano y Sanz, whose *Apuntes para una biblioteca de escritoras españolas* provides invaluable biobibliographical information about scores of Spanish women writers.

3. Serrano y Sanz, *Apuntes,* 241–42. All translations are my own.

4. Jiménez, Introducción to "Doña Mariana de Caravajal y Saavedra. *Navidades de Madrid y noches entretenidas, en ocho novelas,*" 11. A shortened version of Jiménez's introduction may be found in his "Doña Mariana de Carvajal y Saavedra, mujer y escritora en la España de los Felipes." *Explicación de Textos Literarios* 6, no. 2 (1978): 205–13.

5. Jiménez, ed. *Navidades de Madrid,* 22.

6. Welles, "María de Zayas y Sotomayor and Her *Novela Cortesana:* A Re-evaluation," 301.

7. See Serrano y Sanz, *Apuntes,* 242–43, and Bourland, *The Short Story in Spain in the Seventeenth Century,* 150, 170–71, for a complete bibliographical description of editions.

8. Jiménez's edition is based upon a copy of the 1663 edition found in the Hispanic Society of America.

9. Serrano y Sanz, *Apuntes,* 243.

10. González de Amezúa y Mayo, *Formación y elementos de la novela cortesana,* 99; Bourland, "Aspectos de la vida del hogar en el siglo XVII según las novelas de Doña Mariana de Carabajal y Saavedra," 331; Pfandl, *Historia de la literatura nacional española en la*

Edad de Oro, 370–73; and Sainz de Robles, *Ensayo de un diccionario de mujeres célebres,* 214.

11. Goytisolo's stimulating essay, "El mundo erótico de María de Zayas," first appeared in *Cuadernos de Ruedo Ibérico* 39–40 (October 1972–January 1973): 3–27, and was reprinted in *Disidencias.* Although it is the prologues Amezúa wrote for editions of María de Zayas's short story collections which come under attack here, the same position can be found in Amezúa's earlier *Formación y elementos de la novela.* For a more modern, if less cogent, analysis of the *novela cortesana,* see Palomo, *La novela cortesana.* A useful overview of the *novela* form can be read in Clements and Gibaldi, *Anatomy of the Novella;* Pabst, *La novela corta en la teoría y en la creación literaria;* and Krömer, *Formas de la narración breve en las literaturas románicas hasta 1700.* See also Willard F. King, *Prosa novelística y academias literarias en el siglo XVII* (Anejo X. Madrid: BRAE, 1963), for the relationship between literary academies and the framed tale.

12. Welles, "María de Zayas," 301.

13. Dunn, *Castillo Solórzano and the Decline of the Spanish Novel,* xi.

14. Ibid., 59. Thus Doña Mariana writes in her preface, "To the Reader," that she hopes to provide "good, honest entertainment for amusing oneself during the long, idle nights of freezing winter."

15. For an example of the first point of view, see de la Torre Rodríguez, "Una exploración sobre la novela cortesana española del Renacimiento y Barroco," 654–55; for an example of the second, see Chevalier, *Lectura y lectores en la España de los siglos XVI y XVII,* 28–29. See also Pacheco-Ransanz, "Varia fortuna de la novela corta," 407–21.

16. I am citing from the English translation by Pine-Coffin: *Galateo; or The Book of Manners,* 68. The Spanish adaptation may be found in Gracián Dantisco, *Galateo español,* in the section called "De las novelas y cuentos" (On Novels and Stories), 155–70.

17. By 1665, Bourland notes, new stories "almost entirely ceased to be written, although several of the old collections were reprinted more than once and indeed continued to be reissued all through the eighteenth century" (*The Short Story in Spain,* 10).

18. Serrano y Sanz also thought Doña Lucrecia might be "Doña Mariana's ideal after her husband died" (*Apuntes,* 243).

19. Jiménez also notes the use of interiors as settings in Doña Mariana's work, adding that "the scenes at the beginning and end of the collection are veritable exponents of home life among the privileged classes of the period" (*Navidades de Madrid,* 20).

20. In keeping with this idea, Della Casa remarks that "it is certainly true that we generally listen with greater pleasure and keener imagination to stories about people whom we know, if the incidents fit their characters, than to tales about strangers who are unknown to us" (*Galateo,* 70).

21. Abel, "(E)Merging Identities: The Dynamics of Female Friendship in Contemporary Fiction by Women," 417, 434, 415. See also the subsequent critical exchange between Abel and Gardiner in the same issue.

22. Pfandl, *Historia de la literatura,* 371.

23. Melveena McKendrick describes *la mujer esquiva* of Spanish drama as "the woman who, for some reason, is averse to the idea of love and marriage." The type, which proliferated in theater from the turn of the seventeenth century until approximately 1660, has its roots in the Petrarchan tradition and classical literature and is thought to be a creation of Lope de Vega. See McKendrick's "Women Against Wedlock: The Reluctant Brides of Golden Age Drama," 115–46.

24. Bourland, "Aspectos de la vida del hogar," 364. Florence Yudin notes that "the tendency of literary genres to overlap and blur formal differences characterizes many Golden Age works. Without confusing their separate aims, playwrights and novelists shared many stylistic and structural principles" ("The *novela corta* as *comedia:* Lope's *Las fortunas de Diana,*" 181). Nor should we forget Doña Mariana's twelve lost *comedias.*

25. Gracián, *The Art of Worldly Wisdom,* 173.

26. See Ordóñez, "Woman and Her Text," 6–7, for an analysis of Zayas's more overtly feminist posture in effecting "reader identification with the cause of women."

27. See McKendrick, "Women Against Wedlock," 118.

28. Ibid., 116.

29. See Gardiner, "The (US)es of (I)dentity," 436.

30. Andrist, "Male/Female Friendship in *Don Quixote,*" 158–59. I should mention here Ruth El Saffar's work on reinterpreting the shadowy presence of the feminine in Cervantes's later fiction such as the *Persiles*. She notes that, once recuperated, the lost woman "brings back into the society from which she had been stolen or ejected, health, prosperity, harmony, and wholeness." Thus, male heroes "while redeeming her . . . are [themselves] redeemed" (*Beyond Fiction,* xii).

31. As this article was going to press, I ran across Evangelina Rodríguez Cuadros's edition of *Novelas amorosas de diversos ingenios del siglo XVII* (Madrid: Castalia, 1986), in which she includes Carvajal's "La Industria vence desdenes" (pp. 235–79). See also pp. 39–41, 67 of her introduction, for comments on Carvajal.

Novella 5. Virtue Is Its Own Reward

After serving eight years in Flanders, a Cordovan gentleman named Don Alonso de Saavedra, with the royal peace ratified and armies withdrawn, asked permission of his general to return home.[1] This granted, and accompanied by a slave whom he'd taken with him from Spain and two servants retained in Flanders, he disembarked at Seville in the dead of winter. He decided not to warn his family of his arrival in order to give them the sudden joy of reunion. As he headed toward the cathedral to hear mass, he ran into a mule driver with whom he had traveled in the old days and called over to him. When the man stood before him, he asked if he still arranged passage. He replied "certainly" and said that he was now an independent because he had his own mules. Don Alonso was delighted to see him getting on so well, saying he had need of him because he had to go to court, passing through Cordova along the way. He would of course pay him handsomely regardless of the sum. To which Francisco responded that he would go to the ends of the earth with him. Much pleased with his answer, he determined to set off immediately, despite the inhospitable weather. And so their provisions made ready, they left Seville on the eighth of November.

On the second day of their journey, nearly in sight of his home, a storm came upon them so suddenly that the sky darkened, the heavens hurled hail thick as frozen spears, blinding them with thunder and lightning and wind. In a very short time it turned into such a heavy rain they thought they would drown in it. Beset by such unexpected fury, Don Alonso decided, before night should close its dusky doors, to try for a thick patch of olive grove a quarter of a league from the road. Spurring on their mounts with the greatest speed, they went in looking for a place of refuge and were cheered somewhat by the protection the thick and abundant trees offered after they made a canopy of their capes hoisted over the leafy branches. To judge from the unfortunate travelers, the downpour lasted until past eleven that night. As it slackened, lovely Cynthia[2] revealed her silvery face, and by the dim rays of her hazy light, Don Alonso discovered that they were near a ditch, a boundary which divided it from other olive groves.

Shortly after this they heard the neighing of horses approaching from the other side. Fearing thieves and making certain of their weapons, they paid close heed. They saw two horses come near, and, from one, two men dismounted. One of them went over to the second horse and pulled off a woman who was crying, while the man with her slipped off after her. In a low voice the weeping woman pleaded: "Oh sir, pity. How is it possible for this noble breast to be so cruel?" To which he answered: "I'll have no more weeping. Those false and deceitful crocodile tears offend even more my outraged heart." And he said to the others: "Make haste while this wretched night protects us." Without answering, they grasped the spades which they had brought with them and began to dig at the foot of a thick tree trunk.

Shocked at the pitiful and unexpected turn of events, Don Alonso was determined not to allow such great treachery, so he said very quietly to his servants and slave: "Throw yourselves with your swords bared against these wretches, while I take advantage of the moment to steal away this woman and place her in safekeeping." He ordered Francisco to make ready the two mules on which they'd come, because they would be going to the court now that it was no longer possible to enter Cordova; and said to his slave Rodrigo that he would wait for them at the Inn of the Saints.

As he was giving this order, one of the men digging said: "Sir, I think the hole is deep enough now." The man came over to look and answered: "Dig to the very center of the earth, and leave my injury and vengeance buried in it." It seemed to the noble Cordovan's servants they ought not to give him the opportunity to do so. They went after him in relentless pursuit, struggling to keep him away from the lady. While they were all fighting together, Don Alonso came out and, seizing the woman by the arm, said to her: "Come; while you are with me, no one will hurt you." He could very well be a bandit, she thought, but that did not stop her from following him; for she considered that she would be better off in the hands of thieves than in the cold clutches[3] of the horrifying death which awaited her.

Francisco was already there with his mule. Lifting the woman up and placing her side-saddle, Don Alonso got on his own mount, and they took a shortcut to arrive more quickly at the inn. Knowing by the noise that his master had escaped, Rodrigo decided to make short business of the danger they were in. So taking out two small pistols he was carrying, he fired one, wounding one of those digging, and firing the other, he did the same to his companion. The cruel man, fearing the same, begged him to spare his life. To which Rodrigo replied: "Then go to that thicket over there and be thankful I didn't kill you." Seeing the two horses, he and his companions killed them so that they couldn't be followed. Then turning to where their mules stood, they mounted and went to the inn where they were expected.

The driver had given the innkeepers to understand that he was taking the woman to serve a lady to whom she had been recommended, and asked that they please give her a bed. Meanwhile some servants of the gentleman would be arriving, for with the storm they had gotten lost. Don Alonso asked if they had enough provisions. The innkeeper's wife replied that they certainly did; they had excellent chicken and a great deal of game and fruit in season. She ordered four chickens to be cooked and well seasoned, and rabbit and partridge to be prepared for a bite to eat, since they would be going soon afterward. This was done, and the servants having arrived, without even asking about the woman, they ate, made ready what they had to take, and left, fearing pursuit. At a league's distance from the inn, they left the royal highway and entered some steep hills. Don Alonso wanted to know whom he was protecting so that he could understand the danger he was in, for the cloaked lady was also wearing a small mask. After they had dismounted, he said to her: "Now my lady, you've seen how we have all placed our lives in danger to defend yours, and if this good will merits any consideration, I beg of you, reveal yourself, and tell me who you are and where you would like me to take you. My journey was to the court, but now it will only be what you desire until I know you safe from harm."

She answered him by removing the mask to reveal a face of such rare beauty that it left them astonished and Don Alonso even more bewildered, for in her honest bearing she showed herself to be a lady of quality. So he gave her to understand, saying she could not deny the truth to him. To which she answered: "I would be ungrateful if I did not grant your desire. I will not say who I am; it is enough to tell you the reason for my unhappiness. I am from Cordova and of such well-known high birth that one of the leading noblemen of the city set his sights upon me. When I tell you his name is Don Luis de Saavedra, I am telling you his rank. He courted me with such ardent and continual attentions that he earned that place in my heart which he will not lose unless I lose my life. At night I would speak to him through a low window. One night, as he spoke of his great love for me, I answered that his attentions were wanting. Since we were equal in rank and nobility, why did he not ask my father for my hand in marriage? He answered to my satisfaction that he was waiting for a brother who was in Flanders, and he would not be content if he too were not present to celebrate his good fortune. I assure you he gave me such a desire to know his brother that much of our conversation together dealt with his imminent arrival. But to my misfortune it happened that, while at the town council, my father and my lover both being councilmen,[4] the two of them found themselves at odds over trying to draw lots for court representative. Burning with anger my father implied certain things about Don Luis, and Don Luis, offended, forgetting that I reigned in his heart, struck my father in the face with his hat. Now unrestrained, they drew swords, wounding one another so gravely that we feared for their lives.

"To tell you the pain I felt would be impossible, because all of my family became my enemy, and there was no one I could trust to find out how he was. To add to my unhappiness, when it came to making peace, my father declared himself his sworn enemy and that included his family and anyone who counted himself his friend. Everyone became so stirred up that we very nearly divided into two camps. The magistrate asked Don Luis to make himself scarce for a while, pretending to be going to Valladolid while all along he was lying low at a country house two leagues from the city.

"Shortly before, fearful that I would change my mind in anger, he left me a letter, entrusting it to a servant who knew of our affection. I was just as fearful and, seeing the servant one day, I summoned him without considering the risk I was taking. I asked about his master. He told me where he was staying and, giving me the letter, he waited for a reply. I told him to come back that night to the window where I used to talk with my lover. Then retiring to my room, I found the letter contained some lines of verse. . . .

"Determined to put his fears to rest, I replied that he offended me in doubting my good faith and that I had had the same fear, and I asked that he write back to soften the pain of his absence, for I could not live without him. When the servant came that night, I gave him the note, charging him to make haste. He replied that he would be leaving forthwith, and that I should take care to arrange another day for him to speak with me. The next day at noon, I rushed to the window, certain that my father was taking a nap. Seeing that Don Luis was waiting for me I called out, taking the letter and charging him to return that night. I retired to my room to see what he had written me. After many expressions of gratitude esteeming my reply, he went on to say that, if my love was as firm as I had said it was, then I should determine to leave my home since it was no longer possible to marry with my father's consent. I answered that he should come for me tomorrow night; that, once we were married, my father would relent; and that, in the event he did not, nothing else mattered except being with him.

"I have, to my regret, a bastard brother, the fruit of my father's affair with a household slave so beautiful that I assure you, without the brand,[5] she could compete with the most perfect lady. My father has publicly recognized Leonardo, having implied that his mother is someone else. This has given him so many airs that nobody can curb his excesses. Just as I was about to fold the paper to which I have referred and, with my lover's letter lying on the desk, he burst into my room so suddenly that I had no time to hide the letters. He tore them from my hands, read them and having seen what they contained, treated me so badly by word and deed that he even laid hands on this face before you. Overcome by anger, I told him he was a wretched slave, a son of a whore. He flinched, swearing I would pay for it. As he took the papers with him to my father's room, it was my good fortune (if it's true I have any) that, engrossed in his vengeance, he did not notice the door was ajar.

I went to a neighbor's house across the street. That same night my father came looking for me and, as he embraced me, said he couldn't be angry over such a small thing, not with a daughter whom he loved so very much. After bringing me home, he remained alone with me, saying: 'I don't want this marriage with Don Luis. I promise to leave you so well fixed you will want for nothing. While I decide which husband I will choose for you, I want to take you to Seville and leave you in a convent. Take off those fancy clothes and put on some modest thing, because we are leaving here tonight and I don't want anyone to know you are missing.' I answered that his will was mine, but with the intention of warning Don Luis so that he could rescue me from the convent.

"Night fell, and accompanied by Leonardo and another slave with as bad a character as his, we reached that place where it was certain I would have died by his cruel hand if your bravery had not defended me." She ended these words in tears, and Don Alonso said to her: "My Lady Esperanza, dry those lovely eyes. I know who you are from my brother's letters. I am Don Alonso, whom you so wanted to know, and the happiest man in the world, since after being so long away from home, Providence brought me here to save your life. What I fear is that your father, believing your abduction to be on the orders of Don Luis, will seek new treachery out of revenge. Tell me, dear lady, where you wish me to leave you, for I must make haste to return to Cordova."

The lovely lady embraced him out of sheer happiness. She asked if he could take her to the court where she had an aunt, her mother's sister, who was also a nun in the Reformed Carmelites. Don Alonso ordered provisions to be brought out and, after they had eaten, they remounted, determined to ride with all speed. At the court, leaving her at an inn, he went to the convent and asked for the prioress. There, he gave an account of what had happened, asking her to call in the aunt. In return, they told him to bring Doña Esperanza while they would ask permission to receive her. To the noble Cordovan it was unseemly to bring her dressed so badly.

So, seeing a clothes merchant, he purchased a dress of gold brocade and, returning to the inn, had her put it on, asking the innkeeper meanwhile to find horses for him.

He handed her over to the aunt and, departing at top speed, reached his house, where he found his mother and all the servants weeping. Without letting on how worried he was, he asked the reason. His mother, prudent as always, recounted to him Don Luis's love affair and his troubles with the town council, finishing off with this: "Doña Esperanza's been missing from home for eight days, and Don Alvaro has quarreled with your brother, accusing him of dishonoring his daughter, robbing his house, and making off with property worth more than twelve thousand ducats. Someone revealed that he was hiding in a country house and the magistrate had him brought back a prisoner and he has him in jail and nobody can see him and, if Doña Esperanza doesn't show up, we'll see him on the scaffold."

He responded that there was a remedy for everything, for had he not come to console her? Giving her to understand that it was in his power to do so, and donning a black suit which he'd requested, accompanied by his servants he went to the house of the magistrate, who was happy to see him. Don Alonso begged leave to speak with him in private. When the servants had retired he gave an account of Don Alvaro's treachery and, telling him everything, observed that the servants could not change their story in such a short time and would be the best witnesses that he was telling the truth. The magistrate sent for a clerk to make an arraignment against Don Alvaro, taking the statements of Don Alonso and of his servants. Having examined the witnesses, he called in a captain, asking for his support and aid in surrounding Don Alvaro's house. Accompanied by his bailiffs, he went into the house. Don Alvaro became agitated upon seeing him and asked what he wanted. In order to set him at ease, he [the magistrate] answered that he was looking for some delinquents who had been seen leaping from roof to roof around here. He ordered the constables to search the house even though Don Alvaro resisted it. They found the servants and, making them get dressed, he had them put in jail. Taking Don Alvaro to the magistrate's office, he advised him to account for his daughter's whereabouts because, as he understood it, Don Alvaro had killed her. Don Alvaro replied that they were false witnesses and that Don Luis could account for her since she was in his hands. Leaving him imprisoned with the order that no one should speak to him, the magistrate went to the jail, resolved to torture the two prisoners. Fearful of being put on the ropes,[6] they confessed the whole truth. They were asked if they recognized the men who abducted her. Leonardo replied he did not; by the light of the moon, he noticed only that it was a mulatto who fired the pistols.

As the case was judged publicly, there were witnesses to testify that they had found the horses dead. The motive verified, the clerk went to take

Don Alvaro's testimony. He replied with a second denial, saying that the afflicted men, fearful of the torture, had given in to whatever was asked of them. The magistrate was troubled, since Don Alvaro was a powerful man and of such high birth. Having made a transcription of the authorized proceedings, he sent a trusted servant to deliver it to the council magistrates, saying in a letter to the Right Honorable President of Castile that the parties were most noble and powerful and that he could not decide on sentence in the case without an order from His Honor.

The papers having been examined at the council, a court secretary went to the convent to take Doña Esperanza's statement. The servant had brought her a letter from Don Alonso, in which he advised her to declare that it was he who had defended her and brought her there. When the secretary arrived, as she was already prepared to do so, she declared everything to the letter. The secretary then returned to the council with the statement. Seeing that it agreed with what was written, a royal decree was dispatched to the magistrate, as the judge best qualified to do the sentencing ordered in the letter: "That mindful there had been no death issuing, he should try to patch up the quarrel by marrying off Don Luis to the lady mentioned in the proceedings."

With the servant's arrival in Cordova, the magistrate, as he was content with the dispatch, went to the offices of the town council and, taking Don Alvaro out from where he was, he let him know what the royal decree said. He also read him his daughter's statement, explaining that he had orders from His Majesty to marry her to Don Luis and to pass sentence in this case; that his crime merited taking his head off his shoulders and that, by exercising compassion, he [the magistrate] thought it would be better to admit the charge, obey the royal decree, desisting from the present quarrel since it was unjust, and if not, that he would proceed with all due severity against him. Don Alvaro was persuaded and ashamed that his affair with the slave might be made public, so he responded that he would comply with the order. The magistrate, who appreciated his prudence, confronted them all, and the stipulations were agreed upon under forfeit of life for anyone who broke the peace.

With this the order was given for his release. In the company of friends and kinsmen, they then prepared to go to the court for Doña Esperanza. In the time it took to return to Cordova, the magistrate, like a good judge, sentenced Leonardo to six years' hard labor and the slave to the galleys for life, to labor in vain. With the newly betrothed happy lady having returned to Cordova, the magistrate sent for Don Alvaro, warning him that within fifteen days he must sell the female slave outside the city limits, because it wasn't seemly that a gentleman of quality should give such a bad example. He promised to comply, although he was very sorry to do so.

When he arrived home, he called the slave[7] and said to her: "Well,

Juliana, you'll now have your way; your wish, which you have asked of me so many times, to give you freedom, will be granted. The magistrate has informed me that I am to sell you outside Cordova. You know by now of the love I have felt for you, and I should be very sorry if, once beyond my power, you conducted yourself wantonly. I shall have to find a fellow who is an honest man to marry you. Tomorrow I will give you your freedom; and beyond what you have acquired in my house, I will give you five hundred ducats. Make ready everything that is yours while they find me something appropriate, because I have only fifteen days' grace and then you must leave Cordova." And without giving her time to reply, he called his steward and told him to bring a surgeon to remove the brand and to look for an honest man to marry her, reminding him that he must not reside in Cordova. He answered that he knew such a man, a carpenter from Granada. Don Alvaro replied: "Well, speak to him then because this must be done quickly."

The steward went to strike a deal with the carpenter's master. When they had explained the marriage to the man, he accepted with alacrity, saying that so long as they made good on their promises, he would carry out his word, and asked that his master make the arrangements with the lord. So it was done. When they stood before Don Alvaro, he sent for a clerk and told him to prepare two documents, a letter of manumission and an article of marriage; and taking out the five hundred ducats, he put them with the article of marriage along with the jewels she had to make a sum of one thousand. With this he went to the vicar-general and begged him to give permission to marry them without the marriage banns. As the vicar-general knew about the past vexations, he agreed, and, the blessings received, the couple left the next day for Granada.

The story ended, Doña Lucrecia said: "I gave to this occurrence when Don Antonio told it to me the title of 'Virtue is its own Reward.' " The great valor and prudence of Don Alonso were the reason for its happy ending, his brother enjoying the abundant fruit of his well-employed resolve and everyone living afterwards in lasting and secure friendship.

Novella 6. Love Conquers All

Narcisa, a Milanese lady and mistress over many, as illustrious of blood as she was conceited, was of such rare beauty that she surpassed all other women in her country. She lived so free of love's cares that she gloried in being cruel and disdainful with all those who sought her hand in blessed matrimony. The most powerful nobles of Milan wooed her, proclaiming themselves in love with her beauty. Among her many suitors, those who stood out most confident of their power and contemptuous of their rivals were the Duke Arnaldo and the Count Leonido.

Arnaldo was ugly of face and haughty of manner. He took offense at Narcisa's indifference, going out of his way to annoy her by saying that no one would enjoy her beauty if he couldn't, because all her lovers were nothing but poor gentlemen unworthy of her esteem. With this kind of attitude there were some scandalous and violent quarrels. Leonido did not lag behind in getting even with her disdain, talking spitefully about the honest lady with the intention of tarnishing her honor.

Narcisa was so distressed that she was determined to complain to the viceroy. He responded that he entirely agreed with her, she was quite right, but titled persons of that sort were so powerful that he simply had to turn the other cheek and pretend not to see. And he advised her to act with prudence, since she possessed so much of it. She was so disgusted that, to vent her anger, she treated them with even harsher contempt. As in Milan the competition between the two men was public knowledge, a Spanish gentleman who had taken up residence there decided not to declare his love for her, believing that Narcisa was so haughty and severe she would not esteem his love since she disdained so many lovers and noblemen. It wasn't because he was not worthy of her hand. Don Duarte was, after all, the fortunate descendant of the illustrious house of the dukes of Cardona and so close to inheriting the estates that, if his uncle died without heirs, there was no other kinsman closer by blood to inherit. He feared only her anger, seeing that she seemed to be offended by those who served her. The gallant Spaniard was despondent, as much in love as he was melancholy. It was some comfort to follow her during public ceremonies, without letting slip his vigilance, especially in church where she would go to hear mass, accompanied by a cousin of hers called Clori, a lady of such quality who, had she not been by Narcisa's side, was equally worthy of being loved.

Narcisa had a villa a quarter of a league from Milan, an amusing place with pleasant gardens and situated close to a lovely grove well stocked for hunting. Her friends, especially two titled ladies, liked going there for relaxation sometimes, for Narcisa was beloved by all her women friends, something which is rarely seen. She prided herself on being as courteous and affable with the women as she was cruel with the men, and her loving affection allowed no room for envy.

She had her church pew near a chapel; and Don Duarte upon entering it, gloried in seeing and hearing his adored mistress without arousing the suspicion of the other suitors. One day while her two lady friends were with her, after hearing mass Madame Rosana asked when they would have the pleasure of going to the villa again. At once, she told them, if they desired amusement. Laurencia said to hold off until tomorrow, since she had a visitor that afternoon and wanted to go with them.

As soon as Don Duarte heard the conversation, anxious to see her without the restraints of public behavior, he left the church, went to his house, and put on the garments and cloak of rough cloth that he used for soldiering. Then he went to the villa and asked the gardener if he could put him up for a couple of days there, because he was on the road and ill. Taking out a few small coins, he gave them to him. Content with his payment, the gardener took him to a dwelling that was in the gardens, arranging a bed for him so that he could rest. The next morning a page came by to tell him not to let anyone enter, because his ladyship was coming with some other ladies. As the gardener saw Don Duarte in ordinary clothes, he didn't bother to throw him out.

They came that very afternoon, sitting beneath a lovely bower until it was time to go to the grove. There they asked for some baskets of flowers to entertain themselves by making bouquets. Narcisa took a great quantity of flowers and, weaving a garland, put it on her head. They all applauded her, celebrating her beauty. At that moment a great noise was heard, and when they asked who was causing it, a servant replied: "Count Leonido and two servants have entered by force, and we were unable to detain them." As they approached the ladies, Narcisa angrily said: "I simply do not understand, Lord Leonido, the reason for such insolence. And you could apologize, knowing as you do my express wishes, that I do not esteem your attentions." The count smarted at being belittled in front of the other ladies, and he answered: "The insolence is yours, since you treat a man like me in this fashion. So much vanity already goes beyond arrogance." "How convenient," said Narcisa, "that you should speak to me in the garden, for if you were in Milan there would be someone to avenge my displeasure." Not wanting to miss an opportunity, Don Duarte emerged from where he had been standing, leaping out with his sword unsheathed, and said: "There is indeed someone at the villa to serve you." The count and his servants drew out their swords, but Don Duarte gained the advantage and with a slash cut much of Leonido's face, slightly wounding as well the head of a servant. Thus he obliged them to make a hasty departure, as they feared he might kill them all. He followed in their stead and, because he didn't want to be recognized, went to Milan, arriving before the servants.

Everyone was amazed at his great courage, and Narcisa asked the gardener: "Who was that man?" To which he replied that he didn't know. The day before, he'd asked if there was some work for him, so he had taken him in to care for the gardens. With the unexpected trouble no one wanted to go out hunting. Back in Milan, Narcisa said to her cousin that she had her suspicions about that man, because so much boldness could not come from a man of low birth. "So it seems to me," said Clori, "without doubt he loves you and, fearing the severity of your temper, doesn't dare to declare himself." Narcisa replied: "I assure you that his lively grace has left me so piqued I would give anything to meet him." Clori laughed, saying: "I'd take care what you do, for such solicitude is the onset of passion, and I am astonished to say this when I see you so free of love." "Well, don't be astonished," Narcisa said, "for if I was born free of love, I am not free of having been born a woman."[8]

At the time this trouble was brewing, Arnaldo had left to visit his estates. When he returned and his friends told him the count had been wounded, he replied that like them, he was suspicious about the two cousins, Narcisa and Clori. Doubtless Narcisa secretly favored one of her suitors and feared Arnaldo's anger, as he could prevent her from marrying. Burning with jealousy, Arnaldo determined to satisfy his doubts by haunting her street at night, cloaked so as not to be recognized. As Don Duarte thought that Arnaldo was away and Leonido, though improved, had not yet risen out of bed, he wanted to celebrate in some verses the garland Narcisa had worn in the garden. So, accompanied by a page who carried the instrument, Don Duarte went to her street. Seeing that Don Duarte was going to sing, Arnaldo waited first before interrupting the music, for he wanted to be sure it really was his rival. . . .

Arnaldo in his cloak came up to [Don Duarte], saying: "You might well apologize for such daring, for surely you are not unaware that the Duke Arnaldo serves this lady and is paying her court." To which he answered: "I am not preventing his wooing, although I adore Narcisa. If you don't like it, let us leave this street quietly to a place where I can answer you in kind." The duke drew out his sword, saying: "I have no need to leave the street in order to throw you out of it," aiming to wound him in the head. Don Duarte parried the blow with his instrument which broke into pieces, and grasping the neck in his hand he delivered two or three blows which knocked him to the ground, saying: "For the sake of the lady's reputation you have offended, I won't kill you." With this he left the street before anyone could come to the rescue, just as lights were appearing in windows. The two cousins were standing at the window and, as they left, Clori said: "Without doubt our suspicions are confirmed, for this man seemed to me to be the one in the garden since he was celebrating the garland you wore." "It obliges me all the more," said Narcisa, "to look after my own honor than to rely on the love he holds for me; and if his rank is equal to his courage, do not doubt that he will be master of my will. His industry in serving me without revealing his name has so conquered me that I know it will cost me sleepless nights." "It won't be easy," warned Clori, "to find out who he is if he does not wish it." "That doesn't bother me," she answered her, "for his very love will deliver him into my hands."

Arnaldo was several days in bed, but, angered by the thrashing, he wanted to challenge the unknown lover to see if he would show himself in public. He went to the church to wait for Narcisa and when the lady went to take holy water, as she removed a glove to receive it, he tore it out of her hands violently, saying: "Send the fortunate man after to fetch it." Narcisa considered her lovers once more and, seeing they were at odds, she said somewhat harshly: "I do well not to esteem those who serve me, since they do not dare to punish such insolence." Arnaldo laughed, as though in mockery, and with that departed. When night fell, Don Duarte armed himself to the teeth and, donning a mask, went to the duke's house. Giving a note to a page, he told him he would wait for the answer. The page went up to give it to the duke; and, when Arnaldo saw it was a challenge, he took a pistol with the intent to kill him. Going out to the street, he said to him: "Are you the one looking for me?" Don Duarte answered: "I am; follow me if you dare." He followed him closely so that he wouldn't suspect he was going to kill him. They reached a deserted spot, and Don Duarte said: "I've come for the article of clothing you took from a lady today." Arnaldo took out the glove, saying: "You see it here; see if you dare to take it," and putting it inside his hat, he fired at him with his pistol with such bad luck that he missed his target. The valiant Spaniard flung himself at him and, piercing his breast with one thrust, laid him at his feet. He removed the duke's hat and, seeing that the glove was inside, turned his back on him, saying: "Twice I have spared your life, and if you persist in offending our mutual acquaintance, your life is forfeit."

With this he departed and, reaching Narcisa's house, he sent for the steward, who came out to see who was looking for him. Giving him the hat and glove, he said to him: "Tell your mistress that the duke remains in such a state he will not dare to bother her again. And ask whether she wishes to command her adoring servant in anything." The steward went up to deliver the message. Excited, the cousins told him to come up, because they wanted to see him. He went looking for Don Duarte again and seeing that he did not appear, [the steward] went up again to say he had already gone. Narcisa was so upset that she knew herself lost, saying to Clori: "Such cleverness does this man possess to win my heart, for see how he serves me and obliges me without giving himself away. I am determined to return to the country in order to avoid the scandal the duke's wounds may cause. Perhaps there we'll have more luck in satisfying my doubts, for surely he will not fail to follow us." To which Clori replied: "Well, he is a country fellow, and it's no more than two leagues. You do well to avoid such troubles and from there we shall know if Arnaldo is in any danger, for a man with such nerve has me worried." "That is why I wish to leave tomorrow," said Narcisa, "and I shall leave publicly so that our destination is known and my unknown lover will not endanger his life to defend me."

With this decision made, the next day they left Milan. Don Duarte did not want to follow them by day, to lessen the suspicions of the duke's friends and kinsmen. He would go see them at night, as they came out to enjoy the lovely grove within sight of the villa, and return at daylight to Milan, entertaining his thoughts with the desire that night come soon. Narcisa's friends, meanwhile, felt her absence and, as the place was so nearby, they wanted to pay a visit. Accompanied by other ladies, they went to the villa with the intention of staying two days. They were well received by the two cousins, while the country girls and farmers invented various dances and games to entertain them. At night they lit up a good many bowls of perfume[9] and, by their illumination, put on masquerades and silly costumes.[10] As Don Duarte would go every night, he did not want to pass over in silence the splendid merriment, so he wrote some verses. Coming over to a female dwarf[11] whom Narcisa much esteemed for her talents as a musician, he gave her the paper and a ring, saying: "Do me the favor of singing this ballad before your mistress and trust me that I shall well reward the favor." She promised to do so, content with the reward, and withdrew to rehearse. [Then] she was called to the hall to sing. . . .

Everyone applauded the words and Narcisa asked her who had given her the song. She answered [that it was] a country fellow, whom she didn't know. Laurencia said: "You'll no longer think us flatterers when even the peasants praise your beauty." The favor was esteemed, and the next day the ladies decided to return to Milan, asking her to go with them. She answered that, to free herself from the duke's persistence, she would stay for two more months in the country.

Arnaldo kept to his bed and, much improved, intimated that he was going to his estates. He left Milan openly with the design of gaining by force the object of his desire; and remaining concealed, he sent out spies to warn him when his adored and ungrateful object was to return to Milan, so that he could waylay her on the road and achieve his villainous intentions.

Her friends wrote her, telling her of the duke's absence and begging her to come back to Milan, because they found themselves very lonely without her. Rosana dispatched a servant with the letter. When he reached the villa, Narcisa answered that within two days she would grant their wish, for it was she who would gain the pleasure of their beloved company. The duke's spies having informed him and accompanied by six men, he went to wait for her by the side of the road. He ordered that, if the servants attending her resisted, they should be taken to the grove so that they could not defend her. That way the coach could arrive without their knowing what had happened. When the dwarf sang Don Duarte's verses, the two cousins suspected he was in the country. They refused any more attendants than a manservant and the coachman, in order to give the unknown lover the opportunity to speak with them, in the freedom of the countryside. To achieve this end, they left at nightfall.

The fortunate gentleman was coming along unmindful of his good luck when, feeling tired from the weight of his arms, he withdrew to the hollow of some rocks in sight of the road. After a little while he heard the sound of a coach, and, as he did not know of his mistress's intentions, he presumed it must be bringing some ladies to visit her that day. He decided to wait for the coach to pass and stationed himself in the darkest corner. As it came nearer, he saw the men waiting for her to emerge from the grove. Then Arnaldo came along, saying: "Since she has almost no one to attend her, take those two who are with her to the thickest part of the woods and tie them there so that they can't go for help from the peasants. Do not return until I give a whistle." Don Duarte knew very well that the injury was aimed at Narcisa, but he did not want to show himself yet in order to give the duke time to be alone and to make sure she realized how much she owed him. At this point the coach arrived, and three of the six men rushing it reached the footboard to make the manservant step down, threatening him with death if he cried out. The other three did the same with the coachman, carrying the two of them off pinioned, to the thickest part of the woods. Then the duke arrived, saying: "So shall I triumph over your cruel tyranny, for when I have enjoyed your beauty I shall force you to give me your hand." The women were so agitated they could not answer him. Don Duarte emerged from his hiding place just as the duke was about to pull down the footboard and, giving him a stinging blow with the flat of his sword that stunned him, said to him: "Wretch, you might well have taken your pleasure had these ladies no one to defend them." Although the duke was still reeling he took out his sword, but Don Duarte returned with a parry, cutting off his hand completely. The shocked ladies took heart at this, begging him not to kill the duke for their honor was at stake. He answered them, "I would long since have killed him had it not been for your honor." And springing onto the mules in haste, he returned to the villa, managing the coach with such liveliness that he made them laugh.

As the duke's henchmen were on the lookout and saw the coach coming, they feared some new surprise, thinking that the duke had not carried her off. Leaving the two prisoners tied up, they ran to find out the reason. Stunned at seeing him wounded, they asked him why he hadn't whistled or called them. He answered: "The lucky fellow defending her gave me a blow to the side of the head which left me senseless. Take me away from here quickly, for since he has returned to the villa, they will come after us." He was not mistaken in his thinking. Everyone was upset seeing the ladies return, especially when they found out what had happened. Narcisa ordered the peasants to go as quickly as possible to the deepest part of the woods and rescue the two servants from some men who had come to rob the coach. And then they went on, accompanied by their new coachman.

When they arrived at the hall, they recognized him from the many times he had been in the church. Bidding him sit down, Narcisa said to him: "Only you, Sir Duarte, could free me from such a great trial, and the industry with which you have served and obliged me has been so powerful that it has won over my unattached heart, for without offending me you have placed your life in danger to defend me. I should not be who I am were I not grateful, and if the reward for your kindness consists in giving you my hand in marriage, be certain that none other shall be the master of my heart. I shall only wait to see what becomes of Arnaldo's wounds, for I would not want to risk your life now that I esteem it." Don Duarte was so overjoyed that he could not find the words to reply. But when he asked leave to return to Milan, she said that he should stay that night in the villa, because she feared the traitors would surprise him on the way home.

The next day they went to Milan. There the steward told them how the duke had come back that night wounded, and how people were saying that only a league from Milan some thieves had shown up to rob him. This made them happy, judging that by concealing his crime he had not made public the truth. For the attempt to force her on a country road was sufficient to remove his head from his shoulders. In the time it took to dine, the valiant Spaniard enjoyed many favors from the grateful cousins.

As soon as the duke had improved, seeing that he was pursuing an impossible dream and that Narcisa had a secret lover, he no longer wanted to place his life in any greater danger. So changing his intentions, he became betrothed to a cousin to whom he owed many kindnesses, although he had been so blind he had not noticed her favors. Feigning indifference to Narcisa's rejection of him, he was determined to celebrate his marriage with royal entertainment and public merriment. When they told her the news freeing her from such a painful trial, Narcisa became so cheerful that she wanted to show her pleasure. So she ordered that a window near the duke's be rented; she dressed in court finery and, accompanied by her cousin and friends, went to see the revelry. The duke became so incensed seeing her content and carefree that his wife discovered the blow he had been dealt. The festivities over, she asked him as a favor that they retire to his estates and, seeing no more hope to his claims to Narcisa's heart, he thought it well to please her.

After the duke had gone, Narcisa gave her hand to Don Duarte to the great delight of all her friends and even greater admiration for the noble courage and prudent industry of the gallant Spaniard, for Narcisa told them everything that had happened. After eight months Count Leonido returned and, his friends having told him of the duke's absence and Narcisa's marriage, [and] believing that Don Duarte would distrust him for the episode in the garden, he tried to ask for the lovely Clori's hand. He sent word to her how happy he would consider himself to be connected with such an illustrious gentleman [as Don Duarte], and then he wrote, seeking permission to pay her a visit. Don Duarte esteemed the courtesy and, coming forward, performed his duty. The marriage effected, the count showed his generosity by sending his wife rich and costly garments, and living for many years afterward in complete peace and harmony. . . .

[The story ends with a reference to the next narration.]

NOTES TO THE TRANSLATIONS

1. The unrest occasioned by Calvinist uprisings in the Spanish-ruled Low Countries, which had plagued much of Philip II's reign, returned under Philip IV (1621–1665), with Spain's participation in the Thirty Years' War. Although the Peace of Westphalia in 1648 gave independence to the Low Countries, conflict again arose in Flanders in the form of territorial struggles between Spain and France until the Peace of the Pyrenees in 1659. Carvajal could be referring to either peace treaty, though I think it more likely she chose the 1659 date, which is closer to the time she wrote the story.

2. Cynthia, or the moon. Cynthus was the mountain birthplace of Apollo and Artemis, who were therefore also called Cynthius and Cynthia. Artemis, a universal mother figure and goddess of childbirth, was also associated with the moon.

3. In the original, Carvajal uses the phrase *brasas duras,* or "hard coals," but *brasa* also means "thief" in the underworld vocabulary of criminals.

4. Doña Esperanza's father and lover were both *Veinticuatros,* councilmen, as they were known in a number of cities in southern Spain under the ancien régime.

5. It was still quite common to own slaves, male and female, in seventeenth-century Spain. The brand most frequently used to mark slaves was the S and a nail (*clavo*) on both cheeks. In Carvajal's stories there exists a good deal of familiarity and even affection between master and slave, a situation which could lead to abuses. See also Bourland, "Aspectos de la vida del hogar," 347–50; and Deleito y Piñuela, *La mujer, la casa y la moda,* 143–47.

6. Pfandl explains the *cordeles,* or torture by ropes, in these terms: "The rope torture consisted in tying to the accused's bare arm a fine cord and, turning it several times, thus tightening more and more" (*Cultura y costumbres del pueblo español de los siglos XVI y XVII,* 87).

7. Illicit relations between master and slave were not unusual, although as Deleito y Piñuela remarks, such a liaison was considered a shameful secret and could be prosecuted by law (*La mujer, la casa y la moda,* 147). See also note 5.

8. This note of implicit nonconformity with a woman's lot, which one expects to read in María de Zayas, strikes a rare chord in Carvajal. Talens seems to think she was familiar with her predecessor's work (*La escritura como teatralidad,* 168).

9. This kind of perfume was called *cazoleta,* taking its name from the receptacle itself.

10. In the original, *hacían moxigangas*. During carnival time especially, this was a form of public merriment in which extravagant costumes and masks, often representing animals, were worn.

11. Dwarfs often provided entertainment for the nobility. In the royal court they were passed on from one owner to the next. Velázquez would paint several of these jesters, including two—Maribarbola and Nicolás de Portosato—who appear in *Las Meninas* (The

Ladies-in-Waiting, 1656). See José Moreno Villa, *Locos, enanos, negros y niños palaciegos.* Mexico: La Casa de España en México, Ed. Presencia, 1939.

BIBLIOGRAPHY

Primary Works

Carvajal, Mariana de. *Navidades de Madrid, y noches entretenidas, en ocho novelas.* Madrid: Domingo García Morrás, 1663.

______. *Novelas entretenidas.* Madrid: Imprenta y Librería de Don Pedro Joseph Alonso de Padilla, 1728.

Jiménez, Julio A., ed. "Doña Mariana de Caravajal y Saavedra. *Navidades de Madrid y noches entretenidas, en ocho novelas.* Edición crítica y anotada." Ph.D. diss., Northwestern University, 1974.

Related Works

Abel, Elizabeth. "(E)Merging Identities: The Dynamics of Female Friendship in Contemporary Fiction by Women." *Signs* 6 (Spring 1981): 413–35.

______. "Reply to Gardiner." *Signs* 6 (Spring 1981): 442–44.

Andrist, Debra D. "Male/Female Friendship in *Don Quixote.*" *Cervantes* 3, no. 2 (1983): 149–59.

Bourland, Caroline B. "Aspectos de la vida del hogar en el siglo XVII según las novelas de D.ª Mariana de Carabajal y Saavedra." In *Homenaje ofrecido a Menéndez Pidal,* 2: 331–68. Madrid: Librería y Casa Editorial Hernando, 1925.

______. *The Short Story in Spain in the Seventeenth Century.* 1927. Reprint. New York: Burt Franklin, 1973.

Chevalier, Maxime. *Lectura y lectores en la España de los siglos XVI y XVII.* Madrid: Turner, 1976.

Clements, Robert J., and Joseph Gibaldi. *Anatomy of the Novella.* New York: New York University Press, 1977.

Deleito y Piñuela, José. *La mujer, la casa y la moda.* 3d ed. Madrid: Espasa-Calpe, 1966.

Della Casa, Giovanni. *Galateo; or The Book of Good Manners.* Translated by R. S. Pine-Coffin. Harmondsworth: Penguin Books, 1958.

Dunn, Peter N. *Castillo Solórzano and the Decline of the Spanish Novel.* Oxford: Basil Blackwell, 1952.

El Saffar, Ruth. *Beyond Fiction: The Recovery of the Feminine in the Novels of Cervantes.* Berkeley: University of California Press, 1984.

Gardiner, Judith Kegan. "The (US)es of (I)dentity: A Response to Abel on '(E)Merging Identities.'" *Signs* 6 (Spring 1981): 436–42.

González de Amezúa y Mayo, Agustín. *Formación y elementos de la novela cortesana. Discursos leídos ante la Real Academia Española.* Madrid: Tipografía de Archivos, 1929.

Goytisolo, Juan. "El mundo erótico de María de Zayas." In *Disidencias,* 63–115. Barcelona: Seix Barral, 1977.

Gracián, Balthasar. *The Art of Worldly Wisdom.* Translated by Joseph Jacobs, 1892. New York: Frederick Ungar, n.d.

Gracián Dantisco, Lucas. *Galateo español.* Edited by Margherita Morreale. Madrid: CSIC, 1968.

Krömer, Wolfram. *Formas de la narración breve en las literaturas románicas hasta 1700.* Madrid: Gredos, 1979.

McKendrick, Melveena. "Women Against Wedlock: The Reluctant Brides of Golden Age Drama." In *Women in Hispanic Literature: Icons and Fallen Idols,* edited by Beth Miller, 115–46. Berkeley: University of California Press, 1983.

Ordóñez, Elizabeth J. "Woman and Her Text in the Works of María de Zayas and Ana Caro." *Revista de Estudios Hispánicos* 19, no. 1 (January 1985): 3–15.

Pabst, Walter. *La novela corta en la teoría y en la creación literaria.* Madrid: Gredos, 1972.

Pacheco-Ransanz, Arsenio. "Varia fortuna de la novela corta en el siglo XVII," *Revista Canadiense de Estudios Hispánicos* 10 (1986): 407–21.

Palomo, María del Pilar. *La novela cortesana (Forma y estructura).* Barcelona: Planeta, 1976.

Pfandl, Ludwig. *Cultura y costumbres del pueblo español de los siglos XVI y XVII: Introducción al estudio del Siglo de Oro.* 2d ed. Barcelona: Araluce, 1942.

———. *Historia de la literatura nacional española en la Edad de Oro.* 2d ed. Barcelona: Editorial Gustavo Gili, 1952.

Sainz de Robles, Federico Carlos. *Ensayo de un diccionario de mujeres célebres.* Madrid: Aguilar, 1959.

Serrano y Sanz, Manuel. "Carvajal y Saavedra (Dª Mariana de)." In *Apuntes para una biblioteca de escritoras españolas desde el año 1401 al 1833,* 1: 236–44. Madrid: Est. Tip. Sucesores de Rivadeneyra, 1903.

Talens, Jenaro. *La escritura como teatralidad.* Valencia: Universidad de Valencia, 1977.

de la Torre Rodríguez, Ventura. "Una exploración sobre la novela cortesana española del Renacimiento y Barroco." *Cuadernos Hispanoamericanos,* no. 357 (March 1980): 650–56.

Welles, Marcia L. "María de Zayas y Sotomayor and Her *Novela Cortesana:* A Reevaluation." *Bulletin of Hispanic Studies* 55 (1978): 301–10.

Yudin, Florence L. "The *novela corta* as *comedia:* Lope's *Las fortunas de Diana.*" *Bulletin of Hispanic Studies* 45 (1968): 181–88.

PART FIVE

ngland

WOMAN OF LEARNING

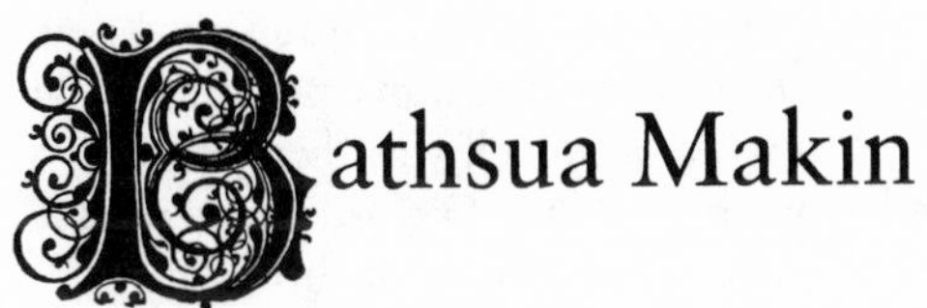athsua Makin

FRANCES TEAGUE

In the early years of the seventeenth century, a clergyman named John Pell wed Mary Holland. They lived at Southwick in Sussex and, by 1610 or so, had a family of three children: two boys, Thomas and John, and a girl, Bathsua.[1] The name "Bathsua" is a variant of "Bathsheba," who was the beautiful mother of Solomon the Wise (2 Samuel, 11–12). No doubt John and Mary Holland Pell hoped that their daughter would be physically attractive—since a seventeenth-century woman's life was in marriage—and the mother of wise sons whose intellectual achievements would ensure her lasting fame. Ironically, Bathsua Makin's reputation is today ensured by her own intellectual achievement; although she married and had a son, nothing definite is known of either husband or child.

By the 1630s, the Pell family had dispersed. In 1616, John, Sr., died; the following year, Mary died also. Their oldest boy, Thomas, served Charles I as a Gentleman of the Bedchamber for awhile, but in 1635 he emigrated to America. John, Jr., was educated at Trinity College, Cambridge, entering in 1623 when he was only thirteen (he was two years ahead of Milton). By 1630, John had received his M.A. and was praised for his mastery of nine foreign languages. A mathematician, an educator, and a clergyman, he began teaching in Amsterdam. Bathsua also became a teacher.

Perhaps her own education had been undertaken by her brother John or by friends of her family after her parents' deaths; perhaps her mother had lived long enough to teach her the rudiments of what she should know. Since there was no education for women outside the home in the early seventeenth century, the knowledge that later earned Bathsua Makin the reputation of being the most learned woman in England must have been acquired privately. Probably John had some hand in her education, for she, like him, knew Latin, Greek, Hebrew, French, Spanish, and Italian well enough to teach those languages (*Essay,* 42).

She probably married Makin in the 1630s. A letter written in 1668 by her brother John mentions her son, but if she had other children, we know nothing about them. *Alumni Cantabrigienses* mentions no student at Cambridge named Makin or Machin while John Pell was there, although a Thomas Machon matriculated from Hart Hall, Oxford in 1655. He might be her son, in which case her husband was John Machon, "clerk."[2]

Evidently her husband either died or was imprisoned soon after their marriage. Bathsua Makin began to work as a governess in the 1630s and was well enough known in this profession by 1640 to be governess to Charles I's daughter, the Princess Elizabeth. In her work, *An Essay to Revive the Antient Education of Gentlewomen* (1673), Makin discusses the extent of Elizabeth's learning at age nine in 1644, presumably the last time that Makin saw her royal pupil.[3] The *Essay* also refers to ". . . Dr. *Loves* Daughters; Their Worth and Excellency in Learning is yet fresh in the Memory of many Men" (p. 10). One scholar has speculated that these pupils were the daughters of Dr. Nicholas Love, a London clergyman; his children would have received their education in the 1630s.[4]

In the years before the Civil War, then, the young widow was forced to draw on her own intellectual resources to earn enough to keep herself and her child. Makin was already teaching the Princess Elizabeth in 1640, for a letter written then by Anna Maria van Schurman to Makin asks about the royal pupil.[5] After the war began, Princess Elizabeth was taken into custody by Parliament, and, in October of 1642, she wrote a letter to Parliament asking to be allowed to keep her attendants.[6] This would explain why Makin continued to teach her until 1644. Makin's job at court probably came through her brother Thomas's royal connection; but if this be the case, her position with the Love family is more difficult to understand. That family was allied with the Puritans and a son (also Nicholas Love) served as one of the judges at Charles I's trial in 1649, although he did not sign the king's death warrant.

Whatever the case, Makin's world must have been a frightening one in the 1640s. One brother, loyal to the crown, had left for America in 1635; the other, who would ally himself to Cromwell, left for Amsterdam in 1643. Without her brothers, Makin remained in England with her son, teaching Parliament's prisoner, the Princess Elizabeth, while the king, her student's father, battled for his country and his life. Soon after Makin left her job in 1644, she was struggling to help someone in her life imprisoned for debt, although there is no indication of who that person was. In the middle of the Civil War, Makin had to do what she could to have him released. The misery she endured in the process led to her first publication: *The Malady and . . . Remedy of Vexations and Unjust Arrests and Actions.*

Dated September 24, 1646, this pamphlet complains bitterly of laws imprisoning men accused of being in debt. The pamphlet begins with a brief historical section in which Makin speaks of the importance of individual liberty. Next she introduces her subject, "some late Statutes, made upon fair and specious pretences for the imprisoning men's bodies for debt."[7] After several pages that rehearse the unjust and oppressive nature of the practice, the pamphlet concludes with a series of six proposals: the first, that men imprisoned for debt should be set free; the next five, that those who have brought false accusations for debt should be punished severely. As Makin argues, "The Sheriff may not seize and take the beasts of the plough upon any execution for debt, . . . much less in all reason and equity the body of the man who is master, owner, and guider of the beast." The closing paragraph points out that because of false accusations some people have been imprisoned for years "for want of access to a full hearing of their causes"; furthermore, after "eleven or twelve years' suits and imprisonments, . . . some of us have been damnified divers thousands of pounds, and others quite ruined and undone."

While the victim of imprisonment is unknown, the pamphlet makes little sense unless Makin has in mind a case in which she herself has been involved. Only a strong personal interest would justify so audacious a proceeding as a seventeenth-century woman's writing and publishing a political pamphlet. In paragraph six, she writes of the hardship inflicted on the debtor's "wife and children left desolate and forsaken"; in paragraph ten, she writes about the debtor's "wife and family" and his "wife and children." If she is writing of her own situation at the end of the pamphlet when she speaks of "eleven or twelve years' suits and imprisonments," she may be referring to either her husband or her brother Thomas. In the former case, the repeated references to "wife and children" make sense: her husband did not die in the early 1630s but was instead thrown in prison; his death in 1646 led to Makin's protests against imprisonment for debt. In the latter case, the pamphlet suggests one reason that Thomas may have left England so abruptly for the New World in 1635; his case was not settled until 1646, eleven years later. In either case, Makin clearly believes that the accusers lied about the debt and should be punished for their perjury.

While these speculations are tempting, several factors suggest that the pamphlet actually makes no direct reference to the facts of Makin's case. To begin with, she did not put her name on the pamphlet. Moreover, she assumes the persona of a male who speaks "as a free commoner of England." He complains "on behalf of myself and many thousands of free-born of this nation, spoiled of their birthright and liberty, now languishing in prisons." Thus it is the imaginary persona who has been imprisoned for eleven or twelve years. Makin's assumption of this persona of the male prisoner is further complicated by the fact that the persona himself assumes a persona on occasion, pretending to be a Roman citizen and addressing the pamphlet to "noble Senators and grave Consuls." While these features make it impossible for one to assess the relevance of the pamphlet to Makin's own life, they do suggest that well before she wrote her *Essay,* she had considered the problem of assuming a persona, as well as the rhetorical strategy necessary if she were to marshal arguments in a way that would persuade a largely male audience. She would use similar techniques in her *Essay.*

From the publication of *The Malady and . . . Remedy* in 1646 until an unsuccessful petition to the Council of State in 1655, no specific information on Makin's life exists. Presumably she continued her work as a governess of young ladies. Most scholars think, for example, that an entry in John Evelyn's diary describes a project in which Makin was involved. Evelyn writes of a jaunt on the river: "Went to Putney by water, in the barge with divers ladies, to see the schools, or Colleges, of the young gentlewomen."[8] Judging from a reference in his *Numismata* to John Pell, Evelyn may have known the family; given Makin's interest in the education of women, an affiliation with such a school would make good sense.[9]

During the 1650s Makin probably resided with Lucy, the Countess of Huntington, teaching both the countess and her daughter Elizabeth. This relationship was evidently a close one. During her time with the Countess of Huntington, Makin taught the mother as well as the daughter, for in *Essay* she employs *præteritio* to say: "I am forbidden to mention the Countess *Dowager* of *Huntington* (instructed sometimes by Mrs. *Makin*) how well she understands *Latin, Greek, Hebrew, French* and *Spanish;* or what a proficient she is in Arts, subservient to Divinity, in which (if I durst I would tell you) she excels" (p. 10). The passage is a charming one, as Makin praises her student despite the countess's modesty that forbids such praise.

On March 28, 1664, Elizabeth died, two years after her marriage to James Langham. Simon Ford, who had preached at the funeral, published a book that included his sermon as well as memorial verses from Elizabeth's friends and admirers. An anecdote in Ford's sermon suggests that he had spoken to Makin before he wrote about his subject: ". . . she was known once in her younger days to address herself to her *Governess* with tears, intreating her pardon for that in her very child-hood *she was conscious that she had been defective in affection to her, for she thought, that then she did not love her.*"[10] Ford's book includes a 39-line elegy that Makin wrote May 2, 1664. Makin praises Elizabeth's noble birth and her virtue in conventional terms; less conventional are the lines that praise Elizabeth's learning:

Her hours were all precisely kept, and spent
In her devotions; and her studies meant
To share some for her languages, which she
In Latin, French, Italian happily
Advanced in with pleasure; what do I
Recount her parts? her memory speaks more
Than what can be, or hath been said before.

Here is the voice of the devoted and loving teacher; Elizabeth Langham had been the kind of student who takes pleasure in her language lessons.

If Makin's time with the Countess of Huntington was generally happy, the 1650s brought disappointment as well. In August of 1655, the Council of State refused Makin's petition that she receive an annual pension of £40 for her attendance on the Princess Elizabeth. Her work as a royal governess went unrewarded by the Puritan Commonwealth, nor is there any indication that the royal family was more generous after the Restoration. Financial trouble was accompanied by family trouble two years later. While he was teaching on the Continent, John Pell wrote his wife Ithumaria, complaining that she was too friendly with his sister Bathsua: "I could wish that you had made an end with your sister Makin. You know she is a woman of no small impatience. She will not strike to rail at me and you, where ever she comes."[11] The reason for John Pell's displeasure remains obscure. Perhaps Makin had tried to use his connections with the government to obtain her pension; perhaps she had sought financial help from him. Since Pell would return to England for good by 1658, Makin may have interfered in some way with his plans for his homecoming. According to the *DNB*, his other letters to his wife "are harsh and contemptuous in tone, and suggest that Ithumaria was a foolish woman, though a devoted wife"; so his comment on Bathsua may simply be an outburst of bad temper.

By the end of the 1650s, then, it seems likely that the Countess of Huntington no longer needed a governess, since her daughter Elizabeth would marry in 1662; that Bathsua Makin's family was, for some reason, annoyed with her; and that she was having financial troubles. Her hopes for a steady income from a government pension had been dashed, and her future seemed dreary. She would spend her life as a servant who taught young ladies the usual subjects—dancing, singing, music, writing, and keeping accounts—and who tried to interest her charges in her own love of such languages as Latin, Greek, and Hebrew. Yet nothing in her *Essay* or in the few details of her life suggests that Makin was in the least dismayed. Indeed, she seems to have shown great enthusiasm and energy in writing a European ally who valued education for women as she did.[12]

In 1659 a new book appeared in London: *The learned Maid, or Whether a Maid May be a Scholar?: A logick exercise,* Clement Barksdale's translation of *De Ingeniis Muliebris* (1641) by Anna Maria van Schurman, the finest woman scholar in Europe and a correspondent of Makin. Makin had evidently read the original Latin book with enthusiasm, for she and Schurman had written (in Greek) since 1640.[13] They admired each other. Anna Maria van Schurman wrote: "Now, it is wonderful that you are cheerful while attending to your many household cares, rarely being in the company of philosophy, and in no way having a taste of your Muses, voiceless in the midst of the noise of armed men. . . . [F]or this reason [love of learning] you lend your talent in the education of the royal girl." In a later letter she assures Makin that "we share all the same difficulties."[14] In her turn, Makin refers throughout the *Essay* to Schurman's learning and virtue, and it was she who helped Schurman make the epistolary acquaintance of Sir Simonds d'Ewes.[15]

Both of them shared a hunger for knowledge and the deep-seated belief that women as well as men should be educated. Such a conviction was anomalous in the seventeenth century, for despite the remarkable achievements of women during the English Civil War, women were generally regarded as incapable creatures that could not or should not be educated. Any education they received was at home or from such servants as governesses. Thus in her *Essay,* Makin had no difficulty summarizing the arguments against the education of women; she had, undoubtedly, heard them often:

> *Women do not much desire Knowledge; they are of low parts, soft fickle natures, they have other things to do they will not mind if they be once Bookish. The end of Learning is to fit one for publick Employment, which Women are not capable of.* Women must not speak in Church, *its against custom. Solomon's good House-wife is not commended for Arts and Tongues, but for looking after her Servants; And that which is worst of all, they are of such ill natures, they will abuse their Education, and be so intolerably Proud, there will be no living with them: If all these things could be answered, they would not have leisure.*[16]

What we know of the rest of Makin's life suggests that she spent most of her time doing what she could to fight such notions and to work for the education of women. In ancient times, she believed, "Women were formerly Educated in the knowledge of Arts and Tongues, and by their Education, many did rise to a great height in Learning" (*Essay,* 3). In her own day, she looked to the example of Anna Maria van Schurman's learning, as well as her own knowledge and that of her students. The evidence from the past and from her own experience showed clearly that women deserved education.

By 1663 Makin was calling for the sort of rigorous curriculum for women that Schurman's book recommended.[17] She had moderated her ambitions ten years later when she actually opened one of the first schools for women. Her 1673 *Essay* serves two functions: to set out her ideas and arguments about the education of women and to advertise her new school to interested parents. It is a remarkable document in two ways, then, for it not only offers an exposition of seventeenth-century theory about women's education but also gives a fairly specific outline of how such theory was put into practice.

The *Essay* is in the form of a series of unsigned letters written by different personae. The first letter is a reverent dedicatory epistle to Princess Mary (later the queen), the oldest daughter of James II, then Duke of York. The second letter, "To the Reader," declares that men should not *"prejudge and cast aside this book upon sight of the title": An Essay to Revive the Antient Education of Gentlewomen*. The persona declares, "*I am a Man myself.*" He insists that he is working for the improvement of men, for if women are educated, men will have to be more diligent to keep up with them; furthermore, "*to scoff at Women kept ignorant . . . savours not at all of a Manly Spirit.*" As she did in *The Malady and . . . Remedy,* Makin simply sidesteps any question of the propriety of a woman's writing a pamphlet; the use of the male persona allows her considerable freedom. Moreover, she takes pleasure throughout in using inverted arguments, turning masculine arguments against her position inside out, so that she may use them to her advantage. A third letter purports to come from another man, a skeptic who denies that women have any capacity or time for education. The quality of prose in it is notably below that of the other two letters, again a skillful use of rhetorical strategy. On page 7 the *Essay* proper, an open letter to the skeptic, begins.

In a short introductory section (pp. 7–8), the sympathetic male persona proposes that education leads to improved intellect and morals; he further reasons that women, who are more vicious than men, have a greater need for education. Here is a good example of Makin's use of the inverted argument: if antifeminists have argued that women are fundamentally less virtuous than men, so be it—all the more reason to educate women! A long section follows (pp. 8–22) in which the persona catalogues the women who have excelled in learning. Languages, oratory, philosophy, mathematics, poetry, and divinity are included in this section; the examples of learned women come from the Bible and classical literature, as well as from medieval and Renaissance Europe. Anna Maria van Schurman is mentioned in five categories, while Makin herself is only mentioned in conjunction with the learned ladies she has taught: Lucy, Countess of

Huntington, and the Princess Elizabeth. Among the many other notable European women, Makin mentions a few names repeatedly: Rosuida (Hroswitha), Elizabeth of Schonangia, Constantia and Baptista Sforza, Queen Christina of Sweden, Lady Jane Grey, and Queen Elizabeth of England. The technique of the inverted argument again appears in connection with Makin's favorite subject, languages: "It is objected against Women, as a reproach, that they have too much Tongue: but it's no crime they have many Tongues; if it be, many Men would be glad to be guilty of that fault. The Tongue is the only Weapon Women have to defend themselves with, and they had need to use it dextrously" (p. 11). The passage is wittily ironic, particularly in the mouth of a male persona.

The next section of the essay (pp. 22–29) is given the subtitle, "*Care ought to be taken by us to Educate Women in Learning*." The opening section begins with a concession to those hostile to the education of women: only "R I C H" women "*Of good natural parts*" should receive education. Such women of social rank and power ought to be taught, however, because untaught women are, unfortunately, frivolous creatures. Putting to good use the standard antifeminist arguments, Makin writes: "Meerly to teach Gentlewomen to Frisk and Dance, to paint their Faces, to curl their Hair, to put on a Whisk [a neckerchief], to wear gay Clothes, is not truly to adorn, but to adulterate their Bodies; yea, (what is worse) to defile their souls" (p. 22). Later she extends her argument. It is not the wicked nature of women that necessitates their education, but the noble nature of men. "Had God intended Women onely as a finer sort of Cattle, he would not have made them reasonable. Bruits, a few degrees higher than Drils [mandrills] or Monkies, (which the *Indians* use to do many Offices) might have better fitted some mens Lust, Pride, and Pleasure; especially those that desire to keep them ignorant to be tyrannized over" (p. 23). In short, men who are opposed to the education of women would probably enjoy bestiality with apes; decent men, however, recognize that women are reasonable creatures who can and should be taught. Good men deserve educated wives.

The *Essay* goes on to detail the advantages of education for women. Women who have been taught are able to keep themselves if they must, as some wives had to do in the Civil War and as poor spinsters or widows must do. Furthermore, education keeps women contented at home, protects them against heresies, and enables them to help their husbands. One of the greatest benefits that would arise from educating women is that children would be educated, learning from their mothers or nursemaids. (One notes that, by this point of the essay, Makin's earlier concession that only rich women of good parts be educated has gone by the board. Instead she envisions educated women in all walks of life—from the fine lady to the lowly nursery maid.) She ends the section by arguing that if women are improved by education, their families and nation will be better also.

Next (pp. 29–42), Makin refutes all the objections to education for women that she can think of. The pamphlet ends with an advertisement for her new school at Tottenham. Whether the school at Tottenham was a success we do not know. Nor do we know anything of the rest of Makin's life. The only hint of how she ended her days comes from an undated letter to her brother John. In it she asks him to send her some information about "the new comet"—probably a reference to either the Great Comet of 1680 or Halley's Comet of 1682. Thus, the letter may have been written when brother and sister were old and poor. Such straitened circumstances would explain two offers she makes. First she says that she will copy some documents for him, a generous offer if he were short of funds or unable to copy the papers himself for reason of health. Further, she sends him "some raisins which are the best breakfast you can eat, if you spit out the stones."[18] She seems to have been thoughtful, but also a bit officious, as a sister should be.

Bathsua Makin's life is not well-documented. Aside from a few clear facts, her biography is a series of speculations and questions. It is, nonetheless, an exemplary life in some ways. She was clearly a remarkable teacher: her pupil, the Princess Elizabeth, mastered five languages in the middle of a threatening civil war; she was able to teach both a countess and her daughter, giving all parties satisfaction. In her own lifetime and after, Makin was mentioned by contemporaries as a model of learning. Her reputation must have made it easier for other women who desired education to defend their wishes. Her influence extended to Anna Maria van Schurman in Utrecht, who was cheered by the way that Makin endured hardship. Her *Essay* may have provided a model for Mary Astell, whose *Serious Proposal to the Ladies for the advancement of their true and greatest interests* (1694 and 1697) advocated a seminary for women in which they could study such subjects as philosophy and languages.

Her writing has more than historical value, however. The sharp wit and ironic arguments of the *Essay* have merit in themselves. Her arguments remain fresh, and she anticipates modern feminist scholars by looking to history for the example of other learned women. To find herself in such a volume as this would have given her great joy.

NOTES

1. The information about John and Thomas Pell is taken from *The Dictionary of National Biography* (*DNB*) and the 11th edition of the *Encyclopædia Britannica* (*EB*), s.v. "John Pell." The information on Bathsua Makin's life comes from the DNB, s.v. "Bathsua

Makin"; Moira Ferguson, *First Feminists;* Mary R. Mahl and Helene Koon, *The Female Spectator;* Myra Reynolds, *The Learned Lady in England;* Doris Mary Stenton, *The English Woman in History;* and Hilda L. Smith, *Reason's Disciples.*

2. *Alumni Cantabrigienses,* compiled by John and J. A. Venn, s.v. "John Pell" and "Thomas Machon."

3. [Bathsua Makin], *An Essay to Revive the Antient Education of Gentlewomen* (1673), Wing M309; hereafter cited as *Essay.* A facsimile edition was prepared in 1980 by Paula L. Barbour for the Augustan Reprint Society, no. 202.

4. See Reynolds, *The Learned Lady in England,* 277; *DNB,* s.v. "Nicholas Love."

5. The letters are printed in Greek in Schurman's *Opuscula* (1650), 164–66. I am grateful to Thomas Poss for translating them for me; see my note, "New Light on Bathsua Makin," 16.

6. *EB,* s.v. "Elizabeth (1635–1650)."

7. *The Malady and . . . Remedy of Vexations and Unjust Arrests and Actions* (1646), Wing 310. I quote from the edited text in Mahl and Koon, *The Female Spectator,* 118–24.

8. John Evelyn, *Diary,* 1:250.

9. Evelyn, *Numismata,* 265; scholars generally accept Makin's affiliation with the Putney school.

10. Simon Ford, *A Christian's Acquiescence* (1665), Wing F1485, 111. Makin's poem is on 162–63. I quote the poem from Mahl and Koon, *The Female Spectator,* 124–25; they edit from Huntington Library M.S. H.A. 8799 rather than from Ford.

11. Mahl and Koon, *The Female Spectator,* 116.

12. For further information about Schurman, see Stenton, *The English Woman in History;* Reynolds, *The Learned Lady in England;* J. R. Brink, *Female Scholars;* and the bibliography on Schurman contained in this volume.

13. Schurman, *Opuscula,* 166.

14. Ibid., 164–66; Thomas Poss's translation.

15. Stenton, *The English Woman in History,* 193.

16. Makin, *Essay,* 6. All quotations are cited from a microfilm of the original. After finishing this chapter, I encountered Mitzi Myers's interesting analysis of Makin's *Essay* in the article "Domesticating Minerva: Bathsua Makin's 'Curious' Argument for Women's Education," 173–92.

17. Antonia Fraser, *The Weaker Vessel,* 323; I do not know Fraser's source for this statement.

18. Mahl and Koon, *The Female Spectator,* 116.

From An Essay to Revive the Antient Education of Gentlewomen

[In the earlier part of her *Essay,* Makin has discussed the function of education, given a catalogue of learned women, and explained the importance and advantages of educating women.]

Before I mention the Objections, I shall state the Propositions I have endeavoured to prove; That which I intend is this, That Persons of competent natural parts, indifferently inclin'd and disposed to Learning, whom

God hath blessed with Estates, that they are not cumbred[1] in the World, but have liberty and opportunity in their Childhood; and afterwards, being competently instructed in all things now useful that concern them as Women, may and ought to be improved in more Polite Learning, in Religion, Arts, and the knowledge of things, in Tongues also as subservient to these, rather than to spend the over-plus time of their youth, in making Points for Bravery, in dressing and trimming themselves like *Bartholomew*-Babies,[2] in Painting and Dancing, in making Flowers of Coloured Straw, and building Houses of stained Paper, and such like vanities.

Object. *No Body means Gentlewomen should be thus educated in matters of meer vanity; but in practising their Needle, in knowing and doing those things that concern good Housewifery, which is Womens particular qualification.*

Answ. I know not what may be meant, but I see what is generally done. In most Schools for educating this Sex, little more is proposed by the Undertakers,[3] or expected by the Parents. As far as I can observe, the less any thing of solidity is taught, the more such places are frequented. I do acknowledge, in the state of the Question, that Women should be accomplished in all those things that concern them as Women. My meaning is, The over-plus time may be imployed in polishing their minds with the knowledge of such things as may be honourable, pleasant and profitable to them, and their Relations afterwards.

Before I proceed further to Answer the remaining Objections, I desire this may be taken notice of, That what-ever is said against this manner of Educating Women, may commonly be urged against the Education of Men.

Object. *If we bring up our Daughters to Learning, no Persons will adventure to Marry them.*

Answ. 1. Many men, silly enough, (God knows) think themselves wise, and will not dare to marry a wise Woman, lest they should be over-topt.

2. As some Husbands, debauched themselves, desire their Wives should be chast, and their children vertuous: So some men, sensible of their own want, (caused by their Parents neglect) will chuse a learned Woman, in whom they may glory, and by whose prudence their defect may be supplyed.

3. Learned men, to be sure, will chuse such the rather, because they are sutable. Some Men marrying Wives of good natural parts, have improved themselves in Arts and Tongues, the more to fit them for their converse.

4. Many Women formerly have been preferred for this very thing.[4]

Athenais, Daughter to *Leontius* the Philosopher, left destitute by him, was entertained by his Sister *Placida* for her Learning, and was after married to the Emperor *Theodosius*, charmed by her worth, being fitted by her education for that high place; she is recorded for an excellent Empress. Upon her being baptized, she was called *Eudocea*.

Constantine married *Helena* the daughter of *Lois*, more for her Learning, than for other accomplishments.

We may probably imagine *Hortensia, Terentia, Tullia*, and divers others had never been married to such brave men, had not their Education preferred them.

If this way of educating Gentlewomen should now be set on foot, there will not be so great a number bred; but (as degenerate as times are) there would be found learned men enow, to whom they may be preferred for their very Education.

Object.[5] Solomon'*s good Housewife is commended for rising early, imploying her Servants, making Garments, by which her Husband was known in the Gate. It seems she was of quality, she had so many Servants, and her Husband a Magistrate; their Courts of Judicature were at the Gate: no mention is made of Arts or Tongues.*

Answ. It seems Persons of Quality were more industrious in those times than they are now. I do not intend to hinder good Housewifery, neither have I called any from their necessary Labour to their Book. My design is upon such Persons whose leasure is a burthen.

Further, if *Solomon*'s good House-wife was accomplished with Arts and Tongues, she would have more reverence from her Servants, and by her knowledge in Economicks, know better how to manage so great a Family.

Solomon describes an industrious Woman. I am suggesting what persons ought to do that are about these things. Those that deny this, deserve no Answer, but are to be thought on with scorn, as that Duke that thought Women wise enough that knew their Husbands Doublet and Breeches asunder.

If there be any persons so vain, and are yet pleased with this Apish kind of Breeding now in use, that desire their Daughters should be outwardly dressed like Puppets, rather than inwardly adorned with Knowledge, let them enjoy their humour; but never wonder if such Marmosets married to Buffoons, bring forth and breed up a generation of Baboons, that have little more wit than Apes and Hobby-Horses. I cannot say enough against this Barbarous rudeness, to suffer one part, I had almost said the better part, of our selves to degenerate (as far as possible) into brutality.

Object. *Women are of ill Natures, and will abuse their Education: They will be proud, and not obey their Husbands; they will be pragmatick, and boast of their Parts and Improvements. The ill Nature that is in them, will become more wicked, the more wit you furnish them with.*

Answ. This is the killing Objection, and every thick-skull'd Fellow that babbles this out, thinks no *Billingsgate* Woman can Answer it.[6] I shall take the Objection in pieces.

1. *They will abuse Learning.*] So do men; he is egregiously simple, that argues against the use of a necessary or very convenient thing from the abuse of it. By the Argument no men should be liberally brought up; strong Drinks should never be used any more in the World, and a hundred such like things.

2. *They are of ill Natures.*] This is an impudent calumny; as if the whole Sex of Women, or the greatest part of them, had that malice infused into their very Natures and Constitutions, that they are ordinarily made worse by the Education that makes Men generally better.

——Ingenuas didicisse fideliter artes
Emollit mores, nec sinit esse feros.[7]

The Heathen found, that Arts wrought upon Men, the rougher Sex. Surely it is want of fidelity in the Instructor, if it have not the like effect upon softer and finer Materials.

3. *They will be proud, and not obey their Husbands.*] To this I Answer; What is said of Philosophy, is true of knowledge; a little Philosophy carries a Man from God, but a great deal brings him back again;[8] a little knowledge, like windy Bladders, puffs up, but a good measure of true knowledge, like Ballast in a Ship, settles down, and makes a person move more even in his station; 'tis not knowing too much, but too little that causes the irregularity. This same Argument may be turned upon Men; what-ever they answer for themselves, will defend Women.

Those that desire a farther Answer, let them peruse *Erasmus* his Dialogue, of the *Ignorant Abbot* and the *Learned Woman.*[9] An ignorant Magistrate, or Minister, may as well plead against improvement of Knowledge in all below them, lest they should be wiser than themselves, and so deride them. Do not deny Women their due, which is to be as well instructed as they can; but let Men do their duty, to be wiser than they are. If this doth not please, let silly Men let wise Women alone; the rule is, All should be (as near as they can) equally yoked.

Object. *The end of Learning is publick Business, which Women are not capable of. They must not speak in the Church; and it is more proper for men to Act in the Common-Wealth than they.*

Answ. They may not speak in the Church, but they may inquire of their Husbands at home; it is private instruction I plead for; not publick Imployment. Yet there is no such contradiction in the terms: *Miriam* and *Deborah* were extraordinarily called forth by God, as well as *Aaron* and *Barak.*[10] Sometimes Women may have occasions for publick Business, as Widows, and Wives when their Husbands are absent; but, especially persons born to Government. The *Salique* Law[11] hath not prevailed all the

World over, and good reason too; for Women upon Thrones have been as glorious in their governing, as many Men, as I have shewed before. But lay all this aside; there are other ends of Learning, besides pleading in the Hall, and appearing in the Pulpit. Private Persons (as I have before shewed) may many ways please themselves, and benefit others. This Objection also will turn the Point upon all Men that are in a private capacity.

Object. They will not mind their Household Affairs.

Answ. Men are judged to be more capable of Countrey business by liberal Education. Most ingenious Contrivances, even in Husbandry and Trades, have been invented by Scholars. You may as well say, a Gentleman that hath Countrey Affairs to manage, ought not to be a Scholar, because he will be poring upon his Book, when he should be looking after his Plowmen.

Object. *They have other things to do.*

Answ. Those which have, may mind those things for ought I have said: The Question is of persons at leasure, Whether these had not better be imployed in some good Literature, than in pilling Straws,[12] or doing nothing, which is the certain Seed of doing mischief?

Object. *Women do not desire Learning.*

Answ. Neither do many Boys, (as Schools are now ordered) yet I suppose you do not intend to lay Fallow all Children that will not bring forth Fruit of themselves, to forbear to instruct those which at present do not thank you for it.

But I have said, there is in all an innate desire of knowing, in Women as well as Men: if the wayes to the Temple of *Pallas* be so tedious and intricate, that they confound or tire her Servants; or, if you dress up learning in such an ugly and monstrous shape, that you afright Children; I have nothing to say to such, but that they should reform their Schools, or else all will think they have no desire any, either Male or Female, should be instructed.

Object. *Women are of low Parts.*

Answ. So are many Men; we plead only for those which have competent parts. To be sure, some Women are as capable of Learning, and have attained to as great height in it as most Men; witness those Examples before produced.

If this be true, their Parts generally are lower than Mens, there is the more need they should by all convenient means be improved. Crutches are for infirm persons.

Object. *Women are of softer Natures, more delicate and tender Constitutions, not so fixed and solid as Men.*

Answ. If their Natures are soft, they are more capable of good Impressions; if they are weak, more shame for us to neglect them, and defraud them of the benefit of *Education,* by which they may be strengthened.

Object. *It is against custom to educate Gentlewomen thus; those that do attempt it, will make themselves ridiculous.*

Answ. This Argument might have been used to the *Irish;* not to use Traces at Plow and Cart, but to draw their Horses by their Tails, which was a general custom amongst them. Bad Customs (when it is evident they are so) ought to be broken, or else good Customs can never come into use. That this is a bad Custom, is evident, continued upon a bad ground. Let Women be Fools, and then you may easily make them Slaves.

Object. *What need Women learn Tongues, there are Books enow in English for them to peruse?*

Answ. The great Thing I design is, the Knowledge of things; as Religion; the Names and Natures of Herbs, Shrubs, Trees, Mineral-Juyces, Metals and Precious Stones; as also the Principles of Arts and Sciences before mentioned. The learning of Tongues is only subservient to these. Was all Learning in *English,* as it is now in *French,* I think those dead Languages would be of little use, only in reference to the Scriptures. My opinion is, in the educating of Gentlewomen, greater care ought to be had to know things, than to get words. If one must be neglected, it's better to neglect Tongues than Arts; though it is best where both may be had.

Object. Solomon's *vertuous Woman,* Prov. 31. *is commended for good Housewifery, not for Arts and Tongues; yet her Husband was a Person of Quality, he sat amongst the Elders of the Land in the Gate.*

Answ. It seems Persons of Quality were more industrious in those times than now they are. Our Ladies would count it a great disparagement to them to do as she did; to seek Wool and Flax, and to work willingly with their own hands, *vers.* 13. to lay their hands to the Spindle, and to take hold on the Distaff, *vers.* 19. to rise while it is Night, and to give Meat to her Household, and a Portion to her Maids, *vers.* 15. It's like the necessities of those times were greater, and the way of living far different from that which is now in use. The Duke of *Florence* is a great Merchant; Noblemen in England, and Gentlemen in France, think it disparagement to them to be so.

Answ. 2. I plead that our Ladies should have but the same Abilities this vertuous Woman had; not to labour as she did, but to understand as she did. I am sure to do all those things well that she performed, so as to be reverenced of her Servants, that her Children should rise up before her, and call her Blessed, and that her Husband should praise her, requires knowledge in Arts and Sciences, which were hardly got in those days without the knowledge of Tongues; if they then were, or can be now, I am contented without them.

To buy Wooll and Flax, to die Scarlet and Purple, requires skill in Natural Philosophy. To consider a Field, the quantity and quality, requires knowledge in Geometry. To plant a Vineyard, requires understanding in

Husbandry: She could not Merchandize, without knowledge in Arithmetick: She could not govern so great a Family well, without knowledge in Politicks and Œconomicks: She could not look well to the wayes of her Houshold, except she understood Physick and Chirurgery: She could not open her Mouth with Wisdom, and have in her Tongue the Law of kindness, unless she understood Grammar, Rhetorick and Logick. This seems to be the description of an honest, well-bred, ingenious, industrious Dutch-woman. I desire our Women (whose condition calls them to business) should have no other breeding, but what will enable to do those things performed by this Woman.

As for those that are above these, I am sure the highest breeding imaginable will be useful to them. I believe the men of our times would say, it's pity any Woman should have so much Authority as this Woman had, she would be so masterly there would be no living with her.

Object. Another Objection that seems unanswerable, is this; *How shall time be found to teach Children these things here proposed? Boyes go to School ordinarily from seven till sixteen or seventeen, and not above one in four attain so much knowledge in the Tongues, as to be admitted into the University, where no great accuracy is required; and they learn nothing else usually, besides a little History: Gentlewomen will not ordinarily be sent out so soon, nor is it convenient they should continue so long. Further, half their time, it is supposed, must be spent in learning those things that concern them as Women. Twice as many things are proposed to be taught Girls in half the time, as Boyes do learn, which is impossible.*

Answ. This Objection makes the whole Contrivance seem idle, unless a satisfactory Answer be given.

I say therefore, The learning of things will be no hinderance to the getting Words. Words are the marks of things, and they are learnt better together than asunder. As a man shall sooner remember Names, if he see the persons, so a Girl shall much easier fasten in her memory the names of Herbs, Shrubs, Mineral-Juyces, Metals, Precious Stones; as also the names of Birds, Beasts, Fishes; the parts of Man's Body; if she see the things themselves in *specie;* or the Pictures and Representations, where the things themselves cannot be had. This is a great Truth, (if there be any such things as a concatenation of Notions, as doubtless there is) the thing being perceived, Words freely follow. Besides to learn words thus, will be very pleasant and delightful, even to Children. As the eye is not satisfied with seeing, if it be an Object it can reach and distinguish: So the mind of a Child is not satisfied with understanding, if it be a thing he can apprehend. Let those that do believe this, try a Child of four years old in plain Pictures of Men, Beasts, Birds, or Fishes, they will see how inquisitive he will be; or, let them shew Herbs, Flowers, Stones, or any thing rare, and see whether it is any burthen to the Childs understanding or memory to learn the name when he sees the thing.

Let no Body be afrighted, because so many things are to be learnt, when the learning of them will be so pleasant; how profitable I need not tell you.

If any doubt how this may be done, or what Authors we shall use, that words and things may be learnt together;

I answer, *Comenius* hath prepared *Nomenclatures* for this purpose. His *Orbis Pictus,* contains all the Primitive Latine words, and the representation of most things capable of being set out by Pictures; it may be learnt by beginners in three months, and is as a System of his *Janua Linguarum.*

[Makin describes the *Janua Linguarum* and how to use it to teach vocabulary. She then explains a method of teaching accidence and grammar.]

Those that do not understand these short hints, may peruse a *Grammar* and an *Apology;* to which is added Rules for Pointing and Reading Grammatically; Composed by M. *Lewis,* Sold by *Thomas Parkhurst,* at the Bible and three Crowns in *Cheapside,* in which these things are more largely discussed. Or they may speak with M. *Lewis* himself any *Thursday* in the Afternoon, between three and six of the Clock, at the Bolt and Tun in the *Fleetstreet.*

I will not trouble you with his Discourse, how this Method is founded upon the general rule of Speaking, that goes through the World, and how the English Tongue is one of the most regular Languages spoken upon the face of the Earth. The *Grammar* of this being known, it may be a Standard to measure all other Languages by.

If you peruse his *Apologie,* you will see how the *English* is a foundation to the *Latin,* the *Latin* to the *Greek,* you may there see how he demonstrates, to learn to decline *Greek Nouns,* and form *Greek Verbs,* hath not a fourth part of the difficulty in it, as there is in the *Latin.*

Let not Persons rashly censure these Proposals, before they have examined the *Hypothesis,* and heard what the Author can say in defence of it.

Let no Person be discouraged, because Grammar, Words, and Things, are proposed to be learnt in so short a time; the plainness and shortness of the Grammar, the seeing the Things, and having the Words in so short a compass, will make the Work easie and very delightful.

If all I have said may conveniently be done, I expect many will deride this Design. I am contented, let them abound in their own sense, and have Wives as silly as themselves desire, over whom they may tyrannize.

I hope I shall by this Discourse perswade some Parents to be more careful for the future of the Breeding of their Daughters. You cark and care to get great Portions for them, which sometimes occasions their ruine. Here is a sure Portion, an easie way to make them excellent. How many born to good Fortunes, when their Wealth hath been wasted, have supported themselves and Families too by their Wisdom.

I hope some of these Considerations will at least move some of this abused Sex to set a right value upon themselves, according to the dignity of their Creation, that they might, with an honest pride and magnanimity, scorn to be bowed down and made to stoop to such Follies and Vanities, Trifles and Nothings, so far below them, and unproportionable to their noble Souls, nothing inferior to those of Men, and equally precious to God in Christ, in whom there is neither Male nor Female.

Let a generous resolution possess your minds, seeing Men in this Age have invaded Womens Vices, in a noble revenge, reassume those Vertues, which Men sometimes unjustly usurped to themselves, but ought to have left them in common to both Sexes.

POSTSCRIPT

If any enquire where this Education may be performed, such may be informed, That a *School* is lately erected for Gentlewomen at *Tottenham-high-Cross,* within four miles of *London,* in the Road to *Ware,* where Mris. *Makin*[13] is Governess, who was sometimes Tutoress to the Princess *Elisabeth,* Daughter to King *Charles* the First; Where, by the blessing of God, Gentlewomen may be instructed in the Principles of *Religion;* and in all manner of sober and Vertuous Education: More particularly, in all things ordinarily taught in other Schools:

As, *Works of all Sorts,*
Dancing,
Musick,
Singing,
Writing,
Keeping Accompts,
} Half the time to be spent in these Things.

The other half to be imployed in gaining the *Latin* and *French* Tongues; and those that please, may learn *Greek* and *Hebrew,* the *Italian* and *Spanish;* In all which this Gentlewoman hath a competent knowledge.

Gentlewomen of eight or nine years old, that can read well, may be instructed in a year or two (according to their Parts) in the *Latin* and *French* Tongues; by such plain and short Rules, accommodated to the *Grammar* of the *English* Tongue, that they may easily keep what they have learned, and recover what they shall lose; as those that learn Musick by Notes.

Those that will bestow longer time, may learn the other Languages, afore-mentioned, as they please.

Repositories also for Visibles shall be prepared; by which, from beholding the things, Gentlewomen may learn the Names, Natures, Values, and Use of *Herbs, Shrubs, Trees, Mineral-Juices, Metals,* and *Stones.*

Those that please, may learn *Limning, Preserving, Pastry* and *Cookery.*

Those that will allow longer time, may attain some general Knowledge in *Astronomy, Geography;* but especially in *Arithmetick* and *History.*

Those that think one Language enough for a Woman, may forbear the Languages, and learn onely *Experimental Philosophy;* and more, or fewer of the other things aforementioned, as they incline.

The Rate certain shal be 20£. *per annum:* But if a competent improvement be made in the Tongues, and the other things aforementioned, as shall be agreed upon, then something more will be expected. But the Parents shall judge what shall be deserved by the Undertaker.

Those that think these Things Improbable or Impracticable, may have further account every *Tuesday* at Mr. *Masons* Coffee-House in *Cornhil,* near the Royal Exchange; and *Thursdayes* at the Bolt and Tun in *Fleetstreet,* between the hours of three and six in the Afternoons, by some Person whom Mris. *Makin* shall appoint.[14]

NOTES TO THE READING

I have retained the original spelling, punctuation, italics, and capitals. Although her usage seems odd to a modern reader's eyes, Makin follows standard seventeenth-century usage. I have changed her swash *s* to normal lowercase *s* and omitted catchwords.

1. cumbred: encumbered or burdened.
2. *Bartholomew*-Babies: dolls sold as souvenirs of Bartholomew Fair, an annual London festival held near St. Bartholomew's Hospital.
3. Undertakers: those who administer the school.
4. Constantine was Roman emperor in the early fourth century; Theodosius in the late fourth century. Hortensia, daughter of Quintus Hortensius Hortalus, was an orator in her own right; Terentia was Cicero's first wife, and Tullia was Cicero's daughter.
5. See Proverbs 31:10–31.
6. *Billingsgate* Woman: a woman using coarse and unsuitable language.
7. Ovid, *Epistulae ex Ponto,* 2.9.47–48: "Faithful study of the liberal arts makes one's manner gentle and does not let it be arrogant."
8. Francis Bacon, "Of Atheism," *Essays:* "A little philosophy inclineth men's mind to atheism, but depth in philosophy bringeth men's minds about to religion."
9. Erasmus, *Abbatis et eruditae.*
10. See Exodus 15:20–21, Judges 4–5.
11. *Salique* Law: sixth-century Frankish or Salian collection of laws that said no woman could be a royal heir.
12. pilling Straws: peeling or picking up straws, *i.e.,* an idle pastime.
13. Mris.: Mistress.
14. Presumably the person appointed was a Mr. Lewis; earlier Makin says that those who are curious about a textbook he wrote may question him at the Bolt and Tun any

Thursday afternoon. Wing lists a series of grammar texts by Mark Lewis that were published from 1661 on (Wing L1842–L1850).

BIBLIOGRAPHY

Primary Works

Ford, Simon. *A Christian's Acquiescence* (Wing F1485; 1665).

Makin, Bathsua. *An Essay to Revive the Antient Education of Gentlewomen* (Wing M309; 1673).

———. *An Essay to Revive the Antient Education of Gentlewomen.* Edited by Paula L. Barbour. Augustan Reprint Society, no. 202. Los Angeles: William Andrews Clark Memorial Library, 1980.

———. *The Malady and . . . Remedy of Vexations and Unjust Arrests and Actions* (Wing 310; 1646).

Schurman, Anna Maria van. *Opuscula.* 1650.

Related Works

Alumni Cantabrigienses, compiled by John and J. A. Venn. Cambridge: Cambridge University Press, 1924. S.v. "John Pell" and "Thomas Machon."

Brink, J. R. *Female Scholars.* Montreal: Eden Press, 1980.

Dictionary of National Biography (*DNB*). S.v. "Nicholas Love," "Bathsua Makin," "John Pell."

Encyclopædia Britannica (*EB*), 11th edition. S.v. "Elizabeth (1635–1650)"; "John Pell."

Evelyn, John. *Diary.* London, 1850–1852.

Evelyn, John. *Numismata.* London, 1697.

Ferguson, Moira. *First Feminists.* Bloomington and Old Westbury: Indiana University and Feminist Press, 1985.

Fraser, Antonia. *The Weaker Vessel.* New York: Knopf, 1984.

Mahl, Mary R. and Helene Koon. *The Female Spectator.* Bloomington and Old Westbury: Indiana University and Feminist Press, 1977.

Myers, Mitzi. "Domesticating Minerva: Bathsua Makin's 'Curious' Argument for Women's Education." In *Studies in Eighteenth-Century Culture,* edited by O M Brack, Jr., 14: 173–92. Madison: University of Wisconsin for the American Society of Eighteenth-Century Studies, 1985.

Reynolds, Myra. *The Learned Lady in England.* Boston: Houghton Mifflin, 1920.

Smith, Hilda L. *Reason's Disciples.* Urbana: University of Illinois Press, 1982.

Stenton, Doris Mary. *The English Woman in History.* London: Allen and Unwin, 1957.

Teague, Frances. "New Light on Bathsua Makin." *Seventeenth-Century News* 45 (1986): 16.

A "WISE, WITTIE AND LEARNED LADY"

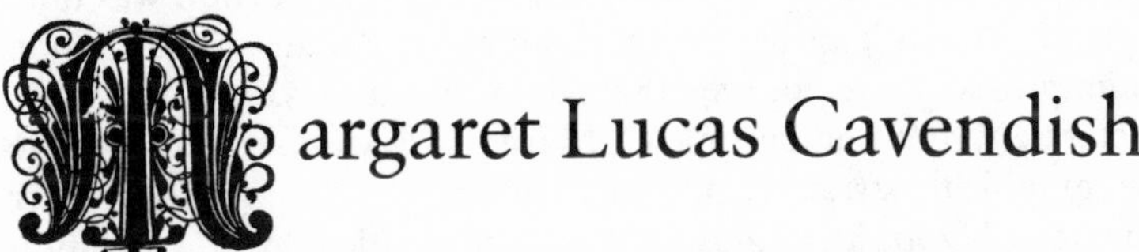

Margaret Lucas Cavendish

MOIRA FERGUSON

The writings of Margaret Lucas Cavendish, Duchess of Newcastle, span a tumultuous era in British history when the aristocracy fought unsuccessfully to retain political power—from the Interregnum after the execution of Charles I in 1649 until eight years after the Restoration of his father, Charles II, in 1660.[1] A dying feudal system had finally succumbed to the new bourgeois patriarchal order. Born in 1623, the duchess was the last child of the "largest landowning family in Colchester," Essex. The family Lucas "had risen to the ranks of the gentry during the previous century."[2] Through her marriage to the wealthy Duke of Newcastle she rose dramatically on the social scale, although both their families were financially ruined during the Civil War. Colchester itself was "one of the hotbeds of puritan sentiment"—so much so that, when the Parliamentary forces overran the town, both "officers and men" entered the family tomb and cut off the hair of the duchess's recently deceased mother and sister. The duchess's inability to comprehend the actions and demands of Parliament's supporters characterizes all her political writings. One of her biographers attributes her blindness to a "lack of a proper historical consciousness."[3]

The duchess's adult life was fundamentally affected by the seventeenth-century revolution. As maid-of-honor to Queen Henrietta Maria, she lived at the court-in-exile in France to which other British exiles were drawn. There, at the end of 1645 after a clandestine courtship, she married the fifty-two-year-old William Cavendish, everyone's idea of an urbane cavalier, a devotee of the arts, a writer, and later a nobleman, the Duke of Newcastle. (He had arrived in Paris in the spring of 1645 but first went elsewhere on the Continent.) A Royalist commander, he had fled England after Parliament trounced his army at York in July 1644, a defection that seriously demoralized the Royalists.[4] Shortly afterward, he was proscribed by Parliament and banished. For twenty-year-old Margaret Lucas, the match was socially advantageous, since "her portion was only two thousand pounds"; given the fact that most Royalist estates were being summarily sequestered, even that sum was dubious.

An inveterate writer and chronicler, Margaret Lucas Cavendish wrote an autobiographical narrative, published as the eleventh section of her twelve-part text, *Nature's Pictures*. In that section, titled "A True Relation of my Birth, Breeding and Life," the Duchess straightforwardly narrates her eventful personal history, displaying a devoted sense of family and predictable anger and scorn toward class adversaries. The entire section is a valuable index to her character and attitudes. Her own account, in "A True Relation," of events until her marriage speaks for itself:

> My father was a gentleman, . . . and though . . . not a peer of the realm, yet there were few peers who had much greater estates, or lived more noble therewith. . . . Towards the latter end of Queen Elizabeth's reign, . . . he unfortunately killed one Mr. Brooks in a single duel. [And because of that] . . . his exile was from the time of his misfortunes to Queen Elizabeth's death. . . . But King James of blessed memory graciously gave him his pardon, and leave to return home to his native country, wherein he lived happily, and died peaceably, leaving a wife and eight children, three sons, and five daughters, I being the youngest child he had, and an infant when he died.
>
> As for my breeding, it was according to my birth, and the nature of my sex; for my birth was not lost in my breeding. For as my sisters was [sic] or had been bred, so was I in plenty, or rather with superfluity. Likewise we were bred virtuously, modestly, civilly, honourably, and on honest principles. . . . After my father's death the estate was divided between my mother and her sons, paying such a sum of money for portions to her daughters, either at the day of their marriage, or when they should come to age; yet by reason she and her children agreed with a mutual consent, all their affairs were managed so well, as she lived not in a much lower condition than when my father lived. . . . Also we were bred with respectful attendance, every one being severally waited upon, and all her servants in general used the same respect to her children (even those that were very young) as they did to herself; for she suffered not her servants, either to be rude before us, or to domineer over us, which all vulgar servants are apt, and ofttimes which some have leave to do. . . . Neither were we suffered to have any familiarity with the vulgar servants, or conversation: yet caused us to demean ourselves with an humble civility towards them, as they with a dutiful respect to us. Not because they were servants were we so reserved; for many noble persons are forced to serve through necessity; but by reason

the vulgar sort of servants are as ill bred as meanly born, giving children ill examples and worse counsel.

As for tutors, although we had for all sorts of virtues, as singing, dancing, playing on music, reading, writing, working, and the like, yet we were not kept strictly thereto, they were rather for formality than benefit; . . . As for my brothers, . . . they were bred when I was not capable to observe, or before I was born; likewise the breeding of men were after different manner of ways from those of women. . . .

As for the pastime of my sisters when they were in the country, it was to read, work, walk, and discourse with each other. . . . I observed they [my brothers and sisters] did seldom make visits, nor never went abroad with strangers in their company, but only themselves in a flock together, agreeing so well that there seemed but one mind amongst them. And not only my own brothers and sisters agreed so, but my brothers and sisters in law, and their children, although but young, had the like agreeable natures and affectionable dispositions. For to my best remembrance I do not know that ever they did fall out, or had any angry or unkind disputes. . . . I had a great desire to be one of her maids of honour, hearing the Queen had not the same number she was used to have. Whereupon I wooed and won my mother to let me go; . . . When I was gone from them, I was like one that had no foundation to stand, or guide to direct me, which made me afraid, lest I should wander with ignorance out of the ways of honour, so that I knew not how to behave myself. . . . In truth, my bashfulness and fears made me repent my going from home to see the world abroad. . . . But my mother advised me there to stay, although I put her to more charges than if she had kept me at home, and the more, by reason she and my brothers were sequestered from their estates, . . . So I continued almost two years, until such time as I was married from thence. For my Lord the Marquis of Newcastle did approve of those bashful fears which many condemned, and would choose such a wife as he might bring to his own humours, and not such a one as was wedded to self-conceit, or one that had been tempered to the humours of another; for which he wooed me for his wife; and though *I did dread marriage, and shunned men's company as much as I could* [my italics], yet I could not, nor had not the power to refuse him, by reason my affections were fixed on him, and he was the only person I ever was in love with. (pp. 275–88)

After a description of her "not amorous [but] honest and honourable" love for her husband (and no mention of the thirty-year age difference), the duchess devotes the next fourteen pages of the forty-page narrative to the effect of the Civil War on the couple's lives. The duke spent sixteen years abroad, the duchess fourteen and a half. She describes their exile—the first two years in Paris and the remainder in Rotterdam and Antwerp, the duke choosing the latter "for the most pleasantest and quietest place to retire himself and ruined fortunes in" (p. 296). The duchess presents a tender portrait of her mother who "lived to see the ruin of her children, in which was her ruin and then died" (p. 294), as well as vignettes of siblings and of a much-loved brother-in-law, Sir Charles Cavendish, with whom the duchess traveled to England "to seek for relief" over the sequestration of "my Lord's estate." Such an action was not uncommon, a similar one having been undertaken by Lady Verney and by other exiled women aristocrats.[5]

In describing this onerous task, from which she had mistakenly thought that she stood to benefit financially, the duchess makes the reader privy to her political opinions (p. 296).[6] She reserves particularly scathing remarks for the female sectaries (members of radical sects) who struggled so vocally and visibly for female autonomy during the Civil War. Since their bid for independence was not dissimilar to the duchess's lifelong resistance to cultural and social norms for women—evident in her prolific literary output and in her creative wardrobes—she rationalizes her disapprobation of their activities and displaces personal tension in the process. She attributes "vulgarity" to their persistence in petitioning, smugly insisting that she would never exhibit herself as a "beggar [*i.e.*, petitioner] at the Parliament door" (p. 297). Rumors that she was frequenting Parliament angered her greatly. The duchess denies her political solidarity with Nonconformist women because her class antagonism overrides or enables her to deny any such bond.[7] On gender issues throughout her works in general, the duchess's reasons for her attitudes are often less clearcut and sometimes actually contradictory.

The final section of the narrative affirms and explains the duchess's love of writing and contemplation, a predisposition caused by a number of factors: the "comfortable cocoon" of her family upbringing with no "pressure towards conformity"; their reliance on self and one another without need of external interaction; her shyness and love of fame, the former leading to aesthetic introspection, the latter to public display and promotion. The duchess seems oblivious to this contradiction, yet its existence undergirds her narrative and helps to explain both her immersion in private writing and her love of sartorial extravagance.[8] The duke's example and encouragement also mattered mightily to her, almost as if he and his writing gave her the permission she felt she needed to fulfill her own inclination to write and publish. The duke's praise of her literary pursuits and his defense of their authenticity make his support abundantly evident. On the other hand, she accentuates his artistic preeminence over herself in almost suspect statements of self-belittlement: "Also he recreates himself with his pen, writing what his wit dictates to him, but I pass my time rather with scribbling than writing, with words than wit" (p. 306).

This wide-eyed disclaimer about her "scribbling" raises a critical issue in all her texts about the way she presents herself. Elaine Hobby's observation (concerning another text written by the duchess) that there are three "Margaret Cavendishes" seems especially pertinent here.[9] The duchess's "authentic self" is difficult to fathom, even elusive, while the character she openly "presents" often appears torn by conflict. These conflicts, as Hobby further argues, are produced "by the gender constructs that operate on all women writers."[10] In "A True Relation," for example, as in earlier and later works, she constantly refers to her bashfulness and reclusive style of living. By contrast, she trumpets her need for (and right to) fame, delights in stunning the public with gorgeously elaborate costumes, and states repeatedly to that public—so that her desire cannot be misunderstood—the intensity of her ambition and longing for fame.

Psychologically speaking, the duchess seems shy and eager to be noticed but has no wish to converse or interact with people. Her writings and dress enable her to express her talent and the extroverted side of her personality, which seems in continual conflict with an introverted nature and an eagerness to withdraw. Her intelligence and willfulness enable her to harmonize these apparently dissonant aspects of her personality. She is not ashamed, she asserts in "A True Relation," "of my mind or body, my birth or breeding, my actions or fortunes" (p. 300). It is a statement with an overly defensive tone. She further understands, or rationalizes, that the reconciliation of these sides of her personality enriches her literary output:

> For my part I had rather sit at home and write, or walk, as I said, in my chamber and contemplate; but I hold necessary sometimes to appear abroad, besides I do find, that several objects do bring new materials for my thoughts and fancies to build upon. Yet I must say this in the behalf of my thoughts, that I never found them idle; for if the senses bring no work in, they will work of themselves, like silk-worms that spins out of their own bowels. Neither can I say I think the time tedious, when I am alone, so I be near my Lord, and know he is well. (pp. 309–10)

While the duchess was on the Continent, the strain of financial and familial worries caused her health seriously to deteriorate. She was diagnosed as melancholic because she scarcely moved. Her diet was also rigorous and obsessive, being linked in her mind to mental capacity:

> As for feasting, it would neither agree with my humour or constitution, for my diet is for the most part sparing, as a little boiled chicken, or the like, my drink most commonly water; for though I have an indifferent good appetite, yet I do often fast, out of an opinion that if I should eat much, and exercise little, which I do, only walking a slow pace in my chamber, whilst my thoughts run apace in my brain, so that the motions of my mind hinders the active exercises of my body; for should I dance or run, or walk apace, I should dance my thoughts out of measure, run my fancies out of breath, and tread out the feet of my numbers. ("A True Relation," 308–9)

Her attentiveness to dress might also be considered compulsive, delighting as she did in a "singularity, even in accoutrements of habits" (p. 312). The "greatest physician" of the time, Sir Thomas Mayerne, who had been consulted earlier because she had not become pregnant in the first two years of marriage (a blow to the duke's expectations), was again summoned. He severely disapproved of her self-diagnosis and self-prescription that called for constant purging and bleeding "and without doubt too much, since it hath been done by her own directions, as often at least as by the advice of her physicians, a thing to be noted but not imitated."[11] He especially chastised her about her favored cure—strong laxatives—and reminded her that in "too often scouring a kettle it is at last worn out to holes."[12] In light of contemporary knowledge of these symptoms and habits, we might well wonder if the Duchess of Newcastle had an early, undiagnosed case of anorexia and bulemia. She may also have been amenorrheic because of her diet. Her repression of her suffering, her lack of even veiled reference to her sexuality or to her sexual compatibility with the duke may point to a certain sexual reluctance on her part that is often symptomatic of the "binge and purge" illness.[13] There is very little veiled or unveiled sex expressed in women's writings of this period, however. In one recent study, Marilyn Lawrence discerned "a struggle for autonomy," the quest for identity, as a common factor in all cases of anorexic women. The duchess's marriage to her first suitor, the distinguished Duke of Newcastle—a marriage that had to take place in a foreign country where she was severed for the first time from an emotionally self-supporting family—was probably a strain. At least in the beginning, she may have felt overwhelmed. No such feelings, however, are disclosed in her autobiography, which she probably censored heavily. Coincidentally or not, it was just after Dr. Mayerne's fulminations that the duchess journeyed to England, leaving her husband behind for sixteen months. Very quickly, she pursued an extremely energetic literary career with a view toward publishing her manuscripts. There was a veritable outpouring from her pen: she wrote verse throughout 1652, as if revivified and inspired to find a pleasurable release for her energies. After eight years abroad from 1643 to 1651, she was delighted to be in England among her closely knit family.

After King Charles II returned to England from exile, the Duke of Newcastle hurriedly left Antwerp to pay his allegiance. The duchess remained behind at Antwerp, "in pawn" for the duke's debt. Several months after their reunion they retired to Welbeck Abbey in Nottinghamshire in 1660, the duke deeply disappointed at having been passed over by a king immersed in the Restoration settlement and implementing a new dispensation. Hence in the biography of her husband the Duchess of Newcastle skates over this episode in a few sentences, although their semi-imposed new life on northern estates seems to have suited her: "Wherefore, for my pleasure and delight, my ease and peace, I live a retired life, a home life, free from the entanglements, confused clamours, and rumbling noise of the world, for I by this retirement live in a calm silence, wherein I have my contemplations free from disturbance, and my mind lives in peace, and my thoughts in pleasure."[14] To make amends (one suspects) the king bestowed on the marquis the title of duke.[15]

Delightedly absorbed in natural philosophy, the duchess responded to contemporary philosophers, among them Thomas Hobbes, René Descartes, and Henry More, in *Philosophical Letters* (1664). One recent biographer pronounces her an "outspoken" materialist philosopher, in her insistence that "matter itself is both cause and effect and [in her] making an absolute and Baconian distinction between the natural and supernatural."[16] She followed the publication of *Observations upon Experimental Philosophy* in 1666 with a visit to the Royal Society in 1667.

The Duchess of Newcastle died unexpectedly in 1673 in her fiftieth year, "having undermined her health by her sedentary life and her habit of doctoring herself."[17] Too old to attend the funeral, the duke undertook to publish in 1676 all commendatory letters and poems accorded the duchess. To commemorate them both, he wrote an epitaph for the tombstone in Westminster Abbey that gives pride of place to the fact of "noe issue": "Here lyes the Loyall Duke of Newcastle and his Dutches, his second wife, by whome he had noe issue; her name was Margarett Lucas, youngest sister to the Lord Lucas of Colchester; a noble familie, for all the Brothers were Valiant and all the Sisters virtuous. This Dutches was a wise, wittie and learned Lady, which her many Bookes do well testifie; she was a most Virtuous and a Loving and carefull wife, and was with her Lord all the time of his banishment and miseries, and when he came home never parted from him in his solitary retirements."

IN ANY TIME PERIOD, the quantity and length of works that the duchess wrote would be prodigious, but for the seventeenth century they were decidedly remarkable: twelve works (in folio) and seven reeditions or translations. The limited number of modern reissues tells the tale of posterity's burial of Margaret Cavendish, Duchess of Newcastle. No reissue appeared before 1969 except for the second edition of the duke's *Life* in 1675.

All her works were printed and published in London. If their prefaces are to be believed, her first two published works, *Poems and Fancies* and *Philosophical Fancies,* were written during the sixteen months she spent in England between November 1651 and March 1653. Most of the texts were written before 1660 while the duchess was living abroad with her exiled husband.[18] Although Cavendish had not published anything until her visit to England (*Poems and Fancies* and *Philosophical Fancies* did not appear until just after she had left), she had written voluminously in her youth and after her marriage had turned to essays and "opinions." These writings were published as *The Worlds Olio* in 1655, a literary potpourri or "stew" (olio) that comments on a host of not distinctly connected topics. In *Philosophical Fancies* she mentions these writings to the reader and declares that she had "not originally intended to publish them."[19] Her virtuosity and ability to flout convention needled contemporaries into branding her more than "a little distracted"; how could she be, wrote Dorothy Osborne, "so ridiculous else as to venture at writing books and in verse too?"[20]

The duchess's focus on contemporary science casts a remarkable slant on her writings. In *Poems and Fancies* the first section explores her ideas about an atomic theory of matter, which she repudiated the following year for a more complex but equally materialistic theory that assumed nature was divided into animate (rational and sensitive) and inanimate (gross and senseless) matter.[21] The possibility that the duchess wrote only two works—the biography of her husband and her most scientific work, *Observations upon Experimental Philosophy*—after her return from exile also deserves note, though she probably revised works after her return. In any event there is little way of determining exactly what she wrote in the 1650s and 1660s. Possibly she decided not to write herself into her works so much after exile, but preferred rather to concentrate on topics and people external to (though ultimately connected with) herself. Certainly she wanted the acclamation of posterity but drew back from or was cautioned against continuing earlier confessional forms—about herself and women's collective concerns. She does not exactly defeminize her own discourse, because writing biographies and investigating scientific phenomena are creatively autonomous acts and feminist pioneering ones by definition. But she does devote less time to matters concerned strictly with women.

On the other hand, even the multilayered apparatus to *The Life of William Cavendish,* which includes epistles heaped upon prefaces, addresses, sections entitled "To the Readers," and the like, tells a pointed story about veiling and proclamation simultaneously. The dedicatees or addressees are Charles II and the duke himself, as well as the duchess in an epistle from John Rolleston, the duke's secretary. But there is also a twelve-page preface written by the duchess in which she elaborates on her decision to write, her sources, her choice of approach, and her imperfections as a chronicler. These twelve pages add up to a late autobiographical sketch that begins with the duchess alleging that she obeys the duke's orders because she is so ignorant about writing histories:

> When I first intended to write this history, knowing myself to be no scholar, and as ignorant of the rules of writing histories, as I have in my other works acknowledged myself to be of the names and terms of art; I desired my Lord, that he would be pleased to let me have some elegant and learned historian to assist me; which request his Grace would not grant me; saying, that having never had any assistance in the writing of my former books, I should have no other in the writing of his life, but the informations from himself, and his secretary, of the chief transactions and fortunes occurring in it, to the time he married me. I humbly answered, that without a learned assistant, the history would be defective: but he replied, that truth could not be defective. I said again, that rhetoric did adorn truth: and he answered, that rhetoric was fitter for falsehoods than truths. Thus I was forced by his Grace's commands, to write this history in my own plain style, without elegant flourishings, or exquisite method, relying entirely upon truth, in the expressing whereof, I have been very circumspect; as knowing well, that his Grace's actions have so much glory of their own, that they need borrow none from anybody's industry. (p. liii)

Despite such rigorous reservations, this history is severely doctored; we are not informed how the duke lost York and subsequently fled without consulting the king. She ends with a "humble," transparently conventional, plea to be forgiven for her inadequacy: "Nobody can certainly be more ready to find faults in this work, than I am to confess them; being very conscious that I have, as I told my Lord I should, committed many for want of learning, and chiefly of skill in writing histories. But having, according to his Lordship's commands, written his actions and fortunes truly and plainly, I have reason to expect, that whatsoever else shall be found amiss, will be favourably pardoned by the candid readers, to whom I wish all manner of happiness" (p. lxiv). Obviously hurt and perhaps humiliated by the fact that Charles II neither invited them to be part of his court nor, from their point of view, compensated them appropriately, the duchess offered herself as the duke's hagiographer. At another level, she offered the duke and the public an heir.

Recurring commentaries in the Duchess of Newcastle's works speak to her motivation in writing and her complex attitudes toward other women. Equally formidable is her eclectic literary range: poems and "fancies" (fables and short moral discourses); fantastic explorations like early science fiction tales; scientific probings that the seventeenth century delighted in, especially those that probed the elements of matter; numerous plays and fragments of dramas or one-act plays; and biography and autobiography. Not last or least are her innumerable prefaces, dedications, and passages "to the reader" that amount to layer upon layer of prefatory apparatus; in these she explains herself, seems to fortify herself, and exposes her opinions. Collectively, they reveal (and conceal) an extraordinarily complex woman.

The guiding assumptions of "Female-Orations" (part 11 of *Orations of Diverse Sorts,* 1622), for example, tell us how keenly the duchess observed sexual politics in her society. In keeping with the form of an oration, the "opposition" subsequently argues against those assumptions:

> Ladies, Gentlewomen, and other Inferior Women, but not less Worthy; I have been industrious to Assemble you together, and wish I were so Fortunate, as to perswade you to make frequent Assemblies, Associations, and Combinations amongst our Sex, that we may unite in Prudent Counsels, to make our selves as Free, Happy and Famous, as Men: whereas now we Live and Dye, as if we were produced from Beasts, rather than from Men: for, Men are happy, and we Women are miserable; they possess all the Ease, Rest, Pleasure, Wealth, Power, and Fame; whereas Women are Restless with Labour, Easeless with Pain, Melancholy for want of Pleasures, Helpless for want of Power, and dye in Oblivion, for want of Fame. Nevertheless, Men are so Unconscionable and Cruel against us, that they endeavour to barr us of all sorts of Liberty, and will not suffer us freely to Associate amongst our own Sex; but would fain bury us in their Houses or Beds, as in a Grave. The truth is, we live like Batts, or Owls, labour like Beasts, and dye like Worms. (1:239–40)

Because she wrote abundantly, readers can easily be selective with the duchess's texts and find passages in which she exclusively praises or upbraids women. Her contradictions signify internal and external dilemmas over the question, although undoubtedly she sympathizes with more than criticizes women and the tribulations they face, especially in matters of marriage and educational deprivation. Such ardent advocacy is inevitable in a woman chagrined at ridicule and her lack of formal education, particularly obvious in the early texts. Even more important she highlights scenarios, notably in her plays, that demonstrate the potential of women and show how some of them "take on" the patriarchal structure. The central characters of her plays are women, often of exceptional ability: heroic women like Lady Victoria of *Bell in Campo,* independent women like Orphant in *Loves Adventures,* or scholars like Sanspareille in *Youths Glory and Death Banquet.* The main plot of *Bell in Campo,* for example, illustrates a strong woman "laying down the law"; Lady Victoria, declining to be left behind when her husband goes to war, organizes an army of women—"a warlike body"—who join the men. She becomes the "general of a female army of 'Heroickesses,' . . . saves her country, and her husband, in battle . . . and permanently improve[s] the lot of all women" by her example.[22] Lady Victoria insists that women are not innately inferior and, if given an education equal to men's, would prove—despite any physical weakness—just as capable as men. By contrast, the subplots of the duchess's plays portray the more realistic world in which women are dependent upon and exploited by men. The main plots generally project the strength of women; the subplots underscore the weaknesses of their plight.[23]

Outside the duchess's sympathies lie the female petitioners of the Civil War, but these women symbolize class enemies who (from the duchess's aristocratic standpoint) disrupted her life. At no point in her narrative does she concede any justice to Parliament's position. She also scorns female idleness, but these remarks could have sprung just as easily from her frustration at the limitations of women's lives. In many texts—the orations, plays, and *Nature's Pictures,* for example—where she winces at drunken, shiftless husbands and difficult childbirths, she is displaying a deliberate compassion about experiences she never endured.

Flauntingly obvious in the first "Female-Oration" is the admixture of autobiography with wish projection: "I have been industrious to Assemble you together, and wish I were so Fortunate, as to perswade you to make frequent Assemblies, Associations, and Combinations amongst our Sex . . . to make our selves as Free, Happy and Famous, as Men" (p. 239). In *Nature's Pictures* she offers a series of vignettes about and for women. This combination of autobiography, concern for herself and for other women seems to flow naturally from her early upbringing. The duchess grew up in "frequent assemblies, associations, and combinations amongst our sex," with her sisters and mother, and then was reimmersed in a comparable pattern in Queen Henrietta Maria's entourage. By marrying a distinguished aristocrat (arguably a father figure of sorts) enamored of her disposition and talents, she enjoyed a certain leisure and privilege and was able to exercise her talents freely for most of her married life. She also attempted to gain more wealth by petitioning personally for the return of the duke's sequestered lands. Fame was the spur to her writings, or at least a major goal: that fact she states over and over.

In later orations, she tells women to appreciate inaccessible tasks such as treasure-seeking previously reserved for men. She also responds to her own charge about the lack of female wit and physical strength by exhorting women to "hawk, hunt, race, and do the like exercises that men have." In the fourth "Female-Oration," she recommends that women should expropriate or reappropriate all male activities and privileges: ". . . and let us Converse in Camps, Courts, and Cities; in Schools, Colleges, and Courts of Judicature; in Taverns, Brothels, and Gaming-Houses; all which will make our Strength and Wit known, both to Men, and to our own selves: for, we are as Ignorant of our Selves as Men are of us. And how should we know our Selves, when as we never made a trial of our Selves? or, how should Men know us, when as they never Put us to the Proof? Wherefore, my Advice is, we should Imitate Men, so will our Bodies and Minds appear more Masculine, and our Power will Increase by our Actions" (pp. 242–43). The next two orations take issue with women who emulate men, thus further emphasizing the necessity she perceived for a female reappropriation. In the course of these debates, she also subtly spotlights women's advantages over men in discourse, bearing, and self-preservation (because they expose themselves less foolishly to danger); she summarizes these advantages in the final, seventh *Female Orations* as "Beauties, Features, Shapes, Gracefull Demeanour . . . and such Insinuating and Enticing Attractives, as Men are Forc'd to Admire us, Love us, and be Desirous of us, in so much as rather than not Have and Injoy us, they will Deliver to our Disposals, their Power, Persons, and Lives, Inslaving Themselves to our Will and Pleasures: also, we are their Saints, whom they adore and worship, and what can we desire more, than to be Men's Tyrants, Destinies, and Goddesses?" (p. 246). Though this conclusion reinforces the idea of the pedestal as desirable, the duchess is also manipulating a rigid seventeenth-century role stratification to women's best advantage. She calls for women to wrest as much power from men as they can and to take control of their own lives, her skill consummate in making this argument highly acceptable in terms of seventeenth-century discourse. It is also possible to argue that the duchess represents a variety of viewpoints in *Orations* and subscribes to none. Her feminist ideas elsewhere, however, suggest a political correspondence with the "feminist" orations.

I have discussed at some length the duchess's attention to women in *Orations* and elsewhere. The excerpts that follow this essay elucidate her other abiding preoccupations and leitmotifs: her concern with public image and the many forms it took; her private feelings in love letters to the duke; her commitment to scientific pursuits and ambition; her desire for contemporary fame and posterity's approval (she dedicated more than one text to the universities of Oxford and Cambridge); and perhaps most obviously her absorption in the act of writing, her concern with style, with her role as an author, with her varied readerships.

Finally, what can be said of the duchess's writings and self-presentation that in a sense defy classification? She was a political outlaw, a materialist in an age of ardent belief, her husband a relic of sorts, non grata to the Parliamentary side and perhaps to some of his Royalist friends on account of his unexpected flight. She was scarcely part of court circles and remained detached from Restoration debauchery and social gaiety. Consequently, she mixed only infrequently with women of her own class, let alone independent, middle-class women. But she observed and read and engaged herself—at a measured and deliberate distance—with contemporary culture, science, and politics. She witnessed the growth of the Royal Society, which she wanted desperately to join. She decried the Civil

War victory, yet was personally attracted to some aspects of revolutionary ideology. She was a stranger in a known land and (from her own perspective) a well-known person in an alien society.

The Duchess of Newcastle and her ideas, her sense of fashion, and her deportment were both orthodox and hugely unorthodox. She fit and she did not fit. Her writings reflect consistently contradictory attitudes, her reclusive yet ostentatious way of life. They hide and display, show off and peep through cracks. She seems intellectually proud but also shy about her interest in science. The only consistency is her virtuosity and rich imagination, her talent and courage. The duchess is not an enigma, however, because such a term mystifies her more than need be; after all, she was very much in the business of explaining, either directly or through a mass of ironic subtexts.

Nonetheless, she was a complex woman living in tumultuous times, part of a political rearguard and a cultural vanguard, possibly much more self-conscious than present biographical knowledge reveals. The Dutch years are still a mystery, but we know that Anna Maria van Schurman was corresponding with Bathsua Makin, who herself was tutor to Queen Henrietta Maria's daughter. Links between them and the Duchess of Newcastle may eventually come to light. The Duchess may possibly have toned down a bourgeois-tending feminist consciousness for fear of affronting her class. What we do know is that the Duchess of Newcastle was a woman trying to chart intellectual and feminist depths, hunting for new ways to talk about the world, for acceptable ways to be herself and publicize her thoughts. In all these ventures, she was ahead of her time.

NOTES

1. Throughout the essay I use the titles by which the pair are more popularly known (the Duke and Duchess of Newcastle), although Newcastle did not receive a duchy until 1661.

2. Elaine Hobby, "The Fame of the Honest Margaret Cavendish," 47; Mary Ann McGuire, *Margaret Cavendish, Duchess of Newcastle, on the Nature and Status of Women,* 194. I want to thank Elaine Hobby for sharing with me her Master of Arts dissertation on the Duchess of Newcastle, as well as sections of her forthcoming book, *Women in Print 1642–1660* (Virago Press, 1988–89). I also thank Professor Hobby for a valuable reading.

3. Douglas Grant, *Margaret the First: A Biography of Margaret Cavendish, Duchess of Newcastle, 1623–1673,* 48–49.

4. Ibid., 54–87.

5. Hobby, "The Fame of Margaret Cavendish," 8.

6. See also Grant, *Margaret the First,* 109.

7. Dolores Palomo points out, however, that in *Social Letters* the duchess was rebuked for friendship with women on the "other side" and states that women did not start the war. In *Female Academy,* the middle-class women speculate that someday all women, not just those of gentle birth, will be able to enter the academy. And in *The Convent of Pleasure,* the

duchess is aware of the tribulations experienced by women of all classes. The same is true of her refusal to report on the private life of a woman servant in a reference in *Social Letters.* I want to thank Professor Palomo for an incisive reading of this text; her forthcoming biography of the duchess will set the record straight in a number of critical and still perplexing areas.

8. Grant, *Margaret the First,* 41.

9. In her forthcoming biography, Dolores Palomo will elaborate on the idea that the duchess's public posture may be more of a construct than formerly thought.

10. Comments received in a private communication to the author by Elaine Hobby.

11. Grant, *Margaret the First,* 103–4.

12. Ibid., 96, 103–5.

13. See, for example, Marilyn Lawrence, *The Anorexic Experience* (London: Women's Press, 1984), 32–39 and passim; Suzanne Abraham and Derek Llewellyn-Jones, *Eating Disorders: The Facts* (Oxford University Press, 1984); and Felicia Romeo, *Understanding Anorexia Nervosa* (Springfield, Ill.: Charles Thomas, 1986).

14. Grant, *Margaret the First,* 228.

15. See note 1. In recognition of Cavendish's services during the Civil War, the king had created him Marquis of Newcastle in October 1643 (Grant, *Margaret the First,* 61, 183).

16. Grant, *Margaret the First,* 198.

17. Grant, *Margaret the First,* 237.

18. The duchess explains the chronology of her writings in *The Life,* 303–4.

19. Hobby, "The Fame of Margaret Cavendish," 30.

20. Grant, *Margaret the First,* 116, 196–200.

21. Ibid., 111.

22. Pearson, "Women may discourse," 35.

23. Ibid., 35, 36.

From Poems and Fancies

TO POETS

And if I be out of the Fashion, because Women do not generally write; yet, before you laugh at me, let your Reason view strictly, whether the Fashion be not usefull, gracefull, easie, comely, and modest: And if it be any of these, spare your Smiles of Scorne, for those that are wanton, carelesse, rude, or unbecoming: For though her Garments are plaine, and unusuall, yet they are cleane, and decent. Next, Truth tells you, that Women have seldome, or never, (or at least in these latter ages) written a Book of Poetry, unlesse it were in their Dressings, which can be no longer read then Beauty lasts. Wherefore it hath seemed hitherto, as if Nature had compounded Mens Braines with more of the Sharp Atomes, which make the hot, and dry Element, and Womens with more of the round Atomes, which Figure makes the cold, and moist Element: And though Water is a usefull Element, yet Fire is the Nobler, being of an Aspiring quality. But it is rather a Dishonour, not a Fault in Nature, for her Inferiour Workes to move towards Perfection; though the best of her Workes can never be so Perfect as her selfe; yet she is pleased when they imitate her; and to imitate her, I hope you will be pleased, I Imitate you. Tis true, my Verses came not out of Jupiters Head, therefore they cannot prove a Pallas: yet they are like Chast Penelope's Work, for I wrote them in my Husbands absence, to delude Melancholy Thoughts, and avoid Idle Time. The last thing Truth tells you, is, my Verses were gathered too soon: wherefore they cannot be of a Mature growth; for the Sun of time was onely at that height, as to draw them forth, but not heat enough to ripen them; which makes me feare they will tast harsh, and unpleasant; But if they were strew'd with some Sugar of Praises, and Bake'd in the Oven of Applause, they may passe at a generall Feast, though they do not relish with nice, and delicate Palates; yet the Vulgar may digest them: for they care not what the Meat is, if the Crust bee good, or indeed thick: for they judge according to the quantity, not the quality, or rarity: but they are oft perswaded by the senses of others, more than their owne. Wherefore if it be not worthy of Commendations, pray be silent, and cast not out severe Censures; And I shall give Thankes for what is Eaten.

OF EARTH

Why Earth's not apt to move, but slow and dull,
Is, Atomes flat no Vacuum hath' but full.
That Forme admits no empty place to bide,
All parts are fil'd, having no hollow side.
And where no Vacuum is, Motion is slow,
Having no empty places for to go.
Though Atomes all are small, as small may bee,
Yet by their Formes, Motion doth disagree.
For Atomes sharp do make themselves a Way,
Cutting through other Atomes as they stray.
But Atomes flat will dull, and lazy lay,
Having no Edge, or point to make a Way.

MORAL DISCOURSES. A DISCOURSE OF LOVE, THE PARENT OF PASSIONS.

No Mind can think, or Understanding know,
To what a Height, and Vastnesse Love can grow.
Love, as a God, all Passions doth create,
Besides it selfe, and those determinate.
Bowing downe low, devoutly prayeth Feare,

Sadnesse, and Griefe, Loves heavie burthens beare.
Anger Rage makes, Envie, Spleene, and Spight,
Like Thunder roares, and in Loves quarrels fight.
Jealousie, Loves Informer is t'espie,
And Doubt its Guide, to search where'ts Foe doth lye.
Pity, Loves Child, whose Eyes Teares overflow,
On every Object Misery can shew.
Hate is Loves Champion, which opposeth all
Lovers Enemies, their Ruine, and their Fall.

OF AMBITION

Ten Thousand Pounds a yeare will make me live:
A Kingdome, Fortune then to me must give.
I'le conquer all, like Alexander Great,
And, like to Caesar, my Opposers beat.
Give me a Fame, that with the World may last,
Let all Tongues tell of my great Actions past
Let every child, when first tis taught to speak,
Repeat my Name, my Memory for to keep.
And then great Fortune give to me thy power,
To ruine Man, and raise him in an Houre.
Let me command the Fates, and spin their thread;
And Death to stay his sithe, when I forbid.
And, Destiny, give my your Chaines to tye,
Effects from Causes to produce thereby.
And let me like the Gods on high become,
That nothing can but by my will be done.

THE CLASPE

Give Mee the Free, and Noble Stile,
Which seems uncurb'd, though it be wild:
Though It runs wild about, It cares not where;
It shewes more Courage, than It doth of Feare.
Give me a Stile that Nature frames, not Art:
For Art doth seem to take the Pedants part.
And that seemes Noble, which is Easie, Free,
Not to be bound with ore-nice Pedantry.

THE HUNTING OF THE STAG

There was a Stag did in the Forrest lye,
Whose Neck was long, and Hornes branch'd up high.

His Haunch was broad, Sides large, and Back was long,
His legs were Nervous, and his Joynts were strong.
His Haire lay sleek, and smooth upon his skin,
None in the Forrest might compare with him.
In Summers heat he in coole Brakes him laies,
Which grew so high, kept of the Suns hot Raies.
In Evenings coole, or dewy Mornings new,
Would he rise up, and all the Forrest view.
Then walking to some cleare, and Christall Brook,
Not for to Drink, but on his Hornes to look:
Taking such Pleasure in his Stately Crowne,
His Pride forgets that dogs might pull him downe.

. . . .

Besides, a company of Men were there,
If Dogs should faile, to strike him every where.
But to the last his Fortune hee'll try out:
Then Men, and Dogs do circle him about.
Some bite, some bark, all ply him at the Bay,
Where with his Hornes he tosses some away.
But Fate his thread had spun, so downe did fall,
Shedding some Teares at his owne Funerall.

ALSO FROM "POEMS AND FANCIES"

I know, those that are strict and nice about Phrase, and the placing of words, will carp at my Booke: for I have not set my words in such order, as those which write elegant Prose. But I must confesse ingenuously, my shallow wit could not tell how to order it to the best advantage; besides, I found it difficult, to get so many Rhythmes, as to joyn the sense of the Subject: and by reason I could not attaine to both, I rather chose to leave the Elegance of words, then to obstruct the sense of the matter. For my desire was to make my conceit easie to the understanding, though my words were not so fluent to the eare. Againe, they will finde fault with the Numbers; for I was forc'd to fewer or more, to bring in the sense of my Fancies. All I can say for my selfe is, that Poetry consists not so much in Number, Words, and Phrase, as in Fancy. Thirdly, they will finde fault at the Subject; saying, it is neither materiall, nor usefull for the Soule, or Body. To this I answer, My intention was, not to teach Arts, nor Sciences, nor to instruct in Divinity, but to passe away idle Time; and though Time might be better spent: yet 'tis oft spent worse amongst many in the world.

I Language want, to dresse my Fancies in,
The Haire's uncurl'd, the Garments loose, and thin;

Had they but Silver Lace to make them gay,
Would be more courted then in poore array.
Or had they Art, might make a better show;
But they are plaine, yet cleanly doe they goe.
The world in Bravery doth take delight,
And glittering Shews doe more attract the sight;
And every one doth honour a rich Hood,
As if the outside made the inside good.
And every one doth bow, and give the place,
Not for the Mans sake, but the Silver Lace.
Let me intreat in my poore Bookes behalfe,
That all may not adore the Golden Calf.
Consider pray, Gold hath no life therein,
And Life in Nature is the richest thing.
So Fancy is the Soul in Poetrie,
And if not good, a Poem ill must be.
Be just, let Fancy have the upper place,
And then my Verses may perchance finde grace.
If flattering Language all the Passions rule,
Then Sense, I feare, will be a meere dull Foole.

A Poet I am neither borne, nor bred,
But to a witty Poet married:
Whose Braine is Fresh, and Pleasant, as the Spring,
Where Fancies grow, and where the Muses sing.
There oft I leane my Head, and lift'ning harke,
To heare his words, and all his Fancies mark;
And from that Garden Flowers of Fancies take,
Whereof a Posie up in [ ] I make.
Thus I, that have no Garden of mine owne,
There gather Flowers that are newly blowne.

Epistle to Nature's Pictures

BOOK XI. AN EPISTLE.

I have heard, that some should say my wit seemed as if it would overpower my brain, especially when it works upon philosophical opinions. I am obliged to them for judging my wit stronger than my brain: but I should be sorry that they should think my wit stronger than my reason:

but I must tell them that my brain is stronger than my wit, and my reason as strong as the effeminate sex requires.

Again, I have heard some should say, that my writings are none of my own, because when some have visited me, though seldom I receive visits, they have not heard me speak of them, or repeat some of the chapters or verses; but I believe, if they should desire the best orator to repeat his orations or sermons that he hath spoke *ex tempore,* he shall not do it although but an hour's discourse: for I believe Tully, who I have heard was an eloquent orator, yet could not repeat them over to his auditory. The same is in writers; for I do believe Homer, as great and excellent poet as it is said he was, could not repeat his poems by heart, nor Virgil, nor Ovid, or any other; nor Euclid repeat his demonstrations, numerations, and the like without book, nor Aristotle, who, I have heard, was a great philosopher, the explanations of his opinions by heart; for I have heard that his memory failed in the writing, for that he hath sometimes contradicted himself; and my Lord, who hath written hundreds of verses, songs, and themes, could not repeat three by heart; and I have heard him say, that after he hath writ them, he doth so little remember any part in them, that when they have been a short time by, and then read them over, they are new to him. But he is not so forgetful of other things, for he hath an extraordinary memory for received courtesies, or to do any timely good or service, not only to friends, but to strangers. Also he hath an excellent memory concerning the general actions of and in the world. But certainly they that remember their own wit least, have the most of it; for there is an old saying, and surely true, that the best wits have the worst memory, I mean wit-memory; for great memories are standing ponds that are made with rain; so that memory is nothing but the showers of other men's wits; and those brains are muddy that have not running springs of their own, that issue out still fresh and new. Indeed, it's against nature for natural wits to remember; for it is impossible that the brain should retain and create; and we see in nature, death makes way for life; for if there were no death there would be no new life or lives.

But say I were so witless I could repeat some of my works, I do think it would seem self-conceitedness to mention them; but since that report, I have spoken more of them than otherwise I should have done, though truly I condemn myself; for it is an indiscretion, although I was forced to that indiscretion, and I repent it both for the disfiguring of my works, by pulling out a piece here and a piece there, according as my memory could catch hold; also for troubling, or rather vexing the hearers with such discourses as they delight not in.

Besides, it hath been a long and true observation, that every one had rather speak than listen to what another says; insomuch as for the most part all mankind run from company to company, not to learn, but to talk, and like bells their tongues as the clappers keep a jangling noise all at once, without method or distinction.

But I hope my indiscretion in speaking of my works to my hearers is not beyond a pardon, for I have not spoke of them, nor parts in them, much nor often, nor to many, but to some particularly, as those I thought did understand poetry, or natural philosophy, or moral philosophy, though I fear not always according as their capacities lay. For I have observed, some understand commonwealths, customs, laws, or the like; others, the distinguishments of passions, and understand nothing of law; others, divinity, that understand nothing of temporal government, and so the like of many several studies; and some may have a rational capacity to most sciences, yet conceive nothing of natural philosophy, as of the first matter, or innated matter, or motions, or figures, or forms, or infinites, or spirits, or essences, or the like; nay, for the most part they conceive little further than an almanac to know the time by, of which I am ignorant, for I understand it not. And for poetry, most laugh at it as a ridiculous thing, especially grave statists, severe moralists, zealous priesthood, wrangling lawyers, covetous hoarders, or purloiners, or those that have mechanic natures, and many more, which for the most part account poetry a toy, and condemn it for a vanity, an idle employment; nor have they so much fancy of their own, as to conceive the poetical fancies of others; for if they did, they must needs love poetry; for poetry is so powerful, and hath such an attractive beauty, that those that can but view her perfectly, could not but be enamoured, her charms do so force affection. But surely those that delight not in poetry or music, have no divine souls nor harmonious thoughts. But by those weak observations I have made, I perceive that as most men have particular understandings, capacities, or ingenuities, and not a general; so in their discourses some can speak eloquently, and not learnedly; others learnedly and not eloquently; some wittily, and neither learned nor eloquent; and some will speak neither learnedly, eloquently, wittily, or rationally. Likewise, some can speak well, but 'tis but for a time, some a longer, and some a shorter time, like several sized candles, are longer or shorter ere they come to a snuff; where sometimes some objects or conceits, unexpected objections or questions, or the like, do prove as a small coal got into the tallow of their wit, which makes it bleer out sooner than otherwise it would do. Also some will speak wisely upon some subjects, and foolishly upon others.

Likewise some will speak well as it were by chance; others in one discourse speak mixtly, now rational, then nonsensely, at least weakly or obstructedly. But they are great masters of speech that speak clearly, as I may say, untangled, which can wind their words from off their tongue without a snarl or knot, and can keep even sense, like an even thread, or can work that thread of sense into a flourishing discourse; and they have a quick wit that can play with, or on any subject, which doubtless some can do of those things they never heard, saw, or thought on, but just when they speak of it. And some have great capacities, as may be perceived in their discourse: but yet their speech is like those that are lame, which limp and halt, although the ground whereon they go is even, smooth, and firm. But some have such large capacities, elevated fancies, illuminated souls, and volubility of speech, that they can conceive, create, enlighten, and deliver with that abundance, curiosity, facility, and pleasure, as their conversible company is a heaven, where all worldly delights reside.

But to return to the ground of this Epistle. I desire all my readers and acquaintance to believe, though my words run stumbling out of my mouth, and my pen draws roughly on my paper, yet my thoughts move regular in my brain; for the several tracks or paths that contemplation hath made on my brain, which paths or tracks are the several ways my thoughts move in, are much smoother than the tongue in my mouth, from whence words flow, or the paper on which my pen writes; for I have not spoke so much as I have writ, nor writ so much as I have thought. For I must tell my readers, that nature, which is the best and curiousest worker, hath paved my brain smoother than custom hath oiled my tongue, or variety hath polished my senses, or art hath beaten the paper whereon I write; for my fancy is quicker than the pen with which I write, insomuch as it is many times lost through the slowness of my hand, and yet I write so fast, as I stay not so long as to make perfect letters.

But if they will not believe my books are my own, let them search the author or authoress: but I am very confident that they will do like Drake, who went so far about, until he came to the place he first set out at. But for the sake of after ages, which I hope will be more just to me than the present, I will write the true relation of my birth, breeding, and to this part of my life, not regarding carping tongues, or malicious censurers, for I despise them.

MARGARET NEWCASTLE

From Bell in Campo

PART I, ACT 2, SCENE 9

Enter the Lady Victoria and a number of women of all sorts with her, she takes her stand upon a heap of green turfs, as being in the Fields before the Garrison Town, and then speaks to those women.

Lady Victoria. Most Heroical Spirits of most chast and loving Wives, Mistrisses, Sisters, Children or Friends, I know you came not from your several Houses and homes into this Army meerly to enjoy your Husbands, Lovers, Parents and Friends in their safe and secure Garrisons, or only to share of their troublesome and tedious marches, but to venture also in their dangerous and cruell Battels, to run their Fortunes, and to force Destiny to joyn you to their Periods; but the Masculine Sex hath separated us, and cast us out of their Companyes, either out of their loving care and disire of preserving our lives and liberties, lest we might be distroyed in their confusions, or taken Prisoners in their loss, or else it must be out of jealousy we should Eclipse the fame of their valours with the splendor of our constancy; and if it be Love, let us never give the preheminence, for then we should lose that Prerogative that belongs to the Crown of our Sex; and if it be thorough Jealous mistrust of their Fame, it were poor for us to submit and quit that unto men, that men will not unto us, for Fame makes us like the Gods, to live for ever; besides, those women that have staid at home will laugh at us in our return, and their effeminate Lovers and Carpet Knights, that Cowardly and Luxuriously Coin excuses to keep and stay them from the Wars, will make Lamporis of us for them to sing of our disgrace, saying, our Husbands, Lovers, and Friends were so weary of us, as they were forced to take that pretence of affectionate love to be rid of our Companyes; wherefore if you will take my advise, let us return, and force those that sent us away to consent that we shall be partakers with them, and either win them by perswasions, or lose our selves by breaking their decrees; for it were better we should dy by their angry frowns, than by the Tongue of Infamy.

(*All the women call to her.*)

All the women. Let us return, let us return.

(Lady Victoria waves her hand to them to keep silence.)

Lady Victoria. Noble Heroickesses, I am glad to hear you speak all as with one voice and Tongue, which shows your minds are joyned together, as in one piece, without seam or rent; but let us not return unfit to do them service, so we may cause their ruin by obstruction, which will wound us more than can their anger, wherefore let us strive by our industry to render our selves usefull to their service.

All the women. Propound the way, and set the Rules, and we will walk in the one, and keep strictly to the other.

Lady Victoria. Then thus, we have a Body of about five or six thousand women, which came along with some thirty thousand men, but since we came, we are not only thought unusefull, but troublesome, which is the reason we were sent away, for the Masculine Sex is of an opinion we are only fit to breed and bring forth Children, but otherwise a trouble in a Commonwealth, for though we encrease the Commonwealth by our breed, we encomber it by our weakness, as they think, as by our incapacities, as having no ingenuity for Inventions, nor subtill wit for Politicians; nor prudence for direction, nor industry for execution; nor patience for opportunity, nor judgment for Counsellers, nor secrecy for trust; nor method to keep peace, nor courage to make War, nor strength to defend our selves or Country, or to assault an Enemy; also that we have not the wisdome to govern a Common-wealth, and that we are too partial to fit in the Seat of Justice, and too pittifull to execute rigorous Authority when it is needfull, and the reason of these erronious opinions of the Masculine Sex to the Effeminate, is, that our Bodyes seem weak, being delicate and beautifull, and our minds seem fearfull, being compassionate and gentle natured, but if we were both weak and fearfull, as they imagine us to be, yet custome which is a second Nature will encourage the one and strengthen the other, and had our educations been answerable to theirs, we might have proved as good Souldiers and Privy Counsellers, Rulers and Commanders, Navigators and Architectors, and as learned Sholars both in Arts and Sciences, as men are; for Time and Custome is the Father and Mother of Strength and Knowledge, they make all things easy and facil, clear and propitious; they bring acquaintance, and make friendship of every thing; they make Courage and Fear, Strength and Weakness, Difficulty and Facility, Dangers and Securities, Labours and Recreations, Life and Death, all to take and shake as it were hands together; wherefore if we would but accustome our selves we may do such actions, as may gain us such a reputation, as men might change their opinion, insomuch as to believe we are fit to be Copartners in their Governments, and to help to rule the World, where now we are kept as Slaves forced to obey; wherefore let us make our selves free, either by force, merit, or love, and in order, let us practise and endeavour, and take that which Fortune shall profer unto us, let us practice I say, and make these Fields as Schools of Martial Arts and Sciences, so shall we become learned in their disciplines of War, and if you please to make me your Tutoress, and so your Generalless, I shall take the power and command from your election and Authority, otherwise I shall most willingly, humbly, and obediently submit to those whom you shall choose.

All the women. You shall be our Generalless, our Instructeress, Ruler and Commanderess, and we will every one in particular, swear to obey all your Commands, to submit and yield to your punishments, to strive and endeavour to merit your rewards.

Lady Victoria. Then worthy Heroickesses, give me leave to set the Laws and Rules I would have you keep and observe, in a brass Tabler.

All the women. We agree and consent to whatsoever you please.

(Exeunt.)

ACT 4, SCENE 16

Enter two women like Amazons.

1 Woman. Our Generalless seems to be troubled, perceiving how heavily this Female Army takes their losses.

2 Woman. She hath reason, for it may hinder or at least obstruct her high designs.

(Exeunt.)

ACT 4, SCENE 17

Enter the Lady Victoria and her Amazons, She takes her stand and speaks to them.

Lady Victoria. Noble Heroicks, I perceive a mourning veil over the Face of this Female Army, and it becomes it well; for 'tis both normal and human to grieve for the Death of our friends; but consider constant Heroicks, tears nor lamentations cannot call them out of the grave, no petitions can perswade Death to restore them, nor threats to let them go, and since you cannot have them alive being Dead, study and be industrious to revenge their quarrels on their enemies lives, let your justice give them Death for Death, offer upon the Tombs of your Friends the lives of their Foes, and instead of weeping Eyes, let us make them weep through their Veins; wherefore take courage, cast off your black Veil of Sorrow, and take up the Firematch of Rage, that you may shoot Revenge into the hearts of their Enemies, to which I hope Fortune will favour us; for I hear that as soon as the Masculine Army have recovered strength there will be another Battel fought, which may be a means to prove our loves to our Friends, our hate to our Enemies, and an aspiring to our honour and renown; wherefore let us imploy our care to fit our selves for our march.

All the women. We shall follow and obey you, where, and when, and how you please.

PART II, ACT 1, SCENE 3

Enter the Lady Victoria, and her Heroickesses.

Lady Victoria. Noble Heroickesses, I have intelligence that the Army of Reformations begins to flag, wherefore now or never is the time to prove the courage of our Sex, to get liberty and freedome from the Female Slavery, and to make our selves equal with men: for shall Men only sit in Honours chair, and Women stand as waiters by? shall only Men in Triumphant Chariots ride, and Women run as Captives by? shall only men be Conquerors, and women Slaves? shall only men live by Fame, and women dy in Oblivion? no, no, gallant Heroicks raise your Spirits to a noble pitch, to a deaticall height, to get an everlasting Renown, and infinite praises, by honourable, but unusual actions: for honourable Fame is not got only by contemplating thoughts which lie lasily in the Womb of the Mind, and prove Abortive, if not brought forth in living deeds; but worthy Heroickesses, at this time Fortune disires to be the Midwife, and if the Gods and Goddesses did not intend to favour our proceedings with a safe deliverance, they would not have offered us so fair and fit an opportunity to be the Mothers of glorious Actions, and everlasting Fame, which if you be so unnatural to strangle in the Birth by fearfull Cowardize, may you be blasted with Infamy, which is worse than to dye and be forgotten; may you be whipt with the torturing tongues of our own Sex we left behind us, and may you be scorned and neglected by the Masculine Sex, whilst other women are preferr'd and beloved, and may you walk unregarded untill you become a Plague to your selves; but if you Arm with Courage and fight valiantly, may men bow down and worship you, birds taught to sing your praises, Kings offer up their Crowns unto you, and honour inthrone you in a mighty power.

May time and destiny attend your will,
Fame be your scribe to write your actions still;
And may the Gods each act with praises still.

All the women. Fear us not, fear us not, we dare and will follow you wheresoever and to what you dare or will lead us, be it through the jawes of Death.

Lady Victoria. Great Mars thou God of war, grant that our Squadrons may like unbroken Clouds move with intire Bodyes, let Courage be the wind to drive us on, and let our thick swell'd Army darken their Sun of hope with black despair, let us poure down showers of their blood, to quench the firy flames of our revenge.

And where those showers fall, their Deaths as seeds
Sown in times memory sprout up our deeds;
And may our Acts Triumphant garlands make,
Which Fame may wear for our Heroicks sake.

(Exeunt.)

ACT 3, SCENE 8

Enter the Lady Victoria, and many of her Amazons, then enters a Messenger from the Masculine Army.

Messenger. May it please your Excellence, our Lord General and the rest of the Commanders have sent you and your Heroicks a Letter, desiring it may be read in a full Assembly.

Lady Victoria. One of you take the Letter and read it.
(One of the women takes the Letter and reads it to all of the Company.)

To the most Excellent of her Sex, and her most worthy Heroickesses.

You Goddesses on Earth, who have the power and dominion over men, 'tis you we worship and adore, we pray and implore your better opinions of us, than to believe we are so unjust as to take the Victory out of your fair hands, or so vain glorious as to attribute it to our selves, or so ungratefull as not to acknowledge our lives and liberties from your valours, wisdoms, and good fortune, or so imprudent as to neglect your power, or so ill-bred as to pass by you without making our addresses, or so foolish as to go about any action without your knowledge, or so unmannerly as to do anything without your Leave; wherefore we entreat you and pray you to believe that we have so much honour in us, as to admire your beauties, to be attentive to your discourses, to dote on your persons, to honour your virtues, to divulge your sweet graces, to praise your behaviours, to wait your commands, to obey your directions, to be proud of your favours, and we wear our lives only for your service, and believe we are not only taken Captives by your Beauties, but that we acknowledge we are abound as your Slaves by your Valours; wherefore we all pray that you may not misinterpret our affections and care to your persons, in believing we sent you away because we were weary of you, which if so, it had been a sin unpardonable, but we sent you away for your safety, for Heaven knows your Departure was our Hell, and your Absence our Torments; but we confess our errours, and do humbly beg our pardons, for if you had accompanied us in our Battels, you had kept us safe, for had we fought in your presence, our Enemies had never overcome us, since we take courage from your Eyes, life from your smiles, and victory from you good wishes, and had become Conquerours by your incouragements, and so we might have triumpht in your favours, but hereafter your rules shall be our methods, by which we will govern all our actions, attending only wholy your directions, yet give us leave humbly to offer our advise as Subjects to their Princess if you think fit, we think it best to follow close the victory, lest that our Enemies recruit their forces, with a sufficient strength to beat us out of what we have gained, or at least to hinder and oppose our entrance, and hopes of Conquering them, where if you will give us leave we will besiege and enter their Towns, and rase their Walls down to the ground, which harbour their disorders, offending their Neighbours Kingdoms; yet we are not so ambitious as to desire to be Commanders, but to join our forces to yours, and to be your assistants and as your Common Souldiers; but leaving all these affairs of War to your discretion, offering our selves to your service,

We kiss your hands, and take our leaves for this time.

(All the women fall into a great laughter, ha, ha, ha, ha.)

Lady Victoria. Noble Heroickesses, by your valours, and constant, and resolute proceedings, you have brought your Tyranes to be your Slaves; those that Commanded your absence, how humbly sue your presence, those that thought you a hindrance have felt your assistance, the time is well altered since we were sent to retreat back from the Masculine Army, and now nothing to be done in that Army without our advise, with an humble desire they may join their forces with ours: but gallant Heroickesses, by this you may perceive we were as ignorant of our selves as men were of us, thinking our selves shiftless, weak, and unprofitable Creatures, but by our actions of War we have proved our selves to be every way equal with men, for what we want of strength, we have supplied by industry, and had we not done what we have done, we should have lived in ignorance and slavery.

All the Female Commanders. All the knowledge of our selves, the honour of renown, the freedome from slavery, and the submission of men, we acknowledge from you; for you advised us, counselled us, instructed us, and encouraged us to those actions of War: wherefore to you we owe our thanks, and to you we give our thanks.

Lady Victoria. What answer will you return to the Masculine Army?

All the commanders. What answer you will think best.

Lady Victoria. We shall not need to write back an answer, for this Messenger may deliver it by word of mouth; wherefore Sir pray remember us to your General and his Commanders, and tell them, that we are willing upon their submissions to be friends, and that we have not neglected our good Fortune, for we have laid siege to so considerable a Fort, which if taken, may give an easy passage into the Kingdome, which Fort we will deliver to their forces when they come, that they may have the honour of taking it; for tell them, we have got honour enough in the Battel we fought, and victory we did win.

(Exeunt.)

From The Description of a New World, called the Blazing-World

TO THE READER

All do ground their Opinions upon Reason; that is, upon rational probabilities, at least, they think they do: But Fictions are an issue of man's Fancy, framed in his own Mind, according as he pleases, without regard, whether the thing, he fancies, be really existent without his mind or not;

so that Reason searches the depth of Nature, and enquires after the true Causes of Natural Effects; but Fancy creates of its own accord whatsoever it pleases, and delights in its own work. . . .

The Emperor perceived her grief by her tears, and examining the cause thereof, she told him that she had received Intelligence from the Spirits, that that part of the World she came from, which was her native Country, was like to be destroyed by numerous Enemies that made War against it. The Emperor being very sensible of this ill news, especially of the Trouble it caused to the Empress, endeavoured to comfort her as much as possibly he could; and told her, that she might have all the assistance which the Blazing-World was able to afford. She answered, That if there were any possibility of transporting Forces out of The Blazing-World, into the World she came from, she would not fear so much the ruin thereof: but, said she, there being no probability of effecting any such thing, I know not how to shew my readiness to serve my Native Country. The Emperor asked, Whether those Spirits that gave her Intelligence of this War, could not with all their Power and Forces, assist her against those Enemies? She answered, That Spirits could not arm themselves, nor make any use of Artificial Arms or Weapons; for their Vehicles were Natural Bodies, not Artificial: Besides, said she, the violent and strong actions of war, will never agree with Immaterial Spirits; for Immaterial Spirits cannot fight, nor make Trenches, Fortifications, and the like. But, said the Emperor, their Vehicles can; especially if those Vehicles be mens Bodies, they may be serviceable in all the actions of War. Alas, replied the Empress, that will never do; for first, said she, it will be difficult to get so many dead Bodies for their Vehicles, as to make up a whole Army, much more to make many Armies to fight with so many several Nations; nay, if this could be, yet it is not possible to get so many dead and undissolved Bodies in one Nation; and for transporting them out of other Nations, it would be a thing of great difficulty and improbability: But put the case, said she, all these difficulties could be overcome; yet there is one obstruction or hindrance which can no ways be avoided: For although those dead and undissolved Bodies did all die in one minute of time; yet before they could Rendezvouze, and be put into a posture of War, to make a great and formidable Army, they would stink and dissolve; and when they came to a fight, they would moulder into dust and ashes, and so leave the purer Immaterial Spirits naked: nay, were it also possible, that those dead bodies could be preserved from stinking and dissolving, yet the Souls of such Bodies would not suffer Immaterial Spirits to rule and order them, but they would enter and govern them themselves, as being the right owners thereof, which would produce a War between those Immaterial Souls, and the Immaterial Spirits in Material Bodies; all which would hinder them from doing any service in the actions of War, against the Enemies of my Native Countrey. You speak Reason, said the Emperor, and I wish with all my Soul I could advise any manner or way, that you might be able to assist it; but you having told me of your dear Platonick Friend the Duchess of Newcastle, and of her good and profitable Counsels, I would desire you to send for her Soul, and conferr with her about this business.

The Empress was very glad of this motion of the Emperor, and immediately sent for the Soul of the said Duchess, which in a minute waited on her Majesty. Then the Empress declared to her the grievance and sadness of her mind, and how much she was troubled and afflicted at the News brought her by the Immaterial Spirits, desiring the Duchess, if possible, to assist her with the best Counsels she could, that she might shew the greatness of her love and affection which she bore to her Native Countrey. Whereupon the Duchess promised her Majesty to do what lay in her power; and since it was a business of great Importance, she desired some time to consider of it; for, said she, Great Affairs require deep Considerations; which the Empress willingly allowed her. And after the Duchess had considered some little time, she desired the Empress to send some of her Syrens or Mear-men, to see what passages they could find out of the Blazing-World, into the World she came from; for, said she, if there be a passage for a Ship to come out of that World into this; then certainly there may also a Ship pass thorow the same passage out of this World into that. Hereupon the Mear- or Fish-men were sent out; who being many in number, employ'd all their industry, and did swim several ways; at last having found out the passage, they returned to the Empress, and told her, That as their Blazing World had but one Emperor, one Government, one Religion, and one Language, so there was but one Passage into that World, which was so little, that no Vessel bigger than a Packet-Boat could go thorow; neither was that Passage always open, but sometimes quite frozen up. At which Relation both the Empress and Duchess seemed somewhat troubled, fearing that this would perhaps be an hindrance or obstruction to their Design. . . .

After the view of these Glorious and Magnificent Buildings, which the Duchess's Soul was much delighted withall, she resolved to take her leave; but the Emperor desired her to stay yet some short time more, for they both loved her company so well, that they were unwilling to have her depart so soon: Several Conferences and Discourses pass'd between them; amongst the rest, the Emperor desir'd her advice how to set up a Theatre for Plays. The Duchess confessed her Ignorance in this Art, telling his Majesty that she knew nothing of erecting Theatres or Scenes, but what she had by an Immaterial Observation, when she was with the Empress's Soul in the chief City of E. Entring into one of their Theatres, whereof the Empress could give as much account to his Majesty, as her self. But both the Emperor and Empress told the Duchess, That she could give directions how to make Plays. The Duchess answered, That she had as little skill to form a Play after the Mode, as she had to paint or make a Scene for shew. But you have made Plays, replied the Empress: Yes, answered the Duchess, I intended them for Plays; but the Wits of these present times condemned them as uncapable of being represented or acted, because they were not made up according to the Rules of Art; though I dare say, That the Descriptions are as good as any they have writ. The Emperor asked, Whether the Property of Plays were not to describe the several Humours, Actions and Fortunes of Mankind? 'Tis so, answered the Duchess. Why then, replied the Emperor, the natural Humours, Actions and Fortunes of Mankind, are not done by the Rules of Art: But, said the Duchess, it is the Art and Method of our Wits to despise all Descriptions of Wit, Humour, Actions and Fortunes that are without such Artificial Rules. The Emperor asked, Are those good Plays that are made so Methodically and Artificially? The Duchess answer'd, They were Good according to the Judgment of the Age, or Mode of the Nation, but not according to her Judgment: for truly, said she, in my Opinion, their Plays will prove a Nursery of whining Lovers, and not an Academy or School for Wife, Witty, Noble and well-behaved men. But I, replied the Emperor, disire such a Theatre as may make wife Men; and will have such Descriptions as are Natural, not Artificial. If your Majesty be of that Opinion, said the Duchess's Soul, then my Playes may be acted in your Blazing-World, when they cannot be acted in the Blinking-World of Wit; and the next time I come to visit your Majesty, I shall endeavour to order your Majesty's Theatre, to present such Playes as my Wit is capable to make. Then the Empress told the Duchess, That she loved a foolish Farse added to a wife Play. The Duchess answered, That no World in Nature had fitter Creatures for it than the Blazing-World: for, said she, the Lowsemen, the Bird-men, the Spider- and Fox-men, the Ape-men and Satyrs appear in a Farse extraordinary pleasant. . . .

One time the Duchess chanced to discourse with some of her acquaintance, of the Empress of the Blazing-world, who asked her what Pastimes and Recreations her Majesty did most delight in? The Duchess answered, That she spent most of her time in the study of Natural Causes and Effects, which was her chief delight and pastime; and that she loved to discourse sometimes with the most Learned persons of that World: . . .

And sometimes the Empress goes abroad by Water in Barges, sometimes by Land in Chariots, and sometimes on Horse-back; her Royal Chariots are very Glorious, the Body is one intire green Diamond; the four small Pillars that bear up the Top-cover, are four white Diamonds, cut in the form thereof; the top or roof of the Chariot, is one intire blew Diamond, and at the four corners are great springs of Rubies; the Seat is made of Cloth of Gold, stuffed with Ambergreece beaten small: the Chariot is drawn by Twelve Unicorns, whose Trappings are all Chains of Pearl; and as for her Barges, they are onely of Gold. Her Guard of State (for she needs none for security, there being no Rebels or Enemies) consists of Giants, but they seldom wait on their Majesties abroad, because their extraordinary height and bigness does hinder their prospect. Her Entertainment when she is upon the Water, is the Musick of the Fish- and Bird-men; and by Land are Horse and Foot-matches; for the Empress takes much delight in making Race-matches with the Emperor, and the Nobility; some Races are between the Fox- and Ape-men, which sometimes the Satyrs strive to outrun; and some are between the Spider-men and Lice-men. Also there are several Flight-matches, between the several sorts of Bird-men, and the several sorts of Fly-men; and Swimming-matches, between the several sorts of Fish-men. The Emperor, Empress, and their Nobles, take also great delight to have Collations; for in the Blazing-world, there are most delicious Fruits of all sorts, and some such as in this World were never seen nor tasted; for there are most tempting forts of Fruit: After their Collations are ended, they Dance; and if they be upon the Water, they dance upon the Water, there lying so many Fish-men so close and thick together, as they can dance very evenly and easily upon their backs, and need not fear drowning. Their Musick, both Vocal and Instrumental, is according to their several places: Upon the Water, it is of Water-Instruments, as shells filled with Water, and so moved by Art, which is a very sweet and delightful harmony; and those Dances which they dance upon the Water, are, for the most part, such as we in this World call Swimming-Dances, where they do not lift up their feet high: In Lawns, or upon Plains, they have Wind-Instruments, but much better than those in our World: And when they dance in the Woods, they have Horn-Instruments, which although they are of a sort of Wind-Instruments, which although they are of a fort of Wind-Instruments, yet they are of another Fashion than the former: In their Houses they have such Instruments as are somewhat like our Viols, Violins, Theorboes, Lutes, Citherins, Gittars, Harpsichords, and the like; but yet so far beyond them, that the difference cannot well be exprest; and as their places of Dancing, and their Musick is different, so is their manner or way of Dancing. In these and the like Recreations, the Emperor, Empress, and the Nobility pass their time.

THE EPILOGUE TO THE READER

By this Poetical Description, you may perceive, that my ambition is not onely to be Empress, but Authoress of a whole World; and that the Worlds I have made, both the Blazing- and the other Philosophical World mentioned in the first Part of this Description, are framed and composed of the most pure, that is, the Rational parts of Matter, which are the parts of my Mind; which Creation was more easily and suddenly effected, that the Conquests of the two famous Monarchs of the World, Alexander and Cesar. Neither have. I made such disturbances, and caused so many dissolutions of particulars, otherwise named deaths, as they did; for I have destroyed but some few men in a little Boat, which dyed through the extremity of cold, and that by the hand of Justice, which was necessitated to punish their crime of stealing away a young and beauteous Lady. And in the formation of those Worlds, I take more delight and glory, that ever Alexander or Cesar did in conquering this terrestrial world; and though I have made my Blazing-world a Peaceable World, allowing it but one Religion, one Language, and one Government; yet could I make another World, as full of Factions, Divisions and Warrs, as this is of Peace and Tranquility; and the Rational figures of my Mind might express as much courage to fight, as Hector and Achilles had; and be as wise as Nestor, as Eloquent as Ulysses, and as beautiful as Hellen. But I esteeming Peace before Warr, Witt before Policy, Honesty before Beauty; instead of the figures of Alexander, Cesar, Hector, Achilles, Nestor, Ulysses, Hellen, etc. chose rather the figure of Honest Margaret Newcastle, which now I would not change for all this Terrestrial World; and if any should like the World I have made, and be willing to be my Subjects, they may imagine themselves such, and they are such, I mean in their Minds, Fancies or Imaginations; but if they cannot endure to be Subjects, they may create Worlds of their own, and Govern themselves as they please. But yet let them have a care, not to prove unjust Usurpers, and to rob me of mine: for, concerning the Philosophical-world, I am Empress of it my self; and as for the Blazing-world, it haveing an Empress already, who rules it with great Wisdom and Conduct, which Empress is my dear Platonick Friend; I shall never prove so unjust, treacherous and unworthy to her, as to disturb her Government, much less to depose her from her Imperial Throne, for the sake of any other, but rather chuse to create another World for another Friend.

Three Letters of Margaret Lucas to William Cavendish

1. For my lord of Newcastll,

My lord,

Ther is but on acsident, which is death, to mak me onhapy ether to my frindes or fame or your affeetion, tho the last I prefer equall to the firest;

but I fear others foresee we shall be unfortunat, tho we see it not our seleves, or elles ther would not be such paynes taking to unty the knot of our affeetion. I must confes, as you have had good frindes to counsell you, I have had the like to counsell me and tell me they heer of your profesions of afeetion to me, which they bed me tak hed of, for you had ashured your selfe to many and was constant to non. I answred that my lord Newcastll was to wis and to honest to ingag himself to many; and I hard the Qeene should tak it ell that I ded not mak her aquainted befor I had resolved. I asked of what? they sayed of my resolution to you. I asked if I should aquant the Qeene with every conplement that was bestod on me, with many other idell descouersce, which would be to long to wright; but pray doe not think I am inquisitive after such frivolus talk, for I avoyd company to avoyd ther descours. For the King and Qeene's favour, my lord, I think you will never be in danger of loosing it, for I never hard that any body perfeetly had it. For my lord Jermyne, I think you know your self to well to seek so loe; tho I will not say but pollisee sometimes makes ues of inferiours, but it is the glorie of the inferiours to neglect when they get the advantag of ther superiours. They they [*sic*] that tould you of my mother has beter inteligenc then I; and shur, my lord, I threw not my self away when I gave my self to you, for I never ded any act worthy of prays before; but tis the natur of thos that cannot be happy to dessir non elles should be so, as I shall be in haveing you; and will be so in spit of all malles, in being, my lord, your most humbell sarvant,

MARGREAT LUCAS.

Pray lay the falt of my wrighting to my pen.

18. For my lord Newcastll,

My lord,

I shold be sory if your busnes be not acorden to your dissir, and pray, me lord, consider well wither marring me will not bring a troubl to your self; for beleve me, I love you to well to wesh you unhapy, and I had rather lose all hapnes my selfe then you shoud be unfortunat. But if you be resoveled, what day soever you ples to send for me I will com. My lord, I know not what counsell to give consering the Quine, but I fear she will tak it ell if she be not mad aquanted with our intenshoins; and if you ples to right a leter to her and send it to me I wil delever it that day [*deleted:* we be marred,] you send for me. I think it no pollese to desples the quine, for though she will doe us no good she may doe us harme. I have sent my mayd about som busnes and she and my lady Broune shal agre about the other things you spak of. I understand the parswashon of some againest your marreg; [su]er thay would not p[ers]wad you but for your good; but if you think you have don unadvisedly in promesis your self to me, send me word and I will resing up all the intrist I have in you, though unwillingly; but what would I not doe for any thing that may condues to your content; for heerafter, if you should repent, how unfortunat a woman should I be. I have bene very ell this thee [*sic*] days, but health can not be so plesing to me as knowing my self to be, my lord,

your most umbell sarvant,
MARGREAT LUCAS

Pray, me lord, doe not messtrust me for telling of any thing that you have commanded my silance in, for though I am a woman I can keep counsell; but I hav not power ofer the emmaganacions of others.

[*deleted:* Pray remember I have ennemyes] Pray consider I have enemyes.

19. For my lor[*sic*] of Newcastll.

My lord,

It can be in no bodyes powr to ues me ell if you ues me well. I have not ben with the Qeen as yet be reson I am not well, but I heer she would have me acknowledg my self in a falt and not she to be in any; but it will be hard for me to accuse my self and to mak my self guilty of a falt when I am innocent; but if it be the duty of a sarvant to obaye all the commandes of mestres, tho it be against my self I will doe it, if it be but to bring my self in to ues of obedience against I am a wife. For the hindirance of our marrag, I hop it is not in ther power; I am sure they can not hinder me from loving, for I must be and will be and am, my lord, your admiring, loving, honouring, humbell and obedient sarvant,

MARGREAT LUCAS

BIBLIOGRAPHY

Primary Works

Cavendish, Margaret. *Poems and Fancies*. London. Printed by T. R. for J. Martin, and J. Allestrye at the Bell in Saint Pauls Church Yard, 1653.

———. *Philosophicall Fancies*. London. Printed by Tho Roycroft, for J. Martin, and J. Allestrye, at the Bell in St. Pauls Churchyard, 1653.

———. *The Worlds Olio*. London. Printed for J. Martin and J. Allestrye at the Bell in St. Pauls Church-Yard, 1655.

———. *The Philosophical and Physical Opinions*. London. Printed for J. Martin and J. Allestrye at the Bell in St. Pauls Church-Yard, 1655.

______. *Natures Pictures Drawn by Fancies Pencil to the Life*. London. Printed for J. Martin, and J. Allestrye, at the Bell in Saint Paul's Churchyard, 1656. The eleventh (autobiographical) section is titled "A True Relation of my Birth, Breeding, and Life."

______. *Playes*. London. Printed by A. Warren, for John Martin, James Allestry, and Tho. Dicas, at the Bell in Saint Pauls Churchyard, 1662.

______. *Orations of Divers Sorts, Accommodated to Divers Places*. London. Printed 1662. (The recent *Norton Anthology of Women's Literature,* edited by Sandra Gilbert and Susan Gubar, contains a section.)

______. *CCXI Sociable Letters*. London. Printed by William Wilson, 1664.

______. *Philosophical Letters: or, Modest Reflections Upon some Opinions in Natural Philosophy, maintained By several Famous and Learned Authors of this Age, Expressed by way of Letters*. London. Printed 1664.

______. *Observations upon Experimental Philosophy, To which is added, the Description of a New Blazing World*. London. Printed by A. Maxwell, 1666.

______. *The Life of the thrice Noble, High and Puissant Prince William Cavendishe, Duke, Marquess, and Earl of Newcastle*. . . . London. Printed by A. Maxwell, 1667. (A second edition of the English version was published in 1675.)

______. *Plays, Never before Printed*. London. Printed by A. Maxwell, 1668.

______. *Poems, and Phancies*. The Second Impression, much Altered and Corrected. London. Printed by William Wilson, 1664.

______. *DeVita et Rebus Gestis Nobilissime Illustrissimique Principis, Guilielmi Ducis Novo-castrensis, commentarii*. London, 1668.

______. *Observations upon Experimental Philosophy: To which is added, The Description of a New Blazing World*. The Second Edition. London. Printed by A. Maxwell, 1668.

______. *The Description of a New World, called the Blazing-World*. London. Printed by A. Maxwell, 1668.

______. *Poems, or Several Fancies in Verse: with the Animal Parliament, in Prose*. The Third Edition. London. Printed by A. Maxwell, 1668.

______. *Orations of Divers Sorts, Accommodated to Divers Places*. The Second Edition. London. Printed by A. Maxwell, 1671. (Part 11: "Female Orations," first edition 1662.)

______. *Natures Pictures Drawn by Fancies Pencil To the Life*. The Second Edition. London. Printed by A. Maxwell, 1671.

Grant, Douglas, ed. *The Phanseys of William Cavendish Marquis of Newcastle addressed to Margaret Lucas and her Letters in reply*. London: Nonesuch Press, 1956.

Related Works

Ballard, George. *Memoirs of British Ladies, who have been Celebrated for Their Writings*. Oxford, 1752. Reprint with introduction by Ruth Perry. Detroit: Wayne State University Press, 1985.

Brink, Jeanine R., ed. *Female Scholars: A Tradition of Learned Women Before 1800*. Montreal: Eden Press, 1980.

Camden, Carroll. *The Elizabethan Woman: A Panorama of English Womanhood, 1540–1640*. Houston, Tex.: Elsevier Press, 1952.

Cotton, Nancy. *Women Playwrights in England ca. 1363–1750*. Lewisburg, Pa.: Bucknell University Press, 1980.

Delany, Paul. *British Autobiography in the Seventeenth Century*. London: Routledge & Kegan Paul, 1969.

Ehrenreich, Barbara, and Deidre English. *Witches, Midwives and Nurses: A History of Women Healers*. Old Westbury, N.Y.: Feminist Press, 1973.

Gagen, Jean. "Honor and Fame in the Works of the Duchess of Newcastle." *Studies in Philology* 56, no. 3 (July 1959): 519–38.

———. *The New Woman: Her Emergence in English Drama, 1600–1730.* New York: Twayne, 1953.

Gartenberg, Patricia, and Nena Whittemore. "A Checklist of English Women in Print, 1475–1640." *Bulletin of Bibliography and Magazine Notes* 34 (1977): 1–13.

George, Margaret. "From Goodwife to Mistress: The Transformation of the Female in Bourgeois Culture." *Science and Society* (1973): 152–77.

Grant, Douglas. *Margaret the First: A Biography of Margaret Cavendish, Duchess of Newcastle, 1623–1673.* Toronto: University of Toronto Press, 1957.

Hampsten, Elizabeth. "Petticoat Authors: 1660–1720." *Women's Studies* 7 (1980): 21–38.

Hill, Christopher. *The World Turned Upside Down.* New York: Viking, 1975.

———. *Milton and the English Revolution.* New York: Viking, 1977.

Hobby, Elaine. "The Fame of the Honest Margaret Cavendish." M.A. thesis, Essex University, 1979.

Hogrefe, Pearl. *Tudor Women: Commoners and Queens.* Ames: University of Iowa Press, 1975.

Hurd-Mead, Kate Campbell. *A History of Women in Medicine from the Earliest Times to the Beginning of the Nineteenth Century.* New York: Haddam Press, 1938.

Irwin, Joyce L., ed. *Womanhood in Radical Protestantism: 1525–1675.* Lewiston, N.Y.: E. Mellen, 1979.

Jones, Marcia Bell. "Self Images: A Study of Female Autobiography Written in England from 1660–1800." Ph.D. diss., University of North Carolina, 1978.

Kanner, Barbara S., ed. *The Women of England: Interpretive Bibliographical Essays.* Hamden, Conn.: Archon Books, 1979.

Kelso, Ruth. *Doctrine for the Lady of the Renaissance.* Urbana: University of Illinois Press, 1956.

Labalme, Patricia H. *Beyond Their Sex: Learned Women of the European Past.* New York: New York University Press, 1980.

MacFarlane, Alan. "Lawrence Stone, *The Family, Sex and Marriage in England:* Review Essay." *History and Theory* 18 (1979): 103–25.

McGuire, Mary Ann. "Margaret Cavendish, Duchess of Newcastle, on the Nature and Status of Women." *International Journal of Women's Studies* 1, no. 2: 193–206.

Palomo, Delores. "Margaret Cavendish: Defining the Female Self." *Women's Studies* 7 (1980): 55–66.

Pearson, Jacqueline. "'Women may discourse . . . as well as men': Speaking and Silent Women in the Plays of Margaret Cavendish, Duchess of Newcastle." In *Tulsa Studies in Women's Literature* 4, no. 1 (Spring 1985): 33–45.

Richetti, John J. "The Portrayal of Women in Restoration and Eighteenth-Century English Literature." In *What Manner of Woman,* edited by Marlene Springer, 65–97. New York: New York University Press, 1977.

Shepherd, Simon. *Amazons and Warrior Women: Varieties of Feminism in Seventeenth-Century Drama.* New York: St. Martin's Press, 1981.

Smith, Hilda. *Reason's Disciples: Seventeenth-Century English Feminists.* Urbana: University of Illinois Press, 1982.

Stone, Lawrence. *The Family, Sex and Marriage in England: 1500–1800.* New York: Harper and Row, 1977.

———. "Literacy and Education in England, 1640–1900." *Past and Present* 42 (1969): 69–139.

Wiley, Autrey Nell. "Female Prologues and Epilogues in English Plays." *PMLA* 48 (1933): 1060–79.

TORY WIT AND UNCONVENTIONAL WOMAN

phra Behn

MARY ANN O'DONNELL

The "first woman to earn her living by her pen." The "producer of detestable trash" and "dramatic sewage." The "first abolitionist." Damned for the wrong reasons, praised for the wrong reasons, Aphra Behn the woman has obscured Aphra Behn the writer, and the myth has eclipsed the achievement. Stock responses appear in criticism after criticism, fostering a literary tradition that hides the sensitive, creative writer behind shocked moralizing or uncritical patronizing. Until recently, Aphra Behn's considerable talents as dramatist, novelist, poet, and translator were ignored in literary histories and genre studies, because critics found it easier to attack the biography than to face the canon and simpler to promote banalities than to examine a complex writer and her work.

A cold marble slab on the floor of the Cloisters of Westminster Abbey bears witness to Aphra Behn's death in April 1689. But her birth is obscure, her family and early life untraceable, her marriage a mystery. Verifiable facts of Behn's life are meager, yet enough exist to flesh out a fascinating, forthright, and talented woman. Three early biographies appeared between 1696 and 1698,[1] within ten years of her death, and these can be supplemented by Behn's own statements about herself in some of her works.

The biographies taken together establish Behn as a gentlewoman, born a Johnson in Canterbury, Kent.[2] Her family was related to Lord Willoughby of Parham, a kinship that earned her father the appointment as lieutenant-general of Surinam even though he died at sea before reaching his post. Also presented are details of her spying mission in the Netherlands and a brief reference to her marriage to one Mr. Behn, a

Dutch merchant from London; conspicuously absent, however, are intimate details of her life and literary circle and assessments of her literary works. Because the biographical accounts, especially the 1698 "Memoirs," are filled with what appear to be fanciful sketches for plays or short stories, the memoirs have been attacked as complete fiction; but these attacks have long since been discredited.[3]

The name Johnson was never disputed after Behn's death. In fact, as Maureen Duffy reports, the name Johnson is validated by Thomas Culpepper, who wrote in his manuscript "Adversaria" that Behn was born a Johnson in Canterbury or Sturry and that she was "foster sister to the Colonell [that is, himself] her mother being the Colonell's nurse."[4] Duffy traces one Eaffrey Johnson, daughter of Bartholomew and Elizabeth Denham Johnson, whose baptism appears in the register of St. Michael's Church, Harbledown, for December 14, 1640, and suggests Mrs. Johnson was wet nurse to Culpepper and his sister.[5]

Another approach to the Culpepper relationship is currently being studied by Sharon Valiant, who connects Aphra Behn to Culpepper through Culpepper's mother Barbara Sidney, whose first husband was Thomas Smyth, Viscount Strangford. Valiant suggests that Behn's mother may have been the illegitimate daughter of Lady Mary Sidney Wroth by Wroth's cousin William Herbert, third Earl of Pembroke. It is not known where Culpepper and his younger sister were raised after the untimely death of their parents in 1643, but the Sidneys or the Herberts may have accepted the children. This theory helps explain Behn's connections with the Howard and Willoughby families and establishes for Behn a lineage of literary women from the Countess of Pembroke through Lady Mary Wroth.[6]

When Behn speaks about herself in her prose fiction, even allowing for a fictional *persona* as narrator, she does not contradict any information provided in the early biographies, but her autobiographical statements are often as interesting for what is not said as for what is.

In *Oroonoko* she speaks of her father's appointment to Surinam and his death at sea, but she also alludes to her mother, her sister, and her brother.[7] In the same novel, she affirms a connection to the court and to the theater, in statements that her detractors never challenged, when she writes that she returned from Surinam with "some rare Flies, of amazing Forms and Colours," which she gave to "His Majesty's Antiquaries," and a set of Indian feathers that she gave "to the King's Theatre, and it was the Dress of the *Indian Queen,* infinitely admir'd by Persons of Quality; and were unimitable."[8] She openly states in *The Fair Jilt* that she was sent to Antwerp by King Charles.[9] In yet another passage that could be autobiographical, the narrator in the oddly bitter opening of *The History of the Nun: or the Fair Vow-Breaker* discusses continental convents and religious orders, confiding: "I once was design'd an humble Votary in the House of Devotion," but chose otherwise.[10]

Her dedications and occasional poems add a few more pieces to the puzzle. In her 1683 dedication of *The Young King,* Behn entrusts the work to "Philaster," fearing "the reproach of being an *American.*"[11] Her Tory politics and her strong support of the Stuarts echo through her works, especially in her dedication of *The Second Part of The Rover* to James, Duke of York, and in her poems on the death of Charles II, the coronation of his brother, and the "happy birth" of the Prince of Wales. Even when James is supplanted by his daughter Mary and her husband, William of Orange, Behn's dying voice welcomes Mary—but only as daughter of a great father. Her devotion to the Howards of Norfolk is heard in several of her works. In her 1682 dedication of *The City Heiress* to Henry Howard, Lord Mowbray (and later Duke of Norfolk), she effusively praises "the great *Howards* of *Norfolk* and *Arundel,*" claiming to have come "into the World with a Veneration for [Howard's] Illustrious Family, and [been] brought up with continual Praises" for the premier Catholic family in England.[12] In the same dedication, she lauds Mowbray's stand in defense of his beleaguered great-uncle, William Howard, Viscount Stafford, who was executed as part of the Popish Plot.[13] Recalling the death of Stafford in her poem to Sir Roger L'Estrange in 1689, Behn provides strong evidence that she was a Catholic at the time of her death.[14]

Behn never refers to a husband, and no records yet confirm her marriage, although several candidates have been advanced. All that can be surmised for now is that in 1664 or 1665 Aphra Johnson married one Mr. Behn, a Dutch merchant, and that before she served as Royal spy in the Netherlands, she was widowed, perhaps in the plague of 1666.[15] In the fall of 1666, Behn was sent to the continent as liaison for her alleged former lover William Scott to report, sometimes in her own code, on Dutch naval movements.[16] Impoverished by her efforts to gather information, spurned in her requests for needed money, Behn returned at the end of 1666 to a London devastated by plague and fire. The documents in her own words from this period are few: three petitions for £150 to repay one Edward Buttler so that she might escape debtors' prison are the only records we have of Behn from 1667 to 1670,[17] when her first play, *The Forc'd Marriage,* was produced.

Whether Behn suffered the indignities of debtors' prison or was redeemed at the last minute is not known; nor can we trace her career between 1667 and 1670. While some suggest that she became mistress to some well-placed courtier—Buckingham, Rochester, and even Charles II have been advanced with no evidence—more likely Behn found a niche in the theater through Thomas Killigrew. It was to Killigrew's King's Men that she gave the Indian feathers on her return from Surinam, although she produced *The Forc'd Marriage* with the rival Duke's Men. With her known attractiveness and vivacity, she might have tried acting; but more likely her sophistication and wit led her to begin as an anonymous adapter of old plays. Such employment would explain her extensive use of earlier works and the occasional charges of plagiarism leveled against her later, charges she was to answer in the postscript to *The Rover* and the preface to *Sir Patient Fancy.*

Whatever Behn's activities between her retirement from spying in 1667 and her emergence as a dramatist in 1670, she began and ended her professional career the same way—plagued by debt. From her own writings, autobiographical and otherwise, and from the few contemporary records, it is clear that Behn found herself troubled from the beginning of her literary career not only by financial difficulties but by political, religious, social, and personal problems as well. Nonetheless, she transcended her problems, transcended her sex and the traditional role of women. Impelled by the need to survive, refusing to submit to the role of wife or mistress, assured that even without a classical education she could write with the best of the wits, Behn chose for herself as untraditional a role as she could: professional writer. She also chose a second untraditional role—especially in her prologues, epilogues, and dedications—as unabashed Tory and faithful supporter of the Stuart kings and their circle.

Behn's literary career not only parallels the shifting social and political fortunes of the Stuarts but also reflects her own tensions and the changing tastes of Restoration theater-goers. The golden age of her dramatic career spans the years 1670 to 1682, during which time she saw thirteen plays produced, most quite successfully. The first phase of her theatrical career lasted two years, from 1671 to 1673, beginning with *The Forc'd Marriage*[18] and *The Amorous Prince* and ending with the disastrous *Dutch Lover.* In *The Forc'd Marriage* and *The Amorous Prince,* Behn addressed the audience's taste for multiplot poetic tragicomedy with music and masques to divert and entertain. Although Behn quickly sensed that poetic drama was not her métier, these first two plays show the strong sense of stagecraft, character movement, plot pacing, and spectacle that mark her later successes. The plays of this first phase also illustrate some themes that came to dominate her work, especially her hatred of arranged marriages and her dramatic plea to allow lovers the right to choose their own spouses.

With her first two plays, the critics may have bemusedly tolerated the woman who dared write for the stage, but on her third try, *The Dutch Lover,* they struck. They probably had good reason because *The Dutch Lover* fails in its overplotted and heavy-handed attempt to satirize the witless Dutchman. In addition to poor construction, the play was destroyed in production, as Behn charges in her address to the "Good,

Sweet, Honey, Sugar-candied READER," by inattentive acting, ad-libbing, poorly designed costumes, and an inferior epilogue. Her defense of one of her poorest plays provided the occasion for Behn's first literary preface, a spirited attack on her critics and an insightful exposition of her literary theory. In this treatise, Behn satirizes the laborious production of "Learning," defends drama from claims that it must contribute to general morality, and maintains that she writes to entertain. Her treatise climaxes with the portrait of the "white, ill-favour'd wretched Fop" who attacks the play because the author is a woman.[19] Yet, after so lively a defense of her sex and her art, Behn failed to produce another play for three years. Perhaps she was stung by the attacks on *The Dutch Lover* or engaged in revising plays not worthy of her name—or perhaps she had even withdrawn temporarily from the theater.

When she returned to the boards in 1676 with *Abdelazer,* she began her most prolific period of dramatic writing, a period that ended in 1682 after the production and publication of ten successful plays.[20] Her only pure tragedy, *Abdelazer,* a probing study of lust and revenge, shows Behn's maturing sense of staging and her carefully timed use of music.[21] The most praised dramatic moment of this play is its opening scene in which Abdelazer sits sullenly while soft music plays and Behn's most famous lyric, "Love in Phantastique Triumph sat," is sung. In this play especially, the theme that was to inform so much of her prose fiction of the next decade—the power of uncontrolled sexual passion to dehumanize and destroy—is very much in evidence.

In this second, highly productive phase, Behn experimented with less complicated plots and less exotic settings and also intertwined elements of the comedy of manners with the comedy of intrigue and classic romance. Particularly successful were her four "London" plays: *The Town-Fopp,* produced in the fall of 1677; *Sir Patient Fancy,* in January 1677/8; *The Roundheads,* in December 1681; and *The City-Heiress,* in the spring of 1682. Behn's facility with political comedy and her quick eye and ear for London eccentricity combined to form fast-paced satire of Whiggish foibles, especially of the *senex amans* and greedy *bourgeois* merchants and knights. But beneath this sparkle, a darker side appears when characters are married against their will. In *The Town-Fopp* the mismatched lovers solve their problems through divorce, and at the end of *Sir Patient Fancy* the young, long-suffering Lady Fancy openly mocks her hypochondriacal old husband as a cuckold and goes off with a sufficient settlement to live with her impoverished lover. This bitter edge to her plays provoked criticism and afforded Behn the opportunity to publish another preface, this one to defend herself from charges of bawdiness, in *Sir Patient Fancy.*

Several other conventions and motifs appear in this second phase of Behn's playwriting. Behn's plays abound with mistaken identity and disguise, but the plays of this period use cross-dressing of women as a political statement. In *The Town-Fopp* and *The Feign'd Curtizans,* as well as in *The Rover,* women present themselves dressed as males, by no means a novelty in English theatre. But in each case, the male garb allows the women to experience the freedom to move outside rigid norms and strict conventions forced on them by women's dress. In *The Town-Fopp* male disguise allows Behn to skirt the edge of lesbian attraction when Diana, scorned by her husband on their wedding night, finds her rival Celinda disguised as a boy and begins to channel her sexual frustrations toward the smooth-cheeked "lad." Cross-dressing, like masquerade and carnival, provides a comic festival of misrule, and like the festival of misrule it can be allowed only as a temporary aberration. Another alternative for her women characters seeking to escape oppression is the brothel, which Behn ironically juxtaposes to the convent that many of her young women are expected to enter. In Behn's highly romanticized brothel, young women may choose their votaries and live apart from the cruel demands of a patriarchal society while experiencing pleasures that parallel those of the libertine male. Like male dress, however, brothels in Behn's plays provide no permanent refuge.

The brothel as symbol for woman's transitory freedom appears most powerfully in *The Rover,* with the ironically named courtesan Angelica Bianca, who spurns all who cannot meet her price. But Angelica's unlicensed freedom is countered by the purity of Hellena, who tames Willmore and marries him. Angelica is the most fully delineated of Behn's stage characters, and the portrait of the rejecter rejected tempers the exuberance of the rest of the comedy. *The Rover* affirms conventional marriage (but to a partner of one's choice), validates the worth of the pure woman, and explores the suffering of the woman who chooses to live an unconventional life.

With *The Rover,* Behn's most popular play, the critics found a new charge—plagiarism. In an era that accepted borrowings and adaptations, this odd charge surely nettled Behn, who acknowledged her source in Thomas Killigrew's closet drama *Thomaso.* But for the first time she hesitated to put her name on the title page; as a result, the first two issues of the play (both 1677) were published without her name, even though they did include a feisty postscript to answer the charges of plagiarism. Pride of authorship probably got the best of her, and the third issue (also 1677) added Behn's name to the title page.[22] Defiantly, Behn returned to Killigrew's *Thomaso* for *The Second Part of The Rover* late in 1680. Here her dark side reappears, and she again opts for the unconventional with Willmore, now a roving widower, choosing this time the prostitute, La Nuche, as the play celebrates love untrammeled by ceremony or public vows.

The City-Heiress was the last play Behn wrote in her golden years of dramatic writing. Following the publication, four years after staging, of *The Young King,* the first play she ever wrote, Behn produced nothing for the stage for four years. After this hiatus, she returned with two more plays before her death, *The Emperor of the Moon* and *The Luckey Chance.* After her death *The Widdow Ranter* was produced late in 1689 and *The Younger Brother* in the winter of 1695/6, neither with much success. These four plays were probably written in the early 1680s. In the dedication to *The Emperor of the Moon,* Behn asserts that this play was "calculated for His Late Majesty of Sacred memory," Charles II,[23] and Charles Gildon claims to have cut a number of references to Whigs and Tories from *The Younger Brother* while preparing it for the stage in 1695;[24] both references suggest composition in the early 1680s. These plays continue to explore the power of love and expose the silliness of willful old men, especially rich Whigs. The great popularity of *The Emperor of the Moon* stems from its reliance on French farce and Italian *commedia dell'arte* sources for good-natured comedy of trumpery, ridiculous disguise, and music-filled pageant. But in *The Luckey Chance,* Behn returns to hard-edged libertine comedy as two poor sparks take on the establishment by tricking two wealthy aldermen, one of whom loses his wife's virtue to his rival in a card game and assists at his own cuckolding.

While she was writing primarily for the theater, Behn probably lived comfortably. But 1682 seems to have been the turning point in her career. The Popish Plot spread fear and paranoia among many who were patrons of the arts, and Behn found the senseless execution of William Howard, Lord Stafford, straining her Tory loyalties and intensifying her hatred of the Whigs. Playgoing had fallen off in these baleful times when there was much real tragedy to engage the public's interest and little to amuse. Early in 1682 Behn's company, the Duke's Men, subsumed the weaker King's Men, and dissension between members of the former rival companies may have prompted Behn to take a sabbatical. In August, political trouble struck when the lord chamberlain issued an arrest warrant accusing Behn of slurring James, Duke of Monmouth, the bastard son of Charles II, in the epilogue to the anonymous play *Romulus and Hersilia.*[25] It is likely that Behn left the country at this time or even before it, not returning until late 1683.[26] It is also possible that around 1682 Behn experienced the onset of the sclerotic or dystrophic disease that was to sap her physical strength, although not her spirit, reduce her to penury, and provide the impetus for a great literary outpouring in the last two years of her life.

Before 1682, Behn had already begun to publish some poetry and translations. Early in her career, she had written her first dedicatory poem—for the publication of Edward Howard's play *The Six Days Ad-*

venture[27]—and had probably edited *The Covent Garden Drolery.*[28] In 1680 Dryden invited her to paraphrase Ovid's "Oenone to Paris" for his collected translation of *Ovid's Epistles;* although in subsequent editions Dryden superseded Behn's paraphrase with John Cooper's translation of the same work, he never withdrew Behn's poem from the collection.[29]

As early as 1673, Behn's songs began to show up in broadsides and miscellanies, a tribute to their popularity. By 1682, with the theaters in financial difficulty, Behn in political trouble, and the public's taste rapidly changing, miscellanies offered the possibility of making a small income, though hardly in the range of a third-night's take.[30] The first collection of her poems, *Poems upon Several Occasions* (1684), contains several songs previously published in her plays and three poems that first appeared in Rochester's poems,[31] but it also includes many original poems, most notably her salute to "The Golden Age," her long *poème à clef* "Our Cabal," and her response "Written in a Fit of Sickness" to Anne Wharton, Rochester's cousin, whose earlier poem had complimented Behn's elegy on Rochester's death. To this collection is attached her first lengthy translation from the French, *A Voyage to the Isle of Love* by the Abbé Paul Tallemant. This work is more than simple translation, since Behn rewrote Tallemant's prose and poetry into English poetry that improves on the French original. In her second collection, her *Miscellany* of 1685, Behn interspersed among the works of other poets a dozen of her own poems and appended her translation of La Rochefoucauld's maxims. Translation became her chosen form through this period; in addition to French love poetry and epigrams, Behn translated some of the works of Fontenelle, thus being one of the first to bring to England this influential writer's scientific, religious, and philosophical theories.[32]

In Behn's lyric and occasional poetry and in her prose fiction, her personal voice emerges more clearly than it did in her dramatic works, prompted perhaps by the less-public nature of the prose and verse, perhaps by her increasing poverty and illness and her despair about the political and religious chaos in England.

Her most open support of James, Duke of York, began when he acceded to the throne on the death of King Charles in 1685. Between 1685 and her own death four years later, she published ten occasional poems. The first three mourn the death of Charles II, console Charles's widow, "the Great Patern of Piety and Virtue, Catherine Queen Dowager," and celebrate the coronation of James II. A second group of three celebrates first the pregnancy of James's queen, Mary of Modena, and then her happy delivery of a Prince of Wales, and later defends the royal mother against the attacks of "Bavius," the hack poet John Baber, who had openly mocked the royal birth in his poem *To the King*. Others observe disparate events: the Duke of Albemarle's governorship of Jamaica and Sir Roger L'Estrange's publication of the third part of *The History of the Times*. Even as she was dying in the early spring of 1689, Behn was able to write her last two occasional poems, the welcome to Queen Mary, and her six-stanza reconciliation with Bishop Burnet, who had urged her to welcome Mary and may have arranged for the poem's publication.

About the same time Behn turned to translation, she also started to write prose sketches. That Behn found the one outlet closest to the challenge of theatrical writing is evident from the dramatic power of her first published work of fiction, the three parts of *Love-Letters between a Noble-Man and His Sister* (1682–1687). Because she based the *Love-Letters* on the unfolding saga of the elopement of ardent Monmouth supporter Ford, Lord Grey with his sister-in-law, Lady Henrietta Berkeley, Behn was able to write "to the moment" as each new chapter developed. Part 1 thus ends with Philander (as she called Grey) under arrest while Silvia (the *nom de clef* given to Lady Henrietta) escapes to Holland. When Behn resumed the story in 1685, she had little factual material to follow; so her imagination ranged freely, complicating the story with a noble Dutchman, Octavio, who loves Silvia and whose sister is seduced by the faithless Philander. Finding the epistolary technique limited in moral expression and narrative expansiveness, Behn experimented in this second part with a new voice, which begins to realize its power at the end of part 2 and finds full control in part 3 as all pretensions to the epistolary are dropped in favor of the eyewitness narrator. Part 3 was determined by historical events, particularly the Duke of Monmouth's abortive revolt against his uncle, King James. Although part 2 turned away from political satire to concentrate on the love interest, Behn was forced by the facts of the unfolding story to return to the combination of the two in part 3, where Behn's realistic depiction of Monmouth's rebellion subordinates the love story, splitting the narrative. Despite the split, Behn is writing at her best. The psychological study of the debased Silvia plotting to revenge herself on all men, of the repentant Octavio entering a Bernardine monastery to find a higher happiness, and of the traitor Philander in a final twist betraying the rebellion to save himself is unsurpassed in Behn's writing, with the possible exception of *Oroonoko*.

The themes that Behn first examined in *Love-Letters between a Noble-Man and His Sister* recur in her other fiction. While her plays focus on satirizing forced marriages, Whiggish pretensions, and the power of love to regenerate the rake, her fiction probes the psychology of passion, explores the sensational and the exotic, and satirizes larger segments of society and social mores. The stories can be grouped into those with an "English" setting and those without. The English stories—"The Adventure of the Black Lady," "Memoirs of the Court of the King of Bantam," "The Unhappy Mistake," *The Unfortunate Bride*, "The Unfortunate Happy

Lady," and *The Wandring Beauty*—balance romance and realism with light satire, and the narrator's voice is more the simple storyteller's than that of the insistent eyewitness heard in the third part of *Love-Letters.* Behn's foreign settings encouraged her development of sensational incident, from the unintentional bigamist's premeditated murder of her two husbands in *The History of the Nun: Or, The Fair Vow-Breaker* to the mutilation of Oroonoko. Behn's exoticism and her biting satire developed together.

Best known are *The Fair Jilt* and *Oroonoko,* in which folk and fairy-tale motifs combine with stark realism and an ambivalence about the protagonist as each story explores the destructive power of love. With the antiheroine Miranda in *The Fair Jilt,* Behn continues the study of deviant female psychology that began with Isabella in *Abdelazer* and Silvia in *Love-Letters between a Noble-Man and His Sister.* Embedded in the larger story is the fairy-tale-like story of Prince Henrick, betrayed by his brother and forced to save himself by becoming a Franciscan priest. Miranda's attempt to seduce Henrick replays the Biblical tale of Joseph and Potiphar's wife, while the miraculous escape of Miranda's lover, Prince Tarquin, from the executioner's ax carries the force of legend.

In *Oroonoko,* Behn overlays three separate worlds. The conspiratorial court of Oroonoko's kingly grandfather in Coramantien and the supposedly secure English world of the reader are satirically juxtaposed against Surinam, with its rebellious black slaves, their sadistic white masters, and the menacing Carib Indians. While on the surface this is a story of love and brutal hatred, more deeply it contends with power and powerlessness, with authority and subversion. The powerless slave Oroonoko performs the Herculean tasks of killing enormous wild animals and protecting the narrator and her family, yet at the same time he is a debased slave who cannot protect his pregnant wife and unborn child from violation and further enslavement except by killing them. The narrator, too, is powerless; although she is one of the most important personages in Surinam, her father, the designated lieutenant-general of the colony, had died en route to his assignment. Without strong male protection, the woman, like Oroonoko, experiences complete powerlessness, and she fails to save the royal slave, because of her sex and her ambivalent fear of him.

Behn's own sense of powerlessness and frustration grew as she became physically weaker and her beloved James II was deposed. Poor, politically alienated, Behn concentrated her final efforts on fiction and poetry, and in these last works she did not mask her feelings. She became increasingly aware that men would write for money and fame, but because of her sex she could hope for neither. Earlier in her career, in the Epistle to the Reader in *Sir Patient Fancy* (1678), she defended herself against charges of bawdiness as one "who is forced to write for bread and not ashamed to owne it."[33] In one of her last works, her powerful longing for fame interrupts Cowley's consideration of the laurel tree in her paraphrased translation of the last book of his *Six Books of Plants,* when she pleads in her own voice

> Let me with *Sappho* and *Orinda* be
> Oh ever Sacred Nymph, adorn'd by thee;
> And give my Verses Immortality.[34]

Torn between immediate need for money and deep craving for recognition, Behn labored for two decades in the theater, and in fiction, translation, and poetry. The underlying tension in all her works results from her desire to please a libertine theater audience and a puritan reading public, to garner praise and payment from pleased and flattered nobility and their hangers-on and at the same time entice middle-class readers to purchase the play they might not bear to see staged or the novel of passion and violence they could read only while sequestered in their closets. Despite her need to please a difficult audience, Behn's eye on immortality infused her stylized plays with a humanity that transcends Restoration manners and morals and developed in her novels the conflicts between self and society that were later to inform the traditional English novel.

Behn has a valid claim to immortality. She wrote plays as powerful and as well-constructed as those of the male Restoration dramatists who are still read and admired today, and her early novels helped shape realism, characterization, and narrative stance in later novels. This was the woman who asked for "the Priviledge for my Masculine Part the Poet in Me" and stoutly maintained: "I am not content to write for a Third day only. I value Fame as much as if I had been born a *Hero;* and if you rob me of that, I can retire from the ungrateful World, and scorn its fickle Favours."[35]

This was Aphra Behn.

NOTES

1. The first biography was published in 1696 as "An Account of the Life of the Incomparable Mrs. Behn," in her *Younger Brother.* Later that same year, a fuller account appeared as "Memoirs on the Life of Mrs. Behn" by "A Gentlewoman of her Acquaintance," in her *Histories and Novels.* An embellished sixty-page version of the "Memoirs" by "One of the Fair Sex" was published in the expanded third edition of *All the Histories and Novels* in 1698 and in subsequent editions.

2. There is no basis for the persistence of the maiden name "Aphra Amis." While checking a birth record for "Aphra Johnson" found in Wye by Edmund Gosse, Montague Summers learned that the name found by Gosse should have been reported as "Aphra Amis"

(*Works,* 1:xvii–xviii). This second misidentification has persisted despite A. Purvis's report that "Aphra Amis" died shortly after her baptism ("Mrs. Aphra Behn," inside front cover). To date, no verifiable birth record for Aphra Behn has been found.

3. Ernest Bernbaum's attacks appeared in "Mrs. Behn's Biography a Fiction," *PMLA* 28 (1913): 432–53, and "Mrs. Behn's *Oroonoko,*" *Anniversary Papers by Colleagues and Pupils of George Lyman Kittredge* (Boston: Ginn, 1913), 419–35. For refutations of Bernbaum, see the correspondence from Behn's spying mission in the Netherlands edited by William Cameron, *New Light on Aphra Behn,* and studies related to her stay in Surinam, particularly Harrison Platt, "Astrea and Celadon: An Untouched Portrait of Aphra Behn," and B. Dhuicq, "Further Evidence of Aphra Behn's Stay in Surinam."

4. Quoted in Duffy, *The Passionate Shepherdess: Aphra Behn 1640–1689,* 19. Duffy (p. 293) locates Culpepper's *Adversaria* in the British Library, Harley MS 7587-605, vol.2.B.

5. Duffy, *The Passionate Shepherdess,* 19–23. Although it is difficult to reconcile Behn's highly placed connections at court with a wet-nurse mother, Duffy's candidate deserves attention.

6. I am most grateful to Sharon Valiant for her extensive genealogies supporting this theory, a theory far better developed than I can indicate here.

7. Page 148 of the 1688 London edition mentions her father, page 167 speaks of her brother, and page 238 notes her mother and sister (see pp. 177–78, 184, and 208 in vol. 5 of Summers's *Works*). In a letter now in the Public Record Office, probably written in 1667, she mentions her mother (Summers, *Works,* 1:xxvi), and in several other PRO documents relating to her spying mission in the Netherlands Behn refers to her brother (Cameron, *New Light on Aphra Behn,* passim).

8. London (1688), 4–5 (Summers, 5:130).

9. London (1688), 60 (Summers, 5:98).

10. London (1689), 6 (Summers, 5:265). Religious orders for men and women were frequently mentioned in her work; for example, *The Fair Jilt* discusses Beguines and Cordeliers knowledgeably; part 3 of *Love-Letters between a Noble-Man and His Sister* presents Octavio's first vows as a Bernardine; and convents figure in *The History of the Nun, The Nun,* and *The Lucky Mistake.* Even in *Oroonoko,* the narrator mentions that she amused Imoinda and Oroonoko with "Stories of Nuns."

11. London (1683), a1^{v} (Summers, 2:105).

12. London (1682), A2^{r}–A3^{r} (Summers, 2:199). In 1685 she again praises Henry Howard, Duke of Norfolk, as "*Generous, Gay,* and *Great*" in her *Pindarick Poem on the Happy Coronation of . . . James II* (p. 15). There are two versions of this work, different enough to be considered separate editions, but her praise of Howard appears in both on the same page.

13. Behn neither names Stafford, calling him only the "great sufferer," nor specifies Mowbray's action except to note that he "cry'd, *Not guilty*" when "Truth and Innocence was [sic] criminal" (A2^{v}; Summers, 2:200).

14. In her *Poem to Roger L'Estrange* she writes that Stafford "like a *God,* dy'd to redeem *Our Faith*" (London, [1689], 4). For further information on the possibility that Behn was a Catholic see Gerald Duchovnay, "Aphra Behn's *Oroonoko*: A Critical Edition," and his "Aphra Behn's Religion," *N&Q* 221 (1976):235–37; also M. A. O'Donnell, "Experiments in the Prose Fiction of Aphra Behn," (Ph.D. diss., Fordham University, 1979), 14–24. An early suggestion also appeared in "England's First Lady Novelist," *St. James's Magazine* 7 (1863):351–58.

15. Henry A. Hargreaves, "A Case for Mr. Behn," *N & Q* 207 (1962):203–5; and Duffy, *The Passionate Shepherdess,* 48–51. It is even possible that there was no Mr. Behn and that Aphra Johnson assumed a surname in much the same way that she appropriated the sobriquet "Astrea." It is not beyond Behn's playfulness to change from "Johnson" to a name probably pronounced "Ben."

16. As noted before, her reports from Holland are in the Public Record Office and have been edited by William Cameron, *New Light on Aphra Behn.*

17. These documents were first published by the pseudonymous "Ithuriel" ("Aphara Behn," *N&Q,* 2d ser., 8 [1859]:265–66). Montague Summers (1:xxvi–xxvii) reproduces Behn's petition indicating that her arrest was to be executed on the following day. See also Cameron, *New Light on Aphra Behn,* 33.

18. Her friend Thomas Otway made so inauspicious a stage debut as the king in *The Forc'd Marriage* that he almost wrecked the production the first night and never returned to the stage again. John Downes recounts the story in his *Roscius Anglicanus* (London: For H. Playford, 1708).

19. London (1673), A2[r]–a2[r] (Summers, 1:221–25).

20. See O'Donnell, *Aphra Behn: An Annotated Bibliography of Primary and Secondary Sources,* A4–A15.

21. Behn's source, *Lust's Dominion,* dictated plot, tone, and characterization, but Behn's extensive revisions made the play her own. See Henry Allen Hargreaves, "The Life and Plays of Mrs. Aphra Behn"; David Wilfred Meredith, "Borrowing and Innovation in Five Plays by Aphra Behn"; and De Ritter, "The Gypsy, *The Rover,* and the Wanderer."

22. In the third issue, she also added an interpolation "especially of our Sex" in her defense against "the Criticks, who are naturally so kind to any that pretend to usurp their Dominion, especially of our Sex." Some copies of the second issue also carry the interpolation.

23. London (1687), A2[v] (Summers, 3:391).

24. "Epistle Dedicatory" in *The Younger Brother* (London, [1696], A3[r]; Summers, 4:317).

25. *The True Protestant Mercury,* August 12–16, 1682.

26. No works by Behn were entered in the *Term Catalogue* between Trinity term 1682 and Michaelmas 1683, suggesting that Behn may have been out of the country at this time. For further discussion on this point, see O'Donnell, *Aphra Behn: An Annotated Bibliography,* 6–7.

27. London (1671), a2[r]–a3[r]. Behn reprinted this poem with variants in her 1684 collection *Poems upon Several Occasions.*

28. Behn's link to this work has been studied by G. Thorn-Drury in his reprint of it (London: Dobell, 1928).

29. In his preface, Dryden notes Behn's translation is "in Mr. Cowleys way of Imitation" and that he "was desir'd to say that the Authour who is of the Fair Sex, understood not Latine. But if she does not, I am afraid she has given us occasion to be asham'd who do" (a4[r]).

30. Two letters from this period, first printed in *Gentleman's Magazine* in May 1836 (pp. 481–82), indicate Behn's financial problems. The first, undated but probably 1684, asks Jacob Tonson for an additional five pounds for *Poems upon Several Occasions.* The second, dated August 1, 1685, assigns to Zachary Baggs six pounds from her next profits if her debt has not been paid. The first letter, the original of which has dropped from sight, appears in a transcript of Tonson's letters (now in the Beinecke Library) and is reprinted in Summers, 1:xlv–xlvi; the second is in the Folger Library with manuscript transcript in the same Beinecke collection.

31. *Poems on Several Occasions by the Right Honourable, The E. of R——* (Antwerp, 1680). These three poems were once attributed to Rochester. See David M. Vieth, *Attributions in Restoration Poetry: A Study of Rochester's Poems of 1680* (New Haven: Yale University Press, 1963), 448–50, and O'Donnell, *Aphra Behn: An Annotated Bibliography,* 250–52.

32. In 1686, she translated *La Montre,* Balthazar de Bonnecorse's poetry sequence of love-longing and breathless anticipation of the physical joys of love. When Behn returned to

the Abbé Tallemant's prose-poems, she translated his *Second voyage de l'Isle d'Amour* as *Lycidus* (1688), adding to it a "Miscellany of New Poems by Several Hands," including another ten of her own. In addition, she translated Fontenelle's discourses on *The History of Oracles* and *A Discovery of New Worlds,* both in 1688; to the latter she appended a translator's preface in which she discussed the problems of translation from French.

33. London (1678), Al[v] (Summers 4:7).

34. London (1689), 143.

35. *The Luckey Chance* (London [1687], al[r]; Summers, 3:187).

Song from Abdelazer (1677)[1]

Love in Phantastique Triumph sat,
  Whilst Bleeding hearts around him flow'd,
For whom fresh pay[n]s he did create,
  And strange Tyrannick pow'r he shew'd;
From thy bright Eyes he took his fires,
  Which round about in sport he hurl'd;
But 'twas from mine he took desires,
  Enough t'undoe the Amorous world.

From me he took his sighs and tears,
  From thee his pride and cruelty;
From me his languishments and fears,
  And ev'ry killing Dart from thee:
Thus thou, and I, the God have arm'd,
  And set him up a Deity,
But my poor heart alone is harm'd,
  Whilst thine the Victor is, and free.

Epitaph On the Tombstone of a Child, the last of Seven that died before[2]

This Little, Silent, Gloomy Monument,
Contains all that was sweet and innocent;
The softest pratler that e'er found a Tongue,
His Voice was Musick and his words a Song;
Which now each List'ning Angel smiling hears,
Such pretty Harmonies compose the Spheres;
Wanton as unfledg'd Cupids, ere their Charms
Had learn'd the little arts of doing harms;
Fair as young Cherubins, as soft and kind,

And tho translated could not be refin'd;
The Seventh dear pledge the Nuptial Joys had given,
Toil'd here on Earth, retir'd to rest in Heaven;
Where they the shining Host of Angels fill,
Spread their gay wings before the Throne, and smile.

The Counsel. A Song[3]

I.

A Pox upon this needless Scorn:
Sylvia, for shame the Cheat give o'er:
The End to which the Fair are born,
Is not to keep their Charms in store:
But lavishly dispose in haste
Of Joys which none but Youth improve;
Joys which decay when Beauty's past;
And who, when Beauty's past, will love?

II.

When Age those Glories shall deface,
Revenging all your cold Disdain;
And Sylvia shall neglected pass,
By every once-admiring Swain;
And we no more shall Homage pay:[4]
When you in vain too late shall burn,
If Love increase, and Youth decay,
Ah Sylvia! who will make Return?

III.

Then haste, my Silvia, to the Grove,
Where all the Sweets of May conspire
To teach us ev'ry Art of Love,
And raise our Joys of Pleasure higher:[5]
Where while embracing we shall lie
Loosly in Shades on Beds of Flow'rs,
The duller World while we defie,
Years will be Minutes, Ages Hours.

To the fair Clarinda, who made Love to me, imagin'd more than Woman[6]

Fair Lovely Maid, or if that Title be
Too weak, too Feminine for Nobler thee,
Permit a Name that more Approaches Truth:
And let me call thee, Lovely Charming Youth.
This last will justifie my soft complaint,
While that may serve to lessen my constraint;
And without Blushes I the Youth persue,
When so much beauteous Woman is in view.
Against thy Charms we struggle but in vain
With thy deluding Form thou giv'st us pain,
While the bright Nymph betrays us to the Swain.
In pity to our Sex sure thou wer't sent,
That we might Love, and yet be Innocent:
For sure no Crime with thee we can commit;
Or if we shou'd—thy Form excuses it.
For who, that gathers fairest Flowers believes
A Snake lies hid beneath the Fragrant Leaves.

Thou beauteous Wonder of a different kind,
Soft Cloris with the dear Alexis join'd;
When e'r the Manly part of thee, wou'd plead
Thou tempts us with the Image of the Maid,
While we the noblest Passions do extend
The Love to Hermes, Aphrodite the Friend.

From A Paraphrase on the Lords Prayer[7]

Our Father,

O Wondrous condescention of a God!
To poor unworthy sinful flesh and blood;
Lest the high Mistery of Divinity,
Thy sacred Title, shou'd too Awful be;
Lest trembling prostrates should not freely come,
As to their Parent, to their native home;
Lest thy incomprehensible God-head shou'd
Not by dull Man be rightly understood;
Thou deignst to take a name, that fits our sense,
Yet lessens not Thy glorious Excellence. . . .

Give us this day our daily Bread,

For oh my God! as boasting as we are,
We cannot live without thy heavenly care,
With all our Pride, not one poor Morsel's gain'd,
Till by thy wondrous Bounty first obtain'd;
With all our flatter'd Wit, our fanci'd sense,
We have not to one Mercy a pretence
Without the aid of thy Omnipotence.
Oh God, so fit my soul, that I may prove
A pitied Object of thy Grace and Love;
May my Soul be with Heavenly Manna fed,
And deign my grosser part thy daily bread.

And forgive us our Tre[s]passes,

How prone we are to Sin, how sweet were made
The pleasures, our resistless hearts invade!
Of all my Crimes, the breach of all thy Laws
Love, soft bewitching Love! has been the cause;
Of all the Paths that Vanity has trod,
That sure will soonest be forgiven of God;
If things on Earth may be to Heaven resembled,
It must be love, pure, constant, undissembled:
But if to Sin by chance the Charmer press,
Forgive, O Lord, forgive our Trespasses.

As we forgive them that Trespass against us.

Oh that this grateful, little Charity,
Forgiving others all their Sins to me,
May with my God for mine attoning be.
I've sought around, and found no foe in view,
Whom with the least Revenge I would pursue,
My God, my God, dispense thy Mercies too.

Lead us not into Temptation

Thou but permits it, Lord, 'tis we go on,
And give our selves the Provocation;
'Tis we, that prone to pleasures which invite,
Seek all the Arts to heighten vain delight;
But if without some Sin we cannot move,
May mine proceed no higher than to love;
And may thy vengeance be the less severe,
Since thou hast made the object lov'd so fa[i]r.

But deliver us from Evil.

From all the hasty Fury Passion breeds,
And into deaf and blinded Error leads,
From words that bear Damnation in the sound,
And do the Soul as well as Honour wound,
That by degrees of Madness lead us on
To Indiscretion, Shame, Confusion;
From Fondness, Lying, and Hypocrisie,
From my neglect of what I ow to thee;
From Scandal, and from Pride, divert my thought,
And from my Neighbour grant I covet nought;
From black Ingratitude, and Treason, Lord,
Guard me, even in the least unreverend word.
In my Opinion, grant, O Lord, I may,
Be guided in the true and rightful way,
And he that guides me may not go astray;
Do thou, oh Lord, instruct me how to know
Not whither, but which way I am to go;
For how should I an unknown passage find,
When my instructing Guide himself is blind.
    All Honour, Glory, and all Praise be give[n]
    To Kings on Earth, and to our God in Heaven.

—Amen.

A Song in Dialogue[8]

She. Silvio, when will you be kind,
    Ah, Silvio, when will you be kind.
Sil. When Constancy in Swains I find,
    Ah, when Constancy in Swains I find.
She. Ah my Silvi[o], you're too Fair,
    E'er to give me cause to change,
    Ah! do not let me then despair,
        For my Heart's not given to range.
Sil. Men will Sigh, Protest, and Weep,
    Ah! what a coyle with love you'll keep,
        Till our Blushes you o'er-come:
    Ah! till the blessing you have won,
        Which, having once obtain'd, you fly:
    Or if, by chance, you linger on,

Can see us Sigh, can see us Dye,
And Triumph when we are undone.
She. Oh! may my Flocks forget to feed,
And Wolves into my Sheepfold break:
May heaven forget me in my need,
And thou disdain me when I speak,
If ever I thy Love betray,
Or with false Vows they faith repay.
Sil. Then take my hand, which ne'er to Swain
Was render'd, on the score of Love:
But, oh! I give it you with pain,
For fear you shou'd Inconstant prove.

Another Song[9]

Morpheus, Morpheus, God of Sleep,
This Hero from all danger keep,
Let soft Dreams around him rove,
Dreams of kind delights in Love.
What-ever toyls pursue the day,
Do thou at Night chase all away.
Make soft Garlands for his Head,
With Roses and with Poppies spread.
Let soft Musick fill his Ears,
Musick from the Tuneful Sphears,
While Cupids round his Couch still play,
And wanton in the breaking day.

From A Pindarick Poem on the Coronation of His Most Sacred Majesty James II (1685)[10]

I.

Arise my Muse! Advance thy Mourning Head!
And cease lamenting for the Mighty Dead!
Quench all the Funeral Tapers in your Tears,
And as the fainting flames expire,
Let your soft falling Tides retire;
While you behold the Prospect that appears

In the vast Glories of succeeding years!
Advance! and throw thy sable weeds away!
And string thy Lyre for some Harmonious Lay,
Worthy the Celebration of this Mighty Day!
Come ye soft Angels all, and lend your aid,
Ye little Gods that tun'd the Spheres,
That wanton'd, sung, and smil'd and play'd,
When the first World was by your Numbers made;
And Danc'd to order by your Sacred Ayrs!
Such Heavenly Notes as Souls Divine can warm,
Such wond'rous touches as wou'd move
And teach the Blest to Sing and Love!
And even the Anger of a GOD wou'd Charm!
O Tune it high, and strike with bold success,
But sweet and gentle, every strain,
As that which once taught by the Charming Swain,
By its soft force the Spirit dispossest
From the great King and Prophets raging Breast. . . .

To the Unknown Daphnis on his Excellent Translation of Lucretius (1683)[11]

Thou Great Young Man permit amongst the Croud
Of those that sing thy Mighty Praises Loud
My humbler Muse to bring her Tribute too;
Inspir'd by Thy vast Flights of Verse
Methinks I should some wonderous thing Reherse
Worthy Divine Lucretius, and Diviner You!
But I of feebler Seeds design'd,
While the slow moveing Atoms strove
With Careless Heed to Form my Mind,
Compos'd it all of softer Love:
In Gentle Numbers all my Songs are drest:
And when I would Thy Glories sing,
What in Strong Manly Verse should be exprest
Turns all to Womanish Tenderness within;
Whilst that which Admiration does Inspire,
In other Souls, kindles in Mine a Fire.
Let them Admire thee on—whilst I this newer way
Pay thee yet more than They,

For more I ow, since thou hast taught Me more,
Than all the Mighty Bards that went before;
Others long since have pauld the vast Delight,
In Duller Greek and Latine satisfi'd the Appetite:
But I unlearn'd in Schools disdain that Mine
Should treated be at any feast but Thine.

Till now I curst my Sex and Education,[12]
And more the scanted Customs of the Nation,
Permitting not the Female Sex to tread
The Mighty Paths of Learned Heroes Dead:
The Godlike Virgil and Great Homers Muse
Like Divine Mysteries are conceal'd from us,
We are forbid all grateful Theams,
No ravishing Thoughts approach our Ear;
The Fulsom Gingle of the Times
Is all we are allow'd to Understand, or Hear.

But as of old when Men unthinking lay,
Ere Gods were worship't, or e're Laws were fram'd
The wiser Bard that taught 'em first t'obey,
Was next to what he taught Ador'd and Fam'd;
Gentler they grew, their Words and Manners chang'd,
And Salvage now no more the Woods they rang'd:
So Thou by this Translation dost advance
Our Knowledge from the state of Ignorance;
And Equallst Us to Man! Oh how shall We
Enough Adore, or Sacrifice enough to Thee!

The Mystick Terms of Rough Philosophy
Thou dost so Plain and Easily Express,
Yet Deck'st 'em in so soft and Gay a Dress,
So Intelligent to each Capacity;
That They at once Instruct, and charm the Sense
With heights of Fancy, Heights of Eloquence;
And Reason over all unfetter'd Plays,
Wanton and undisturb'd as Summers Breeze
That gliding Murmurs o're the Trees,
And no hard Notion meets, or stops its way;
It Peirces, Conquers, and Compells[13]
As strong as Faiths resistless Oracles,
Faith the Religious Souls content,
Faith the secure Retreat of Routed Argument. . . .[14]

From the Epistle to the Reader in The Dutch Lover (1673)

Good, Sweet, Honey, Sugar-candied READER.

Which I think is more than any one has call'd you yet. I must have a word or two with you before you do advance into the Treatise; but 'tis not to beg your pardon for diverting you from your affairs, by such an idle Pamphlet as this is, for I presume you have not much to do, and therefore are to be obliged to me for keeping you from worse imployment, and if you have a better, you may get you gone about your business: but if you will mispend your time, pray lay the fault upon your self; for I have dealt pretty fairly in the matter, and told you in the Title Page what you are to expect within. Indeed, if I had hung out a sign of the Immortality of the Soul, of the Mystery of Godliness, or of Ecclesiastical Policie, and then had treated you with Indiscerpibility, and Essential Spissitude (words, which though I am no competent Judge of, for want of Languages, yet I fancy strongly ought to mean just nothing) with a company of Apocryphal midnight tales cull'd out of the choicest Insignificant Authors . . . I were then indeed sufficiently in fault; but having inscrib'd Comedy on the beginning of my Book, you may guess pretty near what peny-worths you are like to have, and ware your money and your time accordingly.

I would not yet be understood to lessen the dignity of Playes, for surely they deserve a place among the middle, if not the better sort of Books; for I have heard that most of that which bears the name of Learning, and which has abus'd such quantities of Ink and Paper, and continually imploys so many ignorant, unhappy souls for ten, twelve, twenty years in the University (who yet poor wretches think they are doing something all the while) as Logick, &c. and several other things (that shall be nameless, lest I mispel them) are much more absolutely nothing than the errantest Play that e'er was writ. . . . I am my self well able to affirm that none of all our English Poets, and least the Dramatique (so I think you call them) can be justly charg'd with too great reformation of mens minds or manners, and for that I may appeal to general experiment, if those who are the most assiduous Disciples of the Stage, do not make the fondest and the lewdest Crew about this Town; for if you should unhappily converse them through the year, you will not find one dram of sence amongst a Club of them, unless you will allow for such a little Link-Boys Ribaldry, thick larded with unseasonable, oaths & impudent defiance of God, and all things serious. . . .

. . . And therefore to return to that which I before was speaking of, I will have leave to say that in my judgement the increasing number of our latter Plays have not done much towards the amending of mens Morals, or their Wit, than hath the frequent Preaching, which this last age hath been pester'd with, (indeed without all Controversie they have done less harm) nor can I once imagine what temptation any one can have to expect it from them: for, sure I am, no Play was ever writ with that design. If you consider Tragedy, you'l find their best of Characters unlikely patterns for a wise man to pursue: . . . for Playes were certainly intended for the exercising of mens passions, not their understandings, and he is infinitely far from wise, that will bestow one moments private meditation on such things: And as for Comedie, the finest folks you meet with there, are still unfitter for your imitation, for though within a leaf or two of the Prologue, you are told they are people of Wit, good Humour, good Manners, and all that: yet if the Authors did not kindly add their proper names, you'd never know them by their characters; for whatsoe'er's the matter, it hath happen'd so spightfully in several Playes, which have been prettie well receiv'd of late, that even those persons that were meant to be the ingenious Censors of the Play, have either prov'd the most debauch'd, or most unwittie people, in the Companie: nor is this error very lamentable, since as I take it Comedie was never meant, either for a converting or confirming Ordinance: In short, I think a Play the best divertisement that wise men have; but I do also think them nothing so, who do discourse so formallie about the rules of it, as if 'twere the grand affair of humane life. This being my opinion of Plays, I studied only to make this as entertaining as I could, which whether I have been successful in, my gentle Reader, you may for your shilling judge. . . .

Indeed that day 'twas Acted first, there comes into the Pit, a long, lither, phlegmatick, white, ill-favour'd, wretched Fop, an Officer in Masquerade newly transported with a Scarfe & Feather out of France, a sorry Animal that has nought else to shield it from the uttermost contempt of all mankind, but that respect which we afford to Rats and Toads, which though we do not well allow to live, yet when considered as a part of Gods Creation, we make honourable mention of them. A thing, Reader—but no more of such a Smelt; This Thing, I tell ye, opening that which serves it for a mouth, out issued such a noise as this to those but sate about it, that they were to expect a woful Play, God damn him, for it was a womans. . . .

From Act 5 of The Rover (1677)

[Angelica, scorned by Willmore, threatens his life.]

Ang. [T]ell me,
How many poor believing Fools thou hast undone?
How many hearts thou hast betray'd to ruin?

—Yet these are little mischiefs to the Ills
Thoust taught mine to commit: thoust taught it Love?
Will. Egad 'twas shrewdly hurt the while.
Ang. —Love, that has rob'd it of its unconcern
Of all that Pride that taught me how to value it.
And in its room
A mean submissive Passion was convey'd,
That made me humbly bow, which I nere did
To anything but Heaven.
—Thou, Perjur'd Man, didst this, and with thy Oaths,
Which on thy Knees, thou didst devoutly make,
Soften'd my yielding heart—And then, I was a slave—
—Yet still had been content to've worn my Chains:
Worn 'em with vanity and joy for ever,
Hadst thou not broke those Vows that put them on.
—'Twas then I was undone.
[All this while follows him with a Pistol to his Breast.]
Will. Broke my vows! Wh[y], where hast thou lived?
Amongst the Gods? for I never heard of mortal Man,
That has not broke a thousand Vows.
Ang. Oh, Impudence!
Will. Angellica, that Beauty has been too long tempting,
Not to have made a thousand Lovers languish,
Who in the amorous Favour, no doubt have sworn
Like me: did they all dye in that Faith? still Adoring?
I do not think they did.
Ang. No, faithless Man; had I repaid their Vows, as I did thine,
I would have killed the ingrateful that had abandon'd me.

Will. This old General has quite spoil'd thee, nothing makes a Woman so vain, as being flatter'd. Your old Lover ever supplies the defects of Age, with intollerable Dotage, vast Charge, and that which you call Constancy; and attributing all this to your own Merits, you domineer, and throw your Favours in's Teeth, upbraiding him still with the defects of Age, and Cuckold him as often as he deceives your Expectations. But the Gay, Young, Brisk Lover, that brings his equal Fires, and can give you dart for dart, you'l [find] will be nice as you sometimes.

Ang. All this thou'st made me know, for which I hate thee.
Had I remain'd in innocent security,
I shou'd have thought all men were born my slaves,
And worn my pow'r like lightening in my Eyes,
To have destroy'd at pleasure when offended:
—But when Love held the Mirror, the undeceiving Glass

Reflected all the weakness of my Soul, and made me know
My richest treasure being lost, my Honour,
All the remaining spoil cou'd not be worth
The Conqueror's Care or Value.
—Oh how I fell like a long-worship't Idol
Discovering all the Cheat.
Wou'd not the Insence and rich Sacrifice,
Which blind Devotion offer'd at my Alters,
Have fall'n to thee?
Why wou'dst thou then destroy my fancy'd pow'r. . . .

From Act 4, Scene 1 of The Feign'd Curtizans (1679)

[With his friend Galliard, Fillamour enters what he believes to be a brothel and meets one of the "feign'd curtizans," his beloved Marcella, whom he fails to recognize.]

Mar. What on your guard my lovely Cavalier! lyes there a danger
In this Face and Eyes, that needs that rough resistance?
—Hide hide that mark of anger from my sight,
And if thou woud'st be absolute conqueror here,
Put on soft looks with Eyes all languishing,
Words tender, gentle sighs, and kind desires.

Gall. Death! with what unconcern he hears all this? art thou possest—pox, why dost not answer her?

Mar. I hope he will not yield,— [*Aside*
—He stands unmov'd,—
Surely I was mistaken in this face,
And I believe in charms that have no power.

Gall. S'death thou deservest not such a Noble creature,—
I'le have 'em both my self.— [*Aside*

Fill. —Yes! thou hast wondrous power,
And I have felt it long. [*Pawsingly*

Mar. How!

[*Fill.*] —I've often seen that face—but 'twas in dreams:
And sleeping lov'd Extreamly!
And waking—sigh't to find it but a dream,
The lovely Phantom vanish't with my slumbers,
But left a strong *Idea* on my heart;

Of what I finde in perfect Beauty here,
—But with this difference, she was Virtuous too! . . .
Fill. Oh, I coud talk Eternity away,
In nothing else but Love!—cou'dst thou be honest?
Mar. Honest! was it for that you sent two thousand Crowns.
Or did believe that trifling sum sufficient,
To buy me to the slavery of honesty.
Gall. Hold there my brave Virago.
Fill. No, I wou'd sacrifice a Nobler Fortune,
To buy thy Virtue home!
Mar. What shou'd it idling there!
Fill. Wh[y]—make thee constant to some happy man,
That wou'd adore thee for't.
Mar. Unconscionable! constant at my years?
—Oh 'twere to cheat a thousand!
Who between this and my dull Age of Constancy,
Expect the distribution of my Beauty.
Gall. 'Tis a brave wench,— [*Aside.*
Fill. Yet charming as thou art, the time will come
When all that Beauty like declining flowers,
Will wither on the stalk,—but with this difference,
The next kinde Spring, brings youth to flowers again,
But faded Beauty never more can bloom. . . .

From The Amours of Philander and Sylvia (*Part 3 of* Love-Letters between a Noble-Man and His Sister, 1687)

[The gentle Octavio, who befriended and loved the jilt Silvia, abjures the world and enters a Bernardine monastery in a ceremony witnessed by Silvia and the unnamed narrator, who describes the event in most sensuous terms.][15]

'Twas this Order that Octavio had chosen, as too delicate to undertake the Austerity of any other; and in my opinion 'tis here a Man may hope to become a Saint, sooner than in any other, more perplext with Want, Cold, and all the necessaries of Life, which takes the thought too much from Heaven, and afflicts it with the Cares of this World, with Pain and too much Abstinence: and I rather think 'tis Necessity than Choice that makes a Man a Cordelier, that may be a Jesuit or a Bernardine, two the best of the Holy Orders. But to return, 'twas upon a Thursday this Ceremony began; and as I said there was never anything beheld so fine as the

Church that day was, and all the Fathers that officiated at the High-Altar; behind which a most magnificent Scene of Glory was opened, with Clouds most rarely and Artificially set off, behind which appear'd new ones more bright and dazling, till from one degree to another, their lustre was hardly able to be look'd on; and in which sat an hundred little Angels so rarely dress'd, such shining Robes, such Charming Faces, such flowing bright Hair, Crown'd with Roses of White and Red, with such Artificial Wings, as one would have said they had born the Body up in the Splendid Sky; and these, to soft Musick, turn'd their soft Voices with such sweetness of Harmony, that for my part, I confess, I thought my self no longer on Earth; and sure there is nothing gives us an Idea of real Heaven, like a Church all adorn'd with rare Pictures, and the other Ornaments of it, with what ever can Charm the Eyes; and Musick, and Voices to Ravish the Ear; both which inspire the Soul with unresistable Devotion; and I can Swear for my own part, in those Moments a thousand times I have wish'd to Die; so absolutely I have forgot the World, and all its Vanities, and fixt my thoughts on Heaven. While this Musick continued, and the Anthems were singing, Fifty Boys all in White, bearing Silver Censers, cast Incense all round, and perfum'd the Place with the richest and most agreeable Smells, while two hundred Silver Lamps were burning about the Altar, to give a greater Glory to the open'd Scene, while other Boys strow'd Flowers upon the inlaid Pavement, where the gay Victim was to tread; for no Crowd of Gazers fill'd the empty Space, but those that were Spectators, were so placed, as rather served to adorn than disorder the awful Ceremony, where all were silent, and as still as Death; as awful as Mourners, that attend the Hearse of some lov'd Monarch. While we were thus listening, the soft Musick playing, and the Angels singing, the whole Fraternity of the Order of St. Bernard, came in, two by two, in very graceful Order; and going up to the shining Altar, whose Furniture that day, was Embroidered with Diamonds, Pearls and Stones of great Value; they bow'd and retired to their Places, into little gilded Stalls, like our Knights of the Garter at Windsor: After them fifty Boys that sang, approach in order to the Altar, bow'd, and divided on each side; they were dressed in white Cloth of Silver, with golden Wings and rosy Chaplets: After these, the Bishop in his pontifick Robes, set with Diamonds of great Price, and his Mitre richly adorn'd, ascended the Altar; where, after a short Anthem, he turn'd to receive the young Devotee, who was just entered the Church, while all Eyes were fix'd on him: He was led, or rather, on each side attended, with two young Noble-men, his Relations; and I never saw any thing more rich in Dress, but that of Octavio exceeded all Imagination, for the gayety and fineness of the Work. . . . In his Approach to the Altar, he made three Bows; where, at the Foot of it on the lower Step, he kneel'd, and then High-Mass began; in which were all sorts of different Musick, and that so excellent, that wholly ravished with what I saw and heard, I fancied myself no longer on Earth, but absolutely ascended up to the Regions of the Sky. All I could see around me, all I heard, was ravishing and heavenly; the Scene of Glory, and the dazling Altar; the noble Paintings, and the numerous Lamps; the Awfulness, the Musick, and the Order, made me conceive myself above the Stars, and I had no part of mortal Thought about me. After the Holy Ceremony was performed, the Bishop turn'd and bless'd him; and while an Anthem was singing, Octavio, who was still kneeling, submitted his Head to the Hands of a Father, who with a pair of Sissors cut off his delicate Hair; at which a soft Murmur of Pity and Griefs fill'd the Place: Those fine Locks, with which Silvia had a thousand times play'd, and wound the Curles about her snowy Finger, she now had the dying Grief, for her Sake, for her Infidelity, to behold sacrificed to her Cruelty, and distributed amongst the Ladies, who at any Price would purchase a Curl: After this they took off his Linen, and his Coat, under which he had a white Sattin Wastcoat, and under his Breeches Drawers of the same. Then the Bishop took his Robes, which lay consecrated on the Altar, and put them on, and invested him with the Holy Robe: The Singing continuing to the end of the Ceremony; where, after an Anthem was sung (while he prostrated himself before the Altar) he arose, and instead of the two noble Men that attended him to the Altar, two Bernardines approach'd and conducted him from it, to the Seats of every one of the Order, whom he kissed and imbraced, as they came forth to welcome him to the Society. It was with abundance of Tears that every one beheld this Transformation; but Sylvia swouned several times during the Ceremony, yet would not suffer her self to be carried out. . . .

NOTES TO THE READINGS

The texts are given as they appear in the sources cited. Spelling, capitalization, and punctuation are maintained, but italics and small caps are ignored. When there is more than one source for a text, the texts have been compared and only changes in wording identified in the notes; variant spelling, capitalization, and punctuation are ignored.

1. Text from *Abdelazer.* Behn reprinted it in her *Poems upon Several Occasions* (1684).
2. From *Miscellany* (1685).
3. Text taken from *Poems upon Several Occasions* (1684) where it is noted "Set by Captain Pack." This first appeared in Act 4 of *The Second Part of The Rover.*
4. The original line in *The Second Part of The Rover* reads:
   And we can only pity pay,
5. The original line in *The Second Part of The Rover* reads:
   And raise our Charms of Pleasure higher;

6. From the "Miscellany" published in *Lycidus* (1688).

7. From *Miscellany* (1685).

8. Attributed to Mrs. Behn ("By Mrs. A.B.") in *The History of Adolphus* (1691), where it was published by George Granville along with several other known Behn poems. This has not been reprinted since 1691.

9. Attributed to Mrs. Behn ("By Mrs. A.B.") in *The History of Adolphus* (1691), where it was published by George Granville along with several other known Behn poems. This has not been reprinted since 1691.

10. Two separate issues of this appeared in 1685, identical in title page and contents until D1. From D1 to the end, type was reset with enough variation that the two must be considered separate editions. This first stanza is the same in both editions. This poem has not been reprinted since 1685.

11. The text is that of the original dedicatory poem, which appeared in Thomas Creech's translation of Lucretius's *De Natura Rerum* (2d ed., Oxford: L. Lichfield, 1683). The text differs in two major passages from that which Behn later published in *Poems upon Several Occasions* (1684). Until now, this original version has not been reprinted.

12. When Behn reprinted this poem in *Poems upon Several Occasions* the following year, she changed a number of accidentals and substantives, but two changes greatly alter the poem. In the revised edition, line 25 reads:

> Till now, I curst my Birth, my Education,

13. In the revised version in *Poems upon Several Occasions,* lines 55–59 read:

> It Pierces, Conquers and Compels
> Beyond poor Feeble Faith's dull Oracles.
> Faith the despairing Souls content,
> Faith the Last Shift of Routed Argument.

14. The poem goes on to praise Wadham College of Oxford University for producing three great sons: Bishop Thomas Sprat; John Wilmot, Earl of Rochester; and Thomas Creech, the Daphnis of this poem. There are no further variants that alter meaning in the remaining poem.

15. *The Amours of Philander and Sylvia,* 334–42.

BIBLIOGRAPHY

Primary Works

Abdelazer. London: Printed for J. Magnes and R. Bentley, 1677. 2d ed. 1693.

"The Adventure of the Black Lady." In *All the Histories and Novels,* 3d ed., 1698, and subsequent editions.

Agnes de Castro. London: Printed for William Canning, 1688. Translated from the French of M. de Brilhac. Reissued in *Three Histories,* 1688. Reprinted in *The Histories and Novels,* 1696 and subsequent editions.

The Amorous Prince. London: Printed by J.M. for Thomas Dring, 1671.

The Amours of Philander and Silvia. [Part 3 of *Love-Letters between a Noble-Man and His Sister.*] London: Printed and sold by most Booksellers, 1687. 2d ed. 1693. Numerous eighteenth-century editions.

The City-Heiress. London: Printed for D. Brown and T. Benskin, 1682. 2d ed. 1698.

A Congratulatory Poem to Her Most Sacred Majesty on the Universal Hopes of All Loyal Persons for a Prince of Wales. London: Printed for Will. Canning, 1688. Reissued in *Two Congratulatory Poems,* 1688; 2d ed. 1688.

A Congratulatory Poem to Her Sacred Majesty Queen Mary upon Her Safe Arrival in England. London: Printed by R.E. for R. Bentley, 1689.

A Congratulatory Poem to the King's Most Sacred Majesty on the Happy Birth of the Prince of Wales. London: Printed for W. Canning, 1688. 2d ed. 1688; reissued in *Two Congratulatory Poems.*

The Counterfeit Bridegroom. London: Printed for Langley Curtiss, 1677.

Covent Garden Drolery. Collected by A.B. London: Printed for James Magnes, 1672.

The Debauchee. London: Printed for John Amery, 1677.

A Discovery of New Worlds. London: Printed for William Canning, 1688. Reprinted in *Histories, Novels, and Translations* (1700) as *The Theory of System of Several New Inhabited Worlds.* Translation of Bernard le Bovier de Fontenelle's *Entretiens sur la pluralité des mondes.*

"The Dumb Virgin." Published in *Histories, Novels, and Translations* (1700).

The Dutch Lover. London: Printed for Thomas Dring, 1673.

"An Essay on Translation and Translated Prose." The "Translator's Preface" from *A Discovery of New Worlds.* Reprinted in *Histories, Novels, and Translations* (1700).

The Emperor of the Moon. London: Printed by R. Holt for Joseph Knight and Francis Saunders, 1687. 2d ed. 1688.

The Fair Jilt. London: Printed by R. Holt for Will. Canning, 1688. Reissued in *Three Histories,* 1688. Reprinted in *The Histories and Novels,* 1696 and subsequent editions.

The False Count. London: Printed by M. Flesher for Jacob Tonson, 1682. Two issues 1682; third issue 1697.

The Feign'd Curtizans. London: Printed for Jacob Tonson, 1679.

The Forc'd Marriage. London: Printed by H.L. and R.B. for James Magnus, 1671. 2d ed. 1688, reissued 1690.

The Histories and Novels. London: Printed for S. Briscoe, 1696. Another issue (2d ed.?) 1696. Third edition issued as *All the Histories and Novels.* 3d ed. with additions. London: Printed for Samuel Briscoe, 1698. 4th ed. 1699, reissued 1700. Numerous eighteenth-century editions.

The Histories, Novels, and Translations. The Second Volume. London: Printed by W.O. for S.B. and sold by M. Brown, 1700. Several eighteenth-century editions.

The History of Oracles and the Cheats of the Pagan Priests. London: 1688. Translation of Bernard le Bovier de Fontenelle's *Histoire des Oracles.* Reprinted in *Histories, Novels, and Translations* (1700).

The History of the Nun: Or, The Fair Vow-Breaker. London: Printed for A. Baskervile, 1689.

"The Lady's Looking Glass." In *The Histories and Novels,* 1696 and subsequent editions.

Love-Letters between a Noble-Man and His Sister. London: Printed and sold by Randal Taylor, 1684. 2d ed. 1693; reissued 1694. Numerous eighteenth-century editions.

Love Letters from a Noble Man to His Sister. [Part 2 of *Love-Letters between a Noble-Man and His Sister.*] London: Printed for the Author, 1685. 2d ed. 1693. Numerous eighteenth-century editions.

"Love Letters [to a Gentleman]." In *The Histories and Novels,* 1696 and subsequent editions.

The Luckey Chance. London: Printed by R.H. for W. Canning, 1687.

The Lucky Mistake. London: Printed for R. Bentley, 1689. Reissued in Bentley's *Modern Novels,* 1692. Reprinted in *The Histories and Novels,* 1696 and subsequent editions.

Lycidus: Or The Lover in Fashion. London: Printed for Joseph Knight and Francis Saunders, 1688. Translation of the Abbé Paul Tallemant's *Le second voyage de l'Isle d'Amour.* Includes a miscellany of Behn's poems.

"Memoirs of the Court of the King of Bantam." In *All the Histories and Novels*, 3d ed., 1698 and subsequent editions.

La Montre, Or The Lover's Watch. London: Printed by R.H. for W. Canning, 1686. Translation of Balthazar de Bonnecourse's *La Montre*. Reprinted in *The Histories and Novels*, 1696 and subsequent editions.

Miscellany, Being a Collection of Poems by Several Hands, Together with Reflections on Morality, or Seneca Unmasqued. London: Printed for J. Hindmarsh, 1685.

"The Nun, or The Perjur'd Beauty." In *All the Histories and Novels*, 3d ed., 1698 and subsequent editions.

"Oenone to Paris." *Ovid's Epistles*. London: Printed for Jacob Tonson, 1680.

"Of Trees." Translation of the sixth book of *Six Books of Plants*, by Abraham Cowley. London: Printed for Charles Harper, 1689.

"On the Death of E. Waller." *Poems to the Memory of that Incomparable Poet Edmond Waller Esquire*. London: Printed for Joseph Knight and Francis Saunders, 1688.

Oroonoko, Or, The Royal Slave. London: Printed for Will. Canning, 1688. Reissued in *Three Histories*, 1688. Reprinted in *The Histories and Novels*, 1696 and subsequent editions. Numerous eighteenth-century editions and translations.

A Pindaric Poem to the Reverend Doctor Burnet. London: Printed for R. Bentley and sold by Richard Baldwin, 1689.

A Pindarick on the Death of Our Late Sovereign. London: Printed by J. Playford for Henry Playford, 1685. 2d and 3d eds. 1685.

A Pindarick Poem on the Happy Coronation of His Most Sacred Majesty James II and His Illustrious Consort Queen Mary. London: Printed by J. Playford for Henry Playford, 1685. Another ed. 1685.

Plays Written by the Late Ingenious Mrs. Behn. 2 vols. London: For Jacob Tonson and R. Wellington, 1702. Several eighteenth-century editions.

A Poem Humbly Dedicated to the Great Patern of Piety and Virtue Catherine Queen Dowager on the Death of Her Dear Lord and Husband King Charles II. London: Printed by J. Playford for Henry Playford, 1685. 2d ed. 1685.

A Poem to Sir Roger L'Estrange. London: Printed for Randal Taylor, 1688.

Poems upon Several Occasions. London: For R. Tonson and J. Tonson, 1684. Reissued 1697.

A Prologue to Like Father, Like Son. London: Printed by J.V., 1682.

Prologue to Romulus. London: Printed by Nath. Thompson, 1682.

Prologue to Valentinian. [London]: Printed for Charles Tebroc, [1684]. Reprint, *Valentinian: A Tragedy*, by the Earl of Rochester. London: Printed for Timothy Goodwin, 1685.

The Revenge. London: Printed for W. Cademan, 1680.

The Roundheads. London: Printed for D. Brown and T. Benskin, 1682. Two issues 1682; 2d ed. 1698.

The Rover. London: Printed for John Amery, 1677. Three issues 1677; 2d ed. 1697. Numerous eighteenth-century editions.

The Second Part of The Rover. London: Printed for Jacob Tonson, 1681.

"Seneca Unmasqued." Translation of the *Maximes* of La Rochefoucauld. In her *Miscellany*, 1685.

Sir Patient Fancy. London: Printed by E. Flesher for Richard Tonson and Jacob Tonson, 1678.

To Poet Bavius. London: Printed for the Author, 1688.

To the Most Illustrious Prince Christopher Duke of Albemarle on His Voyage to His Government of Jamaica. London: Printed for John Newton, 1687.

The Town-Fopp. London: Printed by T.N. for James Magnes and Rich. Bentley, 1677. 2d ed. 1699.

The Unfortunate Bride. London: Printed for Samuel Briscoe, 1698, [*i.e.*, 1700]. [Includes *The Unfortunate Happy Lady* and *The Dumb Virgin*.] Published in *Histories, Novels, and Translations* (1700).

"The Unfortunate Happy Lady." Printed with *The Unfortunate Bride*. Published in *Histories, Novels, and Translations* (1700).

"The Unhappy Mistake." Published in *Histories, Novels, and Translations* (1700).

The Wandring Beauty. London: For Samuel Briscoe, 1698 [i.e., 1700]. Published in *Histories, Novels, and Translations* (1700).

The Widdow Ranter. London: Printed for James Knapton, 1690.

The Young King. London: Printed for D. Brown and T. Benskin, 1683. 2d ed. 1698.

The Younger Brother. London: Printed for J. Harris and sold by R. Baldwin, 1696.

Collected Editions and Selected Modern Editions

The Plays, Histories, and Novels of the Ingenious Mrs. Behn. 6 vols. London: J. Pearson, 1871.

The Works of Aphra Behn. edited by Montague Summers. 6 vols. London: Heinemann; Stratford: A. Bullen, 1915. Reprint. New York: Phaeton, 1967; New York: Blom, 1967.

The Novels of Mrs. Behn. London: Routledge, 1905; Westport, Conn.: Greenwood, 1969.

Selected Writings of the Ingenious Mrs. Behn. Edited by Robert Phelps. New York: Grove, 1950. Reprint. New York: Greenwood, 1969.

The City-Heiress. Edited by Maria Antonini. Bologna: Centro Stampe Baiesi, 1978.

———. Hersey, William R. *A Critical Old-Spelling Edition of Aphra Behn's "The City Heiress."* New York: Garland, 1987.

The Emperor of the Moon. In *Ten English Farces*. Edited by Leo Hughes and A. H. Scouten. Austin: University of Texas Press, 1948. Also in *Zwei englische Farcen*. Edited by Alfred Behrmann. Frankfurt am Main: Athenaeum, 1973.

The History of the Nun, Or, The Fair Vow-Breaker. In *Restoration Prose Fiction, 1666–1700*. Edited by Charles C. Mish. Lincoln: University of Nebraska Press, 1970.

Love-Letters between a Noble-Man and His Sister [Part 1]. In *The Novel in Letters: Epistolary Fiction in the Early English Novel, 1678–1740*. Edited by Natascha Würzbach. Coral Gables: University of Miami Press, 1969.

Love-Letters between a Noble-Man and His Sister. Edited by Maureen Duffy. Harmondsworth, Eng.: Penguin/Virago, 1987.

The Lucky Chance. Edited by Fidelis Morgan. New York: Methuen, 1984. Also reprinted in *The Female Wits*. London: Virago, 1981.

———. Edited by Jean Coakley. New York: Garland, 1987.

Oroonoko. Edited by Lore Metzger. New York: Norton, 1973.

———. Duchovnay, Gerald. "Aphra Behn's *Oroonoko*: A Critical Edition." Ph.D. diss., Indiana University, 1971.

———. Translated into Dutch by H. D. Benjamins as "Een Koninklijke Slaav in Suriname." *De West-Indische Gids* 1 (1919): 477–95; (1920): 52–70, 339–60, 443–62.

———. Translated into Dutch by Albert Helman as *Oroenoko*. Amsterdam: Arbeiderspiers, 1983.

The Rover. Edited by Frederick M. Link. Lincoln: University of Nebraska Press, 1967.

———. Translated into Italian by Viola Papetti as *Il Giramondo*. Milan: La Tartaruga, 1981.

———. Adaptation by The Royal Shakespeare Company, Swan Theater. Commentary by

Simon Trussler. London: Methuen, [1986]. Cuts about 550 lines of original and adds about 350 lines from other sources.

The Unfortunate Bride. In *The Female Spectator*. Edited by Mary M. Mahl and Helene Koon. Bloomington: Indiana University Press, 1977.

Related Works

Armistead, J. M. *Four Restoration Playwrights: A Reference Guide to Thomas Shadwell, Aphra Behn, Nathaniel Lee, and Thomas Otway*. Boston: G. K. Hall, 1984.

Benjamins, H. D. "Is Aphra Behn in Suriname Geweest? Met Nog Iets Over de Schrijfster." *De West-Indische Gids* 8 (1926–1927): 451–62.

______. "Nog Eens: Aphra Behn." *De West-Indische Gids* 2 (1921): 517–38.

Brownley, Martine Watson. "The Narrator in *Oroonoko*." *Essays in Literature* 4 (1977): 174–81.

Cameron, William J. *New Light on Aphra Behn*. Auckland: University of Auckland Press, 1961. Reprint. Darby, Penn.: Arden Library, 1978.

Day, Robert Adams. "Aphra Behn and the Works of the Intellect." In *Fetter'd or Free? British Women Novelists 1670–1815*, edited by Mary Anne Schofield and Cecilia Macheski, 372–382. Athens: Ohio University Press, 1986.

______. "Aphra Behn's First Biography." *Studies in Bibliography* 22 (1969): 227–40.

______. *Told in Letters: Epistolary Fiction before Richardson*. Ann Arbor: University of Michigan Press, 1966.

De Ritter, Jones. "The Gypsy, *The Rover*, and the Wanderer: Aphra Behn's Revision of Thomas Killigrew." *Restoration* 10 (Fall 1986): 524–26.

Dhuicq, B. "Further Evidence of Aphra Behn's Stay in Surinam." *N&Q* 224 (1979): 524–26.

Duchovnay, Gerald. "Aphra Behn's *Oroonoko*: A Critical Edition." Ph.D. diss., Indiana University, 1971.

Duffy, Maureen. *The Passionate Shepherdess: Aphra Behn 1640–89*. London: Cape, 1977.

Goreau, Angeline. *Reconstructing Aphra: A Social Biography of Aphra Behn*. New York: Dial, 1980.

Guffey, George. "Aphra Behn's *Oroonoko:* Occasion and Accomplishment." *Two English Novelists*. Los Angeles: Clark Library, 1975.

Hargreaves, Henry Allen. "The Life and Plays of Mrs. Aphra Behn." Ph.D. diss., Duke University, 1960.

Hill, Rowland M. "Aphra Behn's Use of Setting." *Modern Language Quarterly* 7 (1946): 189–203.

Jerrold, Walter, and Clare Jerrold. *Five Queer Women*. New York: Brentano's, 1929.

Langdell, Cheri Davis. "Aphra Behn and Sexual Politics: A Dramatist's Discourse with her Audience." In *Drama, Sex, and Politics*, edited by James Redmond, 109–28. Cambridge: Cambridge University Press, 1985.

Link, Frederick M. *Aphra Behn*. Twayne English Authors Series. New York: Twayne, 1968.

MacCarthy, B. G. *Women Writers: Their Contribution to the English Novel, 1621–1744*. Cork: Cork University Press; Oxford: Blackwell, 1944.

McKeon, Michael. *The Origins of the English Novel*. Baltimore: Johns Hopkins University Press, 1987.

Mendelson, Sara Heller. "Aphra Behn." In *The Mental World of Stuart Women: Three Studies*, 116–84. Amherst: University of Massachusetts Press, 1987.

Meredith, David Wilfred. "Borrowing and Innovation in Five Plays by Aphra Behn." Ph.D. diss., Kent State University, 1976.

Messenger, Ann. "Novel into Play: Aphra Behn and Thomas Southerne." In *His and Hers: Essays in Restoration and Eighteenth-Century Literature*, 41–70. Lexington: University of Kentucky Press, 1986.

O'Donnell, Mary Ann. *Aphra Behn: An Annotated Bibliography of Primary and Secondary Sources.* New York: Garland, 1986.

Platt, Harrison. "Astrea and Celadon: An Untouched Portrait of Aphra Behn." *PMLA* 49 (1934): 544–59.

Purvis, A. "Mrs. Aphra Behn." *Amateur Historian* 1, no. 9 (December 1953–January 1954), inside front cover.

Ramsaran, J. A. "'Oroonoko': A Study of the Factual Elements." *N&Q* 205 (1960): 142–45.

Sackville-West, Vita. *Aphra Behn: The Incomparable Astrea.* New York: Viking, 1928.

Salzman, Paul. *English Prose Fiction, 1558–1700: A Critical History.* Oxford: Oxford University Press, 1985.

Siegel, Paul. *Aphra Behns Gedichte und Prosawerke.* Ph.D. diss., Leipzig, 1901. Halle: Max Niemeyer, 1901. Reprinted in *Anglia* 25 (1902): 86–128, 328–85.

Spencer, Jane. *The Rise of the Woman Novelist: From Aphra Behn to Jane Austen.* Oxford: Blackwell, 1986.

Two Centuries of Testimony in Favour of Mrs. Aphra Behn. London: J. Pearson, 1872.

Woodcock, George. *The Incomparable Aphra.* London: Boardman, 1948.

PART SIX

enmark and Sweden

THE DANISH PRINCESS

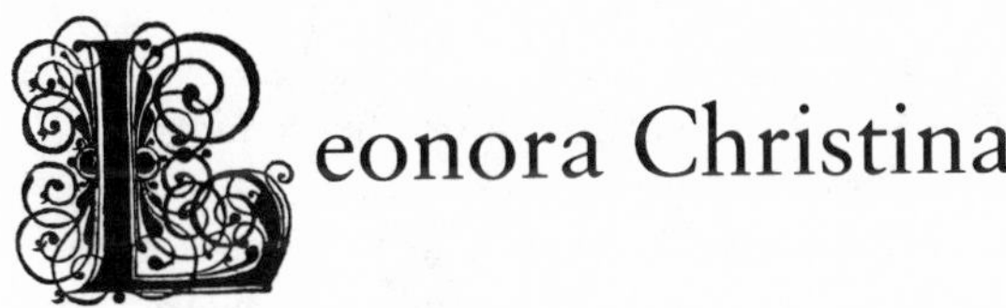eonora Christina

SVERRE LYNGSTAD

When Leonora Christina's *Memory of Sorrow* was discovered in 1868 by the Austrian count Johann Waldstein, a descendant of her youngest son, Leo, and published the following year, a writer of the first rank appeared overnight in Danish literature. *Memory of Sorrow,* conceived and largely written in prison, is the greatest monument of Danish prose in the seventeenth century and the most moving memoir in the language.

Daughter of Christian IV, a Renaissance-style king with a voracious appetite for work, pleasure, and artistic splendor, and his morganatic wife, Kirstine Munk, Leonora Christina (1621–1698) received an excellent education, facilitated by a first-rate mind and an extraordinarily retentive memory. As a child, she wrote in her French autobiography, she could "at one and the same time recite a hymn from memory, copy another, and follow the conversation."[1] She read widely, especially in literature and history, and spoke several languages. Her fluency in French passed muster at the court of Anne of Austria, widow of Louis XIII. She knew Italian, Spanish, even some Latin, and the dialogue in *Memory of Sorrow* shows a perfect command of High and Low German. She also played several musical instruments, could draw and paint, and became a skilled artisan in a variety of media. In prison she learned turning in amber and ivory, and she grew famous for her exquisite needlework with improvised tools and materials.

Leonora was attractive, tall and graceful, and had a gift for repartee. The well-known memoirist Madame de Motteville described her on her visit to the French court in 1647: "Her face was very beautiful, and with her beauty went dignity. . . . She spoke frequently, and always sensibly, with a straightforwardness that had a tinge of her country's coldness, but in which there was nothing common or trifling. . . . We talked about nothing but the Danish lady all day, of her sweet seriousness, of the grace manifest in all she did, and the wit and understanding she displayed."[2]

Though flattering enough, the portrait omits Leonora's boundless curiosity, her independence of mind and taste for adventure. These qualities are illustrated by her views on women's equality, which place her at the cutting edge of contemporary thought. In the preface to her feminist work "Ornament of Heroines," she states that both sexes possess in equal measure a "rational mind" and that sex should yield to merit: "The mind pays no heed to sex and is not changed through external form or figure." She says, further, that not all men perform men's deeds, "but often women acquit themselves heroically. How often does one not see effeminate hearts in men's bodies and, on the contrary, virile strength in weak vessels. It is unfair to measure the deed by the person and not to esteem the person by the deed."[3] She delights in mocking male superiority, smilingly drawing a bodkin from her hair against the sword of Adolph Fuchs, her jailer at Hammershus Fortress, and ridiculing the three vociferous males against whom she defended her husband in Malmø, Sweden, in 1659: "'Messieurs, with your permission, let one speak at a time, for I am but one and cannot answer three at once.' At which they all looked somewhat ashamed."[4] In all things she asserted her equality with men, just as she enjoyed the manly sports of riding, hunting, shooting, and ball playing more than most ladies of her time; she wore men's clothes not only for convenience or disguise but also out of preference.

Yet the destiny of this king's daughter of staunchly independent character was shaped by her husband, Corfitz Ulfeldt, to whom she was married at the age of fifteen. Ulfeldt, fifteen years her senior, rose to the pinnacle of power toward the end of Christian IV's reign; as High Steward of the Realm (*Rigshovmester*), he combined the offices of premier and minister of finance. The High Steward was ex officio chairman of the Council of the Realm (*Rigsraad*), the highest ruling body, and was in charge of both state revenues and the king's treasury. From 1643 to 1650, Ulfeldt was the most powerful man in Denmark, next to the king; up to 1648, the year of Christian IV's death, Leonora Christina was the First Lady of the Danish capital, since Denmark was without a queen at the time. But the Ulfeldts were poised on disaster, actors-to-be in a medieval tragedy of fall from greatness.

Ulfeldt had clearly misused his authority in the days of Christian IV, but in his repeated conflicts with the aging monarch the latter usually gave in to him. His relations with the new king, Frederik III, Leonora's "cold and suspicious" half-brother (JM, xiii), and Leonora's with the queen, Sophie Amalie, were strained from the very beginning. In 1650, the King no longer honored Leonora's title of countess, which Christian IV had conferred upon all his daughters by Kirstine Munk, and in the same year he decided to investigate Ulfeldt's financial administration. Ulfeldt had long been suspected of mismanagement and corruption, especially in his handling of defense contracts. In 1651, after the Ulfeldts were accused of plotting to poison the King and Queen, the situation came to a head. Though the accuser, a disreputable woman named Dina Vinhofvers, was tried and executed, the Ulfeldts decided to escape abroad, thus sidestepping the imminent investigation. This escape, first to Holland and later to Sweden, signaled the beginning of a life of exile that ended only with Leonora's imprisonment in 1663 and Ulfeldt's death in 1664. In 1652 Ulfeldt lost the office of High Steward of the Realm, usually held for life, and in 1653 lost his fiefs as well; in general, Frederik III aimed to reduce the power of the "sons-in-law," the spouses of Christian IV's daughters by Kirstine Munk, and to resist their claim to a privileged position within the Danish nobility.

Henceforth Ulfeldt was ruled by revenge. He agitated abroad for war with Denmark, lent fabulous sums of money to Queen Christina of Sweden, and served on the Swedish side when Denmark declared war on Sweden in 1657. He offered valuable advice to King Charles X Gustavus and urged the Jutland nobility to join the Swedish cause. Chief negotiator for Sweden at Roskilde in 1658, Ulfeldt gloated over the Danish debacle; Denmark lost large territories to Sweden, while Ulfeldt regained his forfeited estates though he continued to live in Sweden. Leonora Christina seems to have disapproved of her husband's active participation in the Swedish campaign (JM, xiv), yet she interrupted her quiet two-year residence in Barth, Pomerania—received from Sweden's Queen Christina as security for a large loan from Ulfeldt in 1654—and followed him to Denmark, apparently from a sense of wifely duty. After the war they settled in Malmø.

Arrogant, excessively ambitious, and at times quite irrational, Ulfeldt soon became disenchanted with the Swedish king, who had enfeoffed him and put him in charge of pacifying the Danish nobility in the conquered provinces. To an ardent believer in aristocratic privilege whose slogan was *Ubi bene ibi patria* (where one is happy, there is one's homeland),[5] this was a repugnant task; Ulfeldt found the status of the Swedish nobility demeaning. When Sweden renewed the war, Ulfeldt decided a further reduction in Danish power was not in his interest; his sympathies having turned around, he put out feelers to Frederik III. In May 1659, Ulfeldt was accused of treason by King Charles, largely on the ground of his alleged betrayal of the plan for the (unsuccessful) storming of Copenhagen in February the same year. Since he was laid low by a stroke, his defense was undertaken by Leonora. But despite her heroic effort—dauntless courage, unfailing presence of mind, and skill in argumentation, as well as a readiness to depart from the truth—in December 1659,

Ulfeldt was sentenced to death and she herself "incurred the King's disfavor."[6]

King Charles may have intended to pardon them, for the sentence was never proclaimed; but in February 1660, he died. Anxious about the future and alarmed by rumors that they would be transported to Finland for life imprisonment, the Ulfeldts decided to flee—in disguise, as usual. Since the Peace of Copenhagen, concluded on May 27, 1660, seemed to confirm the Ulfeldt clause in the Roskilde Treaty, permitting them to live in Denmark, they determined that Leonora would attempt a reconciliation with King Frederik while Ulfeldt went to Lübeck. To her horror, Ulfeldt showed up in Copenhagen. They were arrested and brought to Hammershus Castle on the island of Bornholm.

Their imprisonment at Hammershus lasted from July 1660 until December 1661. Leonora wrote an account of it at the time, which has been lost. But she gives a vivid description of the ordeal in her French autobiography, especially the daring escape attempt she masterminded; she also gives a scathing portrait of their notorious jailer, Major General Adolph Fuchs, murdered in 1662 by their eldest son, Christian. To obtain their freedom and permission to reside in Denmark, they had to renounce most of their Danish properties and make other painful concessions. Leonora's learning and greatness of mind are evident from her epigrammatic reply to her husband's question whether to sign the final "document of submission" and live, rather than die in prison: "Rebus in adversis facile est contemnere mortem, / Fortius ille facit, qui miser esse potest. / Accidit in puncto, quod non speratur in anno" (adapted from Martial: In adversity it is easy to make light of death; / He who is apt to be unhappy does so even more readily. / What couldn't be expected in a year happens in a moment). They went to stay at Ellensborg, Fyn, Leonora's estate.

By this time Ulfeldt was more or less insane (JM, 335).[7] Soon his restlessness returned; under the pretext of visiting a spa for his health he received the King's permission to leave the country and went to Amsterdam, Bruges, and Paris, as usual accompanied by his wife. His mind was seething with plans for revenge: he spoke to representatives of the Elector of Brandenburg and had audiences with Louis XIV. The Elector reported his treasonous proposals to his Danish ally. On July 24, 1663, Ulfeldt was found guilty of *lèse-majesté* in the highest degree and sentenced, in absentia, to a most ignominious death. Leonora Christina, in England to collect an old debt from Charles II, her cousin once removed whom they had befriended in his French exile, was decoyed by the English authorities into the hands of the Danish envoy and taken to Copenhagen. Thus began Leonora's captivity in the Blue Tower, which was to last for nearly twenty-two years.

LEONORA CHRISTINA was no stranger to writing when she began *Memory of Sorrow.* Besides helping Ulfeldt compose several apologias, she had done translations from the French and Spanish and written a number of autobiographical accounts. Most important is the French autobiography, which contains much interesting information about Leonora's childhood and youth. Written in the Blue Tower in 1673, it was a prelude to the weightier work, *Memory of Sorrow.* In her own judgment "Ornament of Heroines," a celebration of "heroic women," was her most important project; it was started in prison, and three parts were allegedly completed there (JM, 275; M, 295). But only the first part, dealing with "valiant heroines," has been preserved and published.[8] Compared to *Memory of Sorrow,* it seems conventional. In prison Leonora also composed hymns, both in German and Danish, as well as other verse, and in her retreat at Maribo Manor, a former monastery, she wrote a play that was performed by her household.[9]

Leonora's recollections of prison life were addressed to her children, of whom seven grew to maturity and were eventually scattered all over Europe; but she may also have had an audience of her peers in mind. Like so much prison literature, they are steeped in self-justification. However, *Memory of Sorrow* contains distinct elements of fictionality usually absent both from apologia and from straight reminiscence. Though the text was written at different times, mostly after her release from prison, the adopted point of view, including the use of the present tense, insinuates that the entire work—except for a few final pages—was composed in prison.[10] This narratological artifice is significant: the effect of suffering recorded live, so to speak, differs notably from past suffering recollected in tranquillity. Leonora may, in fact, have wished to confirm her self-image as "Christ's crossbearer," a role she attributed to herself from her "youth up" (JM, 97; M, 89).

Despite this personal myth, the book's aesthetic reflects the changing circumstances of composition. The first part, written in prison, concentrates on the author's plight in the "Dark Church," where she was oppressed by prison sickness and subjected to repeated interrogations, and on her ensuing religious crisis. The language is literary and marked by German syntax, with a more colloquial style in passages of free indirect discourse *(erlebte Rede).* Once the judicial and spiritual agon is past, Leonora shifts her attention outward, to the minute experiences of everyday life and her relationships with the common people. Though the first part may seem superior to the rest,[11] the two main narrative blocks are integral to each other and assume definite contours of theme, mode, and tone.

Memory of Sorrow proceeds on two levels: that of ordinary human consciousness, ignorant of and anxious about a menacing future, and that of a religious enlightenment rooted in the Book of Job. The literary expression of the former is drama; and the first part of the book, with its allegedly innocent suffering, hunger strike, death wish, and spiritual anguish, is marked by the conflicts and suspense of tragedy. Initially, we see Leonora wrestling with her accusers for the soul of her husband; when she can no longer shut her eyes to his crimes, she starts wrestling with God for her own soul, for the meaning of a seemingly failed life. Leonora's Job-like dispute with God is the turning point of the story, radically shifting the point of view from tragedy to divine comedy.

This shift is signaled by the introduction of glaring incongruities that undercut the tragic tone. Thus, at a time when Leonora lives on the plane of tragic suffering, taking no food and wishing only to die, a shocking rhyme in the text plunges the action from the sublime to the ridiculous: annoyed with the castle steward, Leonora utters an imprecation in the tradition of French tragedy, "Dieu vous punisse," at which he, misunderstanding, says to the attendant, "She wants to piss." The ludicrous nature of the farcical intrusion is noted by Leonora herself, who then perceives, for the first time, that her "stomach desired food." Similarly, in the moment of religious breakthrough, when she awakens with comforting verses from Luther's Bible on her lips ("whom the Lord loveth he chasteneth," etc.), her attendant believes that she has mentioned her stockings in her sleep (JM, 148–50; M, 153, 155). Even the moment of recognition, therefore, is riddled with ambiguities worthy of a cosmic ironist: natural needs and mundane concerns, couched in a suitably low, vernacular style, shift the perspective from tragedy to parody and divine comedy.[12]

From this point on, a transcendent, nontragic vision informs the narrative, the Book of Job functioning as the overall paradigm.[13] This paradigm gives meaning to Leonora's life as well as coherence to her autobiography. The centrality of the Book of Job is evident from the preface, where she mentions six earlier afflictions from which God delivered her, adding that he will not let her "perish" in the seventh (JM, 100; M, 94). The allusion is to Job 5:19: "He shall deliver thee in six troubles: yea, in seven there shall no evil touch thee." Leonora's ability to break out of her self-obsession and raise herself to an ironic God's-eye view saves her from utter despair; it also liberates her narrative drive, enabling her to depict life and people with sympathetic interest and humorous detachment.

As narrative, *Memory of Sorrow* exhibits several features that could be considered modern. In fact, its style has been called literary impressionism, which flourished in Denmark in the 1870s, immediately after the appearance of Leonora's masterpiece. Finn Stein Larsen defines its cardinal traits as phenomenological perception and dramatization. Leonora's narrative is marked by objectivity, with a minimum of direct commentary; by a basically scenic structure in which dialogue becomes part of the action through indirect discourse and *erlebte Rede;* by frequent use of parataxis, forcing the reader to become a co-creator of the text. The incident with the castle steward which takes place on August 9, 1663, illustrates these features. Here Leonora presents a series of concrete observations, visual and auditory, in which the verbal exchanges are part of the action. Narrative omniscience is limited ("though he must have known," "it seemed to me"), and a causal explanation of the castle steward's erratic behavior is suggested only at the end of the scene. Finally, her opinion of the steward is not stated directly but instead is conveyed through nuance, tone, and the unfolding of the scene. While not the only style in *Memory of Sorrow,* this is certainly the predominant one. Larsen attributes its genesis chiefly to Leonora's character and unique predicament: a proud aristocrat confronted with a hostile or vulgar environment evoking caution and contempt.[14] The distance and objectivity characterizing the narrative attitude, with its impressionistic corollary, may indeed be due partly to the circumstances of the book's composition.

The impressionistic method enabled the author to portray character with vivid realism. There are no formal portraits; characters are depicted through their behavior, their words and actions. The successive castle stewards and women attendants are individualized through carefully selected details. Leonora's naturalistic picture of Cathrina is worthy of Frans Hals, a near contemporary; and the squirt incident, with its caustic, grotesque representation of Johan Jäger, recalls Flemish genre painting (JM, 228–30, 201–2; M, 244–46, 213–14). Her portrayal of Christian—a death-row inmate whose life is absurdly spared because his victim's wife refused to pay for his execution and who is free to wander at will in the prison—is no less vivid for turning into a full-scale crime novelette, too complex to be usefully excerpted.

Still, the most fascinating character in *Memory of Sorrow* is Leonora Christina herself. Her personality can only be described in contraries: pride and humility, contempt and compassion, severity and kindness. With all her vengefulness and her self-righteous assumption that Providence is working on her side to defeat her enemies, she commands our respect and sympathy because of her steadfast strength in the face of terrible suffering.

More than anything, perhaps, one is struck by the dialectic of power and eros: the desire to control people and the need for affection and intimacy. Her sense of decorum, of what the world owes her as an aristocrat, a king's daughter, never leaves her. She *must* be in control, even in a situation where she is powerless and given over to the whims of sordid, mean, and cruel people of the lowest moral character. She cows her jailers into following her tune, as in her firm refusal of Mr. Jäger's sexual advances and her exposure of Chresten, who is shamed into resignation (JM, 202, 252; M, 214, 270). She tames, or gets rid of, any attendant who refuses to shape up. In order to control others, she is even prepared to relax self-control and vent her temper in physical violence. To inspire awe in Karen, the daughter of Ole, she tells her, "I can strangle the strongest fellow with my bare hands, if I get hold of him unawares." Sorely provoked by Inger, she slaps her "so that the blood flowed from her nose and mouth," and adds that, if "really angry," she would "mutilate" her (JM, 181, 245; M, 190, 261–62). Her effective handling of the touchy Christian, a quasi-Dostoyevskian demon of spite, guilt, and near-madness, is a subtle mixture of outspokenness and restraint, straightforward dealing and deviousness. She defeats the very ambiance of confinement, transforming it into an arena of triumphant martyrdom. And the way she stages her exit from prison is in perfect keeping with the rest of her conduct during the captivity.

While very conscious of her high birth and wary of a hostile world, Leonora Christina has a common touch that enables her to share her knowledge, wisdom, and human warmth with others. Though her women attendants are generally dissolute and guilty of crime, especially infanticide, and cast a lurid light on the morals and living conditions of commoners in seventeenth-century Denmark, Leonora is able to communicate with several of them. She cannot redeem them, but she can perform a variety of helpful, supportive roles: as mentor, comforter, confessor, and tutor. She is a constant mentor to Karen, the daughter of Nels, a sixty-year-old whom she teaches to read using a subtle, nondirective approach that would pass muster with any modern educator (JM, 205–6; M, 217–18). The situation is touching but also funny, and both student and teacher know it.

From a higher, diachronic perspective, *Memory of Sorrow* shows the metamorphosis of a Renaissance woman deprived of all external supports. The book's first part dramatizes the collapse of reason and of individual self-sufficiency. Leonora sees her former life reduced to nothingness: all is vanity. She evokes a medieval image of human worthlessness, calling herself "shameful dung." What saves her from total despair is the ethical absolute of conjugal fidelity, sanctified by Christian marriage. Such fidelity had always been a centripetal force in her life, not surprisingly in view of her background and experience: the mutual recriminations of her parents, who became estranged when she was a child of seven or eight, and her sisters' scandalous sexual behavior. Writing from prison, she sees her duty as a wife as the only value on which a sense of identity can be based; everything else, even truth, becomes trivial: she consistently denies any awareness of treason, though most scholars think she must have known a great deal.[15]

Strangely enough, her conversion experience, polarizing her existence between spirit and dung, brings her back to the world of nature and people. It embodies a truly Baroque paradox. Though there is little evidence of Baroque style in *Memory of Sorrow*, the experiential tensions and ambiguities it manifests are characteristic of the Baroque. The same applies to Leonora's sense of humor, truly incongruous under the circumstances: the king's daughter can laugh amid the filth of prison. She learns to laugh not only at the absurdities of the world, illustrated by her comment that the executed effigy of her husband "didn't utter a sound" (JM, 160; M, 167), but at herself as well.

Still, the Renaissance spirit persists in Leonora's fascinated interest in everything around her, animate or inanimate, animal or human. She studies the reproductive habits of fleas and the vagaries of caterpillars, reports like a professor of medicine on a "peculiar malady" caused by a "large stone" in her intestine, and gives a rational explanation of witchcraft (JM, 289–91, 269, 173–74; M, 323, 328, 288–89, 181–82). Moreover, her inventiveness in finding ways of passing the time, in a situation where all materials and tools were denied her for fear she would take her own life, harbingers a hero of the following century, Robinson Crusoe, with whom she was compared by Johannes V. Jensen.[16] The comparison may seem farfetched but is quite valid, for in the Blue Tower Leonora had to invent her life anew. Thus, Leonora Christina, poised between Renaissance and Baroque, foreshadows modern attitudes. Contrary to the traditional "saintly" image enhanced by Kristian Zahrtmann's paintings,[17] she was a person to whom nothing human was alien. No wonder she has been celebrated in other arts as well, by writers, sculptors, and composers.

A brief selection from *Memory of Sorrow* can only hint at its richness. In this translation, I have tried to include a variety of scenes, characters, themes, moods, and styles so as to suggest the scope and movement of the narrative. The Bunnett translation, while flawed, is recommended to those who would like to read this curious and deeply moving work in its entirety.

NOTES

1. *Leonora Christina Comtesse d'Ulfeldt Autobiographie 1673*, ed. C. O. Bøggild-Andersen, 2c/9 (marginal comment; the numbers refer to the French text and the Danish translation respectively; each leaf of the French manuscript is equal to four pages in the book: a,b,c,d); *Memoirs of Leonora Christina*, trans. F. E. Bunnett, 37. Further references to the Bunnett translation (M) will be given in the text.

2. Mme de Motteville, *Mémoires*, ed. M. F. Riaux (Paris: Charpentier, 1855), 1:338–39; C. O. Bøggild-Andersen, *Jammers Minde og andre selvbiografiske Skildringer*, ed. Johs. Brøndum-Nielsen and C. O. Bøggild-Andersen, xii. Further references to the latter work (JM) will appear in the text.

3. *Hæltinners Pryd*, ed. Christopher Maaløe, 20–21.

4. *Autobiographie 1673*, 9d/40, 9a/35; JM, 33, 29; M, 61–62, 65–66.

5. J. A. Fridericia, *Adelsvældens sidste Dage: Danmarks Historie fra Christian IV's Død til Enevældens Indførelse, 1648–1660*, 163.

6. S. Birket Smith, *Leonora Christina Grevinde Ulfeldts Historie*, 1:387.

7. While this view is generally accepted, a hypothesis proposed by Johannes Helweg, M.D. ("Var Korfitz Ulfeldt sindssyg?" 1020–37) that Ulfeldt's progressive mental decline—whose beginnings Dr. Helweg traces to the last years of Christian IV's reign—was due to general paresis, has not been seriously considered by historians and critics.

8. *Hæltinners Pryd*, ed. Maaløe.

9. Most critics are skeptical about the hypothesis of Egill Rostrup ("Leonora Christina's Skuespil," 103–13) that this play was *Den beklagelige Tuang* (The Unfortunate Coercion), an adaptation of Isaac Vos's *De beklaeglijcke dwang* (1648), in turn adapted from a play by Lope de Vega. Carl S. Petersen seems to lean toward the view that it was a little Shrovetide play (*Fra Folkevandringstiden indtil Holberg*, 840).

10. Otto Glismann has examined the manuscript of *Memory of Sorrow*, using such criteria as watermarks, script, ink color, number of lines per page, spelling, and so forth. He concludes that part one (up to page 85 of the manuscript), a clean copy that ends abruptly with Leonora Christina's religious breakthrough at the end of August 1663, was written in prison in 1674, though based on earlier notes; part two, a working manuscript covering the period from 1663 to about 1674, the original end-point of the planned narrative, was probably started around New Year's Day 1693, more than seven years after her release; part three, a draft characterized by a more random narrative, may have been written in 1695 or 1696 ("Om Tilblivelsen af Leonora Christinas Jammers-Minde," 72–102).

11. See, for example, the judgment of Petersen, *Fra Folkevandringstiden indtil Holberg*, 840.

12. For a more extensive treatment of these modal shifts in *Memory of Sorrow*, see Jens Aage Doctor, "Sandhedens rolle," 17–20.

13. Ibid., 20–23.

14. Finn Stein Larsen, "En impressionist fra baroktiden? En tekstlæsning i Leonora Christinas Jammersminde," 23–25.

15. See, in particular, the following exchange in the late 1950s: Svend Aakjær, "Leonora Christinas Skyld—Et Aktorat," 233–48, C. O. Bøggild-Andersen, "Kongedatteren for historiens domstol. Nogle bemærkninger til Svend Aakjærs aktorat mod Leonora Christina," 24–39, and Aakjær's rejoinder, "Leonora Christinas Dommer," 40–44.

16. According to Jensen, Leonora Christina lived a "Crusoesque life within the walls of a castle" (quoted by Doctor, "Sandhedens rolle," 35).

17. See Karl Madsen, "Kristian Zahrtmanns Leonora Christina-Billeder," 524–43, and Nicolaus Lützhöft, "Zahrtmann's Leonora Christina Pictures," 749–55.

From Memory of Sorrow; or A Recollection of What Happened to Me, Leonora Christina, in the Blue Tower, from August 8, 1663, to May 19, 1685.[1]

My dearest children:[2]

The past can seldom be recalled without sadness, for it was either better or worse than the present. If it was happier, more joyful and honorable, its recollection naturally saddens us, all the more so as the present might be unhappy, grievous, and ignominious. If former times were sadder, more miserable, and more deplorable than the present, their recollection is equally grievous, for we encounter and feel at once, as it were, all the past misfortunes and adversities we suffered time and again. But inasmuch as all things have two handles whereby they may be hefted, as Epictetus says, one handle by which they may be borne, the other by which they may not,[3] it is up to our will which handle we lay hold of, the bearable or the unbearable one; if we grasp the one by which they may be borne, we can recall all that is transitory, however sad and painful it may have been, with joy rather than with grief; wherefore I will grasp the bearable handle and in the name of Jesus run through my memories, recollecting all the misery and woe, all the grief, scorn and adversity, the insult and injury, which have befallen me in this place, and which I have overcome by the grace of God, and not at all grieve over it but, on the contrary, remind myself at every step of the goodness of God, giving thanks to the Most High, who has always been present with His mighty help and comfort; who has governed my heart, that it did not depart from God; who has preserved my mind and my reason, that it did not start wandering; who has maintained the strength and natural vigor of my limbs; who has even vouchsafed me, and still does, peace of mind and contentment. Glory and praise be to Thee, incomprehensible God, forever and ever!

And now to my purpose: . . . When the boat docked at the small pier near the office of the Treasury, Captain Alfeldt[4] landed, gave me his hand, and conducted me up to the castle bridge. In Castle Square, regiments of horse and foot were drawn up, and musketeers were standing on both sides as I walked forward. On the castle bridge stood Jokum Waldburger, the castle steward, who went ahead of me, and since the people had formed a line on both sides up to the King's Stairs, the castle steward acted as if he were going that way but turned around sharply and said to Alfeldt, "This way," and so saying walked to the gate of the Blue Tower, stood there fumbling with the key for a while and pretended he couldn't open it, in order to make me a spectacle to the people as long as possible. . . . (One incident I will not omit to mention, namely, that when I raised my eyes to heaven, a screaming raven flew over the Tower, followed by a flock of doves which were flying in the same direction.) . . . The castle steward went up the stairs and showed Alfeldt the way to a prison for malefactors which was called the "Dark Church." . . .

The clock was striking half-past four when Jokum closed the door of my prison. Before me I saw a small low table, on which stood a brass candlestick with a lighted candle, a high chair, two small chairs, a bedstead of deal without posts and with old, hard bedding, a commode and a chamber pot. Wherever I turned I was assailed by stench; and no wonder, for three peasants who had been imprisoned there and had been removed and placed elsewhere that very day, had relieved themselves around and against the walls. . . . [While] the door of my prison was closed for a moment, [after a visit from the King's officials], I took the opportunity to hide here and there in holes, and among the debris, a gold watch, a silver pen which gave ink and was filled with ink, and a scissors-case of silver and tortoiseshell.

This was scarcely done when the door opened again and the Queen's Mistress of the Robes, her Woman of the Bedchamber, and the wife of the stores clerk, Abel Catharina, entered. . . . They didn't greet me. Abel Catharina did the talking and said: "It is Her Majesty the Queen's will that we take away your clothes and that you shall wear these instead." I replied, "In God's name!" Then they removed my hair pad, in which I had sewn up rings and many loose diamonds. Abel Catharina felt all over my head to see if anything was hidden in my hair; then she said to the others, "There is nothing there; we won't need the combs." . . . She stripped me completely. I had hidden some ducats under the broad gold lace of my petticoat, a small diamond jewel in my silk camisole, some jacobuses[5] in the feet of my stockings, and some sapphires in my shoes. When she wanted to remove my shift, I asked to be allowed to keep it. No, she swore upon her soul she dared not. They stripped me completely, and the Mistress of the Robes gave Abel Catharina a nod, which she didn't at once understand, so the Mistress of the Robes said: "You remember your orders, don't you?" Thereupon Abel Catharina searched my body in its most secret place and said to the Mistress of the Robes: "No, by God, nothing there." I said: "You act toward me in an unchristian and unseemly manner." . . . After they had thus despoiled me, and dressed me in the clothes they brought, a servant of the Mistress of the Robes came in, searched everywhere with Abel Catharina, and found everything I had hidden. But God blinded their eyes so that they didn't notice my diamond earrings, and some ducats I had sewn into a leather strap around one of my knees; I also saved a diamond worth two hundred rix-dollars,[6] I had bitten it out of the gold on the ship and thrown the gold overboard; the stone I had kept in my mouth. . . . When they had searched thoroughly everywhere, they took all my clothes, except a taffeta cap for my head, and left. . . .

Then the table was laid and four dishes were brought in, but I had no appetite, though I had eaten little or nothing the whole day. An hour after the dishes had been taken away, a girl named Maren Bloks came in, saying that she had orders from the Queen to stay the night with me. . . . She said that the Queen couldn't find anybody who dared to be alone with me, because I was supposed to be evil; it was also rumored that I was very wise, and knew the future. I replied, "If I had that kind of wisdom, I hardly think I would have ended up here, because then I could have been on my guard against it." Maren said we might know things and still not be on our guard against them. . . . She said further: "The Queen knows quite well that my reason was unsettled during a fever, that's why she wanted me to stay with you; but even if you hit me, I wouldn't hit you back." Whereupon she threw her arms around my neck as I sat there and caressed me in her manner, saying, "Hit me, dear heart, hit me! I won't," she swore, "hit back." I was rather alarmed, fearing the onset of madness. She said, further, that when she saw me coming up from the pier, she felt as if her heart would burst. . . . I accepted her unusual caresses, since I couldn't help it at the time, smiled and said it would be extremely unfair to offer blows to someone who showed such great affection as she had done, for one of her own sex at that; I had no idea how the Queen could imagine I hit people, since I had never even slapped a chambermaid.

. . . My thoughts prevented me from sleeping. I kept thinking about my present condition and was utterly unable to reconcile myself to it, or fathom the reason for such a great misfortune. . . . After lying a long time with my face to the wall, I turned around and noticed that Maren was secretly weeping to herself, so I asked her the reason for her tears. At first she denied that she was weeping, but afterward confessed that this whole affair had given her much to think about. It occurred to her that she had heard so much about Lady Leonora and her splendor, etc., about how the King [Christian IV, her father] loved her and everybody praised her, etc., and now she was locked up in this accursed thieves' prison, where the light of day never entered and the stench was enough to poison somebody who just came in and left, let alone those who had to remain there. I thought she wept perhaps because she was going to be shut up with me in this terrible prison, so I comforted her and said she would stay only until somebody else had been assigned to me, since she was in service elsewhere; but that I, for my part, was not thinking about former times, the present gave me enough to attend to; if I were to recall the past, I would also remember the unhappy fates of great men, emperors, kings, princes, and other high personages, whose splendor and prosperity had far exceeded mine and whose misfortunes had been even greater than mine; for they had fallen into the hands of tyrants, who had treated them inhumanly, but this king [Frederik III] was a Christian king and a man of conscience; he would probably think better of it when he had time to reflect, my enemies left him no time to do so at the moment. When I said this, she wept even more than before but said nothing, thinking to herself (as she revealed to me some days afterward) that I didn't know about the infamous sentence that had been passed upon my late lord,[7] which she feared would befall me too, and weeping all the more because I trusted the King so well. We went on talking through the night.

On the morning of August 9, [1663,] at six o'clock, the castle steward came in, said good morning and asked if we would like some brandy. I didn't answer. He asked Maren whether I was sleeping. She replied that she didn't know, came up to my bed and put the same question to me. I thanked her, it was a kind of drink I had never tasted. The castle steward chatted with Maren, was extremely merry for such an early hour, and told her his dreams, which he no doubt invented merely for the sake of talking. He told her, secretly, that she should go to the Queen, and ordered her to say aloud that she wanted to go out a little. He said he would stay with me until she returned, which he did, speaking to me occasionally and asking me if I wanted anything, if I had slept, if Maren had watched well. But he didn't get an answer, so time began to fall heavy on his hands. He walked up and down the stairs, sang a morning hymn, shouted for somebody, then for somebody else, though he must have known they weren't there.

At that time, a man named Jon used to help Rasmus, the tower warden, bring up the meals; to him he called more than forty times, in a singing tone that he changed from high to low, sometimes screaming as loudly as he could and answering himself: "Tut, he's not there, by God, he's not there!" Then he roared with laughter at himself and started shouting again, either for Jon or for Rasmus, so that it seemed to me he had been nipping at the brandy. . . .

At six o'clock in the morning August 10, the castle steward opened the door, to the great delight of the women [Anna and Catharina], who were sincerely longing for him, especially Catharina, who was very plump; she couldn't stand the stuffy atmosphere and was sick almost the whole night. When the castle steward had inquired about their health, about how they were doing and whether they were still alive, and they had complained about their condition, he offered them brandy, which they eagerly accepted. When it was seven o'clock, they asked to go home, which they did; but they first reported to the Queen what had occurred during the half-day, and the night. The castle steward remained with me.

When it was almost nine o'clock, he brought in a chair without saying a word. I could tell from this that visitors were coming, and so they did, for shortly afterward there entered Count Rantzov, the Prime Minister; the Chancellor, Mr. Peter Retz; Treasurer Christoffer Gabel; and Secretary Erik Krag, all of whom shook hands with me and sat down by my bed.[8] Krag, who had paper, pen and ink with him, sat down at the table. . . . The Chancellor said, "Your husband has offered the kingdom of Denmark to a foreign lord."[9] I asked if the kingdom of Denmark belonged to my husband, that he could thus offer it, and since nobody answered I continued and said, "Gentlemen, you all know my lord; you know that he has been esteemed a man of intelligence, and I can assure you that when I parted from him he was still in his right mind. Well, it stands to reason that no sensible man would offer that which didn't lie within his power and was not his to dispose of. He is holding no office, he has neither the authority nor the means, so how could he be so foolish as to make such an offer, and what lord would accept it?"

Count Rantzov said: "Yet it is so, Madame; he has offered Denmark to a foreign potentate, you know it well." I replied, "As God is my witness, I know of no such thing." "Oh, yes," said Count Rantzov, "your husband kept nothing secret from you, therefore you know it perfectly well." I replied, "My husband certainly didn't conceal from me anything that concerned us both. I never troubled myself in former days with that which related to his office; but he never concealed from me anything that affected us both, so I am sure that, if he were planning anything of the sort, he wouldn't have kept me in the dark about it. And I can truly say I am not at all aware of such a thing." Count Rantzov said: "Madame, confess while the King is still asking you to do so." I answered, "If I knew it I would gladly say so, but as surely as God lives I do not know, nor, God help me, can I ever believe my husband would have been so foolish, because he is in delicate health. . . . He couldn't walk up a short flight of stairs without resting to catch his breath; how, then, could he undertake an enterprise that demanded such a great effort? I can truly say that not a week goes by without an attack, of one kind or another. . . . You can do with me what you will; what I do not know, I cannot say." . . . [After more questioning] they left, having spent nearly three hours with me, and then the castle steward and the women entered.

. . . Anna attended to the light during the night, for she was more alert than Catharina. I read aloud to them from Anna's book, commended myself to God and lay down to sleep. But my sleep was very light, the promenading of the rats would wake me, and there were great numbers of them. Hunger made them bold, they ate the candle as it stood burning. Besides, Catharina felt very uncomfortable all night, so that this also prevented my sleeping.

Early in the morning on August 11, the castle steward came as usual, bringing brandy with his compliments, although they had a whole bottle already. Catharina complained a lot, said she couldn't stand the oppressive air; she felt as if she would suffocate as soon as she came through the door; if she had to stay there a week, she was convinced she would be carried out dead. The castle steward laughed at this. . . .

On August 13, after [another interrogation], . . . the Chancellor said: "There is now nothing further to do than to let you know what sort of husband you have, and to let you hear his sentence." . . . Then followed the reading of the unheard-of and illegal sentence which, without a hearing, had been passed on my lord. It was as unexpected and grievous as it was ignominious, and unjustifiable before God and all men who love justice. No documents were brought forward on which the sentence had been based. There was no mention of indictment or defense, there was no other basis but mere words: that he had been found to be a criminal, having offered the crown of Denmark to a foreign sovereign and made him believe he had the support of ecclesiastical and lay magnates, who had proven by their signed protestations that this was not the case, for which reason he was condemned as a criminal.

. . . Anyone can easily imagine how I felt, but few or none can understand how it was I didn't choke at that unexpected misfortune, or didn't lose my mind. I couldn't utter a word for wailing and weeping. . . . When all had been read, I lamented with deep sighs and mournful tears that I had lived to see this sad day and begged them, for Jesus' sake, to let me see what the harsh sentence was based on. Count Rantzov answered, "Of course, Madame, there are documents that we have gone by; some of your friends are in the Council." "Yes, worse luck!" I said. "Won't you let me see the documents, I beg you for God's sake!" . . . Count Rantzov answered as before, that there were documents and that some of my friends sat in the Council, adding that they had all been agreed, not one had had any objection. I dared not say what I thought. I knew quite well how things are done in such absolute governments; nobody dares to contradict, they simply tell you, "Sign, it's the King's will, and do not ask why, or you will be condemned as well."[10] I was silent and bewailed my ill fortune, which was irremediable. When Krag read the minutes, it appeared he had written, when I was asked if I would like to be a party to my husband's sentence, that I had answered I would consider it. I asked, "How was that?" The Chancellor immediately replied, "No, she did not say that, but she requested to know the charges brought against her husband." I repeated my words again,[11] but I don't know whether Krag wrote them down; for a large part of what I said was not put down in writing. Krag let himself be swayed too much by his feelings, and would gladly have made bad worse. He is now gone where no false writings avail. God suddenly snatched him away in an unclean place, called him to judgment without warning.[12] And Count Rantzov, who was the prime mover and originator of that illegal sentence, the like of which was never known in Denmark, didn't live to gloat over the execution of a wooden image.[13] When this was done, they got up and shook hands with me. This painful visit lasted more than four hours. . . .

[Following the fourth interrogation, August 17, in a room on the floor above,] the castle steward came in and said to me: "Now you are to remain here, it is a nice room and has been freshly whitewashed; you may now be contented." . . . I will here describe my prison. The room is seven of my paces long and six wide; it has two beds, a table and two chairs. It was freshly whitewashed, which caused a terrible smell; besides, the floor was so thickly covered with dirt that I thought it was made of mud, though it was really laid with bricks. It is eighteen feet high, with a vaulted ceiling, and at the very top is a window which is two feet square. Before it are extra heavy iron bars, besides a lattice-work, which is so close that one couldn't put one's little finger into the holes. The lattice-work had been thus ordered with great care by Count Rantzov (as the castle steward afterward told me), so that pigeons couldn't slip a letter through, which he had probably seen done in a novel he had read. I felt faint and deeply grieved in my heart, awaiting a merciful deliverance and an end to my sorrow, was quiet and uncomplaining, answering little when the woman [Karen, the daughter of Ole] spoke to me. . . .

When I felt that my stomach desired food and could retain it, I grew impatient that I couldn't die, but had to go on living in such misery; I began to dispute with God and wanted to justify myself to him. . . . I said with Job, "Show me wherefore thou contendest with me. Is it good unto thee that thou shouldest oppress, that thou shouldest despise the work of thine hands?" I didn't forget to mention any of Job's many arguments when he tried to justify himself, and it seemed to me I could reasonably apply them to myself. With him and Jeremiah, I cursed the day I was born and was very impatient, though I kept it to myself and didn't speak aloud; if, at times, a word escaped me unawares, it was in German (since I had mostly read the Bible in German), so that the woman couldn't understand what I was saying. . . . I never felt better than at night, when I noticed that she was sleeping; then I could let my tears flow freely and give vent to my thoughts. Then I called God to account. I enumerated everything I had innocently suffered and endured during my life, and remonstrated with God: Had I deviated from my duty? Should I have done less for my husband than I had done? Was this my reward for refusing to abandon him in his adversity? Was I to be tortured, tormented, and mocked for this now? Weren't the many unspeakable misfortunes which I had endured with him enough, that I had to be preserved for this great and irremediable calamity? I won't conceal my unreasonableness. I will confess my sins. I asked: Could there still be something worse in store for me, for which I was to live? Was there any misery on earth that could be compared to mine? I prayed God to put an end to it, for it didn't at all redound to his credit to let me live and be constantly tormented; I was not made of iron and steel, after all, but of flesh and blood. I prayed to be given an inspiration, or to be informed in a dream, what I was to do to shorten my misery.

When I had disputed thus for a long time and wearied my brain, and also wept so bitterly that it seemed there were no more tears left, I fell asleep, but awoke in terror, for I had awful, unspeakable fantasies in my dreams, so that I dreaded going to sleep and began again to bewail my misery. At length God looked down upon me with an eye of mercy, so that on August 31 I had a night of quiet sleep, and at the very break of day I awoke with the following words on my lips: "My child, faint not when thou art rebuked of the Lord; for whom the Lord loveth he chasteneth, and scourgeth every son whom he receiveth." I uttered the last words aloud, thinking that the woman was sleeping; she may have awakened at that very moment, and she asked me if I wanted something. I answered, "No. . . . I don't want anything."

I then lay quietly collecting my thoughts. I realized and confessed my folly, that I, who was only dirt and clay, dust and ashes, nay, shameful dung, wanted to justify myself before God, most high and most incomprehensible, to dispute with my creator, and criticize and contradict his decrees. I burst into a flood of tears, prayed sincerely and fervently for mercy and forgiveness. . . . If I had uttered foolishly the words of Job, I also said, with him, that I had done unwisely and spoken about things that were too high for me and that I didn't understand. I threw myself on God's mercy, relying on his great compassion. . . . The power of God was working within me. Many comforting sayings from Scripture came to mind, chiefly these: "If so be that we suffer with Christ, we may also be glorified together." Also: "All things work together for good to them that fear God." Also: "My grace is sufficient for thee, for my strength is made perfect in weakness." I thought especially often about Christ's words in St. Luke: "Shall not God save his own elect, which cry day and night unto him, though he bear long with them? I tell you that he will save them speedily." I felt in my affliction how useful it is to have learned hymns and Bible passages in youth. Believe me, my children, it has been a great comfort to me in my misery. . . .

. . . A decision was made to execute a wooden effigy, and [November 12] in the morning, the outer room was opened, swept, cleaned, and strewn with sand.[14] When the door opened at noon and the woman had talked with the coachman on the stairs, she entered, came over to my bed, acted dismayed and said hurriedly, "Oh, Jesus! Lady, they are bringing your husband!" The news terrified me, which she easily noticed; for as she uttered it, I sat up in my bed and stretched out my right arm and hand, and was unable to bring it back again at once. She may have felt sorry the very same moment, because I kept sitting like that without a word, and so she said, "My dearest lady, it's your husband's image." . . .

The next morning, at about nine o'clock, the effigy was woefully treated by the executioner, but it didn't utter a sound. At the midday meal the castle steward told the woman how the executioner had cut off its head and dismembered the body into four quarters, which were then broken on the wheel, while the head was exhibited on the city hall. The castle steward stood in the other room, telling the story in a loud voice so that I could hear it, and repeating it three times. . . . I lay there quietly, without a word, grappling with my own thoughts. . . . The mockery I didn't care about, for in France there were too many instances of nobles whose effigies and portraits had been burned by the executioner, and who were restored to favor again afterward.[15] . . .

In the month of March [1664], the castle steward came in, affected a quite gentle manner and said, among other things: "Now you are a widow, now you can tell the truth about everything." I replied with a question: "Can widows tell the truth about everything?" He smiled and said, "I don't mean that; I mean this treason." I answered, "You can ask others about that, those who know about it; I do not know of any treason." And as it seemed to him that I didn't believe my husband was dead,[16] he took out a newspaper and let me read it, perhaps chiefly because my husband was harshly portrayed in it. I didn't say much about it, only remarked, "Scribblers for newspapers don't always tell the truth." He could take it any way he pleased. I lay there hoping it might be so, that my husband had escaped his enemies by death; and I thought to myself with the greatest astonishment: that I should have lived to see the day when I wished my lord dead! Then I became absorbed in sorrowful thoughts once more and didn't feel like talking. The woman believed I was sad because my lord was dead and comforted me, quite sensibly in fact, but her comforting only intensified the memory of former times, so that I couldn't regain my peace of mind until long afterward. I was worried by your plight, my dearest children. . . . I sat up whole nights in my bed, for I was unable to sleep, and when I have a headache I cannot lay my head on the pillow. I prayed fervently to God for a merciful deliverance. It hasn't pleased God to grant this, but he gave me patience to bear my heavy cross. . . .

[The woman] showed in many ways that she, as well as Maren Bloks, believed I could practice sorcery. In fact, my own remarks at times gave occasion for this opinion. I remembered how my late lord used to say (when in his younger days he wanted to make somebody believe he understood black magic) that people feared those of whom they had this opinion, and never dared to do them harm. It happened one day at the midday meal, while the castle steward sat talking with me, that the woman was chatting away on the stairs with some people about the witches who had been arrested in Jutland; the superior court judge in Jutland at the time sided with the witches, saying that there were no witches. When the doors were locked, we talked at length about witches, and she said: "This judge is of your opinion, that it is a science and not magic."[17] I said, as I had said before, that some had more knowledge than others, and that some used their knowledge for doing harm; although it might happen naturally and not by means of the devil's art, still it was not permitted in the Word of God to use nature for doing harm; nor was it fair to give an honor to the devil which wasn't his due. We went on talking until she got angry, lay down and went to sleep, and that was the end of her anger. . . .

I was always looking for something to divert my thoughts, and since I noticed that the potter had left a piece of clay outside in the other room when he put up the stove, I asked the woman to give it to me. . . . I mixed the clay with beer and made various articles, which were often done over again; among other things, I made figures representing the castle steward and the woman, and small mugs and bowls. And as it occurred to me to try to make something on which I might inscribe a few words to the King without the castle steward's noticing . . . , I molded a cup over one-half of the pint goblet in which I was given wine, made it round underneath and placed it on three knobs, then wrote the King's name on the side, and under the bottom these words: *"S'il y a un Sinna, soyez un Auguste."*[18] . . . [When the castle steward found out about these things,] he requested to see them. . . . He said at once: "I will take all this with me and let the King see it; perhaps you will then be permitted some pastime, something to keep your hands busy." I was well satisfied.[19] . . . The next day he said to me: "Well, my dear lady, you almost got me into trouble!" "How is that?" I asked. "I brought the King a petition from you. The Queen didn't notice, but the King saw it at once and said, 'So, you are now bringing me petitions from Leonora?' I was paralyzed with fright and said, 'Gracious King! I haven't brought you anything in writing!' 'Look here!' said the King, showing me there was something, in French, under the bottom of the cup. The Queen asked why I had brought something in writing I didn't understand. I swore I hadn't noticed it and begged their pardon. The good King stood up for me, and the caprice did not displease him." . . .

The castle steward [from 1665 on, Johan Jäger] . . . was full of mad pranks and played tricks such as boys enjoy; he tried dallying with the woman [Karen, the daughter of Nels], but she wouldn't join the game. He was drunk almost every day when he came up at dinnertime. . . . He tried to dally with me too, opened his mouth and wanted me to throw something, to see if I could hit his mouth. I laughed and said, "How stupid you are!" and asked him to come closer; then I would see if I could hit it. "No, no," he said, "then I would really be stupid. You would probably give me a box on the ear." Once at noon he came up with an odd kind of squirt, round like a ball, and he put a tiny spout in it, barely noticeable; it was quite pretty. When it was pressed in some place the water squirted out, quite high and at some distance. He got fresh and squirted me. When he saw that I was angry, he brought the squirt to me, then rushed back and sat down again, opened his mouth as wide as possible and asked me to squirt into it, if I could. I didn't want to start playing with him, because I knew his coarseness very well from the stories he told, and gave the squirt back to him. When Karen was bringing in the roast, the castle steward had the squirt between his legs, and though he sat on a low stool, he could still squirt into the woman's face; he was at some distance from her, and the ball was no bigger than a small apple. . . . She knew nothing of the squirt (she has a rather quick tongue, though) and said, "May God heap shame on you, Mr. Steward! Are you peeing on me?" The castle steward laughed like crazy, he was so pleased. . . . One evening he was drunk, or behaved as such, [and] tried in his usual way to caress me and feel my knee, then grabbed the edge of my petticoat. I pushed him away with my foot and just said: "When you are tipsy, stay away from me and don't come in here, I'm telling you." He didn't say a word, got up and left; and, in fact, he didn't come in afterward when he was tipsy but remained outside in the other room, lying in the window, where there was a broad stone bench; he would take a nap after my doors were locked, then the coachman and Chresten [the tower warden] came and dragged him down. . . .

[When sometime in 1669 the new woman, Cathrina, was dissatisfied with the way she had been confessed by our pastor,][20] I comforted her as best I could, read and sang to her, told her she should repent and be sorry for her sins and work to mend her ways, and not be irritated by the want of devotion in the pastor; she should take possession of Christ's redemption and merits for the forgiveness of her sins, for the pastor had given her Christ's body and blood in the bread and wine. "Yes," she replied, "with God's help I'll reform." I said, "Will you keep what you have promised me?" Her vow was that she would never drink herself as tipsy as she had done once. I won't omit to relate this episode. She received . . . a pint of French wine with each meal, and I a pint of Rhine wine. She could drink both portions without getting quite intoxicated; for she drank the French wine with her food and afterward lay down; and when she got up in the afternoon she drank my wine. In the evening she saved my wine for breakfast, but once she kept the wine from my supper in a jug along with her own, so that she had two quarts of wine with dinner; she sat there drinking it on the sly, so quietly, and I didn't notice, was just pondering a pattern I wanted to knit. Finally I looked at her, since she waited so long before going to bed; then she turned over all the vessels, one after another, and there was nothing in them. I spoke to her and said, "How come? Have you drunk all the wine?" She could barely answer, tried to stand but couldn't. "To bed, you drunken sow," I said. . . . She crawled along and fell onto the bed, flat on her face, while her feet were on the ground. . . .

She slept a couple of hours in this position, but still didn't quite sleep it off; for when she wanted to clean up, herself as well as the room, she just sat there awhile on a low stool, the broom between her knees and her hair about her ears. She took off her bodice to wash it, and so she sat in her shift, which was open in front, with two ugly, blackish-brown breasts hanging out; she moaned and prayed to God to help her: she was dying. I was angry, yet couldn't help laughing at this sad picture. When her moaning wouldn't stop, I said angrily, "Well, may God help you, you besotted devil; to the guard-house with you. I won't have such a boozer around me. Go and sleep it off, and don't let me hear you talk about God when you are tipsy, because then God is far away from you, and the devil is with you!" (I laughed at myself afterward.) She lay down again, and about four o'clock she was quite sober, cleaned up everything and sat weeping quietly. Then she suddenly threw herself at my feet and, embracing my legs, blubbered and howled, begging me for God's sake to forgive her this once—it would never happen again. . . .

At the end of April [1670][21] . . . my door was opened one afternoon, and the castle steward came in with some ladies. . . . First entered a young lady whom I didn't know. Next appeared Lady Augusta, Duchess of Glücksburg, whom I recognized well enough, because she hadn't changed much. And then the Electoral Princess of Saxony, whom I recognized from her likeness to her noble father, and last of all our most gracious Queen,[22] whom I chiefly looked at. . . . Lady Augusta said: "Phew, what a hideous room! I couldn't live a day in it. I'm surprised you have been able to endure it for so long!" I replied, "The room is such as pleases God and His Majesty, and as long as it is God's will, I'll be able to endure it." . . . She asked me if I had fleas. I replied that I could furnish her with a regiment of fleas, if she wanted them. She replied quickly with an oath, and swore she didn't want them. Her question made me rather sarcastic, and I was annoyed at the delight she betrayed at my miserable condition, so when she asked me if I had crab-lice or bugs, I answered her with a question, asking if my brother-in-law Hannibal Sehested was still alive.[23] This question silenced her for a moment, because it made her realize that I knew her. She did not answer. The Electoral Princess . . . had probably heard of my brother-in-law's intrigue with Lady Augusta. . . . The gracious Queen looked downcast the whole time and said nothing. When Her Majesty gave me her hand, I kissed it and, holding onto it, begged Her Majesty to intercede for me, at least for some alleviation of my captivity.[24] Her Majesty didn't answer with words, but with a flood of tears. The virtuous Electoral Princess did the same; she wept very sorrowfully. And when they had reached the other room and my door was closed, both the Queen and the Electoral Princess said, "It is a sin to treat her thus!" . . . Lady Augusta urged them to leave and afterward complained about them to the Queen Mother, who said that I had myself to thank for it; I had deserved to be treated worse than this.[25] . . .

To describe all the mean conduct I endured would be too lengthy, and not worth the trouble. I still want to mention one thing concerning Chresten, the tower warden, who caused me all sorts of annoyance at the end of this tenth year of my imprisonment [1673]. Among other annoyances, he once struck my dog, so that it cried. . . . I was highly displeased. He just laughed and said, "It's only a dog." I gave him to understand that he struck the dog because he couldn't get at me. He laughed heartily at that and said, "I don't care about your anger as long as the castle steward is my friend." (This conversation took place while I was at the table, with the castle steward seated next to me, and Chresten stood in the doorway leaning his arms on the doorjambs.) I said, "I could get the castle steward and you into serious trouble, if I chose to; do you understand that, you people?" (I knew about too many things they wanted to hide, in more than one respect.) The castle steward looked as though he were deaf and dumb and remained seated, but Chresten sneaked off, somewhat ashamed, without saying a word. Afterward he was a little scared of me, when he wasn't too drunk, because then he didn't care what he said, about either high or low. Later he abused the woman, said he would strike the dog before my very eyes. This, however, did not happen. Chresten's foolhardiness increased, so that Peder Tøtzløf [the castle steward's deputy] told the steward about his bad behavior, that I had complained about the wild doings of the prisoners, who made such a noise at night that it kept me awake, for Chresten spent the night at home and let the prisoners do as they pleased. . . . [Soon after], on April 24, 1674, [he resigned]. . . .

Jonatha, who . . . [has] attended me [since 1682,] . . . is weak in many respects. Sometimes she is doubtful about her salvation and enumerates all her sins. . . . She makes a sin of that which is no sin, and what is sin she refuses to regard as sin. She says it is a sin to kill a dog, a cat, or a bird—the innocent animals don't do any harm; it is an even greater sin to starve the poor beasts. I asked her once if it was a sin to eat meat. "No," she answered, "it's the one who killed the animal who sinned." She swears that if she were obliged to get married and had to choose between a butcher and an executioner, she would prefer the latter. She has told me about several quarrels she has had with people who either beat or starved their own animals. One story I will not omit to mention, as it is very funny. One day, she said, she sold some pigs to a butcher. When the butcher boy was about to strap the animals' feet and carry off the pigs on a pole, she felt sorry for the poor things and said, "What, are you going to kill them? No, I won't allow that!" and she threw the money back at them. I asked her: Didn't she know that pigs were butchered? Why did she think the butcher had bought them? "Yes," she said, "I knew that quite well. Had he let them walk on their own legs, I wouldn't have cared; but to tie up the poor beasts in that way and to hear them scream, that I couldn't stand." It would take too long to describe all the extravagant whims she related of herself. But with all this she is not stupid, and I believe she is true to anyone she loves. She served me very well, and with great care. . . .

On May 2, [1685], it was talked about openly that I would probably come out of prison, and several people asked the tower warden [Ole] if I had been freed the evening before, and at what time, so that Ole began to get worried and couldn't put up as brave a front as he would have liked. He said to me in a sad voice: "My good lady, you'll certainly be freed. Some people think you are free already." I said, "That is in God's hands." "Yes," he said, "but what's to become of me?" I answered, "You will remain tower warden, as you are now." "Sure," he said, "in fine style!" He turned around, unable to hold back his tears, and left. Then Jonatha perceived that my deliverance was drawing near, tried to hide her sorrow and said, "Ole is very sad, but I am not." (And the tears were standing in her eyes.) "Anyway, people say the King is definitely going away the day after tomorrow. If you are to be let out, it will be today." I said, "God knows." Jonatha remarked that there was at least some hope. I said that, ever since the first day of my imprisonment, I had been hopeful that God would at last have mercy on me and look upon my innocence. . . .

. . . At eight o'clock [on May 19] Tøtzløf came up to me and told me that the Lord Chancellor, Count Allefelt,[26] had sent the castle steward a royal order that I was to be released from my imprisonment and could leave whenever I pleased. . . . Tøtzløf asked if I wanted him to lock the doors, as I was now free. I replied, "As long as I remain within the doors of my prison, I am not free; besides, I want to leave in style. Lock the door and inquire what my sister's daughter, Lady Anna Catharina Lindenow, says, whether His High Excellency sent any message to her (as he promised) before he left.[27] When Tøtzløf was gone, I said to Jonatha, "Now, in Jesus' name, this evening I'll be freed." . . . She thanked God with me, and when the doors were opened at noon and I dined, she laughed at Ole, who was very sad. I told her that Ole might well sigh, his cabbage would be missing its nice piece of bacon. . . .

At about ten o'clock in the evening, the castle steward opened the door for my sister's daughter. (I hadn't seen him for two years.) He said courteously: "Well, are we going to part now?" I replied, "Yes, now the time has come." Then he gave me his hand and said, "*Ade* [Farewell]." I answered with the same word, and my niece laughed heartily.

Shortly after the castle steward had left, my sister's daughter and I walked out of the tower. Her Majesty the Queen had wanted to see me as I came out and had gone to a balcony. But it was rather dark; moreover, I had a black veil over my face. Castle Square, up to the bridge and beyond, was so jammed with people that we could barely push our way through to the coach.

The time of my imprisonment was twenty-one years nine months and eleven days. . . .

My dearest children! . . . I now live in the hope it may please God and the King's Majesty that I show you this account myself. God in his mercy grant it.

NOTES TO THE TRANSLATION

1. The original concluding date was June 11, 1674, which Leonora Christina thought was her birthday.

2. This is how Leonora Christina begins the preface to *Memory of Woe* (JM 95; M, 87). According to one critic, Otto Andrup, who wrote the introduction to the facsimile edition of *Memory of Sorrow,* the memoir was written so that Leonora's children might inherit her property. Andrup attributes its expansion into a general account of her imprisonment partly to a desire for camouflaging her purpose and partly to her literary disposition (*Den fangne Grevinde Leonora Christinas Jammers Minde,* 21).

3. *Encheiridion,* chap. 43 (in some editions, chap. 65).

4. Bendix Ahlefeldt, captain in the Life Guard Regiment.

5. Jacobus: An English gold coin first used by James I; it was current at twenty shillings.

6. Rix-dollar: any of various large silver coins, now nearly obsolete but used widely for centuries in Germany, the Netherlands, and Scandinavia. At the currency reform in Denmark in 1873, it was valued at two kroner.

7. Ulfeldt was sentenced to death in absentia on July 24, 1663, a couple of weeks before Leonora's imprisonment in the Blue Tower. She refers to her husband as her "late" lord because even though Ulfeldt was still alive at this point, he was dead by the time Leonora wrote the memoir.

8. Christian Rantzau, Count of the Empire, German-born; Peder Reedtz; Christoffer Gabel, the King's treasurer; Erik Krag, head secretary in the Danish chancellery.

9. The "foreign lord" here referred to is Friedrich Wilhelm, Elector of Brandenburg.

10. Marginal note: "It had happened as I thought: there were some in the Council who refused to sign, one because he hadn't been present at the time of the trial, another because he hadn't seen what the sentence was based on; still they had to sign with the others, on the peril of the King's displeasure."

11. In the margin is added, "and asked whether I was permitted to appeal the sentence; they were all silent."

12. Krag died in 1672, two years before this part of *Memory of Sorrow* was completed.

13. Count Rantzau died before the execution of Ulfeldt's effigy, which took place on November 13, 1663.

14. Marginal addition: "The Queen wanted this wooden image to be brought into the outer room and placed in front of the door in such a way that it would tumble into my room when my inner door was opened; but the King would not hear of it."

15. It is interesting that Leonora thinks of France in this connection. Most of the noblemen involved in the Fronde (1648–1653), a rebellion during the minority of Louis XIV, were later pardoned, including its leader, Louis II de Bourbon, the Great Condé, who was Ulfeldt's model.

16. Ulfeldt spent the last months of his life in Basel, Switzerland, where three of his sons

attended the university. Having caught pleurisy, he died fleeing down the Rhine on February 20, 1664, after hearing a rumor that the King's men were on his tracks.

17. The name of this judge was Villum Lange, known as a progressive. In a letter from 1670 about this very trial, he expresses the same views as are here attributed to him.

18. "If there is a Ciina, be an Augustus." Allusion to Corneille's tragedy of 1643, published under the title *Cinna ou la clémence d'Auguste*. Cinna, who headed a conspiracy against Augustus in A.D. 4, was pardoned and made a consul. From then on, Cinna was loyal to the Emperor.

19. Marginal addition: "The castle steward told me afterward that the clay articles were placed in the King's art cabinet, beside a rib from a lamb roast I used as a knife which he also gave to the King, hoping (he said) in this way to obtain a knife for me."

20. Hieronymus Buck, pastor of St. Peter's Church, Copenhagen.

21. This visit is dated too early by Leonora Christina, since Princess Anna Sophie, eldest daughter of Frederik III and future Electoral Princess of Saxony, did not arrive in Copenhagen until August. She became Electoral Princess only in 1680.

22. Charlotte Amalie of Hessen-Kassel, wife of Christian V. Though not beautiful, she was gifted as well as friendly and tactful.

23. Lady Augusta is believed to have had a love affair with the statesman Hannibal Sehested, who had married Leonora's sister Christiane. Leonora must have been well aware that her brother-in-law had died several years ago.

24. Soon after the death of Frederik III in February 1670, Leonora Christina's circumstances improved. In 1671, she received an additional room, and in 1672 she was granted a modest annual pension, enabling her to purchase practically anything she wanted—clothes, books, even a clavichord. She kept pets, including a short-tailed rat in a cage, until a woman burned it to death with a candle.

25. The Queen Mother's vendetta against Leonora Christina, superior to her both in beauty and accomplishments, ceased only with her death in February 1685, the year of Leonora's release from prison.

26. Frederik Ahlefeldt.

27. His High Excellency was the title of the natural sons of the King, in this case Ulrik Frederik Gyldenløve, son of Frederik III. Gyldenløve, Governor of Norway, had long served as Leonora Christina's spokesman with Christian V.

BIBLIOGRAPHY

Primary Works

Aakjær, Svend, comp. "Breve fra Kirstine Munk og Leonora Christina." *Danske Magazin,* ser. 8, vol. 1 (1957–61): 81–113. Chiefly letters to Leonora Christina from her mother during the turbulent years 1653–58.

Den fangne Grevinde Leonora Christinas Jammers Minde. Facsimile edition. Introduction by Otto Andrup. Copenhagen: Levin & Munksgaards Forlag, 1931.

Hæltinners Pryd. Introduction and commentary by Christopher Maaløe. Copenhagen: Reitzel, 1977. Biographies of "valiant women."

Jammers Minde og andre selvbiografiske Skildringer. Edited by Johs. Brøndum-Nielsen & C. O. Bøggild-Andersen. Copenhagen: Rosenkilde & Bagger, 1949. Standard edition of *Memory of Sorrow* and other autobiographical writings.

Leonora Christina Comtesse d'Ulfeldt Autobiographie 1673. Facsimile edition. Introduction, translation, and commentary by C. O. Bøggild-Andersen. Copenhagen: Forening for Boghaandværk, 1958. French and Danish text and commentary.

Memoirs of Leonora Christina. Translated by F. E. Bunnett. New York: E. P. Dutton & Co., 1929.

"Nogle Breve fra Korfits Ulfeldt og Leonora Christina." Compiled by J. A. Fridericia. *Danske Magazin,* ser. 5, vol. 2 (1889–92): 69–83. Letters.

"Nogle Breve til Oplysning af Corfitz Ulfeldts og hans Families Historie i Aarene 1662 og 1663." Compiled by J. A. Fridericia. *Danske Samlinger* 6 (1870–71): 221–43. Letters.

Related Works

Aakjær, Svend. "Leonora Christinas Dommer" (L.C.'s Judge). *Jyske Samlinger,* n.s. 5, no. 1 (1959): 40–44.

______. "Leonora Christinas Skyld—Et Aktorat" (L.C.'s Guilt—A Prosecution). *Jyske Samlinger,* n.s. 4, no. 4 (1958): 223–48.

Billeskov Jansen, F. J. "En kongedatters memoirer," in *Fra Runerne til Thomas Kingo.* Vol. 1 of *Dansk litteraturhistorie,* edited by P. H. Traustedt, 406–17. Copenhagen: Politikens Forlag, 1976. A recently published Danish literary history.

Bjørn, Hans. "Leonora Christina—Christian IV's datter." In *Leonora Christina: Historien om en heltinde,* ed. Anne-Marie Mai, 9–57. *Acta Jutlandica* 58, Humanistisk Serie 57. Aarhus: Arkona, 1983. Stresses the profound differences between the early literary work and *Memory of Sorrow.*

Bøggild-Andersen, C. O. "Kongedatteren for historiens domstol. Nogle bemærkninger til Svend Aakjærs aktorat mod Leonora Christina" (The King's Daughter Before the Judgment of History: Some Observations on Svend Aakjær's Prosecution of L.C.). *Jyske Samlinger,* n.s. 5, no. 1 (1959): 24–39.

Dalager, Stig, and Anne-Marie Mai. "Leonora Christina. Et forsvar for kvindekønnet." In *Danske kvindelige forfattere,* 1: 35–64. Copenhagen: Gyldendal, 1982. Focuses on the literary development of L.C. from a feminist perspective.

Doctor, Jens Aage. "Sandhedens rolle" (The Role of Truth). *Kritik,* no. 16 (1970): 5–36.

Fridericia, J. A. *Adelsvældens sidste Dage: Danmarks Historie fra Christian IV's Død til Enevældens Indførelse, 1648–1660.* Copenhagen: P. G. Philipsen, 1894. A notable Danish historian's interpretation of the transition from "rule by the nobility" to absolute monarchy.

Friese, Wilhelm. *Nordische Barockdichtung.* Munich: Francke Verlag, 1968.

Glismann, Otto. "Om Tilblivelsen af Leonora Christinas Jammers-Minde" (On the Genesis of L.C.'s *Memory of Sorrow*). *Acta philologica Scandinavica* 28, nos. 1–2 (1966): 75–102.

Helweg, Johannes. "Var Korfitz Ulfeldt sindssyg?" (Was C.U. Insane?). *Tilskueren,* October 1913: 1020–37.

Lange, Julius. "Contra Leonora Christina." *Tilskueren* 5 (1888): 721–39. Reprinted in *Udvalgte Skrifter,* ed. G. Brandes & P. Købke, 1: 366–81. Copenhagen: Nordiske Forlag, 1900–1903.

Larsen, Alf. "Jammers Minde," in *Den kongelige kunst,* 154–96. Oslo: Dreyers Forlag, 1948. Highly personal, idealized portraits of both Leonora Christina and her husband.

Larsen, Finn Stein. "En impressionist fra baroktiden? En tekstlæsning i Leonora Christinas Jammersminde" (An Impressionist from the Baroque Period? A Reading of L.C.'s *Memory of Sorrow*). *Kritik,* no. 25 (1973):17–33.

Lützhöft, Nicolaus. "Zahrtmann's Leonora Christina Pictures." *American-Scandinavian Review* 11 (1923): 749–55.

Madsen, Karl. "Kristian Zahrtmanns Leonora Christina-Billeder." *Tilskueren* 2 (1885): 524–43. Discussion of Zahrtmann's paintings on subjects from the life of L.C.

Mai, Anne-Marie, and Stig Dalager. ". . . et eventyr, som er værdigt en roman." In *Leonora*

Christina: Historien om en heltinde, 58–86. Discusses *Memory of Sorrow* as confessional literature that experiments with style and genre in ways that have become paradigmatic in women's writings.

Petersen, Carl S. *Fra Folkevandringstiden indtil Holberg.* Vol. 1 of *Illustreret dansk litteraturhistorie,* by Carl S. Petersen and Vilhelm Andersen, 833–50. Copenhagen: Gyldendalske Boghandel, 1929. Standard Danish literary history.

Rostrup, Egill. "Leonora Christina's Skuespil" (L.C.'s Play). *Litteraturen* 1 (May 1918): 103–13.

Schmalensee, Lisa, and Lene Torp. "Leonora Christina Ulfeldt: *Jammersminde* 1663–1685." In *Analyser af dansk kvindelitteratur: Litteratur & Samfund* 31 (1980): 6–29. Ideological feminist criticism emphasizing the alleged contradiction between L.C.'s conception of gender and her view of marriage.

Smith, Sophus Birket. *Leonora Christina Grevinde Ulfeldts Historie. Med Bidrag til hendes Ægtefælles og hendes nærmeste Slægts Historie.* 2 vols. Copenhagen: Gyldendalske Boghandelsforlag, 1879–81. The standard biography of Leonora Christina.

Stæhr, Claus Pico. "Leonora Christina og 1600-tallets europæiske litteratur—en oversigt." In *Leonora Christina: Historien om en heltinde,* 89–96. Characterizes *Memory of Sorrow* as a "unique" work in the context of seventeenth-century European literature.

SOVEREIGN BETWEEN THRONE AND ALTAR

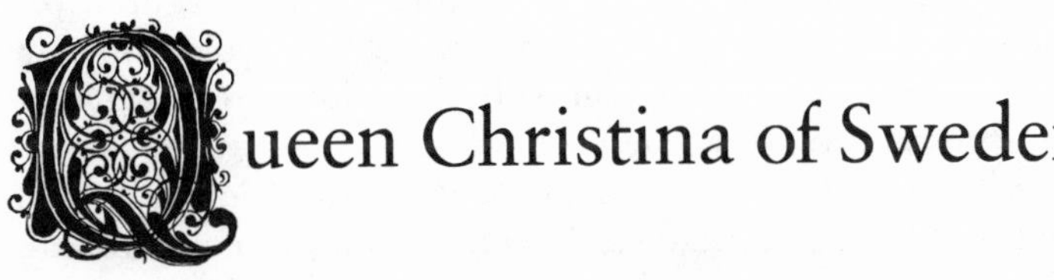

Queen Christina of Sweden

JEANETTE LEE ATKINSON

Christina of Sweden (1626–1689) is one of history's most enigmatic figures. A study in contradictions, she baffled and fascinated her contemporaries as well as historians of succeeding generations. Christina's controversial career hinges on two stunning acts and their relation to each other. In June 1654, only ten years after she had begun ruling one of Europe's most powerful nations and not even four years after her elaborate coronation, Christina abdicated in favor of her cousin Carl Gustav and left her country. On November 3, 1655, she formally declared herself a Roman Catholic and proceeded to make a widely publicized entry into Rome. Not only was Christina the daughter of Protestantism's great champion Gustav Adolf, but a victor in the Thirty Years' War she was also regarded as the leader of the Protestant world. She could scarcely have set off a greater shock in seventeenth-century Europe, ravaged and dominated as it was by religious strife. Her change of faith unleashed a flood of polemics and panegyrics that to some extent color the perception of Christina to this day.

Under Christina, Stockholm had become a center of feverish intellectual and cultural activity. The Swedish ballet rivaled that of France, and the first flowering of Swedish as a literary language was underway.[1] Christina had assembled a magnificent library, and scholars at her court included Nicolaus Heinsius, Isaac Vossius, and Descartes. Reveling in the booty from a successfully concluded war, Sweden at mid-century was at the crest of its glory. To the rest of the world, Christina, the "Pallas of the North," personified her burgeoning nation.

Startling though it was, Christina's abdication was a calculated act which she had taken years to engineer. Indeed, the young monarch had raised the issue before she was crowned. Christina's actions are not devoid of logic, but her personal idiosyncrasies add an undeniable aura of irrationality. Her other motives aside, Christina's abdication and change of faith became a dramatic spectacle for which she was author, principal actor, and appreciative audience. She conceived of her abdication as a grand, heroic gesture which would win worldwide acclaim and admiration. It became in her eyes her greatest achievement.

Christina was the only surviving child of King Gustav Adolf of Sweden and his beautiful but neurotic and sickly wife, Maria Eleonora of Brandenburg. Christina was mistaken for a boy at birth, but Gustav Adolf admitted no disappointment. A close, affectionate bond developed between father and daughter, whereas the relation between Christina and her mother was always awkward. When Gustav Adolf was killed in the Battle of Lützen in 1632, Christina was only six years old. Until her eighteenth birthday Sweden was governed by a regency designed by the brilliant statesman Axel Oxenstierna, the king's trusted chancellor.

From the moment of her birth Christina's life was marked by polarities and discrepancies. Her sex was among the most troublesome problems, and the circumstances of her upbringing exacerbated the conflict. Before his departure, Gustav Adolf had taken pains to have Christina's right to the succession affirmed by the Estates, and had also left detailed instructions for his daughter's education. After his death the Estates lost no time in reaffirming Christina's right to the throne, in order to forestall any mischief-making on the part of Sweden's old enemies, Denmark and Poland. The Polish Vasas, Catholics, represented a particularly keen threat, because their claim to the Swedish throne had some legitimacy and they had substantial support among Swedish sympathizers. The regency followed Gustav Adolf's directive that Christina be given a purely masculine upbringing as the only means of investing her with the authority necessary to overcome the disadvantage of her sex.[2] Such a training was eminently suitable to Christina, who proved herself an assiduous student and ardent sportswoman.

Christina's education was scarcely tempered by any feminine influence. Upon her husband's death, Maria Eleonora confined her daughter with her in such a protracted and psychotic show of grief that Oxenstierna and the regents removed Christina from her care in 1636, to the child's vast relief. Christina then spent two years with her father's sister Catherine, and, after Catherine's death, was supervised by various courtly ladies. Political instruction began early for Christina, who did not miss the significance of the fact that the king had specifically excluded his wife from any participation in government.[3]

By the standards of her day, Christina became a notoriously unfeminine woman, who had "neither the face, nor the beauty, nor the inclinations of a woman." A contemporary observed in 1653: "There is nothing feminine about her save her sex. Her voice, her manner of speaking, her gait, her mien and her manners are those of a male." At times she wore masculine clothing, and, with few exceptions, she avoided the company of women. Yet Christina quickly charmed most of her contemporaries, men and women, with her "sweetness," intelligence, and lively wit.[4] Christina was not ignorant of the discrepancies between her gender and her persona. One of her dearest companions in Sweden was the lovely Countess Ebba Sparre, whose beauty must have served as a constant reminder of her own lack of traditional feminine charm. Christina criticized herself for ignoring the good qualities of her sex, but at the same time she felt unfairly censured for "faults" which would not have been held against a man. Whatever the causes, she became an unflinching misogynist, her own considerable accomplishments notwithstanding.[5]

Christina received an exemplary education, though it too contained the seeds of conflict. The guidelines for her upbringing, promulgated by the Estates in 1635, stipulated that she be reared within the bounds of Lutheran orthodoxy. Yet her tutor, the urbane and tolerant theologian Johann Matthiae, was consistently at odds with the religious establishment. Avoiding sectarian and dogmatic issues in his religious instruction, Matthiae inadvertently laid the groundwork for his charge's dissatisfaction with the intellectual confinement of Swedish Lutheranism. Christina's political education was primarily the work of her chancellor, Axel Oxenstierna, a homespun Swedish aristocrat and consummate statesman. Ever mindful of the threat from the Polish Vasas, Oxenstierna regarded an unchallenged religious orthodoxy as a bulwark of the state. He sided with the church in the 1647 trial and condemnation of Matthiae for the Unionist sympathies expressed in his book *Idea boni ordinis in Ecclesia Christi* (Items of Good Order in the Church of Christ). Christina was unable to protect her tutor from any but the direst consequences arising from this trial.[6] Her abdication and apostasy hastened the death of her chancellor and signaled the end of her tutor's clerical career.

The common ground between Christina's two mentors was a solid foundation in the literature and philosophy of Greek and Latin antiquity and of the Renaissance, which they imparted to their eager pupil. By her sixteenth birthday Christina had an international reputation for her prodigious intellect. She was proficient in modern foreign languages in addition to Latin, was thoroughly at home in philosophy, literature, and history, and followed the latest discoveries in chemistry and astronomy.[7] Inspired by the stoic tenor of her education, and indeed of the seventeenth century in general, Christina placed extraordinary demands on herself, making a fetish of stoic "virtue." She became a restless, driven young woman. When not studying, she rode horseback for hours on end. She ate and drank little.[8] Chronic poor health was the price of such frenetic activity.

Christina began to sit in on government meetings at age sixteen and ascended the throne when she turned eighteen. However posterity may judge her tenure as queen, her contemporaries regarded her as a powerful and able ruler. Jealous of her prerogatives, Christina ruled with an absolutism hitherto unseen in Sweden, no mean achievement in view of the long period of regency control.[9] But on the other hand, a pervasive self-indulgence and concomitant lack of perspective are also evident in the queen's dealings. The stoic self-control which she believed she exercised so perfectly over her thoughts and actions left no room for self-criticism or moderation. While her generals were threatening mutiny for lack of money, she lavished huge sums on her ambassador to France, Magnus Gabriel de la Gardie. She became such an ardent Francophile that the French took advantage of her diplomatically. Eager to have an end to the war, Christina chafed under her chancellor's determination to safeguard Swedish interests in the negotiations leading to the Peace of Westphalia, and she deliberately undercut one of her own representatives, Oxenstierna's son Jean.[10] Christina's financial policies threatened to impoverish the nation and sow the seeds of revolution. Sweden at the height of its glory was a poor country faced with an acute civil crisis.[11]

It was in this setting that the drama of Christina's abdication and conversion began to unfold. Religion did not force Christina to relinquish her throne; instead, her decision to abdicate paved the way for her change of faith. The issue of marriage provided the motivating force. In fact, Christina's solution to the problem of marriage became the dominant factor in her domestic policy and shaped her nation's future. From around age sixteen, Christina was subjected to increasing pressure to marry and provide an heir. Although the old-guard Swedish aristocracy, including the Oxenstiernas, were opposed to the Palatine family, it became the general consensus that Christina would marry her cousin Carl Gustav. As a young girl she had promised him her hand. But the marriage was not to take place.

There is no simple explanation for Christina's instinctive aversion to marriage and childbearing, though it developed at an early age. The delicate state of her health and her mother's poor record in childbearing gave Christina ample reason to doubt her ability to produce a normal heir. Moreover, the very idea of pregnancy was repugnant to her. Yet Christina was attracted to men; she portrays herself in her autobiography as a passionate woman who was drawn strongly to the "pleasures of love" but abstained from them. Christina enjoyed the power and prestige of her position and tolerated no conventional restraints on her behavior. Marriage appeared to her an unbearable subordination, a step unworthy of a woman of her talents.[12] Ironically, in Italy Christina seems to have experienced a painful, humiliating passion for the influential and handsome Cardinal Azzolino.[13]

The matter was further complicated by Christina's deep commitment to the principle of hereditary monarchy, still a relatively new concept in Sweden. It was, then, as vital to Christina's interests as to the stability of her nation that she provide an heir, but she found it impossible to do so in the conventional manner. Abdication, strictly on her terms, was her way of cutting the Gordian knot. Christina determined to make Carl Gustav crown prince, with the right of succession vested in his male heirs. Against all odds, she got her way through delaying tactics, dissimulation, parliamentary maneuvering, and political blackmail. When she was crowned in 1650, in the most elaborate ceremony ever staged in Sweden, Christina had already laid the groundwork for relinquishing her throne.

She did not follow through on her design for almost four years, in part because she was having second thoughts. Nonetheless, forces were in motion that inexorably propelled her toward abdication. Ruling itself seemed to become increasingly unbearable and burdensome.[14] At the same time, Sweden was beginning to seem too small a stage for Christina, who at least for a time saw herself in the role of a world peacemaker. The foreign artists and musicians as well as the diplomats at her court instilled a longing in the restless young queen to see the world, especially Italy and France. The idea of a grand, heroic sacrifice held strong appeal for Christina, who, taking her stoic self-image to extremes, liked to place her crown beneath her feet and proclaim that "virtue" was man's sole happiness.[15]

While religion was not the reason Christina had labored so single-mindedly to install Carl Gustav as crown prince, it was a major factor in her abdication itself. By education, temperament, and experience, Christina was ill-suited to Swedish Lutheranism, which had long since stagnated in a narrow orthodoxy. She had always detested its tedious harangues and fire-and-brimstone sermons. She was fascinated by questions of ethics and religion. Nothing dealing with religious controversy escaped her, and her librarians scoured all of Europe to obtain the obscure and heretical books and manuscripts she requested. The breadth and depth of Christina's philosophical perspective put her on a collision course with the intellectual confinement of Protestantism. She was particularly intrigued by questions of religious certainty, a matter with acute political ramifications in her age. The sectarian strife and dogmatic squabbles endemic to Protestantism invalidated its claim to represent the "true religion" from the start.

The immediate consequence of Christina's delving into religious issues was a pervasive skepticism, and for a time she moved away from Christianity altogether.[16] Around 1649 Christina's court, which harbored a number of French intellectuals displaced by the Fronde, had become a center of libertinism and freethinking. However, the early libertine and freethinking literature remained within the formal framework of Catholicism. A similar situation prevailed with respect to stoicism. Though stoicism is fundamentally incompatible with Christianity, this incongruity was not readily apparent to the seventeenth century, particularly among Catholic intellectuals.[17]

There was no need to proselytize Christina in the conventional sense. Indeed, any overt attempt to convert her would likely have been rebuffed. But Christina was receptive to Catholicism in the last years of her reign, and the Catholics seized the opportunity. The French ambassador Chanut, who enjoyed a close relation with the queen, was among the first to sense her religious disquietude. He worked subtly and patiently to augment her sympathy for Catholicism, as much for diplomatic as for religious reasons. During this period Christina also engaged in extensive discussions of religion with the Spanish ambassador and with the Jesuit confessor of the Portuguese ambassador. Sweden's harsh laws against Catholics necessitated the strictest secrecy in all these dealings. Though it was Christina who contacted the Jesuits in 1651, her turn to Catholicism was very much a manifestation of the Counter-Reformation.

The Catholics with whom Christina associated represented the intellectually tolerant, moderately skeptical modern wing of the church. The two Jesuits sent to instruct her in Catholicism were not rigid theologians, but a mathematician–natural scientist and a humanist. Instead of pressing the queen on points of dogma and confession, they assured her that there was no innate conflict between the Catholic faith and her intellect. Whether Christina's conversion was the result of a profound religious experience, or a rational, though somewhat naïve, attempt to create a more liberal intellectual environment for herself, afterwards she remained loyal to the Catholic church, if not to individual popes.[18]

Though Christina relinquished her crown ostensibly to devote herself to the *vita contemplativa,* her subsequent actions show that she was not prepared to give up her power.[19] The document setting forth the terms of her abdication established her in the unique position of sovereign without a country, answerable to God alone.[20] Christina not only was a queen without a nation but, because of Sweden's financial hardships and perennial unrest in her appanage, was often a queen without money. The fact that she was able to maintain her sovereign status without the financial or dynastic means to back it up testifies to the power of her personality and her political skill.

Christina thought she would have the world as her stage, and initially her expectations were fulfilled. She had decided to settle in Rome in order to be free from all secular authority. Pope Alexander VII planned a grandiose welcome for the Swedish queen in order to demonstrate the power and triumph of the Catholic church. His massive propaganda apparatus, along with numerous diplomatic reports, ensured that the world missed no detail of Christina's elaborately stage-managed passage to Rome. This reception of Christina as a world power, however, accorded her disproportionate status and influence.[21] She soon embroiled herself in Vatican politics and its European ramifications. Christina had ambitions of raising and commanding her own army and of becoming queen of Naples—ambitions that were thwarted. In 1657 she set off an international legal and diplomatic storm by executing her retainer Monaldesco while she was a guest of Louis XIV at Fontainebleau. In the 1660s she intrigued unsuccessfully to become queen of Poland. After Carl Gustav's death in 1660, her tentative efforts to reassert her claim to the Swedish throne were firmly rebuffed.[22] Christina gradually retired to the position of a Roman Maecenas, founding at least two academies and supporting musicians, artists, and scholars. She commissioned and produced Scarlatti's first opera and was a patron of the theater. Christina remained a dominant personality in Roman cultural life until her death in 1689.

Christina's enigmatic career will never be fully explained. Her biography is an amalgam of the loftiest and pettiest motives, the most extraordinary and most pathetic traits. Her self-absorption and lack of moderation were her strength and her undoing. She convinced herself that her abdication was a stunningly glorious, heroic act. But she failed to take the fickleness of fame into account. For a time she remained at the heart of European politics, but her real contribution was on the cultural, not the political level. The queen who could tolerate no constraints, not even those imposed by her high position, found her place in the annals of history as a puzzling, fascinating footnote.

Christina was widely admired for her epistolary skills, no small achievement in an age which valued letters as a literary form. Throughout her life she was intimately involved in literary affairs as a critic and patron. In Italy she was a leading opponent of Marinism, an ornate Baroque style traditionally criticized as artificial.[23] Christina apparently did not compose any literary works per se until late in life. Her oeuvre, neither large nor innovative, reflects the tastes and styles of her time. Though Christina composed her letters in at least five tongues, French was her language of choice for her prose works. She composed well over a thousand maxims, collected in her "Ouvrage de Loisir" (Work of Leisure) and her "Sentimens" (Opinions). The former is more worldly in tone, while the latter is more religious and contains many affirmations of loyalty to the Catholic church. Vossius reportedly possessed a collection of her maxims called "Apothegms," but the existence of this document has never been verified.[24] Christina's "Réfléxions diverses sur la Vie et sur les Actions du Grand Alexandre" reveals her notions of heroism and virtue. It contains her philosophy that the faults of great men, like spots on the sun, serve only to highlight their brilliance.[25] Her "Réfléxions sur la Vie et les Actions de César" is a shorter portrait along similar lines. Christina tried her hand at more belletristic endeavors as well. Around 1687 she contributed the theme and some embellishments to a verse drama composed by her protégé Alexander Guidi. She also may have written several poems.[26]

Christina's autobiographical fragment, "La Vie de la Reine Christine faite par Elle-même, dédiée à Dieu," was written around 1681.[27] The selections for translation are taken from this document, the most revealing and original of Christina's works. Following the convention of the time, Christina dedicates and addresses her work to God—a practice that lends authority to her account. In spite of the posing and self-justification, the autobiography gives a remarkably intimate view of a haughty seventeenth-century monarch. Christina was neither a great stylist nor a very original thinker. Her works can be tedious, repetitive, and unclear but at their best are characterized by a frank and vigorous style. Her compositions merit study not only as historical documents but also as examples of the literary fashions of courtly society.

NOTES

1. Heinz Kindermann, *Das Theater der Barockzeit,* vol. 3 of *Theatergeschichte Europas* (Salzburg: Otto Müller, 1959), 573–76. Georg Stiernhielm, the "father of Swedish literature," was poet laureate at Christina's court, where he composed some of the most important works of his career.

2. "La vie de la Reine Christine," 24, 52–53 (hereafter "Autobiography"); Johann Arckenholtz, *Mémoires concernant Christine,* 1:23–24 (hereafter Arck.); Curt Weibull, *Drottning Christina,* 88. Almost a century later Habsburg Emperor Charles VI had to make significant concessions to ensure that the succession of his daughter and heir Maria Theresa would be honored. The so-called "Pragmatic Sanction" was violated less than two months after Charles's death by Frederick II of Prussia.

3. "Autobiography," 62–67; Arck., 1:30, 3:52. W. H. Grauert attributes Christina's subsequent persona to the combination of masculine education and absence of sustained, positive female influence. Moreover, her mother was out of the country from 1640 to 1648 (*Christina Königinn von Schweden und ihr Hof,* 1:39–40, 57–58 [hereafter *CKvS*]).

4. Arck., 1:89, 428, 551; Sven Stolpe, *Drottning Kristina,* 1:67–68 (hereafter *DK*).

5. "Autobiography," 58–59, 67–69. For a discussion of Christina's problematical relation to Ebba Sparre, see Stolpe, *DK,* 1:77–88, 97, and Christina's letters to Ebba Sparre, Arck., 1:528–29, 559–60.

6. Arck., 1:32–33; Grauert, *CKvS,* 2:38, 30; Sven Olofsson, *Drottning Christinas tronavsägelse och trosförändring,* 38–39 (hereafter *DCt*); Michael Roberts, "The Swedish Church," 148–49; Weibull, *Drottning Christina,* 83–98.

7. Arck., 1:160, 345–46.

8. Arck., 1:221–22; 426–28; "Autobiography," 54; Ernst Cassirer, "Descartes und Königin Christina von Schweden," 219–23 (hereafter "DKC"); Sven Stolpe, *Från Stoicism till Mystik,* 95–111 (hereafter *FStM); Weibull, Drottning Christina,* 127–31.

9. Arck., 1:89, 425, 429–30, 447; Grauert, *CKvS,* 1:154, 192–93; Olofsson, *DCt,* 54, 59.

10. Arck., 1:88–115, 191–203; Grauert, *CKvS,* 1:153–60, 213–41; Olofsson, *DCt,* 44.

11. Arck., 1:203ff., 373–77; Åström, "The Swedish Economy and Sweden's Role as a Great Power 1632–1697," 73; Olofsson, *DCt,* 206, 75–77, 168–72; Roberts, "Queen Christina and the General Crisis of the Seventeenth Century," 111–37; Weibull, *Drottning Christina,* 51–73. In her comments to "Histoire de ce qui s'est passé après la mort du Grande Gustave, . . ." (Arck., 3:163), Christina hotly denied that Sweden faced any difficulties at all when she abdicated.

12. Arck., 1:166–67; "Autobiography," 56–58 ("mon tempérament ardent et impéteux ne m'a pas donné moins de penchant à l'amour que pour l'ambition,") 57; Grauert, *CKvS,* 1:317–22; Stolpe, *DK,* 1:70–74, 166–68; 2:99–105; Stolpe, *FStM,* 211–19.

13. Stolpe, *DK,* 2:106–19. Olofsson interprets Christina's apparently passionate letters to Azzolino in terms of "the Baroque period's exaggerated and ornate phrases" (*DCt,* 145). Carl Bildt deciphered the chiffres in these letters (*Christine de Suède et le cardinal Azzolino: Lettres inédites, 1660–1668* [Paris, 1899]).

14. Arck., 1:404, 447; Grauert, *CKvS,* 1:569–71.

15. Matthiae interpreted rumors about Christina's conversion as evidence that she was undertaking a great work of religious reconciliation (Grauert, *CKvS,* 2:29; "Autobiography," 3).

16. Arckenholtz blames Christina's conversion on the Jesuits (1:463). Though several points in Cassirer's essay on Christina and Descartes have been refuted by subsequent historians, it remains one of the best treatments of the philosophical foundations of seventeenth-century religious questions; Grauert emphasizes the role of Matthiae's tolerance and Christina's general intellectual—not necessarily theological—receptivity to Catholicism. Deliberately leaving the issue of the sincerity of her conversion open, he stresses that her decision to abdicate came first (*CKvS,* 2, 28–67). Olofsson concentrates on the diplomatic maneuvering behind Christina's abdication and conversion and stresses that the rigidity of the Lutheran establishment precluded any attempts on Christina's part to work for reform (*DCt,* 35–41). Stolpe denies that Christina's conversion was essentially a religious experience, while Weibull proceeds from the assumption that Christina became a devout Catholic and abdicated in order to gain religious freedom (*Drottning Christina,* 117–21).

17. Stolpe, *DK,* 1:192–214; *FStM,* 163–79; Cassirer, "DKC," 228–36.

18. Stolpe, *DK,* 1:215–32; 2:18; Stolpe, *FStM,* 140–42. In 1660 and 1666 Christina returned to Sweden to obtain a better arrangement of her economic affairs. Her insistence on practicing Catholicism openly created great problems and humiliations for her (Arck., 2:43–50, 82–115; Grauert, *CKvS,* 2:104–308).

19. See Christina's letter to Chanut, January 1654, in Arck., 1:395–97.

20. Text of this act in Weibull, *Drottning Christina,* 161–62; Arck. preface to vol. 3, x.

21. Weibull, *Drottning Christina,* 162–63. Among those who reacted favorably to Christina's abdication, there was some sentiment "que cette Princesse en quittant la Couronne de Suède, meritoit celle du monde entier" (Arck., 2:433).

22. Arck., 2:43–50, 82–115. Grauert interprets these claims in light of Christina's desire to preserve hereditary monarchy in Sweden, and as efforts to safeguard her economic arrangements; he denies that she actually sought to regain the Swedish crown (*CKvS,* 2:157, 171–73, 299).

23. Stolpe, *DK,* 2:134; Ernst Meyer, "Om drottning Kristinas literära verksamhet i Italien," 90 (hereafter "LVI").

24. Arck., 2:2; Meyer, "LVI," 101.
25. See p. 58. Neither "Alexandre" nor "César" is complete.
26. Stolpe, *DK*, 2:159; Meyer, "LVI," 114.
27. This fragment consists of nine chapters. On page 45 Christina refers to the death of Count Brahe "one year ago." Since Brahe died in 1680, 1681 is taken as the date of composition of the autobiography. See Meyer, "LVI," 113. Stolpe places the beginning of the project in 1660 (*DK*, 2:112, 248).

From The Life of Queen Christina, Written by Herself, Dedicated to God

CHAPTER 4

The queen my mother assured me that in being confined with me, she was confined with a boy. She had some dreams that she believed mysterious, and the king had the same kind.[1] The astrologers, who are always ready to flatter princes, assured him that the queen was pregnant with a male successor. Thus they humored themselves, they hoped, they deceived themselves, and finally it came to the time, Lord, which you have prescribed for all those who enter into life. The court had already returned to Stockholm. The king was there also, but he was seriously ill, and the astrologers who were there asserted unanimously that the moment of my birth, . . . was such that it was impossible for it not to cost the life of the king, the queen, or the child.[2] They also asserted that if this child was able to survive the first twenty-four hours it would be somebody truly extraordinary. It was in such a constellation of the stars that I came to the world on December 18, 1626.[3] . . . I was born cauled from the head to the knees, with only my face, arms, and legs free. I was completely hairy; I had a deep and strong voice. All these things made the midwives believe that I was a boy. They filled the palace with a false joy, which deceived the king himself for awhile. Hope and desire helped mislead everybody, but it caused great consternation for the women when they realized that they were wrong. They were at a loss how to disabuse the king. Princess Catherine, his sister, took that errand upon herself. She carried me in her arms in such a position for the king to see me and to make him perceive what she did not dare say to him. She gave the king the means to disabuse himself. That great prince did not express any surprise at all; he took me in his arms and made me as welcome as if he had not been wrong in his expectation. He said to the princess, "Let us thank God, my sister. I hope that this girl will well be worth a boy to me. I ask God to preserve her for me, since he has given her to me." The princess, in order to soothe him, tried to flatter him that he was still young, that the queen was too, and that she would give him a male heir before long, but the king responded to her once more, "My sister, I am content. I ask God to preserve her for me." After that he sent me back with his benediction, and appeared so contented that he astonished everybody. He ordered that a Te Deum be chanted and that all the festivities customary at important births of the first males be carried out. In short, he appeared as great in this occasion as in all times of his life. Meanwhile they hesitated to disabuse the queen until she was in a state to bear such disappointment. I was given the name Christina. The Lutheran minister who baptized me (it was the great chaplain of the king) traced the sign of the cross with the baptismal water on my forehead and enrolled me, without knowing what he was doing, in your militia from that happy moment. For it is certain that what he did was contrary to the customary Lutheran ceremony.[4] People made a fuss as if it had been an act of superstition, and he had to extricate himself from it as best he could. The king used to say about me in jest, "She is going to be clever, because she fooled us all." So I was born, I gave the solemn lie to the astrologers, because the king recovered, the queen gave birth successfully, I was in good health, and, moreover, I was a girl.

It is necessary here, Lord, that I give you thanks contrary to those of that great man, who in times of old thanked you for having had him born a man, and not a woman. Because I, Lord, thank you for having had me born a girl, all the more so because you did me the favor of not allowing any weakness of my sex to pass into my spirit, which you by your grace made completely virile like the rest of my body.[5] You used my sex to preserve me from the vices and debaucheries of the country where I was born; and after having condemned me to the weaker sex, you desired to exempt me from all its ordinary weaknesses. You also emancipated me from all its dependencies by having me born on a throne where I was obliged to command alone. You also chose to make me understand, from the cradle, the advantage of this great independence, which I have been able to preserve and which I shall preserve until my death. If you had had me born a man, perhaps custom and example would have perverted me. Perhaps I would have drowned all the virtues and talents which you gave me in wine, as many others do. Perhaps my temperament, fiery and impetuous, would have carried me away into debauchery with women, from which it would have been more difficult for me to free myself. Perhaps that *versatile* spirit (I can't find another term to express what I am thinking) which you have given me, and which makes me so adaptable to the manners of all the nationalities with which I live, would have overcome finally that horrible aversion which I have for wine, for the dissolute life, and that instead of making my subjects cease these detestable vices, I would have made myself accustomed little by little to their defects in order to make myself more agreeable to them. At the least I would have run the risk that women would have occupied the time which I have used for study and for the search for truth, through which I have prepared myself to receive your guidance.[6] Suffer me to admire your goodness, which has favored me in so many ways, that it has meant to form for me a kind of merit, or rather of destiny, out of my greatest defect.

The queen my mother, who had all the weaknesses as well as all the virtues of her sex, was inconsolable. She could not abide me, because she said that I was a girl and ugly; and she was not greatly in the wrong, because I was as swarthy as a little Moor. My father loved me very much, and I responded accordingly to his love in a manner which surpassed my age. It seemed that I perceived the differences in their merits and their feelings, and that I began to do justice to them from the cradle.

It happened, a few days after my baptism, that a heavy beam fell and nearly crushed the cradle where I was sleeping, without injuring me in the least. Besides that accident, there were still other attempts on my life. I was purposely allowed to fall, and a thousand other tricks were attempted to make me perish, or at least to cripple me. The queen my mother had a lot to say on the subject and could not be disabused of her notions. Be that as it may, no other injury remains with me except a slight irregularity in my stature which I could have been able to correct had I wanted to take the trouble.[7]

. . . You had me born surrounded by laurels and palms. I slept under the shelter of their shadows; my first sleep was nourished among trophies; it seems that victory and fortune used to play with me. In short, the throne served me as a cradle, and I had scarcely been born when I had to mount it. The king my father assembled the Estates for this purpose a few months afterward. He had homage paid me, and Sweden kneeling adored me in my cradle.

CHAPTER 5

There was nothing remarkable in the first years of my childhood other than a deadly illness which struck me during a trip the king was making to the mines. A courier was dispatched to inform him of my sickness. He made such extraordinary haste to be near me that he arrived in twenty-four hours, something which a courier had never done. He found me in a desperate condition and seemed inconsolable, but at last I recovered, and he showed a joy proportionate to his grief. He had the Te Deum chanted. After that, the king took me on his trip to Kalmar, where upon arrival he put me to a little test which greatly increased his affection for me. I was not even two years old when he went to Kalmar. The people there didn't know whether to fire salvos from the garrison and from the cannons of the fortress to salute him according to custom, because they were afraid of frightening such an important child. So as not to be lacking in respect, the governor of the palace requested the order from the king. The king, after a slight hesitation, said, "Carry on, fire. She is the daughter of a soldier; she has to get used to it." That was done; they fired the salvos in due form. I was with the queen in her carriage, and instead of being terrified . . . I laughed and clapped my hands . . . ordering them in my way to fire still more. This little adventure greatly increased the king's fondness for me, because he hoped that I had been born as intrepid as he. Afterward he always took me with him to see him make his troop inspections, and everywhere I gave him such signs of courage as could be demanded at such a tender age of a child who scarcely talked. He took pleasure in playing with me. He used to say to me, "Run along, leave me alone. I shall take you someday to places where you will be contented."[8] But unfortunately for me, death prevented him from keeping his word to me, and I did not have the good fortune of making my apprenticeship under such a good master.[9] When he departed I was a little bigger, and had been taught a little compliment which I was supposed to recite to him. But he was so busy that he could not play with me. Seeing that he was not listening to me, I pulled at his boot-top, and made him turn toward me. When he saw me, he took me in his arms and embraced me, and could not hold back his tears, according to what the people present have told me. They have also assured me that, when he left, I cried so hard for three whole days without stopping that it did so much damage to my eyes that I was on the verge of losing my sight, which was very weak, just like that of my father, the king. My tears were taken as evil omens, especially because I normally cried little and rarely.

CHAPTER 8

The king had directed all of the people concerned to give me a completely masculine education, and to teach me everything which a young prince must know, in order to be worthy of reigning. He declared emphatically that he did not want anyone to inspire me with any of the sentiments of my sex save those of honesty and modesty. In all else he desired that I be a prince, and that I be instructed in everything which a young prince ought to know. My inclinations supported his plans marvelously, because I had an aversion and an invincible antipathy for everything which women do and say.[10] Moreover I had an insurmountable incapacity for all their handcrafts. They never found a way to teach me any of them. But in exchange I learned with a marvelous facility all the languages, sciences, and exercises in which I was to be instructed. But since then I have learned still others without the aid of any teacher, and it is certain that I never had any for German, French, Italian, or Spanish, no more than for Swedish, which is my native language.[11] It is the same with the exercises. I was taught only a little about dancing and how to mount a horse. Nevertheless I can do the exercises, and I make use of all arms reasonably well without having been taught completely how to handle them. In short, between what I was taught and what I wanted to know by myself, you did me the favor, Lord, of making me capable of everything which a prince must know and of everything which a girl can learn with honor. Moreover, I was indefatigable. I often would sleep in the dew on the hard ground. I ate little and slept less. I used to spend two or three days without drinking, because I was not permitted to drink water and because I had an almost invincible aversion for wine and beer. The queen my mother once gave me a whipping because she surprised me secretly drinking the rosewater which she used to wash her face. That made people let me drink some "small beer," which is considered to be so bad that nobody but the basest rabble among us drinks it.[12] But finally I drank some of it by necessity, always preferring it to beer and wine. I believe that they inflamed my entrails and burned so strongly inside that it caused me a great many ailments of the bile; since my bile burned my blood in a strange manner. I would never drink except when forced by an extreme necessity. I would be hungry in the same way, when it was necessary. But for eating, everything tasted good to me except ham and everything that comes from swine, for which I have an invincible antipathy. I bore heat and cold with no difficulty. I used to take long journeys on foot. I rode horseback without ever tiring. I led such an extraordinary life in spite of everybody. People did everything possible to prevent me, but they had to be patient and let me go. I loved study passionately, but I did not love hunting, racing, gaming less. I loved horses, dogs; but no pleasant entertainment has ever made me lose a moment of my studies or of my duties, and you know, Lord, that by your grace I have nothing to reproach myself about in that regard. As much as I might have loved hunting, I was not cruel, and I never killed an animal without having felt a keen compassion for it. The women and men who were in waiting on me used to despair, because I fatigued them terribly and did not give them any rest, day or night; and when my women tried to deter me from such a fatiguing way of living, I would make fun of them and would say to them, "If you are sleepy, go rest. I don't need you." The hours of my days were occupied with business, studies, and exercises.[13] On holidays there were games, or people went on a chase, or there was some other entertainment of which my age was capable.

After his return to Sweden (in the year 1636) the chancellor used to spend three or four hours with me every day, in order to instruct me in my duty. It was from him that I learned in part what I know about the art of ruling. You intended, Lord, for one of the greatest men in the world to give me the first lessons, and that is not one of the lesser debts that I owe you, because having taken the king my father away from me, you chose that this great man remain to instruct me. I took extreme pleasure in hearing him speak, and there was no study, game, or amusement which I would not gladly cease in order to listen to him. In return he took an extreme pleasure in instructing me, and we used to spend some three or four hours, and often more, together, very content with each other; and if I dare say it without offending modesty, that great man was forced more than once to admire a child in whom you had placed such talents, as well as a desire to be taught and a capacity for learning, which he admired without comprehending, since it was so rare in a child of my age.

My preceptor [Johann Matthiae] took the same pleasure. I was assiduous. I loved beautiful books. I read them with pleasure. I had an insatiable desire to know everything. I was capable of everything. I learned everything with no difficulty. . . . In short, all my teachers were very satisfied with me. My preceptor was my confidant.[14] I told him all my little sorrows, and I made observations with him which used to surprise him. We would reason together about the government. He would tell me everything that happened, and I made my observations on everything with him. . . .

In such a felicitious birth, in so many fine talents, which are the gifts of your grace alone, Lord, corrupt nature had mixed some faults which I shall not conceal.[15] I was mistrustful, suspicious, and also ambitious to excess. I was irascible and hotheaded, vain and impatient, scornful and jeering. I would never give quarter to anybody: and these faults, instead of diminishing with age and fortune, got so much worse that they made me recognize only too clearly that the defects stemmed from my personality and not from my destiny, and very recently I have felt these faults more keenly and more intensely in bad fortune than in good. Because it seems that the calm of good fortune in some way lulls the fierce beasts to sleep, whereas bad fortune piques and awakens them. I know well that I can suppress them when I wish. But I do not know if I have ever tried seriously to tame them completely. It is your grace alone, Lord, which has prevented them from carrying me away as much as they could have, and, if you occasionally gave them rein, you never permitted them to throw me.[16] I used to be unbelieving and not very devout,[17] and my hot and impetuous temperament did not give me less inclination for love than for ambition. Into what misfortune would such a terrible propensity have cast me, had your grace not used my faults themselves to correct me. My ambition, my haughtiness, incapable of submitting to anyone, and my pride, scornful of everything, served me as marvelous preservatives; and by your grace, you added to them a fine delicacy, through which you guarded me from an inclination so perilous to your glory and my happiness; and however close I may have been to the precipice, your powerful hand pulled me away. You know, whatever slander might say, that I am innocent of all the falsehoods with which it would blacken my life.[18] I avow that had I not been born a girl, the inclination of my temperament would perhaps have dragged me to terrible debauchery. But you, who made me love glory and honor all my life more than any other pleasure, you preserved me from misfortunes where the circumstances, the license of my station, and the ardor of my temperament would have thrown me. I would have gotten married without a doubt, if I had not recognized in myself the strength which you gave me to abstain from the pleasures of love. I know the world too well not to be aware that a girl who intends to amuse herself needs a husband, especially a girl of my quality, who does not wed a husband without making herself a subject, or rather a slave of his wishes and caprices. I was born in a station and in such a destiny that I could have chosen from all the men the one who would have been the most to my taste: because there was not any one of them in the world who would not have believed himself happy if I had wanted to give him my hand. I was too aware of all my advantages not to have the inclination to use them. Had I felt in myself any sort of weakness, I would have known how, like so many others, to get married in order to amuse myself, . . . and I would not have had that invincible aversion (of which I have given so many striking signs) against marriage,[19] if it had been necessary for me. But you gave me a heart which should not be occupied except by you. You formed it with such an admirable and vast capacity, that nothing could replenish it except you alone. You were to be the sole object of my desires. This heart was yours from the moment it beat in my being. You had, unknown to myself, instilled a secret intelligence in it. You alone did miracles in this heart, which make you so much more glorious because they have you alone for spectator and witness. You made my sins and defects, which are mine, serve this admirable relationship no less than all the virtues and talents with which you have been so generous to me. I contributed nothing to all that except my unworthiness, and nothing more remains for me but to observe you with respect and silence, to let you act and admire you.

I have yet a defect of which I almost forgot to accuse myself; it is that of having scorned the decorum of my sex too much, and it is that which has often made me appear more guilty than I am; but I recognized this defect too late to be able to correct it, and I did not want to take the trouble. I myself am convinced that I would have done better to have freed myself from it altogether, and it is the sole weakness of which I accuse myself, because . . . I should have set myself free from it entirely, as my station and my disposition demanded.

I have still other faults which certain people of one or the other sex, who were near me in my childhood, gave me through their bad examples, of which I am completely corrected by your grace. Children are like monkeys; they do everything that they see done; they are like wax, susceptible to all the forms which are imprinted on them. Our nation has vices of its own, as all other nations have theirs. You preserved me from the one of debauchery, but you allowed the vice of swearing to infect me by contagion; but by your grace, Lord, I am entirely rid of it. This is to be excused in some way nevertheless, because I was born in a country and in a century where this defect reigned equally among both sexes in Sweden, where nobody knew how to talk without swearing.[20] As soon as I was capable of recognizing my defect, I worked to rid myself of it, and I succeeded through your grace. I have still two other defects, which are that I laugh too often and too loudly and that I walk too quickly.[21] But since I never laugh at the wrong time, I have neglected this defect as well as the one of walking too quickly, which is a consequence of the impetuosity of my character, enemy of everything sluggish. All these defects would be only of little consequence if they had not been present in a girl. My sex makes them more inexcusable, for they diminish in part the value of all my good qualities and talents, . . .

It is without doubt inexcusable of me, Lord, for not having corrected myself of all my great and small faults, because among the many talents which your generous hand has poured on me, you gave me the one of an admirable and absolute power over myself, so that I can make of myself anything I desire. You know, Lord, that I am speaking the truth. Nevertheless, . . . some defects slipped in, which I was aware of even at the time, and I did not recognize some others until later when they had become irremediable. Some of them are the fault of people, others of the country, others of the age. I am passing over them in silence, because nothing is perfect in this world.[22] I can boast moreover, by your grace, that few princes in Sweden had a better education. It is true that good manners, which are so necessary to distinguish genteel people from the others, were not yet known in Sweden at that time.[23] It is not possible to give good breeding to oneself, and I should not be blamed for this defect. Be that as it may, I owe you, Lord, everything that I am, and I confess that I am indebted for it, after you, to all the great men who reared me. I do not think I was ever ungrateful to them, and I would rather die than ever have been ungrateful to you.

CHAPTER 9

At almost the same time, the queen my mother arrived.[24] She was received in due form. I went in person with all the senate and all the nobility of both sexes from the court to meet her. The tears and laments renewed themselves at this sad sight. I embraced the queen my mother. She drowned me in her tears, and nearly suffocated me in her arms. The body of the king was placed in a vault in the castle. All the ceremonies were conducted according to the fashion of the country to honor the memory of the greatest king who had ever reigned in Sweden. I had to put up with many sermons and harangues, which were more insufferable to me than the death of the king, my father, from which I had recovered completely a long time before, since I did not realize my misfortune. But I strongly fear that I would not have consoled myself so soon had I been in a state to understand it. Because children who await the succession of a crown recover quickly from the loss of a father. But nevertheless, mine was so pleasant, and I loved him so much, that I believe that my fortune would not have comforted me completely had I been capable of perceiving my loss. But . . . it had been almost two years since his death, and I grew tremendously weary of the long and sad ceremonies. But what gave the finishing stroke to my affliction was the lugubrious life which my mother was leading. At once, when she had arrived, she shut herself up in her suite, which was completely covered with black cloth from the ceiling to the floor. The windows of this apartment were sealed with a material of the same color. You couldn't see a thing, and nothing but wax tapers were burned, day and night, which made only the sad objects of mourning visible. She cried almost day and night. . . . I had a great respect and very tender love for her. But this respect made me uncomfortable and became troublesome to me, especially when she took possession of me in spite of my tutors, and when she tried to close me up with her in her apartment. She began at once to find fault with the education I had received up to then. She even had some sort of quarrel with the regency about it. But the respect they had for her made them give her a certain leeway in that regard for some time. They let her care for me in her way, although the regency had been taken from her. For the rest, they believed that they owed her this indulgence. That allowed her to send my aunt away from me too, saying that she wanted to be my governess herself. She tried other changes too, but she was quite justly opposed. However, she loved me tenderly, the more so because she used to say that I was the living image of the late king. But by dint of loving me, she made me despair. She made me go to bed with her and scarcely let me out of her sight. It was with difficulty that I was able to get permission to go study in my quarters and do my exercises there.

You, Lord, have made the weaknesses of the queen my mother serve me, to my advantage; because this constraint that I suffered in being around her served to attach me to study with greater ardor, and that was the reason I made such great and surprising progress in my studies, because I used that pretext to escape from the queen my mother, to leave her sad abode, for which I had such a profound aversion.[25] . . .

Meanwhile the queen-mother had several arguments over the subject of my education with my tutors, who, showing great respect for her, did not allow her to ruin me completely, as she doubtless would have, had she been allowed. For she was a princess who had many good qualities, but she did not have any of the ones which are so necessary for ruling, and she was not able to teach me what she did not know.

. . . .

I feel obliged to state here my opinion on the conduct of the regency in that time, and I shall not hesitate to say that they were correct not to give any part of the regency to the queen my mother. . . . My feeling is that women should never reign; and I am so convinced of this that I would have, without a doubt, taken away all right of succession from my daughters, had I married. Because I would doubtless have loved my kingdom more than my children, and it is treason to allow the succession to fall to girls. I ought to be believed all the more because I am speaking against my own interest. But I make a habit of saying the truth at my expense. It is almost impossible for a woman to be able to discharge the duties of the throne properly, whether she govern for herself or for her ward. The ignorance of women, the weakness of their souls, their bodies, and their spirits make them incapable of reigning. All the women I have seen, in histories and in the world, who have ruled, or who have claimed to do so, have made themselves ridiculous in one way or another. I do not make an exception of myself, and I am ready to call attention to my faults later, if there are any in me. Nevertheless if any women have ever succeeded in fulfilling their duty with dignity, they should not be counted. These examples are so rare, that they ought not to be drawn into a precedent favorable to the sex, and my example less than any other, because I was brought up from the cradle expressly for that purpose.[26] Nonetheless my own experience has taught me that the defect of sex is the greatest of all. It is not that my mother would not have been as capable of governing as all the queens and princess-mothers whom we have seen in our century. But to speak the truth, they were as little capable as she to govern. And regardless of what their flatterers may be able to say about them, I have not seen any who would have been better than she. But I consider her fortunate for not having been involved in this terrible business. To exclude her from it was doubtless the keenest sign of love that the king my father could give her, because she would have doubtless spoiled everything, like all the others who have mixed themselves up in it. But if I praise, as is just, the regency for not having accorded her any part in affairs, I cannot deny that there was a little harshness in separating her completely from me, as I shall reveal later.[27]

NOTES TO THE TRANSLATION

1. After having lost two children at birth, and a daughter who lived less than one year, Queen Maria Eleonora conceived Christina.

2. "This vermin of astrologers had already migrated to the farthest part of the North, as it was found at that time . . . in almost all the courts of Europe. . . . Even prelates were . . . infatuated with this vain science" (Arck., 3:20; Grauert, *CKvS*, 1:122).

3. This date accords with the calendar in use at the time.

4. The chaplain was Matthiae. Arckenholtz doubts the veracity of this anecdote (3:23). Christina is interested in demonstrating that she was predestined for the Catholic church.

5. Christina uses the word *femme* ("woman") to refer to women in general, but in her autobiography she consistently uses the term *fille* ("girl") to refer to herself. Her comment about the virility of her body has given rise to much speculation. Stolpe cites it as evidence that she was a "pseudohermaphrodite"—that she had the sexual organs of a female but the secondary sex characteristics of a male (*DK*, 1:63–65).

6. Literally "to receive your touches" (3:24).

7. One of Christina's shoulders was higher than the other. Arckenholtz and some of Christina's contemporaries claimed that she was able to mask this defect (Arck., 1:550; 3:24), while others were less charitable. One wrote that her jacket was "so badly fitted to her body that the shoulder which was larger than the other stuck out completely on one side" (Arck., 1:543). Arckenholtz attributes this deformity to a fall and cites the possibility that Polish sympathizers were in the court (3:24).

8. Christina uses the formal form of address, *vous*, here, surprising in view of the family relation and the fact that she was just a small child.

9. Arckenholtz notes that Christina makes it clear in this passage that since childhood her greatest desire had been to take part in a battle or to lead an army (3:27; 4:348–93).

10. Arckenholtz notes the difficulty of explaining this aversion but suggests that her masculine education could have contributed to it (3:52; 1:167ff.); Grauert, *CKvS*, 1:40, 58; Stolpe, *DK*, 1:70–73.

11. Arckenholtz claims that Christina was reading Thucydides and Polybius in the original language at age eighteen (Arck., 1:30), but Grauert shows that Christina learned Greek relatively late in her life and probably read the works cited above in Latin translations (*CKvS*, 1:267). Arckenholtz doubts the validity of a contemporary report that Christina spoke French without any accent or mistakes. Further, he discounts her claim that she had no teachers, citing French exercises which Matthiae gave his pupil (3:53); Christina herself claimed that she had "many language teachers," in her notes to "Mémoire de ce qui s'est passé durant la regne de la Reine, avec des notes ajoutées par elle même l'an MDCXXXII (Arck., 3:183).

12. Small beer (*la petite bière*): a weak, diluted beer.

13. Christina's account of her life is corroborated by the report sent by the French Ambassador Chanut to his court in 1648 (Arck., 3:54).

14. Arckenholtz notes that Christina's confidence in Matthiae aroused jealousy in the senate and may have contributed to his humiliation after her abdication (3:55).

15. Tilting at Christina's critics, especially d'Alembert and Holberg, Arckenholtz praises Christina's "frankness and sincerity" in revealing her own faults (3:56). Holberg had published a critique of Arckenholtz's *Mémoires concernant Christine* in 1753.

16. This imagery is interesting in view of Christina's great skill as an equestrienne.

17. Arckenholtz praises Christina's sincerity in referring to her period of religious skepticism, which he blames on the influence of "miserable libertine savants (*persone irreligiosamente letterate*)" at her court (3:56–57). After Christina left Sweden, but before she formally converted, she shocked her contemporaries with her seemingly irreligious actions and statements.

18. Rumors of scandalous sexual escapades plagued Christina even in Sweden, and they still persist in more popular treatments of her life. She was slandered, especially after her abdication, by French and Spanish writers, sometimes for diplomatic reasons. There is no evidence to support the notion that Christina's "immorality" consisted of more than her refusal to behave according to conventional notions of piety and female decorum.

19. Arckenholtz suggests that Christina is referring to her refusal to marry, even to secure the Polish crown [though she was prepared to lie about this] (3:57).

20. Arck., 1:547; Stolpe, *DK*, 2:17–18.

21. In the seventeenth century, inappropriate or loud laughter was considered a serious breach of decorum.

22. Arckenholtz comments that one would indeed have preferred that the queen name these defects (3:60). Other than her pride, irascibility, and religious skepticism, the defects Christina mentions here have more to do with etiquette than character.

23. Arckenholtz criticizes "good breeding" as it was practiced in Christina's day, contrasting it unfavorably with the "simplicity and sincerity" of older customs (3:60); Sweden was still quite provincial until the later years of Christina's reign, when the French influence predominated.

24. Upon Gustav Adolf's death the queen had traveled to Germany and remained with the body on its slow journey to Sweden.

25. As was still the fashion in European courts, Queen Eleonora kept a number of jesters and dwarves in her quarters, which horrified the child (3:66).

26. Christina was aware of the illustrious career of Countess Amalia-Elisabeth of Hessen, who ruled during her son's minority. Christina wrote an admiring letter to her when Amalia retired (Arck., 1:156ff.). As part of her education, Christina studied Camden's work on Queen Elizabeth of England (Grauert, *CKvS*, 1:44).

27. Christina's autobiography ends here.

BIBLIOGRAPHY

Primary Works

Christina's works are included in Johann Arckenholtz. *Mémoires concernant Christine, reine de Suède, pour servir d'éclaircissement a l'histoire de son règne et principalement de sa vie privée . . . suivis de deux ouvrages de cette savante princesse, qui n'ont jamais été imprimés. . . .* 4 vols. Amsterdam and Leipzig: P. Mortier, 1751–1760. Microfilm. New Haven, Conn.: Research Publications Inc. History of Women, 31.1, 1975.

Vol. 1: *Mémoires pour servira a l'histoire de Christine Reine de Suède,* 1751 (main body of biography).

Vol. 2: *Mémoires . . . ,* 1751 (conclusion of biography, various supporting materials); "Ouvrage de Loisir" (aphorisms, c. 1680, 52 pp.); "Réfléxions diverses sur la Vie et sur les Actions du Grand Alexandre" (essay, date unknown, 19 pp.); "L'Endimione di Erilo Cleono" (pastoral verse drama by Alexander Guidi, based on ideas furnished by Christina and with embellishments and verse by Christina, c. 1687, 12 pp.).

Vol. 3: *Mémoires . . . ,* 1759 (further supporting material; two brief histories of Sweden with notes and commentary added by Christina: "Historie de ce qui s'est passé après la mort du Grand Gustave, . . ." and "Mémoire de ce qui c'est passé durant la Regne de la Reine, . . ."); "La Vie de la Reine Christine faite par Elle-même, dédieé à Dieu" (autobiography, c. 1681, 69 pp.).

Vol. 4: *Mémoires . . . ,* 1760 (letters, supporting materials, additions and corrections, lists, appendix of supporting materials); "Réfléxions sur la Vie et les Actions du César" (essay, date unknown, 7 pp.); "Sentimens" (aphorisms, c. 1680, 41 pp.).

English Translations

The Works of Christina of Sweden. Containing Maxims and sentences in twelve centuries, and Reflections on the life and actions of Alexander the Great. Now first translated from the original French. To which is prefix'd an Account of her life, character, and writings, by the translator. London: D. Wilson & T. Durham, 1753.

Taunton, Margaret T. *Christina, Queen of Sweden. A brief notice of her life, conversion, and death, with her Maxims, etc.* 1862.

Birch, Una, trans. *Maxims of a Queen* . . . (selections). London: John Lane Co., 1907.

Related Works

Arckenholtz, Johann. *Mémoires concernant Christine, reine de Suède,* . . . (See Primary Works.)

Åström, Sven-Erik. "The Swedish Economy and Sweden's Role as a Great Power 1632–1697." In *Sweden's Age of Greatness, 1632–1718,* edited by Michael Roberts, 58–101. Problems in Focus Series. London: Macmillan, 1973.

Bjurström, Per. *Feast and Theatre in Queen Christina's Rome.* Nationalmusei Skriftserie, 14. Stockholm: Bengtsons litografiska AB, 1966.

Callmer, Christian. *Königin Christina, ihre Bibliothekare & ihre Handschriften: Beiträge zur europäischen Bibliotheksgeschichte.* Stockholm: Kungl. bibl., 1977.

Cassirer, Ernst. "Descartes und Königin Christina von Schweden." In his *Descartes: Lehre, Persönlichkeit, Wirkung,* 177–301. Stockholm: Bermann-Fischer, 1939.

Franckenstein, Christian Gottfried. *The History of the intrigues and gallantries of Christina, queen of Sweden. And of her court, whilst she was at Rome.* Faithfully render'd into English, from the French original. London, printed for Richard Baldwin, 1697. Ann Arbor: University Microfilms. English Books 1641–1700, 106:7, 1963.

Grauert, W. H. *Christina Königinn von Schweden und ihr Hof.* 2 vols. Bonn: Eduard Weber, 1837, 1842.

Gualdo Priorato, Galeazzo. *The History of the Sacred and Royal Majesty of Christina Alessandra queen of Swedland, with the reasons of her late conversion to the Roman Catholique religion* . . . London: Printed for T. W., 1658. Ann Arbor: University Microfilms. English Books 1641–1700, 72:4, 1962.

Gustafsson, Lars. Review of *Från Stoicism till mystik,* by Sven Stolpe. *Samlaren,* n.s. 39 (1958): 120–26.

Masson, Georgina. *Queen Christina.* First American edition. New York: Farrar, Straus and Giroux, 1969.

Meyer, Ernst. "Om drottning Kristinas literära verksamhet i Italien." *Samlaren* 5 (1884): 65–114.

Mitchell, Stephen A. "The Autobiographies of Agneta Horn and Queen Christina Compared." Chapter 4 of *Job in Female Garb: Studies on the Autobiography of Agneta Horn,* 72–77. Skrifter utgivna av Litteraturvetenskapliga institutionen vid Göteborgs universitet, 14. Published with the financial assistance of the Swedish Council for Research in the Humanities and Social Sciences, 1985.

Olofsson, Sven Ingemar. *Drottning Christinas tronavsägelse och trosförändring.* Diss., Stockholms Högskola, 1953. Uppsala: Appelbergs Boktryckeri AB, 1953.

Roberts, Michael. "Queen Christina and the General Crisis of the Seventeenth Century." In his *Essays in Swedish History,* 113–37. London: Weidenfeld and Nicolson, 1967.

———. "The Swedish Church." In *Sweden's Age of Greatness, 1632–1718,* edited by Michael Roberts, 132–73. Problems in Focus Series. London: Macmillan, 1973.

———, ed. *Sweden as a Great Power, 1611–1697: Government: Society: Foreign Policy.* Documents of Modern History. New York: St. Martin's Press, 1968.

Setterwall, Monica. "Queen Christina and Role Playing in Maxim Form." *Scandinavian Studies* 57, no. 2 (1985): 162–73.

Stolpe, Sven. *Från Stoicism till Mystik: Studier i Drottning Kristinas Maximer.* Diss., Uppsala, 1959. Stockholm: Bonniers, 1959.

———. *Drottning Kristina.* 2 vols. *Den svenska tiden* (I), *Efter tronavsägelsen* (II). Stockholm: Bonniers, 1960, 1961.

Weibull, Curt. *Drottning Christina.* 2d ed. Stockholm: Natur och Kultur, 1934.

PART SEVEN

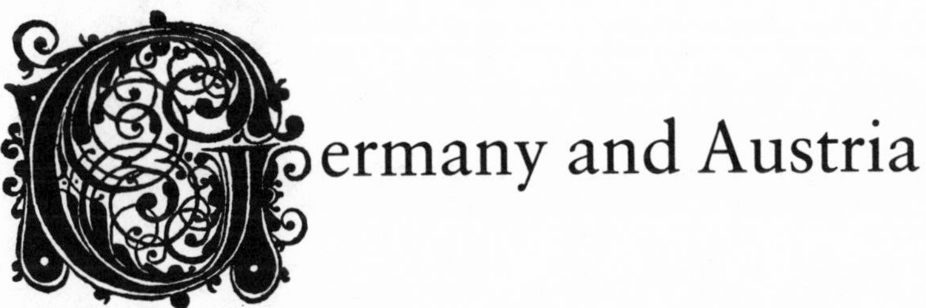

Germany and Austria

PRODIGY AND FEMINIST

ibylle Schwarz

SUSAN L. CLARK

Despite the disruption accompanying the Thirty Years' War, Sibylle Schwarz managed to publish sonnets, numerous "occasional" poems, a Susanna-drama, a verse tragedy, a bucolic novelette, and letters in a time when few women read, wrote, or passed on their thoughts in print.[1] Sibylle's seventeenth-century contemporaries found her work astonishing and praised her highly, at the same time viewing her as an anomaly. In subsequent centuries, however, she gradually disappeared from literary histories and lexicons, even those dealing with women writers, and recent volumes on German Baroque literature rarely mention her.[2]

Sibylle was born to upperclass parents on February 14, 1621, and died seventeen years later of dysentery on July 31, 1638. Raised in Greifswald, Pomerania, in northern Germany on the Baltic Sea, she was the youngest daughter of Regina Völschow and Christian Schwarz, who brought up four sons and three daughters in the Protestant Church.[3] Her mother was a member of a prominent family that had produced numerous civil servants for the city and professors for its university. Her father was a lawyer in civil service who had received university training at Greifswald, Helmstedt, and Jena; his grandmother had been a mayor's daughter and his grandfather a successful businessman. In short, as Helmut Ziefle writes, "Sibylle's parents belonged to the most prominent society in Greifswald."[4] Because of her family's high social status and expectations, Sibylle was sent to school and educated to the extent that learning was accessible to women at that time, perhaps four hours a day for a period of two years. Her schooling consisted of reading, catechism, music, mathematics, and the memorization of psalms.[5] That this brief exposure to learning was not sufficient for Sibylle's inquiring mind is evident from the amount of information she gleaned in further study with her brothers and mentors, by whom she was tutored and with whom she exchanged books. In any event, we learn from her letters and from internal evidence in her work that she read and wrote German, could translate Dutch, had studied Latin and made translations from Ovid's *Metamorphoses,* and was thoroughly familiar not only with contemporary German Baroque poetry but also with figures and myths from classical antiquity. Her brothers were university educated, although Sibylle herself was not.[6] In addition the Schwarz children were fortunate to find companions and mentors in university professors who were friends of the family, among them mathematics and medicine professor Johann Schöner, logic and metaphysics professor Alexander Christian, and theology professor Barthold Krakewitz. Christian Schwarz's various civil service positions also brought him into contact with royalty and members of the nobility. Several of Sibylle's poems accordingly celebrate various events in the lives of her day's rich and famous, as, for example, the matriculation of Duke Ernst von Croy at the University of Greifswald.

Just as social status gained for the Schwarz children a superior education and powerful connections, so did the family's relatively comfortable economic position provide a buffer against extreme hardship in the Thirty Years' War. When imperial troops and then Swedish forces descended on Greifswald, the latter viewed as liberators, Sibylle and other young children were sent to safety at a recently acquired country estate, Fretow, which she idealizes and eulogizes in several of her poems, letters, and dramas. Sibylle considered Fretow the most beautiful place on earth and transformed it in her poetry into a symbol of friendship and the virtuous life.[7] The loss of Fretow—it was burned to the ground in the course of the war—was as traumatic for Sibylle as the sudden death of her mother on January 25, 1630. Her father was posted at Stettin for three years from 1629 to 1631, and the Schwarz children, left in Greifswald, had effectively to make do as orphans. Care of the household was turned over to the eldest daughter, Regina, who had returned home after the death of her husband, merchant Christoph Bünsow, just six days after their wedding in 1629. Regina remarried (her second husband was the pastor of the Nikolai Church in Greifswald) in 1631, leaving the second sister, Emerentia, to run the household. Sibylle took over this task in the months before Emerentia's marriage to Dr. Herman Queren. Emerentia's nuptials took place on the day Sibylle died.

In her time Sibylle Schwarz enjoyed an unusual reputation both within the German literary establishment and among the local citizenry, whose familiarity with her poetic accomplishments is evident from her reaction to their comments and from the great number of poems she wrote commemorating events in their lives (births and deaths to name-days and journeys). She corresponded with the writer Samuel Gerlach, who edited and published her work after her death. Gerlach lived in Danzig, and he was Sibylle's link to the Baroque critic and poet, Martin Opitz, with whom he was in contact when the latter was Polish court historiographer.

Sibylle's poetry found considerable favor with contemporary Baroque poets, as witnessed by the dedicatory poems and letters contained in Gerlach's edition, but it also set her apart as an oddity in less learned Greifswald society. Some friction must have occurred on the local scene, for Sibylle inveighs against those who she believes "envy" her. Gerlach vigorously supported her against her detractors, who seemed to have felt that women should not write; she, while noticeably irked, referred to them as "enemies of the noble lyre," but Gerlach was less charitable and elegant in his phrasing.[8] The publication of his two volumes in 1650 made Schwarz's work available to a wider audience, and soon literary historians began to include her in their compendia, as either an oddity or a *Wunderkind.* Gerlach as a critic and editor maintained a balanced view of her talents; though he praised her, he frankly admitted that she made spelling errors and wrote occasional murky passages and that allowances had to be made because of her youth, dialect, and "poetic license."[9] His highest praise—that Sibylle was "the tenth Muse"[10]—would have pleased her, for she demands in defense of women's writing, "Weren't the Muses women, too?"[11]

The literary critical establishment first included Sibylle Schwarz in its ranks in Daniel Georg Morhof's 1682 work, *Unterricht von der teutschen Sprache und Poesie.* Morhof is hesitant to say that "we have women [literally: women-persons, *Frauenpersonen*] in Germany whose poetic skills would put men to shame," but he nevertheless calls her "a wonder of her time, for, during a period of time between her thirteenth year and her seventeenth year, when she blissfully passed away, she wrote verses that are without compare, not only for one of her tender years but also for one who is a virgin. Many men who live out a normal span and have quite a reputation in the field of poetry have not achieved as much."[12] Morhof's assessment, interesting in and of itself, is central to the process whereby Sibylle Schwarz was relegated to the status of a "forgotten woman," for critics following him often speak more to Morhof than to her work. For example, Christian Franz Paullini paraphrases Morhof in his 1705 treatise on educated women, and Johann Caspar Eberti pays homage in 1706 more to Morhof than to Schwarz herself, already following the trend of citing other critics to establish literary reputations. In 1715 Georg Christian Lehms plagiarizes Morhof, taking whole sentences from the earlier critic's assessment of Sibylle. By 1751 Gottlieb Christian Jöcher includes Sibylle in his lexicon but trivializes her contribution by stating that even at thirteen years of age she wrote "a beautiful verse" and died in 1638. J. C. C. Oelrichs paraphrases Morhof, but at least identifies his source, in his 1767 history of educated inhabitants of Pommern.[13] From this point on, Schwarz gradually fades from the literary landscape. Ziefle rationalizes the fact that her name appears fewer and fewer times in literary lexicons of the nineteenth century by contending that the scholars who did mention her wrote in a more accurate fashion of her gifts; at the same time he notes that some of these assessments came into print in secondary works that have since been proved quite unreliable. He also documents the rare mentions of her in the twentieth century.[14] Ziefle's reasons for studying Schwarz may have been as timely as seeing a link between conditions in our own age and that of the Baroque,[15] but there are other compelling grounds for bringing Schwarz forward from the ranks of "forgotten women"—reasons directly related to her gender and her achievements in a time when women were in fact discouraged from writing and when their writings were most often not preserved.[16]

Schwarz was mourned extensively not only in her immediate family but also in the larger community she joined when she became a poet. A prodigy in her prolific writing, she left as her legacy two substantial volumes of verse and prose totaling over one hundred fifty pages in the Faber du Faur collection.[17] Yet today's literary histories of the German Baroque routinely omit her—among females, only Catharina von Greiffenberg seems to merit mention—and only a handful of scholars like Schoolfield have given Schwarz's literary work the wider exposure it deserves.[18] Of the few dozen women who contribute to the massive Faber du Faur collection, Catharina von Greiffenberg alone boasts a corpus as lengthy and varied as that of Schwarz. To be sure, on occasion Schwarz's efforts fail to rise above predictable themes and clumsy rhyme patterns, but the major part of her work is notable for finely honed metrical skill, intense communication of personal feelings, variety of poetic voices, and mastery of such versification techniques as oxymoron, personification, and *Häufungen* (the piling up of metaphors and similes). She demonstrates considerable familiarity with classical literature, evidenced by her frequent mythological allusions. She often praises Opitz, the dean of German Baroque poetry, and sees herself as consciously emulating him and drawing from his legacy. Her achievement as a writer in the German Baroque period should be reassessed, not only because she is a nearly forgotten woman writer but primarily because her work has outstanding literary merit. Moreover, this achievement must be cast against the background of the unusually daunting circumstances under which she wrote.

Why has Schwarz remained relatively obscure? The critical works that mention her, from Morhof to Ziefle, take pains either to describe her as an anomaly or to fit her into a tradition, literary or societal. I would contend that in the seventeenth century Schwarz did *not* "fit in," as evidenced by contemporary astonishment at her writing skill, and in the twentieth century she still has not "fit in" because women's studies—and studies of Baroque women—are only now gaining wider acceptance. The German Baroque, an age of ornamentation that did not look kindly upon women who wanted to be more than ornaments, produced women writers who gained acceptance by a male literary establishment, yet who wrote "in a different voice."[19]

Schwarz's work is multifaceted. Like other German Baroque poets, her range extends from sonnets to *Gelegenheitsdichtung* (occasional poetry); but it is her deviations from the poetic models under which she was schooled that prove to be most fascinating to the critic and reader. These deviations are tied to her consciousness that she was a woman, and, more than that, a woman writing in an age when women did not write.

This awareness of being female in an overwhelmingly male literary community cuts both ways. On the one hand, Schwarz's curiosity status gave her access to a group of writers, foremost among them Opitz, who were critics as well and were therefore capable of judging what constituted good and publishable material. On the other hand, the little girl dubbed "the Pomeranian Sappho"[20] must have been viewed by many in somewhat the same manner as Samuel Johnson's walking dog ("a woman preaching is like a dog walking on his hind legs. It is not done well: but you are surprised to find it done at all," *Life of Johnson*). Yet the tone of Gerlach's eulogy as well as the monument he left to her in her two published volumes does not smack of that attitude in the least. Nonetheless, consciousness of this anomalous status sounds again and again in Schwarz's poems, from protestations that she ought not to be denied the pen ("Weren't the Muses themselves women?") to repetitive allusions to the "Neid" she must daily encounter. *Neid* is a term that can refer to simple enviousness of others, who in her case are jealous of a poetic skill they do not possess, as well as to a general sense of invidiousness, a feeling that the world itself is hostile. This sense of having to do physical battle with a war-torn and transient world, as well as verbal battle with detractors who feel she should not be writing—or should not receive recognition for something she is unqualified to do—informs Schwarz's poetry.

In fact, the sense of opposition that characterizes the woman writer in the world clearly manifests itself in Schwarz's work in both overt and covert ways. She often complains of her detractors and of the self-destructive "Neid" that she must suffer, but one can find additional evidence that the "wronged woman" stance appears in other guises. For example, in Schwarz's Susanna-drama a woman defends herself against lying and unjust detractors; this tale was extraordinarily popular in the Renaissance, Reformation, and Baroque periods.[21] Furthermore, in Schwarz's "Faunus" fragment, a woman has no choice but to marry a man against her will, because of a prior agreement her father had arranged whereby the daughter/bride was but a piece of property conveyed from one man to another.

A typical woman, in Schwarz's eyes, lives first as a daughter, then as a companion to other young girls, then as a wife and mother, then as a widow, and she finally dies before her time. Such was the life of Schwarz's mother, the housekeepers of prominent citizens in Greifswald, and the first wife of Schwarz's mentor, Schöner, as well as Schwarz herself. The exceptional woman, in Schwarz's eyes, is the female writer who chronicles the lives of others (including other women) but does not live a similar life herself and who, through her work, outlives them all. Significantly, Schwarz writes of other women's engagements, marriages, and the christenings of their children, but she herself died, unengaged and unmarried, a contrast to her sisters and her good friend Judith Tanck.[22] Her life-plan did not follow the prescribed course of most of the upper-middle-class women around her. In short, she chronicled important events in the lives of many women but did not participate in the same rites of passage. Her personae—invariably intense, non-passive, and enthusiastic—often consciously cut themselves off from certain types of female experiences, such as encounters with "Amor." Perhaps Schwarz feared the emotional and physical involvement that love brings, but it seems more in keeping with the many indications in her verse that she felt distanced from a conventional love experience precisely because of her status as a woman poet. Her personae refuse to be confined within the narrow enclosures, metaphoric and real, that encompassed women in the Baroque era. "Amor" may have access to all lands and continents, as she claims in one of her sixteen sonnets, but her personae have the wide-ranging powers of the mind and poetic imagination on their side. Refusing to be bound by "Amor," her personae imagine or describe certain experiences and then repudiate them; in effect, Schwarz rebels *by* writing and *in* her writing.

The sample of her work presented here is both representative and selective. I have included samples of her occasional poetry, a religious song, and a polemic against envy, as well as all sixteen of the sonnets, arguably her best work. There are also epigrams, a translation from the Dutch, a "Fretow"-poem, and one dramatic offering (a marvelously abbreviated Susanna-drama that places a different focus on Susanna's plight in that it gives greater voice to Susanna than to her detractors).

In the translations, I decided against mimicking Schwarz's rhyme and rhythmic patterns in favor of a more natural English rendering. Her language is quite amenable to translation into English, because of her lucidity of expression, recurrent themes, and vocabulary. Her German style is easy and flexible, adapting itself to a variety of situations. Her sonnets present the greatest difficulty to the translator, on account of the compression of meaning necessitated by that form, while her funeral poems offer relatively few *cruces*. Gerlach, whose edition is the only one available, occasionally tidies Schwarz's orthography and grammar; his is therefore a solid working edition for a translation. Nevertheless, a current edition and translation of her complete works are long overdue to provide greater convenience and accuracy for Baroque and women's studies scholars.

In the final analysis, Schwarz offers a window into female experience in the Baroque age, a window that has long been covered. One finds in her writings conventional Baroque sentiments that echo in the works of her male contemporaries—life's transience, God's destructive and restorative powers, the pains and pleasures of love, and the pleasant existence of shepherds and shepherdesses—as well as adherence to the formal elements that prescribed and described Baroque prose and verse. But there are additional dimensions to her writing that came about because she grew up female and died young in an age not noted for its enlightened attitude toward women and in a country devastated by war.

NOTES

1. The sole edition of Schwarz's work has been out of print but is available on microfilm in the Faber du Faur collection (see note 17). Volume one: Sibyllen Schwarzin, Vohn Greiffswald aus Pommern, *Deutsche Poetische Gedichte;* volume two: Sibyllen Schwarzin, Von Greiffswald aus Pommern, *Ander Teil Deutscher Poëtischer Gedichten*. The first volume paginates numerically, and the second uses a combination of alphabetical ordering and numbers; in citing poems from the latter I list letter and number with *recto* and *verso* as necessary.

2. There is no mention whatsoever of Schwarz in Gerald Gillespie, *German Baroque Poetry;* in *Deutsche Barocklyrik,* ed. Martin Bircher and Alois Haas; in *German Baroque* Literature in the European Perspective, ed. Gerhart Hoffmeister; in *Deutsche Barockforschung: Dokument einer Epoche,* ed. Richard Alewyn; in Robert M. Browning, *German Baroque Poetry 1618–1723;* in A. G. De Capua, *German Baroque Poetry: Interpretative Readings;* or in *Deutsche Dichter des 17. Jahrhunderts: Ihr Leben und Werk,* ed. Harald Steinhagen and Benno von Wiese. The latter massive volume contains only Catharina von Greiffenberg and Elisabeth Charlotte von Orléans, who are given a total of 45 of the 921 pages of text. When Schwarz is mentioned, references are perfunctory at best. Marian Szyrocki, *Die deutsche Literatur des Barock,* once cites her as a member of the "Hirtenorden" (p. 169); Gerhart Hoffmeister, "Barocker Petrarkismus, Wandlungen und Möglichkeiten der Liebessprache in der Lyrik des 17. Jahrhunderts," in *Europäische Tradition und deutscher Literaturbarock: Internationale Beiträge zum Problem von Überlieferung und Umgestaltung,* p. 21, notes Schwarz's predilection for trochaic quadrameter; and Richard Newald, *Die deutsche Literatur: Vom Späthumanismus zur Empfindsamkeit 1570–1750,* counts her among "die dichtenden Frauen" (p. 248) but oddly assigns her to the Nürnberg school (p. 212).

3. Sibylle's poems are peppered with religious allusions but are not extraordinarily religious in tone. Secular themes predominate, so that her verses with central religious themes are far outnumbered by her occasional poetry. Like most poets of her time, she alludes frequently to God in her occasional poems, which often treat deaths, funerals, and mar-

riages (sacramental subjects), as well as departures—times when God can provide consolation or protection.

4. Helmut W. Ziefle, *Sibylle Schwarz, Leben und Werk,* p. 6. Ziefle's work is the most recent and by far the most encompassing on Schwarz and her achievements. Tremendously useful in providing biographical background and explanations for many of Schwarz's abbreviations in dedicatory titles, Ziefle's study still falls into many of the traps of late nineteenth- to mid-twentieth-century scholarship. It falls prey to sentimentalism (see note 15), but its major fault is circularity of deductions: the poems are used to create important parts of a biography, which is then used in turn to explicate the poems.

5. Ziefle, *Sibylle Schwarz,* p. 13.

6. This state of affairs was hardly uncommon. One needs only to look at the difference education produced in the refined writings of the Lessing brothers, compared to the inadequate prose of their sister, to see the opportunities given to men and denied to women. Virginia Woolf, of course, has written the seminal text on this type of discrimination in *A Room of One's Own,* where William Shakespeare's advantages are contrasted to the circumstances of a fictitious sister Judith.

7. Ziefle, *Sibylle Schwarz,* 8.

8. See Schwarz, 1: 2.

9. See Ziefle, *Sibylle Schwarz,* 45.

10. See Schwarz, 1: 10.

11. Schwarz, 1: 8.

12. Daniel Georg Morhof, *Unterricht von der teutschen Sprache und Poesie,* 438–39, cited in Ziefle, *Sibylle Schwarz,* 46.

13. See Ziefle, pp. 46–47, for quotes, from Christian Franz Paullini, *Das hoch- und wolgelahrte Frauenzimmer* (Frankfurt, Leipzig: Stoeßeln, 1705), pp. 130–31; Johann Caspar Eberti, *Eröffnetes Cabinet deß gelehrten Frauen-Zimmer, Darinnen die berühmtesten dieses Geschlechts umbständlich vorgestellet werden* (Frankfurt, Leipzig: Rohrlach, 1706), 325–27; Georg Christian Lehms, *Teutschlands galante Poetinnen* (Frankfurt: S. T. Hocker, 1715), 221–25; Gottlieb Christian Jöcher, *Allgemeines Gelehrten-Lexikon. Unveränderter Nachdruck der Leipziger Ausgabe von 1750–1897* (Hildesheim: Olms, 1960–63), 4:408; and J. C. C. Oelrichs, *Historisch Diplomatische Beyträge zur Geschichte der Gelahrtheit, besonders im Hertzogthum Pommern* (Berlin: Im Verlage der Buchhandlung der Realschule, 1767), 20–22.

14. Ibid., 48, 50.

15. Ibid., p. 52: "Als Mensch und Dichterin war Sibylle inmitten einer unruhigen Zeit Verkünderin wahrer Freundschaft und Menschlichkeit, die sich auf inneren, ewigen Werten aufbauten und in ihrer Auswirkung zeitlos sind. Sie spricht in ihrer Echtheit und Einfachheit ganz besonders zum Menschen unseres Jahrhunderts, weil er sich inmitten seiner Krisen—Krieg, technische Versklavung, Umweltverseuchung und Sittenzerfall—vielleicht mehr als je zuvor nach einer höheren und sinnvolleren Lebensgestaltung sehnt."

16. My interest in Schwarz as a "forgotten woman" began when the campus bookstore was unable to obtain enough copies of texts for my Baroque seminar, and I, frustrated, checked out anthologies from the library to provide students with texts. Three of Schwarz's sonnets happened to be included in Schoolfield's anthology (see note 18). Further research produced "Sibylle Schwarz: Sex and the 17th-century Single Girl," presented at the 1985 South Central Modern Language meeting in Tulsa, Oklahoma, where the paper was retitled "Sibylle Schwarz: Gender and a Baroque Woman Writer."

17. Kurt von Faber du Faur, *German Baroque Literature: A Catalogue of the Collection in the Yale University Library.* The Faber du Faur collection is available on microfilm at most major research libraries. Schwarz's work is contained in volumes 271 and 272 of that collection.

18. George C. Schoolfield, *German Baroque Lyric*, 273–75.

19. See Carol Gilligan, *In a Different Voice: Psychological Theory and Women's Development.*

20. Henry and Mary Garland, *The Oxford Companion to German Literature*, state: "In the hyperbolic fashion of the age, she was sometimes termed 'die pommersche Sappho'" (p. 787).

21. Ziefle, *Sibylle Schwarz*, 257, perceptively notes the link between the attempted rape of the woman and the destruction of the land.

22. Schwarz dedicates many of her poems to Judith Tanck, but it seems to me that Ziefle has overemphasized Tanck's relationship to Schwarz, or at the very least placed a skewed focus on it. He sees Tanck as a mother-substitute or perhaps a love-object, but then contends that Sibylle never experienced love (p. 318). Ziefle, who believes that we live "in einer unsicheren Epoche" (p. 323), wavers between speculations about Sibylle's sexual orientation—was she overly dependent on Tanck in perhaps a homoerotic way, or did she actually want to become the second Frau Schöner?—and decided backpedaling. The whole matter of Schwarz's sexual orientation seems to me unrelated to a critical evaluation of what she wrote and how she wrote it.

Sonnets

1[1]

Had all wooers only some recourse,
Venus would not bestow on them so unequally
The reward of sweet love. She would then give mind to
What heartfelt loving is. Now one lover does this,

The other that; one wagers his blood,
The other does not. One commends himself to
Hope and patience, and the other resolves to hang himself.
Venus gives rewards according to merit; she is good to the true ones,

False to the false. How can she do otherwise,
Just because this one laments and weeps, and that one usually laughs?

Love has made me cold, and yet I burn as if I were a light.
Yet this is my custom: I keep quiet
About my pains, and do not vent
That which is within my heart: I both love and do not love.

2

If love is a fire and can make iron malleable,
And I am full of fire and the pain of love,

What then is the nature of my dearest one's heart?
If it were iron, I would have power over it;

If it were golden, I could shape it
With my glowing heat; what, however, if it is fashioned from flesh?
Then I conclude: it is a stone made of flesh:
Nevertheless a stone cannot deceive me as she has.

Is it then like frost, like cold snow and ice?
But if so, then how can she draw from me love's ardor?

It seems to me that her heart resembles laurel leaves
That are undisturbed by a strong thunderclap.
Cupid, she derides your arrows
And thus escapes love's stormy weather.

3

If questioning were worth anything, I might well ask:
Who brings me my pain? What is the reason for my loving and for
This love of mine, which is such a dear discomfort?
Cupid, have you brought my heart into such distress?

I accordingly want to bring suit against you, Cupid, and your bow.
But if my fiery desire causes hard-going on my part,
Is the virtue of the one whom I desire to blame?
But how then can I say contorted things about Venus?

Amor cannot be so strong as to touch my heart.
Caritas[2] led me to assume this burden.

My loving has assumed the manner wooers employ.
Amor is responsible for this; but it will make no impression on me,
Because you and I, my love, are only good friends,
Where then since time eternal has friendship sprung?

4

Love is blind, and nevertheless she can see.
She has vision and is yet glassy-eyed.
She is called great and is still a small child,
Steady on her feet and yet unable to walk.

Yet one must understand this in another fashion:
She cannot see, because her reason melts away

And because the eye that the heart possesses has grown dim,
So that she herself cannot see what has happened to her.

That which she loves has nothing wanting,
However often—even more than others—he fails.

That which she loves has no apparent weakness;
Yet because nothing here is without error,
So I conclude: love sees and is yet blind:
She cannot see herself and yet can give visions.

5

How can love's yoke be sweet and lovely,
When many a heart is accustomed to tell of love's pains
And lament its burdens and deep wounds?
How is that sweet that brings pain to all,

That acts upon hearts as a strong poison,
That strangles many a hero, daunting many of them;
How can it drive away joy and pleasure?
No, no, love's drink is the bitter wine of melancholy.

Still, love is by the same token sweet, because many are given
A pleasant life on account of her sweetness.

Accordingly I conclude that love is a pleasant pain
(However seldom it occurs that contrary characteristics
Can accrue simultaneously to one thing).
The nature of love is sweet bitterness.

6

Love does not spare the gods.
She can overcome everything;
She can bind fast all hearts
With the clear light of her eyes.

Even Apollo's heart breaks,
His clarity eclipsed.
He can find no rest,
For the arrow still lodges in him.

Jupiter himself is bound;
Hercules is overcome

With bittersweet pain.
How then can the hearts
Of mere mortals
Expect to be spared this pain?

7

To love is not to stand idle.
Love runs both day and night.
A heart in love resounds as it breaks
And nearly expires from distress.

Love ought not to be viewed as lazy.
Whether when sleeping or waking, love is
Considerate of the favor of the loved one.
Come what may,

Nothing can seem burdensome to love
Except the difficult pain of love.

One could call love an effort.
Amor is a fiery yoke
That extinguishes itself after awhile;
Otherwise it would consume too much.

8

Alas, Amor, take your heavy yoke from me.
If it is possible, take away love's cares.
Your yoke is cumbersome and accordingly I cannot bear it.
You are too sweet, and as a result I bring suit against you.

Take away the burden that rapidly oppresses me;
What should I say about your pills
Which are so bitter and yet suit me so well?
Caught up in doubt, I both stop and go.

Where should I go? When I am alone,
I only think: ah, if I could be with her!

If I am with her, departure is on my mind.
If she loves me, which I so desire,
The sweetness is yet too much of a burden.
I'd rather suffer death than love.

9

Cloris, your rosy cheeks,
The brightness of your eyes,
And your crimson visage
Now no longer imprison me.

I cannot continue to depend on you,
Because you take no pity
Even if my heart is breaking.
The magnificence of your disdain and arrogance

And your mocking disposition
So sicken my youthful temperament

That I gladly intend to avoid you,
Except that my Galatea,
Who occasions such sweet pain in me,
Wants to suffer in its service.

10

O might I now sing beautifully of your beauty!
O noble demi-goddess! Your lofty virtue
Shines like the sunlight, and fairly takes my breath away.
I will raise your high praise to the very roof of heaven.

There you shall move beyond envy and all misfortune.
Your beautiful glance breaks forth like the sun.
Your crimson visage and everything else about you
Is divine throughout. You can well have mastery over hearts.

Your mouth is rosy red, your breast alabaster.
You, O Galatea, might well be a second Venus.

Your virtue testifies to that, your lovely glance, your smile,
You are a handmaiden to the nymphs; a woman who
Can kill a man with love as soon as he beholds her.
There is not the like of the splendor of your beauty.

11

It is well and good to treasure chaste love.
It is goodness itself. Whoever gives himself over to it completely
Is loved in return, and loves. He loves and is loved.
He can delight eternally in sweet desire.

In the end he even escapes death's grim embrace
And as long as he lives experiences no discomfort,
Because he possesses joy. If he practices love,
Misfortune cannot injure him at any time.

He lives in true peace, in constant unanimity.
He has no need of battlefields, for his sweet battles are fought elsewhere.

Who would not be pleased by this delightful state of affairs
That nourishes us as bread does? He would have to be inhuman,
Who dies in the process of living. He is a clod, a stone,
A wooden image with a heart of metal.

12

If love is chaste, what then accounts for adultery?
If love is good, with nothing evil to be found in it,
How can its fire consume so many?
If love is joy, what then explains its burdens?

Whoever loves loving sails on a sea of lust
And lets himself be bound up in death's net,
Which does not tear. He loves only sin.
Loves vanity, and is empty of virtue.

He is dead to things eternal
And sees his predicament only when he sees his grave.

Whoever now is found in love's ardor,
May he soon behold and hate whom he loves;
I love sweet to him? He will accordingly be distressed.
Is love his bread? May he give it to the dogs.

13

I will go away into the forest and hunt with Diana!
I love, and that I love pleases me in no way,
For love is an endeavor that destroys all good things.
My misery is too encompassing. I am so tormented

That my conscience sickens and yet everlastingly clings to longing
For that which I cannot have. The mean-spirited gout of love,
The painful sickness of irrationality have so caught hold of me
That I am no longer myself. Now I will cast off love

As much as I can, for unfounded loyalty
Is never a peaceful thing and brings—often too late—rue;

Love is a consuming fire that never burns itself out,
Is blindness, is wind, and consuming fire. It is a spoiler of youth.
Love is a good badness and a burdensome virtue;
Be what it may, love has caused me to be listless and burned out.

14

They say that there is no place where Amor is not to be found.
There is no desolate forest or any part of the world
Where this great prince does not hold court.
They say that there is no one whom he cannot master.

Yet he will not be able to overcome my spirit,
Because at no time do I favor his despicable behavior.
Even if he were to set up his tent however far from here,
He would always be found in Arabia.

Europe is certainly his; he sits in Africa;
He lives in Asia, and is familiar with America.

To sum up, no house is closed to him,
No human heart unmoved by him.
He, however, cannot infect me, even if he is near,
For if he is in the village, I will be found in the city.

15

Alas, will you leave me,
O dearest Galatea?
You are of the opinion that I must hate one
Whom I do not see?

No, my love is of such degree
That I would die for you
And melt like the snow
That Apollo is wont to thaw.

You are my joy and bliss
And the sun of my heart.

Ah, see, I am committed
To that which you little love,
And the lifestyle of happy Venus
Distresses me so.

16

My all is gone, my comfort in pleasure and pain,
My second self is gone, my life and my adornment,
My dearest in the world is gone, is already gone from here.
(Love is indeed bitter, but parting even more so).

I cannot be away from you. I cannot avoid you entirely.
O, dearest Dorile! I am no longer by myself.
I am not what I am, if I am not now with you.
Run on, you hours! Will you, too, still envy me?

Apollo, do not rein in your horses!
Quickly, quickly, you days! Come quickly, moonlight!

A day to me seems like a year in which I cannot see
My second sunshine! Quickly, quickly, idle time! Lift your sails
And bring my love today,
And when she is here, then you, time, may pass quite slowly.

On the Blessed Passing of Herr J. Jaeger's Housekeeper[3]

Even if the false tongues
That have spoken against me
Have succeeded
In silencing the strings
Of my lyre,
And ennervating me,

I still cannot leave off writing.
I shall grasp my pen,
Come what may.
Alas, it is a pity that
Those whom all ought to love readily
Have instead become victims.

Her cheeks have paled,
The warm spirit has slipped away,
The windows of her mind[4] are closed,
And no limb stirs.

The pulse that once pounded
Now rests at peace.

I am told that there is great pain
In loving and parting.
Thus, your pain,
Herr Jaeger, goes right to my heart.
Your agony grieves me
More than if it were mine.

I picture your laments
And your words in my mind:
"Where, where is my treasure?"
How much you must grieve,
How often you must think of her
And speak these words:

"You used to light the lamps.
You used to walk with me."
There she stood by the door.
As soon as she'd sit down beside me,
She'd busily be up and about.
Now she's never coming back.

"The house is too small for me.
I do nothing but cry.
I don't go to meals,
As food and drink
And all that is pleasurable are forgotten.
Neither meat nor fish have any taste for me anymore."

Oh, if I could ban you, death,
You father of tyrants
And mother of distress!
You may take away with you
The ringing sounds of lamentation,
You insatiable death!

Nevertheless be comforted, Herr Jaeger,
Even though distress is now at its greatest.
Certainly a day will come
When we will be reunited

With those who have been taken from us.
We follow them, in any event, soon enough.

Wherever I myself turn,
Things are drawing to a close.
War consumes so many lives.
And there so many who are ill,
Who, even while still in life's confines,
Are moving steadily toward their goal.

Give yourself over to God's will!
These pills prescribed for us are indeed bitter.

A Daughter Gives Suck to Her Mother[5]

O mother, you lie under such heavy bonds,
In iron and steel, bound hand and foot,
Brought to great distress by hunger and thirst,
That nothing may help you other than eventual death.
What should I do for you? You have raised me.
I will give you back what you have given me: you have suckled me.
Come, let me give you suck. Come, take bread and wine.
We both can be mothers and daughters.

Some Epigrams[6]

1. CONCERNING THOSE WHO SEEK TO BECOME FAMOUS BY TRAVELING WIDELY

He who would be well-traveled should journey far and wide
In the Holy Scripture. Those roads lead to blessedness.
He who would be well-traveled should journey through the Bible's
books,
For the whole world can be seen there.
He who holds a passport to travel in God's lands
Has no need of any other type of travel.

2. WHO CAN PLEASE EVERYONE?

Even though the Almighty's hand has created the whole world
So that nothing therein is lacking, still there is yet to be

Born in this world a person who can please everyone,
And the world would indeed have to end before such a person were born.

3. VIRTUE ENDURES

Even though virtue is totally scorned by man,
It ultimately wears a crown made by God.

A Song Against Envy[7]

If envy had a thousand tongues
And had stuck out more than a thousand at me,
And were to attack me,
I would nevertheless not be frightened.
Whoever trusts God in all things
Will triumph over the world, envy, and death.

All around me I hear
The songs of most poisonous Sirens.
Their lovely, clear, and yet sickening tones
Shall nevertheless not vanquish me.
I shall stop up my ears
And rise far above these Sirens.

If you do not find pleasant
My poor work and the noble sap my pen contains,
Then you can quickly stop reading it
Before it causes you further distress.
That which I write, I assert from the beginning,
Will remain no false friend.

Do you know me to be given to prattling,
To abandon my lyre,
To delight in seeing
Industrious people going idle?
Drop this slander with which
You intend to wear me down.

I know that it is second nature to you
To be ill-disposed toward the Muses.
Yet my Apollo has never lost
His brilliant visage on account of your treachery.

Virtue shall nevertheless remain
Even after you and all other things pass away.

A vicious animal has raised you, and
The goddesses of Hell have
Given you suck at their granite breasts,
And Momus[8] announces himself as your father.
Your country of origin is desert waste,
Where basilisks and owls nest.

Should I on your account hate
Ever-green Helicon?
Were I to descend to your level,
I would indeed suffer bad fortune.
No, I will remain on Parnassus' heights,
While you may sit in Pluto's kingdom.

What indeed would my Phoebus say
If I were to snatch the laurel wreath
From my head
And toss it into the dust?
Euterpe would be annoyed
If her handmaiden were cast out.

Thalia would take umbrage
And Clio[9] would be greatly angered
If I were to abandon my worthy lyre
And love envy and calumny more than it.
Accordingly, may you leave off with the wrangling
In which you engage to make the worst of my tender years?

Does it not occur to you that it is fitting
That the female sex also
Has access to the Pindus?[10]
So it is equally right that all who approach him with humility
Are well-received by Phoebus Apollo.

I need not go further
And introduce strong evidence,
As you can see well enough
That the Muses themselves are maidens.
All who live should honor virtue
And no one should be driven from it.

All of Holland knows well to describe
Its flowers day and night.

You might well ask Herr Cats,[11]
Who first introduced me to these flowers.
Cleobulina[12] will certainly be
Described by many clever pens.

What sort of a woman among women Sappho was,
Which I do not now describe.
You can read that elsewhere.
I know fifty-eight of these heaven-enshrined females
Who never disappear
And who count their places in the starry firmament.

If I were to praise
My poetic voice too high,
Then a more clever person would surely inform me
That everything finally disintegrates.
Who can twist thread so artfully
That it doesn't come to pieces?

Bring from all corners of the earth
All that humans have considered
And all that has been made known afar
From the hands of clever masters,
And let it remain a thousand years.
It will disintegrate on its own.

Where then is Diana's place of worship?
Jupiter's image is gone from it.
Was it not earlier that the thick walls of Babylon
Were erected?
All that was earlier held to be valuable
Now counts as ash and dust.

Yet that written by Naso[13]
And uttered by Aristotle
Is still available to us today
And has not been hunted into an early grave.
These works live still, although dead,
And have earned eternal praise.

All that the multitude of clever people teaches us
Is communicated through the power of the pen,
Depends on the pipings of Fama,[14]
And is reported to us as news.

Her praise resounds near and far
Until all passes away.

Even if the whole world were
Made up of black ink,
That which one finds written
By those whose winged thoughts
Did not stray from the path of wisdom
Could not be blotted out.

My Opitz[15]—he who has earned the praise
That Germany has given to him
On account of his magnificent language and his poetic lyre,
For he laid the foundation for German poetry—
Is well described above
By those who love art and virtue.

His reputation will not be obscured.
No envy clouds praise of him,
For all who live
Are amazed at his artistry.
Oh, if I could sing only half as well
And coax from my lyres such tones as his!

Envy, cease your calumny!
I know that I am better off without you.
Even if I wrote no more poetry
And left all this behind,
I could deal confidently with the future.
You shall not oppress me.

I will henceforth trust in God,
From whom all poetry comes.
Thus I cannot fear you.
I say once again and with justification:
He who trusts God in all things
Will overcome this world, envy, and death.

The Happiness We Had at Fretow[16]

Even if the whole world were abloom,
There still would be something else that could promise delight,
And even if one could completely scorn that world,
Something pleasing would still retain its hold,

Something that would still be praised and cherished: no sorrow, no lament
Is so great that it can give the lie to that chosen thing
That delights the mind's eye; after sighing, oh, and pain,
Nevertheless comes again to me that chosen time, rich in joy,
That quickens heart and mind; it is just as when we
See Apollo shining more brightly after rain. Joy shares the scales
With sorrow. One would have to be inhuman
Not to find something that is so personally pleasing
And that is self-chosen. Even as I write this,
I see Fretow before me, and I find such delight in it,
This meadow where friendship still blooms, this transformer of distress,
Inexorable mortality's death, where the Muses come into their own
And the soul gains its wings. Another might praise goods;
I, however, praise and love only our faithful mothers, the Muses
Who chose Fretow. The meadow and the beautiful valley,
Are adorned throughout with friendship—
That place, the most beautiful of all places, where near the cool springs
The Muses offer delight and commence their dance.
Fecund[17] Pan himself plays about so dearly with
The nymphs, as is his rogue-like wont, as long as
All are favorably inclined. Here too one sees
The entire host of satyrs and groups of naiads running about.
It is said that Venus fell in love here for the first time.
Accordingly she gives us this place to inhabit,
So that love might stay here, in this place, and
Be ruler here. I shall therefore write
Of the delight of this place. Here one sees in every bush
Love's image, at every fountain, too.
Here true friends walk, and there the gods sit
Who protect our dear meadow from enemies.
The host of clever sister Muses sing so sweetly here
That a mortal could never hear the like better.
Here the worthy Muses keep watch
Over what friendships their children establish.
Heaven itself smiles, because it too
Is pleased with the loyalty and honesty that has
Come here from all; hill and mountain
Are covered with flowers; one hears echoes;
Even the dead live there; one sees nothing other than delight,
Which cityfolk eschew completely.
Now you ask what it is that
Each and all came running

To our company and called the crooked leaping calves the sun's cattle,
Of which Homer writes. They are pastured here
And the sheep live here too
That Ulysses relied upon when he hid under their bellies;
Here too the white cows that Argus tended and ran with
Down to the meadows. And this clear air delights
None other than joined here. We see gods when
Apollo draws his mist over us.
The craft of writing makes us all sit together nearly every day
And listen eagerly on the heights of Parnassus
To the threefold triple choir of the Muses that fuses heart and mind
And draws us from the earth even unto the stars.
And could anyone question us
Who is not knowledgeable of this pleasure,
Who lives only in the city, where nothing but war and strife
Alternate in dreadful rumors and hard, ironlike times?
These times lend their name in fact to this village.
Its name is not of Greek origin,
Or Arabic, for that matter, for Fretow is a word
That belongs ultimately to simple people, to farmers,
For it first passed people's lips
And stuck to this village
When farmers in their fields only thought of their ploughs
And did not hold much with words,
Because that was not their calling; the names should stay.
But were it necessary, one could give many names to this place,
Many names of which it is worthy and which it fully deserves.
It is a place where one can lay aside care's burden. It is
An abode of all delight, chosen by Pallas,
A masterpiece of nature. It is a magnificent existence
That pleases the gods, a place that nurtures friendship
And casts aside all enmity and strife.
If it could be described rightly, one could freely say:
A place where one can wager an entire well-being
And all sensibilities, a place praised by the gods
And chosen for their dancing, an earthly paradise,
A steadfast fortress of friendship. For friendship is and remains
The same impetus that drives my pen.
This friendship is my consolation. It is my counsel.
This friendship, which has nearly been my undoing,
Is my highest pleasure. Oh, if God could grant
That He would love my Fretow as I love it.
Damon and Pythias, who were the first ones to wear the radiant

Crown of friendship, should not be as famed for it
As is the radiant friendship that illuminates Fretow.
Alas, I wish, if I only could, alas, I would
Go then to my friends. There I would be in complete peace
And totally without distress. On account of the gifts that this friendship
 has conferred,
Fretow ought well to take its rightful place in the firmament
And be valued above all things, however great,
That are held in esteem on this earth,
And that this earth supports. To be sure, Fretow boasts no advantages
That cater only to surface, rather than to inner beauty.
In Fretow there is no fool's gold;
Friendship here is golden, despite the lack of gold.
Here there are no buildings that reach up toward Heaven
And yet barely retreat from Hell,
For that is actually lowliness that is elevated
And is arrogance toward God, who Himself sits above in humility,
And is quite far removed from pride. Here are no walls
Thirty ells thick. Here instead have the farmers
Built us a hedge of bushes to ring our friendship,
So that the enemy cannot tread on this sand,
Which can bear only the weight of friendship. Here there
Are no monuments to be seen that take twenty years or longer to build.
No artificial representation of the sun has been created,
Which is said to be precious and yet does not endure.
Diana's temple is also not to be found here,
In which one hardly knows, after lo these many years, how to perform.
Here no image of Jupiter has been constructed,
Which, although it is indeed handsome, still will crumble.
Here is no artificial mechanism
That is given like a sign to ships so that they might reach port
As soon as they spy the light set within it
That keeps them from straying in the darkness.
Here is no magical mountain that spews forth boiling resin
As did Vesuvius, wildly sending its flames
Toward Heaven. Here one sees no crypts
That are gold-encrusted beyond belief.
There is here, however, a monument upon which nature has set its seal,
A good masterwork, well worth the praise it has
Earned and that ought to be celebrated in books: this is my Fretow,
Where simplicity itself dwells much better
Than in those places where one can find beautiful works of art.
Here, here are love and loyalty that do not pass away as easily

As the efforts of man. As a result one finds Fretow
In full bloom and flourishing, as long as there are books
And virtue above. Here virtue has
Chosen an abode and has joined with us in marriage.
Virtue cannot abide deception or treachery or falseness
And prefers to view simplicity's clarity
Rather than a magnificent castle. Virtue intends to honor us,
Since we have rigorously traveled her path.
Thalia is even now in the process of making us a laurel wreath.
Friendship deserves this well-earned reward.
Blessed be those who could stay here only
And pass the remainder of their days here in loyal friendship!
What then can death threaten, or envy, for that matter,
To those freed of all that is mortal?
Alas, if I could just graze sheep here forever,
How gladly I would take on the name of a shepherd!
Make a grave for me here, for Fretow is my goal,
And when I am there, only there, I am then where I want to be.

Susanna[18]

Each time Eurimedes, a judge, sees Susanna coming and going about her business, he discusses her with Heracleon, an unscrupulous judge who also lusts after Susanna. Eurimedes determines that he and Heracleon suffer from the same heartsickness.

Eurimedes. How can I be silent concerning such distress?
How long can one heart's anguish, bittersweet pain,
And consuming fire remain hidden?
Two hearts—mine and yours—have fed
This fire until it has blazed
And become a conflagration that draws from a single intent.
Whenever we meet, we cannot remain silent
Concerning the fire of our ardent desire for Susanna—we must
Reveal to each other our need and pain,
And if anything is to help us, it would certainly be death.

Has not this image of beauty, this Susanna, captivated us?
Has not Amor now assailed two men's minds
At the same time? Her very demeanor attests to this desire
As she goes about her business. Those dazzling rays
Illuminate our inward desire,

Where our dawn rises. The very sun with his speedy horses
Does not rush by as quickly as our own eyebeams
Chase after this sun, Susanna, who gives us such pain.
But what is one to do when one is in such great distress?
We both love. Accordingly the same medicine
Applies to us both—it will kill or cure us both.
We seek the same reward and would gladly do the same deed.

We know that not a day goes by
That Susanna does not bathe. So we can easily
And secretly go to her and hide ourselves on the grounds.
Certainly we cannot keep silent about our desire.
We'll climb her garden wall
And hide among the trees,
And when we see that she is alone
We can then satisfy our common desire.
Let us then remain very quiet and await her here.
We suffer from a discomfort
That none other than Susanna can assuage.

Heracleon. Look, does she not approach, she whom I most desire?
We can now set our plan into motion.

Susanna to her maidens. Fetch me what is necessary for my bath,
The balsam,
The soap and everything else I need.
Shut the gate, so that no one disturbs me here.
Go, my maids, and
Bring me what I have requested.

Eurimedes and Heracleon come out of the corner where they had hidden themselves, unbeknownst to Susanna, and embrace her.

Eurimedes. Oh, lovely one, your beauty's power
Has brought us to this enterprise
Upon which we are now engaged.
Oh, think of our burden!
Might we enjoy your favors,
As we are so smitten with you?

Note, O beautiful one, that we
Are here with you in secret
And that we cannot live
Unless you grant us love's reward

And the possession
Of your chaste crown of virtue.

What? You turn your delightful countenance
Away from us,
This visage that heartens us so?
You attempt to flee?
Consider then that we
Already have you in our arms.

If you are not obedient to our will,
Pain can easily bring you
Around to our way of thinking.
A false "discovery"
Might change your mind.
Yes, we can take it so far

That life or death
Might seem equally pleasurable
Or painful to you.
We'll invent a lover,
A stranger to this neighborhood,
To whom you were in the process of granting your favors!

And add what follows to this:
That you regularly reserved
This respite in your day for him.
He ran away in a great rush
And left you, I shall contend,
In the lurch.
Susanna. My God! Oh, I turn pale!
How have I deserved this?
Which is better: the fictitious desire of a young man
Or the preservation of my chastity?
If I decide that it is necessary to sacrifice my chastity,
Then falsehood will be the ruin of me.
Yet if I uphold my chastity, I effectively choose death.
Still, still, we all must die sometime.

That I stand here, bereft of my clothes,
And that I stand ashamed before evil-doers,
Increases and even doubles my pain,
And I am, poor me, alone.
Nevertheless, because falseness eventually cannot hold its own,
I shall abandon my cowardice completely.

After all, those who carry out "justice" on this earth will desire
Despicable beauty as long as it exists.

Oh, you evil-doers, let me go!
Be aware that God, who sits above us all,
Does not tolerate shame and in fact protects chastity.
Listen to my request, my lamenting entreaty!
Consider, *consider,* that God
Will reward you for this!
If I give up my chastity, I will be scorned.
Help, oh help me, my servants! Soon I shall take cold.
Eurimedes calls the servants. Come, everyone, see the shame
This "chaste" one has called upon herself,
For you will never find anything so scandalous
In all the land.
Throw wide the garden gate
And spread the word
To all whom you see.
Heracleon. Look how it is with this "chaste" one!
She believes that she can
Earn praise for bad behavior.
But because of what we have seen here,
Justice must be served.
Come, everyone, come and see
What has never been seen before.
The Populace. What is all this commotion about?
Oh, what has happened to
Susanna, most virtuous of women?
Heracleon. Tell it, bring it before her husband
That she did not want to preserve her chastity,
As a woman ought.
We saw her here,
With a young man beside her,
Who, as soon as he became aware of us,
Ran off hastily.
Therefore let it be formally charged
That this "chaste" one has engaged in unsuitable behavior.
Let us gather here tomorrow
So that she may be damned and condemned.
Susanna. My God, against whom no human has power,
Must judge today, because these judges are
Acting unjustly. Still, still, why do I lament so much?
Friend and enemy contend here: chastity is my goal,

Which fights against beauty. If these,
Who are never allies, behave as if they were allies,
Then the sun would have to shine at night.
Joaichim. Oh, this sight!
Oh, this red mouth! Then death is certainly here
Where life once was. Oh, my most beautiful one, oh, my joy!
If you are lost to me, I see no sunshine
And I must live without light.
Susanna. No, if it pleases God,
I am neither your sunshine nor your whole world.
I see them already, coming toward us,
Those robbers of my honor, who spread their lies about me so boastfully,
As if they were pure golden truth. Nevertheless I await them here.
They can take only my body, and I shall retain my soul.
Eurimedes. Let this despicable woman come forth,
The one who accepted the foolish reasoning
That chastity is tantamount to death.
Seize her and bring her to judgment.
This is no fabricated story.
Rather, it is the truth.
Susanna. So be it! I have been told
That a complaint has been lodged against me,
And that I must come before the court.
God, O judge of all the world!
Since truth is dear to you,
Take away my earthly adornments.
My parents, my relatives, come!
Come with me, my friends and acquaintances.
Watch the "death" of chastity,
Which is condemned to death on account of its appearance.
Watch it disappear before your eyes.
But it can never perish.
Eurimedes. Is that not she approaching,
She who has earned the death penalty?
Now she shall rightly receive
What justice metes out
As a vile reward to
Women who so contrive.
Heracleon. Tear off her veil
And let her stand uncovered,
Because she will see
Her own grave before her today.

Therefore let all see
Her face.

Come before the court,
In order that judgment may be rendered,
That one might hear
Whether this accusation stems from Hell
Or if Heaven's course can
Bear such a burden.
Eurimedes. And I shall place my hand upon her head
And swear before all concerning her evil ways.
Susanna. I trust in God,
Who never deceives,
He who has ordered
Life and death according to His will.
Eurimedes. Often as we strolled at her garden's edge,
Enjoying the splendor of its flowers or its fruits,
This demented woman bathed, as she was wont to do,
And as soon as she had cast off her clothes
And commanded her maidens to withdraw,
We saw a young man stand beside her
In great sexual excitement. We concluded that
We could see nothing virtuous going on there
(And we attest to this). As soon as they became aware of us,
This young man, whoever he was, ran off hastily.
We brought her here, however,
So that someone, in any event, might soon be punished.
The Populace. How can judges themselves lie?
We all agree: judges' testimony must stand.
Susanna's evil behavior is apparent to all.
It is just that she should be condemned to death.
Susanna. It is up to you, God, to rectify this,
And I trust you completely.
You can see everything that is hidden.
I will stand fast,
Since I have no fear of death.

To you the secrets of all hearts
Are open and
Uncovered.
You see all things
That have occurred,
And you can also recognize envy.

Even as much as Eurimedes has condemned me to death,
No one has asked or asks
If I am innocent.
Still you, my God, know that
These judges' claims
Far outstrip reality.
Daniel. Stop! And pay good heed
And listen
To all that I shall reveal.
Leave this chaste one in peace.
My soul cannot bear the burden of
Any harm done to this woman.

(End of fragment)

NOTES TO THE TRANSLATIONS

1. The sonnets are found in vol. 2, pp. O3–P3.
2. *Caritas* may be defined as spiritual rather than carnal love (*cupiditas*).
3. Vol. 1, pp. 23–25.
4. Schwarz's words here are "der Stirne Fenster," which I have freely translated.
5. Vol. 2, pp. K1v–K2r. Poem is translated from the Dutch.
6. Vol. 2, pp. D4v–D4r.
7. Vol. 1, pp. 6–10.
8. Momus is "fault-finding personified" (*Oxford Classical Dictionary,* 2d ed. [1970], 697).
9. Euterpe is the Muse of Music, Thalia the Muse of Comedy, and Clio the Muse of History.
10. The Pindus is a mountain range in Greece.
11. Sibylle here refers to the Dutch poet Jacob Cats, *Alle de Wercken, so ouden als nieuwe* (Amsterdam: Schipper, 1655).
12. Cleobulina was the daughter of Cleobulus, the Tyrant of Lindus and one of the seven sages of Greece in the 6th century B.C. Cleobulus was famed for his riddles, and his daughter invented a riddle each year for thirty years.
13. Naso is an alternate name for Ovid.
14. Fama is rumor.
15. The reference is to Martin Opitz (1597–1639), author of *Das Buch von der deutschen Poeterey,* in which he contended that German as a language was just as suitable for poetry as French or Italian.
16. Vol. 1, pp. 13–15.
17. The literal meaning here is "green Pan."
18. Vol. 2, pp. M4r–N4r.

BIBLIOGRAPHY

Primary Works

Faber du Faur, Kurt von. *German Baroque Literature: A Catalogue of the Collection in the Yale University Library.* New Haven: Yale University Press, 1958–69.

Schwarz, Sibylle. *Deutsche Poetische Gedichte.* 2 vols. Danzig: Georg Rheten Witwen, 1650. (Volume one: Sibyllen Schwarzin, Vohn Greiffswald aus Pommern, *Deutsche Poetische Gedichte.* Volume two: Sibyllen Schwarzin, Von Greiffswald aus Pommern, *Ander Teil Deutscher Poëtischer Gedichten.*)

Related Works

Alewyn, Richard, ed. *Deutsche Barockforschung: Dokument einer Epoche.* Cologne: Kiepenheuer und Witsch, 1965.

Bircher, Martin, and Alois Haas, eds. *Deutsche Barocklyrik.* Bern: Francke, 1973.

Browning, Robert M. *German Baroque Poetry 1618–1723.* University Park, Pennsylvania: Pennsylvania State University Press, 1971.

Crusius, Daniel R. "The Concept of the Poet in Baroque Literature." *Monatshefte* 47 (1955): 393–99.

De Capua, A. G. *German Baroque Poetry: Interpretative Readings.* Albany: State University of New York Press, 1973.

Garland, Henry and Mary. *The Oxford Companion to German Literature.* Oxford: Clarendon Press, 1976.

Gilligan, Carol. *In a Different Voice: Psychological Theory and Women's Development.* Cambridge: Harvard University Press, 1982.

Gillespie, Gerald. *German Baroque Poetry.* Twayne's World Authors Series, 103. New York: Twayne, 1971.

Hoffmeister, Gerhard, ed. *German Baroque Literature in the European Perspective.* New York: Ungar, 1983.

———. "Barocker Petrarkismus: Wandlungen und Möglichkeiten der Liebessprache in der Lyrik des 17. Jahrhunderts." In *Europäische Tradition und deutscher Literaturbarock: Internationale Beiträge zum Problem von Überlieferung und Umgestaltung.* Bern: Francke, 1973.

Leighton, Joseph. "Deutsche Sonett-Theorie im 17. Jahrhundert." In *Europäische Tradition und deutscher Literaturbarock,* edited by Gerhart Hoffmeister. Munich: Francke, 1973.

Morhof, Daniel Georg. *Unterricht von der teutschen Sprache und Poesie.* Kiel: J. Reumann, 1682.

Newald, Richard. *Die deutsche Literatur: Vom Späthumanismus zur Empfindsamkeit 1570–1750.* Munich: Beck, 1965.

Schoolfield, George C. *German Baroque Lyric.* University of North Carolina Studies in the Germanic Languages and Literatures, 19. Chapel Hill: University of North Carolina Press, 1961. Reprint. New York: AMS Press, 1966.

Steinhagen, Harald and Benno von Wiese. *Deutsche Dichter des 17. Jahrhunderts: Ihr Leben und Werk.* Berlin: Schmidt, 1984.

Szyrocki, Marian. *Die deutsche Literatur des Barock.* Stuttgart: Reclam, 1979.

Wehrli, Max, ed. *Deutsche Barocklyrik.* Basel: Schwabe, 1963.

Wilms, Heinz. "Zur Lyrik des 17. Jahrhunderts." *Doitsu Bungaku* 35 (1965): 91–103.

Ziefle, Helmut W. *Sibylle Schwarz: Leben und Werk.* Bonn: Bouvier, 1975.

PROTESTANT CLARION IN THE HABSBURG EMPIRE

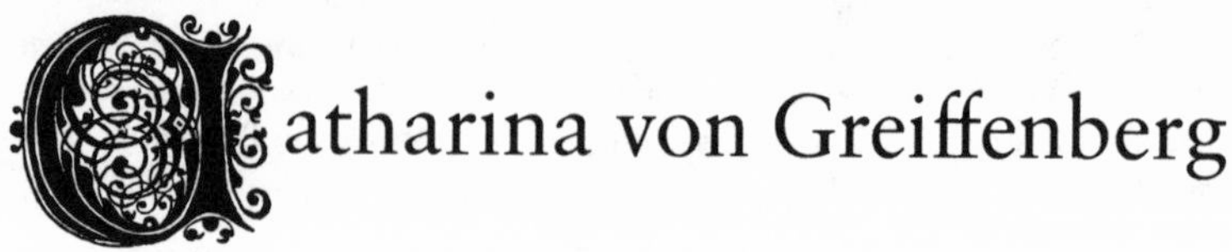

Catharina von Greiffenberg

HELENE M. KASTINGER RILEY

Catharina von Greiffenberg was twenty-eight years old when her *Geistliche Sonnette / Lieder und Gedichte / zu Gottseeligem Zeitvertreib* appeared in 1662. The volume contained 250 sonnets, 52 "songs" (*Lieder*), and 48 additional poems—all of varying quality and apparently selected from a corpus of lyric poetry which Catharina had written over the years. The collection was not her first published work, but poems that appeared earlier did not bear her name; the custom of the time frowned on female authors.[1] Consequently, problems of authorship and questions concerning the arrangement of the poems in the *Sonnets* occupy a substantial part of scholarly inquiry dealing with Greiffenberg's work.[2]

The publication of a woman's work in the seventeenth century is in itself noteworthy, but Catharina was also highly praised by her peers. The poet Sigmund von Birken of Nuremberg, who had edited and sponsored her manuscript for publication, hailed Catharina as the "German Urania."[3] He, in turn, had become acquainted with Catharina's work through her literary mentor, Johann Wilhelm von Stubenberg, whose residence at Burg Schallaburg in Lower Austria was not far from Catharina's familial castle Burg Seissenegg. Stubenberg was a personal friend of Harsdörffer and Birken—the founders of the *Pegnesische Blumenorden*—and was himself a member of the *Fruchtbringende Gesellschaft*. These two literary societies, the so-called Floral Order of Pegnitz and the Fruitbearing Society, were among the foremost of numerous *Sprachgesellschaften* founded in the seventeenth century to further studies in German philology and poetics. Stubenberg was also an active literary dilettante and translator. In the midst of the Counter-Reformation, he and his literary circle of Protestants in Lower Austria supported Catharina's poetic mission to convert Austria's imperial house from Catholicism.[4] While Catharina never clearly stated this intent, the *Sonnets* contain a number of veiled references to it, for example, the statement in sonnet 34 that God, the almighty and all-powerful, can aid the speaker in a "supremely grand task" ("ein eusserst hohe sach"). Stubenberg's letter to Birken of November 13, 1659, also gives some clues. He writes about Catharina: "She has created almost life-sized images of a crown, scepter, sword, orb and eagle, composed entirely of verse, for the emperor of the Holy Roman Empire." The visual aspect remained an important part of her technique. Had she succeeded in converting the emperor to the Protestant faith, of course, she would have attained instant recognition. Given these religiously motivated political ambitions, combined with the seclusion in which she wrote and the acclaim she received, it is no surprise that another large segment of Greiffenberg research covers biographical concerns, her comparative place among peers, and her interaction with her contemporaries.[5]

Yet Catharina von Greiffenberg had no peers among men. Like other women of her time with keen intellectual qualities, she acquired her education outside the mainstream of learning, in spiritual isolation, and subject to the haphazard methods of autodidacticism. When Brinker-Gabler calls her the "most significant poetess of the Baroque formal tradition,"[6] Catharina's accomplishment must be viewed from within the context of opportunities available to her at the time. Brinker-Gabler delineates the governing criteria for literary "acceptability":

> Opitz, who had first published a poetic for German literature in 1624 with rules for metrics, choice of terms, syntax, and verbal embellishment, had several successors in the same century. Among them were Zesen, Schottel, Harsdörffer, Buchner, and Birken. Without exception it was men who decided what skills a poet had to learn, and the institutions of learning and education which taught these skills were open only to men. The universities first encouraged the new style. There was scarcely a poet (and that is true for the following centuries as well) who did not attend a university, make contacts, find friends and benefactors, and who did not travel to continue his education. The literary societies [*Sprachgesellschaften*] which spread quickly in the 17th century also saw their task in the encouragement of education and especially of German language and poetry. Women were denied entry to both institutions. (p. 31)

Some of the *Sprachgesellschaften* later made exceptions to the rule excluding women. The first of these societies was the *Fruchtbringende Gesellschaft,* which accepted the chairman's wife in 1668. She remained the sole female member. Phillipp von Zesen, founder of the *Deutschgesinnte Genossenschaft* (German-minded Association), admitted two female members, of whom the first was Catharina von Greiffenberg. Catharina also belonged to an Austrian association of poetry-writing women, the *Ister-Nymphen-Gesellschaft* (Ister-Nymphs Society), and later became a member of Harsdörffer's and Birken's *Pegnesischer Blumenorden.* Clearly, Catharina had gained acceptance among the leading stylists and formalists of her time, although she "belonged to no school" and her work "escaped the normalizing effects of poetizing as a form of social intercourse."[7] This independence of thought, spirit, and craftsmanship she shared with most creative women of the seventeenth, eighteenth, and nineteenth centuries. Their innovative and fresh approach to art grew out of the restricted educational opportunities they encountered—a positive development from a negative influence. The absence of epoch-defining characteristics in women's literary creations has frequently been interpreted as evidence of their "modernity." A recent study ascribes this trait to Catharina's work as well.[8]

Still, Catharina received a careful upbringing and education within the limits set for women in the seventeenth century. She was born in 1633 into a Protestant family of country nobility, and her religion became an extremely important aspect of her personality and striving. Her early childhood was spent with her younger sister under the supervision of her mother at Burg Seissenegg, a property near Amstetten in Lower Austria which her grandfather had acquired after ennoblement. Her father died when she was still a child, and her father's half brother, Hans Rudolf, became her guardian. Hans Rudolf, who reputedly was in love with her even during her childhood, personally took over her education with great care.

Catharina was a very devout person with two superb gifts: a fine intelligence and a talent for writing, both of which she dedicated to the service of God. Besides the instruction she received from Hans Rudolf, she devoted her time to secluded religious contemplation[9] and to reading and studying in private. Out of this personal contemplative thought grew her first poems. Hans Rudolf's benevolent support of his niece must soon have become insufficient for her intellectual development, for he was not knowledgeable about literary endeavors.[10] To a considerable extent Catharina must have taught herself, a fact mentioned repeatedly in letters among her various supporters.[11] Eventually Johann von Stubenberg became her literary mentor. In his letter of November 13, 1659, Stubenberg wrote to his friend Sigmund von Birken in Nuremberg that "Miss von Greiffenberg . . . is not only well known to me, but in a way she has been my pupil; she lives four miles from me at Seisenekk in Austria wherefore on earlier occasions she often . . . sent me her work for correction. Now the pupil has surpassed the master."[12] It is likely that Stubenberg rather than Hans Rudolf acquainted Catharina with the rules of Baroque poetics. By the time Catharina was in her twenties, she also knew Latin, French, Spanish, and Italian; in the 1680s, after her move to Nuremberg, she tackled Hebrew and Greek as well.

The death of her younger sister in 1651 and a subsequent vision Catharina had in the family's place of worship are customarily cited as the experiences that triggered a poetic sublimation of her grief. Without doubt Hans Rudolf's ardent devotion to her and his desire to marry her also created some tension at home. For a considerable time she resisted his wish. One of her early poems seems to mirror her attitude toward love in a rejoinder to Cupid. Her heart cannot be pierced by his arrows. She wants a poet's crown, not the thorny splendor of roses (love) or the modest beauty of myrtle (the traditional wedding flower of the bride): "Der Lorbeer soll mich zieren, / nicht deine Dornen-Ros' und Myrten-Sträuchelein."[13] These lines call into question the assumption of Kimmich and others that "at the time of their composition" Catharina had no intention of publishing her poems.[14]

Hans Rudolf von Greiffenberg heeded the wish of his beloved niece. Although the preface which introduced the first printed volume of Catharina's poems was signed with Hans Rudolf's name, he most likely did not write it.[15] He probably planned the publication with the help of Stubenberg, who was already acquainted with the quality of Catharina's work and had connections to Birken and his literary society in Nuremberg. Letters with Catharina's poems were written to Birken first by Stubenberg, then by Hans Rudolf between the fall of 1659 and the spring of 1660. Birken apparently liked the poems and offered to publish them. On June 5, 1660, Hans Rudolf replied, thanking Birken for his offer: "In accordance with your advice I will arrange the approx. 300 sonnets and other poems in a proper order and have them published under my name. However, a *printed preface* is to state that she [i.e., Catharina] wrote the poems and that I had them printed *without her knowledge* and to her honor. I have spoken with Mr. Endter who will print them at his own expense, and I will send him the work from Linz on the coming Bartholomew's Day." Hans Rudolf also asked the "Father of Poetic Arts" in his letter to correct the errors in his niece's poems where necessary and to honor the edition with a sonnet of his own and the "rich rhyme" of some other well-known Nurembergers.[16] Thus, Catharina von Greiffenberg's *Geistliche Sonnette / Lieder und Gedichte / zu Gottseeligem Zeitvertreib* were published in the spring of 1662 by Michael Endter in Nuremberg. The arrangement of the poems, their range of quality and the variety of structural composition, their use (or omission) of such conventions as asyndeton, "Baroque catalogue," metaphor, simile, and allegory, etc. have been discussed by literary critics. Catharina has been called unprofessional, a gifted amateur, an innovator, a master of poetic rhetoric, and the most notable female poet of the formal Baroque tradition. No doubt elements to support all these judgments can be found in her poems. Her first work clearly attracted attention among the knowledgeable then and now, and Catharina had her laurel wreath. Two years after the publication of the *Sonnets* in the fall of 1664, she married Hans Rudolf with the dispensation of the margrave of Bayreuth.

In the 1660s Catharina continued her writing in seclusion. She translated du Barta's *Triomphe de la foy,* which was later published under the title *Der Glaubens-Triumf* as an appendix to *Sieges-Seule der Buße und des Glaubens,* (Victory-Support of Penitence and Faith), 1675. The *Sieges-Seule,* begun shortly after the publication of the *Sonnets,* concerned a topic of such timely interest that it was clearly written to attract public attention. Catharina began this epic in alexandrines at the time of the second Turkish invasion in 1663. Horst Frank explains that it is "in the greater part a history of Islam in its interaction with Christianity, beginning with Mohammad and based on careful historical studies." Catharina develops this interaction of Islam with Christianity "as a history of evil in its worldly contest with sacred belief."[17] In addition to its religious didacticism, the epic also has the strongly patriotic orientation befitting the times of strife during which it was written.

The books that won her the greatest public acclaim and made her famous within her own lifetime were the devotionals (*Andachtsbücher*), the only literary production of her later years. These works, highly successful with the general public, consisted of reflections on, and interpretations of, biblical passages, interspersed with poems of her own suited to the text. Although these devotionals established her name as a public figure, literary scholars and standard reference works have passed them over.[18] De Boor/Newald, for instance, claims that Greiffenberg's twelve reflections on the Passion are "the most perfect poetic representation of *Jesusminne,*" but he says nothing further about them.[19] Only recently have Germanists and musicologists begun to ask whether the established artistic criteria on which scholars base the selection of their research topics (criteria which frequently exclude literary and musical works that were highly popular with audiences) do not in fact distort the history of creative endeavors in the arts.[20] Greiffenberg's devotionals, for instance, employ the mixing of genres that was later to become one of the characteristic features of German Romanticism. With the religious tomes of Clemens Brentano, one of the foremost representatives of that school, Catharina's devotionals may share not only the neglect but the significance as well.[21]

As a Protestant in a largely Catholic country during the Counter-Reformation, Catharina experienced considerable economic and religious difficulties as well as pressures from her non-Protestant peers. She had to defend both her confession and, after the death of her husband in 1677, her legal rights and her property.[22] To regain some peace, she left the ancestral castle at Seissenegg in 1680 and went to Nuremberg into voluntary exile. This decision in mid-life also marked the end of the spiritual and personal isolation to which the country estate in Austria had subjected her.

The last years of her life until her death in 1694 Catharina spent at the St. Egidienhof in Nuremberg. Pastor Georg Albrecht Hagedorn of St. Lorenz rendered the funeral sermon. The respect and adoration she was able to command could not be more clearly expressed than in the epitaph:

Schau hier am Stand Verstand die Edleste der Frauen
das Engel-Tugend-Bild den Wunder-Kunst-Pallast
Die doch in JESUnser hatt Ihre Ruh und Rast
Wer mehr wil Ihres Ruhms mag Ihre Schrifften schauen.
Aus unendlicher *Devotion* gesetzt von
L. Stockflethen, Kirchen-Rath u: Superint.[23]

(View on this pedestal Intellect, the noblest of Women,
the Image of Angelic Virtue, the Magical Palace of Art,
who yet has Peace and Repose in our Lord Jesus.
Let him who wants to know more of her Glory see her Writings.
Placed here in eternal devotion by
L. Stockflethen, Church Counselor and Superintendent.)

The poetry selections were chosen from several different collections to illustrate the diversity of form, technique, and metaphor of which Greiffenberg was capable.

NOTES

1. Joachim Rachel, Catharina's contemporary, claimed that women poets like Sappho endangered society with immoral behavior and wrote in his satirical poems published in 1664 that "the pen and the beard" are the sole prerogative of the male ("Zuletzt kein Männerwitz hat bey den Weibern Art/ Den Männern nur gehört die Feder und der Bart." [*Teutsche Satyrische Gedichte,* 8, Frankfurt: Vogel, 1664]). All translations from the German in this essay are mine.

2. Martin Bircher and Peter Daly, "Catharina Regina von Greiffenberg und Johann Wilhelm von Stubenberg: Zur Frage der Autorschaft zweier anonymer Widmungsgedichte," 17–35; Horst Frank, *C. R. v. Greiffenberg: Untersuchungen zu ihrer Persönlichkeit und Sonettdichtung,* 146–47; and others.

3. Flora Kimmich explains that "Birken furnished the volume with an emblematic etching and an explanatory poem, a poem in Catharina's honor, and a long 'Vor-Ansprache,' in the main an apologia for a female author" (*Sonnets of Catharina von Greiffenberg. Methods of Composition,* 13 n. 18).

4. Horst Frank, *Catharina Regina von Greiffenberg: Leben und Welt der barocken Dichterin,* attempts a reconstruction of this personal mission (see pp. 73–87 and passim).

5. Peter M. Daly, "Catharina Regina von Greiffenberg," 615–39; Lucy Jean Price, *The*

Emblematic and Meditative Poetry of John Donne, George Herbert, Andreas Gryphius, and Catharina Regina von Greiffenberg; Urs Herzog, "Literatur in Isolation und Einsamkeit: C. R. von Greiffenberg und ihr literarischer Freundeskreis," 515–46; Xaver Stalder, *Formen des barocken Stoizismus. Martin Opitz, Andreas Gryphius und Catharina Regina von Greiffenberg;* Martin Bircher, *Johann Wilhelm von Stubenberg und sein Freundeskreis,* esp. 198–204.

6. Gisela Brinker-Gabler, *Deutsche Dichterinnen vom 16. Jahrhundert bis zur Gegenwart,* 32.

7. Kimmich, *Sonnets,* 10.

8. Jane M. Mehl, "Catharina Regina von Greiffenberg: Modern Traits in a Baroque Poet," 54–63.

9. Horst Frank, *Leben und Welt,* describes her devotionals (pp. 91, 95).

10. The cumbersome style and haphazard orthography of his letters show him to be singularly unacquainted with the higher forms of writing.

11. See Kimmich, *Sonnets,* 9 n. 3.

12. Ibid., 11. See also Blake Lee Spahr, *The Archives of the Pegnesischer Blumenorden,* who describes the archives' holdings pertaining to Greiffenberg (pp. 38–50); and the primary source, Sigmund von Birken's papers in the archives of the *Pegnesische Blumenorden* (Germanisches Nationalmuseum, Nürnberg), which contains letters from Catharina, Hans Rudolf von Greiffenberg, and Stubenberg, as well as other pertinent correspondence from the years 1659–1681.

13. "Tugend-übung / Sieben Lustwehlender Schäferinnen" (A Practice in Virtue by Seven Shepherdesses Choosing Pleasure, 1658), in *Sieges-Seule der Buße und des Glaubens / wider den Erbfeind Christlichen Namens* (Victory-Support of Penitence and Faith / Against the Arch-Enemy of the Christian Name), 348.

14. Kimmich, *Sonnets,* 11.

15. In a letter dated September 12, 1661, Stubenberg advises Birken that it would be asking too much to expect Hans Rudolf to edit or correct the preface, "for if he were able to improve on it, he would undoubtedly have done so" (Bircher, *Stubenberg,* 202).

16. Kimmich discusses details about the edition (*Sonnets,* 11–14).

17. Frank, *Leben und Welt,* 50–51.

18. Frank briefly mentions Catharina's *personal* devotionals (ibid., 91, 95). De Boor/Newald points out in the section on Greiffenberg that "her later works surely are not to be viewed as reveries and signs of a declining talent," but "ought to receive long-deserved attention" (*Geschichte der deutschen Literatur,* ed. by Helmut De Boor and Richard Newald+ [Munich: C. H. Beck, 1967], 5:250).

19. De Boor/Newald+, ibid. The reference, not further identified, is to Greiffenberg's *Des Allerheiligst- und Allerheilsamsten Leidens und Sterbens Jesu Christi Zwölf andächtige Betrachtungen* (Twelve Devotional Contemplations on the Most Holy and Most Wholesome Suffering and Death of Jesus Christ).

20. Reinhart Meyer, ed., *Die Hamburger Oper. Eine Sammlung von Texten der Hamburger Oper aus der Zeit 1678–1738* (Millwood, N.Y.: Kraus Reprint, 1984), 4:2, 8, and passim.

21. Scholars have only recently pointed to the political significance of Brentano's religious work, which was highly popular in his time but has received little attention by literary critics. See Helene M. Kastinger Riley, *Clemens Brentano* (Stuttgart: Metzler, 1985), 141–45.

22. Brinker-Gabler, *Deutsche Dichterinnen,* 91.

23. Ibid., 90.

From Twelve Devotional Contemplations on the Most Holy and Most Wholesome Suffering and Death of Jesus Christ, Meditation 6

EXPLANATION OF THE ETCHING (TOWARD THE SUN)[1]

I watched the moon, / spiritually thinking,
and fell asleep so doing. In dreams I seemed to see
the moon, / as if a crown, / before the sun to be
yet the dark disk toward earth with light not blinking.[2]
I thought / what's this? And soon I did recall
what never I forget. Your passion is this star
my greatest treasure! A heav'nly king you are
supreme in glowing shimmer / not recognized by all.
You look at faith / your sun so bright.
Your crown and splendid regal dress
(dark and disdained in man's vainness)[3]
invisible: it's seen only by faith's delight.
You are the king, alas, of clarity / in truth:
standing before the judge already bound.
When you walk past / your misery turns around[4]
and clarity is shown / when full moon woos
the heavens' regal crown. Yet what is thine
unseen, it's known by faith. Invisible but true,
so much is clear, is splendor that is you:
in presence of the sun: who deigns to rob its shine?

(ON SUFFERING AS A PATH TO GOD)[5]

1. Thou, all loveliness' temptation,
restoration: dear distress!
pleasurable God-Way-Station,[6]
Jesus' messenger no less
Sacred secret-filled desire
mercy-sweetened wisdom's fire!
Suffering for Jesus' sake
is a heavenly pleasure-stake.

2. Suffering's enjoyment here,
utter clarity your gloom.
amusement is the word for fear,[7]
consolation call your doom.
Crosses crown, a burden's pleasure,

if sweet Jesus is your treasure;
for to suffer for His sake
is a heavenly pleasure-stake.

3. Good misfortune, tender rage,
restful striving, happy strife!
when your Jesus comes t' assuage
anxiously fear-free[8] is life.
Within is totality,
shows its wondrous beauty me:
'tis, to suffer for His sake
truly is a heaven-stake.

4. As transfigured is the Highest
by affliction's somber mood:
feel, my heart, as thou desirest,
now the all-pervasive good:
that the spirit's joyful, too,
when misfortune is on you.
See, to suffer for His sake
is a heavenly pleasure-stake.

5. Gall is now all sweetness' root,
loss of pleasure pleasure-spoils,
poverty is heaven's loot,
scorn, disgrace are honor's foils.[9]
Worldly honors honor not
he who Jesus' honor sought,
knowing that for Jesus' sake
suffering's heavenly pleasure-stake.

6. God transforms[10] for His believers
to contentment their torment,
He enlightens all the grievers
turns to praise and thanks lament.
Takes the poison from their cross[11]
that for health there be no loss,
so that suff'ring for His sake
be a heavenly pleasure-stake.

7. Divine spirit, crosses' crowner,[12]
pain-remover, misery's end,[13]
you bring radiance to the frowner,
conqueror, from heaven sent.
Show yourself in need abroad,
God in us and us in God

and how pain for Jesus' sake
is a heavenly pleasure-stake!

8. Innocence bright sunlight is,
a clear conscience the moon's rays,
spirit's spark, reflection's bliss,[14]
here are shiny starlit ways;
heaven's bright blue citadel,
the faithful constant, never fell:[15]
showing that for Jesus' sake
suffering is a heaven-stake.

9. Full of joy and full of fun
full of God and full of mind[16]
full of angels, full of sun
shines a splendor of this kind.
Full of fortune is this heist:
suffering for Jesus Christ.
Thus in short: for Jesus' sake
pain is heaven's pleasure-stake.

From Sacred Sonnets, Songs, and Poems

PRAYER FOR DIVINE HELP AT THE OUTSET

Lord God / Thou who givest to all / that which Thou has not Thyself!
Entirely free Thou art of / what Thou art to others.
My very beginning and that of the whole world is of Thee
because Thou practised Thy communicative power by our creation.
In Thy book of providence Thou hast written all worldly being.
Thy abundance was equipped with benevolence
that gives to us divine riches always.
Though everything comes from Thee / yet Thou remainest whole.
All things / save Thou / have a beginning
Be with / in / and beside me / when I begin the book.
May Thy inceptive spirit of protection[17] linger upon this work
and yield my song of Thy miracles in clear voice.
My Lord / I now begin / to praise Thee without end:
Let me, commencing well, show Thee without commencement.

That which thou shaltst speak of God,[18]
let Him nurse thee with its pleasure.
What shall magnify the heavens

must flow from His artful treasure.
That which is to laud His honor
has its origin above.
And the light that shall enlighten
takes its clarity from His love.
Therefore, Lord, my good beginning,
Alpha and Omega, Thou![19]
Flow and pour and shine upon me,
Inspire me[20] with Thy power now:
So that I shall sing Thy praise
In unprecedented ways.[21]

TO A TRANQUIL NIGHT[22]

1. Heav'nly throne, star-spangled bright,
And thou, moon, the crown of night!
Shine, for sunrays (though your peer)[23]
Hide behind the earthly sphere.

2. Silence, grave of all my thought![24]
Bring my woe and grief to naught.
Stillness, quiet, calm in me
All desire for movement be!

3. Now that music in the 'sphere
Sleeps in hollow tree-trunks here,
Rest! and do not enter in
Through my thirst for praise-begin.

4. O sweet nectar of God's grace,
In my sleep yield fortune's face,
Nourish knowledge in my dreams
Of what welfare is and seems![25]

5. Shadow, friend of quiet peace,
Night, thou time of troubles' ease![26]
Ne'er so dark shall be your glow
As to blind laudation's flow.

6. And Thou, sovereign of my soul,
Hither come, my tranquil goal.[27]
Resting-chamber be for me,
That I, sleeping, wake for Thee.

7. Eyes of mine, close up for me,
Rich in fruitful rest now be!
Spirit of mine, contemplate!
Praise the Lord at midnight's gate.[28]

ON THE MOST HIGHLY MENTIONED DAY OF MIRACLES[29]

O ne'er-observed event! a virgin-mother rocks
the source, the movement's fountain-head.
As place of rest He chose a tiny stead.
He who embraces earth now shares the crib of flocks.
For this mean stable he left heaven's charms.
Alas, my heart! If you were but swaddling clothes,
embracing loving-strong your Christ who knows:
Would, that I'd cradle Him once in my arms!
O ox and ass, leave me to take your place!
that I may serve my darling in this space.
How wrongful! that the maker of down and quill[30]
on hardest straw must sleep without them still.
my heart is quilling high,[31] takes toward its savior flight:
O honor it so mightily and rest in it tonight!

ON JESUS, THE CRUCIFIED[32]

See the king of kings here hanging,
Sprinkling us all with his blood.
His inflictions are the fountains
from which spring salvation's flood.
See, his hands he stretches out, to embrace us all; sweet desire
just to clasp us and to squeeze us rules his heart of love and fire.
Yea, to kiss us eagerly with passion shows his dear head's inclination,
All his gestures, his behavior, he directs to our salvation.
There! his side, gaping apart,
Lets us see his gracious heart.
When we let our senses win,
we can see ourselves therein.
For every weal and every wound
that on his body could be found
for our soul he would us till
blessing sources, 'twas His will.
Sacrificed he wished to be
'tween heav'n and earth for you and me
that God be reconciled thus;
to give us strength, he died for us.
Yea, his death has given life
to me and to a world of strife.
Jesus! May your death and pain
forever in my heart remain!

ON THE MERRY AND MAGNIFICENT RESURRECTION OF CHRIST[33]

The earth, it seems, could not retain
Him by whose word she was; yet neither see
decay where life's arch-spirit was to be:
How could the sun-fount, primal heat, so wane?

To th' core it fled, by radiant beams 'twas cleft:
To save the Prince of Life from death's realm.
Atlas'd be vanquished by His breath's sweet balm.
His awesome power's both in and on earth deft.

What are to Thee—a mighty lion—death's trivial teeth,[34]
When Thou hast conquered tigers', dragons' jaws,
Sin's and the devil's furious hosts? Bequeathe

That we might find in death life's laws.
Thy resurrection mends my unmade tomb,
And mortal man receives immortal bloom.

ON MY NEVER-ENDING MISERY[35]

O unjust fortune! where's your fickle way,
Your old inconstant stance?
You torment me now with untiring hands?
Where is the change that held so long your sway?

Shall tears replace my heart's most precious blood?
You but untie the joyous, not the mournful strands,
I'm left to sorrowfully drown in misery's sands.
Too deep to measure is misfortune's flood.

No rescue here, nor from the anguish flight:
In front the sea, sideways the rocks, in back the enemy.
If God not beckons with His wonder-might

I'm done for; yet My Friend I see!
Let come what may, I so delight in Thee.
A brave heart conquers every misery.

From A Practice in Virtue by Seven Shepherdesses Choosing Pleasure

AGAINST CUPID[36]

Let the little tyrant toy, with arrows flirt in vain:
no matter what he cannot win, alas, the tiny knave.
Against his arrow-barbs, you see, a diamond-heart[37] I have.
He does not make me smart at all, I dare not feel the pain.

Just let him try a thousand tricks, my heart shall remain free
A ginger-bread I gave to him, the blind child, so renowned:
O easily deluded boy! He thinks my heart he found.
Revenge I'll wreak on you, my dear, your gullibility.

This rock with golden arrow blast, and do not look forlorn.
How do you like it? Look, my dear! Laurels shall please
and grace me here, not myrtle-branch, nor rose and thorn.[38]

You think it is but jest, my boy, I only wish to tease?
No! No! Sweet peace shall be my lover, repose be my defense,
just freedom and tranquillity my brave heart ought to sense.

NOTES TO THE TRANSLATIONS

1. The etching shows the motto "Der Sonne zu" above three vertically aligned spheres in a clouded sky. The uppermost sphere is clearly identified by rays as the sun; the lowest (and in scale largest) sphere is only partially shown and identified by continents and seas as planet earth. Directly between sun and earth, larger than the sun but smaller than earth, is the moon; only a crescent-shaped edge shows the light it receives from the sun. The largest part of the moon is in darkness as seen from earth and casts a shadow upon her. A crown adorns the moon. The constellation appears to depict a solar eclipse. The etching is reproduced in *Epochen der deutschen Lyrik,* ed. Christian Wagenknecht, 4:278.

2. "blinking": in German "fanken" (funkeln) is used to rhyme with "Gedanken."

3. Greiffenberg interprets the constellation as the new (dark) phase of the moon and likens the moon to Christ: an intermediary between humanity (earth) and God (sun), Christ (moon) faces toward and basks in the glory of God, while remaining unseen and unrecognized by those on earth who are without faith.

4. Reference is made to the other phases of the moon when it is visible to earth. The comparison is to Christ's passion when He appeared bound and mocked before Pilate, then was resurrected again to splendor after His crucifixion.

5. Pages 172–74. The poem's first line is "Lockung aller Lieblichkeiten," and it has no title. The last two lines of each strophe are the (slightly varied) refrain, "Ach! um Jesu willen leiden / ist ein Himmel voller freuden." The moral conclusion of the poem is the promise,

"Kurz: um Jesu willen leiden / bringt im Himmel volle Freuden." In this poem Greiffenberg leads the reader progressively from strophe to strophe to the recognition that earthly suffering can be pure pleasure because it is a sure path to heavenly bliss. A *coincidentia oppositorum* explains this oxymoron (strophe 2); to achieve the reversal of meaning on a lexical basis, Greiffenberg works with alliteration and word-manipulation ("ver*luste lust*-gewinn," strophe 5). It is impossible to find English equivalents in each case.

6. "angenehmes Gott-zu-leiten": Reference is made both to Jesus' Calvary experience (stations of the cross) and to human suffering as its equivalent, but also to Greiffenberg's didactic poetic intention.

7. The original shows enjambment and *apokoinu*: "Angst wird man ergetzung müssen / nennen / tröstung alle pein."

8. Greiffenberg uses alliteration and repetition here and throughout the poem ("sanftes stürmen," "zeiget ihre wunder-zier"). A version of the oxymoron ("Glücklichs unglück," "ängstig angst-befreyt") expresses the magical transformation of reality by the mystical union with God.

9. "schmach und hon ein' ehren-zinn": Not a literal translation, but the English word "foil" can mean both to adorn (act as a foil to something) and to bring to naught. It thus illustrates the technique of ambivalence and dual meanings with which Greiffenberg works in this poem.

10. "Gott verwandelt / seinen Lieben . . .": The term "verwandeln" can have magical connotations and the noun ("Verwandlung") can also mean metamorphosis.

11. "Er nimt ihrem kreutz das gifft." Reference is made to the phrase, "O death, where is thy sting?"

12. "Creuz-begräntzer": The spelling permits the interpretation of this word both as "Bekränzer" (nominal form of "to crown with a wreath") and as "Begrenzer" (nominal form of "to set a limit"). God's spirit both glorifies the cross and limits the suffering it causes.

13. "weh-verweher / elends-End" (alliteration, play with words).

14. "Geistes-fank gedanken-wonne": a reference to the "Seelenfünklein" and the *unio mystica* in the Meister Eckhart tradition.

15. "und die blaue Himmels-fest / ist beständigkeit gewest": The past participle "ist . . . gewesen" (a shift in tense) and the term "hier" (a spatial indicator) in this strophe show a change of perspective; earthly concerns are now seen from a point in time and space where pain has been transcended. Transfiguration or spiritual metamorphosis as in the mystical union with God has taken place.

16. "Voller freuden / voller wonne / voller Gottheit / voller Geist": The term "Geist" and its derivations defies definitive interpretation in this pithy phrase. It may mean "geistvoll" (of brilliant mind, full of spirit, witty) but also "filled with spirit," "filled with the Holy Ghost," and "vergeistigt" (transfigured, spiritualized, intellectualized).

17. "Dein Anfang-Schirmungs-Geist." The prayer is versified in the original.

18. "Das, was man von GOtt soll sagen," 385.

19. The first and last letters of the Greek alphabet. The German "Drum mein alles guten Anfang / Ziel und End mein A und O!" signifies Greiffenberg's confession of God's all-encompassing importance in her life.

20. "fließ und gieß / bestrahl / erleuchte mich mit deiner Krafft also": The images of water and sunlight (the elements necessary for the creation and sustenance of life) are merged in the verbs Greiffenberg uses; both water and sunlight may "flow," "stream" and "pour." This type of metaphor is common in medieval mysticism (*unio mystica*), where the influx of divine light into the human soul signifies union with the spirit of God.

21. The original text is more modest: "auf fast-nie erhörte Weise."

22. "Auf die ruhige Nacht-Zeit," 381.

23. The parenthetical insertion is not in the original: "leuchtet / weil den Sonnen-Strahl / uns benimmt der Erden Ball."

24. This verse is rich in alliterating *s* and *g* sounds and their use results in a "magic-chant" quality:

Stillheit / der Gedanken Grab!
stelle Sorg' und Grämen ab.
Stille / stille / still' in mir
alle Herzbewegungs-Gier!

Note also the repetition of the word "still" in its various forms (nouns "Stillheit" and "Stille," adverbial and imperative constructions "stille" and "still'") and the alternation between "stille" and "stelle" which also emphasizes the hypnotic, chantlike, persuasive quality of this stanza. This has been lost in my translation.

25. "fliesse mir in Träumen ein / meiner Wolfahrt Schein und Seyn!" The topic of truth versus deceptive appearance ("Schein und Sein") is common in Baroque literature.

26. "Nacht / du Müh'-Ergetzungs-Zeit!" This line is ambiguous in its meaning and can denote nighttime both as a period of relief from troubles (during sleep) and also as a time when troubling thoughts abound (for insomniacs).

27. "meiner Ruhe Ruh": The constant repetition of words in this poem does not signify a lack of poetic insight or ability. It is supposed to produce a lulling, somnolent effect in accordance with the topic of the poem.

28. "lobe Gott um Mitternacht!" Midnight signifies in Romantic and pre-Romantic literature not only the depth of night (and, symbolically, despair) but also the dawning of new hope (the end of one day and the beginning of another). The "witching hour" is also associated with death and resurrection (the end of earthly and the beginning of eternal life). The notion of sleep as a form of temporary death is common in literature and in this poem. The first reference to it occurs in strophe 2: "Stillheit / der Gedanken Grab!"

29. Page 112. Reference is made to the birth of Christ.

30. Greiffenberg uses the German word "Feder," which may mean feather (as in "featherbed"), quill (as in "feather" and in "pen"), and spring (as in "bed-spring"). She combines these meanings in this and the following two lines: Christ should lie on a bed of feathers (downs); her heart is a soft bed for Christ (feather-soft) and is also made full by means of her own quill (writing); it takes to the wing (like a bird with feathers) in a flight of adoration. There are many plays on words in this poem. In lines one and two, the term "movement" connotes both the rocking movement (the cradle) and Christ as head of the Christian "movement"; in lines three and four the word "spannen" is used to signify a small span or narrow space ("ein spannbreit Ort"), and "to span the world" ("die Erd' umspannt"), etc.

31. "Mein Herz ist feder-voll / fliegt dir mein Heiland zu": This is a paraphrase of a Lutheran metaphor in Luther's Bible translation ("Wes Herz voll ist, dem fließet der Mund über"): the effort of her pen has given her heart wings. See above for the several meanings of "Feder."

32. Page 403. Another, not versified translation by Peter Daly is printed in his book *Literature in the Light of the Emblem,* 131. Daly reprints Greiffenberg's original version with its cross shape and varying type-fonts on the facing page (p. 130). The poem's visual shape is intended to engage the senses along with the intellect: line five marks the cross bar to which Jesus' hands were nailed and coincides with the phrase "Seht / Er strecket seine Händ aus." Greiffenberg's attempt to "shape" her poems according to their content strikes the reader as a rather modern device, employed more commonly in the nineteenth and twentieth centuries among poets such as Christian Morgenstern and representatives of "concrete poetry" (Gomringer and others).

33. Page 169. "Auf die Frölich-und Herrliche Auferstehung Christi."

34. The original adds to the animal symbols in this strophe that of the mouse: "Was wolt dir / starker Leu / der Tod das Mäußlein seyn / nach dem du Drachen schon und Tyger überwunden." The story of the lion and the mouse appears in Aesop's fables.

35. Page 51.

36. Brinker-Gabler gave the poem this title.

37. Peter M. Daly discusses the meaning of such Baroque emblems as the diamond, the stone, and the rock, as well as their religious implication (Christ), with some specific references to Greiffenberg's poems. He does not refer to this specific one from the bucolic tradition. See *Literature in the Light of the Emblem,* 42–43.

38. The triplet reads in the original: "Schau, wie gefällt dir das! trotz, spräng mir diesen Stein / mit deinem goldnen Pfeil. Der Lorbeer soll mich zieren, / nicht deine Dornen-Ros' und Myrten-Sträuchelein." Refer to the text for a possible nonreligious interpretation.

BIBLIOGRAPHY

Primary Works

Birken, Sigmund von. Papers in the *Archiv des Pegnesischen Blumenordens,* Germanisches Nationalmuseum. Nürnberg (letters, drafts, etc.).

Brinker-Gabler, Gisela, ed. *Deutsche Dichterinnen vom 16. Jahrhundert bis zur Gegenwart.* Frankfurt/Main: Fischer, 1978.

Greiffenberg, Catharina Regina von. *Geistliche Sonnette / Lieder und Gedichte / zu Gottseeligem Zeitvertreib.* Nuremberg: Michael Endters; Druck: Bayreuth: Johann Gebhard, 1662.

——— *Des Allerheiligst- und Allerheilsamsten Leidens und Sterbens Jesu Christi Zwölf andächtige Betrachtungen.* Nuremberg: Johann Hofmann; Druck: Johann-Philipp Miltenberger, 1672.

——— *Tugend-übung / Sieben Lustwehlender Schäferinnen* (1658). In *Sieges-Seule der Buße und des Glaubens / wider den Erbfeind Christliches Namens.* Nuremberg: Johann Hofmann; Druck: Christoff Gerhard, 1675.

——— *Sämtliche Werke,* 10 vols. Edited by M. Bircher and F. Kemp. Millwood, N.Y.: Kraus, 1983.

Wagenknecht, Christian, ed. *Epochen der deutschen Lyrik. 1600–1700.* Vol. 4, dtv 4018: 246–49; 275–84. Munich: Deutscher Taschenbuch Verlag, 1969.

Related Works

Bircher, Martin and Peter M. Daly. "Catharina Regina von Greiffenberg und Johann Wilhelm von Stubenberg: Zur Frage der Autorschaft zweier anonymer Widmungsgedichte." *Literaturwiss. Jb. der Görres Gesellschaft* 7 (1966): 17–35.

Bircher, Martin. *Johann Wilhelm von Stubenberg und sein Freundeskreis: Studien zur österreichischen Barockliteratur protestantischer Edelleute.* Berlin, 1968.

——— "Unergründlichkeit." In *Dt. Barocklyrik: Gedichtinterpretationen von Spee bis Haller,* edited by M. Bircher and Alois M. Haas, 185–223. Bern: Francke, 1973.

Black, Ingrid, and Peter M. Daly, eds. *Gelegenheit und Geständnis: Unveröffentlichte Gelegenheitsgedichte als verschleierter Spiegel des Lebens und Wirkens der Catharina Regina von Greiffenberg.* Canadian Studies in German Language and Literature 3. Bern: Lang, 1971.

Brinker-Gabler, Gisela. *Deutsche Dichterinnen vom 16. Jahrhundert bis zur Gegenwart,* 32, 414. Frankfurt/Main: Fischer, 1979.

Daly, Peter Maurice. *Die Metaphorik in den "Sonetten" der Catharina Regina von Greiffenberg.* Diss., Zürich, 1964.

______ "Vom privaten Gelegenheitsgedicht zur öffentlichen Andachtsbetrachtung. (Zu C. R. von Greiffenbergs 'Trauer Liedlein')." *Euphorion* 66 (1972): 308–14.

______ "Emblematic Poetry of Occasional Meditation." *German Life and Letters* 25 (1972): 126–39.

______ "Emblematische Strukturen in der Dichtung der Catharina Regina von Greiffenberg." In *Europäische Tradition und dt. Literaturbarock,* edited by Gerhart Hoffmeister, 189–222. Bern: Francke, 1973.

______ *Dichtung und Emblematik bei Catharina Regina von Greiffenberg.* Studien zur Germanistik, Anglistik und Komparatistik 36. Bonn: Bouvier, 1976.

______ "Catharina Regina von Greiffenberg und Honoré d'Urfé: Einige Bemerkungen zur Frage von Catharinas Rezeption der Schäferdichtung." In *Schäferdichtung,* edited by Wilhelm Vosskamp, 67–84. Dokumente des Internat. Arbeitskreises für Dt. Barockliteratur 4. Hamburg: Hauswedell, 1977.

______ *Literature in the Light of the Emblem: Structural Parallels Between the Emblem and Literature in the 16th and 17th Centuries.* Toronto: University of Toronto Press, 1979.

______ "Catharina Regina von Greiffenberg." In *Deutsche Dichter des 17. Jahrhunderts: Ihr Leben und Werk,* edited by Harald Steinhagen and Benno von Wiese, 615–39. Berlin: Schmidt, 1984.

De Boor, Helmut and Richard Newald+. "Catharina Regina von Greiffenberg." In *Die deutsche Literatur vom Späthumanismus zur Empfindsamkeit, 1570–1750,* 248–50. Munich: C. H. Beck, 1967.

Fässler, Vereni. *Hell-Dunkel in der barocken Dichtung: Studien zum Hell-Dunkel bei J. Klaj, A. Gryphius und C. R. von Greiffenberg.* Europäische Hochschulschriften 44. Bern: Lang, 1971.

Frank, Horst-Joachim. *Catharina Regina von Greiffenberg. Untersuchungen zu ihrer Persönlichkeit und Sonettdichtung.* Diss., Hamburg, 1958.

______ *Catharina Regina von Greiffenberg: Leben und Welt der barocken Dichterin.* Göttingen, 1967.

Handels, Nancy Porter Ferguson. *Catharina Regina von Greiffenbergs Lieder und Sonette, das Problem von Dichtung und Mystik.* Diss., Stanford, 1975.

Herzog, Urs. "Literatur in Isolation und Einsamkeit: C. R. von Greiffenberg und ihr literarischer Freundeskreis." *Dt. Vierteljahrsschrift für Literaturwiss. und Geistesgeschichte* 45 (1971): 515–46.

Kimmich, Flora. *Sonnets of Catharina von Greiffenberg: Methods of Composition.* Chapel Hill: U.N.C. Studies in German Language and Literature, no. 83, 1975.

Liwerski, Ruth. "Ein Beitrag zur Sonett-Ästhetik des Barock: Das Sonett der Catharina Regina von Greiffenberg." *Dt. Vierteljahrsschr. für Literaturwiss. und Geistesgeschichte* 49 (1975): 215–64.

Mehl, Jane M. "Catharina Regina von Greiffenberg: Modern Traits in a Baroque Poet." *South Atlantic Bulletin* 45, no. 1: 54–63.

Möller, Hilke. *Thränen—Samen und Steckdosenschnauze: Linguistische Beschreibung von Neubildungen Catharina Regina von Greiffenbergs und Wolfdietrich Schnurres.* Zürich: Juris, 1975.

Price, Lucy Jean. *The Emblematic and Meditative Poetry of John Donne, George Herbert, Andreas Gryphius, and Catharina Regina von Greiffenberg.* Diss., University of North Carolina, 1977.

Scheitler, Irmgard. *Das geistliche Lied im deutschen Barock.* Berlin: Duncker & Humblot, 1982.

Schürk, Ingrid. "'Sey dennoch unverzagt': Zwei barocke Sonette von der Bewältigung des Schicksals." In *Aus der Welt des Barock,* edited by Richard Alewyn. Stuttgart, 1957.

Slocum, Malve K. *Untersuchungen zu Lob und Spiel in den Sonetten der C. R. von Greiffenberg.* Diss., Cornell, 1971.

Spahr, Blake Lee. *The Archives of the Pegnesischer Blumenorden: A Survey and Reference Guide.* Berkeley, 1960.

Stalder, Xaver. *Formen des barocken Stoizismus. Martin Opitz, Andreas Gryphius und Catharina Regina von Greiffenberg.* Studien zur Germanistik, Anglistik und Komparatistik 39. Bonn: Bouvier, 1976.

Sullivan, John H. *The German Religious Sonnet of the Seventeenth Century.* Diss., Berkeley, 1966.

Uhde-Bernays, Hermann. *Catharina Regina von Greiffenberg. Ein Beitrag zur Geschichte des dt. Lebens und Dichtens im 17. Jht.* Diss., Berlin, 1903.

Villinger, Leo. *Catharina Regina von Greiffenberg. Zu Sprache und Welt der barocken Dichterin.* Diss., Zürich, 1952.

Wehrli, Max. "Catharina Regina von Greiffenberg." *Schweizerische Monatshefte* 45 (September 1965): 577–82.

Wiedemann, Conrad. "Engel, Geist und Feuer: Zum Dichterselbstverständnis bei Klaj, Greiffenberg und Kuhlmann." In *Literatur und Geistesgeschichte. Festgabe für Heinz Otto Burger,* edited by Reinhold Grimm and Conrad Wiedemann, 85–109. Berlin, 1968.

GERMAN RELIGIOUS POET

udamilia Elisabeth

BRIGITTE EDITH ZAPP ARCHIBALD

German literature during the seventeenth century was dominated by the baroque, which towards the end of the century developed into a pseudoclassicism that prepared the way for Gottsched and Lessing. Literary critics make a distinction between an earlier stage of Baroque literature, close to an urbane classicism, and a later stage characterized by a more difficult and "obscure" rhetoric.[1] In the early part of the seventeenth century, Germany reestablished its links with the European Renaissance, reintegrated itself into the European artistic community, and rather belatedly competed with the aesthetic achievements of the French, Dutch, English, Italians, and Spanish.

The Thirty Years' War (1618–1648) annihilated the German bourgeois class with its earthy strength and folk-tone, devastated the majority of the German cities, and effected a renewed taste for greater sobriety and economy in daily life and art.[2] Realism and fanaticism intensified by the horrors of the Thirty Years' War at first seemed to present an insurmountable front against acceptance of the rules of French Classicism. In actuality, however, French Classicism had spread and continued to spread through the efforts of well-bred diplomats, courtly administrators, noblemen, and erudite lawyers who remained to establish the fashionable *Sprachgesellschaften* (literary societies) that flourished in the latter half of the century.[3]

The German Baroque, because of the Thirty Years' War, is known as the age of violent trends and countertrends which produced a literature tortured by doubts and crises. Its dramas and poems were constantly oscillating between the sensual and the spiritual, between worldliness and other-worldliness. The political-historical situation of the times drove the poets either into religious ecstasy and mysticism or into coarsest eroticism. Protestants and Catholics alike groped for a firm hold in a strife-torn world, where all faith and traditions seemed to have lost their former values.

Ludamilia Elisabeth, Countess of Schwarzburg-Rudolstadt belonged to this era of uncertainty. As a product of her time, living in the aftermath of the Thirty Years' War, Ludamilia belonged to that group of writers who demonstrated an earnestness and fervor—at times a mystical approach—to her faith in God. She was an aristocrat who dared to break the rules of convention by engaging her talents in literary work. Although today she is considered a minor poet of the seventeenth century, her poems were quite popular in her own day. They were included in the Protestant and Lutheran hymnals and were memorized and sung by the general populace, thereby contributing to the emergence and spread of the religious language and ideas of Germany.[4]

Ludamilia Elisabeth was born toward the end of the Thirty Years' War, on April 7, 1640, to Ludwig Günther and Emilie Antonie, Count and Countess of Schwarzburg-Rudolstadt in idyllic southern Thuringia.[5] Ludamilia's mother, as well as being educated in the arts and languages,[6] especially Latin and Greek language and literature, was also widely read in contemporary literature and familiar with the works of poets and thinkers of the day. Such a broad education was, of course, unusual for a woman of that era. It was reported of Emilie Antonie and her family that they sought to practice Christianity in every aspect of their lives. They gave to the poor, visited the sick, helped orphans and widows, and never allowed any visitor to depart from their house empty-handed.[7] Ludamilia, under her mother's care, was reared in the elite tradition of the day. She received an education under the tutelege of private scholars and was encouraged to read philosophical and theological works by earlier mystics.[8] Her father died when she was only six years old; her mother and other family members then retired to the seclusion of the Heidecksburg, a castle near Schwarzburg-Rudolstadt, where Ludamilia spent the rest of her life. In 1671, when she was thirty years old, Ludamilia was formally betrothed to Count Christian Wilhelm of Schwarzburg-Sonderhausen. In several poems written upon the occasion of her betrothal, she considers herself married to Christ and demonstrates a reluctance toward marriage because it would conflict with her relationship to God. A short time thereafter, in 1672, one of Ludamilia's sisters was smitten with the measles and eventually died. Ludamilia, thinking herself immune to the disease, nursed her sister until she too contracted measles. On March 12, 1672, shortly after the death of her sister, Ludamilia also died, never having married and never having published any of her poems. Aemilia Juliane, Ludamilia's cousin who married her brother and became the Countess of Schwarzburg-Rudolstadt, published Ludamilia's poems posthumously in

1697 under the title, *Die Stimme der Freundin, das ist: Geistliche Lieder Welche, aus brünstiger und biß ans Ende beharreter* JESUS *Liebe verfertiget und gebraucht Weiland Die Hochgebohrne Gräfin und Fräulein, Frl. Ludamilia Elisabeth, Gräfin und Fräulein zu Schwartzburg und Hohnstein u.s.w.* (The Voice of a Friend; that is, Spiritual Songs, which have been written in fervent love for Jesus and in anticipation of his Second Coming by the late high-born Countess and Young Lady, Miss Ludamilia Elisabeth, Countess and Lady of Schwarzburg and Hohnstein, etc.)[9] This first edition, printed by Benedicti Schultzens, was housed in the Hofbibliothek (court library) in Rudolstadt. The most readily available edition of her poetry was included in an anthology entitled *Geistliche Sängerinnen der christlichen Kirche deutscher Nation* (Spiritual Singers of the Christian Church in the German Nation), edited by Wilhelm Schircks in 1856. Volume 3 containing Ludamilia's poetry is entitled *Der Gräfin Ludamilia Elisabeth von Schwarzburg-Rudolstadt geistliche Lieder in einer Auswahl nach dem Originaltexte* (The Countess Ludamilia Elisabeth of Schwarzburg-Rudolstadt's Spiritual Songs selected from the original text). J. D. Sarnighausen, who made the selections for this volume, chose to include seventy-eight of Ludamilia's poems. Sarnighausen also wrote a short introductory note and included a table of contents with headings for the poems based upon liturgical observances.

Another edition compiled at the same time is more comprehensive. *Die Stimme der Freundin: Geistliche Lieder Ludamilien Elisabeths, Gräfin und Fräulein zu Schwarzburg und Hohnstein usw.* (The Voice of a Friend: The Spiritual Songs of Ludamilia Elisabeth, . . .) was edited by Wilhelm Thilo and published by Liesching Verlag in 1856. Thilo also included a table of contents and topic headings, but they differ from the Sarnighausen headings. As a basis for my translations I have used the Sarnighausen/Schircks edition of Ludamilia's poetry, since it is more readily available and more concise.[10]

Ludamilia's poems demonstrate a rebellion against a deteriorated seventeenth-century orthodoxy[11] and strive instead to view Christianity as a total way of life. Her poems stress the individual's relationship to God; divine redemption; obedience to God; a deep faith in the Bible as the word of God; and a worthy receiving of the Christian's responsibility to forsake sin, to turn to Christ and to the inner recesses of the heart. Above all else, Ludamilia's poems stress the divine indwelling of Christ within the heart of the believer. She can thus be termed a seventeenth-century mystic.

In Ludamilia's choice of words and especially in her use of compounds, her preoccupation with the mystical concepts of the indwelling Christ is evident. The poems superabound with compounds emphasizing the heart and Christ's indwelling: *Herzensschrein, Herzensthür, Herzensräumlein,*

Herzerbarmen, Herzbegiehr, Herzandacht, Herzenschifflein, Herzensgärtlein, Herzenssonne, Herzenssternlein, Herzensgrund, Herzenswunde. The importance of the heart (*Herz*) as the source of life and hence, figuratively, of the inner life is emphasized not only in the Bible but also in the works of such mystics as Johann Arndt and Johann Valentin Andrae, works that Ludamilia had read and studied.[12]

Ludamilia's poems were most likely written with familiar tunes in mind, or melodies were subsequently composed for them. It is therefore no wonder that one often finds the poet employing the common measure of the hymnal stanza (four iambic lines containing respectively eight, six, eight, six syllables and often with an abab rhyme scheme). Besides the common measure, Ludamilia also uses the long measure (octosyllabic iambic lines throughout a four-line stanza). Very often too, she modifies, varies, and recombines common and long measures—sometimes adding lines and substituting trochees for the iambs and sometimes changing the rhyme scheme. There are several instances of poems with alternating hexta-heptasyllabic lines of varying stanza length, or alternating tetra-heptasyllabic lines, or alternating deca-pentasyllabic lines with an aabb rhyme scheme. In his preface to *Die Stimme der Freundin,* Thilo points out that Ludamilia is more concerned with content than with form.[13] Her poems as a whole are quite lengthy; some extend over several pages. There are 205 in the Thilo edition, 78 of which are included in the Sarnighausen/Schircks edition.

Ludamilia's poems, many still in present-day hymnals, are predominantly drawn from the Bible and from mystical writers of the fourteenth and fifteenth centuries. The poems express common religious feelings. The Psalms, understandably, serve as a major source, but scriptural passages from both the Old and New Testaments are quoted, paraphrased, and alluded to throughout the poems. Ludamilia's poems show the heart, as a symbol of the believer, in its relationship to God—either in union with or in alienation from God. The heart is often described as a dwelling place for God and as a place of meeting for God and the soul. Often the union takes the form of a marriage feast for the bride (the believer) and the bridegroom (Christ). The death motif is depicted in a dual fashion: the natural human fear of death and the Christian yearning for death. Often death is viewed as the pathway to life eternal, to God, and to Heaven. Love always overcomes the fear of death.

NOTES

1. René Wellek, "The Concept of Baroque in Literary Scholarship," 86. I use "obscure" in Wellek's sense of "a form of artistic ugliness" or "that artistic perversion, dominated by a desire for stupefying. . . ." Friedrich Werner feels that the last Baroque poets in Germany

lacked the religious earnestness of the earlier generation and that they "therefore dealt in horror and eroticism for their own sake" (Friedrich Werner, *History of German Literature,* 48).

2. When the Peace of Westphalia ended the Thirty Years' War in 1648, Germany was completely devastated and depopulated. Of 400,000 inhabitants of Würtemberg, 48,000 survived; in the Palatinate only 200 peasants were said to be alive at the end of the war. In the histories of the time, terrible images of death emerge. No one can be seen for miles on end; the houses are filled with dead bodies; the plague is everywhere, and worms, wolves, dogs, and vultures feed on the carrion. To write, at such a time, a playful poem of love and desire or to discuss the niceties of a particular verse form required an extraordinary dedication to the arts, perhaps more than the devastated country could produce. Much, or most of the tortured energies of German Baroque art derive from the artists' experiences in a world torn apart by war, sickness, and disease. Seen against this horror, many Baroque achievements have an almost heroic quality which does not necessarily appear on the printed page. See Georg Winter, *Geschichte des 30. jährigen Krieges,* for a complete description of the Thirty Years' War and its effects on Germany.

3. Strangely enough, it was by means of the Thirty Years' War that the foreign words and ideas came into Germany. Opitz, a mediocre poet, was of great importance because he imported French concepts and rules, including the classical French Alexandrine meter of twelve syllables. Many Baroque poets banded together to establish academies for the advancement of culture and the arts. In 1617 Prince Ludwig of Anhalt founded the *Fruchtbringende Gesellschaft;* Philipp von Zesen, another Baroque poet, founded the *Rosenorden,* and Johann Rist the *Elbschwanenorden.* Ludamilia, together with her sisters and tutor, founded a literary society called *Die Fruchtbringende Gesellschaft der Jesus-Liebe,* which was probably modeled after the earlier societies but also emphasized Christian conduct as a stimulus to the writing of poetry.

4. Her poems are mostly found in older hymnals, some of which are still in use. *The Gesangbuch für die evangelisch-lutherische Kirche im Fürstentum Schwarzburg-Rudolstadt* contains seven of Ludamilia's poems; the *Gesangbuch für die vereinigte protestantische evangelische christliche Kirche der Pfalz* contains two; the present-day hymnal of the German Lutheran Church in America, the *Kirchengesangbuch für evangelische-lutherische Gemeinde* contains three of Ludamilia's hymns. One hymn is found in the hymnal for the Dutch Reformed Church in America, the *Deutsches Gesangbuch: Eine Auswahl geistlicher Lieder aus aller Zeiten der Christlichen Kirche.*

5. Biographical material is largely taken from the *Allgemeine Deutsche Biographie* and the introduction to the Sarnighausen/Schircks edition of Ludamilia's poems, *Geistliche Sängerinnen.*

6. Emil Frommel, *Ludamilia Elisabeth von Schwarzburg-Rudolstadt und Marie von Lippe Schaumberg,* 6f.

7. Frommel, *Ludamilia,* 7.

8. Wilhelm Thilo, *Ludamilia Elisabeth, Gräfin zu Schwarzburg-Rudolstadt,* 13.

9. Thilo, *Ludamilia Elisabeth,* 25.

10. The original edition is still available on microfilm from the British Museum. See *British Museum General Catalog of Printed Books,* photolithographic edition to 1955, vol. 241. There are spelling discrepancies and heading irregularities in all the editions.

11. D. A. Tholuck, *Das kirchliche Leben des 17. Jahrhunderts,* 142ff.

12. See Ernest Stoeffel, *The Rise of Evangelical Pietism,* for a description of Andrae's and Arndt's mysticism.

13. Thilo, *Ludamilia Elisabeth,* lxii. Thilo felt that, in contrast to the typical Baroque poet's emphasis on strained metaphor and on bombastic, superlative, inflated, unbalanced, and antithetical language, Ludamilia was more interested in experiential subject matter and did not strive for special effects in the use of her language.

From The Voice of a Friend

WELCOMING THE SAVIOR[1]

1. Now, hosanna, David's son,
Thou who comest from Heaven's throne
To all poor sinners:
March on, march on, for thee
The door and gate are fully open
Here to thy poor children.

2. My heart wants to love thee,
Thou God's Son, thou David's Star,
Thou true Son of Man,
Thou Shiloh, Savior, Shepherd, and Salvation,
My Brother, Throne of Grace and Portion[2]
Come in the name of the Lord.

3. Come King, Prince of Peace and Hero,
Redeemer, Mediator and Ransom,
Thou Light and Comfort to the heathen.
O Savior, Help and Shelter,
Protector, Counsel, Prophet and Defense,
March into my heart with joy.

4. O be praised, Immanuel,
Who overcomes death and hell,
Thou effacer of my sins.
I pray, come into me
Although thou mayest find
A humble little room as thy dwelling place.

5. For thou art Lord of all Lords,
I, ashes and dust, nothing more;
Wouldst thou lie therein?
The house is not worthy of thee;
I poor human, I poor earth,
How shall I satisfy thee?

6. I should no longer ask thee
But thou desirest it,
Thou speakest: give me thy heart
If thou wouldst have it, so be it thine.
The heart cannot be better
Than by the Candle of Life.

7. Thou wouldst have it all alone;
O may it be completely pure and free
From all strange guests!
Thou bringest righteousness
In the Holy Spirit, Peace and Joy,
Is that not for the best?

8. Take in, through my poverty,
Love, honor, fear and humility
And composed will.
My faith hangs on thee,
Thereby thou wouldst dwell in me.
O could that but repose thee.

9. O but all is too weak,
Where thou dost not assist:
Therefore be thou entreated,
O repudiate all
That which displeases thee in this house;
Satan be accursed.

10. Then receive what thou hast made;
Take possession of my heart, take care of it.
It is given to thee completely.
Now let it continually be thy resting place
And lock the doors after thee;
Welcome, O my life!

CONFESSION AND ABSOLUTION

1. Now untie the bonds
Through thy powerful bonds,
Lord Jesus, dishonor that which
Creates so much pain!
Here is the misery of sin
Which binds me so tightly,
Here Satan, world and death
Do not cease to restrain.

2. My tears bind thee,
My heart does not release thee.
Till thou all my longing,[3]
The sins small and great
Which lie heavily upon me,
Have been graciously averted

With thy Jesus-hand
Because I repent of them.

3. With the arms of my faith
I now clasp thy heart,
Embrace thy mercy
And the grief of thy bonds.
I cry timidly:
Deliver me[4] from guilt
And bind me tightly
Through the bond of thy grace.

4. Pass over to thy Father
With thy ornament's bond;
Be thou, Jesus, my counselor
And help me from my sins,
Speak the word again:
Forgive, my Father, please!
Deliver me from my torment
And the yoke of thy anger.

5. Thou permittest thyself to be bound
My Helper and Savior,
With my heavy sins
How can the fetters now
Again bind me . . . ?
Thou rendest them asunder;
Therefore now declare me
From all sins free.

6. No longer let Satan laugh
Who thinks that I am his;
Show this hellish fiend
That I am thine alone.
Announce to death
That he has no part of me
And that what thou hast done
Be his downfall and my salvation.

7. But for this let me live
In the bonds of thy favor,
Knit together and encircled
With thy passionate love.
Therefore may I, my treasure,
Wherever I can,

Always, to my neighbor
Be devoted.

8. From the bonds of the cross
Doth my flesh shrink as a foe,
But because it is consecrated
By thy bonds, my friend,
Dress me only
In this livery,
According to thy love divine
Which knows how weak am I.

9. O, please revoke,
Lord, my confidence,
The foe's bonds and fetters,
For I do not belong to him.
Let the multitude of my sins
Be evermore drowned
In the sea of thy blood
Yes, yes, let it be thus.

SONGS FOR THE EUCHARIST

1. Dearest Jesus, I salute thee,
I welcome thee, thou worthy guest;
In faith I kiss thee now.
And in humility embrace thee,
Thou comest, wouldst give thyself to me,
Wouldst feed me and quench my thirst.
Here is thy flesh and blood;
Hail thee, thou highest good!

2. Poor, I salute thee,
Jesus, beautiful visage,
Eyes and ears be fitted
To receive thy mercy.
O speak, Jesus, for my well being:
Thy sins be forgiven thee.
Eat and drink my flesh and blood:
Hail thee, thou highest good!

3. I salute thee, heart of Jesus,
Now a sinner is knocking;
O, he is coming with repentance and sorrow,

Be thou wide open.
Believingly he would sink himself
In thee and let himself be satiated;
Satisfy him, thou blood of Jesus:
Hail thee, highest good!

4. I salute thee, wound of love,
Which in his side there
My Lord Jesus did feel;
Open, thou door of grace,
Gush forth, spring of blood,
Jesus' blood, run strong and pure;
Satisfy me, O blood of Jesus:
Hail thee, highest good!

5. I salute thee, hands of Jesus,
Which would adroitly administer
Jesus' flesh and blood to me,
Open thy wounds here
Which are engraved by the nails.
O, how thou wouldst revive me,
Flow into me, blood of Jesus:
Hail thee, highest good!

6. I salute thee, feet of Jesus,
Walk with me to the altar,
Where I will enjoy Jesus' body,
When I drink his blood there,
Which was shed for me,
As He was stabbed so hard.
O that would satisfy me, O blood:
Hail thee, highest good!

7. I salute thee, Good Shepherd,
Bridegroom of my soul,
Pious Jesus, shepherd me,
Come here, thou Lamb of God,
In the house of my heart,
Let me worthily receive
Thy most holy flesh and blood:
Hail thee, highest good.

AFTER PARTAKING OF THE LORD'S SUPPER

1. Say, where has thou been,
That thou art so well recovered,
My soul, o where?
Who has cheered thee?

2. Who has imparted counsel?
Which physician hath healed thee?
Who has been thy host,
O who thy guide and thy shepherd?

3. Who has bestowed nourishment upon thee?
Which fountain has quenched thy thirst?
Who has granted thee protection?
Who was thine enemies' offense?

4. Wandering, I saw thee
From the mass of sheep
Far from thy shepherd away,
And yet thou hast found him.

5. Thy wounds were bloody,
All have been dressed
And healed in the fundus,
Thou art now refreshed and healthy.

6. Hungry saw I thee there,
Now thou hast been fed;
Thou didst go out thirsty,
Satisfied thou didst return.

7. All those conspired to kill thee
And to devour thee cruelly
Who are against thee,
But thou art living here.

8. He who sees all pain
And it was the heart of Jesus
Has certainly seen thee
Full of sins going astray.

9. It has searched for thee.[5]
When thou cursedst thy sins
And didst repent of them,
Then Jesus became new therein.

10. He, the physician, imparted mercy
Quickly dressing thee,
His Word and His consolation alone
Have washed the wounds of thy sins.

11. O, upon his pasture of flesh
And to the dew of his blood
Hath led thee so wondrously,
Thy dearest bridegroom.

12. Thy proud enemies' yawning abyss
Was not permitted near thee,
Jesus' hand was ready
Always to rescue thee.

13. I bid thee welcome from the trip,
From the physician, from the nourishment,
From the potion and from the site,
Where thou wast refreshed.

14. Blessed now and ever for thee
Be Jesus' pasture of life
And the refreshing potion, his blood,
Indeed, all delightful good.

15. May all that flourish in thy life,
Which is given to thy life,
Say: yes, thou treasure of my soul,
To thee Jesus, be praise evermore.

DESIRE FOR ASSISTANCE AND A POWERFUL INFLUENCE OF JESUS' LOVE

1. Love of Jesus, faithfulness of Jesus,
This child of Jesus desires thee,
Love of Jesus, O, I cry,
Come and be mine eternally!
I cannot be without thee,
Dearest love, love thou me,
Influence me and penetrate me,
Fill me and encompass me.

2. Love above all loves,
What I am, that thou art to me;
Love of Jesus, encircle me
And what thou hast given me.

Because a member stirs,
O rouse thyself along,
Let my soul, heart, and thoughts
Continually live in thy boundary.

3. Let me not feel anything but thee,
Lead thou the way of my life,
O keep me from sin,
Raise me up when I fall.
Blow upon my wick of faith,
Which can so easily be extinguished;
When I confess my sins to God
And hear his Word, give me light.

4. Love of Jesus, contend for me,
Drive off all enemies;
Love of Jesus, prepare me,
When I eat Jesus' flesh,
When I drink Jesus' blood,
Lend devotion, strength, and courage,
Convert to thee all my senses,
Whatever I do, think and begin.

5. When I pray, speak from me;
When I speak, speak into me;
When I suffer, come to me
And sweeten the pain.
Go with me to work;
If I travel, be near;
Be there, when I drink and eat;
If I sleep, do not forget me.

6. Be in my heart and in my mouth,
May my heart and mouth be full of thee.
Now and in the hour of death
Direct my thoughts
Toward that which thou hast performed;
Turn away Satan's power,
Take me, when I depart,
Love of Jesus, my joy.

RESTING IN GOD

1. O look, my soul,
There stands opened

A wondrous grotto.
Who is that Man
Who beckons so friendly
And entices thee continually?
It is he, methinks,
Who loves thee.

2. O, in faith haste thee
Into Jesus' house,
He it is who furnishes
His heart for his dove.
It is standing open,
Thy Noah presents
His hand, O come
Through penitence to rest.

3. I lay thee down here,
Where thy rest is,
Come back to Jesus,
From whence thou hast come.
He will never again die,
In him is complete pleasure,
He will not see corruption:
O there, there it is good.

4. There thou canst find:
Refreshment in trials and need,
Forgiveness of thy sins,
Deliverance from hell and death;
There thou canst enjoy
Rest for thy spirit,
A calm conscience
And what thou needst for peace.

5. My Noah, my rest,
Now thy dove is here.
My soul, with all that
Is within me,
I now give altogether to thee.
Let her live in thy house,
From thy heart,
Let her nevermore part.

6. She wanted to nest
Once in the world

In vain deeds and lusts,
There she often fell
Victim to birds of prey,
When thou didst not
Reveal the danger,
Falseness, and evil ways.

7. Now she completely disdains
The world, sensuality, and riches
Because of thee and looks
In thy heart through thy blood.
Let her not forfeit that,
Be in me eternally,
I am in thy heart:
O, how well I am resting.

FRIENDSHIP WITH JESUS

1. O, guess, who is my friend,
Who gives me his heart,
Whose intentions are the best,
And who loves my heart?
Shouldst thou say, it is the world,
Her worthless riches, her vile money,
Then thou hast missed the mark:
Another has been chosen.

2. Thinkest thou that it is
A mere man upon this earth;
Then name him, who is faithful
And cannot become unfaithful,
Else thy opinion were wrong.
Speakest thou, however, it is
Thy Jesus full of grace,
Then hast thou guessed aright.

3. He it is, he it is! Dost thou know
Where we exchanged our friendship?
At that fount over there,
The baptismal, where we pledged ourselves.
We became near relations,
When my friend from heaven's land
Did come down to me
And took upon him flesh and blood.

4. I tell thee: My friend is mine!
It cost him his life,
To buy me for himself alone
And shed his blood,
When the well-deserved torment
And my enemies altogether
Would seize me.
He is a friend indeed!

5. We entered into a friendship pact
In those green pastures
And are getting to know each other,
When we meet each other there.
His flesh must I then eat,
His dear blood must satisfy me:
Can one find more constancy,
Can one be more affianced?

6. My friend does not depart from me;
He hath given to me
The cord of faith, that I here
May hold onto Him therewith;
It girds us tightly together,
That one will not forsake the other.
Anon when there is weakness,
He is here and strengthens.

7. To him I bring my sorrows,
I know he is a keeper of secrets;
To him I whisper in the ear
And bring him my request.
He gives me an answer forthwith
By his spirit and his word,
Lets me see his help always
Lets me not go comfortless.

8. We have everything in common,
No one can ever separate us:
My misfortune, distress, and pain are his,
His suffering and death are mine,
All his merit, righteousness,
And resurrection will enable me
To reach the joy of heaven:
He who has this friend can boast.

9. Now I have the greatest good,
Because I have this friend;
Heart, mind, and spirit thank him
For such noble gifts.
Now thou knowest who my friend is,
He is named and is Jesus Christ.
Now know and also believe,
That Jesus will remain my friend.

PLEASURE IN JESUS

1. Who can live more satisfied
Than he who has given himself
To Jesus completely?
O he will be always satisfied,
In all things,
That God does ordain.

2. Has he not upon the earth,
Wherewith he can become great,
Riches, honor, beauty, and power,
Bliss and many good days?
He does not lament,
Day and night he lives content.

3. That wherewith he desires to refresh himself
Can be found in Jesus,
Complete forevermore.
In the world's goods and treasures
Cannot be found perfect rest;
All is vanity.

4. My soul surrenders itself
To her Jesus, whom she loves,
She grips him firmly by faith.
Jesus is mine, O delight!
I have enough; he may direct
My life as he will.

5. Jesus' being in me is honor
And treasure, which I covet,
My beauty and my joy.
That he calls himself my God

And acknowledges me as his child,
Of this joy I am conscious.

6. Jesus is my abundance,
For his dress of righteousness
Gives me a covering.
Jesus is my meat and drink;
As an overflowing torrent
He fills me with good things.

7. There are riches to be acquired,
Which cannot be stolen by thieves
Nor consumed:
In the noble deep fundus
Of Jesus' wounds, there will I find
Grace and blessing sufficient for me.

8. Though I cannot with precious stones
And with pearls appear,
Nor enter in with scarlet robes,
Jesus' tears of blood can crown
Much better than pearls.
His blood shall be my scarlet robe.

9. And if the world rejects me,
I am lifted up in God;
If she curses, he will bless.
If she[6] does not want to house me:
O, in Jesus' side wound
Is my dwelling; what more do I want?

10. Jesus, strengthen my faith,
Let not my trust diminish.
And if I experience a need,
Give me what is pleasing to thee,
And I will be blessed here and there.
I have thee, O, I am rich!

EVENSONG

1. Thanks be to God that another day
Of my life hath ended,
In which sickness, necessity, and vexation
For me thou hast prevented.

2. Forgive and cover thou my sins,
My father, which I have committed,
And permit sweet evening rest
To me, thy child.

3. Where do I find a bed and a place
For my feeble bones?
I search here, I search there:
Where is my guardian?

4. In this world nothing is certain;
Where can I rest?
Therefore I pray thee, Lord Jesus,
To grant me a place.

5. I lay my heart into thy heart;
Thy blood, Jesus, shall cover me,
And I fall asleep in thy wounds:
In spite of him, who would terrify me!

6. Into thy faithful hand will I
Commit my body, soul, honor, and life,
And those who are friends and relatives,
To thee now.

7. Guard, faithful watchman of Israel,
Guard, Jesus, when we are asleep,
Over house, court, and that which I commend to thee,
Keep from all evil.

8. May it be, that even tonight
I will not suffer pain of death:
Yet thy will shall be my will;
Help me to contend faithfully.

9. Reveal, Lord, thy suffering, blood, and death,
Then sin will be silent;
I remain thine in distress and in death,
Satan must retreat.

10. I live and die alone for God,
Nothing can separate me from him:
I am lying in the shrine of his heart
And sleep in the side of Jesus.

SONGS OF DEATH: WILLINGNESS TO DIE

1. Say, my soul, indeed,
If thy God has commanded,
That his faithful servant
Shall fetch thee out of this world:
Do not flee from him,
Wilt thou go with him?
Yea, yea, I will go with him.

2. Thy dear God permits
His Son to woo thee,
His Servant is death:
Wilt thou die willingly,
Wilt thou leave thy fatherland
And wander his streets?
Yea, yea, I will go with him.

3. Wilt thou bid all friends
Here now farewell
And gladly seize
All those treasures, which
To thee the servant brings.
Then prepare thee for the trip:
Yea, yea, I will go with him.

4. It is well known,
That my father is in heaven;
There is my fatherland,
And not here in this world's turmoil.
There, there is where Jesus reigns;
Death leads me to him:
Yea, yea, I will go with him.

5. Shall I not wish
To see anon my Jesus
Who through his blood and wounds
Hath permanently bound himself to me,
At the baptismal fount?
Shall I not go with death?
Yea, yea, I will go with him.

6. O, were the time at hand
For death to escort me there,
Where the Trinity resides,
Which I gladly would see,

Where I would delight in heaven's joy!
After the suffering here below:
Yea, yea, I will go with him.

7. O, that my bridegroom already
Came to meet me,
To take me to heaven's throne
In his tabernacle;
How he would revive me!
His servant shall be told:
Yea, yea, I will go with him.

8. My God, prepare me aright,
Forgive all my sins
That death, thy servant,
May find me here, as thou wilt,
That I may be, as is proper,
Prepared by word and works:
Yea, yea, I will go with him.

YEARNING FOR HEAVEN

1. O, to be in heaven
Dear God, with thee, with thee!
Do hear, my creator, do hear,
And leave me no longer here!
I must be where thou art,
Where my darling, my Jesus, is;
I must away from the tumult of life
Because my solace is in heaven.

2. Here I cannot find fulfillment
In the wretched world of evil,
For it is full of transgressions,
Its total essence displeases me.
Envy, persecution, scorn, and mockery
Are its greatest reward:
O, you despicable worldly turmoil,
Would I were away from you in heaven.

3. How well it were with me,
If I could always behold
The godhead in three persons
And its trinity in unity.
When I see God, the light,

God's holy visage:
O, would I away from worldly turmoil,
With God dwelling in heaven.

4. No rest have I here
In this temporal life;
Can sensual pleasure, money, possessions delight?
Away, away, with vanity!
It is mere impertinence;
O, home, home to my fatherland!
Home out of this worldly turmoil
To my rest in heaven!

5. There no friend can harm me,
No fear, danger or distress,
For I am in God's grace,
God is in me and I am in him,
In him I attain my goal;
Therefore I will do God's will:
Therefore, away, worldly turmoil;
I choose heaven.

6. Sickness, hunger, thirst, frost, heat,
Anxiety, fear, and constant strife
Often cause me stress,
Which heaps sorrow upon sorrow.
All this, however, will end
When I finish my course:
O, what are you, turmoil of this world?
Would I were away from you in heaven.

7. How sweet it will sound,
When I sing the hallelujah
With all the angels:
O, were I there already!
In the meantime let the shrine of my heart,
My Lord, be thy heaven,
Lead me from the turmoil of this world
To thee in heaven, to praise thee.

8. E'en though joy be here,
Mourning be not far away;
But there is joy without sorrow
Over there in eternity.
Retreat, imperfection!

Over there is blessedness.
Good night, turmoil of the world!
My one and all is in heaven.

9. Must I, though, wander
Longer in this time,
Then help me live saintly,
My God, prepare me,
Show me, how to live,
How to die gently and well,
And let not this turmoil of the world
Turn me from heaven.

10. Because thou art in my heart,
I am already in heaven;
But my heart mourns
Its sinful proclivities.
Preferably I would be sinless
In the castle of heaven:
O, take out from the turmoil of the world
Thou me to thee.[7] Thou art my heaven.

11. Stretch thine arms and hands
Out to me; I will go therein.
Come quickly, my bridegroom,
I want to be thine alone.
Forgive all my sins,
Open the heavens' portals:
I am out of the turmoil of this world,
In hope already in heaven.

NOTES TO THE TRANSLATIONS

1. In his edition of Ludamilia's poems, Thilo lists the poems according to a numbering system similiar to that of the hymnbooks. In the Sarnighausen edition, the poems have been given headings or titles according to the content and the occasion for which they were written: A. Festlieder (Songs for liturgical observances), I. Advent, 1. Bewillkommnung des Heilandes (Welcoming the Savior), II. Weihnachten (Christmas), III. Neujahr (New Year's), 1. Von den Wohlthaten Gottes (Of God's Blessings), 2. Neujahrstrost (New Year's Consolation), IV. Epiphanias (Epiphany), V. Passion (The Passion of Christ), 1. Danksagung für das Leiden Christi (Praise for the suffering of Christ), 2. Bitte um Genießung des Leidens Christi (Request for the tasting of Christ's suffering), 3. Vom Blute Jesu (The blood of Christ), VI. Ostern (Easter), VII. Himmelfahrt (Ascension), VIII. Pfingsten (Pentecost). Along with the liturgical poems, there are occasional poems for preparation for prayer, confession, and

absolution, poems for the Eucharist, etc. Ludamilia probably did not give a heading or title to her poems, but most likely she did intend a certain melody for each one; she seems to have included the melodies for the poems. I have used the translations that Sarnighausen gave to particular poems; and, in the cases where no heading was given, I have taken the title Sarnighausen used for that particular set of poems. These have all been translated into English.

2. "Portion" is a term often used by religious writers to signify their oneness with Christ. Its origin is biblical (Psalm 73:26): "God is the strength of my heart, and my portion forever."

3. She will bind Christ to herself until he has granted her the longing of her heart, *i.e.*, the removal of all her sins which lie heavily upon her.

4. Ludamilia uses the words *binde/entbinde* as contrasts.

5. It (the heart of Jesus) has searched for the wandering soul.

6. The poet has personified the world as a woman who has rejected the soul and whom the soul has rejected in favor of Jesus' wounds as a dwelling place.

7. Although she already has Christ here in this world in her heart, she would prefer to have Christ take her out of the turmoil of this world to be with him.

BIBLIOGRAPHY

Primary Works

Schircks, Wilhelm, ed. *Geistliche Sängerinnen der christlichen Kirche deutscher Nation. Nach den Original Texten in Verbindung mit mehreren Hymnologen.* Volume 3: *Der Gräfin Ludamilia Elisabeth von Schwarzburg-Rudolstadt geistliche Lieder in einer Auswahl nach dem Originaltexte herausgegeben von J. D. Sarnighausen.* Halle: Julius Fricke Verlag, 1856.

Thilo, Wilhelm, ed. *Die Stimme der Freundin. Geistliche Lieder Ludamilien Elisabeths, Gräfen und Fräulein zu Schwarzburg und Hohnstein u.s.w.* Stuttgart: Liesching Verlag, 1856.

Related Works

Allgemeine Deutsche Biographie. General German Biography, edited by the Bavarian Academy of Sciences. Published by R. von Liliencron and F. X. Wegele, 1884. Vols. 1, 8, 19, 22. Reprint. Berlin: Duncker and Humbolt, 1969.

British Museum General Catalogue of Printed Books. Vol. 146. Photolithographic edition to 1955. London: Trustees of the British Museum, 1962.

Deutsches Gesangbuch: Eine Auswahl geistlicher Lieder aus aller Zeiten der christlichen Kirche. Cleveland: Central Publishing House, 1889.

Frommel, Emil. *Ludamilia von Schwarzburg-Rudolstadt und Marie von Lippe Schaumberg. Zwei Stillleben aus dem 17. und 18. Jahrhundert.* Berlin: n.p., 1874.

Gesangbuch für die evangelisch-lutherische Kirche im Fürstentum Schwarzburg-Rudolstadt. Rudolstadt: Fürstlich Hofbuchdruckerei, 1901.

Gesangbuch für die vereinigte protestantische evangelische christliche Kirche der Pfalz. Speyer: Zechnersche Buchdruckerei, 1928.

Kirchengesangbuch für evangelische-lutherische Gemeinde. St. Louis: Concordia, 1892.

Koch, Eduard Emil. *Geschichte des Kirchenliedes und Kirchengesangs.* Vol. 4. Stuttgart: Chr. Belser Verlag, 1868.

Lemcke, Carl. *Von Opitz bis Klopstock.* Leipzig: Seemann Verlag, 1882.

Merker, Paul and Wolfgang Stammler. *Reallexikon der deutschen Literaturgeschichte*. Vol. 2. Berlin: De Gruyter Verlag, 1926/28.
Müller, Günther. *Deutsche Literatur von der Renaissance bis zum Ausgang des Barock*. Potsdam: H. Gunther Verlag, 1957.
Schöne, Albrecht, ed. *Die deutsche Literatur: Texte und Zeugnisse*. Vol. 3. Munich: C. H. Beck, 1963.
Stoeffel, Ernest F. *The Rise of Evangelical Pietism*. Leiden: E. J. Brill, 1971.
Tholuck, D. A. *Das kirchliche Leben des 17. Jahrhunderts*. Berlin: Wiegandt und Grieben Verlag, 1861.
Wellek, René. "The Concept of Baroque in Literary Scholarship," *Journal of Aesthetics and Art Criticism* 5 (December 1946): 77–109.
Wentzlaff-Eggebert, Friedrich W. *Deutsche Mystik zwischen Mittelalter und Neuzeit*. Berlin: Walter De Gruyter Verlag, 1947.
Werner, Friedrich. *History of German Literature*. New York: Barnes and Noble, 1948.
Winter, Georg. *Geschichte des 30. jährigen Kriegs*. Berlin: G. Grote Verlag, 1893.

PART EIGHT

Hungary

LYRICIST OF THE SOUL

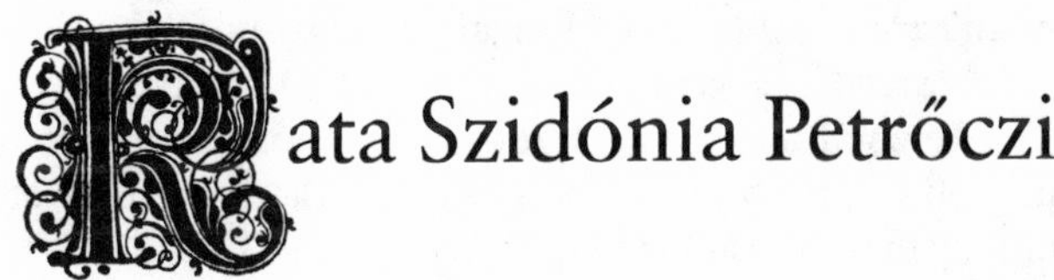

ENIKŐ MOLNÁR BASA

Kata Szidónia Petrőczi was born in 1662 to Baron István Petrőczi (or Petróczi) and Erzsébet Thököly, a first cousin of Imre Thököly, leader of the Hungarian forces in Upper Hungary.[1] This connection to one of the leaders of the Hungarian and Transylvanian forces against Habsburg domination marked her life. Kata Szidónia's mother had died shortly after her birth, most likely as a result of complications from childbirth. The child lived on the Petrőczi estates, centered on Kaszavár in the county of Trencsén (now Trenčin, Czechoslovakia) until the political activities of her father placed the family in imminent danger. In 1670 István Petrőczi was forced into exile for his part in the Wesselényi Conspiracy, an attempt to resist absolutist Habsburg rule. He sent his daughter to Sztrecsény and the care of Zsuzsanna Bakoss, wife of László Wesselényi, while he himself fled with his sons to Transylvania. Because László had not been involved in the conspiracy, his household was expected to be safe from retribution. However, the Habsburg court soon extended punishment to all family members of the conspirators, and Kata Szidónia was forced to flee with her guardians. They went to the Polish estates of the Wesselényi family, also taking with them the treasures that István Petrőczi had left in their care with his daughter. It was here that Kata Szidónia was raised. Judging from her letters and poems, she was not on the best of terms with her guardians, who freely helped themselves to the valuables her father had entrusted to their protection.

In 1681 she married Lőrincz Pekry, a supporter and friend of Imre Thököly, as well as a schoolmate of one of her brothers. She was eighteen at the time and had only recently left Poland to go to Transylvania, not to her native region of Upper Hungary. While the marriage was probably arranged for family and political reasons, it might have been happy at first. She and Lőrincz certainly shared many goals, not the least of which was commitment to the anti-Habsburg political forces. In fact, her family's dedication to the independence movement was broadly based; not only was her father an early champion of Hungarian constitutional rights but her brothers also served as generals in the opposition armies of Thököly and later of Ferenc Rákóczi II (1676–1735). Thus, in later life, in spite of her husband's opportunism, she never lost the protection of Prince Rákóczi. Initially they lived at Ozd, the Pekry estate in Transylvania, although she felt unprotected and cut off from family and friends. Both the letters and the poems of this time give evidence that she was unhappy here, all the more so as her husband's connections to Thököly were viewed with suspicion by Chancellor Mihály Teleki. She requested permission to move to Northern Hungary, but the request was denied.[2]

In 1686 Teleki had Pekry arrested for suspected complicity in Thököly's attacks on Transylvania. Even though his wife was able to gain his freedom in time, it cost them large sums of money and the loss of much of their holdings. Kata Szidónia's poems of these years contain references to the persecutions, the loss of property, and separation from loved ones. Willful, ever-changing Fortune is often the topic, though in a few poems there are references to "her enemies." By 1688, however, Teleki found it expedient to ally himself with the emperor, and Pekry proved a suitable emissary. Pekry's opportunism in serving Teleki was difficult for his wife to accept, for it meant not only a change of political alliances but also conversion to Catholicism. Though Pekry later asserted that he never really converted but only followed the forms outwardly, this conformity gained him the return of his lands and his wife's inheritance, as well as the title of count and positions of increasing importance.

Kata Szidónia herself was Lutheran,[3] and this inheritance left a strong mark on her. Her religious sincerity made compromise with the militant Counter-Reformation difficult but did not hinder her relations with the families of Upper Hungary and Transylvania. There was religious freedom in Transylvania, particularly while it was free of Habsburg domination, and the Protestant confessions were accepted; furthermore, freedom of conscience was the law. Her bitterness at her husband's sham conversion thus has to be seen in the context of Habsburg efforts to re-Catholicize the nation. Her poem on the lost convert to Catholicism shows the deep fear she felt for the spiritual welfare of such people. Moreover, she went so far as to disinherit a daughter who converted and also left specific orders to be buried according to the Lutheran rite.[4]

In the troubled years, as in the more prosperous ones during her husband's mid-career, Kata Szidónia stood by Pekry, although she could not always share his ambitions. She bore him eleven children—five girls and six boys—but only the girls survived. Although troubled by his infidelity and careerism, she nevertheless continued to exert an influence over him throughout his life. While she had not been active in his relocation to Habsburg-ruled Upper Hungary, the sojourn in this area, which at the time (1690/1694) was a center of cultural and literary activity, had a salutary effect on the development of her talents. Kata Szidónia and her husband settled in Besztercze-Váralja, near her birthplace of Kaszavár, and participated actively in the social life of Upper Hungary. She met others like herself—aristocratic men and women versed in literature and writing literary works themselves. The effect of this interaction is evident in the enriched vocabulary and imagery, as well as the more complex construction, her poetry assumed during this period.[5]

Her husband's opportunism continued to be a source of despair, as the themes of her poems, as well as her preoccupation with pietistic writings, testify. The height of his career came in 1702. The following year, Pekry became a prisoner of Prince Ferenc Rákóczi II and changed sides again. Although his abilities allowed him to rise in Rákóczi's service also, he was never fully trusted. Count Bercsényi wrote to Rákóczi: "I feel true sorrow over Pekry, although I do not know his perfidy. . . . His wife, who rules over him, is a wise and good soul, and the good Hungarian will turn to her."[6]

Pekry's return to the cause espoused by Kata Szidónia, as well as his assertion that he had never really embraced the Catholic faith, might have consoled his wife to some extent; still, it was at the loss of relative security and ease. Caught up in the turmoil of the War of Liberation, she was imprisoned by the Habsburg general Rabutin for over ten months in 1704. In the "more than unusually strict captivity" she suffered a stroke, yet also prepared her translation of Johann Arndt. Though eventually liberated by the Kuruc[7] forces, she spent the rest of her life as a refugee in one or another of Rákóczi's estates. She died in Beregszentmiklós, a Rákóczi castle, on October 21, 1708, and was buried next to her two sons at Ozd, the Pekry family estate, as she had instructed in her will.[8] Her husband died shortly thereafter and was buried beside her.

KATA SZIDÓNIA was known for over a century only as a translator of German pietistic writings. She published a collection of translations from Friedrich Johannes Mayer under the title *The Agony of the Acquaintances of Those Lutheran Souls Who Have Converted to Catholicism* . . . , written at least partly in response to her husband's opportunistic conversion but also for all who were similarly affected. The fact that she published this work at her own expense in 1690 in Hamburg attests to her conviction that the public needed to read it, for she never published her more personal poems. It was a time of militant re-conversion in the Habsburg-controlled Hungarian lands, and she rose to meet a need. Later, during her imprisonment in Szeben, she again turned to the German pietists and translated poems from Johann Arndt, which she then published in two volumes. The first came out in 1705 in Kolozsvár (now Cluj, Romania) under the title *Twelve Fragrant Lilies that Revive the Hearts Wearied Under the Heavy Weight of the Cross* and was reprinted by her granddaughter Polixena in 1764, also in Kolozsvár. In 1708 she published another collection of Arndt's poems and prayers, this time from Huszt (now Chust, USSR), her "fourth place of exile"[9] as she states on the title page. The volume is entitled *The True Heart Smoking with Good Fragrance*, a reference to the incense burner—an appropriate Baroque image.

The original poems of Kata Szidónia were not discovered until the late nineteenth century and were not published in their entirety until the twentieth. Critical evaluation has been slow; most often she has been merely mentioned or anthologized as one of the contributors to the literary and cultural milieu of her age. She deserves further evaluation in her own right as a poet.[10] The poems discovered in her manuscript book are personal ones, unpublished. Even though they might have been known in manuscript form—copied into letters, as was fashionable, and circulated among her friends—there is no evidence that they had any particular impact. The booklet of poems was continued by others, perhaps her daughters or granddaughters, who used it for much the same purpose.

The poems are often religious, for Kata Szidónia sought comfort in religion from her personal agonies, primarily her husband's infidelity. Some poems seem to refer to the trials brought on by war; others are vague about the cause of her distress, but certainly her hard life and the loss of her sons played a part. The poems reveal stages of her primary grief—her effort to cope with her husband's betrayal, her anger at the husband and the other woman, her resignation and deepening religious faith as her only comfort. She drew on the traditions of Hungarian poetry, using a variety of forms and meters. There are occasional echoes of the style of Bálint Balassi (1554–1594), but hers is not slavish adaptation. Even in the translations she paraphrased and even supplied new material. A modern tension and restlessness is apparent in her original poems.[11] At first she refuses to accept her betrayal and addresses her husband in reproachful but spirited verses. Later, she rebels against her fate, even while accepting it as God's will.

The small number of themes creates a certain monotony, which is not surprising since the poems were never intended for publication but simply as a solace for herself and possibly others in a similar situation. On the other hand, the images are fresh, often taken from nature to which she responded sensitively. They are also ornamented with allusions to classical gods and mythical beings, as well as with the machinery of Protestant religious poetry, providing a good idea of the intellectual milieu in which she moved.

The little handwritten volume containing Kata Szidónia's poems had forty-five that were undoubtedly hers; this seems to have been the bulk of her personal poetry. (Some poems have lines missing, and the copiers made notes about a page missing here or there.) Thirty-six were in her own hand, while nine were copies, probably made by her daughter Polixena. The collection also contains poems of a later date written by others, probably a daughter or granddaughter. Although the dates of composition are not marked, the first four poems are early ones, written before 1686. Number 5, according to internal evidence, was written in 1686, and the bulk of her poetry between 1690 and 1694. Numbers 31–35 were written after 1695, and number 33 shortly before 1700.[12] In the early poems the sorrows are generalized and seem to refer to the religious and political persecutions she suffered rather than to the later theme of her husband's infidelity.

The manuscript was discovered by Countess Clara Rhédey, a great-granddaughter of Kata Szidónia, who sent it to Kálman Thaly and Pál Gyulai, leading literary scholars of the nineteenth century. Copies were made by Ferenc Toldy, professor of Hungarian literature at the University of Budapest, and by Thaly. Subsequently, the manuscript was lost until 1952 when it was rediscovered during an inventory at the Hungarian Academy of Sciences.[13] This has allowed for a reexamination of the texts based on Thaly's and Toldy's copies.

The poems translated below follow the numbering in the first complete printing of the poems in the *Irodalomtörténeti Közlemények*. Number 3 is written in the four-stress, twelve-syllable line known as the "Hungarian alexandrine," with the quatrain rhyme Kata Szidónia often favored. It shows her mastery of poetic forms. The longer poem 4 expands on the theme of her sad, unfortunate childhood. While her fresh use of natural imagery is not lost in translation, the melody of the lines cannot be reproduced. Each six-line stanza contains three full and three half lines, but only the half lines rhyme; the shorter lines have three stresses. Through meter and content, the half lines carry the meaning, forming an effective unit.

Perhaps her best-known poem is the one that introduces the post-1690 group—number 12, which has received the title "Dear Violet." It gives a survey of the affair from *her* perspective. Pekry seems to have been quite callous, or perhaps he deluded himself into thinking she was unaware of his flirting. He sought her advice even at this time, which bears out Bercsényi's comment that she had influence over her husband, who respected her judgment if not her feelings. The woman in question was one of Kata Szidónia's own relatives, the wife of Miklós Apponyi,[14] so the hurt was even more poignant. The faithfulness she professed all through her trials seems to have been accompanied by real love, for in this poem she addresses her husband in old terms of endearment. The reproach and anger in poem 12 is replaced by resignation and hope of heavenly consolation in poem 15, while poem 18 shows defiance and a reluctance to let herself be an object of pity and gossip. References to classical mythology are linked carefully with the imagery of nature to enrich it. This use of nature to parallel the speaker's emotional state is found in other Hungarian lyrics of this and earlier periods and has been preserved in the folk songs down to modern times. The poet's mastery lies in the novelty yet appropriateness of the image. Poem 32 is a brief prayer, a sigh for help from God; it is included as an example of several such invocations scattered throughout the manuscript.

Kata Szidónia Petrőczi's love poems are significant for their technical mastery and their view of a deeply religious, emotional woman facing the problems of a turbulent time. They are also important because Kata Szidónia was the first in Hungarian poetry to delineate the psychological state of the deserted yet still-loving woman, the hurt and accusing yet still-devoted wife.[15] Her piety inspires with a grandeur lacking in the lighter Rococo poems of her contemporaries. Piety and patriotism add to the seriousness, but also to the emotional, lyrical quality, of her poetry. Love, piety, and patriotism are intertwined in most of her verses, as indeed they were in her life.

The last selections are both religious and patriotic. Entitled "New Hymn. Tune: 'What does the World Trust,'" the first is actually written to the music of a Catholic hymn. It is unusual in that the form changes after the first four stanzas, from five lines rhymed aaabb, with the fifth line generally a half-line, to a six-line form rhymed aaabbb in which the last three lines are half-lines. In each case, however, the second half of the poem answers the first, forming either a plea to God for aid or a comment on the sufferings of God's people described in the first part. Written in 1702–1703, it is based upon a turbulent time not only in her own life but in the Hungarian war of independence also. Poem 39 touches upon the same political and religious problems but has a patriotic rather than a religious orientation. Also written in the form of a hymn, this time in the popular rhymed quatrain using the shorter eight-syllable line of three stresses, it is meant to be an anthem. The poem concludes with "Amen," indicating the prayerful intent. Poem 42 is another of the quatrains in which she distills her sorrow. A leave-taking, it comes almost at the end of the collection.

These translations are based on the printed version by Harsányi and Gulyás, who took the most authentic version from the Toldy and Thaly copies. I have given basically line-by-line prose translations, since the metrical pattern and rhymes could not be reproduced without loss of meaning. To the extent possible, I have sought to capture the feeling of the poems but have concentrated on re-creating the meaning and images.

NOTES

1. Upper Hungary (A Felvidék) was a separate region, though not a separate country. At the time under discussion, it was administratively under Habsburg rule and, along with parts of Transdanubia, formed Royal Hungary. Transylvania and some counties of northeastern Hungary known as the Partium formed the independent Principality of Transylvania. The rest of the kingdom was under Turkish occupation. The borders were not well-defined, and the former unity of the country was not destroyed at all levels: language and culture remained the same, and there was close interaction among the three parts of the country. Also, the wealthier nobles often owned estates in both the Transylvanian and the Royal areas of Hungary. The Rákóczis were the wealthiest landowners of Upper Hungary, yet several of the members of the family served as princes of Transylvania. Thököly, too, was a landowner in Upper Hungary, yet a prince of Transylvania.

2. Biographical information is based on István Harsányi and József Gulyás, "Petrőczi Kata Szidónia versei," 193–94; *A Magyar irodalom története 1660–töl 1772-ig,* ed. Tíbor Klaniczay, 2:353; Jenő Pintér, *Magyar irodalomtörténete,* 3:299–302; Margit S. Sárdi, *Petrőczi Kata Szidónia költészete;* Jenő Sólyom, "Petrőczi Kata Szidónia életrajzához," 358; József Szinnyei, *Magyar írók életes és munkái,* cols. 1052–55. Petrőczi is used both with a final *i* and a final *y;* I have kept the spelling as found in my sources in the notes and bibliography but have used the former spelling in my text, following the usage of the Academy's history of Hungarian literature.

3. *A Magyar irodalom története,* 194.

4. Harsányi and Gulyás, 194, and her will, Bálint Kis, "Gróf Pekry Lőrinczné végrendelete," 736.

5. Pintér, 301; S. Sárdi, 22–23.

6. Kis, 736; Harsányi and Gulyás, 194.

7. *Kuruc,* a term first used in 1673, was the name given to the Hungarian forces that opposed Habsburg rule, fighting under both Imre Thököly from approximately 1679 to 1691 and Prince Ferenc Rákóczi II of Transylvania from 1705 to 1711. They were irregular troops engaged chiefly in guerrilla warfare aimed at national defense and generally united by anti-Habsburg or anti-Austrian feelings. By this time the Turkish power was weak, and Habsburg slowness in waging a decisive campaign against the Turks led many to see the hope of liberation in these forces. Protestants in Upper Hungary as well as in Transylvania sided with them because of the Habsburg persecutions, and their victories were gains for religious tolerance, at least on a limited scale. Political opposition to Habsburg efforts to treat Hungary merely as another hereditary province—or worse, a buffer zone for the Austrian lands—also increased their ranks, particularly under the leadership of Rákóczi. The name might have connotations of "wanderer" or "wandering in exile."

8. Kis, 732–37; Harsányi and Gulyás, 194; S. Sárdi, 35.

9. Pintér, 300.

10. Margit S. Sárdi's work analyzes Petrőczi's poetry in detail and considers the influences on her work. Most of the volume concentrates on detailed examinations of the poems. It is probably the best work on Petrőczi but is also the only monograph that I have been able to locate with the exception of early, chiefly biographical works.

11. *A Magyar irodalom története,* 354.

12. I have used the summary given by Harsányi and Gulyás, 195. S. Sárdi (pp. 49–51) gives these dates: 3, after 1681; 4, probably around 1683; 5, in 1686; 11 and 12, after 1690; 17, 25, 29, 30, after 1690; 20, probably between 1690 and 1694; 31–35, probably after 1695; 33, before 1700; 41 and 44, after 1694; 38, in 1704; 37 and 39, between 1704 and 1705; and 42, 43, and 45, after 1704, probably after 1706. Poems not dated contain no indication of their dates, and thus can only be given approximate times of composition.

13. In 1952 the original manuscript was found during inventory of the Academy's library, and it has been restored. S. Sárdi notes that some corrections were thus possible, and certain passages could be made clearer. Since I did not have access to the manuscript, I had to rely on the Harsányi-Gulyás version. The account of the adventures of the text is based on Harsányi and Gulyás, 190–93.

14. Endre Antalffy, *Petrôczy Kata Szidónia élete és munkái,* 53, cited in Harsányi and Gulyás, 195.

15. *A Magyar irodalom története,* 354.

Poems

3. Poem

Lamentable, I know, was my birth,
Lamentable, orphaned was my upbringing,
Lamentable, mournful my taking to wing,
Lamentable, to my death, will be my mourning.

For my heart, as in deep smoke, smothers in sorrow,
Behold, to the fates I have been exposed,
And this cruelty ceases not, but only renews,
Unfortunate I am, and my sorrow's flame inflames.

4. New Songs. Tune: "Like the Entrapped Orphan"

My poor head, my days pass in sorrow,
From all sides merciless cares surround me,
Ah, ceaselessly, my hours pass in sadness
There is no hope—I pine with great sorrows.

I had hoped, lying in my bed at night,
Perhaps in the morning I would come to joy,
I would rejoice as the dice turned to six,
—But my heart's pain turns blind.

In childhood already I had come to grief
Being left orphaned by my mother.

A bitter, frightening helplessness,
My expected joy turned to sorrow.

Oh, who can ever be in such sorrow,
Who have part in so much care?
Abandoned in great carelessness,
My cause in such sorrowful fate.

My enemies rule over me, even now
Of my goods they have deprived me,
To such a defenseless state have I sunk,
To my enemies' wicked tongues have I been delivered.

There are many who rejoice at my sorrow,
And increase, hourly, my grief,
Nor do they pity my terrible shedding of tears
But rather laugh at my hapless state.

8. Another. To the Tune of "Fortune Turns"

Swift floods, fierce winds,
 I feel their harsh roar,
My heart's pain, its staggering agony,
 Tears dropping from my eyes;
I cannot stop it, I lament hourly
 The change in my fortunes.

For daily they grow, never do they cease,
 The flood of my sorrows;
My wounded heart, my abandoned mind,
 The winds of my sadness
Lay siege to me frightfully, their fateful torment
 Suffocates my life.

All my hopes are gone, no happy hours
 Do I expect;
Rather, day and night I languish
 In great sorrow:
And since thus I am on the rack, and waste horribly,
 I wish for my death.

There is no medicine, no solace for my heart
 Pining in sorrow;
Few are its pitiers, none its comforters,
 Woe to such a hapless one.

There can be neither reliever nor helper
  For my case.

Therefore wholeheartedly, with great readiness,
  I wish to move away
From this wicked world and its transience;
  I gladly take leave.
If God so wills it, let not the hour delay:
  I'm prepared to die.

For death for me can be my aid, and
  Let me forget my sorrow;
It could relieve and bandage my wounds
  And cure all my pains.
It takes from my heart, wipes from my eyes
  My often-shed tears.

12. Another. To the Tune of "Flow My Tears"

Oh my dear Violet, how shall I broach my subject?
My just complaints to you, my dear;
How shall I bring before you my pain
So I hurt you not, yet you know my grief?

In you only my heart found peace,
Without you I never had joy;
How did you change so, why do you hate me so,
Why do you not remember my great faithfulness?

Do you not fear God, for having often
Broken your faith for another's love?
Truly you hate me because of one person,
And wish your wife's death for her pleasure.

For what reason is she worthy of your love?
Was it her wealth or her person that touched your heart?
Her birth or her virtue that forces you to this?
That my own person has come to be hated.

In no way do I hold her better than myself,
And surely my faithfulness is worth more than gold,

Which I know, dear heart, you do not find with her,
For certainly another is dearer there than you.

For already, foreboding that you inclined towards her,
I watched, no matter where you were,
I knew, I truly knew, no matter what you said
I took it hard that you should hate me so.

Not a word did I say, only with many sighs
I continued my life, with tears shed in secret.
Not willing to offend her with my reproaches,
For she seemed to bear friendship towards me.

Shame also restrained me, believe me,
For I had been faithful to you, my sweet,
And I'm not wanted by my true love—
This was the gratitude, this how you paid me.

My dear Violet, my every word you turn around,
You do not even look at me;
You hate so without reason, my one and only Rose,
Is she worthy, that for her you should be angry with me?

When, complaining you remarked to me
That she resents you, you do not know why—
I thought I should die right there, but still endured it;
Why do you touch her knee? But that is not what I answered.

The tile stove must have heard enough:
You made merry with her by it and held counsel,
Thinking, if I see it, you deceive the fool
Often your many words struck my soul.

But perhaps she'll be true to me after all,
She'll not believe your word, will not lean to you,
For I once heard a harsh word of hers addressed to you;
For my good friendship she'll not dig a pit, perhaps.

Not like you, who played before me,
Thinking that I have no suspicions;
But that kiss was more than a joke, and what you whispered—
That is why I watched you, for what you said then.

Her name was your heart, was your soul—I heard—
You promised on oath, too, that you're her true follower;

If I died, should she on my death so desire,
She'd be yours—and you hope my death will not delay.

I'll keep to myself till death all my pains,
Solace my bitterness with these poems;
There is no one to whom I can show my wounds,
Crying, I look only on my written verses.

But truly, you should fear God, my sweet,
For you broke your oath many times;
Truly, He will yet look at my misery,
For my faithfulness surely is in his sight.

I do not complain of these matters to anyone,
Only to Him alone, for I know in all matters
He's the best physician of my sad heart,
And He'll be the protector of my lost cause.

This is not what I deserved from you, my heart,
If you were not afraid of sin, in any case
Shame should at least have kept you from this—
Let God be the assuager of my pain.

15. Another. The Same Tune

Oh my many sighs, when will you cease?
  Why, oh my heart's pain, do you not cease?
  Sorrowful times, why have you no mercy
  On me and my sorrows—why do you rejoice thus?

The many prayers whither my heart
  Tearfully suffering my sorrowful life.
  I weep and torture hourly my soul,
  For I have lost my good hope.

Ah, woe is me, whom the many storms touch,
  Woe to my poor head beset with much care and pain,
  My stuttering, sad tongue dares not speak
  Now that my sad heart no longer has joy.

But if that great Lord looks on me and pities,
  Curing my worldly torment there on high,
  Taking my soul to Heaven, consoling, trusting:
  I know He will not leave me, for I have a good God.

18. Another. Its Tune: "Many Are Saying Now"

My faint heart, be still and soothe your sadness,
And with patience doctor your pains,
For lo, no one pities your many torments,
Ah, there is no one to turn away your sorrows.

Everyone follows his own pleasure and seeks only that,
And everyone laments only his own heart's wounds,
Although all see well your horrible wounds,
Even if they pity, they cannot cure these.

Why then, do you torture yourself? Bear with patience
That which you must, or take it with a good heart,
For it cannot be cured with self-torture and pity—
Trust, rather, your sorrow and your wounds to God.

Not even Orpheus' lute could console you,
The fresh songs of beautiful nymphs are not wanted;
If you walk among pretty flowers and green branches,
You do not gladden, but sigh weeping still.

With sorrowing men, the pretty forest is dearest,
Yet that cannot console either, even that is not wanted;
Flowing waters, beauteous springs, summer's pleasant breezes,
All the many beauties of the world increase your sorrow.

Pretend honey if you swallow poison, do not sorrow;
Let God be your hope and be renewed in that.
He'll aid you and not desert you; turn only to Him;
Give Him your sorrows and fear not but rather be glad.

20. Another. Its Tune: "The Flight of the Muses, or a Similar One"

Woe, my heart's torment, the pain of my wounds
When, oh when, will you cease?
My frequent shedding of tears, my recurrent sighs,
Daily, behold, they increase.
My sorrows dart with ever new arrows into the wounds of my grief,
Into my languishing heart.

I see that never again will it grow happy, for the
Lamentations of my sorrow

Like moss have covered my sorrowful heart, like a fog have
        Obscured my mind.
I increase the clouds with my sighs, oh,
        I decrease my life.

Pity me, granite rocks! Woods, pleasant prairies
        Sorrow over me!
Have pity on me, I ask, for oh, I live in sorrow,
        See what I have become.
Beautiful flowers of the meadows, swift flowing rivers,
        Shed tears over me!

Crowds of forest game, flying birds,
        Hear my repeated cries of pain!
You also, silent Echo, hear how often, oh,
        Cries leave my mouth; you know
The cause of my pain, of my frequent complaints,
        Why have you no compassion?

Oh merciless, hard and cruel
        Tigers and dragons!
By my laments, my horrible pangs,
        You also, oh lions,
Let your hearts be moved, let your tears be shed,
        Poisonous viper-snakes.

Foam of the seas, and its whales and other fishes,
        Understand my pain!
Have pity, I ask you—if only you would give a sign
        And thus ease my pain.
For I no longer have hope that I shall forget
        My distress.

If in the past you listened to Orpheus devoutly,
        How he grieved with his lute
And even Proserpina, the Queen of Hell, had pity;
        Softening her heart,
He won his Euridice
        With his song.

You can justly pity me also, for I, too,
        Grieve without ceasing!
Each night and each day my sad hours pass in woe,
        And into it, by chance,
As into a maelstrom, into the sea's depth,
        I have sunk without hope.

32. Poem

Peaceful patience give me, my sweet Jesus,
That I do not offend you, my saving Christ,
From despair protect me, oh my God,
Let cease, if it please you, my heavy cross.

37. Persecuted Protestants' Invocation New Poem. Tune: "What Does the World Trust?"

Oh merciful God, who are your people's
Defending father; you see how on all sides they come
Against us, your true disciples,
The frightful beasts of prey,
Wolves in sheep's clothing they swallow us.

If you do not help us, we cannot stand,
We stagger horribly in spiritual blindness,
We stand in fear of spiteful fangs aimed at us;
Come, do not let us be lost and despair,
Come, our aid, our succor!

They have determined they will wipe us out,
Off the face of this earth, will annihilate us;
To become lords of our souls, they seek to make us believe
What your holy soul abhors—
Human inventions.

They forbid and distort your Holy Word,
They hate us who revere purely your holy name;
Scorning your holy merits won with the shedding
Of your blood, they persecute your followers,
Forcing them to the same.

They seek other mediators for themselves,
They trust mightily to good deeds,
My loving Jesus, they do not think of you,
They do not bow heads and kneel to you,
They bow heads and knees to the work of hands,
To stone and wood.

Your people's shepherds are driven
From your houses, your holy temples,

Ah, they have no respite, are driven from one place
To the other, are killed.
They spilled much blood
From your believers.

Clapping, they rejoice over our grief,
Their stone hearts harden over our misery
And they domineer over all our goods.
Songs have ceased,
Only groans are heard,
In our streets.

Nowhere can your people stay in peace;
Wherever they go, those with great speed
Find them there, and with great danger,
New strategems, planned marvels,
And weapons,
They consume them.

They entice, seduce the weak of faith,
Imprisoning their souls, driving them
To new inventions.
These only wish
That their goods
Increase.

Instead of your Holy Word, how they trade,
Forgiving future sins for money,
They forbid the Holy Scripture, which they should believe,
Lest they might learn it,
Lest it put an end
To their repentance.

Under the guise of a pure life, behold, how they live!
Licentious revelers who do not fear God.
They consider holy matrimony a great sin
And forbid it;
But they give an example of licentious living to their flock,
An example to their students,
And there is no ban on this.

Our loving Father, have pity in your heart,
You see the distress that your people suffer,
Let your true promise come to your mind,
Saying: Fear not, my people,

Hell's gate cannot
Stand up to you!

We call you to help, as you commanded
Oh, do not let us fall, support our faith,
Strengthen us, I beg you, that as you decreed
We should hope in you,
And not fear them
Who can do us no harm.

For they do not kill the immortal soul;
If through torture they try the body
God will raise it up, and give it eternal life,
After many groans,
And by redemption's way
He shall console us.

39. Another. Light of Our Souls

Light of our Souls,
Good Shepherd of your sheep,
Look down with gracious eyes,
Let your people's word reach you.

Those we send off to you
And with tearful eyes we cry:
Come, save us, our succor,
You see how great is our need.

What have we deserved for our sins?
We fell into your anger,
A foreign nation is upon us,
Oh, how we are oppressed.

Upon us came, as on the Jews,
The horrible Egyptian yoke;
Our life has no safeguards
For we have been provoked to anger.

They destroy our sweet land,
They deprive us of our goods,

Laughing at our misery,
They gnash teeth at us.

Even in our souls they torment us,
For the true faith they hate us,
From one place to the other they chase us.
They expel us from your churches.

Your people are confined into this small space
To honor you purely;
But if your hand does not protect us,
And your heart is not moved to pity us,

They have determined to molest us,
And do not leave us in our faith,
With weapons they force us,
To that which they themselves believe.

Or they have made us into refugees,
Those who stand up to them
They drive out of their houses
To beg, or else they kill them.

In your holy hands are hearts.
You know what efforts
Are made for our ruin,
And this goal which they have determined.

Annihilate their counselors,
Strike to the ground their power,
Scoff at their inventions,
Have pity on our wretchedness.

Restore, for your holy name,
The reverence of your son,
Preserve us for your good being,
Have pity on us for your son's merits.

We ask that your Gospel
Be preached to us;
Remaining pure among us,
Let our souls flow with faith:

So that our children also can see
What the true light is;

That they might learn it truly
And keep it in their hearts.

May they love your Holy Word
That which you left us, let them understand it
And follow it with clean hearts,
Let them praise your holy name.

After their death, however, receive them
In the ranks of the faithful in heaven;
Together with us in great joy,
They shall praise you, Lord, in heaven.

Amen.

42. Another Poem.

Farewell, my frequent vain shedding of tears,
Farewell, my frequent sighs and gnawing at my heart,
Farewell to you also, my frequent sighs,
Farewell I say to you, here and now, my grieving.

BIBLIOGRAPHY

Primary Works

Harsányi, István, and József Gulyás, "Petrőczi Kata Szidónia versei," *Irodalomtörténeti Közlemények* 25 (1915): 190–206, 311–27, 445–57.

Jenei, Ferenc. *Magyar költők*, XVII szazad. Budapest, 1956.

Kis, Bálint. "Gróf Pekry Lőrinczné végrendelete." *Történelmi Tár* (1895), 730–37.

Szász, Béla. "Petrőczi Kata Szidónia és Dálnoki V. Gerzson levelei." *Egyetemes Philológiai Közlöny* 32 (1908): 246–47.

Related Works

Antalffy, Endre. *Petrőczy Kata Szidónia élete és munkái*, 1664–1708. Budapest, 1903.

Ferenczi, Sari. "A Lelki hódolás első kézirata." *Egyetemes Philológiai Közlöny* 31 (1909): 422–33, 596–604.

Harsányi, Ilona. *A XVII. és XVIII. század magyar költőnői*. Budapest, 1935.

Jenei, Ferenc. "Manierista elemek világi költészetünkben Beniczky Pétértől Petrőczy Kata Szidonia-ig." *Irodalomtörténeti Közlemények* 74 (1970): 535–39.

Lakos, Géza. "Hol vannak Petrőczi Kata versei?" *Irodalomtörténeti Közlemények* 21 (1911): 120.

Pintér, Jenő. *Magyar irodalomtörténete; Tudományos rendszerezés*. Vol. 3: *A Magyar irodalom a XVII. században*. Budapest: A Magyar Irodalomtörténeti Társaság, 1931.

Rimeg, Ödön. *Gróf Pekry Lőrinczné, Báró Petrőczy Kata Szidónia élete és költészete.* Marosvásárhely, 1905.

S. Sárdi, Margit. "Baroque et piété dans l'oeuvre de deux femmes de lettres hongroises," *Baroque* 8: 95–104.

———. "Petrőczi Kata Szidónia 'Világi sok búba . . .: A régi magyar vers.' " *Verselemzés.* Budapest: Akadémiai Kiadó, 1979.

———. *Petrőczi Kata Szidónia költészete.* Irodalomtörténeti füzetek, no. 90. Budapest: Akadémiai Kiadó, 1976.

Solyom, Jenő. "Petrőczi Kata Szidónia életrajzához." *Irodalomtörténeti Közlemények* 64 (1960): 358–59.

Sőtér, István, gen. ed. *A Magyar irodalom története.* Prepared in the Magyar Tudományos Akadémia Irodalomtörténeti Intézet. Vol. 2: *A Magyar irodalom története 1660–től 1772-ig.* Edited by Tíbor Klaniczay. Budapest: Akadémiai Kiadó, 1964.

Szinnyei, József. *Magyar írok élete és munkái.* Budapest: Hornyánszki Viktor Könyvkereskedése, 1905.

Thaly, Kálmán. *Irodalom-és míveltségtörténeti tanulmányok a Rákoczi-korból. Toldalékúl kuruczvilági kiadatlan költemények tára.* New ed. Budapest: Ráth Mor, 1899. (1867 ed. lost.)

———. "Báró Petrőczi Kata Szidónia." *Athenaeum* (1874): 1681–91, 1739–55, 1809–22, 2507–21, 2641–58.

Contributors

BRIGITTE EDITH ZAPP ARCHIBALD is an associate professor of foreign languages at North Carolina A & T State University. Her area of interest is German literature of the medieval, Renaissance, Reformation, and Baroque periods.

JEANETTE LEE ATKINSON holds a Ph.D. in Germanic languages and literatures from the University of Pennsylvania. She has written articles on German and Swedish literature and is active as a reviewer, particularly of contemporary Swedish literature.

ENIKŐ MOLNÁR BASA is a cataloger in the Serial Records Division of the Library of Congress. She is interested in Hungarian and comparative literature, particularly the connections between Hungarian literature and the English and German literary traditions.

MAYA BIJVOET is an assistant professor of French and German at the University of Colorado, Colorado Springs. The author of *Liebestod: Its Function and Meaning,* she is particularly interested in European Romanticism and women's studies.

RONALD BOGUE is an associate professor of comparative literature at the University of Georgia. His research interests are seventeenth- and eighteenth-century English and French aesthetics and contemporary critical theory.

SUSAN L. CLARK is a professor in the Department of German and Slavic Studies at Rice University. She works in medieval comparative literature, in German Renaissance, Reformation, and Baroque literature, and in women's studies and detective fiction.

PETER COCOZZELLA is an associate professor of Spanish in the Department of Romance Languages and Literatures at the State University of New York, Binghamton. His numerous publications include studies and translations of outstanding, though little known, works from Castilian and Catalan literatures.

MOIRA FERGUSON is a professor of English at the University of Nebraska, Lincoln, and former chair of the Women's Studies program. Her publications include *Mary Wollstonecraft* (with Janet Todd), *First Feminists: British Women Writers, 1578–1799,* and an edition of "The History of Mary Prince A West Indian Slave Related by Herself."

VALERIA FINUCCI is an assistant professor of Italian at Duke University. Her research interests include feminist critical theory, Renaissance poetry and prose, and nineteenth- and twentieth-century novels written by women.

JOYCE L. IRWIN is a research associate in the Department of Philosophy and Religion at Colgate University. Her research interests include the lives and theology of women within radical reform movements and the theology of music in German Lutheranism.

RUTH LUNDELIUS is an assistant professor of Spanish at the University of Georgia. She has published numerous articles on Spanish drama of the Golden Age, particularly the depiction of women.

SVERRE LYNGSTAD is a professor of English at New Jersey Institute of Technology. His publications include books and articles about Russian and Scandinavian literature, as well as translations from Danish, Norwegian, and Russian.

GLENDA K. MCLEOD is a temporary assistant professor of comparative literature at the University of Georgia. Her publications have primarily concerned early women writers.

MARY ANN O'DONNELL is an associate professor of English and world literature at Manhattan College. She is the associate editor of *Literary Research* and the author of *Aphra Behn: An Annotated Bibliography of Primary and Secondary Sources.*

JEANNE A. OJALA is an associate professor of history at the University of Utah. Her areas of interest include the history of France and the French Revolution and Napoleon.

WILLIAM T. OJALA is an associate professor of English at Arizona State University. His areas of interest are literature and language.

HELENE M. KASTINGER RILEY received her doctorate in Germanics from Rice University and is currently a professor at Clemson University. She is the author of ten books on the German Romantics, Virginia Woolf, Romain Rolland, and creative women in the Age of Goethe.

FRANCES TEAGUE is an associate professor of English at the University of Georgia. Her publications include books on Jonson and Shakespeare, as well as articles on Renaissance drama and early women writers.

NOËL M. VALIS is a professor of Spanish at the University of Michigan, Ann Arbor. She is the author of *The Decadent Vision in Leopoldo Alas, The Novels of Jacinto Octavio Picón,* and *Leopoldo Alas (Clarín): An Annotated Bibliography,* as well as the coeditor of *In the Feminine Mode: Essays on Hispanic Women Writers.*

RIA VANDERAUWERA, who formerly taught at the University of Antwerp, Belgium and the State College of Translation in Maastricht, the Netherlands, is currently working as an editor and freelance translator in Austin, Texas. She has written *Dutch Fiction in Translation: The Transformation of a "Minority" Literature,* as well as various articles on translation.

FRANK J. WARNKE was Franklin Professor of Comparative Literature at the University of Georgia. His many publications include studies of seventeenth-century literature, John Donne, Renaissance women poets, and literary theory and history. He was also coeditor of the *Princeton Encyclopedia of Poetry and Poetics.*

KATHARINA M. WILSON is an associate professor of comparative literature at the University of Georgia. She is the general editor of *Medieval Women Writers* and *Women Writers of the Renaissance and Reformation* (University of Georgia Press, 1984 and 1987) and the author of studies on early women writers, Hrotsvit, and Chaucer.

Index